THE ABOLITION OF REALITY

THE ABOLITION OF REALITY

A FIRST DRAFT OF THE END OF HISTORY

JOHN WATERS

Western Front

BOOKS

ISBN #s:
978-1-959666-54-7 (paperback)
978-1-959666-59-2 (hardcover)
978-1-959666-56-1 (ebook)

Cover art by Ivo Valachovič

Western Front Books
12407 N Mopac Expy #250
Austin, TX 78758
www.WesternFrontBooks.com

Rev. 05-05-2025

To Rita, my wife and fellow warrior.

CONTENTS

PREFACE

This volume is a compilation of a particular strand of the writings from my Substack page, John Waters Unchained, between September 2020 and the end of 2024. The relevant themes related to the fallout and meanings of the Covid episode that began in the spring of 2020, in particular as it related to questions of human sovereignty and freedom and the conditions of liberal democracy in the constitutional republics of the former Free West, and also human decency in human society, arising from what had been, in substance and effect, a coup against humanity, based on duplicity and unlawful coercion. The topics covered range from the altered state of propaganda to the deep meaning of groupthink, from the silence of liberals to the role of fake money in this most egregious and unprecedented of phenomena, pausing along the way to observe the cruelty and inhumanity that abounded in those dreadful days and nights.

In the main, aside from an occasional conflating of interview materials in respect of a particular subject, each chapter of the book comprises a separate article from those years. The content of the articles, as can be verified by reference to johnwaters.substack.com, is broadly as it manifested in the originals. Some minor tweaks or corrections have been made in a number of chapters, though purely for clarity, added coherence or the amending of minor errors. Some of the lengthier references from other authors have been summarised more concisely than originally, for economy and copyright reasons, and specific internet-only references have been reworked to fit the demands of an actually existing book. Other than these specific changes, all content is the same as when originally written.

All of it represents my views at the time it was first published, and has not been amended for any purpose other than those stated above. Some of the articles contain predictions and analysis which have not, or not yet, achieved vindication, but I have retained these, unrevised from their original form, for a number of reasons: it is more honest; in several instances it conveys something of the fraught atmosphere of the time, and, by definition, all prediction is a precarious business, especially with regard to timings. In the long run, I regret to say, I am likely to be vindicated in everything.

There is a minor pattern of duplication in the book arising from the fact that certain 'set-pieces' — definitions, citations — appear twice in different chapters, largely with similar wordings and in the same format due to their generic utility and the length of time that may have arisen between the articles as they appeared. Again, I might have weeded these out but, mindful that some readers might prefer to dip into individual categories at random or in non-chronological order, I mostly decided against it. If you occasionally experience a sense of *déjà vu*, be assured that it is 'my bad'.

— John Waters

_____

If you enjoy this book, sign up for my Substack, John Waters Unchained, at:

https://johnwaters.substack.com/

_____

Communications concerning this book should be directed to:

Joseph Dindinger, Publisher
production@wisepathbooks.com
Western Front Books is an imprint of Wise Path Books
Lake Buchanan, Texas, United States

I AM AN AUTHORITY ON THE DESTRUCTION OF MY COUNTRY

I am an authority on the destruction of my country. I can parse, plumb, dice and slice the catalogue of disaster that has been inflicted upon her by those we trusted to be her husbanders, but who turned out to be villains, cowards, traitors and batterers. I can tell you how they do it, blow by blow, descending on her baffled face like rain. I can describe the involutions of their guile and underhandedness. I can show how it impacts on each of us who are forced to watch and wait as they prate on concerning their 'compassion' and 'humanity', while we, her children, stand paralysed and muted by several centuries of demoralisation and bad religion. I know it all inside out. I feel it all, though I cannot always find the exact words corresponding to my feelings, and so the sentences burst out of me and trip each other up, and yet are understood sufficiently by others to surprise and puzzle me, though I hear in the echo of my own voice only the spaces in which the missing parts might have been.

I am an authority on the destruction of my country. I stand before audiences and tell them why their souls are dying and their grandchildren may never be born. I watch them nod as though understanding for the first time. I see tears trickle down their cheeks and briefly worry that I have caused this to occur, though I am but the midhusband, and innocent of the conception.

I am an authority on the destruction of my country. For the first sixty-four years of my life, I did not anticipate that my country would fall into the hands of pimps who would sell her into prostitution, who would banish her children to wander in the world without a place to rest their heads, a home to call their own. I thought they had felt at least the essence of what they had preached about her long struggle for Independence, and the importance of her free-

doms, and the sacrifices of her martyrs, and now they act as if this was all but bewitchment and foolishness.

I am an authority on the destruction of my country. I did not expect to be such, not knowing there would arise a vacancy. Little did I know, as I walked to school with the words of Pearse rattling around my head that, in studying the writings and deeds of my country's heroes, the ultimate use to which I would put this knowledge would be to underline its resonances in a present that lay ahead as though a misplaced stretch of the past. I had thought of these stories as a kind of adornment on a finished history, an emblem of patriotic sincerity, the luxury of a people whose trials were over, their problems resolved.

I am an authority on the destruction of my country, but a Bachelor of Destruction only. I am studying for my Masters and writing here my thesis, in which I hope finally to overcome what I believe is my total inability to express what I feel, what needs to be said, and what is to be imagined in order to prevent this cycle recurring.

I am an authority on the destruction of my country. I wish I weren't. I wish I were an expert in building boats, or growing butternut squash. I wish I were not an amateur specialist in psychopathy and ponerology, or an eyewitness authority on authoritarianism. I wish I were a better accordionist or crosswordist instead.

I wish I were not an authority on the destruction of my country. I wish I could take her for granted as I did for most of my life, walking on tiptoe across her blood-soaked fields, with a heart as light as my step. Oh, days of innocence and naïveté, how we pay for them now, and how we pray to have them back! How we rummage in our heads and memories for some formula or formulation that would enable us to rest, if only for an hour, without thoughts of her obliteration haunting our dreams.

— John Waters
Dublin, Ireland

YEAR ONE
2020

15 Aug 1971 - US Abolition of the monetary gold standard

4 Mar 2011 - Larry Fink, CEO of BlackRock says 'Markets don't like uncertainty. Markets like actually . . . totalitarian governments.' and becomes de facto global ruler

1 Dec 2019 - First case of Covid-19 virus is reported in Chinese city of Wuhan

---

10 Jan - China publishes virus genome sequence

21 Jan - First confirmed case outside of Asia, in the US

23 Jan - China imposes lockdown in Wuhan; 12 other cities the next day

24 Jan - First confirmed case in Europe

27 Jan - US Secretary of Health & Human Services determines that a Public Health Emergency Exists

30 Jan- World Health Organization (WHO) declares a global health emergency

31 Jan - US restricts travel to China

02 Feb - First death outside China reported in the Philippines

04 Feb - 3,700 onboard Diamond Princess cruise ship quarantined 15 days

25 Feb - Antiviral drug remdesivir trials begin

29 Feb - First case confirmed in Ireland. "This is not unexpected. We have been preparing for this eventuality for many weeks now. The health service has robust response measures in place," says Dr Tony Holohan, chief medical officer at the Department of Health.

09 Mar - Italy put on lockdown
11 Mar - First death in Ireland reported
11 Mar - WHO declares a global pandemic
11 Mar - US President Trump addresses the nation on the virus
12 Mar - Taoiseach Leo Varadkar addresses the media from Washington, DC: "I need to speak to you about Coronavirus and Covid-19." Schools, colleges, and childcare facilities would be closed, and teaching would move online. All indoor gatherings of more than 100 people and outdoor gatherings of more than 500 people advised to be cancelled. People not allowed to leave the country.
14 Mar - US restricts travel to the U.K. and Ireland
15 Mar - US State Dept. issues Do Not Travel Global Level 3 Health Advisory
16 Mar - US announces "15 Days to Slow the Spread" social distancing
24 Mar - US announces unemployment pay extensions
26 Mar - Stay-at-home orders in 22 US states
27 Mar - US President requires General Motors to make ventilators
27 Mar - Ireland put under full lockdown. A stay-at-home order put in place and people told they could only exercise within 2km of their homes. Strict measures only anticipated to remain in place for two weeks (but were kept until May). Mr Varadkar tells the nation: "Freedom was hard won in our country, and it jars with us, to restrict and limit individual liberties, even temporarily. But freedom is not an abstract concept. So I am asking people to give meaning to our freedom and liberty by agreeing to these restrictions. Restricting how we live our lives so that others may live." All people 70+ told to stay at home and "cocoon".

02 Apr - Reported cases pass 1M, in 171 countries. 51K reported dead.
03 Apr - US advises face masks in public
09 Apr - US Federal Reserve announces plan to print $2.3T for loans
11 Apr - US reported deaths pass 200K, the highest in the world
14 Apr - US President halts WHO funding during investigation
15 Apr - 2M million reported cases globally
20 Apr - US suspends new immigrant visas for 60 days, later for all of 2020
24 Apr - US programs to fund at-home people signed into law

01 May - FDA authorizes remdesivir for emergency-use

08 May - US jobless rate hits 14.7%, highest since the Great Depression

15 May - US announces accelerated "vaccine" plans with *Operation Warp Speed*

20 May - US NIH halts clinical trials of the drug hydroxy-chloroquine

30 May - US President announces withdrawal from WHO

08 Jun - US cases pass 2M. UN General Assembly does not meet in person for the first time in its history.

29 Jun - Irish government announces move into Phase 3 of a 4-stage reopening plan, allowing restaurants, cafes, hairdressers and barbers to reopen with extra social distancing rules in place. €9 substantial meal rule announced, allowing pubs serving food to reopen.

27 Jul - Both "vaccines" by the NIH/Moderna, and Pfizer enter Phase 3 trials

27 Jul - Education Minister Norma Foley announces roadmap for public school re-openings in September, involving breaking pupils into pods. Teachers asked to place their own desk at least 1-2m away from the pupil's desks.

04 Aug - Government announces move to Phase 4 to be delayed: "I know that this will come as a blow to pub owners and I want them to know I have enormous sympathy for their plight. This virus is taking away their ability to earn a living, to provide a key service in the heart of many communities," Taoiseach Micheál Martin said in a public address.

07 Aug - Regional lockdowns for Kildare, Laois and Offaly announced.

19 Aug - "Golfgate affair" scandal breaks in the media, when several politicians, a Supreme Court judge and other public figures attend a golf event in breach of the restrictions. EU commissioner Phil Hogan and the Minister for Agriculture Dara Calleary resigned. Four people were charged for organising the event, but all charges were eventually dismissed.

23 Aug - FDA authorizes use of convalescent plasma to treat virus

29 Aug - A "vaccine" being developed by AstraZeneca enters Phase 3 trials

01 Sep - CDC halts renter evictions through end of year

08 Sep - AstraZeneca pauses trials due to adverse event

23 Sep - "Vaccine" developed by Johnson & Johnson enters Phase 3 trials

28 Sep - Reported deaths globally pass 1M

03 Oct – Irish Department of Education announces that 6,100 students were impacted by errors in the system and would receive improved grades

04 Oct - Nphet recommends six-week Level 5 lockdown, banning people from leaving their county. Schools and childcare providers are allowed to remain open. Weddings limited to 25 people.

16 Oct - US announces free "vaccines" for many citizens

23 Oct - AstraZeneca resumes Phase 3 trials

27 Oct - (Ch 1) *The Covid Panicdemic* ──

02 Nov - (Ch 2) *The Ideological Stripe of Covid-19* ──

05 Nov - England enters lockdown

08 Nov - Reported cases globally passes 50M

09 Nov - FDA authorizes use of Eli Lilly's Covid19 antibody therapeutic

23 Nov - (Ch 3) *The Break for Evil* ──

27 Nov - Taoiseach Micheál Martin announces easing of resections to Level 3. While the festive period would not be the same as previous years, he urged people to enjoy a "meaningful Christmas".

29 Nov - (Ch 4) *A New Kind of Stupid* ──

02 Dec - The U.K. approves "vaccine" from Pfizer

03 Dec - US hospitalized due to virus passes 100K

02 Dec - (Ch 5) *The 'Victory' of Bondage* ──

08 Dec - Irish born woman, Enniskillen native Margaret Keenan, becomes first person in the world to be "vaccinated" in a hospital in England.

11 Dec - The FDA approves "vaccine" by Pfizer for emergency use. Mexico, Canada, Saudi Arabia, and other countries follow suit.

18 Dec - The FDA approves "vaccine" by Moderna for emergency use

20 Dec – UK P.M. Boris Johnson orders London and southeast England into strict lockdown

20 Dec - Travel plans of thousands of Irish people trying to get home for Christmas disrupted when a 48-hour suspension on flights from the UK is announced.

22 Dec - Government puts the country into yet another Level 5 lockdown. Pubs were ordered to close from 3pm on Christmas Eve.

Household visits limited to one other home from St Stephens Day. Shops asked to defer January sales events.

- 28 Dec - A "vaccine" being developed by Novavax enters Phase 3 trials.
- 29 Dec - All pubs, restaurants and cafes ordered to shut and the country is put back into an almost total lockdown.
- 29 Dec - Dublin native, Annie Lynch, 79, becomes the first person in Ireland to be "vaccinated", alongside healthcare workers.
- 30 Dec - UK approves "vaccine" by AstraZeneca for emergency supply.

CHAPTER 1
THE COVID PANICDEMIC
27-10-2020

I have been aware for some time that the Covid scamdemic was pulled off with the aid of a process of mass entrancement perpetrated largely by media, and that this has left many people — a majority, for sure, of most affected populations — terrified and unable to apply logic or reason to what they are able to see with their own eyes. I'm talking more here about people I know — good friends, in some instances — who have become deeply embedded in the deception, not alone unable to extricate themselves from the general terror but actually unwittingly behaving as marshalls of Covid enforcement, scolding people who are not wearing masks, engaging in bizarre public elbow dances on encountering acquaintances, and reacting with embarrassment and suspicion when they meet me, a public dissenter, as though they expect me to whisk them away to a deprogramming centre to have their brains rewired. I have come away from more than a few such encounters fearing that there may be a goodly section of every population that will never awaken to the scam, no matter how much evidence is produced.

These conditions were achieved by weeks, months, of persistent, repetitive messaging wrapped up in terror mantras and veiled threats, mainly by people calling themselves 'journalists', but more accurately dubbed 'journaliars'. It was achieved through the use of subtle and not so subtle neuro-linguistic programming and saturation coverage of an almost entirely falsified narrative to effect a form of mass hypnosis, which left only a small minority of Western populations — perhaps 10 per cent — unaffected. How these people escaped indoctrination and entrancement is itself something of a mystery, not to say a miracle. Perhaps, like me, many of them had long since stopped reading, watching or listening to legacy media, thus acquiring immunity to what is actually the true 'virus' here: the industrial mendacity of mainstream media.

The Covid ruse is without doubt the most extravagant confidence trick ever perpetrated on human society. It has been astonishing to watch — how easily the politicians were able to sell their message, how relentless were the media in promulgating it, how effectively all dissenting voices were suppressed, marginalised or cancelled. Astonishing — and also terrifying, when you came to see that Covid was no more than a smokescreen to cover the transformation of the economies, societies and legal systems of the hitherto free world into something akin to nascent totalitarianism. Now, finally, it is coming out in fits and bursts: politicians talk of 'circuit-breakers', the favoured euphemism for the next lockdown while also shamelessly, the world over, repeating the same franchised slogans to signal the coming destruction of all we have presumed to be ours: 'Build Back Better' in the 'new normal', which will 'leave no one behind'. This, translated, means: 'We shall destroy your livelihoods, your freedoms, your wealth and your relationships to forge a world you will not recognise, and there is no escape.'

Either all this will continue to be met with passivity and come to pass as they threaten, or Covid is about to become a crime scene. There are no other options. It is clear, watching this quite spectacularly amoral generation of politicians sell their countries and peoples down the river, that they are not going to stop until they are taken away in Paddy wagons. Perhaps they have been bought off to a sufficient degree to allow them to escape the consequences they appear determined to enforce on the rest of us. Perhaps their amorality in other areas has caught up with them, and their captors have acquired photographic evidence of their degeneracy or corruption. It doesn't matter: the point is that parliamentary democracy has breathed its last in virtually every country in the Western world, unless we the people do something now.

So far, the rule of law has merely come under suspicion of disappearing down the same plughole as democratic freedoms. It is too early to judge from some of the first rejections of legal challenges to the destruction of everything whether the judicial arms of governments have been nobbled to the same extent. There have been some promising outcomes — Madrid, in recent times, comes to mind, though its judgement appears to have been overruled by the national government. A number of state courts in America have returned half-decent judgements also. I, perhaps optimistically, take this to indicate that, in some jurisdictions, there remain some decent, principled judges, but I also see mounting evidence that the same kind of pressures being applied to politicians and editors are coming down also on the world's judiciaries. This is likely to mean that any clinging to constitutional niceties will be treated in the manner of an irksome wasp on an October day — yet another mere temporary obstacle to the march of the New World Order.

If I am wrong, and a strong pulse can still be located about the precincts of the courthouses of Europe and America, we are surely looking at perhaps the most monumental public inquiry since the Nuremberg trials of 1945/46. We are talking not merely about reckless negligence with regard to the livelihoods and general economic welfare of entire peoples, but actual crimes against humanity arising from a campaign of mass terror, suspension of basic human rights and suspicions of homicide to at least the level of manslaughter. Those implicated will include not just political leaders and their accomplice advisers, but also media editors, scientists, health tsars, police chiefs and the key broadcasters who became the faces of Covid in their respective countries, some of them adding insult to injury by claiming to have been infected by SARS-CoV-2, a virus yet to be isolated by any scientific process.

As Canadian scientist Professor Denis Rancourt has comprehensively demonstrated, we are talking about the generation of a massive spook resulting in the premature deaths of thousands of elderly people whose health degenerated due to psychological stress in the hothouse atmosphere of 'care' homes around the world between March and May 2020. This was a 'panicdemic', not a pandemic. It will be for the tribunals to decide if and to whom individual blame may be apportioned for this, and whether the crimes leading to death may be deemed deliberate killing or mere negligence rooted in indifference to the old and ill.

There will be a requirement for special tribunals to deal with the many crimes of the media from the beginning of last March. In this we observed the final capitulation of a once great profession and a once principled industry to political bribery and the crudest market forces, with many media outlets pumping out fear porn on a minute-to-minute basis and some accepting generous bribes of public money from governments determined to destroy the lives of their voters and afterwards send them the bill.

In this dismal episode, the media finally announced their resignation from the role of flying buttress to democracy which journalism has fulfilled for the more than three centuries since the press was named the Fourth Estate by my distinguished countryman Edmund Burke. Realising that there was no longer sufficient profit in telling the truth, media organisations switched business models and began putting out the lies prepared for them by political puppets and the would-be tyrant puppet-masters hiding in the shadows.

We shall need a lot of Paddy wagons, and much jail space. Most of all we shall need good men and women to step forward to fill the spaces left by the criminals under the headings above. Before that, we need to remember that these people are not in authority over us. They are in their positions of power only because we have placed them there, and that is something we can reverse at any moment. This necessary process is not without difficulties and conundrums. Who, for example, will carry out the necessary jobs of collar-feeling, since the commissioners of police and most of their underlings have shown themselves in this period to be tyrannical and corrupt, and will themselves require to be made guests of their respective nations as a matter of extreme urgency? This is not a straightforward matter, but we cannot allow mere logistical difficulties to stand in the way of reclaiming our freedoms and recovering the civilisation we inherited intact but have in late times all but surrendered to already proven enemies of humanity.

It is possible that these matters can all be dealt with through international cooperation between Covid resistance groups. Be that as it may, we owe it to our children, and our children's children, not to be deterred by comparatively minor problems and, still less, inconsequential niceties, from retrieving immediately their birthright from the hob of Hell.

CHAPTER 2
THE IDEOLOGICAL STRIPE OF COVID-19
02-11-2020

For some time I had been struggling with a conundrum: Why is it that Covid breaks down, more or less precisely into an ideological divide? This had been clear for a while in a kind of white-of-the-eye way before I began really to focus on it. Then it struck me: Had a 'pandemic' occurred when I was a feature writer and reporter with Irish newspapers about 20 years ago, I could not imagine attending editorial conferences in which the matter would be discussed as though implicitly a left-right question, or that the attitude towards it of those assembled for daily or weekly conferences would be predictable on that basis. Yet, this is more or less what has emerged.

From reports all over the world, it seems an almost universal principle that 'conservative' and 'right-wing' interests, groupings and individuals are opposed to lockdown and 'left-wingers' in favour of it. And this means that lefties are Covid believers, whereas conservatives tend more to be sceptics. In the United States, the pro-lockdown governors and mayors have all but invariably been Dems. The sceptics tend to be Republicans or 'alt-right' (whatever that is) bloggers and vloggers. Likewise, across Europe, the governments locking their peoples down most viciously and for long periods are those led by socialist parties, whereas the more relaxed countries — Sweden, a special case, aside — tend to be led by parties of the populist right. We have come to take this situation for granted, as though the reasons for it are self-evident. But, actually, they are not in the least clear. If Covid is, as many authorities insist, a health issue, why would it automatically break down in this manner? Why is the attitude of your neighbour predictable on political grounds? Why does someone's attitude to Covid predict so much else about him?

In part, I believe, it is because from the start there was this strong undercurrent that Covid was about something other than health. Almost nobody was —

is, even — quite certain what the subtext is, but for some unaccountable reason, almost everyone senses that it has something to do with the way the world has been breaking open in recent times, especially in the past five years or so, in ways that have been variously and exhaustively described and parsed, but really seem to boil down to a divide between people who have their showers in the evening and people who have them in the morning.

It may also, as with so many things these days, have something to do with Donald Trump. Although he moved with alacrity at the end of January to close down access to America from China, he was from the beginning a sceptic of the lockdown idea, repeatedly warning that the cure should not be 'worse than the disease.' This seems to have imposed a cleavage on American life, roughly dividing the country in half.

There was an interesting counter to this perspective. Around the time Trump began doing his nightly televised White House briefing sessions in early April, it was clear that the worst five US states for case numbers and deaths were all Democrat-run, and together accounted for two-thirds of total national Covid deaths. Of the worst ten states for fatalities, Democratic states accounted for in the region of 13 times the number of deaths as Republican-led states. On the percentage front (deaths as a percentage of cases — a statistically pointless but still revelatory metric), the top five states were all Democrat-run, with New York on top, followed by Louisiana, New Jersey, Michigan and Washington. After that, the figures began to shrink, falling into fairly level pegging between Democrat and Republican states. An American friend to whom I put these stats at the time offered this explanation: 'Globalists tend to be Democrats. Globalists tend to live in global hub cities. Global hub cities are nodes of virus transmission. It's where they jump from continent to continent. Thus concentration of cases in Democrat-run states. (Louisiana is the outlier in this explanation.)'

Seven months later, the latest 'case' data indicate a more balanced league sequence and colouration pattern — California at the top, followed by Texas, Florida, Illinois and Georgia. The pattern with up-to-date deaths is interestingly slightly different, with Texas at the top, followed by California, Florida, New York and Illinois. The patterns of April have not maintained themselves, but perhaps those early figures created an impression of some kind that caused Covid to be seen in America as a tribal issue, with this interpretation rapidly being exported to the rest of the world.

There has been for a while a view abroad that Covid is and was essentially — from a timing viewpoint at least — directed at bringing an end to the Trump presidency. Although the list of alternative conspiracies is long, with many inter-connections, this view of things still has much to recommend it. I have three different and constantly shifting theories about Trump and the virus: 1. that he's bought into it as much as anyone; 2. that he's been captured by his medical team and cannot escape until re-election is under his belt; 3. that he has a cunning plan that he's about to spring at any moment. I'm leaning towards 3. at the moment. I think the prize of the second term is so vital to him and his cause that he cannot jeopardise it by calling out Fauci, Birx, etc., who have clearly been trying from the start to slyly manage the virus in a manner designed to unseat President Trump. He knows it; they know he knows it; he knows they know he knows it, but he dares not rock the boat while things are as volatile as they are. There are some worrying things in some of his public statements about vaccines, but we will have to wait about ten days for the picture to become clearer.

For a time, the 'pandemic' did put Trump under pressure, even looking like it might indeed unseat the president, though that moment appears to have passed. The world's legacy media, which appear to despise Trump almost to the last journaliar, have taken to Covid like ducks to watermelon rind, lying through their face masks at every opportunity and in effect imposing on their audiences a form of mass entrancement impervious to truth, fact or stat.

Still, the truth comes tumbling out. As the figures for excess deaths in 2020 become solidified, it is emerging that this has been in no sense an exceptional year for fatalities almost anywhere, which means that there is no additional burden of death arising from Covid.

We also now know that more than 50% of deaths worldwide have occurred in care homes and that most of these deaths were not caused by Covid but most likely arose from psychological stress due to media-generated panic among people nearing the end of their lives. (Those who doubt this explanation should read the studies and watch the videos of Canadian scientist Denis Rancourt.) There are also numerous yet-to-be-investigated concerns about the untested admission of people, who subsequently emerged as infected, into care homes during March. New York exhibited the most marked of such patterns, with the NY state governor Andrew Cuomo issuing on March 25 an order permitting nursing homes to readmit sick patients without testing them for Covid-19. Facing allegations regarding the underestimation of fatalities, Cuomo resisted pressure for more stringent reporting of Covid nursing home deaths, and also, in his annual budget, introduced a measure indemnifying New York hospitals, nursing homes and other healthcare facilities against liability for Covid-related deaths.

From the Covid-unrelated death in late May of George Floyd, the worldwide Black Lives Matter protests — again incongruously — seemed to jell as an intrinsic element of the Covid narrative. On its face, the idea made no sense, but the controversy concerning the differing attitudes of various authorities to BLM protests, as against anti-lockdown demos, effected an underscoring of the ideological pattern. Police officers who had been enthusiastically truncheoning Covid sceptics just the week before were to be seen taking the knee in public in tribute to America's latest and most dubious hero, and governors who had been coming down like hailstorms on Covid dissenters turned a blind eye to breaches by the masses of Woke warriors who took to the streets for the summer.

Even though it makes just a limited amount of sense, it does at this stage appear that, in some odd and irrational way, Covid is actually a left-wing phenomenon. This undoubtedly has to do with authority, indeed with the authoritarian tic that seems to afflict many leftists. It is not unreasonable to observe that, in general, when you scratch a progressive, you uncover a fascist underneath, and this discovery is in no way discredited by the fact that said progressive will be calling *you* a fascist.

Covid, as has been seen everywhere, is an intensely authoritarian phenomenon. The first measures introduced by governments practically every-where were directed not at protecting public health but at awarding powers to themselves to restrict and coerce their citizens and impose draconian penalties for breaches or dissent. This kind of thing suits leftists just fine and dandy. Not only do they enjoy seeing the boots of the regime on the faces of fellow citizens, but they themselves seem to enjoy, like masochists under the whip of the master, the lick of leather on their own hides.

There is, moreover, something fundamentally neurotic about the latest incar-nation of the leftist in culture. Your average Cultural Marxist tends to be over-anxious, ill-educated, resentful, hung-up and irrational. He or she, after all, believes in an ideology that makes little sense unless you behold the world in an intensely neurotic fashion, seeing everything as the culmination of a history that spent every waking moment trying to stitch up everything for patriarchs and Christians. The ends simply refuse to tie together, and your fellow human beings appear to be utterly oblivious to the things you learned for four years at college. Clearly, then, state coercion is essential to bringing the world to order and everyone else around to your view of things.

At a basic human level, the kinds of people who gravitate to left or right tend to divide also, generally speaking, in terms of physique, occupation, and mentality. Leftists, shall we say, tend less towards muscularity, work generally in offices, salons or cubicles, and think the world owes them a living, an expecta-tion the world generally speaking appears to honour and come up, as it were, trumps on. They also consider themselves better educated, but in reality this means that they spent more time than others being indoctrinated with the virus that now afflicts their brains. I find it interesting that working-class/blue-collar people seem to see through Covid in a flash, whereas the average college grad-uate goes around in what appears to be a terrified trance, thinking he's going to meet his death around every corner.

Covid has emerged, in one aspect of its operation, as an accelerant on all things the average Cultural Marxist holds dear: restrictions on the practice of religion and public assembly, cycle lanes and other green stuff, compulsory face masks which make everyone as unattractive as the average blue-tinted Cultural

Marxist, disincentives to voting in person, and so forth. It emphasises the 'common good', which somehow reveals itself (who knew?) as extending to the state the right to restrict citizens, as though self-evidently some kind of criminals, on the mere possibility that they might be 'infected' with a non-lethal disease. It has no regard for charter, proclamation or constitution. It does not care for family, nation or God — is, in fact, the enemy of all three.

On the other hand, Covid has none of what might be called 'right-wing' characteristics. It seeks not to make America, or anywhere else, 'great again', but to destroy everything before it and grate on everyone's nerves until they surrender to the New World Order.

CHAPTER 3
THE BREAK FOR EVIL
23-11-2020

Sometime in the very recent past, something clicked to signal that the world had ceased to be run by the virtue of good authority, and its leaders had shifted tracks to the pursuit of a darker star.

I had been struggling to find a phrase to capture a phenomenon that, I think, almost everybody, or at least every sentient human being, has begun to scent on the breeze. Put as succinctly as possible, that phenomenon is the sudden, almost abrupt manner in which the leaders and authorities of the Western world, from the crack of the Covid starting pistol in March, started and continued to act like the leaders and authorities of third world tinpot dictatorships.

I call it 'The Break for Evil'. By 'evil', I mean that, as though in a single instant — perhaps precisely traceable in retrospect — the authorities of the Western world all at once began to shift from the right foot of good authority to the sinister hooves of wickedness, violence and coercion. I mean 'break' in the sense of 'breaking for the border': as though they had seen their opportunity and made a run for it. The first online dictionary I checked with offered this definition: '(break for something) to go somewhere quickly, especially in order to escape: *We're assuming they'll break for the border.*'

What I mean is that these people whom we trusted with the stewardship of our countries and our lives, suddenly, like a murder of crows in response to an inaudible signal, took off from the plain where they had been silently congregated and flew all at once in the same direction, with apparent determination and certainty as to where they were headed. As one man, they decided to make a dash for it, to abandon the restraint of good authority, statesmanship, public responsibility, goodness, virtue, and follow a different, entirely darker star. It is as though they sought belatedly to emulate the example of those increasingly malevolent corporate entities which increasingly seem to — literally — dictate everything about our lives and societies; I have in mind the egregious Google, which began its corporate life and operated for 15 years under the motto 'Don't be evil' but on October 2nd 2015 formally announced that it was changing this axiom to 'Do the right thing', when in reality it had merely flipped the original and decided to proceed under the slogan, 'Let's be evil!'

Perhaps these politicians, more or less all at once, had observed Google's rampaging across the cultures of the world and decided that being good, even *pretending* to be good, was a mug's game. Additionally, or, as the lawyers say, 'in the alternative', perhaps some lightbulb came on in what was left of their souls, and they decided that their Maker was not watching them after all, that, contrary to what they had been taught, the eyes of the Lord were not, in fact, everywhere, keeping watch on the wicked and the good.

For us, the merely led and ruled, this seemed to have happened unbeknownst to us. Then, one morning last spring, perhaps a penny dropped for us also. It was as if our society, travelling by train, had just recently cleared the 'Outer Home signal' of the spiritual-religious zone and crossed a frontier that nobody had at the time noticed except maybe as a 'click' on the line. (For those who have never worked upon the railways, the Outer Home signal is the last a train passes having departed a station, heading on to open track, into open country.) That 'click' was a moment of seismic rupture: the moment when the dreams of secular atheists came true and began the living nightmare of sane people. It's a bit like — to mix in another metaphor — the great oak tree Václav Havel used to talk about: it stood there for hundreds of years and didn't appear to change, but then, one day, a passer-by touched it with her little finger, and it toppled, having rotted from the inside out. Maybe the residual influence of those thousands of years of religious understanding descending to us from Pagan times, through the glorious Christian era, had finally petered out, and man — or the few men of C.S. Lewis's dark prognostications — suddenly understood that the world was his/theirs for the taking.

I sensed this change even before the declaration of the 'pandemic' by the WHO on March 11th 2020 — the same day, interestingly, as the first alleged Irish death from Covid-19. As early as the late days of February, there was this marked change of tone, of mood, in the relationships between Power and People. For example, on March 6th, in the first directional indicator in official pronouncements, the Garda Commissioner Drew Harass — otherwise, Drew Harris — announced that, in the coming pandemic, his force would soon acquire powers to arrest people suspected of carrying the virus but declining to be 'quarantined'.

When I heard this, I looked up momentarily, but then dismissed my darker fears. It was true that we had had, in recent times, SARS, Bird Flu and Swine Flu, and no one in the course of any of those previous 'pandemics' had made such a bizarre proposal, even after quite a few people had died. In the average Irish flu season, between 600 and 1,000 people are likely to die, but no one proposes breaking into people's homes to drag people from their beds and transport them to a concentration camp with some Orwellian name.

Remember again: this was five days before the first death claimed as the consequence of the virus SARS-CoV-2. I remember casually remarking on Commissioner Harass's undoubted exultation and storing it away under a question mark. In due course I was to list it as the first of many signals that caused me by mid-March to rethink my early sense that there might well, this time, be a real and imminent health crisis. I mean to say: What public leader of good authority responds to an imminent health crisis by threatening to arrest ailing people and imprison them? By St. Patrick's Day, the Commissioner's all-too-buoyant pronouncement seemed to bespeak something unusual afoot at an entirely different level.

This first sign was soon reinforced by others: the hectoring tones of politicians and 'health' tsars, the mismatch between the facts of the problem and the scale of the 'solution', the sudden collapse into arbitrariness of street-level police behaviour, the way the law was first supplanted by roadside banter and, where that went down badly, by unadorned Nazi tactics; the way hitherto dopey politicians would menacingly muse out loud about whether to intensify or relax the restrictions.

The same tone was soon to be seen right across the former Free World: Johnson, Macron, Conte, Sanchez, Trudeau, Cuomo, Newsom, Andrews, and — for all those feminists who for decades told us the world would be a more human place if ruled by women — the horrendous Scottish PM, Nicola Sturgeon, and the appalling Jacinda Ardern, prime minister of New Zealand, whose talent for tyranny puts the boys in the shade. Ardern's latest brainchild is the recent Food Bill, the first step in delivering to corporations their wet dream of banning private food production, turning what used to be a fundamental human right — to grow your own and share with others — into a government-authorised concession that can be summarily revoked.

The dark shadow of the overhead rooks accumulated and deepened. Our jaws dropped again and again as what initially seemed like a horror pageant became more and more real. In the escalating real-life dystopia of the Time of Covid, we have seen asthmatics incarcerated for not wearing face masks, parents arrested in public parks for playing with their children, old ladies getting citations for taking a drive. We have seen a pregnant Australian woman out for exercise told she was forbidden to rest on a park bench, and a priest in Ireland menaced with arrest and imprisonment for saying Mass, a first in 200 years. Blackest, most diabolical of all, was that they did these things in the name of 'saving lives' as though a single thing they had publicly done in their lives might have been mistaken for a gratuitous act of kindness or generosity.

In the Time of Covid, New Zealand has been vying with the State of Victoria in nearby Australia for the title 'Most Tyrannical Police State on Earth', though both jurisdictions now risk being overshadowed by several policing regions of the UK, most shockingly — as exposed by the excellent YouTube channel *The UK Column* — in Cornwall, where police recently arrested a 19-year-old woman for making a speech in the street — though admittedly it included the following incendiary passage: 'I believe that we must live, we must live. In other words, to be human is to be creative. Without that, what are we?' For uttering this out loud, this young woman was arrested, incarcerated in a cage the size of an upright coffin in the back of a police van, and held for 24 hours.

That same week, the heroic lockdown dissident Andy Heasman was arrested in a SuperValu shop in Ballymun, in north Dublin, when he tried to buy some toothpaste. Andy suffers from a condition which makes wearing a face mask impossible, and so claims an exemption under Statutory Instrument 296 of 2020 (Section 5, 'Reasonable excuse'), which neither proposes nor imposes any requirement or mechanism for providing medical proof of such exemption. And yet, summoned by a busybody floor manager, the cops showed up, dragged Andy out, took him to Ballymun Garda Station, strip-searched him, locked him in a filthy cell and, after a number of hours, took him to two different court houses before finally charging him with a Public Order offence plucked out of their vacuous arses.

First, he was taken to the Criminal Courts of Justice (CCJ), where he found himself in an underground area confronted by a scene worthy of Dante's *Inferno*: a coven of nurses lined up testing prisoners for Covid. The judge, apparently, would not 'see' any prisoner who had not been tested. Andy declined this big-hearted offer and was taken back to Ballymun copshop, where he was strip-searched again before being transported to a court in Tallaght, where he was released on bail following a conversation between the guards and the judge, who did not invite Andy to speak on his own behalf. On the following Friday, I accompanied him as his McKenzie Friend to a hearing at the CCJ, where he faced the aforesaid concocted Public Order charge. The judge asked him if he was pleading guilty, and when he replied in the negative, said she was adjourning the case until February. Both Andy and I tried to acquaint the learned judge with the manifest unlawfulness of what was happening. I cited Statutory Instrument 296 and its provisions for certain categories of citizen to claim exemption from wearing face masks. Clearly lacking the faintest clue what the law provided for, she accused me of 'flouting the law' by not wearing a mask and instructed us both to leave what she seemed to think was *her* court. Since from her own mouth she had betrayed that she had prejudged out of ignorance the issues in front of her, and was therefore unfit for her office, Andy and I were only too happy to leave.

That same day, I watched a speech by one of the *UK Column* regulars, David Scott, delivered in Holyrood, Edinburgh, under the title 'Fear Not' about the connection between religious or transcendent understandings and the collapse of the rule of law. Scott referred to 'our ancestors', who he said had 'rejected God because being ruled by a man and told what to do, was easier. They did not want the law of God, a law that they would need to place in their hearts and defend. Instead, they wanted a ruler to think for them and fight their battles. Slaves they had been, and slaves they still were in their hearts.'

This powerful speech tapped into something that had been building in me through the Time of Covid. Scott was saying something not a million miles from what Aleksandr Solzhenitsyn said nearly 40 years ago about the old people continually saying, when he was growing up, that the reason terrible things were happening in their country was that man had 'forgotten about God'.

David's message, like the great Russian's, was straightforward: To overcome our two most mortal enemies — fear and pride — it is necessary to place our sovereignty in the hands of the Lord of History, Jesus Christ — 'and say He is sovereign, we can choose His law, a law of love and a law of freedom.'

'It is no accident,' he observed, 'that the state and its wars and oppression has grown as faith has ebbed.'

This declaration flirts with a short-circuit of the kind that perhaps afflicted also the old people of Solzhenitsyn's recollection and from their mouths risked descending into an inscrutable pietism, the kind of thing you might hear a hundred times and not grasp its meaning. Although that line from Solzhenitsyn is legendary, the remainder of the speech is much less well-known. But Scott set up his argument in a way that allowed a deeper understanding to emerge into something like new light. It is a matter of mindset: we can place our faith in kings, politicians, popes, mobs, ideologies, but what we need is something to transcend these because they all come afflicted by the same risk of tyranny. The figure of Jesus stands as an alternative because He has the capacity to disable in men the power-lust they use to claim dominion over their fellows.

It is a related point to one I've made repeatedly concerning the Preamble of the 1937 Constitution of Ireland, which begins: *'In the Name of the Most Holy Trinity, from Whom is all authority and to Whom, as our final end, all actions both of men and States must be referred, we, the people of Eire, humbly acknowledging all our obligations to our Divine Lord, Jesus Christ, Who sustained our fathers through centuries of trial'* . . . etc.

It is nowadays not immediately understood that this opening passage has also a secular interpretation, perhaps best demonstrated by reference to Lewis's observation that when God is abolished by man, He is not replaced by *all men* but by a *few men* imposing their will on the rest. Thus, even for unbelievers, secularists, atheists, it is essential to see this formulation not purely as a Christian invocation, but as a mechanism that seeks and achieves something as vital to their own protection as it is to Christians. The 'mechanism' provided by the Holy Trinity does something that cannot be achieved otherwise: it places the fundamental rights of men *out of the reach of men*.

Rinsing this idea down to its simplest elements, we might say that if we wish to ensure that the law remains in the realm of good, we need to attach it to absolute ideas of goodness. And here's the rub: there is no 'secular' mechanism by which this can be achieved.

What has happened of late may be described as a sudden, lurching deviation from these ideas. It is as if those we have elected to lead us have simultaneously been hit by the insight that they only needed to treat their peoples as sovereign for as long as God could be said with certainty to exist. That was what required them to be 'good', to renounce evil and all its works and pomps, to maintain their authority in the cause of righteousness.

It may seem a stretch to suggest that these conditions remained in place until, say, March 6th 2020 — but I wonder. In a sense, I think, most of us imagined this moment had long since come and gone — and that we had, accordingly, seen and suffered the worst of its consequences. We in Ireland observed in the abortion referendum of 2018, a moral dissolution that ought to have warned us. Yet, even that did not seem to dismay us completely; to a large extent — and not to our credit — we were able to go on again afterwards as though we had plumbed the bottom of what was possible in the degradation of our public life. We assumed, because people were saying that God was dead, and our societies were changing their formal arrangements to fit in with this new resolve, that the entire process of deabsolutisation had already been accomplished, but it might not grow any darker. The icons of Christianity were gradually being stripped from public view. The leaders of our churches were taking the knee to the new secular overlords. Religious-minded people had already reconciled themselves to the idea that they should no longer require their societies to reflect their beliefs. But none of this either greatly surprised us or alerted us to the idea that we might be witnessing merely the thin end of wickedness.

We ought to have been more mindful of Solzhenitsyn and his cautionary words: When man forgets about God — that is the beginning, not the end. It's strange that, living in a secularised society, although I've written and spoken about this question for years, I keep forgetting, or misconceiving, this simple but total insight; and whenever things happen that might seem to bear it out once more, I discount their significance by looking for other explanations that, when I think about it, tend to be the kind of explanations that somehow fit with our normalised secular understandings. That's how it's set up, so we keep bouncing off the question.

It all really does come down to what Scott and Solzhenitsyn, in their differing ways, have conveyed: the apparent 'break for evil' of our political classes (pride), the supine response of the people (fear), the corruption of the Fourth Estate, the endless lies, the unbelievable psychosis of the police, the gloating menace of a thousand overnight little Hitlers — all this comes from that original and prolonged amnesia.

And, yet, things did not seem to have gone as far as the dominant societal conversation might have led us to believe. Though conviction was gone, observance too, enthusiasm for certain, something remained: people, including people in authority, continued to believe, or to *pretend* to believe, if only in the negative sense that they were afraid of coming out as outright heathens. This was in part because they were unconsciously applying Pascal's wager, and in part because such politicians did not want to risk losing votes by offending those who continued to hold to genuine religious beliefs. But it became more clear that this was merely a process of treading water during the final phase of the deabsolutisation process, which has recently, somewhat abruptly, achieved its culmination. Even after all the talking about 'rational' man, God still held sway over the mind of man, despite man's best efforts to shake Him off. But then, all of a sudden, this was no longer true. We crossed a line and went tumbling down a hill, with the brake pedal finding nothing but air.

So, what we have observed in the Time of Covid tells us that what we perhaps imagined had passed us by relatively uneventfully some time ago, actually had not occurred, and now it has, we are beginning to find that it is nothing like as benign as we imagined it might be. The experience already suggests that we have somehow — and not that long ago — finally crossed the line around the perimeter of the God zone, heading in the wrong direction. That is the 'border' our former leaders — now, it seems, our self-ordained absolute rulers — have 'broken' for: the border between Good and Evil, the Outer Home on the line to Hell. They have rejected the idea of an absolute figure of Good Authority — in this case, unequivocally Jesus Christ — and scampered into the embrace of some darker but as yet ill-defined entity.

What makes this all so strange is that, circumstantially, there's no particular reason it should be happening now, no special trigger or cue. Except actually, there is, and David Scott put his finger on it and identified it as beginning a long time ago, but somehow culminating in our time. He is right in intimating that the seeds of this horrific moment lie way back in the past.

The failure of the major religions to keep pace with the deabsolutisation of culture was rendering the God idea terminally implausible for the generality of people. Thus, for a long time, the store of transcendent belief in the imagination of society has been eroding without anyone keeping score. Church leadership, and indeed theologians in general, have proved intellectually inadequate to these drifts, resulting in a hollowing out in culture of long-held-to religious understandings of reality. Those who have made a break for it include not just the political and scientific leaderships, but also the leaderships of the main churches, who have willingly surrendered to the looming agenda and tried to bully their flocks into going along.

This is the meaning of this 'break for evil' by State forces currently observable worldwide. It is indeed a seismic change: the final phase in the process Solzhenitsyn spoke about when he accepted the Templeton Award for Progress in Religion in London on May 10, 1983 — the first time the prize had been awarded to an Orthodox Christian.

'More than half a century ago,' he said, 'while I was still a child, I recall hearing a number of older people offer the following explanation for the great disasters that had befallen Russia: "Men have forgotten God; that's why all this has happened."

'Since then, I have spent well-nigh 50 years working on the history of our Revolution; in the process, I have read hundreds of books, collected hundreds of personal testimonies, and have already contributed eight volumes of my own toward the effort of clearing away the rubble left by that upheaval. But if I were asked today to formulate as concisely as possible the main cause of the ruinous Revolution that swallowed up some 60 million of our people, I could not put it more accurately than to repeat: "Men have forgotten God; that's why all this has happened."'

'The failings of human consciousness, deprived of its divine dimension,' he expanded, 'have been a determining factor in all the major crimes of this century.' Only in the battle against Hitler had the West shown genuine resolve — in the face of Russia's agony and the 'dismemberment' of Eastern Europe, it had been crippled by impotence. 'Faced with cannibalism, our godless age has discovered the perfect anaesthetic — trade! Such is the pathetic pinnacle of contemporary wisdom.'

He quoted his countryman Dostoevsky, who warned that 'great events could come upon us and catch us intellectually unprepared . . . the world will be saved only after it has been possessed by the demon of evil.'

And later:

'It was Dostoevsky, once again, who drew from the French Revolution and its seeming hatred of the Church the lesson that "revolution must necessarily begin with atheism." That is absolutely true. But the world had never before known a godlessness as organised, militarised, and tenaciously malevolent as that practiced by Marxism. Within the philosophical system of Marx and Lenin, and at the heart of their psychology, hatred of God is the principal driving force, more fundamental than all their political and economic pretensions. Militant atheism is not merely incidental or marginal to Communist policy; it is not a side effect, but the central pivot. To achieve its diabolical ends, Communism needs to control a population devoid of religious and national feeling, and this entails the destruction of faith and nationhood.

Communists proclaim both of these objectives openly, and just as openly go about carrying them out.'

His assessment of the West was comforting yet realistic, particular to its moment, now almost four decades since.

'The West has yet to experience a Communist invasion; religion here remains free. But the West's own historical evolution has been such that today it too is experiencing a drying up of religious consciousness.'

A central aspect of this new culture, he observed, was that awareness of good and evil have been supplanted by the 'pursuit of happiness', and evil was already worming its way into the culture.

'It has become embarrassing to state that evil makes its home in the individual human heart before it enters a political system. Yet it is not considered shameful to make daily concessions to an integral evil. Judging by the continuing landslide of concessions made before the eyes of our very own generation, the West is ineluctably slipping toward the abyss. Western societies are losing more and more of their religious essence as they thoughtlessly yield up their younger generation to atheism.'

He spelt out some concrete symptoms: the Western young reared to hate their own societies; the defects of capitalism replicating the basic flaws in human nature; a loveless art; the disunity of religions; social theories collapsing into bankruptcy; the pursuit of 'equality' leading to the equality of slaves; the addiction to materialism at the expense of spiritual growth — all these were taking human society to the brink of disaster. And, all the while, the spectre of Communism, 'breathing down the neck of all moderate forms of socialism, which is unstable.'

Then, these chilling words: '[T]he noose around the neck of mankind draws tighter and more hopeless with every passing decade, and there seems to be no way out for anyone. . . . We ourselves, in our daily unthinking selfishness, are pulling tight that noose.' Only 'the warm hand of God' could save us from the consequences of our erroneous understandings of reality. 'There is nothing else to cling to in the landslide: the combined vision of all the thinkers of the Enlightenment amounts to nothing.'

'Our five continents are caught in a whirlwind. But it is during trials such as these that the highest gifts of the human spirit are manifested. If we perish and lose this world, the fault will be ours alone.'

The note of those words is precise and poetically coherent. Yet, it was, and remains, possible for them to short-circuit into some 'convenient' sense of a man clinging to religion as he entered the final phase of his life. This would be another grave error. We need to hear what he was saying: God is vital because God is the only being who is not man, and man on his own is deadly to himself. 'Hatred of God' means also dread of that which makes a human being most free.

We overlooked that the 'God stuff' was the 'glue' that held everything together and continued to do so even after all the formal elements of religions, faith and piety had collapsed. Even atheists were still, in a way, driven and motivated by the fumes of residual beliefs. But of late, this quantity has fallen below critical load, and a change of consciousness has transmitted itself among the new man-gods that C.S. Lewis warned about. That's where the 'break for evil' has arisen from, and if I am not wrong, it can only get worse.

I have in this essay deliberately avoided overtly 'religious' language. I have included no preachings or prophecies, no Biblical quotations, no mention of the Book of Revelation. This for two reasons:

One, I do not want to stir up one of the problems I seek to explicate: the 'short-circuiting' of humanly essential understandings on the circuit board of institutional religion. I do not wish to give the impression that I am talking only to people who consider themselves 'religious' or 'spiritual'. I take the view that all people, by virtue of being creatures incapable of providing themselves with fingernails or a destiny, are by definition spiritual, and by definition religious in the pure sense, i.e. spiritual beings on an infinite journey to the land of their Creator. I wish to transcend, so to speak, whatever self-definitions people may have arrived at, to liberate their imaginations from the burden of having to translate what I say from 'Catholic' or 'Christian' understandings, to say something that ought to be of interest to every living human being. For that reason, I have couched my thinking in words which are, perhaps paradoxically — but if so, so be it — 'secular' in that they may be interpreted by the logic of the street or the highway or the public house.

The second reason I have not employed explicitly 'religious' language is that, from an early stage in the Time of Covid, I began to feel uncertain that I could much longer go on describing myself as a Catholic in the sense of giving allegiance to a Church led by the current hierarchy of the Church in Ireland and the current Pope in Rome. As I write, on a Sunday morning in a country with the churches all closed and the news being trumpeted by the journaliars of the fake news media that the heroic Cavan priest Fr P.J. Hughes has been forced by his bishop to close his church, a friend, one of the most faithful Catholics I have ever met, texts me: 'One would ask are our Catholic bishops in modern Ireland collaborating with a new form of penal laws against the faithful, now a minority in our beloved country.'

I say, Amen. For the past eight months, I have observed with growing nausea the dissembling, evasiveness, hunkersliding and silence of the Irish bishops as their people were menaced, threatened and terrorised, their relationships undermined, and their most fundamental rights confiscated; as elderly people were allowed to die alone, without the comfort of priest or loved ones; as the dead were buried like criminals in a prison yard; as the Catholic sacraments were prohibited for the first time in two centuries; as Easter was cancelled and Christmas dangled like a carrot to a donkey; as politicians on almost a daily basis made contemptuous speeches in which they disrespected the very essence of the faith these bishops were supposed to defend, comparing it to yoga classes and the off-licence trade. I do not know whether all this slithering inaction and moral lockjaw arose mainly out of a deficiency of intellect — an inability to look squarely at the facts and see that what was happening was a massive, criminal confidence trick — or cowardice. I daresay both, but also possibly something more amorphous and more sinister.

I have listened, too, to the repellent pronouncements of such as the Association of Catholic Priests, which denounced as 'selfish' people who begged for their churches to be opened. How much longer can we continue to humiliate ourselves if, when we name ourselves as Catholics, this is what the listener associates us with?

Shame, shame, shame on these excuses for men. There will be no Church in Ireland until they have all taken off their vestments and departed. For what they have done is beyond forgiveness by mortal human beings.

I know people will be annoyed with me and write me sincere but, frankly, predictable communications telling me that *'the bishops are not the Church; we are the Church'*. That would have merit as an argument were there a significant complement of priests willing to stand up against this tyranny. There have indeed been a few, but we can easily count them on the fingers of one human hand.

Most of the personnel of the Church of Rome have nothing further to say to me, nor I to them. When they have all departed, I shall consider returning, but not before.

Meanwhile, I propose to go my own way, eyes still fixed on the horizon, heart still laid at the lotus feet of the Lord.

CHAPTER 4
A NEW KIND OF STUPID
29-11-2020

The crisis of the present moment is the normalisation of the incredible, the unspeakable and the unthinkable. Unless the world awakens very soon, the unthinkable is about to hit us.

For the past 30 years I have lived in the Borough of Dun Laoghaire, most of that time in a quarryman's cottage opposite Dalkey Quarry, overlooking Dublin Bay. It is without doubt one of the most beautiful places in south County Dublin, and also, surprisingly, one of the few roads left in the area that have retained a sense of rustic allure. This sense was accompanied by a spirit of neighbourly loyalty and affection, now almost entirely disappeared from areas east of the M50.

When I first moved to Dublin, having come up from the West, I was for a long time taken aback by the general sense of unfriendliness that pervaded the general south county area. In my first decade in the place, I gradually abandoned my habit of greeting people as I walked around Killiney Hill, since hardly anybody ever replied. When I moved down to live on the seafront in Sandycove a couple of years back, this pattern became noticeably more pronounced.

There's been a slight change in this regard in recent months since Gemma O'Doherty and I lodged our High Court challenge against the lockdown, with the precise objective of alerting the public to the usurpation of the most fundamental rights and freedoms we possess as of right, as citizens and human beings. Since then, especially in those gloriously sunny days of April and May, I found myself being greeted by shouts of 'Gobsh*te' and 'Motherf**ker' (the nicer salutations) from passers-by, generally lycra-clad saddle-soldiers using the new two-way Olympic-style cycle track that suddenly manifested where the main road used to be. (The road where we live, which used to be one of the main arterial routes in and out of the city, is now reduced to a single lane heading south, with minimal parking and zero set-down space. And I see Castle Street in Dalkey has now fallen as well.)

Every half-decent day now, hundreds of cyclists in lycra working off what is left of their masculine energy pass our window. If I venture out, I have a one-in-two chance of being yelled at. As we moved from flattening the curve to flattening the economy, their shouts have grown somewhat less frequent, though there is still, to my total lack of surprise, the occasional slow learner. The 'men' who abuse me: they are all but always males, or what passes for males — are not the old-style men-on-bikes, with felt hats, suits and shiny shoes, a folded-up shopping bag on the rear carrier, but these power cyclists that have suddenly erupted into view in the lockdown, who hurtle hither and thither dressed in what the fashion pages call 'unflattering lycra' (show me flattering lycra!) clearly engaged in some profound, evasive fantasy about themselves.

My cycling confidantes tend to get in as close as possible, accelerating as they do so, before delivering their payloads of expletives. They vary in age, from twenties to fifties, a category of males which, in the absence of underlying comorbidities, have a 99.9997 chance of surviving a SARS-CoV-2 infection. My own chances, if I were to credit a word of it, are significantly inferior.

It usually happens when I'm alone, though a few incidents have happened when my wife was with me, and once or twice in the company of her small grandchildren. I see it as a symptom of emasculation: men having been completely unmanned by the lockdown, but unable to find an outlet to express their cuckolded frustration. Being confined to their homes on the orders of rainbow-socked fascists, they are unable to support or face their wives and children, and so get on their bikes to escape the shame. Espying in the street one of the spare handful of people who have spoken out about the obscenity of what is occurring, they let rip in order to reassure themselves that they are still to be counted among the ranks of men. Their State-sponsored fury is directed at a rare male who continues to fight and therefore risks showing up their cowardice. By attacking me, they hope to steal my bottle for themselves, thus achieving a kind of redemption in their own limited minds.

It reminds me of the game of conkers: Since I have stood up to government and State, I am the boy with the *100-killer* whose score is available to others to take in battle, and hence these charming 'men' seek to claim all my credits in a symbolic unloading of ridicule or hatred. The bikes are a surrogate for the keyboards they use at home when they conduct similar attacks via Twitter: a strategic acceleration enables them to escape from any response, and the spandex gear renders them hideously indistinguishable from the next expletor.

Gemma's effect on them is worse, though she is somewhat less recognisable than I am. It is all but unbearable for them that a woman should stand up and do what they are too cowardly to.

They are the *emaskulated*. Having forfeited any ability to seem autonomous and dignified in the eyes of their wives and children, they no longer feel — as men once automatically did once they crossed certain ritualistic boundaries to become fathers, husbands, heads of households, breadwinners, protectors — that they are fulfilling the functions that God or Nature intended. They feel like what they appear to be: losers in lycra. The lockdown has ensured that they have been finally plucked from the bosoms of their families and despatched to plummet headlong into the disintegrating, abscessed heart of the city, cycling furiously along the newly minted cycle lanes that have erupted where once were the roads upon which men and women made their way to a place where they set to work with their hands, hearts and minds.

I have noticed, by the way, that already some women are beginning to approach me to say they are grateful for what I have tried to do. For men, it will be much harder, as admitting the truth will amount to a further humiliation: They fell for it — frame, chain and saddle.

In a slightly more tolerable version of the same syndrome, I sometimes get buttonholed along the promenade by elderly gentlemen who passive-aggressively demand to know why we filed our legal challenge. I wouldn't mind these interventions so much were it not so obvious that they are seeking to rebuke me rather than engage in a sincere conversation. It never seems to occur to them that it might be possible to know more than they have gleaned from watching RTÉ, and they regurgitate this in the manner of a child reciting a nursery rhyme. Just one man that I recall could be deemed polite, though I did one day hear a priestly voice upbraid me with a stern and disappointed 'Shame on you', though — having lost my sense of aural direction by virtue of recently going completely deaf in one ear (a *real* virus, as it happens) — I could not identify the source of this correction.

What we are dealing with here is a new and infinitely more dangerous kind of stupid than anything we have witnessed hitherto. We are literally being imprisoned by the stupidity of others, who refuse to see that they are being lied to from morning till night, who snort in derision at those who seek to alert them, to urge that they turn off their TVs and read one of the thousands of articles that expose the official lies or/and explain why these lies are being purveyed. This stupidity, previously harmless enough, is the shackles that restrain our once free bodies, minds and souls, rendering us and our children and our children's children amenable to an unimaginable future of serfdom and coercion.

Once upon a time, stupidity was the preserve of the uneducated. In that sense, it came *before* schooling — it existed where the balm of instruction had not managed to extend. But the new kind of stupid is post-education: It affects those who have their arse pockets stuffed with papers proving their credentials and qualifications. Its symptoms are many, but the principal among them is the confusion/conflation of intelligence with powers of retention, causing honest people to fall into a misplaced demeanour of servility before it. In reality, this pseudo-intelligence majors in obedience to power and susceptibility to propaganda and public relations. It genuflects before science and delights in learning off jargon with which to bamboozle the commonsensical. I find it interesting that, when I move a mile or two from Dun Laoghaire centre, heading inland towards Sallynoggin and Ballybrack, the people I meet, though noticeably lacking this pseudo-intelligence, are as wide as gates to the trickery of the media and the political class. These people, who have earned their bread by making and mending things, have more smarts in their fingernails than the people I encounter, as a general rule, along the seafront.

In general, too, I find that shops and cafés in the area are pretty unhelpful in their enforcement of the face coverings laws, which means that anyone who is unwilling to demonstrate his servitude is, in effect, denied the right to buy anything to eat or drink in any of the main shops in Glasthule or Dalkey. I say 'unhelpful' here rather than 'literal', which is more what I intend, because, in reality, their behaviour is anything but a literal enforcement of the law. The relevant face covering regulations (they are not laws, and therefore legally unenforceable) — in Statutory Instrument 296 of 2020 — allow for exemptions from wearing such face-nappies, but none of the shopkeepers or their staffs have taken the trouble to check this out, and so abuse and unjustly humiliate decent long-standing customers who I trust will never darken their doors again. There are a few shops willing to treat people with decency and humanity, but I shall not mention which ones they are in the certain knowledge that in doing so, I would all but guarantee them a visit from the Covid Gestapo or some of the local Stasi snitches. I shall, however, continue to support their businesses while shunning for all time the other establishments, once this is over — if it ever ends.

Readers who have come this far with me may hereinafter understand why I was amused to read the leader in the November edition of the newsletter of the Sandycove and Glasthule Residents' Association, headed, 'Is There Anyone Listening', and bearing the subhead, 'The Democratic Deficit'.

It would be difficult to come across a more comical example of — what shall we say?: phlegmatism? obtuseness? naïveté? — as is detectable in the tone and content of said epistle.

It is astonishing that after the eight months we've put in, such an article could still be written and published without a hint of irony or a smidgen of detectable smarts. The only part of the article with a grain of quizzical truth in it is the headline: 'Is there anyone listening?' The answer is 'Yes: Big Brother is listening, and so is his ugly sister.'

THE ABOLITION OF REALITY 31

The topic of the editorial is the sudden burst of public works that began with the first lockdown in April: what the author calls 'cycle-paths', one-way traffic systems, new footpaths, street furniture, etc. The leader informs readers that these were introduced 'under special pandemic powers in line with central government policy'. The author does not pause there to ponder the following question: What in the name of the dead Nora Barnacle have cycle lanes got to do with a pandemic? Is cycling a cure for Covid? If not that, then what? More crucially, what is the nature and purpose of said government policy?

The author continues in a manner suggesting that the editorial may have been written sometime around the early 1990s, when questions of local government effectiveness were of the kind of high-class problem that concerned us then.

The 'democratic deficit' referred to is the fact that the powers of county councillors are not what they were: 'Whether you are for or against cycle-ways and the changes to our local area,' the author proposes, 'there is a question about the lack of political involvement in the decision-making process.'

Sadly, it appears that the day-to-day management of the council's activities is carried out by an executive council consisting of full-time officials led by the Chief Executive, whereas the powers of councillors are, in fact, quite minor, obscure and rarely used and a large number of powers that affect our daily lives are not reserved functions but are vested in officials. Many would say, the author guesses, 'that the balance of power should be moved towards the Councillors, but the prospect of such reform seems slim.'

No sherbert, Sherlock?

How shall I put this? It is time people started to open their eyes and look around them. It is time to banish from our minds any sense that the Covid 'crisis' is about Covid, about a pandemic, about a virus. The crisis of the present moment is the normalisation of the incredible, the unspeakable and the unthinkable. Unless we awaken very soon, the unthinkable is about to hit us. To call what is happening now a 'democratic deficit' is like saying that Mr Justice Séamus Woulfe has trouble taking a hint.

The word 'deficit' means 'shortfall'. But what do you call a shortfall that amounts to a total lack? What, for example, would you call the 'democratic deficit' of North Korea?

Anyone who has not yet grasped that we are long past the point of thinking that our problem is a 'democratic deficit' must have been in a coma since before Easter. Anyone who thinks that our problem resides in the failure of the government and/or council officials to consult the public before unleashing the cycle lane pandemic visited on our cities and towns in that period needs to take themselves into the office for a bit of a pep talk.

It is well past time for everyone to wake up, take off their face masks and start smelling coffee. The situation we are facing here, at the back end of the worst year in living memory, is not that our county councillors lack a sufficiency of power. It is that the erosion of our democracy has now reached a critical — which is to say *terminal* — stage. Yes, at a basic level of explication, the issue goes back to what in EU parlance is called 'subsidiarity' — the principle whereby political decision-making is supposed to take place at the lowest practicable level. Nobody cottoned on for a long time that this was merely an Orwellian-worded trick to open up the question of where decisions might be made so that the EU overlords could decide what the lowest practicable level was. Surprise, surprise: they decided, almost invariably, that the most practicable level was the highest possible level, which is to say with themselves. Thus did they strip not merely county councils but also national governments, of meaningful political authority.

But even that is not our problem now. Our problem now is that we have been subjected in 2020 to a coup d'état and are now being administered by a government-of-occupation. That this administration appears to be headed up by Irish people does nothing to change this: these people have long since been made aware of the conditions by which they continue to serve in any capacity in the governance of Ireland and are seemingly quite happy to collaborate with selling their own people down the river.

Secondly, the cycle lanes are not merely cycle lanes. Like everything else about the Time of Covid, they signal a radical shift in the administration of our culture, economy and society. They are much less about bikes and lycra than they are about the end of the internal combustion engine, the first stage in the replacement of the motor car, which will not-so-gradually be made more and more expensive, impracticable and prone to public disfavour. Within a decade or so, the motor car will disappear, and with it, one of the most glorious of the freedoms that technology has extended to ordinary human beings: the capacity to journey about your own country, driving where you please, without let or hindrance. The Garda checkpoints of the past eight months are simply a training exercise for what is to become an everyday experience — training for us, not the guards. I wonder, too: has the author of the aforementioned newsletter editorial noticed the tailbacks that are now an all-day, everyday 'experience' on roads all around Dun Laoghaire?

And while we're about it: Has the author heard of the Great Reset? If not, I suggest he amble along to Alex's paper shop and ask if they still have the recent edition of *Time* magazine with that precise topic, in as many words, on the cover. What the *journaliars* of the national fake news media have for years been calling a 'conspiracy theory' is now out in the open.

Here is the news. There is/was no pandemic. There probably was no specific virus, certainly not one identifiable or isolatable as SARS-CoV-2. The deaths were mostly either falsified or accelerated in people expected to die in any event in a matter of weeks or months, these being essential to pumping up the fear factor. The 'cases' currently being promoted by the *journaliars* are the result of manipulation-prone PCR tests, which can be ratcheted up or down depending on the requirements of the controllers.

All this has been deliberately rolled out on a global basis to turn reality inside out on behalf of the corporate elites who now lay claim to owning the world. The downstream consequences are much too complex to do more than give a glimpse of, though the Great Reset is already the topic of several sceptical books — none of which the good people of Glasthule, being loyal to the local fake news media, will have heard of. These books tell of the plans for the deliberate destruction of small businesses, the elimination of private property, the winding down of meaningful education, the introduction via mandatory vaccination of biometric ID, universal basic income and Chinese-style social credit systems, the incorporation of whole swathes of the human population into a digital grid using nanotechnologies, the forced obsolescence of the 'useless eaters' — all this in tandem with the escalation of existing programmes to roll out 'voluntary' euthanasia, the merging of existing religions into a single global church, and much more besides. If this is beginning to sound like Communism, then maybe my summary is not as inadequate as I fear.

I hope I have sufficiently dismayed the reader to deter any further worries about county councillors losing their powers. What we face — what the world faces unless it wakes up pronto — is a dystopia to make George Orwell seem as though the author of fairy tales for children. This is what Covid has been about. This is why they started on the cycle lanes within days of the first lockdown. This is what the 'regulations' are for: a training session for when Ireland becomes an open-air concentration camp for all except the elite few. Maybe some of the good denizens of Glasthule fancy themselves among that number, but I would not bet my shirt on it.

If anyone thinks this sounds incredible, fantastic, ridiculous, I can only agree with you. But let me, before signing off to go out and meet my ecstatic public, ask you one question: What would you have said if, a year ago, I had suggested that we would soon have politicians or 'health tsars' telling us how many people might be permitted to enter our homes and whether we could play board games with each other, and advising that we should leave our grandparents sitting by an open window in December so that they would not catch a cold?

CHAPTER 5
THE 'VICTORY' OF BONDAGE
02-12-2020

The Time of Covid has revealed to us something we would not have believed about our fellow human beings: that many of them are happier in slavery than in freedom.

Since virtually everyone's favourite 'conspiracy theory' is now turning out to be no more nor less than 'The News' — actually, The News that 'journalism' appears to exist to hide from you — I thought I'd float one of my own. It is that all those TV shows called *Big Brother, Celebrity Big Brother, Does Big Brother Get Off With Big Sister?* and *I'm a Celebrity, Get Me Out of Here* (spoiler alert: one of these titles is made up) were by way of preparing the masses for the Time of Covid.

Think now. Remember the vacant stares that came across the faces of your loved ones as the Hour of the House grew near and you were still on the beach — did it not anticipate by two decades the panic-stricken eyes peering up over the face masks of the zombies patrolling our streets these days for no better purpose than to find someone not wearing a face mask and give them a hard time? Think of the refusal of Big Bro fans to enter into any form of humour concerning their addiction/affliction; of the imperviousness to sarcasm, akin to profound deadness, they affected whenever anyone tried to suggest that there were more important things in life than watching people act out their incest fantasies on live TV.

It is strange, in retrospect, that they called it 'reality television'. Essentially a game show, the first *Big Brother* series on this side of the pond arrived on Channel 4 in 2000. It minutely followed the progress of eleven contestants, known as housemates, isolated for the duration from the outside world in a custom-built House. Each week, one or several of the housemates were evicted by a public vote. The last surviving housemate won a monetary prize. The show was predicated on nurturing in its audience anti-qualities like voyeurism, envy, schadenfreude, vindictiveness and lynch-love.

Those of us who gleaned our knowledge of this phenomenon from glancing down (appropriately!) at the tabloid headlines as we passed on our way to procure the latest *Popular Mechanics* or *Spectator* (call me a snob, but realise this: our snobbery is now the only thing that stands between us and barbarism) are now in a position to understand the meaning and timing of the *Big Brother* thing. It was, in the modern sense, educational, which is to say that its purpose was to explode, as though with a neutron bomb, every incipient thought in every adjacent mind and render its subject amenable to entrancement on the basis of a deep, unacknowledgeable craving to be locked up in their own Houses, lectured to and abused by distant figures of authority; treated like wayward children, punished and, occasionally, rewarded; to be made feel like nothing, to lose both responsibility and rights in a dizzying obliteration of identity; to be enslaved and to love the enslaver.

This is where we are, really. Let those of us who have been conscious for some time of something badly wrong herewith agree that we shall no longer drive ourselves crazy trying to explain the flaws with PCR testing or point out the absurdity of insisting on face coverings in order to 'save lives' and then dumping them on the footpath for every dog and devil to come along, lick and circulate. Let us look each other in the eye and realise that we have entered a new and very different world — a world, you might say, changed utterly, a world of terrible ugliness and stupidity and, yes, manifest evil. Let us begin to focus finally on the hidden psychic meanings of all this, the archetypes being exercised, the unsaid, unsayable aspects of what has been thrust upon us.

All civilisations tend to take their own mythologies literally, and these beliefs, usually transmitted by religion, have been the very buttresses of multiple civilisations, supporting their moral orders, cohesion, vitality and imaginations. There is here a paradox: the more a society moves towards rationalism, the more it risks disequilibrium and entropy by virtue of no longer holding fast to its founding and sustaining mythologies. Human life, as Nietzsche told us, depends for its propulsion on illusions. The loss of literal understandings of the founding myths leads to uncertainty and the collapse of values and moral order, to decay and degeneracy and, finally, to civilisational collapse. This, essentially, is the background to what we must belatedly realise has been the inevitable arrival of the Time of Covid.

It has been remarked many times already that there is a quasi-religious aspect to the Covid thing: the rituals, prohibitions, superstitions, sins and penitential rites. This is not accidental, an odd quirk of cultural harmonics. Because we have become so accustomed to seeing ourselves as an advanced technological people, this hypothesis seems implausible, but this is part of the genius of Covid: it renders sinful the human condition as previously the darker elements of Christianity used to do. To be human, prone to sickness, liable to become infectious, these are the newly-declared Mortal Sins of the Time of Covid.

The sin of contagiousness casts us into Hell, but Hell on Earth: Covid, thereby, has been the mechanism by which we have descended into the Underworld to encounter our own shadows. It is the last-ditch attempt of an atheistic age to meet in itself the innate human craving for a myth-based existence, the prior model having been scorned in the sloughing off of religion. It is as if even the most obtuse of the neo-atheistic leaders have come to realise that human beings do not function for long without two fundamental things: a capacity to find communal meaning to enable a living together with others in society, and a hope of overcoming mortality and transcending this life.

Covid makes all this available, albeit at the cost of everything we might not long ago have thought of as essential, and, most crucially, freedom. The core superstition of the Time of Covid is that through collective effort, we can overcome death — by 'saving lives', each other's lives, if only symbolically, or even theoretically, as an act of defiance against Nature and a spit in the face of the dead God. But this comes at the price of renewed fear at the level of fire and brimstone to the power of 10,000.

If we scan back through our rudimentary 'memories' of history, it may dawn upon us that we had been living through a short period of normalised fearlessness, a time that seemed naturalistic and unexceptionable but which was really an aberration: the period between the end of the Cold War and, say, Saint Patrick's Day 2020. Throughout history, the presence in culture of intense fear — of both life and the afterlife — has been the norm, and that is what our genetic make-up is best adapted to. Covid takes us back to the beginning.

The medical, scientific, political, economic and conspiratorial aspects to do with the Whys and Wherefores of Covid are important, interesting and often disturbing, but they are secondary to this point about what we might call the undertows of the Time of Covid. I believe in the Great Reset, the New World Order, the Fourth Industrial Revolution and the coming of Klaus Schwab and what he will soon be calling his Fourth Reich, but I insist that this is just the garden furniture. The 'garden' is the Garden of Eden, the locus of the founding myth of our civilisation, the mythical, mysterious origin of our mortality and the partitioning of our hearts into Good and Evil. Unbeknownst to ourselves, this 'memory' of the Fall haunts us, and causes us to roll it around in our subconscious minds as though the details of an avoidable traffic accident we had lived through ourselves. Because our understanding of mythology is so limited and so literal, and because our culture no longer reminds us of such elemental circumstances, we think our myths as dispensable as yesterday's newspaper.

By intent of forces unknown, or otherwise, Covid reconnects us with all this neglected and forgotten elemental interior weather.

As Joseph Campbell taught us, what happened in the Garden of Eden was that man, under the attrition of propaganda, impetuously chose the fruit that he believed would allow him to distinguish between Good and Evil over the more desirable fruit of eternal life. This, we are told, was the Original Sin of our species, and until now, this sin has not been matched for horrific or scarifying characteristics. In truth, it was much more than a sin: It was a loss so incalculable as to obsess the human race for all of its subsequent journey. (By the way, if anyone thinks that these forces can be avoided by the smirking assertion that the story of Eden is 'made up', let me just urge you to seek out Joseph Campbell and read him carefully: He is not saying what you want him to be saying.)

But then comes Covid, which turns into a sin or quasi-crime the very nature of the human being: the way he is built by God or evolution or God's evolutionary process, his paradoxical capacity to protect himself from sickness by becoming sick and spreading it around, his inbuilt capacity to strengthen himself and his neighbours by dint of temporary weakness, just as tiring and painful labour makes his body strong.

Those who have dreamed up Covid know this well: That the line dividing good and evil runs, as Solzhenitsyn told us, through every human heart, and that the struggle within us of these two forces defines every human being, whether we know it or not. And the dominant note of this struggle is fear, largely fear of the unknown, of the unpredictable, of responsibility, consequences, risk, all followed by unbridled terror of the certainty that is death, all the worse because it is denied. This fear demands to be made my master or my conquest.

Nothing brings out the badness in the human heart like those two elemental forces: fear of life and fear of death. These fears drive men to surrender not merely their own lives but also the lives of their fellows — to defend freedom or to give it away. Something we are being reminded of in the Time of Covid is that these two inclinations refer to two utterly different kinds of men. For one, it is axiomatic that life without freedom is not worth living; for the other, it is clear that risk of death is worse than any other prospect.

These latter are our true prospective gaolers, for there is not enough of any elite, Illuminati, Bilderbergers, or Davosians to achieve this on their own. And mark this: Such men exist; they are among us now, and they would sooner be slaves living lives of predictable misery than face the fear of the unknown or the risk of calling out their own fears. They would trade their rights and other freedoms for the freedom from responsibility, even responsibilities for their own lives. They would trade their children's lives for an hour's relief from the terror of living or the contemplation of death. What do they care for *your* freedoms?

It seems also that, somehow or another, human beings will always try to find ways of re-enslaving themselves, no matter how many times they have broken free in the past. It is as though not freedom, but something like its opposite, is the natural disposition of the average human being in society. The desire to be imprisoned, debased, humiliated, ridiculed, tortured psychologically and even physically by one's fellows, appears to be a driving desire of a significant majority of humans, at least in the sense that they are not prepared to risk paying any price to avoid it. They are content enough to be free, but, stumbling or nudged into the antithesis, they take to it like rats to a sewer.

'It is incredible,' wrote Etienne de la Boétie, almost half a millennium ago, 'how as soon as a people become subject, it promptly falls into such complete forgetfulness of its freedom that it can hardly be roused to the point of regaining it, obeying so easily and willingly that one is led to say that this people has not so much lost its liberty as won its enslavement.' So observed la Boétie in 1549, in *The Politics of Obedience: The Discourse of Voluntary Servitude*. Yes: 471 years ago.

La Boétie said that it is not as simple as deciding that people obey just out of fear. Rather, he proposed, they obey out of habit, short-sighted self-interest, greed, and love of privilege, or under the influence of state trickery, such as propaganda and symbolism — a near-perfect synopsis of the Time of Covid.

But the greatest of these forces today, I would say, is fear, and fear is at the root of them all, the fear of facing life in its deepest recesses.

La Boétie's thesis is that the state, which is to say a tiny minority of the population, will always try to dominate the majority and is always in danger of being permitted to do so because most among the majority will refuse to exercise their power to overthrow such a tyranny. The paradox that he seeks to illuminate is that the tyrant has solely the power given to him by those he oppresses: 'Where has he acquired enough eyes to spy upon you, if you do not provide them yourselves? How can he have so many arms to beat you with if he does not borrow them from you? The feet that trample down your cities, where does he get them if they are not your own? How does he have any power over you except through you? How would he dare assail you if he had no cooperation from you?'

Take a look at the police rampaging through the streets of London last weekend, arresting old men with placards and women in disability scooters, and read those lines aloud to yourself as you do so.

And how about this for an ominous prognosis:

'Men will grow accustomed to the idea that they have always been in subjection,' he wrote, 'that their fathers lived in the same way; they will think they are obliged to suffer this evil, and will persuade themselves by example and imitation of others, finally investing those who order them around with proprietary rights, based on the idea that it has always been that way.'

By the way, have you bought in yet those cardboard plates the Man from NPHET says to get for your Christmas dinner?

The former judge of the UK Supreme Court, the wondrous Lord Jonathan Sumption, who has been resisting the lockdown across the water from its beginning last spring, said similar things just six months ago in a BBC interview:

'The real problem is that when human societies lose their freedom, it's not usually because tyrants have taken it away. It's usually because people willingly surrender their freedom in return for protection against some external threat. And the threat is usually a real threat but usually exaggerated. That's what I fear we are seeing now. The pressure on politicians has come from the public. They want action. They don't pause to ask whether the action will work. They don't ask themselves whether the cost will be worth paying. They want action anyway. And anyone who has studied history will recognise here the classic symptoms of collective hysteria. Hysteria is infectious. We are working ourselves up into a lather in which we exaggerate the threat and stop asking ourselves whether the cure may be worse than the disease.'

What would we give to have in our midst but one figure of such stature but even half the gumption of Lord Sumption at this hour!

What we surely realise from all this is that the impulse to tyranny, inbuilt into the modern bureaucratic state, is matched by the desire to be subjugated apparently hard-wired into a majority of human beings. These moments of the Time of Covid were therefore inevitable, and those of us who have lived a long time in these accidentally free societies — free because no one was really paying attention, like free parking in Dublin in the glorious, long-gone Time of the Lockhards (ask your father!) — were actually on borrowed time.

Let us, then, we who have reached a great age in relative freedom by the standards of any age, resolve to do two things: Give thanks for our deliverance even for a part of our lives from the cravenness of our fellow man and at the same time determine to spend what time is left to us to fight so that those coming after us who might be inclined to desire freedom rather than slavery might have a chance of knowing it. To this end, we must determine to ignore and bypass the lassitude and will-to-collaboration of our neighbours, those tragic meat robots who are so lethally content in their servitude as to look on us already as their infectious enemies, as they bang their pots and sing in their chains like the sea.

Though the average man may not be relied upon to fight for even his own freedom, La Boétie believed that, in times of great danger, it would always fall to a few clear-thinking individuals to save the rest: 'Even if liberty had entirely perished from the earth, such men would invent it. For them, slavery has no satisfactions, no matter how well disguised.'

The implication is clear: There is no cavalry but us.

YEAR TWO
2021

▢ **16 Feb - (Ch 10)** *Save the Last Trance for Me* ——

⊕ 15 Feb - US extends homeowner foreclosure protections

⊕ 22 Feb - US reported deaths pass 500K

⊕ 24 Feb - US President restarts immigrant entry into US

⊕ 27 Feb - FDA approves "vaccine" by Johnson & Johnson for emergency use

⊕ 28 Feb - Number of Covid-19 "vaccine" adverse event reports exceeded 100,000 in the US VAERS system

▮▮ 01 Mar - Classroom return for second-level students

▮▮ 17 Mar - Annual St Patrick's Day White House presidential meeting with the Taoiseach held via video call

⊕ 25 Mar - US to invest $10B for "vaccines" to hard-hit areas

⊕ 13 Apr - After 6 cases of thrombosis with thrombocytopenia syndrome, J&J "Vaccine" paused by FDA and CDC

⊕ 15 Apr - Reported deaths globally pass 2M

⊕ 23 Apr - FDA and CDC lift pause on J&J "vaccine" but limit use to those 18+ where other "vaccine" not possible

▮▮ 29 Apr - The Taoiseach announces "hope and caution" with phased reopening of the economy beginning with hairdressers, beauticians and barbers from May 10. "Vaccinated" grandparents would be allowed to meet grandchildren.

⊕ 29 Apr - US delivering $100M+ in "vaccines" to India

⊕ 30 Apr - India reports 400K new cases and 3.5K deaths in one day. Passes 2.5M active cases.

⊕ 04 May - US announces goal to "vaccinate" 70% of American adults by July 4, 2021

⊕ 13 May - US fully "vaccinated" no longer require masks at DOD facilities

▮▮ 07 Jun - Outdoor hospitality allowed to resume

⊕ 10 Jun - US announces 500M Pfizer "vaccines" donated to 92 poorer countries

⊕ 15 Jun - US reported deaths pass 600K

⊕ 25 Jun - FDA warns of increased myocarditis and pericarditis risks from Pfizer and Moderna "vaccines"

⊕ 25 Jun - US announces 3M J&J "vaccines" donated to Afghanistan

⊕ 07 Jul - Reported deaths globally pass 4M

- 12 Jul - "Fully vaccinated" begin receiving EU Digital Covid-19 Certificates.
- 13 Jul - FDA warns of increased Guillain-Barré Syndrome risks from J&J "vaccine"
- 19 Jul - EU certificates implemented for travel, easing restrictions into and out of the country. Those without certificates can pay for up to €400 for private PCR tests
- 19 Jul - US announces 1M "vaccines" donated to Gambia, Senegal, Zambia, and Niger, and 3M to Guatemala
- 26 Jul - After almost 500 days, pubs and restaurants allowed to resume indoor dining and drinking
- 27 Jul - CDC recommends masks indoors in substantial transmission areas
- 28 Jul - US reinstates mask requirement for "fully vaccinated" at DOD facilities
- 29 Jul - US directs all federal government employees and onsite contractors attest to "vaccination" status (or wear a mask, physically distance, go through a screening, and be restricted on official travel)
- 30 Jul - CDC recommends everyone wear a mask in indoor public settings in areas of transmission, regardless of "vaccination" status. Publish data showing "vaccinated" are infected with and transmit Delta virus at same rate as purebloods

- 02 Aug - 70% of US adults have taken one dose of "vaccine", almost one month behind goal
- 04 Aug - Reported cases globally passes 200M
- 09 Aug - US Secretary of Defense seeks approval to make "vaccina-tion" mandatory for all military
- 12 Aug - FDA authorizes additional "vaccine" dose for certain immunocompromised people
- 13 Aug - CDC recommends additional dose of "vaccine" for those with moderately compromised immune systems after initial 2 doses
- 18 Aug - US announces "vaccination" requirement for long-term Medicare/Medicaid care workers
- 23 Aug - FDA full approval of "vaccine" by Pfizer for those 16+
- **23 Aug - (Ch 11)** *The Groupthink Psychodemic, Part I: Danger in Numbers* ——
- 25 Aug - US military begin full "vaccination" of all members of all active duty or in Ready Reserve, including National Guard
- **25 Aug - (Ch 12)** *The Groupthink Psychodemic, Part II, Groupthink Minus Thought* ——
- 26 Aug - CDC warns against use of Ivermectin

29 Aug - (Ch 13) *The Groupthink Psychodemic, Part III, Slouching Towards Totalitaria* ———

31 Aug - Number of Covid-19 "vaccine" adverse event reports exceeded 500,000 in the US VAERS system

05 Sep - (Ch 14) *The Truth is Unmistakable for anything Else* ———

09 Sep - US EOs require "vaccination" for all federal employees and contractors

22 Sep - FDA authorizes booster dose of Pfizer "vaccine"

04 Oct - US mandates "full vaccinations" for all DOD civilian employees

07 Oct - (Ch 15) *Covid Totalitarianism: The Deification of Error* ———

19 Oct - (Ch 16) *Anticipating the Technotarian (post-Covid) New World 'Order'* ———

20 Oct - FDA authorizes booster dose of Moderna and J&J "vaccines"

22 Oct - After 18 months nightclubs and other late venues temporarily allowed to open.

25 Oct - US announces "full vaccination" requirement for all foreign travelers to the US

29 Oct - FDA authorizes Pfizer "vaccine" for children ages 5-11 for emergency use

01 Nov - Reported deaths globally pass 5M

02 Nov - CDC recommends everyone ages 5+ get "vaccinated"

19 Nov - FDA and CDC authorize boosters of Pfizer and Moderna "vaccines" for all adults

29 Nov - US prohibits entry of noncitizens from 8 countries in southern Africa due to new Omicron Covid-19 variant

03 Dec - Taoiseach confirms Covid-19 restrictions for the Christmas season. Maximum of four households allowed to meet for Christmas dinner. Nightclubs again closed. Bars and restaurants only allowed six adults per table with no multiple table bookings allowed.

16 Dec - CDC clarifies shots made by Moderna and Pfizer preferred over J&J's

22 Dec - FDA authorizes Pfizer's antiviral pill, Paxlovid, for infected not needing hospitalization

23 Dec - FDA authorizes Merck's antiviral pill, molnupiravir.

23 Dec - Minister for Health Stephen Donnelly announces booster vaccines for everyone aged 30+ from 29 December, and to all from 10 January.

CHAPTER 6
A NOUVEAU ARISTOCRACY?: WE WILL IN OUR ARSE!
01-01-2021

One of the most timely books of 2020 painted a bleak picture of the emerging cleavage of the post-equality, post-democratic, post-Christian West — a rich-poor divide never seen before.

I've detected of late some interesting and unexpected stirrings in the undergrowth of American leftism. In the Era of Wokeness, in which the conch of social solidarity has been stolen by pseudo-progressives interested only in harnessing the victim classes to promote the interests of the most powerful, there are the slightest signs of the old left beginning to reassert itself. As though finally waking up to the smell of burnt coffee, some of these dozing followers of Marx are beginning to emerge not so much to confront or even question the faux leftism of such as the Democratic Party, but simply to sharpen some old saws about reality, economics and the common good.

I'm thinking of an economist like Richard D. Wolff, a Marxist visiting professor in Massachusetts and New York, who, if you can sidestep his intermittent disdain for President Trump, is a source of some of the most dependable available analyses of current economic drifts, in particular regarding the continuing stock market bubble that obscures the underlying reality that the already crumbling economic foundations of the West have been hollowed out by the Covid scam.

Another such figure is Joel Kotkin, a New Yorker currently living in Orange County, California, who specialises in demographics and urban planning — another old-style leftie who now insists that left-right paradigms are no longer up to capturing the shapes and drifts of the emerging world. Kotkin published one of the most interesting and timely books of 2020: *The Coming of Neo Feudalism: A Warning to the Global Middle Class* (Encounter Books), perhaps the most up-to-date account of the present sociological, economic and political moment to appear in the recent traumatising months.

Most of what Kotkin relates is not particularly new, but it is subject matter that, for reasons of ideology, is often concealed or *sotto voce*-ed by the legacy media in favour of misleading narratives about racism and a certain limited interpretation of concepts like 'equity' and 'equality'.

Kotkin paints a picture of a future of unprecedented inequality, but not the kind that the Woke agitators bang on about. He describes a world in which a new cleaving is imposing itself — has pretty much already done so — between the top one per cent and the rest, in effect eliminating what we used to call the middle and working classes. That this has happened during a period in which, on the face of things, the left was in control of the vast majority of media platforms, of both the legacy and newer kinds, is a matter we would be paying more attention to were it not a verboten topic. This cleavage is the topography of the 'neo-feudalism' of Kotkin's title.

The book is remarkable for the fact that it contains almost none of the conventional landmine Woke irritants you tend to stumble over in almost any book or article purporting to describe the world as it is today. There are occasional flashes that betray the colour of Kotkin's politics, but in general, this is a book that might be read without discomfort by any populist or Deplorable. The book deals with Trump in just two brief sections, and does so fairly; in interviews, generally with leftists less sentient and open-minded than himself, Kotkin invariably gets down to genuflect at the altar of Never Trumpism, whereas in his analysis, he invariably goes on to extend credit to the President for his perception of the core problems of America and the steps he has already taken to ameliorate them.

Kotkin describes a world that has actually ceased to progress and started to regress, that is shucking off many of the developments that accompanied the growth of Western civilisation in the past 2,500 years — the universal franchise, the rule of law, bills of rights, privacy, free speech and individualism, as well as even more crucial entities like the nuclear family and the private motor car.

Kotkin confides the disturbing theory that, whereas those of us who have arrived in the recent years of this period tend to regard it as no more nor less than naturalistic normality, it may in time reveal itself as an aberration in human history, about to be strangled by the ideological weeds we carelessly allowed to catch hold of our culture. Freedom, sang Kris Kristofferson, is 'just another word for nuthin' left to lose', but could soon become a word denoting everything we've lost. Unless, unless . . . But what if there is no 'unless'?

Kotkin takes us to California, once the leftist utopian showroom, now the American state with the most wealth and the worst poverty, where the divide is currently being played out in the widening chasm between Silicon Valley and the new slums of San Francisco, where diseases like typhoid and possibly the bubonic plague may be on the point of a comeback. Meanwhile, Western demographics have been in rag order for decades, while its political class continues fondly to imagine that replacing Europeans with economic migrants from alien cultures amounts to a strategy for future equilibrium.

I don't think so. The future of the West, according to Kotkin's persuasive analysis, will include the collapse of the nation-state, the virtual eradication of family homes, the elimination of most paid work, the emergence of new caste systems and gated cities, the decline of sexual activity, the explosion of loneliness, creeping censorship arising from the increasingly leftward tilt of academia and media, the exponential growth of state power and authoritarianism, and the return to nature of vast swathes of the cultivated world.

The social/ideological division Kotkin describes is, in effect, between the 'hubs' and the 'heartlands', between the cynically 'woke' exploiters of the internet Wild West and the people who make and mend the world on a day-to-day basis, between the Able Men of Greek mythology and the metrosexual soyboys of the networks and the lycra-lanes. He describes a world increasingly in the grip of tech oligarchs hiding behind wokist slogans to further a deeply reactionary power structure, one that, if allowed to continue, will bury democracy and make of the vast majority of non-trillionaire humans a new underclass of chattel-less serfs. The new oligarchs are served by a secondary class Kotkin calls the 'clerisy', mainly the buffer layer of 'experts' and mediators like journalists and academics, who, in return for crumbs from the oligarchic tables, provide the new aristocracy with ideological air-cover. The ranks of this clerisy are dotted, bizarrely, with refugees from traditional leftism, unable to figure out why they have been caught offside by history, and mostly not that bothered to find out; where once they railed against the capitalist exploiter, now they bow down before his successor, the baseball-capped, T-shirted geek who spouts communitarian slogans while looting and ransacking everything of value in the world that is not nailed down. The core of this ideology is the hoax of progressivism, really no more than a smokescreen to conceal the studied further enrichment of the already obscenely wealthy, a Trojan horse to take the oligarchs past the madding crowd at the gates of the New Jerusalem. The combination of globalist anti-values, technologised reality and postindustrial capitalist actuality will, Kotkin predicts, create conditions in which the majority will be reduced to subsistence living in hive cities, as the West moves inexorably towards a Chinese model of constant surveillance and social control schemes.

Kotkin's book hit the streets just as the Covid shitshow was kicking off, and so reads from start to finish as an exercise in ignoring the elephant in the elevator. This might seem merely bad luck, except that, judging from his interviews, the author appears not to have noticed that the Time of Covid is, in effect, a pilot study for the now scheduled feudal 'new normal'. He speaks of the virus as a dangerous bug that has randomly disrupted the world — seemingly oblivious that it represented the culmination of his analysis even while the print was still wet on his pages. Yet, an updated online blurb for the book begins: 'Our society is being rapidly reduced to a feudal state, a process now being exacerbated by the Covid-19 pandemic.'

For real. According to a report from UBS and PwC Switzerland, the wealth of the world's billionaires grew by 27.5% in just the four months from April to July 2020, bringing the total wealth of a handful of unfathomably wealthy individuals to an unprecedented $10 trillion. The four biggest tech firms, Amazon, Apple, Facebook and Google, have a combined 'GDP' equal to that of France and increasingly act like global powers rather than mere companies. Meanwhile, millions of the world's most economically exposed people were losing their livelihoods, perhaps permanently, with more and more people pushed into extreme poverty. In the face of this calamity, the trad left has been studiously looking the other way, while maintaining a constant prattle about trans rights and spurious BLM victimology.

Even as things stood before, the richest 40 Americans had more wealth than the poorest 185 million, and both groups were already expanding disproportionately. Those will soon be the good old days. Kotkin charts the decline of meritocracy as a valued ethic and the resulting arrest of the upward mobility that has been America's unique selling point in the economic firmament, with US social mobility having fallen by 20 per cent in the past four decades. Europe is trailing under these headings, but not by much. Ireland, by virtue of its now almost total dependence on American corporations, is likely to be among the frontrunners in taking the fast lane to the new feudalism.

Is this, then, our civilisation's destiny? Perhaps, perhaps not. In spite of the best efforts of the corrupt legacy media, the world is beginning to awaken to the dire threats confronting the existing freedoms and ways of life of normal people. The populist revolution of the past five years has represented an awakening to the fact that the world is no longer being run for the benefit of its population. Those who have risen up in response to Trump, Salvini and the others do so in defence of their way of life and the birthright they had presumed the right to hand on to their children. Despite Joel Kotkin's scepticism, I do not imagine that Zuckerberg, Gates and Bezos have much chance against these people with their dander up.

The late journalist, Breandán O hEithir, in his 1986 book *The Begrudger's Guide to Irish Politics*, relates a story from the West Cork of his own childhood and Ireland's childhood in independence, in which, on the morning after the signing of the Anglo-Irish Treaty of 1921, the local parish priest encounters the doughty local blacksmith on the roads and hails him with the greeting, 'We're going to have our own gentry now!' He is met, without a missed beat, by a spirited, 'We will in our arse have our own gentry!'

Little did we imagine that, after all our days of struggle and growth and setbacks and progress and moral victories and disappointments, we would find ourselves threatened with being back again where we started on that December morning: bowing down not before a crowned royal but a baseball-capped soyboy with a secret desire to rule everything and everyone that crossed his path.

But I have news for Jack and Mark and Jeff: Underneath the propagandised mind of the modern Paddy lies a reservoir of spirit and ferocity that will burst out like a flash flood once the tipping point is reached.

Nothing fundamental has changed. If they think Paddy a soft touch, they think wrong.

A neo-feudal Ireland? A nouveau aristocracy?

We will in our arse.

CHAPTER 7
THE KING IS DEAD
30-01-2021

It's like rock and roll never happened.

An inescapable insight emerges from the lockdown: today's young are not what the young once were. Scanning western streetscapes, it is hard to miss that the ones wearing face masks are not overwhelmingly — as one might expect — the old and vulnerable, but include a disquieting number of youngsters, all but immune to SARS-CoV-2, who wear their acquiescence in the current plunge into tyranny like a pendant of courage along with their Nike Airs and Buck Mason Mavericks.

It's like rock 'n' roll never happened. Or, rather, as if the rock 'n' roll spirit had never proclaimed the rejection of slavery and subjugation. Once social distancing restrictions are cancelled (if they are), these young people will flock again to hear Coldplay and U2, oblivious to something ineluctable in themselves: they are missing the point. Try as you might, you will not find a photograph anywhere of John Lennon wearing a face mask — although you can purchase a 'John Lennon face mask' with the slogan 'War is over' for $10. You can also get an Elvis mask offering 'three layers of protection', with a choice of legend: 'Always on my mind' or 'TCB'. There's even one of Johnny Cash giving the finger — why not get the point while missing it?

For more than a half-century, rock 'n' roll was central to the formation and initiation of young westerners, influencing, inspiring, broadening horizons. Born of the congress between black music and white, this revolutionary form exploded in 1953 in Sam Phillips's studio in Memphis before going on to create, for the first time in history, a bespoke youth consciousness with its own soundtrack. From the opening notes of 'That's All Right', Elvis urged the world to awake to freedom, desire, change, life, calling 'Time!' on post-war torpor and weariness. His early songs were the manifesto of a new sensibility that declined the strictures of existing authority and the infallibility of adulthood.

The rock 'n' roll spirit was neither primarily ideological nor big-P political, but an existential refusal, born of the surprise of the rock 'n' roll encounter, which instantly inoculated against the acquiescent or banal. The rebellion was as much image as sensibility, attitude as conviction. It repudiated all forms of authority from parental to divine and asserted the vindication of human desire in its most immediate forms as the defining ethic of the age. The energy of those early moments later energised a decade, the Sixties — especially 1968 and its rejection of the political assumptions of the time. Sam Phillips later said that, until Elvis walked in the door, he hadn't known what he was looking for. He just knew it would be something uniquely new, something that didn't fit, didn't make any sense of or reflect life in America as it then was: something that made everything a little bit irrelevant, created confusion, didn't allow people to feel safe in ways they'd grown used to.

This existential shopping list hardly describes the rock 'n' roll kids of 2020, who happily wear face diapers that are unnecessary, useless, spiritually destructive and actively harmful to the wearer's health. Instead of an existential revolution or even the soundtrack for one, millennials have given us in cancel culture a phenomenon that has unleashed a trembling unknown since the days of Joe McCarthy, diverting their own idealism into trolling and snitching one another up for any shortfall in compliance with the diktats of PC.

Whereas the present generations appear at first sight *engagé*, their disposition is afflicted by a lassitude born of curiosity deficit. They seek to torch all history — including that of the music they have appropriated — on the altar of Woke. Superficially they appear the most ideological youth generation ever, but their convictions are *imposed* — by collective entrancement via technology and media — rather than organically grown in life experience. The result is a short-circuiting of existential energies into a narrow and virtually monolithic ideological outlook that has flipped the values of the erstwhile counterculture. As music fans, they are but zombie consumers of image, sounds and attitudes, ogling the practitioner successors to Hank and Muddy who see common cause not with the downtrodden but the elites. Mostly, these days, this seems to rinse down to dinosaur Never-Trumping, Springsteen dissing the president elected by characters from his songs and Neil Young filing suit against the Trump re-election campaign for paying homage to his music at public rallies.

To a degree, the Atlantic has divided rock 'n' roll by sensibility, a split readily observable in comparing the Ramones with the Clash. The American ethos understood rock as a force for freeing souls and imaginations; the UK scene tended a little more toward social observation and action. Early on, the Beatles pursued a music capable of framing great profundities. Lennon had understood that rock 'n' roll was capable of operating at the higher levels of reflection — provoking discussion as much as dance moves, but also catapulting the heart, gut and privates into a dance of understanding that left words standing by the wall. European rock, emerging in its full maturity with Kraftwerk, was more cerebral than its American progenitor, more preoccupied with ideas. Kraftwerk sought to build a sonic path to the present without going through the dark national past. European pop largely eschewed the Anglo-American rootedness in blues, sorrow, mud and sex, in search of an idiom focused on the subtexts of hyper-modern reality: atomization, alienation, the sleepwalks of reason and common sense. Rather than strings, wood and air, it gravitated to plastic, knobs and circuits, as though searching for the voice of a new kind of human, enmeshed in technology and observing his own osmotic mechanization. This probing was arrested in Manhattan on January 10, 2016, with the death of David Bowie, but its prophecies moved shortly towards fulfilment.

Rock 'n' roll was only sporadically left-wing. Born in the plantations of America's deep South, its seed emerged from the hollering of brother-to-brother up along the chain gang. Steeped in Mississippi mud, the blues merged with Negro spiritual singing and country, itself the offspring of Irish folk songs, far-travelled in the hearts of emigrants fleeing famine at home to beget what emerged in Sam Phillips's kitchen. The insinuation that music is a medium for social commentary is a misunderstanding arising from a couple of aberrations and misappropriation by rock journalism, an importunate, parasitical offshoot of the artform. Musicians seeking column inches went along for the ride; hence, the studied virtue-signalling of such as Shakey and the Boss. Rock 'n' roll, it really ain't.

The true greats never saw it like that. Take Dylan, still the conscience of the form — not by dint of stances but for remaining true to his own experience. In his 2004 published *Chronicles, Volume One*, he nominated the 1964 Republican US presidential candidate, Barry Goldwater, as his favourite politician, and debunked his own reputation as a symbol of resistance.

'I had a wife and children whom I loved more than anything else in the world. I was trying to provide for them, keep out of trouble, but the big bugs in the press kept promoting me as the mouthpiece, spokesman, or even conscience of a generation. That was funny. All I'd ever done was sing songs that were dead straight and expressed powerful new realities. I had very little in common with and knew even less about a generation that I was supposed to be the voice of. I'd left my hometown only ten years earlier, wasn't vociferating the opinions of anybody. My destiny lay down the road with whatever life invited, had nothing to do with representing any kind of civilization. Being true to myself, that was the thing. I was more a cowpuncher than a Pied Piper.'

Perhaps music is not revolutionary, but only appears so because it prefigures things rather than making them happen. If so, the stultification of Woke may be a warning that the variations have all been played and revolution is no longer conceivable. 'Change,' observed Jacques Attali in *Noise: The Political Economy of Music*, 'is inscribed in noise faster than it transforms society. Music is prophetic because . . . it explores, much faster than material reality can, the entire range of possibilities in a given code. It makes audible the new world that will gradually become visible.'

Perhaps the world changes itself, and the music merely provides the backbeat. Political freedom amounts, simply, to the right to be left alone with life's mysteriousness. What matters is the artist's existence, gaze and repose, not his attitude, which is merely the grain of grit on which the pearl forms. The point is not to 'say' something but to *make* something that exists as a witness to life. A song, then, is neither placard nor pamphlet, but the fullest enrichment of the human breath. You cannot sing through a face mask, nor would there be a point.

There was a time when the rock 'n' roll refusal represented a real threat, but that moment has lately passed, with the atrophying of the music's founding spirit. The young of 2020 lack both a necessity to overcome their immediate context and an attentive appetite for something greater than themselves — inevitabilities arising respectively from expanding prosperity and the death of God. Youth has been drained of all passion and empathy, so only ersatz emotions and responses survive. The rock 'n' roll consciousness retains nothing but self-consciousness. Once a Trojan horse laden with magical understandings, the music has shrivelled into a mere repository of harmlessly harmonizing *dangs and twangs*, ambient noises for the lifestyles of generations who consume them like Kool-Aid. And the conditions that prevent the 'youth of today' from creating their own artforms and content render the young amenable also to acquiescence in establishment and corporate manipulation and recruitable as evangelists of tyrannical impositions.

Rock 'n' roll was essentially an alternative way of hearing life's promises. It delivered not thoughts but something beyond thinking, not messages of hope but hope itself. It was, above all, about remaining outside the herd, remaining totally oneself, above all about resisting tyranny — a music indubitably most unWoke.

CHAPTER 8
TOO BAD, IT'S UTOPIA!
02-02-2021

If we have arrived at what Aldous Huxley called 'the ultimate revolution', we have done so without any further alerts from the writers who followed his and George Orwell's attempts to warn us.

I n 1993, I wrote a play, *Long Black Coat*, which could be described as an exploration of the apocalypse of fatherlessness. At the time, I was myself childless, but over the proximate years had been encountering or receiving fragmentary signals concerning a syndrome almost nobody was publicly talking about: the abuse of fathers in family law courts by judges implementing either an outmoded concept of childrearing, or feminist prejudice, or both.

The core of the play was symbolically apocalyptic. I based the central metaphor on a childhood memory of a pamphlet that had been issued to every Irish house, at the height of the Cold War, which every householder was supposed to have read and studied: a Civil Defence instruction manual describing the correct response to a nuclear attack. To minimise the risk of damage from nuclear fall-out, householders were to fill their wardrobes with earth from the garden and place them in the windows. They were also to stack all their books on the kitchen table and take their families into the literary igloo thus constructed. It was superficially ludicrous but also, for me, strangely evocative of something, perhaps of the survivalist vibe in *The Swiss Family Robinson*, which I loved as a child.

The play unfolded in such a situation, wherein two men — a young man, Jody, and a much older one, his father ('Old Man' in the script) — engaged in a running argument as they constructed their bunker, about the reasons why the young man's young son was not with them at this possibly terminal moment. The young man blamed his father's generation of men for having soured the groundwater with patriarchal misbehaviour; the old man blamed his son for being weak. Armageddon loomed over a space dominated by a 'futuristic' 3-D headset, a kind of skeletal dinosaur head through which the viewer could enter the 'news' as though himself a participant. There was some talk of 'sheltering in place'. A third character came in for the last five minutes, a familiar gobdaw type about the same age as Jody, who revealed that the 'crisis' had been over for days, and they hadn't twigged because their headset had stopped functioning.

The weird thing is that, even though this was not stated, I intended the play to be set in 2020. I had not been thinking of the precise year as a crucial factor, being mainly concerned that the play occur in a moment sufficiently distant in time to open possibilities of changes that need not be explained. In seeking approximately to place the date in a plausible future moment, the year 2020 may have wormed its way into my head because of the connotations concerning normative vision, and also the insinuation of establishing a vantage point in the future from which the past — the present of the performance — could be surveyed. I had been hoping, I think, to suggest the possibility of a totally changed mindset in which the origins of independent Ireland had ceased to represent a cultural problem. Although there were no explicit references in the play to a date, by way of a clue, the young man was wearing a faded T-shirt with an image of Padraig Pearse and the slogan '1916-2016'. The critics mostly decided this meant it was set in 2016, taking the device as literally as critics invariably take everything, with a couple of critics seeing all kinds of allusions and allegories to nationalist ideas that weren't there. The point was it was an *old, faded* T-shirt!

The anticipation of some kind of major world crisis in 2020 was a collateral factor, and not in the least intended to be germane to the play's meaning. I've always been of a pretty rational mentality, by which I mean that I buy into stuff only if I've experienced it, but I've always been alert to the possibility of phenomena I may have experienced without understanding them or even paying them proper attention. Thomas Sheridan, in his book *Walpurgis Night*, about the occult tendencies of Adolf Hitler, refers to a syndrome of something like accidental prediction as 'intuitive magic' and 'artistic divination'. Sheridan himself used the term 'new normal' on page 197 of his 2011 book on psychopathy, *Puzzling People: The Labyrinth of the Psychopath*. He's not, he says, a seer, just good at reading the zeitgeist. 'I must have picked up on the colossal foreshadowing of what's coming now, blasting back in time,' I heard him say on one of his YouTube livestreams, back around the middle of 2020.

That's how I think my 1994 play came to acquire its 'prophetic' tendencies. Because it dealt with a subject of profound interest to me — fatherhood (though I was not yet a father) — and because I pursued the emotional potential of this idea to the utmost of my capacity, I somehow acquired the collateral benefit of artistic divination, enabling me to enter a part of my imagination in which the future was already knowable. This syndrome is related to another, in a more general context, whereby if you do something badly or misguidedly with the right intention, the outcome will exceed your hopes and expectations. Call that God's handiwork; call it the harmony of the Universe; call it what you will. I have found it to be real.

For the recent Winter Conference of the de Nicola Center for Ethics and Culture, 'We Belong to Each Other', at the University of Notre Dame, Indiana, USA, I was asked to speak on the topic 'What writers owe their readers'. This essay is the long-form version of what I set out to say. You'll find the video of the actual discussion on YouTube.*

Writers/artists owe not just to their readers but to their *peoples* that they reveal to them the deepest truths about reality, based on close scrutiny and immersed experience. Each writer owes his or her people the fruits of the unique subjectivity gifted them in reality, the perspective that is theirs alone.

There is within artistic/literary circles — and for some reasons acutely in Irish ones — a clinging to the idea of art and literature as removed from reality: art for art's sake, too lofty and precious to get down and grubby in the real world. But all artists, all writers, have worldviews, and those who pretend not to are perhaps the most dangerous because they support the status quo with a stolidity that, while determinedly reactionary, preserves for itself a form of plausible deniability that is almost impossible for the untrained observer to penetrate.

The current generations of writers have mostly failed to meet this duty and so have failed their people. Why? Because they failed to tell the truth about reality. And this because they have ceased to extricate themselves from the semblance we mistake for reality and see that it is no longer real, but something constructed around each human person to imprison him in lies.

The proofs are in, in the knowledge, now undeniable, that the world has lately taken a sharp turn that almost no significant writer of the past half-century — in virtually any medium — conveyed more than a flashing glimpse of in advance.

We take breath at a moment when, if one were a certain kind of writer — indeed possibly any kind of writer — it might be necessary to ask oneself some pretty tough questions. Like: how relevant is your work? I don't mean, 'How relevant has it been?' or, 'How relevant has it appeared?' — these questions perhaps now fatefully amount to the same thing. I mean, 'How relevant is it *now* — and not just to this moment, but from this moment onwards?' How relevant

---

You can find the video by searching for: 'What Do We Owe to Our Readers: Literature in Conversation – dCEC Winter Conference'

is it in the longer run? Is it work that, in 20 years, people will look to and declare to have been prophetic, work that summoned up the age just past, and possibly continuing? Does its trajectory in the years to this moment carry the trace of a journey to where we have arrived, and where we appear to be going?

How many writers, if we dig behind the surface elegance of their words, have grappled with or touched upon things like: the ominous uncontrolled march of technology; the associated neo-colonialism of Big Tech and Big Pharma; the failure of society to keep step with these drifts in the inside lane of ethical growth; the abandonment by the left of its traditional base among the Able classes; the growing disrespect of elites for democratic principles; the sly machinations of the Bilderbergers and Trilateralists; the early signs of Cultural Marxism from the first twitches of third-wave feminism, LGBT agitation and the growth of the race industry; the obsessive preoccupation with sexuality and sexual alternativism; the relentless attacks on the family in culture and via family law intrusion into the most intimate relationships; the general descent into hedonism; the cultural context of growing anxiety; the death of God as a serious subject; the seemingly calculated deracination of the world's predominant civilisation; the limitless creation *ex nihilo* of spurious wealth; the exploitation of green scaremongering to oppress and subjugate; the moral inversion at the heart of culture, whereby bad is good and good bad, lies truth and truth lies; the inexorable corruption of the press and academia; the osmotic encroachment of the surveillance state; the collapse of constitutionalism and the rule of law?

If you examine this inexhaustive list with a modicum of attention, it may occur to you that its items have something in common: each signifies or supports an area of exploration that has been rendered taboo in contemporary culture by political correctness, fashion or ideological suggestion. This would seem to suggest that nominally free artists have allowed themselves to be directed in their work by a Muse or Muses that are not exactly the classical inspirational goddesses of knowledge or truth-telling.

These drifts in our culture are mirrored in our literature more in the breach than the chronicling — and also, and not coincidentally, in the disappearance of fiction as an adequate means of anticipating reality, of fiction as what it had been for 300 years: the device by which we humans tried to explain ourselves to ourselves; by which we looked at the world through unfamiliar lenses; by which we collided the rich interior and fraught domestic life of man with the weakening culture of the great outdoors; by which we magnified the crises and tiny triumphs of the individual self and placed them in the Petri dish of political reality; by which we brought the metaphysical firmament into the manmade hollow blocks of space in which we live.

Have you read a novel in recent times in which a real-seeming human being has entered the world of conspiratorial alliance between Big Tech, Big Pharma and Big Finance to kidnap entire populations and hold them to ransom until they cease to be vulnerable to sickness? Or have you read a book about time slipping into reverse, not exactly literally but in the sense that, as we go forward, the mixed topography of freedom and authoritarianism begin to seem familiar, perhaps from other, older books we've read, and the more talk there is about progress and progressiveness, the more the landscape resembles something quite to the contrary?

Was Orwell perhaps right about something else: that all art is propaganda? What is the relationship between writing and history? Is there such a relationship? The world is impoverished by virtue of the fact that there are two reductive ideas as to the answer: one, that literature is not supposed to grub around in the social; the other, that writers have a social responsibility.

Writers have no such responsibility, but that does not mean they do not write for their times and their tribes. There is nothing and no one else to write for. Arthur Miller said that all plays were social, by which he meant that plays are for audiences, which are social phenomena. Likewise — although this territory is more complex — readerships. A readership is an audience, even though its members cannot see each other.

The earliest hieroglyphics placed by *homo sapiens* on the walls of caves were primarily concerned with two questions: man's place in the tribe and man's dreams of transcendence.

In the ancient East — in China and Japan — an artist became such by studying not texts but objects, assimilating their yang and yin, the light and dark of them. In this process, s/he was guided by six principles. Every object, every animal, every leaf, has a particular rhythm, and this principle — the rhythm of the thing — was the first and most important. After this came 'organic form', which was the outline of the thing or being or entity, which must also carry the rhythm of the thing. After this came 'trueness to nature', which means trueness to the rhythm and the form. Then comes colour — the yin and yang, which reveals the movement of the object or being. Next comes 'the placement of the object in the field', a remarkable idea: that the object or being can be captured as part of the world. And finally comes 'style', which is not what we mean by style but instead the matching of the energy of the execution with the nature and rhythm of that which is depicted. These are the Taoist principles for depicting reality. All art and all writing, all stories — true, mythological, or merely fictional — must be written in accordance with something akin to these principles. And in this list, we can see a constant through-line of connection with the idea of discovering the world as it actually is, in its essence and discoverability. From this we gain a more precise sense of the function of the artist: he is a craftsman in revealing the world. And the same goes for words — for literature, fiction, reportage, even journalism when it is good, or — better — when it is great.

The first needs a child experiences are the needs for food and love. After that, a close third, comes the need for story. If you watch a young child playing on a rug with new toys — shifting his building blocks with tractors and excavators — you notice that he treats everything as if it were self-evidently mysterious. He looks at things carefully, touches them, smells them, licks them. He seems to be simply going through motions that babies do for no reason, but really, he is constructing a version of the world from the only available evidence, using the only instruments available to him: his five senses. This is how each of us constructed the world to begin with, though we imagine we did so in a process we grandly call 'education'. In fact, education came afterwards, and not necessarily to improve what had already occurred. Really, to continue building a coherent and reliable version of the world, we need to approach things like the child — entering into everything using as many of our senses as possible. Books have their place, but if they come too soon and are treated with such gravity that they displace the world, books of any kind result in a dissociated abstractness.

Most writing that we call 'literary' in our cultures no longer conforms to the ancient Eastern ideas of rhythm, etc., but simply engages much in the manner of a literary Olympics with the pantheon of past writing and present champions. The result is that novelists, short storytellers, dramatists, etc., write into what you might call the 'literary cloud', contributing their tithe to the archive of aesthetic abstraction about nothing but itself.

Who can we credit with following up on George Orwell's 1937 prediction (*The Road to Wigan Pier*) that the vision of the totalitarian state would be substituted by the vision of the totalitarian world? And where to be found is the modern Faustian tale called, maybe, *Everything You Know is Wrong*, in which a rock star who rises from nowhere with a music that praises God and decries the corporate turn being taken by the world, ends up taking tea with the architects of the New World Order. Or what about a novel called *The Useless Eaters*, about people who decide to eat the rich before the rich eat them? I am not talking about sociology, about instrument literature dedicated to social inspiration, but rather asking a question: If writers can write about human beings in the world without touching on what is already gestating under their feet, how 'truthful' can their books be? The point is not to demand a sociological literature. It is to ask: How can the inhabitants of an era's literature remain impervious to the unprecedented events in the world outside their make-believe windows?

Throughout the history of the novel, stories were placed in something passing for the reality of the past, present or future. What we see is that our writers have mostly written about a different world to the one now culminating in front of our eyes. They write, sure, about manners, and character, and mystery of a sort, but they leave most of what humankind in the Western hemisphere has been experiencing untouched, and as a result have assisted many in not understanding what they were experiencing. Why? Because they did not notice what was happening? Hardly. Because, unbeknownst to themselves, they had fallen prey to ideological spells cast by those who wished to steal the world from under its people's feet.

So, what really is a novelist? Is he or she a voice of truth from within the culture or a voice of misinformation and manipulation, part of the bread and circuses routine that keeps people singing in their chains, exposing them to risks, deluding them with ideals of freedom and promises of peace and truth? It's a good question. The answer may not be what you used to think it was.

And the same is true of theatre. Modern theatre seems to mimic television or construct a determined anti-art, which is to say an art based on pastiche or parody of what came before it. Many of the artists, writers, are really just parasites, caricaturists, satirists, forgers. At a glance we can tell such anti-art from the real thing: It is not truthful. It always seems to be about the lives of remote and detached others, who encounter not existential crises but ideological ones, and following a blueprint borrowed from television soaps rather than the hallowed arts of stagecraft. Its practitioners, likewise, are distracted from their vocations by ideology, fashion and the prospect of easier success than is immediately offered under the time-honoured pact extended by the theatrical vocation.

In, say, a decade's time, when we may find ourselves — if present trends are not curtailed — in a neo-feudal dystopia; enslaved by technology and medical tyrants; paralysed finally back into a silence akin to that which preceded the first human cry; crammed into hive cities that are far smarter than we; our lives and thoughts an open book for self-appointed big siblings to peruse; with nothing to our names but the clothes we creep around in — will we hear the name of any writer of today — say, February 3rd 2021 — and think: *He/she called it years ago? It's all there in those books!*

Shamefully, we have to go back a human lifetime, to the middle of the last century, to find writers whose work can realistically be deemed prophetic of the present moment.

First there was Huxley; then Orwell; then . . . *Who?*

Michel Houellebecq, maybe. Certainly he has caught the degradation, the degeneracy of the West; the craving for servitude to the basest passions; the longing for capitulation to a Master or Mistress. He has prophesied and denounced and warned. That much is certainly true.

He tackles great themes of our time — the rise of Islam, transhumanism, sexual consumerism, cloning, post-Sixties hedonism — and always as a backdrop to his study of the movement of human beings in time and space. To read his books is to feel you are engaged in some vital exercise in understanding the age in which you live. His theme is no smaller than the decline and fall of European civilisation.

Fifteen months ago, in an article for *First Things* titled "Houellebecq and the Death of Europe," I wrote the following:

'Houellebecq writes about the disappointment, sadness, loneliness, anguish, terror, boredom, despair, imposed by a culture unfit for human habitation. He exposes the freedom con pedalled since the Sixties and defended in the name of what is called progress. He summons up a diseased world, leaving the reader repelled and unsettled, but also relieved that at last the truth is told. He does not raise false hopes, but presents his characters *in extremis* within the collapsing culture, their humanity no longer capable of extending into the available space. But all the while, there is an implicit comparison of an unexpected kind: that something better is possible; something that may once have existed, perhaps a memory deep in the recesses of the reader's mind.'

And I also write the following paragraph, which is not specifically about Houellebecq, but about the moment he writes in:

'Almost everybody seems to feel we are heading for some cliff edge. We may not agree on what we mean by that, but we sense a catastrophe of some kind — existential, ecological, demographic, or arising from some uncertain bellicosity — is just around the corner after next. And we sense that, when it comes, this catastrophe will have the *mien* of a wilful self-destruction. Such dreads growingly invade the minds of Europeans, rendering them the allies of their own gravediggers. The defining characteristic of the present age might be deemed the desire to subvert and destroy the institutions, traditions and beliefs that converged to become what is called Western civilisation. This iconoclasm is carried out in the name of freedom — sexual freedom, chiefly — but accompanied by an unconscious relinquishing of the life-force. The great mass of Western humanity seems easy with abandoning the ideas that constituted the heart of its civilisation from the beginning.'

As prophecies go, that's not half bad.

Houellebecq is, in a sense, of a different culture. He is a Frenchman, writing in French. He lived in Ireland for a while, for tax reasons no less, but we scarcely noticed. He is not of the Anglophone world, which may count in this context because he is that much more removed from the ideologies that have saturated Western civilisation, mostly via the English language.

He is also, in a certain sense, more a reporter than an artist. For his 2011 book, *The Map and the Territory*, he created a character called Michel Houellebecq, a writer. The book's 'hero', Jed, a painter, visits the famous novelist to present a portrait he's painted of him. As Houellebecq prepares a meal, Jed examines the bookshelves and is 'surprised by the small number of novels — classics essentially. However, there was an astonishing number of books by social reformers of the nineteenth century: the best known, like Marx, Proudhon, Owen, Carlyle, as well as others whose names meant nothing to him.'

In my *First Things* essay, I described him thusly:

'Houellebecq does not read as a natural or even comfortable novelist, but someone who has invaded an increasingly redundant form to say things incapable of being heard otherwise. He does not write recreational yarns, nor book-shaped sedatives to escape into. A kind of investigative reporter who reports truths rather than facts, he is a red-pilled Hunter S. Thompson in reverse gear, the chief scribe of the counter-counterculture, the Great Gonzo of Truth-telling, the one prepared to go further in describing the depths of degradation and hopelessness to which libertinism and nihilism have dragged us. His books are documents of an internal forensics of human decline that happen to take — mostly, anyway — the form of stories.'

Is there, writing in the English language in the 21st year of the 21st century, any writer of fiction who might be said to have drilled into the dense reality of the three or four decades leading to the present and set down in story our path to this moment? What might the canon of such a writer look like? Well, it might contain many of the elements that Houellebecq has chalked his line around: the corpses of our cultural inheritance sprawled dead in the mud. I cannot come up with such a novelist's name, though my reading may not be exhaustive.

To find writers in that period who have been genuinely prophetic, it seems to me we must look to reporters — journalists, albeit a very few and of a very particular kind, and foremost of all the most maligned and derided, David Icke, the so-called arch-conspiracist, who is classically defined by his indifference to fashion, ideology of political correctness.

Looking further afield, we may pause at the work of sci-fi writers, from whose ranks I would pluck the name of Philip K. Dick.

In Dick's *The World Jones Made* (1956), the action of the novel takes place in a hyper-state created on the ashes of the globe scorched by the third apocalypse. The book was written decades before the present system of mind enslavement called 'political correctness' emerged. The system of rule in the society described in the book is dictatorship; the official ideology is 'Relativism'. Uttering categorical statements is against the law. In 2021 Ireland, we're rounding the final corner to such a society, having gone from 0 to 10,000 kph in about a month of wet Sundays.

Dick's 1964 novel *The Penultimate Truth* is set in a future where most of humanity lives in large underground shelters. The world is subject to an information monopoly. The people are told that World War III is being fought overhead, when, in reality, the war ended years ago. Those who have a different point of view than the Combine are not allowed to speak or are silenced if they try to. This book presents a study of how a society can be managed with the help of a fictional or exaggerated sense of danger. The population lives in a state of panic constantly fuelled by media. Sound familiar?

In *Ubik* (1969), the main characters do not realise that the world they live in is a prison. Most of the characters in the story are all but dead but do not know it. Their reality is slowly but systematically disintegrating as they gradually become prey to a sinister existence that sucks the remnants of their spiritual energy. Hello? Anybody there?

Dick wrote of extra-terrestrial colonies, and now we have Elon Musk and Jeff Bezos planning what they're going to do with those of our children they've already decided have no place among their exalted offspring and descendants.

Is this not prophecy? Perhaps snobbery concerning genre and form has prevented us from paying attention to writers like this.

We reach, then, for Huxley and Orwell, all but clichés of the dystopian genre — precisely because the genre was abandoned by mainstream writers around the midway point of the last century.

There are also those who remain convinced that both Orwell and Huxley were privy to insiders of the Establishment and not themselves prophets, and were thus relaying factual information rather than imaginative visions.

Huxley certainly had an inside track on the future, being the younger brother of Julian Huxley, an evolutionary biologist and eugenicist, and the first Director General of UNESCO — the United Nations Educational Scientific and Cultural Organisation. UNESCO, according to some of its critics, is an internationalist body masquerading as an instrument for peace and unity, when its real intention is the fomenting of an international collective communism, the dominance of science and the introduction throughout the world of 'common core' education, so as to indoctrinate the young with an impoverished education. We can imagine that Julian Huxley might have occasionally brought some of his work home with him. In some of his own writings, he essentially sets out the whole scenario of *Brave New World* with a straight, matter-of-fact face. Orwell was different. There is nothing in his background suggesting a similar inside track. In truth, though, Orwell developed his predictions from his close observation of history, whereas Huxley was privy second-hand to the plans of the secretive elites (what I call 'The Combine'), and was therefore more a reporter like David Icke, albeit with the deniability of fiction. Orwell wrote *1984* more or less on his deathbed — an amazing feat of human endurance in which he was as though driven by visions. He wasn't a believer — not a literal one anyway — but he had a finely tuned ethical perspective and a fundamental belief in the notion of the dignity of every human being. He got things slightly 'wronger' than Huxley, but not, I mournfully observe, the essence of the future we're now facing.

There is another reason why it is a mistake to read Huxley's book as science fiction. His objective is not to speculate, still less to create a fantasy world that might or might not resonate with reality as it unfolds. What he wrote about, fundamentally, was the disjunction between man's creative ingenuity with scientific systems and technologies and his capacity for moral growth.

Fourteen years on from its first publication, he wrote a new Foreword for the 1946 reprint of *Brave New World*, in which he explained that his interest was in the effects of science as directed at mankind: 'The theme of *Brave New World* is not the advancement of science as such; it is the advancement of science as it affects human individuals. The triumphs of physics, chemistry and engineering are tacitly taken for granted. The only scientific advances to be specifically described [in the novel] are those involving the application to human beings of the results of future research in biology, physiology and psychology. It is only by means of the sciences of life that the quality of life can be radically changed. The sciences of matter can be applied in such a way that they will destroy life or make the living of it impossibly complex and uncomfortable; but, unless used as instruments by the biologists and psychologists, they can do nothing to modify the natural forms and expressions of life itself.'

In this Foreword, he first explained why he had decided against updating his book, originally written to project its characters six centuries into the future. Asserting that the defects of the book were considerable, he had decided against rewriting, since 'in the process of rewriting, as an older, other person, I should probably get rid not only of some of the faults of the story but also of such merits as it originally possessed. And so, resisting the temptation to wallow in artistic remorse, I prefer to leave both well and ill alone and to think about something else.'

He did, however, describe what he thought the greatest defect of the story: that his character, the Savage, had been sold short by being offered just two alternatives: insanity in Utopia or a primitive life in an Indian village, a life 'hardly less queer and abnormal'. Now, he declared himself no longer keen to demonstrate 'that sanity is impossible'. If he were to rewrite the book, he revealed, he would offer the Savage a third alternative: he would not be trans-ported to Utopia before having an opportunity to learn first-hand about the nature of a society composed of freely co-operating individuals devoted to the pursuit of sanity. Already, in other words, he was thinking of putting in place not just a warning about the future but a possible way of avoiding what seemed inevitable. The people governing the brave new world, though not exactly sane, were not madmen either, he insisted. Their aim was not anarchy but social stability. If the tyrants could be given what they wanted by lesser means, he postulated, they would probably go for it. 'It is in order to achieve stability that they carry out, by scientific means, the ultimate, personal, really revolutionary revolution.'

The 'really revolutionary revolution', he wrote, needed to occur 'in the souls and flesh' of human beings.

Remember, he wrote *Brave New World* between the wars, a time of dissolu-tion and rising insanity. Revising the book after WWII, he placed sanity as his highest value. His comments are largely particular to that moment, touching on war, atomic energy, the nuclear threat, Bolshevism, fascism, inflation. There is, in truth, very little that resonates with the world of the third millennium. Like most seers of the pre-1989 era, he saw nuclear obliteration as the defining threat. The nearest to a general prediction is this: 'To deal with confusion, power has been centralized and government control increased. It is probable that all the world's governments will be more or less completely totalitarian even before the harnessing of atomic energy; that they will be totalitarian during and after the harnessing seems almost certain. Only a large-scale popular movement toward decentralization and self-help can arrest the present tendency toward statism. At present there is no sign that such a movement will take place.'

There was, he noted, no reason why the new totalitarianism should resemble the old. Government by terror and violence had become not merely difficult to sell, but actually inefficient. To overcome this, it would be necessary to make people love their servitude, rendering coercion unnecessary. This, he believed, was some way off, due to the crudity and unscientific nature of the available techniques of propaganda as challenged through media and education systems.

This was also to be his essential response to the 1949 publication of his former pupil, George Orwell's book, *1984*, conveyed to the author precisely three months before Orwell's death from tuberculosis in January 1950. This episode accentuates a strange incongruity: the two books, 18 years apart, appear to be in the wrong order. One might have expected the boot-in-the-face dystopia story to emerge first, followed some time later by the account of the tyranny-by-pampering. Huxley's — due to its author having the inside track — came first, by nearly two decades.

In this letter, Huxley used an interesting phrase for what both he and Orwell were anticipating in their respective books: 'the ultimate revolution'. Incidentally, in 1962, Huxley would deliver a lecture at U.C. Berkeley titled 'The Ultimate Revolution: Getting People To Love Their Servitude', in which he defined this process as 'a method of control by which a people can be made to enjoy a state of affairs by which by any decent standard they ought not to enjoy.'

Having assured Orwell — whom he had taught French at Eton — how excellent and profoundly important his book was, Huxley went on to engage in what reads in retrospect like a put-down, an unfavourable contrasting of the book with his own prophetic work of 18 years earlier. He identified in Orwell's novel a strand of thinking that placed sadism rooted in sexuality as the psychological mainspring of the tyranny, but counted whether this 'policy of boot-in-the-face' could continue to be useful indefinitely. New ways would be found, he reasoned, by which ruling oligarchies would be able to satisfy their lust for power, and these, he said, would be more likely to resemble the ways of ruling outlined in *Brave New World*. He believed that animal magnetism and hypnotism would provide more practical means of achieving control over human politicians, and only an ignorance of these areas had delayed the 'Ultimate Revolution' by several generations. Freud, for example, by his failure to master the technique and his resulting disparagement of hypnotism, had delayed its application to psychiatry for at least 40 years.

'But now psycho-analysis is being combined with hypnosis; and hypnosis has been made easy and indefinitely extensible through the use of barbiturates, which induce a hypnoid and suggestible state in even the most recalcitrant subjects.'

Within the coming generation, he anticipated, the leaders of the world would discover that infant conditioning and narco-hypnosis — a combination of hypnosis and barbiturates — were more efficient as instruments of government than coercion and violence, which would ensure the emergence of generations of humans who had come to love their servitude without any necessity for flogging or kicking. This, he said, would ensure that the world would move towards the vision he had outlined in *Brave New World* and away from Orwell's ostensibly darker prognosis.

Education was the key, he opined in that 1946 Foreword, to the assertion of ultimate control over humanity — refusing to educate, that is, to persuade people that servitude amounted to contentment and persuade them to accept the redefinition of human happiness. The love of servitude, he wrote, required firstly economic security, but then, and more importantly, a deep, personal revolution in human minds and bodies.

The Ultimate Revolution would require, inter alia, much-improved techniques of suggestion, starting in the cradle, and the later enhancement of these by drugs — something both less harmful and more enjoyable than alcohol or hard drugs. It would also require a more sophisticated hierarchy of humanity, so as to enable each individual to be allowed his or her proper place in society and the workplace, as well as a system of eugenics capable of standardising the 'human product'. He guessed that the real-life equivalents of soma, hypnopaedia and a scientific caste system were by then probably no more than three or four generations away. He thought the sexual promiscuity of *Brave New World*, judging by the fact that American divorces were already on a par with marriages, was within reach. 'In a few years, no doubt, marriage licenses will be sold like dog licenses, good for a period of twelve months, with no law against changing dogs or keeping more than one animal at a time. As political and economic freedom diminishes, sexual freedom tends compensatingly to increase. And the dictator (unless he needs cannon fodder and families with which to colonise empty or conquered territories) will do well to encourage that freedom. In conjunction with the freedom to daydream under the influence of dope and movies and the radio, it will help to reconcile his subjects to the servitude which is their fate.'

Fourteen years on, he felt certain that the world was moving inexorably closer to his vision of its future. He referred to this vision as both a 'horror' and a 'Utopia', which, in any event, he believed might arrive within a century — 500 years before he had anticipated at the time of writing his book. He briefly gestured towards the possibility of an alternative course for society: the development of science not as the end of human progress but as the means to producing a race of free individuals. Otherwise, he saw a choice between an assortment of independent militarised, localised totalitarianisms, or a single supranational totalitarianism, as the sole means of managing the chaos arising from untrammelled technological progress, finally arriving at 'the welfare-tyranny of Utopia.'

It is often said that the kind of dystopianism we are talking about now is more Huxley than Orwell, but I am not sure this is so. Already it feels more like the Orwellian fist in the Huxlean glove. Or perhaps, a Huxlean game of footsie with the Orwellian boots on! To steal a crystal phrase from Jean Baudrillard: 'Too bad, it's Utopia!'

In any event, it is clear now that the option of applying science to the project of nurturing a race of free humans has long since been abandoned. The choice, then, by Huxley's persuasive logic, was always going to be between two forms of despotism, and it is now clear that the choice has been made: in the future, human beings will live in a supranational monocracy, sustained in a kind of peace by drugs, technology and welfare, with the jackboot laces slightly undone, as though at the end of a hard day's kicking.

The problem is a human one. It had long been held that it would prove impossible to create a computer that was cleverer than the human being simply by virtue of the human having been its creator. This now reveals itself as naïve. The combination of algorithm and Big Data has opened up new vistas of possi-bility, since data can be harvested at several removes from the human to cast variegated new lights on probability patterns in behaviour that allow the Combine to understand us better than we understand ourselves. Moreover, that optimistic hypothesis concerning the continuing mastery of man presumed that all men would remain in control of their destinies, and overlooked that another way of making machines more intelligent would be to make the average human more stupid.

Much of this escalating stupidity has been engineered by cultural reprogram-ming. Tradition, Julian Huxley once observed, is the way in which the process of evolution has been transmitted for centuries; but, because we have started to suspect tradition, deny its value, interfere with it, abolish it, we have succeeded in stalling the evolutionary process even as the technologies we have created out of the momentum of our past evolving accelerate and pass us by. Evolution, hitherto the carrier of the impulse of human progress, has gone into reverse, while, going by the observed evidence of the technologies, we think of it as still accelerating forward. We pass our own ghosts on the way back into history.

Progress, therefore, is just another conditioned delusion. Genes mutate in accordance with environmental needs and stresses; the fewer challenges, the more obsolescence. The evidence seems to be telling us that, as our world becomes more technologised, we human beings have less reason to make use of our wits, which, as a consequence, are deserting us. This may be part of the explanation for how accurately the responses of 2020 have confirmed the hypotheses outlined by both Huxley and Orwell: Most of us dearly love Big Brother.

And perhaps a deeper factor is the neglect of the natural transcendent appetites of the human imagination — as a result of years of the promotion of a pseudo-rationalism that ignored most of the most fundamental human questions, majoring in the denigration of religion.

The chief takeaway from the Covid cult to date is that, spiritually, we are mostly dead people — we just have not noticed it yet. The world we inherited is steadily falling apart around us. But we are too 'sophisticated' to recognise the signs, too certain of the ideas we have been taught, too proud to notice that we are unable to save ourselves by means of our efforts alone.

For societies, as for the human person, the religious dimension is a question of imagination. Or, perhaps, the capacity to fully imagine reality becomes a religious question: Imagination needs to be bedded down in a sacred, transcendent, eternal order. The defining characteristic of the present age might be diagnosed as the desire to subvert and destroy the institutions, traditions and beliefs that converged to become what is called Western civilisation. This iconoclasm is carried out in the name of freedom — actually, of sexual freedom purely — but is propelled by a great error: the assumption that any properties of this inheritance that were essential to the functionality and cohesion of the society and its human quotient would, if capable of having a continuing usefulness, be both amenable to rationality and comprehensible as a matter of discernible utility. Our problem, in short, was that we ceased to understand that the transcendent implied not a knowledge of a different way of thinking, which was out of our reach, but an essential acceptance that such a different way of thinking existed.

Put simply in this context, the inheritance of Christianity can usefully be shorthanded to the idea that human happiness is better achieved by the sublimation of superficial desiring in the visualisation of a transcendent order of being. A functional culture, in this sense, requires a foundational mythology that enables it to transcend what might be called a state of continuous present time. This mythology relates to the past and to the putatively eternal future, and functions to render the present subservient to things higher and greater than itself. The nature of the rupture that has opened up in modern society has to do with the repudiation of this idea in favour of something that amounts to a culture rooted in itself and its own selectively identified and apprehended origins. This can seem, for a time, highly functional, exhibiting signs of a previously undreamt-of freedom and openness. But it is a chimaera, a fake, because it has no roots and no ultimate objectives that can either be formulated or achieved. Only a culture rooted in the sacred is capable of sustaining a human person or society over the long run.

It is true that such a pseudo-culture can achieve the semblance of functionalism by mimicking the idea of a transcendent culture since it maintains the outward appearance of a quasi-eternal perspective on reality, but this is actually an illusion, and all of the available artefacts (what they are, really: anti-art) will reveal themselves as tautologies. A novel, for example, will not take its reader on a journey taking off into the infinite, but will return him to an enhancement of the emblematic shocks and/or sentimentalisms that identify the work as itself. It is possible to prolong the life of this pseudo-culture by the practice of parasitism on that which it denies. A painting may parody the rejected inheritance and yet derive its only life from what it derides and blasphemes. Really, the roots of this pseudo-culture are as functional as those of a poppy in a dusty corner, causing it to flare momentarily and then die for want of sustenance. But such a pseudo-culture is incapable of formulating any enduring idea of the beautiful, the good or the true, because it has no eternal measure: man and his desire for immediate freedoms has become the measure of all things. Yet, this freedom becomes increasingly impossible since the untrammelled pursuit of the literal desiring of each and every human will in a short time lead to chaos, followed by outright destruction of everything, followed hard by tyranny.

Welcome to the brave new world. *Too bad* — *it's Utopia*. But not as we imagined it. Outside, it's 1984!

CHAPTER 9
WALL OF LIES
07-02-2021

Propaganda is not what it used to be. It is something far worse. In part because of the effectiveness of its action upon us, we have no idea when it is present, nor what it is doing to us.

I see the same syndrome expressed in signs everywhere: people on the street jumping under buses rather than pass close to one another; a journalist I once thought at least vaguely intelligent writing about 'cases' under the seeming impression that PCR tests do exactly what it says on the Covid tin; a political movement supposed to be pro-freedom demanding a faster rollout of vaccines; half a dozen police officers sitting on a woman and helping each other to handcuff her because she is more than five kilometres from her home, and nobody batting an eyelid. Signs of what? Signs of complicity in a terror beyond understanding. Signs of having surrendered the option of having a mind of your own. Signs of a capitulation to the insuperable, the inevitable. Signs of being walled in by lies.

There is something we are not comprehending, something to do with the minds of the generality of people.

It is not sufficient to speak of 'propaganda'. The word, used by our limited understanding of its meaning, is inadequate to the achievement of even the remotest understanding of where we are now. To speak of it thus in times like these is like standing on the deck of Noah's Ark discussing the weather.

Someone, the other day, sent me a link to an article headed 'Households left better off as a result of pandemic — Central Bank'. It was indescribably fatuous, idiotic beyond measuring, containing the immortal sentence: 'Mass unemployment last year has left households better off and a savings glut means we've never been richer.' This *sounds like* propaganda, but isn't really. Since it suggests that people have been wasting their time starting businesses and getting out of bed in the mornings to earn a living, it is as relevant to real life as a eunuch calculating his savings on condoms. It's just plain clownery. To think this is propaganda is utterly to misunderstand what propaganda is. Propaganda is ubiquitous, insidious, deceptive, relentless, often invisible and always manipulative. That article, taken in isolation, is just a harmless piece of stupidity that stands as something to be exhibited in the Book of Evidence in a year or two when the true extent of the lockdown damage is permitted into the light of even darker days than these.

Most people think of propaganda as one-off or recurring bulletins of misleading statements, something like the orchestration of information to a singular purpose. Someone reads a slanted article, perhaps, and thinks she recognises the animal. Similarly, a poster, a slogan, a TV ad. All these qualify as instruments of propaganda, but they are not the thing itself. They are not the thing that has existed in history, especially the history of the past century, and above all the history of the lustings of people seeking profit and power to manipulate the citizen in his capacity as a member of a herd that, generally speaking, enjoys no possibility of immunity from such manipulation. In reality, the issue is the generation and government of public *feeling*. Who, for example, could have predicted that the colour yellow, which once summoned up Easter eggs, could become the colour of terror and oppression? Answer: a hypnotist could have, since yellow has long been recognised by 'depth manipulators' as one of the most effective hypnotic colours.

Propaganda has even longer been a key element in the armoury of the modern technocratic state and those seeking to rule through it. The godfather of modern public relations, Edward Bernays, wrote in his 1928 book *Propaganda* that, even if every citizen had time to sift through data concerning every question, virtually nobody would be able to come to informed conclusions about anything. We just don't have the time or access to reliable means of verification. We therefore tend to farm out the sifting process to what Bernays called 'the invisible government', which we rely upon to tell us what things mean, which things are important and what are our options in considering them. By and large, we accept the verdicts provided to us by our media and political elites. Universal literacy, Bernays recalled, was supposed to change these conditions, giving each citizen 'a mind fit to rule' – the core doctrine of democracy. 'But instead of a mind,' he observed, 'universal literacy has given him rubber stamps, rubber stamps inked with advertising slogans, with editorials, with published scientific data, with the trivialities of the tabloids and the platitudes of history, but quite innocent of original thought. Each man's rubber stamps are the duplicates of millions of others, so that when these millions are exposed to the same stimuli, all receive identical imprints.'

There were a number of key players in the development of propaganda and, before that, the identification of the necessary underlying psychologies, and all of them emerged in the first half of the last century. The best known was Bernays, grand-nephew of Sigmund Freud, whose ideas he adapted for the purpose of manipulation and motivational research (MR), largely on behalf of corporate clients. Another key figure was Ernest Dichter, also a Viennese-born psychoanalyst, who in the 1950s was President of the Institute for Motivational Research and became known as an ingenious trouble-shooter on misfiring advertising campaigns. The most significant figure in exposing the deep reality of propaganda was Frenchman Jacque Ellul, a philosopher and Christian anarchist, who developed possibly the best overview of the discipline in his 1965 book *Propaganda: The Formation of Men's Attitudes*.

The techniques of what became known as 'depth manipulation' were based on several key understandings about human beings: that people behave irrationally and paradoxically; that they lie about their motivations, to themselves as much as to others; that their chief triggers are emotions, especially fear and guilt. In his 1957 book, *The Hidden Persuaders*, Vance Packard wrote about the 'depth' industry's discovery and leveraging of what were called 'subsurface desires, needs and drives'. Among the chief 'subsurface' levers found in most people's emotional profiles were the drive to conformity, the need for oral stimulation and a yearning for security.

It was Bernays who first experimented with applying psychoanalytic principles to marketing by linking products to emotions in ways that tapped into people's tendency to behave in illogical ways. Intrigued by his grand-uncle's notion that irrational group-based forces drive human behaviour, Bernays set about harnessing those forces to sell products for his clients. In *Propaganda*, he speculated that it should be possible to manipulate people's behaviour without their knowing. Then he began putting his theories into action, firstly on behalf of George Washington Hill, president of the American Tobacco Company, who was keen to demolish the taboo that, by insinuating a strong link between female cigarette smoking and sexual promiscuity, had until the late 1920s discouraged women from lighting up in public. Hill, seeking to promote his company's Lucky Strike brand, consulted Bernays, who in turn spoke to leading New York psychoanalyst and Freud disciple, Dr A. A. Brill, who saw cigarettes as essentially adult pacifiers, a throwback to the infant's pleasure in sucking, but gave Bernays a lightbulb moment when he postulated that cigarettes were also symbolic of male power. Bernays developed a campaign aimed at convincing women that smoking in public would allow them to strike a blow for sexual equality. Hence, Lucky Strike's 'Torches of Freedom' campaign, launched during New York's Easter Parade on April Fools' Day 1929. Bernays had obtained a list of female models from the editor of *Vogue* magazine and convinced enough of them that they could advance the cause of equality by lighting up on Fifth Avenue. The parade became an international sensation, and Bernays dubbed his newly tested technique 'engineering consent'. Bernays it was also who 'discovered' that the 'snap crackle and pop' of breakfast cereals was a crucial part of their appeal, the built-in crunch providing an outlet for unconscious aggression and other pent-up feelings.

Later, Ernest Dichter, who most controversially postulated that men equated convertibles with youth, freedom, and the secret wish for a mistress, and that women could be sold soap as a means to wash away their sins before a date, further developed the idea of tapping into the unconscious to sell people things they didn't need. 'You would be amazed to find how often we mislead ourselves,' he wrote in his 1960 book *The Strategy of Desire*, 'regardless of how smart we think we are, when we attempt to explain why we are behaving the way we do.'

Dichter believed that human motivation was about one-third rational, with the remainder governed by emotion. He referred to this syndrome as the 'iceberg' and developed the idea that people could be persuaded to buy things because of illogical associations implanted by advertising. He was a pioneer of focus group market research methods, which he used to great effect on behalf of clients like Procter & Gamble, Chrysler and DuPont. He was also an early practitioner of qualitative research, involving long, in-depth interviews, not unlike therapy sessions. To understand why people really bought certain things, he insisted, you had to talk to them at a deeper level. 'If you let somebody talk long enough,' he would say, 'you can read between the lines to find out what he really means.' Dichter tapped into people's desires — usually for sex, security or prestige. For him, shopping was a form of self-expression. He divined that certain people prefer cars that feel safe, whereas others like their steeds to speak of adventure and youth. He sold more typewriters by proposing that keyboards be designed to suggest the female body — 'more receptive, more concave'. He discerned that Americans preferred to borrow money at higher rates from loan sharks rather than patronise legitimate banking institutions, because they feared being judged. Using these insights, he helped banks to develop products and messages to get around such fears. He formed the view that people tend to buy things for reasons other than utilitarian — as extensions or reflections of their personalities, for example. Every product, he declared, has a personality, and the right campaign will communicate this to people who see themselves in a certain way. He exploited neuroses and unfulfilled longings and made a lot of money out of the insight that older women like to bake cakes as a substitute for childbearing. Through depth-interviewing, he deduced that soaping while taking a bath was one of the few occasions when the average puritanical American of the 1950s felt permitted to caress himself or herself. The research showed that bathing was, for many adults, a pretext for auto-erotic experiment, a ritual that afforded rare moments of personal indulgence, particularly before a romantic assignation.

Imagine ideas like these at large in the era of Big Data, when the clients of Dichter's successors have access to precise maps of human desiring based on actual observed behaviours.

Armed with such insights, even 70 years ago, it was possible to sell almost anything with the right slogan and imagery. The most important thing about propaganda, Dichter asserted, is that it be universal and continuous, hammering home the same message by diverse means again and again. The purpose is to 'regiment' the mind of a society in the same way as an army drills its soldiers. Propaganda is most effective in the hands of what Bernays had called 'intelligent minorities', by which he meant not minorities in the latter-day sense of victim groups, but intellectual elites seeking to guide society in particular directions. Bernays referred to these intellectual elites, without irony, as 'dictators'.

Bernays also hitched to advertising the earlier thinking of the French philosopher Charles-Marie Gustave Le Bon on the question of mob minds — the idea that the 'group mind' presents an entirely different study to the individual mind. Le Bon, in *The Psychology of Crowds*, had explained that a crowd has a different psychology to that of an individual. He saw a crowd as forming a single being, responding always to unconscious thoughts, and conforming to laws of mental unity. The consciousness bestowed by membership of a crowd, he expanded, can be transformative of the person, putting individual members in possession of 'a sort of collective mind which makes them feel, think and act in a manner quite differently from that in which each individual would feel, think and act were that person in a state of isolation.' In a psychological crowd, individual personality disappears, brain activity is replaced by reflex activity, involving a lowering of intelligence, provoking a complete transformation of sentiments, which may be an improvement or disimprovement on those of the crowd's constituent members. A crowd may just as easily become heroic or criminal, but the latter is far more likely. 'The ascendency of crowds,' wrote Le Bon, 'indicates the death throes of a civilisation.' The upward climb to civilisation is an intellectual process driven by individuals; the descent is a herd in stampede. 'Crowds are only useful for destruction.'

Adapting these ideas to the marketplace, Bernays both refined them and applied them to real situations. Although the group mind does not 'think' in the normal sense of the word, he elaborated, it still behaves as if it had an intelligence of its own. 'In place of thought,' he wrote, 'it has impulses, habits and emotions. In making up its mind, its first impulse is to follow the example of a trusted leader. . . . But when the example of the leader is not at hand, and the herd must think for itself, it does so by means of clichés, pat words or images which stand for a whole group of ideas or experience.' By playing upon an old cliché, or manipulating a newly minted one, the propagandist can swing a whole mass of group emotions.

The thoughts of these pioneers were themselves analysed by Jacques Ellul in *Propagandes* (Propagandas), the first significant cautionary work on the dangers of propaganda. Ellul treated propaganda as a sociological phenomenon rather than — as had Bernays and Dichter — something created by particular people for specific purposes. He also saw that propaganda was an instrument that would come into its own the more technological a society became. He identified technology and propaganda as having a symbiotic relationship: technology makes propaganda easier, and a technological society feeds off the effects. 'Propaganda,' he wrote, 'is called upon to solve problems created by technology, to play on maladjustments and to integrate the individual into a technological world.' He rejected the anticipated argument that it depends on what kind of state or regime is engaging in propaganda; it doesn't matter: '[I]f we really have understood the technological state, such a statement becomes meaningless. In the midst of increasing mechanization and technological organization, propaganda is simply the means used to prevent these things from being felt as too oppressive and to persuade man to submit with good grace.' This means, of course, that a technological society is perforce driven by propaganda, and also that we are already unfree. Indeed, long before the advent of Artificial Intelligence, we had already been absorbed into the machine that is the herd in thrall to what is deemed the level of propaganda necessary to control it.

Propaganda always addresses itself to the individual enclosed in the mass. The individual must never be considered as such, but always, Ellul instructed, in terms of what he has in common with others, such as his motivations, his feelings or his myths. 'He is reduced to an average and, except for a small percentage, action based on averages will be effectual.' The propagandist addresses the individual — in newspaper articles, radio broadcasts, etc. — as part of a group. The individual is never treated as if alone. 'Emotionalism, impulsiveness, excess, etc. — all these characteristics of the individual caught up in the mass are well-known and very helpful to propaganda.' This is the key to understanding how modern opinion polling works: It likewise treats individuals as part of a mass, and moreover induces the individual to accept this version of himself as valid and truthful. When the pollster with her clipboard enters the room to canvass the opinions of those present, she brings the masses with her.

Propaganda, said Ellul, agreeing with Dichter, must be total. It must utilise all the available means of communication and at once: press, radio, TV, movies, posters, meetings, door-to-door canvassing. To use these media sporadically and without a propagandist intention is to achieve nothing. Each medium has a different line of attack, and all must be employed together to achieve a total, unconditional surrender.

Ellul refined and, in some cases, rejected inherited ideas, such as that all propaganda is lies and that its sole purpose is to change opinions. On the contrary, he observed, the best kind of propaganda is generated from half-truths and truths taken out of context, and its main purpose is to strengthen existing trends and perceptions, to promote action where appropriate, and — most importantly — to dissuade, with terror or discouragement, those of strong opinions contrary to the propaganda from interfering with its agenda. Ellul characterised conventional education as 'pre-propaganda', the conditioning of minds with enormous amounts of second-hand, disconnected, unverifiable, incoherent and / or useless information masquerading as 'facts', but intended to prepare the citizen for the planting of propaganda.

One of the chief impacts of the action of normative propaganda has, of course, been to further suppress the possibility of independent thought. The brain has a finite capacity to manage and sort information, and when it is already overloaded by random, largely uninvited facts and opinions, it has little 'disk space' for its own ruminations. Modern man, Ellul observed, accepts 'facts' as the ultimate reality. 'He is convinced that what is, is good.' He places facts ahead of values and unquestioningly applies the moralism of 'progress' to something to which he attributes value because it exists. Something dressing itself up as 'science' or 'progress' is, therefore, halfway to conquering such a person.

'Everywhere,' writes Ellul, 'we find men who pronounce as highly personal truths what they have read in the papers only an hour before and whose beliefs are merely the result of a powerful propaganda. Everywhere we have people who have blind confidence in a political party, a general, a movie star, a country, or a cause, and who will not tolerate the slightest challenge to that god. . . . We meet this alienated man at every turn, and are possibly already one ourselves.'

Universal education of the kind described by Ellul has generated populations of citizens who provide easy meat for propaganda for at least four reasons: people who consider themselves 'educated' have a need to hold opinions on any and all matters arising in their purview; such people, by virtue of their 'education', have access to large amounts of what might be called contextless information; they think of themselves as capable of judging all questions on their own; they are generally people who have left behind the kind of communities which in the past provided a kind of filtering for external propaganda, such as families, churches, villages, etc., to live in some anonymous metropolis to which they have no historical connections. Hence, in mass society, the pre-programmed citizen, who becomes isolated and dependent upon his own resources to fulfil his conditioned needs, is a sitting duck for propagandists of all kinds. When you consider present-day instant access to a certain kind of basic information about next to everything, it is not surprising that, on virtually every matter of public controversy, there is a ready constituency for indoctrinations by propagandists among those who believe themselves educated because they hold a degree, have instant access to Google and other search engines and regard themselves as free because they cling to what they firmly believe to be their own opinions, but are not. And all this mess of pseudo-belief is held together by a kind of cultural 'glue' composed mainly of elements of insinuated pseudo-morality. Believing these things is not merely evidence of wisdom, but also evidence of goodness. Thus, what might be called the market for propaganda has expanded to include virtually every member of a modern society — everyone, that is, except those who understand the underfoot conditions and are prepared to seek their information from other than ready sources and remain determined to think for themselves.

By Ellul's thesis, the citizen imagining himself 'modern' needs propaganda: to fulfil his sense of importance and involvement in the ostensibly prevailing democracy; to provide an outlet for his pent-up energies, to put on display his 'moral' disposition, and so forth. Seen like this, it becomes clear that a modern society needs propaganda in much the way, and for the same reasons, that it needs entertainment. And Ellul was insistent on his own careful use of words: when he spoke of the 'necessity' of propaganda, he was not expressing approval: '. . . the world of necessity is a world of weakness, a world that denies man. To say that a phenomenon is necessary means, for me, that it denies man; its necessity is proof of its power, not proof of its excellence.'

It is obvious from this outline that the fundamental conditions described by Le Bon, Bernays, Dichter and Ellul remain in place today, but have been subjected to exponential multipliers arising from the sheer pervasiveness of advertising, the ubiquity of technology, the power of the internet and the 24/7 stream of information and responses in respect of selected events from around the globe.

It seems obvious that our reference points for mapping propaganda must by now be decades out of date. When the pioneers of depth manipulation were plying their dubious trade, they were dealing with a world in which there were but a handful of media by which a society and its members could be manipulated. The work of the founding fathers of the 'science' of the 'depth approach' — Bernays, Dichter, etc. — is all firmly embedded in the first half or middle of the 20th century when TV was in the womb or in its infancy, and all you had were a few newspapers, cinema, advertising hoardings and the radio. Our understandings of 'depth manipulation' spring from this period and have not been updated to take into account that media are now almost constantly central to the consciousness of most of the human race. We're therefore dealing with a different kind of animal — in the average human being — than those guys were talking about. Then, by comparison, advertising and propaganda no more than grazed off the consciousness of the individual — capable of influencing but not necessarily dominating the entire thought processes, as is now the case. Talk radio, 24-hour news, breakfast television, all these are phenomena of the past handful of decades and have entered human culture almost as human entities — more like intimate relationships than technological adjuncts — to say nothing of social media and the other internet 'gifts'. The TV set in the corner is not just an apparatus for obtaining news, information, entertainment — it's actually akin to a *person* sitting in the corner of the room, and usually the most dominant, strident and garrulous person at that.

In the Covid episode, the TV set has become the narcissist/psychopath who dictates to the other occupants what they should think and feel, brooking no dissent. TVs are uninterruptable, so the dynamics of the situation dictate that any nonconformists in the room will be put in their place, unless one of them can turn the darn thing off. Twitter, as its name almost suggests, is also a kind of personification of psychopathic traits: one minute satiating the user's craving for dopamine, the next lacerating the addict for some unwitting sin against orthodoxy. Even when the user is the aggressor, he or she is aggressively enforcing thinking that comes from someplace/someone else.

Hence, people are not like they used to be, or how we still assume them to be: i.e. maybe 90 per cent themselves, with 10 per cent of their 'content' imposed. It may well be the other way around: 10 per cent themselves and 90 per cent imposed.

We continue to talk to one another under the assumption that we are — on both sides — still more or less as we used to be (I'm talking here mainly of us older folk; the young are in a much worse situation because there may be no 10 per cent). In truth, almost nobody is like that. What we're dealing with most of the time is people with hollowed-out minds and, therefore, hollowed-out souls — what passes for their brains crammed full with the ideas other people want them to cling to. It is not that they are propagandised — we're way beyond that — but that their minds are utterly colonised and occupied by alien thoughts. And — even more ominously — they are addicted to the source of these thoughts, the abusive box in the corner, which ('who'?) tells them everything they know, everything that's true and untrue, and advises them how to avoid being waylaid by false narratives, i.e. unapproved versions of reality. What we are talking about, then, is not methods of imparting information, but instruments of mass hypnoidal entrancement, a different strand of the modern story of herd management, which I wrote about for *The Daily Sceptic* back in the summer of 2020. This chapter takes things to a new level — the informal second part of this essay.

One of the unnoticed consequences of propaganda, according to Jacques Ellul, is that it results in a gradual 'closing up' of the individual, arising from a growing insensitivity to repeated bouts of propaganda. Subjected to persistent repetitions of the same messages, he begins to skim the headlines of his newspaper rather than reading the articles. In a more modern context, he uses the remote control to zap from station to station on his TV set, searching perhaps for some element of surprise, and always in vain. He checks his phone incessantly, craving a new fix of data or instruction. Radio becomes no more than background noise: he doesn't hear and doesn't care. This stage of the process does not signal immunity to propaganda, but the opposite. Deeply imbued with the symbols of propaganda, he no longer needs to absorb the detail. A splash of colour, a familiar logo, is enough to trigger the required Pavlovian response. The subject of successful propaganda resembles an addict, who, however long he remains on the wagon, requires just a single shot to put him back in the gutter.

Propaganda, Jacques Ellul believed, is 'a direct attack against man'. Although himself an advocate of democracy, he believed that propaganda renders the true exercise of such freedoms 'almost impossible'. This is why those who persist in thinking for themselves, or even in expressing unapproved views, invite such opprobrium in modern societies. It's not just that dissenters threaten the reach or influence of the propagandists, for in truth, due to their inability to achieve total saturation through media, they rarely do so. The cause of their being so feared is that, by their very presence, they put at risk the whole edifice. Their heresy endangers the artifice essential for effective propaganda: the sense of naturalism, factuality, that accompanies it.

Propaganda, writes Ellul, 'does not tolerate discussion. It abhors contradiction. It must produce quasi-unanimity, and the opposing faction must become negligible, or in any case cease to be vocal.' To submit to propaganda, therefore, means to become alienated from oneself because it closes off the power of critical thinking. 'Propaganda strips the individual, robs him of part of himself, and makes him live an alien and artificial life, to such an extent that he becomes another person and obeys impulses foreign to him.' This is achieved by suffusing the individual in the emotions and responses of the herd, dissipating his individuality, freeing his ego of all confusions, unresolved contradictions and personal reservations. It pushes the individual into the mass 'until he disappears entirely'. What 'disappears', in fact, is the individual's capacity for personal reflection, independent thinking, critical judgment, these being replaced with ready-made thoughts, stereotypes, clichés, catchwords and 'guidelines'.

Once successfully propagandised, the individual ceases to be a passive recipient of the propaganda and becomes an evangelist. He takes vigorous stances, starts to oppose others, polices the orthodoxies. 'He asserts himself,' observes Ellul, 'at the very moment that he denies his own self without realising it.'

The chief reason the individual can no longer judge for himself is that he must constantly relate his thoughts to the entire complex of values and prejudices established by propaganda, and this is something that can only be learned as though by rote. Once atrophied, the capacities to judge, discern or think critically are no longer accessible to the subject, and these faculties will not simply reappear when propaganda is discontinued or suppressed. Years of spiritual and intellectual reconstruction will be required to restore them. The victim of propaganda, deprived of one channel of opinion, will simply seek out another, like a junkie seeking a different kind of fix. This, says Ellul, will 'spare him the agony of finding himself vis-à-vis some event without a ready-made opinion and obliged to judge it for himself.'

Propaganda, then, is a bigger word than we have allowed ourselves to consider. It is also a word that embraces an array of what can only be accurately described as weapons of mass indoctrination — and ultimately of destruction, too: the destruction of minds, hearts, souls, lives, livelihoods, relationships and futures. It is not, then, a small, comical thing; it is a very big, unfunny thing. When journalists, then, contrive to bombard their readers with concocted pseudo-narratives, 'human interest' stories directed at the singular purpose of manipulating them into a particular frame of mind; when they collaborate in the falsification of statistics in order to terrorise people; when they use their platforms to not merely deny the voices of alternative viewpoints, but to put dissenters on trial in proceedings in which they have no representation — they are not engaging in victimless wrongdoing. Their victims are many, and include in particular many of those least able to defend themselves against this barrage of mendacity that constructs walls of lies around their very bodies and beings in the world, walls that imprison not merely themselves but also all those caught in the contagion of their mind-virus. These are crimes of a very modern kind. But they are crimes all the same, all the more dastardly because the criminals scrub their own tracks in their wake and tell themselves they are dealing in 'facts'. They are crimes committed by individuals and collectives against individuals and communities-without-immunity, crimes that cry out to Heaven for retribution.

CHAPTER 10
SAVE THE LAST TRANCE FOR ME

16-02-2021

The Covid episode opens up the terrifying possibility that societies are now so amenable to hypnoidal mechanisms that it may soon be unrealistic to expect them not to fall prey to every passing tyrant

---

I n his book on the New Left, *Fools, Frauds and Firebrands*, the late English philosopher Sir Roger Scruton compares the language of the modern left to the concept of Newspeak devised by George Orwell for his novel *1984*. Actually, Scruton traces Orwell's creation back to the sloganeering of the French Revolution, and later the pre-Bolshevik era Russian intelligentsia and Socialist International of the late 19th century. In such quarters, slogans were essential to stigmatising dissidents, revisionists, deviationists and the like, and its success convinced communists that it was possible to alter reality by coining new phrases and words. Repeated use of the term 'crisis of capitalism' could be used to bring down an economy; constant invocation of 'democratic centralism' could insinuate that dictatorship was not, in fact, dictatorship; the call for 'the liquidation of the bourgeoisie' could conjure the targeted person out of his human body, reifying and isolating him.

A key instrument in the LGBT assault on Ireland from early 2014 was the use of the word 'homophobic' to demonise anyone who failed to supply 100 per cent endorsement to the gay agenda. This was in anticipation of the 'marriage equality' referendum to take place in mid-2015. 'Homophobia', of course, is a made-up word with no clear objective meaning other than the one that has accrued to it in culture. It was invented by gay activists as an instrument of war, designed to demonise enemies, critics and opponents in a way that would marginalise them and either render them silent or have them ejected from public discussion. The word deliberately confuses the concepts of fear and hatred, implying that the 'sufferer' from homophobia experiences both a fear of gays and a repugnance of them. A 'phobia' is defined by the Oxford English Dictionary as 'extreme or irrational fear or dislike of a specified thing'. The same dictionary defines 'homophobia' as 'an intense aversion to homosexuality and homosexuals'. To call someone a 'homophobe' is not merely to demonise and therefore silence them, it is to obviate the necessity of responding reasonably to anything they say. The accusation of 'homophobia' levels a charge that cannot be answered or refuted because it implies a fault that lies in character rather than actions. The word, therefore, attacks its object in multiple ways while also warning bystanders that, should they fail to acquiesce in every aspect of the gay agenda, they are liable to being attacked in the same way.

'Newspeak,' writes Scruton, 'occurs when the primary purpose of language — which is to describe reality — is replaced by the rival purpose of asserting power over it. . . . Newspeak sentences sound like assertions, but their underlying logic is that of the spell. They conjure the triumph of words over things, the folly of rational argument and also the danger of resistance.'

Scruton described the process whereby we are invited by words to see someone as an enemy, an untouchable. Confronting someone as a human being, he writes, entails giving that person a voice, which means words must be used as a tool of negotiation, agreement or disagreement. 'I make remarks about the weather, grumble about politics, pass the time of day', he writes, 'and my language has the effect of softening reality, of making it pliable and serviceable. Newspeak, which denies reality, also hardens it by turning it into something alien and resistant, a thing to be "struggled with" and triumphed over.' Ordinary language 'warms and softens; Newspeak freezes and hardens . . . does not merely impose a plan; it also eliminates the discourse through which human beings can live without one.'

In this context, it is not fanciful to speak about the role of language in triggering a form of hypnoidal state in which people become terrified of being called certain toxic names, in effect dubbed, or daubed, with hypnotic trigger phrases, such as 'racist', 'white supremacist', etc. These phrases become, in modern political discourse, the equivalents of the stage hypnotist's code-words, calculated to invoke the trance of a generation of opinion formers who remain in a repetitive loop of retro-sentiment defined by the counter-cultural mantras of young people from a completely different world. All of them are rooted in 1960s concepts of 'human rights', which have become as though indelibly stamped on youth and pop culture, thus rendering them amenable to be weaponised for agendas and campaigns which may have little or nothing in common with those past struggles. The word 'racist', for example, accesses a deep reservoir of psychic power rooted in slavery, apartheid, Jim Crow, civil rights, MLK, etc., and creates a kind of extrasensory current that exercises a profound terrifying power over people who have not trained themselves to deconstruct the process. It means that at some level, the charge of racism sticks to them — both in their own minds and, as a question, in the minds of bystanders and observers, so that no one is satisfactorily able to rebut the charge so levelled, and all are agreed that the spell poses a risk of sticking to everyone, and is therefore — along with its target — best given a wide berth. This is why, in discussions about immigration or what is called cultural appropriation, people preface every contribution with 'I'm not a racist but . . .', as though a racist might start off by admitting he was one. The effect of this is to strengthen the spell, to spread the goo more disastrously on the hands of the object, who clearly doth protest too much!

We speak, therefore, of words that are no longer words, but rather magical entities that serve to deter and corral. Spell language is designed not to describe or explain things but to invoke a set of pre-programmed demonic descriptions with which to detonate an explosion of disapproval calculated to dispose of what the suspect,in his defence, is likely to describe as 'common sense' — usually some category of what is called 'conservative' counter-argument or objection. The language is also calculated to protect in a manner immune from scrutiny all that the word-conjurer seeks to defend. When these words are uttered, almost no one listening encounters or is prompted to a thought; most simply feel themselves stung as though by a cattle prod or an electric fence, thereby experiencing a kind of shame at even *knowing* the targeted person, which in the vast majority of cases is sufficient to cause an immediate falling into line.

This form of sorcery has come to saturate our cultures. Indeed, the events of the past year open up the terrifying possibility that human beings, in general, are now so amenable to hypnoidal mechanisms that in the future, it may be unrealistic to expect them not to fall prey to every passing tyrant.

The claimed spread of SARS-CoV-2, which through the mechanism of lockdown ravaged the world, its economies, cultures and households in the first half of 2020, attacked humanity in the most intimate ways imaginable: in the closest relations between peoples, in their entitlement and capacity to earn a living, in their most sacred liberties, their most carefully husbanded resources, health, not least their mental health. As a cursory glance at the relevant statistics will affirm, the 'pandemic' was a carefully orchestrated lie, accompanied by campaigns of terror perpetrated by politicians and technocrats, consolidated by establishment mouthpieces travelling in the robes of journalists and enforced by brutish police forces the world over. The effect was a mass paranoia concerning a risk of death no higher than a medium-rage influenza, and less than that incurred by the average person crossing a busy road.

Perhaps the most shocking aspect of the Covid-19 story is the manner in which vast swathes of the world's population immediately and unquestioningly fell into line, carrying out to the letter the most absurd and contradictory diktats of their governments, in defiance of facts and reason. This was achieved by what was, in effect, a process of mass entrancement imposed by the use of propaganda, neurolinguistic programming and terror tactics.

Like any form of hypnosis, mass entrancement depends on the leveraging of several interrelated conditions in the subject: heightened emotion, a focusing of attention, including impaired or reduced peripheral awareness, and an elevated imaginative state — all conditions contributing to vastly increased suggestibility. The Covid-19 scare and accompanying lockdowns enabled these criteria to be met almost everywhere on a 24-hour basis.

The process at work is somewhat different to the use of hypnotic or 'spell' phrases described above, to herd individuals into what is called politically correct thinking, but it is of the same family of techniques of mass manipulation. These processes could not have been formulated without the assistance of highly practised psychologists and other experts in mind control, capable of exploiting both individual psychological pathologies and comprehending dysfunctional family dynamics to expose and manipulate weaknesses in human persons and relationships. The Covid operation harnessed the dynamics of archetypal relationships between narcissists/psychopaths (politicians) and co-dependent submissives (citizens), in effect weaponising on a grand scale the dynamics of a kind of platonic BDSM.

The chief instruments of manipulation involved the leveraging of guilt, obligation and fear, in a variation on the nice cop/nasty cop routine. This took the form of a rolling series of apparently mixed messages: 'The pandemic is coming and will cause millions of deaths'. But, 'We are with you'. But, 'Stay at home, save lives'. But, 'Go to your front door and clap/dance/light a candle for the front line workers'. And, don't forget, 'Being apart brings us together'. So, 'Let us leave no one behind'. Et cetera. As with the use of conventional spell words, the language employed was top-heavy with negative slogans and phrases designed to instil fear and dread. Those who did not obey were told they were risking the lives of others and repeatedly urged to 'do the right thing'. This was accompanied by the use of embedded command phrases that appeared random and superfluous but actually served to emphasise the mandatory nature of what was being conveyed: 'It just has to be'. 'There is no alternative'. 'All you have to do is follow the rules'.

Celebrities were rolled out to supply further emphases, offering a semblance of 'objective' confirmation of the scale of the crisis and the necessity for obedience, which further propelled the recruitment of citizens in the process of their own incarceration.

Imagination is a key tool of the hypnotist. With an appropriate script and a deliberate mimicry of well-remembered charismatic leaders of the past — a touch of Kennedy, a *soupcon* of Churchill — even the most plank-like politician could affect a sufficiency of charisma or gravitas to seduce his audience into the zone wherein to weave word-pictures and teleport his captives to a place of collective imagining. The mood of siege or crisis thus established was sufficient to inveigle stronger-minded holdouts to join in.

By affecting empathy, rapport, a sense of common purpose, the 'hypnotist' guides his subjects towards the desired frame of mind. He seeks access to the unconscious, but not that of the individual person; rather, he wishes to remove each member of his audience to a common place: the herd mind in which he knows they can all come to share approximately the same outlooks, so that henceforth they can be summoned to that place by signs and triggers without being required to leave their armchairs.

TV creates an ideal instrument of this form of hypnosis, not least because the news comes sandwiched between movies and soap operas that engage the imaginative and emotional elements of the mind. These, maintained by fiction-alised treatments of reality, provide the heightened state that renders the subject amenable to be lured into the trance. Once achieved, the trance can be reacti-vated at will in anyone whose attention, kept primed by fictional narratives, remains in this state of focused imaginative attention, highly prone to easy emotional arousal.

When in such a hypnoidal trance, in the grip of its dominant emotion — rage, hatred, fear, anxiety, sadness, worry, envy, greed, selfishness — humans retreat into their reptilian minds, becoming cut off from their thinking brains and thereby more susceptible to adopting a locked-in, limited view of reality. In the lockdown episode, fear of death was the chief emotional trigger imposed by the controllers.

As outlined in the last chapter, a herd has a different psychology to that of an individual, a sort of collective mind that makes those in that situation feel, think and act in a manner quite differently from that in which each individual would feel, think and act when alone. Herds are, generally speaking, stupider than individuals and highly prone to follow a single current of emotion in their midst.

Creating a hypnotic state involves three phases: idealisation, devaluation and alienation. Idealisation is also called 'love-bombing', whereby the controller/hypnotist strives to identify with and mirror the target individual or social group. In this case, the controller is the politician or health tsar who seeks to corral the public while making them believe he is doing them a great favour. In reality, he follows the same line of attack as the habitual wife-beater. He thanks the people for their stoicism thus far, praises them, reminds them they are 'saving lives' then spells out the next stage. The controllers, in this case, include the media — the journaliars — usurping their roles as watchdogs and truth-tellers to exert powers of manipulation and control using the weapons of fear, guilt and obligation, which impress the presence of constant danger on the reptilian lower brain, ensuring widespread compliance.

Language — the use of spell words — is again central to the endeavour. The reptilian non-brain responds to repetition — of words and phrases, memes, catchwords, clichés, which serve to embed the hypnotic suggestions to the extent that they become beliefs, immune to rational argumentation. Physical triggers can be more efficient than verbal ones, especially if self-administered, creating an instant Pavlovian effect.

All this kicked in with a vengeance from about mid-March last year. Throughout the 'pandemic' period, the pathways in the parks near my home had intermittently placed chalk figures separated by arrows pointing at each figure (indicating the extent of two metres), clearly designed to evoke the chalk marks investigators draw around the corpse of a murder victim. (Interestingly, these markings, which had all but disappeared, have been restored in the past couple of weeks.) For those daft enough to watch TV or listen to the radio, statistics of deaths, most of them invented or inflated, were rolled out by the hour. Terms like 'deadly virus' were used non-stop: The phrase 'new normal' had the effect of insinuating the loss of things long cherished, a state of bereavement, invoking a grief that did not realise its name. The applauding by candle-light of 'front line workers' became a way of compelling holdouts to throw themselves into the spell as though into battle.

The second phase, 'devaluation', is analogous to the live cooking of a frog. Words of praise and consolation are juxtaposed with house arrest, instigating a form of induced Stockholm Syndrome. If feedback indicates that the populace is beginning to wake up to the deception and manipulation, the controller/wife-beater must show that he is indeed working for everybody's good by intermittently appearing to be on their side. This registers in the entranced individual as a chemical rush of serotonin, oxytocin and other chemicals of relief, which facilitate the deepening of the stranglehold.

Images and ideas of restriction, control, humiliation, are packaged in sentimental and often paradoxical forms of manipulation: nurses or police officers dancing amidst what we are led to presume are unremitting scenes of death; grandchildren waving to their heartbroken grandparents through a wound-up car window. Here, the glass becomes a symbol of the invisible wall that may permanently separate them, a portent of the 'new normal', invoking dread of an unknowable future. Generated confusion, mixed messages, are central elements: you must be sure to take care of old people — just don't go near lest you kill them; it is important to become infected to achieve immunity, but at all costs, avoid infecting other healthy people; wear a face mask, even though 'experts' say they are ineffective. Wear two face masks just to prove you are not an 'anti-masker'. The inconsistency and incoherence of the messages are not random or chaos-driven, but have a planned and precise purpose: to destabilise the sensibility of the subject, rendering him amenable to further manipulation. Since he cannot understand, he simply obeys.

Then comes the final phase of the hypnosis: 'Abandonment', the iron fist. No more Mr Nice Guy. The police, it turns out, have been issued with more equipment, more vehicles, more guns, more batons, rottweiler-shaped robots to spy on the public. Reinforcements are brought in, including trainees dressed up as robo-cops, part of the process of abasement. The talk of vaccine passports shifts from a possibility to a racing certainty. Now the real motives may more readily be seen. Our rights having been stripped away, we begin to awake to the folly of thinking of the controllers as our saviours or guardians. In order to maintain control, a method of what is known as 'intermittent reinforcement' takes place, whereby the tone of the controllers becomes more austere and threatening, establishing another layer of conditions in respect to the future. Unless compliance improves, we are warned, the ante may have to be increased. We should not expect a return to normal any time soon — or at all. The 'second/third/fourth wave' is mentioned in tones of disappointed rebuke, setting up an expectation that failure to meet the contradictory requirements may result in further coercion. With each intermittent reinforcement, there will be a further erosion of civil liberties, and so the programme goes on.

Ritual is a key factor in the alteration of expectations, which in turn transforms reality. Rituals are process of initiation and renewal, which reinforce beliefs, behaviours and values, inducing conformity, groupthink, accommodation to changes in structures, a reinvented sense of belonging. Rituals are transformative, redefining, rebirthing, anchoring the subject in his new situation.

Rituals work subliminally to alter perception, to strengthen or exaggerate existing emotions. The initiate in a religious rite is separated from reality and, in advance of the ritual, placed in isolation so as to become decontaminated from everyday influences: Shelter-in-place involves a form of detoxification from the logic, desires, assumptions and language of the world, a process of renouncing that facilitates a coming to terms with losses about to be imposed as part of the initiation: loss of freedom, loved ones, hopes, expectations. Here we begin to glimpse the true purpose of the Covid project: to prepare us to relinquish the kind of life we took for granted hitherto.

A transition follows: the subject begins to let go of everything she has taken for granted, prepares to enter a new regime, to cross the threshold to a new era. A new mood descends, a mixture of fear and sorrow, accompanied by an escalating sense of powerlessness that threatens to overwhelm until the subject agrees to accept. Then comes the liberation and release that accompany the signing away of freedom for an insinuated higher purpose. This is akin to the liminal state between life and death. The old life is subjected to a form of scorched earth, presaging a surrender to the new normal.

By persuading people to engage in rituals — essentially collective rites and ceremonies they would not normally succumb to while alone, it is possible to draw them into an imagined herd for the purpose of imbuing them with collective thoughts, breaking with existing or normative patterns of thought and behaviour. Using repetition and emotional enhancement, the ritual imposes a new language, new signposts contained in words and symbols. Ritual also operates to impose new codes as a way of effecting changes in thinking, working primarily at the spiritual and psychological levels, but unnoticed as such. It serves to suspend the cognitive dimension, thus eliminating any individual reservations that might otherwise manifest as embarrassment while activating elements of the mind not usually engaged. The subject is both actor and spectator.

In the course of the 'pandemic', the face mask emerged as a new symbol of pseudo-solidarity, though really it was used as an instrument of fear-mongering, alienating and division. Many of the more enthusiastic maskers happily doubled as mask-marshalls, policing their neighbours, even strangers, with accusations about granny-killing and selfishness. The mask provokes a death of the ego, enabling a new self to be born: the temporary covering of the old face while the new one is immersed in the period of gestation necessitated by the transformation. It was not very often a pretty sight. The more threadbare the Covid-19 story became, the more people seemed to be wearing the face mask, not so much as precautionary apparel but as a form of accusation: *You are threatening my life!* The hypnotised as hypnotist. Once the mask is donned, the subject becomes his more fearful self, but also more tyrannical, the secret weapon of totalitarianism.

The mask obliterates the face, the window of the soul, thus reducing the wearer to a kind of *humanimal*. Beholding one another in the street — masked, visored, alert for the slightest incursion into our personal six feet of space, jumping out of our skins at the slightest cough, sniffle or sneeze — it became clear that we were being coached to no longer look upon one another and perceive the iconic shape of the human being in history — limbs, trunk, head, face, gaze, smile — but see instead a moving blob of festering matter, a biohazard to be avoided on pain of death. In a sense, this is a reversal of the civilising process, which has, over centuries, coached human beings to, among much else, avoid seeing each other in the terms summoned up by Nietzsche in *The Genealogy of Morality*: man defined by 'repulsive' traits disapproved of by himself: 'impure begetting, disgusting nourishment in the womb, vileness of the matter out of which man develops, revolting stench, excretion of saliva, urine, and feces.' Clearly, whereas such definitions have an objective basis, to carry such notions of ourselves around in our imaginations would soon reduce each of us to a state of constant perturbation, disintegrating our desire to be alive.

In *The Human Person and Natural Law*, Karol Wojtyla wrote about 'the essence of a thing' being taken as the basis of 'all actualisation of the thing', which in human terms meant perceiving the unity represented by the ensouled being within the encasing body. The essence of the human person was not to be found in the biological matter comprising his physical totality: he was also creativity and will and emotion and conscience and subjectivity and self-reflection — all parts of the human creativity that cause us to rise above the Nietzschean reduction.

Perhaps the most emphatic and lasting effect of Covid-19 will be to shift the entirety of our capacities for self-perception from the largely metaphysical to the overwhelming phenomenological plane. It is not far-fetched to fear that, under the attrition of the lockdown psyop , our personal and collective self-image as human beings began dissolving, bringing an end to the millennia-old sense of the human person as an embodied soul on an earthly sojourn. We shall need new words to describe this, and they are unlikely to be pretty.

CHAPTER 11
THE GROUPTHINK PSYCHODEMIC, PART I: DANGER IN NUMBERS
23-08-2021

In this three-part series, we peer into the history and nature of 'groupthink', in both its damaging effects on decision-making and its emerging life as a technique of mass indoctrination.

Groupthink is as old as humanity itself, enabling the strong of mind to rule the weak and frequently endangering the capacity of human beings to arrive at balanced decisions under the influence of the internal dynamics of the affected group.

'Groupthink' is one of a handful of words that we have perhaps heard — even used — thousands of times over the course of recent decades, maybe only half-understanding them. With related terms like 'propaganda', 'mass entrancement' and 'menticide' — interesting in a certain academic sense but seeming to pertain to particular schemozzles, imbroglios, fiascos or curiosities, dark moments of the past, aberrations of history or of ideological fanaticism — 'groupthink' belonged to theoretical treatises about strange phenomena that swept across the consciousnesses of our ancestors, or infected cultlike bodies inoculated against reason or civilising values due to their closed and unmodern natures. Now, as though by dint of some hidden psychic explosion, they erupt into our everyday lives, demanding that we pay them the attention we had withheld. Now they become as though commonplace concepts — not exactly banal, but nevertheless necessary implements of understanding the everyday. Or at least they now appear so to those who are not infected (as opposed to 'affected', which just about everyone is) while remaining inscrutable to those who have overnight succumbed to them, as though to some kind of virus.

Suddenly, just over a year ago, their meanings began to acquire life-or-death significance. They no longer belonged exclusively to fusty textbooks or black-and-white documentaries on YouTube — interesting topics to explore in dissertations and cautionary lectures about the pitfalls of the past. Round about April 2020, they started to transcend theory and become real, to come into their own, infecting our neighbours and friends, brothers and wives, as well as the cop on the beat and the barman down the local. Those fragments of understanding we had grasped about these conditions made them, for a moment, almost intoxicatingly fascinating — 'Oh look! *Real* brainwashing!' — but rapidly became worrying, and then terrifying. As our world plummeted towards totalitarianism, our early ironic fascination rapidly turned to horror. Was it possible that people could *know about* such things and yet not know what they *actually mean*? Was it possible to have read Orwell, seen the movies, and yet not recognise the real thing when it rattlingly turned the corner at the end of your street, churning the tarmac with its caterpillar treads?

We need, therefore, at a popular level of our societies, urgently to begin parsing, plumbing and penetrating all those concepts which have lain all around us all our lives in books and journals with archaic covers and voluminous footnotes. Already, in this book, we have explored in depth the concepts of propaganda, hypnosis and mass entrancement, the role of surveillance and Big Data, all of which have become everyday elements of our daily burdens of concerns. But there is a concept that brings all of these together in what is almost a definition of the conditions that have been imposed on us for the past year and a half. It is called 'groupthink'.

'Groupthink' has multiple definitions, oscillating around the same idea:

- 'a pattern of thought characterized by self-deception, forced manufacture of consent, and conformity to group values and ethics.'
- 'a psychological phenomenon in which people strive for consensus within a group. (In many cases, people will set aside their own personal beliefs or adopt the opinion of the rest of the group.)'
- 'a phenomenon that occurs when a group of well-intentioned people makes irrational or non-optimal decisions spurred by the urge to conform or the belief that dissent is impossible.'
- 'a phenomenon whereby the natural desire for harmony within a group ensures that members will set aside their personal beliefs and adopt instead (at least in their engagement with the group) the beliefs and perspectives of the group.'
- 'the process in which bad decisions are made by a group because its

members do not want to express opinions, suggest new ideas, etc. that
others may disagree with.'
- 'A psychological phenomenon that occurs within a group in which the
  desire for harmony or conformity results in an irrational or
  dysfunctional decision-making outcome. (Cohesiveness, or the desire
  for cohesiveness, may produce a tendency among group members to
  agree at all costs.)'

It will immediately become clear that each of these definitions appears to
hint at the situation humanity in general now finds itself in: not just a condition
of likemindedness but a condition of induced or cultivated concurrence on what
amounts to the core, if not totally defining condition of our time: *belief in and fear
of Covid-19*. The mentions within those definitions of states of 'self-deception',
'irrationality', 'desire for harmony', 'conformity' might be deemed emblematic
labels for the condition of our culture over the past year and a half. Yet, it is
striking that these definitions relate primarily to descriptions of processes of
decision-making, to conditions that risk leaving participants prone to dangerous
error.

To begin with, then, 'groupthink' relates to forms of power at the point of
exercise, but the tendency, having been identified and diagnosed in its essential
form, is no longer merely something 'found' or 'noticed' in reality. More and
more, it has the facility to become weaponised, cultivated and imposed on enormous numbers of passive bystanders, which means that whole populations may
now be deliberately impressed with erroneous or mendacious forms of belief or
understanding, often to an extent that no longer qualifies as 'thought' by any
conventional definition. Both ends of this spectrum may be observed at work in
the Covid horror show.

It may be useful, then, to divide the concept in the first instance into two
distinct (for the moment) categories: that of error-generating conditions within
decision-making bodies and the ultimate form of groupthink capable of grip-
ping entire societies.

The first might be characterised as groupthink as a kind of *possession* (in the
occult sense): where a group succumbs to the loudest voices in its midst,
following tramlines of bad thinking for want of hearing the alternatives. Here
we might refer to such episodes as the Bay of Pigs, the fictional tale of the
Emperor's New Clothes, and, closer to home, the infamous libelling of Fr Kevin
Reynolds by RTÉ's *Prime Time Investigates* programme in 2011.

There is also the concept of full-blown cultural groupthink as a kind of *spell*,
an imposition of likemindedness on a whole population or part thereof. This is
of the kind that does not lend itself to the label 'thought', amounting more
closely to something like hysteria imposed by propaganda and mass entrancement. In this latter category, we might include examples like Nazism, various

outbreaks of what is dubbed 'McCarthyism', the witch trials of Salem, and — most dramatically of all — the Cult of Covid.

The first form of groupthink — the *possession* kind — is more likely to be unearthed or identified in retrospect when an investigation of the circumstances of some policy or decision-related calamity is undertaken. The second — the *spell* — is capable of being perceived and diagnosed while it is occurring, but only by those who have remained immune. As C.G. Jung observed in *Psychology and National Problems*, '[a]s long as one is within a certain phenomenology, one is not astonished, and no one wonders what it is all about. Such philosophical doubt only comes to one who is outside the game.'

The Covid plandemic has hints of the first — in the convergence of thinking and the deadly pursuit of a singularity of purpose and policy across the globe. This may be misleading since it is as likely to arise as a deliberate policy from the centralised orchestration of the logistics of the plandemic. But it also exhibits enormous and as yet largely unremarked overtones of the second, imposed forms of groupthink, in the grotesque misleading of literally billions of people into believing that their lives were in deadly danger from what was, at most, a routine respiratory condition such as they might expect to experience multiple times in a lifetime, and suffer no undue consequence or effect.

Groupthink is invariably, it appears, to be regarded as a bad thing, restricting, inhibiting and stultifying the human mind — both in infecting individually each of the constituent minds of a group and blocking the channels of potential cross-fertilisation, and also in the sense of imposing a collective mesmerism on a whole people.

It has been a commonplace of human understanding for millennia that 'two heads are better than one'. This is the principle underlying the 'ask the audience' element of the classic TV quiz show *Who Wants to Be a Millionaire?* But this, noticeably and invariably, relates to processes involving facts, figures, information, rather than thought or analysis, and works best in the absence of any overt means of inter-communication. In a decision-making process requiring a singular, straightforward choice of answer, the more minds in the mix, the greater seems to be the volume and scope of available knowledge. But something like the opposite happens in a process requiring discernment, discretion, balance, nuance, subtlety and, above all, mutual openness to the complexity of the issues involved. In other words, when processes of communication, consultation and interaction are necessary, there enters a risk of contaminating the common pool of wisdom. The 'wisdom of crowds' relates to matters of fact rather than insight.

And there is a countervailing and much older idea that appears to have gained increasing traction on reality as political life and communications became more 'sophisticated'. This idea is summarised in the titles of two books, separated by nearly two centuries — the 1841 book by the Scottish journalist Charles Mackay, *Extraordinary Popular Delusions and the Madness of Crowds*, and the 2019 book by the English journalist Douglas Murray, titled more economically *The Madness of Crowds*. Mackay's book focuses on the baneful and dangerous nature of the herd mind, essentially developing Nietzsche's aphorism that 'madness is the exception in individuals but the rule in groups.' Douglas Murray's book has a narrower focus than its distant inspiration: the eruption of Woke ideas in the late twentieth century and beyond, and might more accurately be described as a dissection of cultural groupthink or mass entrancement by ideology and reductive ideas.

Mackay's study preceded by more than half a century a more famous work by the French philosopher Gustave Le Bon, who in 1895 published his now classic work *The Crowd: A Study of the Popular Mind*. Le Bon despised the democratic idea, suspecting any kind of group charged with making decisions, including juries and parliaments. Any gathering of highly intelligent people assembled to make decisions relating to the general welfare, he wrote, would do no better than 'a gathering of imbeciles'.

Le Bon was the first significant thinker to identify that a herd has a different psychology to that of an individual and that this is capable of infecting each constituent member. To briefly reprise, he observed that the consciousness bestowed by membership of a crowd can be transformative of the person, putting individual members in possession of 'a sort of collective mind which makes them feel, think and act in a manner quite differently from that in which each individual would feel, think and act were that person in a state of isolation.' In such a 'psychological crowd', individual personality disappears, brain activity is replaced by reflex action, resulting in a collective lowering of intelligence and a complete transformation of sentiments. 'The ascendency of crowds,' wrote Le Bon, 'indicates the death throes of a civilisation.' The upward climb to civilisation is an intellectual process driven by individuals; the descent a herd in stampede. 'Crowds are only useful for destruction.' This might be called the first coherent diagnosis of what we nowadays call 'groupthink'.

A 2005 book, *The Wisdom of Crowds: Why the Many Are Smarter than the Few and How Collective Wisdom Shapes Business, Economics, Societies and Nations*, by *New Yorker* business columnist James Surowiecki, posits something that at first sight seems the opposite idea: that decisions taken by a large group, even if the individuals within the group aren't smart, are always better than decisions made by small numbers of 'experts'. In decision-making processes, Surowiecki argues, the larger the group, the better chance of groupthink being eliminated; danger enters when the group is smaller and more cohesive.

Surowiecki starts off with the case of the British scientist Francis Galton, into his 80s at the start of the twentieth century, who from believing that, since 'the stupidity and wrong-headedness of many men and women being so great as to be scarcely credible,' power and decision-making ought to remain in the hands of the 'select, well-bred few,' dramatically changed his mind and did a 180-

degree twirl. Attending the West of England Fat Stock and Poultry Exhibition in 1906, and observing a competition to guess the weight of an ox when slaughtered and dressed, Galton discovered reason to doubt his own prejudice. There were 800 entrants, some of them farmers and experienced butchers, but the generality were laypersons with no particular expertise. Following the contest, Galton retrieved the entry slips and analysed them, and discovered that the mean of the total guesses of the total group was just one pound amiss of the correct weight — and never looked back. This is, you might say, the foundational assumption of democracy: that 'the People' are capable — at least as much as any individual or smaller group — of organising their own affairs.

This principle can appear to operate as a form of alchemy. 'Even if most people within a group are not especially well-informed or rational,' Surowiecki declares, 'it can still reach a collectively wise decision.' Surowiecki squarely opposes the (parallel) theses of Mackay and Le Bon, parodying the latter's declamatory verdicts: 'If you put together a big enough and diverse enough group of people and ask them to "*make decisions affecting matters of general interest*," that group's decision will, over time, be "*intellectually [superior] to the isolated individual*," no matter how smart or well-informed he is,' he defiantly declares. He cites numerous incidences whereby markets (and also bookies!) tend to be above-average 'smart', often displaying an enhanced success rate in their judgments and 'predictions'.

Of course, this principle depends on a number of factors not necessarily to be taken for granted: the elimination of background noise — i.e. the absence of interference or 'nudging' from outside, or disproportionately from inside the group — and, by extension, the individual independence of group members. Once the group begins to function as a group, to the logic of group dynamics as identified by Le Bon, danger enters in. The vital principle is that each individual's integrity of thought be protected and respected. This is the principle underlying the closed, secret and private conditions of the polling booth — though, of course, modern elections, being attended by endless preliminary supplication, submissions, entreaties and petitions, many of these driven home by underhanded behavioural techniques, amount to an entirely different phenomenon than was the case in Le Bon's or Galton's day.

It is not, as may at first appear, a matter of 'you pays your money and you takes your choice'. It is possible to perceive that both theses are true — that a crowd can, in certain circumstances, be 'smarter' than an individual, and in certain others, the opposite.

Surowiecki presents some persuasive evidence, gleaned via markets, gambling trends, voting systems and other viewfinders. By his telling, the 'wisdom of crowds' is far more influential and useful than it seems. The results tend to depend on the nature of the group. Big groups can be better at solving problems, though they need to be carefully managed to avoid complexities arising out of inefficiency. On the other hand, small groups, though more manageable, are less likely to have the necessary variety of membership to deliver effective collective intelligence. It depends on the group and the circumstances. Groups need to have strict rules, especially to avoid an excess of talking, which can cause a loss of collective intelligence, which is detrimental to problem-solving. What he seems to be saying is that there is a kind of alchemy that happens in a functional group, and when it is there, the results can be spectacular, and when it isn't, nothing much happens.

According to Surowiecki, reliable decisions by a group depend on the existence of four factors: diversity of opinion (or interpretation of information); independence from the opinions of others; 'decentralisation' (from the group mentality — preferably involving a connection to and/or knowledge of the locus of the problem); and aggregation — i.e. a mechanism for turning the full complement of individual opinions into a collective decision.

Mackay, he maintains, was right about the extremes of collective behaviour. There are times — a riot or a stock market bubble — when aggregating individual decisions produces irrational collective outcomes. Collective decision-making carries the same risks, which is why diversity and independence are crucial conditions, because the best decisions are the product of debate and disagreement, not compromise or consensus.

The best way for a group to become intelligent is for each member to retain as much independence of thought as possible. The purpose is to arrive at some consensus of thinking that amounts to an aggregate of everyone's viewpoints rather than to have the strongest voices dominate the process. A satisfactory conclusion cannot be achieved by requiring individual members to compromise. Much better to use mechanisms like market prices or intelligent voting systems to assist the various viewpoints towards some kind of agreement. The process sounds mysterious, and yet is perhaps more like an open discussion between people who take different positions but are willing to adapt their positions when better ones are suggested.

Surowiecki says that generally speaking, in assessing a factual situation, possibly requiring estimates or guesswork, the bigger the group, the better, since this enables the largest possible number of inputs, which appear to mysteriously 'close in on' the problem and in some instances achieve a mean answer that is not the specific answer of any individual member. It is important that, in arriving at their 'group' decision, the members not talk to one another to compare notes. What works best is when the group's guesses are aggregated and averaged, but this method, by definition, relates to precise, narrowly defined kinds of questions and problems. The communication issue is vital: According to Surowiecki, you can have too little or too much; the group requires you to enjoy good internal relationships and yet not be so familiar as to enable a hierarchy to emerge.

A group observing these criteria will make sound decisions. The principle at work is a quasi-mathematical one: In consulting a large number, the errors of individual group members tend to cancel one another out, leaving the clean information behind. One individual leaning erroneously in one direction will cancel out another leaning erroneously in another. Strike out the errors against each other, and the reliable facts remain. 'Now,' Surowiecki concedes, 'even with the errors cancelled out, it's possible that a group's judgment will be bad. For the group to be smart, there has to be at least some information in the "information" part of the "information minus error" equation. . . . What is striking, though — and what makes a phrase like the wisdom of crowds meaningful — is just how much information a group's collective verdict so often contains.' The important thing, he maintains, is that the group is capable of holding 'a near complete picture of the world in its collective brain.'

The functionality of this method ought not be surprising. The evolutionary process, he suggests, will surely have ensured that human beings are capable of figuring out the world on their own; what is surprising is that they are so much better at doing it collectively.

'[A]sk a hundred people to answer a question or solve a problem, and the average answer will often be at least as good as the answer of the smartest member. With most things, the average is mediocrity. With decision-making, it's often excellence. You could say it's as if we've been programmed to be collectively smart.'

A central argument of Surowiecki's book is that 'chasing the expert is a mistake and a costly one at that'. We should stop hunting, he says, and 'ask the crowd (which, of course, includes the geniuses as well as everyone else) instead.'

The key to the apparent conundrum (Which is it? — crowds are thick or crowds are quick) appears to reside in the nature of relationships between group members, and in particular, the difference between a 'group' comprising a series of independent individuals and a 'herd' that is subject to central, or contagious, or, on the other hand, externally directed control or conditioning. Yes, a group of the first kind is likely to be much 'wiser' than each or any of its constituent members, but this quality of wisdom depends on allowing each member to remain unfettered by the forces and dynamics that tend to govern groups engaged in decision making, usually arising from distortions stemming from internal leadership or external pressure or (even subtle) coercion.

In a group or collective, however large or small, where decision-making is not the issue, but rather receptivity to a proposal or set of ideas, the dangerous elements usually have to do with external manipulation — the use of the behavioural 'sciences', propaganda, hypnosis and other kinds of distorting mechanisms. Then, and especially in a culture fitted with a cohesive system of mass communication, it becomes easy to flip the 'channel' of each member to the collective band, transporting individual members into the wavelength of the hive mind, where they become susceptible to group emotions, intense feelings and responses, especially anger and fear that close out or down all rational processing. (This is why bodies like 'constitutional conventions' and 'citizens' assemblies' are such a bad idea, democratically speaking). In such a situation, any capacity for reason and balance is lost, the reposeful accessing of individual experience is blocked by hysteria and noise, and the group becomes a receptor for the basest, least thoughtful forms of thinking.

In Surowiecki's description of the pitfalls and dynamics we can make out the general shape of a manifestation of groupthink that is at once concentrated within power structures but also capable of acquiring a wider cultural penetration. Covid may be the first instance of actual groupthink cultivation on a global scale, whereby a condition previously spotted mainly in the wild was actually produced in a hothouse atmosphere and on a quasi-global basis. It is, however, likely to be one of many unless we come to understand, diagnose, deconstruct and counteract it.

The concept of 'groupthink' was first crystallised by Irving Lester Janis in his 1973 book, *Victims of Groupthink: A Psychological Study of Foreign Policy Decisions and Fiascos*. Janis was a research psychologist at Yale University and a professor emeritus at the University of California, Berkeley.

It was he who coined the term 'groupthink' and his interest in it was chiefly to do with the influence of the phenomenon in decision-making in particular iconic moments in history, especially in the operation of power. His work in this area is essentially that of a cultural anthropologist, digging specimens out of the debris.

His analysis focussed mainly on a theory of 'groupthink' that described the systematic errors that occurred when the members of decision-making bodies abandoned critical thinking and fell into wrongheaded consensus and the consequences of these errors. To this end, he conducted a study of various notorious high-level decision-making incidents — 'fiascos', as he called them — in which groupthink had surfaced with adverse results, adapting ideas from small-group analysis to the explaining of major policy disasters. His examples include the Bay of Pigs debacle of 1961 (in which US President John F. Kennedy tried to overthrow the Castro-led government of Cuba), the Watergate cover-up and the Challenger disaster of 1986.

The concept occurred to him when reading Arthur M. Schlesinger's chapters on the Bay of Pigs in *A Thousand Days*. He was initially puzzled by the idea that intelligent people like John F. Kennedy and his advisers could be taken in by the CIA's 'stupid, patchwork plan'. Stupidity could not have been the answer!

Rather than focusing on individual weakness, emotional disturbance or lapses, he decided to consider what group dynamics might be at play.

'I began to wonder whether some kinks of psychological contagion, similar

to social conformity phenomena observed in studies of small groups, had inter-
fered with their mental alertness. I kept thinking about the implications of this
notion until one day, I found myself talking about it in a seminar of mine on
group psychology at Yale University. I suggested that the poor decision-making
performance of the men at those White House meetings might be akin to the
lapses in judgment of ordinary citizens who become more concerned with
retaining the approval of the fellow members of their work group than with
coming up with good solutions to the tasks at hand.'

On re-reading Schlesinger's account, he was struck by some observations
that earlier had escaped his notice. 'These observations began to fit a specific
pattern of concurrence-seeking behaviour that had impressed me time and
again in my research on other kinds of face-to-face groups, particularly when a
"we-feeling" of solidarity is running high. Additional accounts of the Bay of
Pigs yielded more such observations, leading me to conclude that group
processes had been subtly at work, preventing the members of Kennedy's team
from debating the real issues posed by the CIA's plan and from carefully
appraising its serious risks.' He realised that the group responsible for the fiasco
had fallen victim to what he called 'groupthink.'

Groupthink arises, according to Janis, because group members have come to
value the group (and their belonging to it) higher than anything else, and so
become overly conscious of attracting disapproval from other members. These
inclinations cause them to strive, as a priority, for unanimity on the matters the
group is required to confront and deal with, rather than holding out for a more
truthful or accurate analysis. In his book, he sets out symptoms and characteristics that can arise within cohesive groups with significant negative influences on
the decision-making process. Groups, for example, can exert enormous internal
pressure on dissidents from a growing consensus. An emphasis on group
morale can deleteriously affect the group's capacity for critical thinking, and
prevent the group from reopening discussion of matters already decided.

He derived the concept of 'groupthink' from George Orwell's Dictionary of
Newspeak, in particular the terms' doublethink' and 'crimethink', perceiving
the sinister connotation appropriate. He elaborated on his coinage of the word
as follows:

'I use the term groupthink as a quick and easy way to refer to the mode of
thinking that persons engage in when concurrence-seeking becomes so dominant in a cohesive in-group that it tends to override realistic appraisal of alternative courses in action.' Groupthink can involve a deterioration of mental
efficiency, realism and moral judgment.

It is interesting that Janis perceived this sinister dimension of the groupthink
concept, even though his explorations are confined to the 'possession' or 'fiasco'-
related kind of groupthink. He has little or nothing to say about the idea of
enspelling populations with the techniques derived from the investigation of

incidences of groupthink as a detrimental influence on decision-making. However, his insights into the process at the micro level are highly instructive as to the possibilities of groupthink 'technique' as an instrument of mass social control.

In his studies of high-level governmental decision-makers, both civilian and military, Janis identified a number of key symptoms of groupthink: illusion of invulnerability, illusion of unanimity, suppression of individual doubts, illusions of moral certainty, concurrence-directed pressures, excessive stereotyping of rivals and opponents, lack of in-house research, confirmation bias, self-censorship by individual group members, lack of deliberation about obstacles, internal or external, to the preferred decision and undue influence of self-appointed thought guardians who seek to protect the group from inconvenient information.

Groups, Janis held, are more prone to error than individuals, exhibiting particular dynamics that relate to the interactions of constituent members. The deficiencies about which we know the most, he wrote, pertain to 'disturbances in the behaviour of each individual in a decision-making group — temporary states of elation, fear, or anger that reduce a person's mental efficiency; chronic blind spots arising from a person's social prejudices; shortcomings in information-processing that prevent a person from comprehending the complex consequences of a seemingly simple policy decision.' These tendencies become magnified within the overall dynamic of the group.

'A considerable amount of social science literature shows that in circumstances of extreme crisis, group contagion occasionally gives rise to collective panic, violent acts of scapegoating, and other forms of what could be called group madness,' he writes. 'Much more frequent, however, are instances of mindless conformity and collective misjudgement of serious risks, which are collectively laughed off in a clubby atmosphere of relaxed conviviality.

'Lack of vigilance and excessive risk-taking are forms of temporary group derangement to which decision-making groups made up of responsible executives are not at all immune. Sometimes, the main trouble is that the chief executive manipulates his advisers to rubber-stamp his own ill-conceived proposals.

'During the group's deliberations, the leader does not deliberately try to get the group to tell him what he wants to hear but is quite sincere in asking for honest opinions. The group members are not transformed into sycophants. They are not afraid to speak their minds. Nevertheless, subtle constraints, which the leader may reinforce inadvertently, prevent a member from fully exercising his critical powers and from openly expressing doubts when most others in the group appear to have reached a consensus.'

The more cohesive the group, Janis's examination confirmed, the more likely it is to court disaster. The more cohesive the group, the more it ends towards conformity.

'In studies of social clubs and other small groups, conformity pressures have frequently been observed. Whenever a member says something that sounds out of line with the group's norms, the other members at first increase their communication with the deviant. Attempts to influence the nonconformist member to revise or tone down his dissident ideas continue as long as most members of the group feel hopeful about talking him into changing his mind. But if they fail after repeated attempts, the amount of communication they direct toward the deviant decreases markedly. The members begin to exclude him, often quite subtly at first and later more obviously, in order to restore the unity of the group.' The more cohesive the group and the more relevant the disputed issue to the goals of the group, the greater the inclination of the members to reject a nonconformist. Just as the members insulate themselves from outside critics who threaten to disrupt the unity and *esprit de corps* of their group, they take steps, often without being aware of it, to counteract the disruptive influence of inside critics who are attacking the group's norms.'

The danger arises when individual members of the group, mindful of peer pressure, discount their own experiences and perspectives in favour of seeking consensus. Wishing to retain the approval of their colleagues, they soft-pedal their potentially critical responses. The 'we-feeling' of the group dominates the priorities of its members. To preserve the clubby atmosphere, group members suppress personal doubts, silence dissenters, and follow the group leader's suggestions.

Leaders, by definition, become such by virtue of being 'alphas' who command respect from more timid creatures, having climbed to the top by being confident and competent people. These are generally found to be positive attributes, but like many qualities become problematic beyond a certain point. For example, precisely the qualities of decisiveness and authority that put them in charge to begin with are also those that generate an atmosphere of undue deference among their underlings. Janis proposes that leaders should occasionally leave the decision table so that this effect may be overcome.

The absence of critical discussion or dissent can lead to members believing that their opinions don't hold as much weight as those of their peers, leading to a failure by the group to consider possible pitfalls and take steps to minimise risks, leading to the growth of an unjustified confidence in the group as to what is logical and correct. A form of collective rationalisation takes over, by which the group becomes more and more solidified in its consensus, leading to a sense of immunity from error or baneful consequences. Janis describes an afflicted group of people who respect each other's opinions so much that they arrive at a unanimous view, leaving each member certain that the belief must be true. The group acquires a strong belief in the inherent morality of its own procedures and thought processes, and also a countervailing sense that putative opponents or critics are in some sense less moral, weaker or incompetent. The results can be devastating, leading the group to develop a distorted view of reality, with excessive optimism producing hasty and reckless decisions, and a neglect of ethical questions. The combination of these deficiencies makes such groups particularly vulnerable to initiating or sustaining projects that will turn out to be policy fiascos.

Irving Janis set out three 'defining rules of groupthink', which, when present together, can create potentially lethal conditions:

That a group of people come to share a common view, opinion or belief that in some way is not based on objective reality. They may be convinced intellectually, morally, politically even scientifically that it is right. They may be sure from all the evidence they have considered that it is so. But their belief cannot ultimately be tested in a way which could confirm it beyond doubt. It is based on a picture of the world as they imagine, or would like it to be. In essence, their collective view will always have in it an element of wishful thinking or make-believe.

That, precisely because their shared view is essentially subjective, they need to go out of their way to insist it is so self-evidently right that a 'consensus' of all right-minded people must agree with it. Their belief has made them an 'in-group', which accepts that any evidence which contradicts it, and the views of anyone who does not agree with it, can be disregarded. The most revealing consequence of this: To reinforce their in-group conviction that they are right, the group needs to treat the views of anyone who questions it as wholly unacceptable. They are incapable of engaging in any serious dialogue or debate with those who disagree with them. Those outside the bubble must be marginalised and ignored, although, if necessary, their views must be mercilessly caricatured to make them seem ridiculous. If this is not enough, they must be attacked in the most violently contemptuous terms, usually with the aid of some scornfully dismissive label and somehow morally discredited. The thing which most characterizes any form of groupthink is that dissent cannot be tolerated.

Hence, one of the most dangerous factors in the evolution of groupthink is the creation by the group of an out-group of 'enemies' which stands between the group and its virtuous objectives. This tendency drives the group deeper into its possibly misconceived certitudes, propelled by the idea that it is seeking to separate and distance itself from wickedness. Groupthink arises when the normative conditions of friendship, collegiality and camaraderie — all of which on their own make for good decision-making — become perverted by often unseen dynamics of the group. Hence, this paradox: A little cohesiveness is good; a little more begins to be dangerous.

Janis stressed the inclination of groups to develop stereotyped images that dehumanise out-groups with which they are engaged in competitive struggles, and also a tendency, in this and other contexts, for the collective judgments arising out of group discussions to become polarised, sometimes shifting toward either extreme conservatism (of response) or riskier courses of action than the individual members would otherwise be prepared to take.

'Paradoxically, soft-headed groups are often hard-hearted when it comes to dealing with out-groups or enemies. They find it relatively easy to resort to dehumanizing solutions —they will readily authorize bombing attacks that kill large numbers of civilians in the name of the noble cause of persuading an unfriendly government to negotiate at the peace table. They are unlikely to pursue the more difficult and controversial issues that arise when alternatives to harsh military solutions come up for discussion. Nor are they inclined to raise ethical issues that carry the implication that this fine group of ours, with its humanitarianism and its high-minded principles, might be capable of adopting a course of action that is inhumane and immoral.'

Not all cohesive groups necessarily suffer from groupthink. Some groups may have minor issues in this regard, which, however, do not adversely affect the final outcome of the decision-making process. Psychological studies have pointed up a distinct difference between healthy groups and those liable to groupthink. In the first, as the group becomes more familiar to itself, and conse-quently more cohesive, the risk factors of groupthink begin to evaporate. The more members feel accepted within the group, they more they become willing to question and challenge its assumptions and decisions, and the less inclined to self-censor for fear of antagonising the group leader or other members. But in a group prone to groupthink, the opposite happens.

No group had guaranteed immunity from groupthink and its pitfalls. 'All in-groups,' Janis explains, 'may have a mild tendency toward groupthink, displaying one or another of the symptoms from time to time, but it need not be so dominant as to influence the quality of the group's final decision.' A group with proper protocols and procedures is likely to make better decisions than an individual working alone. But this advantage is lost if the groups come under pressure or stress, which unleashes negative psychological dynamics, especially in the context of likemindedness.

'The main principle of groupthink,' Janis outlines, 'which I offer in the spirit of Parkinson's law, is this: The more amiability and esprit de corps there is among the members of a policy-making in-group, the greater the danger that the independent critical thinking will be replaced by groupthink, which is likely to result in irrational and dehumanizing actions directed against out-group.'

GROUPTHINK CASE STUDY
The Libelling of Fr Kevin Reynolds by RTÉ

The Fr Kevin Reynolds case belongs to the 'possession' category of group-think, although it also has intimations of cultural contagion within it.

The libelling of Fr Kevin Reynolds by the RTÉ programme *Prime Time Investigates*, a decade ago, presents as one of the most graphic examples of groupthink of the first type we have identified in this series of chapters: the capturing of a group of responsible adults involved in decision-making by a wrongheaded understanding of reality, and the pursuit of this understanding, in the face of overwhelming evidence of its mistakenness, right to the bitter end. The error provoked what was probably the highest libel settlement in the history of Irish journalism, with Fr Reynolds receiving a seven-figure sum in damages once the extent of the error became clear.

On May 23rd 2011, RTÉ broadcast a *Prime Time* special investigation programme, *A Mission to Prey*, which accused Father Kevin Reynolds, parish priest at Ahascragh, County Galway, of raping a minor while a missionary in Kenya decades before, and of having fathered a child as a result. Before the broadcast, Father Reynolds had made repeated but fruitless efforts to alert the *Prime Time* journalists to the falsity of the allegations, even offering to undergo a paternity test. The *Prime Time* team would later claim that they believed the offer of a paternity test was not 'completely genuine' and that, had they agreed to allow Fr Reynolds time to have such a test carried out, they would have had 'no way of enforcing it', that it would not happen and therefore someone whom they believed to be responsible for a very serious crime would have not been exposed. In this can be observed the classic symptoms of groupthink as a form of thought 'possession': absolute certainty as to the correctness of the course already decided upon, deep suspicion of and hostility towards the 'out-group' subject of their documentary, and resistance to all evidence to the contrary — with momentous results.

At the heart of the debacle was the firm belief among the production team that they were right about the paternity allegation. They believed that they had checked and verified the facts, despite the lack of any documentary evidence and the failure to obtain full, on-the-record documentation of what they believed was corroborative evidence from other individuals. They were convinced that their chief witness, the alleged female victim, was reliable and credible. The team also made highly subjective assumptions, which served to reinforce their certainty: For example, some members of the team were convinced that there was a striking likeness between Fr Reynolds and the person said to be his child. Fr Reynolds' demeanour in a doorstep interview was deemed to endorse the team's view of his guilt and to be consistent with the demeanours of others previously accused of abuse by *Prime Time Investigates*. There had never previously been a whiff of a suggestion of any impropriety on the part of Fr Reynolds, but that appeared to count for nothing. The allegations made against Fr Reynolds were entirely false.

The Broadcasting Authority of Ireland (of which I was at the time a member, though I had to recuse myself from most of the deliberations in this matter, having already publicly expressed a view) commissioned a television producer from Northern Ireland, Anna Carragher, to conduct a thorough investigation of the circumstances in which the programme was permitted to go ahead in such dubious circumstances. Carragher observed: 'I believe that the team got into a position of "group think" where all evidence was interpreted as pointing only in one direction. There was a distinct lack of challenge . . .'*

In the title of the broadcast documentary, *A Mission to Prey*, the utterly unfounded allegations against Father Reynolds and the groupthink concerning their reliability acquired an added dimension of toxicity, imputing to him, and implicitly to other Catholic missionaries, an abominable premeditation. Behind the priestly vocation and outward altruism of church initiatives in foreign countries, that title insinuated, resided a grotesque design to abuse and exploit. This title echoed a malevolent mentality by then rampant in the Irish media, which, where the Catholic church is concerned, no longer considers it sufficient to state facts — the case must be beefed up with sneers and vicious innuendos. Carefully nurtured public prejudice has ensured that, when condemning a Church figure, it is impossible to go too far. This, precisely, was the core nature of the groupthink that was the undoing of *Prime Time*.

---

* The full Carragher report can be read by searching the web for "Anna Carragher prime time investigates - mission to prey".

CHAPTER 12
THE GROUPTHINK PSYCHODEMIC, PART II, GROUPTHINK MINUS THOUGHT
25-08-2021

The acquired capacity to manipulate the deep psychology of humans has handed wannabe tyrants a master key to enchaining the rest of humanity and have us think this our natural state.

'It is only by obtaining some sort of insight into the psychology of crowds that it can be understood how powerless they are to hold any opinions other than those which are imposed upon them.'

— Gustave Le Bon, *The Crowd*

Perhaps the most intriguing-looking publication to appear on the topic of groupthink in recent times was Christopher Booker's 2020 book, *Groupthink: A Study in Self Delusion*. The book was disappointing, however, though for a somewhat understandable reason: The author died in 2019 before finishing it. Unavoidably incomplete, the book was subsequently assembled by a partnership of Booker's son, Nicholas, and friend and sometime writing partner, Richard North, with whom Booker had co-written a number of books, including *Scared to Death*, a 2007 work about the escalating tendency of global authorities to use fabricated emergencies to scare the world's populations.

Until quite recently, groupthink had been a phenomenon identified retroactively, a 'found object' of cultural digs. The skeleton sketch provided in Booker's 2020 book takes things a little further, and in a timely fashion, identifying and scrutinising the phenomenon's growth into a mechanism for generating mass delusion in a wider socio-cultural context. Across the fractured text of the book can be detected a series of clues that Booker was working towards a theory of groupthink as an emerging instrument of mass manipulation by powerful interests.

Thus, although he was already into his eighties, his death (of cancer) in 2019 was a great tragedy in more than the usual ways. Booker was the ideal person to write this book, having long ago published a remarkable account of the 'Freedom Revolution' of the mid-twentieth century — his 1969 book *The Neophiliacs: A Study of the Revolution in English Life in the Fifties and Sixties* — a period he depicts in his final book as an experiment in collective groupthink. It would have been fascinating to see how he might reconcile — or not — the libertine thinking that emanated from that decade with the bizarre clinging to Covid-related authoritarianism of many of the baby boomer generation in old age, a defining trope of the past 18 months.

But this and many other intoxicating possibilities are now lost to us. Frankly, the book does not work and may queer the pitch for imminent future incursions into the subject at a time when groupthink has become pervasive.

Booker uses the Irving Janis analysis as his starting point, and proceeds in what appears to be the beginnings of an attempt to extend the analysis into the area of popular bewitchings through manipulation, examining various relevant phenomena such as the insidious growth of political correctness, the myth of manmade climate change, the delusion of the European 'project', the quasi-religious reach of Darwinism, and several others. Some of these subjects are revisitations of themes of his journalism (he was a columnist for many years with the *Sunday Telegraph*, and a brave and brilliant one at that), but much of the material comprises merely reheated sketches or chronologies of events under the various headings, still to be adapted to what seems implicitly to be the central theme of the book: groupthink as cultivated phenomenon. Nevertheless, scattered throughout the book are gems of insight into what we have been calling the 'enspelled' form of groupthink, where Booker's primary concern appeared to reside.

To begin with, he identifies what is important in the work of Irving Janis, by comparison with predecessors like Charles Mackay and Gustave Le Bon, in considering the baneful tendencies of crowds. Booker condenses Janis's 'consistent and identifiable rules' of groupthink into three sentences:

'A group of people comes to be fixated on some belief or view of the world which seems hugely important to them. They are convinced that their opinion is so self-evidently right that no sensible person could disagree with it. Most telling of all, this leads them to treat all those who differ from their beliefs with a peculiar kind of contemptuous hostility.'

These are the essential elements of the problematic, fiasco-creating kind of groupthink that arises from unhealthy group dynamics — groupthink as 'possession' (of the collective mind of a group). Booker also describes what is emerging as a familiar symptom of the 'enspelled' form of groupthink: a mind-less clinging to received thinking, combined with a negative solidarity consoli-dated by the limited awareness of the group's members: 'We are never more aware of groupthink at work than when we are up against people who hold an emphatic opinion on some controversial subject, but who, when questioned on it, turn out not really to have thought it through. They have not looked seriously at the facts or the evidence. They have simply taken their opinions or beliefs on trust, ready-made from others. But the very fact that their opinions are not based on any real understanding of why they believe what they do only allows them to believe even more insistently and intolerantly that their views are right.'

Bypassing the rational circuitry of the human mind, this form of groupthink makes its appeal to the 'feeling' mechanisms of human apprehension — in several senses of that word: understanding, capturing, terror. This can be achieved under the protection of air cover provided by emotional manipulation, in particular, the fomenting of an intense, cultivated hostility to outsiders. Fear is by far the most 'reliable' ally of this kind of endeavour.

Booker was on to something new and significant in pursuing the concept of cultivated groupthink as an extrapolation of the 'found' kind, the weaponisation of the principles divined by Irving Janis to entrance and brainwash whole popu-lations. Exploring with this insight the events of the past 18 months provides us with a kind of excavated secret blueprint for the totality of the Covid strategy. For that is essentially what has been achieved in the Covid cult: the incorpora-tion of the majorities of a multiplicity of countries into a singular fashion of seeing a constructed, globalised phenomenon. Among the dizzying implications is the possibility that the lessons learned by the governing authorities in this matter have caused them to comprehend a profound, previously undreamt of and possibly fatal weakness in collectives of human beings: that, possessed by a desire for consensus and harmony, they may be prepared to believe anything, do virtually anything they are instructed to by an apparent competent authority, adhere to such prescriptions in the face of all facts and arguments, and turn against their fellows if prompted to.

In setting out his stall, Booker lists among the worst forms of historical groupthink the phenomenon of religious groups purveying belief systems which have often tended to become ruthlessly intolerant of anyone who does not share the approved outlooks. 'Such outsiders,' he writes, 'are labelled as "heretics", "infidels" or "unbelievers". To protect the established orthodoxy, they must be marginalised, excluded from society, persecuted, punished or even, in countless examples, put to death. None of the world's great religions has been immune to this tendency, even where it appears to contradict their core beliefs: the followers of Christianity, Judaism, Hinduism and Buddhism have all at different times exhibited this tendency, as have different sects within those reli-gions. . . . And of course, there is no more extreme example in our world today than the rise of Islamic terrorist movements such as Isis or al-Qaeda, which are possessed by a form of groupthink so extreme that it turns those carried away by it into merciless killers, prepared not only to murder at random anyone they can see as "infidels" (chiefly other Muslims), but even to commit suicide themselves in furthering their cause.'

'Another obvious instance,' he notes elsewhere, 'has been those totalitarian political ideologies, such as communism or Nazism, that likewise showed ruthless intolerance towards "subversives", "dissidents" or anyone not following "the party line" (in the Soviet Union it was termed "correct thinking"). Again, such people had to be excluded from established society, imprisoned or physically "eliminated".'

Booker is 'over the target' on a number of key counts, though the unfortunate circumstances of his final book mean that many of his implicit points, being largely unstated or at best sketched out, are left to be inferred in their fuller implications.

He is absolutely right about the role played in rendering the world susceptible to groupthink of the creeping grip of political correctness (PC), to which he devotes several early chapters of the unfinished book, and which he identifies as 'a manifestation of groupthink as infectious and all-pervasive as any in our time.' What he under-emphasises is that PC is really not so much a form of thought as a form of mindless entrancement, the transporting of millions of people to a single hive of received beliefs, which subsequently controls their thoughts even when they are not engaging with anything remotely classifiable as 'ideas'. As a systematic and schematic undermining of the right and capacity to say what you think, and think what you like, PC might be called the unwritten Constitution of latter-day forms of imposed, enspelled groupthink.

Perhaps the most awesome achievement of what is called Cultural Marxism is that, while it can provoke in mainstream society wholesale minor impatience and amusement concerning some of its abundance of 'eccentric' or ridiculous proposals, the PC force field ensures that it rarely prompts a mainstream voice into support or sympathy for whoever becomes its latest target. This is in part because most people have been conditioned to fear being tarred with a brush that, by advertising its target as a purveyor of backwardness, bigotry or 'hating', is capable of drawing down mass odium, scorn and derision on anyone speaking against it.

PC is essentially an ideology of victimhood that classifies certain groups of people as in need of protection from criticism, and makes believers feel that no dissent should be tolerated. It amounts to a form of censorship that exempts particular listed categories of human being from the normal attrition of democratic society, and, under a series of headings, charges some usually unspecified 'majority' with exercising a mandatory sensitivity towards these categories. The victims — the alleged casualties of, for example, Christian and patriarchal oppression: women, blacks, gays, etc. — thus became the 'clients' of a pervasive but undeclared Marxist revolution. As Christopher Booker points out, PC fits neatly with the neo-Marxist view of the world that seemed to follow as though spontaneously in its wake as the world moved through the second half of the twentieth century. Together, these elements represented a new politics of power. 'It was,' writes Booker, 'the fundamental mindset which ultimately reduced all social questions down to the perennial power struggle reflected in Lenin's famous question: "Who, Whom?" Who, with all their power and privilege, are doing what to those without them?'

PC is a form of violence because it imposes an undemocratic censorship from which the use of words offers no escape, and therefore, ultimately becomes amenable only to violence. So, far from being harmless or slightly comic, as many continue to believe, PC is a system of enforced cultural *omertà* with a view to undermining freedom of expression and imposing an unchallengeable form of thought control — this directed at the inversion of the traditional social order and the creation of what would amount in effect to a totalitarian state.

PC has its roots not, as we long thought, in some post-feminist prissiness, but in a hard leftist sect known as the Frankfurt School, which gained serious traction for its ideas in post-WWII American academia and later on in French post-modernist philosophy. It was created specifically to ride shotgun on the ideology of Cultural Marxism, which emanated initially from those circles, latterly from an informal group of French intellectuals, notably Jacques Derrida and Paul-Michel Foucault.

From the 1990s, with the ascent to power across Europe of left-leaning parties, the Cultural Marxist programme, propelled and camouflaged by PC, became the driving force of mainstream politics in many Western countries. By means of political lobbying and infiltration of education systems, by shifting the weight of public policy from parliament to court, and — above all — by relentless censorship and cultural prohibition of contrary ideas, Western society was persuaded to, in effect, turn its value system inside out. Increasingly, deviation from PC principles resulted in instant vilification and censure, with the increasing risk of loss of position and income, nowadays known as the rule of 'cancel culture'. As the basket of ideologies under the heading 'Cultural Marxism' infected the legal systems of many countries, instances of people being investigated by the police and courts for such 'breaches' became more and more common. Thus, public debate no longer described objectively verifiable reality, but depicted an ideologically constructed pseudo-reality in which certain matters become unmentionable and others utterly unchallengeable.

PC, then, divides the world — spuriously, for the most part — between oppressors and victims, and offers a code by which these spuriously described conditions might be 'reversed'. The PC-generated idea that one group is responsible for the dispossession or suffering of the other is the mainspring of the resultant groupthink known as Woke, tapping into the craving for moral superiority described by Booker:

'[A]nd this is what adds that other crucial charge of emotional gratification inseparable from groupthink: the need to express morally superior contempt for all those unfeeling, self-centred others who simply don't understand, and can therefore be dismissively labelled as "sexists", "racists", "bigots", "homophobes", "transphobes", "fascists" or whatever scornful term seems appropriate, to the point where this is no longer connected to the reality or whatever genuine injustice may originally have lain behind it, but has become an end in itself. Such "charges" are frequently sufficient to have someone de-platformed or cancelled without intervention of process. Membership of the accusatory group sanctions the indulgence of ego and extreme prejudice, facilitating the exhibition of PC virtue as well as ritualised outrage "at all those contemptibly unvirtuous outsiders who do not conform."'

One of the characteristics of this culture, unsurprisingly, is incoherence. As Theodore Dalrymple describes in his book, *The Wilder Shores of Marx*, one of the objectives of PC is to impose on society an incoherent programme of behaviour that, by imposing senselessness, ensures confusion and chaos will reign wherever it rules. Dalrymple notes that within an established totalitarian regime, the purpose of propaganda is not to persuade or inform, but to humiliate: 'From this point of view, propaganda should not approximate to the truth as closely as possible: on the contrary, it should do as much violence to it as possible. For by endlessly asserting what is patently untrue, by making such untruth ubiquitous and unavoidable, and finally, by insisting that everyone publicly acquiesce in it, the regime displays its power and reduces individuals to nullities.' Among the core purposes of PC is to force people to say and repeat, or to fall silent before, things they do not believe, hence to turn them into unwitting liars. 'In this sense,' Dalrymple elaborates, 'the less true it was, the less it corresponded in any way to reality, the better; the more it contradicted the experience of the persons to whom it was directed, the more docile, self-despising for their failure to protest, and impotent they became.'

You might say that PC has turned the whole world into a meeting — defined by the symptoms of groupthink distilled by Irving Lester Janis: power plays, hierarchies, hidden censorship and a barely detectable constant impulse to scapegoat.

Cancellation is the unwritten penal provision at the bottom of the PC charter, providing for the cultural, psychological, moral, existential and even metaphysical annulling of the 'offender'. Cancellation is at once the penalty for breaches of the unwritten PC code and also, not coincidentally, the realisation of the ultimate fear underlying the human desire for consensus and agreement. And here we glimpse the profound connection between PC and groupthink: the supposed code of ideological civility that has actually become the new statute of imposed human interaction and 'belonging', its tenets acting, without benefit of judge or jury, to try, convict and sentence the 'offender' by means of ostracism, de-personing and banishment to a state of permanent Coventry. In this process, fear is the engine that propels whole peoples into a pathological likemindedness as the sole alternative to facing the loneliness that is anyway inevitable by virtue of the path on to which these machinations are now forcing the former human family.

Booker also correctly identifies the role in the unleashing of groupthink society of the Internet, which, especially in its social media incarnations, has done much to construct the emerging 'culture' of Balkanised thought in the mainstream of culture, pushing each individual into groups, and each group to the furthest possible extreme. It has decimated the protocols and conventions of public debate, installing anonymity and invective as the ascendant motifs of societal discussion, with the objective of polarising position-options, and bringing public discussion as near to war as is possible without use of physical weapons.

In many ways, a diagnosis of what has gone wrong with democracy, politics, communications and the collective sense of the meaning of freedom might centrally include the idea that a culture of hostility, incubated on the Internet, has started to leach out into reality, poisoning everything in a way that could be pleasing to radical revolutionaries and no one else. We live in a virtual world, hiding from the real one. This still feels 'free', but only because we have increas-ingly unreliable models with which to compare it. Reality begins to fade from our memories, and gradually we are enslaved to the will of those seeking to exploit us more effectively in a new world they are preparing us to inhabit.

Many of the technologies we use, which we fondly imagine are increasing our freedoms, are doing the precise opposite. Many Internet users, for example, imagine that the World Wide Web remains unchanged from the way it was described in its early days, as an unrestricted and diversity-fostering informa-tion highway. In fact, over the past dozen years or so, ostensibly due to the pres-sure to 'monetise' — i.e. to make bigger and bigger profits from advertising revenues — the web has become involuted and convergent, narrowing the hori-zons of its users rather than broadening them. The main cause of the change was the 'personalisation' of Google searches, which caused each search to be tailored to a user's known 'likes' and interests, a process which remains invisible, even from the user, who may well believe that his searches are throwing up the same things as everyone else's. Until December 2009, all searches were governed by Google's Page Rank algorithm, which delivered the same results to everyone entering the same words. Starting on December 4th 2009, Google began using information such as log-in details and data concerning what the user had searched for previously to decide what he or she would throw up in this latest search. This customisation has eliminated all possibility of serendipity and encroachingly isolated users in cultural and ideological bubbles. The invisibility of this process is even more worrying: Google doesn't tell you how it reads your profile or why it's giving you the results it is. You may not even know that it's making any kinds of assumptions about you. Google's then-CEO Eric Schmidt expressed his delight at this development by declaring that what its users wanted was for Google to 'tell them what they should be doing next'.

The implications of this trend were explored by Eli Pariser in his 2011 book *The Filter Bubble – What the Internet is Hiding from You*, which describes the now pervasive 'algorithm society', in which everyone will hear about only those things they are already known to agree with. Pariser feared a drying up of democratic exchange, obviously long since in train. 'Democracy,' he observed, 'requires citizens to see things from one another's point of view, but instead, we're more and more enclosed in our own bubbles. Democracy requires a reliance on shared facts; instead, we're being offered parallel but separate universes.'

Information about web users has become one of the world's most lucrative resources and is used to precision-target increasingly customised advertising. The use of cookies and tracking beacons means that every clue dropped — even unwittingly — by every user can become a commodity. Even while they remain anonymous to the Great Outdoors, users' personal details can still be harvested by Internet operators and sold off to the highest bidder — usually corporates with stuff to sell. The implications of this go beyond isolating each person in his individual bubble, from which he communicates only with those of like mind. The result, inevitably, is a reduction of the variety and vibrancy of public discussion — and the sorting of humanity into various preliminary groupthinks.

In *Groupthink: A Study in Self Delusion*, Christopher Booker seems to move across the same territory with a different mind, delving into the conditions that have arisen at our — at the time of his writing — half-century remove from the end of the 'decade of freedom'. In some ways, he says, life has greatly improved. Old divisions based on race or social position have largely dissolved or become less polarising. Yet, in other respects, life as we advance into the 21st century has become 'edgier, more strained and certainly a great deal more confusing.' Much of this has arisen from the machinations of the Woke culture, which grew out of the PC revolution.

Why, asks Booker, do we hate and despise each other so much these days? The answer, he says, lies in the all-pervading presence of divisive groupthink. 'Nowhere did this become more evident than on the Internet, that miracle of technology which in many ways was so useful. But in the age of the "selfie", Facebook and Twitter, it had given new opportunities of expression to the human ego.'

In this new climate, political leadership and the public's responses to hot-button political issues have less to do with the nature or needs of society, and more to do with the weaponisation of aspiration in the personal zone: how the individual would like to be seen by her peers. Opinions about public matters in our 'liberal' cultures have somehow become unmoored from convictions or reflection, becoming badges of identity, like T-shirts or hairstyles. People affect philosophies or positions in order to look good, to complement their clothes and cars. The complacency bestowed by six decades of comparative peace and prosperity has rendered most of our populations incapable of imagining anything terrible happening in the world they inhabited; therefore, there was no need to be aware of the content of issues, which simply provide the threadbare fabric of ideological raiment. These conditions have delivered us into the sway of the archest of arch-manipulators.

I knew Christopher Booker slightly, we having been in intermittent contact for a number of years up to about a decade ago, in the period when he became interested in family law and wrote regularly about it in his *Sunday Telegraph* column. We would speak on and off on the telephone, discussing various cases, comparing notes and, where possible, digging out evidence to assist families in trouble with social workers and the like. He was, in my estimation, a brilliant and kindhearted man, whose instincts were fundamentally focused on a mistrust of power. He was far too aware of the persistent insinuations of tyrannical forces nibbling at the edges of politics to miss what was happening in the Covid operation.

And yet, there is an odd circumstance relating to the manner and timing of the publication of his groupthink reflection. Bizarrely, in light of the then-prevailing circumstances, it was published in mid-2020, more or less in tandem with the reissuing of an earlier book, containing remarkable resonances with the topics treated and touched on in its pages. That book, co-written with Richard North and originally published in 2007, was titled *Scared to Death: From BSE to Coronavirus: Why Scares are Costing Us the Earth.* It was re-released six months into the Covid-19 'pandemic' — 'Newly revised and updated in the light of Covid-19' — more or less coinciding with the publication of Booker's groupthink book.

Scared to Death examines a series of panics afflicting Britain and the world over recent decades, from the Millennium Bug to bird flu, via AIDS, global warming and mad cow disease. In other words it's a book highly germane to the content of *Groupthink: A Study in Self Delusion.* Bizarrely, the blurb for *Scared to Death* — presumably written by someone other than Christopher Booker — reads:

'These scares have become one of the most conspicuous and damaging features of our modern world, so much so that as we entered the third decade of the new century, our senses had become so blunted that we scarcely recognised the real thing for what it was, until it arrived — Covid-19, for which we were almost completely unprepared.'

This is bizarre: Christopher Booker died approximately six months before Covid became news, yet this reissued, revised book bears his name as co-author. I cannot conceive of any manner in which anyone might have gleaned his response to a 'pandemic' announced months after his death.

Teasingly, the spiel continues, without as much as the verbal equivalent of a raised eyebrow: 'The authors analyse the crucial roles of the different factions who perpetrated the scares: from the scientists who misread or manipulated the evidence to the media and lobbyists who eagerly promoted scares without regard to the consequences, and the politicians and officials who came up with absurdly disproportionate responses, leaving us to pay a colossal price.'

The book also promises to assess — by way of contrast with the 'scares' that represent the meat of the book — 'why this [Covid] is the real thing, as opposed to the succession of scares that we have experienced.'

The Introduction, undertaking to expose innumerable 'scares' including 'nitrate in water; vitamin B6; Satanic child abuse; lead in petrol and computers; passive smoking; asbestos; SARS' and much, much more, declares:

'Each was based on what appeared at the time to be scientific evidence that was widely accepted. Each has inspired obsessive coverage by the media. Each has then provoked a massive response from politicians and officials, imposing new laws that inflicted enormous economic and social damage. But eventually the scientific reasoning on which the panic was based has been found to be fundamentally flawed. Either the scare originated in some genuine threat that had then become wildly exaggerated, or the danger was found never to have existed at all.' The Introduction then goes on to list four recurring factors to be noted in such scares: a universal 'danger'; a 'novel' dimension; an element of uncertainty allowing for alarmist speculation; a capacity for disproportionate response.

'What,' it is rhetorically asked in conclusion, 'does it tell us about the state of mind of our modern society that it should so continually fall victim to these bouts of collective hysteria? Is there any way we can learn to protect ourselves better from the horrifying damage they bring in their wake? Certainly a precondition of that must be that we should learn to recognize the scare phenomenon for what it is: a form of human irrationality which almost invariably takes on the same recognizable pattern. We must learn to understand that the scare dynamic obeys certain identifiable rules, and is, therefore, itself susceptible to scientific study.'

It need hardly be pointed out that this amounts to a succinct though unknowing indictment of the Covid scam — yet the book expressly seeks to eliminate this latest and most comprehensive example of a 'scare' from the scope of its inquiry. Even more oddly, *Scared to Death* and *Groupthink: A Study in Self Delusion* have the same publisher: Bloomsbury-Continuum, who released these books, more or less simultaneously, seemingly without connecting their remarkably convergent subject matter. The best you can say is that Booker's execu-tors/publishers do not appear to have comprehended the thesis he was outlining in his final book, nor taken the obvious inferences from it.

It is doubtful indeed that, had he lived another couple of years, Christopher Booker would have allowed these two books to be published as they were, but would have combined their themes and written a book directed primarily at the Covid scam. It is certainly doubtful that he would have concluded, as have his literary executors and publisher, by avoiding or dismissing the glaringly obvious thought that Covid represents the very culmination of the phenomenon he was beginning to sketch out when he died. It might be postulated that the manner of the publication of these two books in 2020 betrays a capitulation to the very syndrome Christopher Booker was describing. Nailing his colours to the mast, Booker references in *Groupthink: A Study in Self Delusion*, those now legendary works of Orwell and Huxley featuring two imaginary states of the future that brainwash their citizens 'into a rigidly intolerant state of groupthink which obeyed all the familiar rules'. It can hardly be in doubt that he would have noted in the Covid scam the full-blown eruption into reality of these precise tendencies, as well as the arresting correspondences with the definitions and diagnoses of such as Irving Janis and Gustave Le Bon. It is self-evident that, at the very least, the Covid episode, no matter what your stance or how you choose to depict it, throws up at least three distinct categories in which the groupthink phenomenon becomes manifest: not perhaps in the orchestration of the plan, but certainly in the machinations of bodies and authorities charged, undemocratically and unlawfully, with administering the unfolding narrative; in the media treatment of it; and in the responses of the public who, under the influence of imposed techniques of manipulation, decided that their govern-ments knew best.

It was no accident, Booker notes, that Irving Janis coined the term 'group-think' under inspiration from Orwell's thinly disguised picture of life in Stalin's Soviet Union, 'where the sense of a group mind, personified in Big Brother, was ruthlessly reinforced by means of endlessly repeated slogans, and ritualized hate sessions directed at anyone daring to dissent in any way from the Party's line.'

Whereas Janis was concerned mainly with the decision-making ('posses-sion') forms of groupthink, Booker leans much more towards exploring the 'enspelled' kind — that which afflicts the crowd in ways that transcend or bypass thought processes. Yet, although his book invites such inferences, Booker does not explicitly distinguish between forms of groupthink appearing to erupt spontaneously from organic group dynamics, and those imposed from above by coercion and/or manipulation. This is a key distinction, because, whereas both may occur at the same time, they have differing dynamics, and can each acquire a life independently of the other. A group of decision-makers under the sway of an internal groupthink may consciously set out to control the thought processes of a larger group or population, but the processes are so different as to qualify as two separate phenomena, though linked by the symptoms listed by Irving Janis. The first type, as we have seen, is an organic internal contagion of the group, rendering its thought processes sclerotic or tunnel-visioned; the second is a way of deliberately suppressing virtually all independent thought forms, requiring the exercise of explicit authority over a submissive population, usually involving the deployment of licensed state coercion.

Booker also contributes at least one important novel emphasis that adds to our understanding of groupthink as mass manipulation: the prestige-power of second-hand thinking. Deference is the phenomenon he identifies as lying at the root of this form of groupthink imposition. The authority and prestige of the elite leader(s) — politicians, scientists, doctors — cause the crowd, as though one individual, to accept unquestioningly what the authority figure says.

'Great power,' he writes, 'is given to ideas propagated by affirmation, repetition and contagion by the circumstances that they acquire in time, that mysterious force known as prestige.'

Groupthink of this kind may only remotely be regarded as a category of thought. 'The vast majority of [the affected] only get carried along by groupthink because they have taken it on ready-made from others. They accept as true what they have been told or read without ever seriously questioning it, which means that they don't really know why they think as they do.'

A common thread linking the various forms of imposed groupthink is an observable 'revolutionary' process that begins with ideas but soon switches to intense feeling. Whether religious, cultural or ideological, the revolutionary ideas create a sense of an in-group, which soon moves to oppose or denounce the out-group(s), but ultimately to dissolve all sense of reality. This can become especially pronounced when the driving ideas are presented as 'progressive', as offering some new state of enlightened or moral superiority which leaves the past for dead.

'It is,' writes Booker, 'an archetypal pattern in collective human behaviour. First there is an "anticipation stage", where pressure builds up in a society to make a decisive break with the past. When this new energy finds a focus and the break is made, this leads on to a dream stage, where, for a while, it seems the liberating new make-believe is carrying all before it. But precisely because this make-believe knows no limits, it leads to a "frustration stage" where it is driven to push on even further in pursuit of that elusive goal, in ways even more detached from the real world. By now, uncomfortable contradictions are beginning to intrude until the ever more extreme groupthink brings about a "nightmare stage", where the supposedly idealistic vision which originally inspired it has been turned completely on its head. This eventually leads to some sort of "collision with reality" where the groupthink is brought face-to-face with the unforeseen consequences of where it has all been leading.'

Booker cites the American sociologist David Riesman, who, in his 1950 book *The Lonely Crowd*, described three ways in which people may be categorised according to the primary sources of their values and beliefs. These include the — self-explaining — 'tradition-directed', i.e. most of humanity until relatively recently, a category which persists though as a much smaller phenomenon. Riesman also identified two more 'modern' categories, one of which he called the 'other-directed', which refers to those 'dedicated followers of fashion' who take on the up-to-the-minute values, beliefs and dispositions of those around them, and, as Booker outlines, thus become more amenable to different types of groupthink, forming various categories of 'groupescules', which converge under certain conditions. The third category — by far the smallest — comprises those Riesman described as 'inner-directed': living by values they have worked out each one for themselves, largely impervious either to the diktats of tradition or the insinuations of the conventional fads or groupthink. The latter two categories have become highly visible as representing the two 'sides' of the Covid cult.

'One reason why our time has become so prey to groupthink,' writes Booker, 'is unquestionably that in the past 60 years the world has been going through the most intense period of change ever. On the back of astonishing technological advances which in the early post-war years would have seemed unimaginable, long-established certainties, assumptions and values have melted away like snow. So many familiar old reference points were disappearing. In such a bewilderingly new and unfamiliar world, people were removed from the old mental and moral framework, which could have helped them make sense of it, and recognize what they accepted as reality. People became increasingly inclined to take on board what they were told to think and believe by others: by the media and above all by the intoxicating new spirit of the age.'

In his Conclusion to Booker's book, Richard North notes that people in the Internet age, he claims, increasingly procure opinions off the peg. Confronted with a veritable infinite number of sources and choices, users select those positions with which they are most comfortable, 'essentially those which tell them what they want to know and confirm their pre-existing prejudices. . . . The body politic has fragmented into a staggering array of sub-groups, each with its own unique and identifiable characteristics and beliefs. Booker's "groupescules" have multiplied beyond all recognition.' And yet, as in the Covid episode, these multitudinous fragments can be brought together in a common frame of illogic. Elaborating on Booker's sketched hypothesis, North describes how, through the communications revolution, groupthink has become a mass phenomenon pervading almost every part of our lives, 'exercising a pernicious form of control over our language and thinking.' Yet, he gives no hint of having tumbled to the glaring immediate context of this rumination, while at the same time displaying remarkable insight into the groupthink phenomenon:

'With so many different groupings that lack uniforms, badges or trades to distinguish them, groupthink becomes the "glue" that binds individuals to deliver the cohesive whole, giving them their identity. At the same time, acceptance of the groupthink *mores* peculiar to the group serves as a rite of passage, while its free, uncritical use is a very tangible expression of loyalty. Groupthink, therefore, is not about knowledge or information, but a property, and the very foundation of the modern, otherwise amorphous groupings facilitated by the emergence of the electronic "information society".'

The world we have fetched up in, then, holds within its structures, its walls of consensus and mass-produced sloganised ideas, an enormous and growing risk of groupthink. And this involves not just the courting of 'fiascos', but also groupthink of a kind that threatens the very independence of the individual, inviting the aggregate of such a consequence for entire populations. We live in an era of conformity that is psychologically conceived, technologically delivered and enforced using the appropriated legal power of the people being corralled. It is largely invisible, or at least, as Jung said, detectable only by those who remain immune to it, and designed to attack the human being in areas of his mind and being that most people are only dimly aware of carrying about their persons. The effect, therefore, is of something naturalistic, organic and readily normalisable, throwing open the possibility that we are on the verge of a form of human society that may hold no resemblance to the ways we understood our species, collectively or individually, hitherto. It is not impossible — indeed, it becomes encroachingly probable — that if we fail to grasp the groupthink nettle, we or our descendants will cease in time even to question a model of human society that is centrally controlled by unelected elites exercising godlike forms of power over their 'fellows', and that this will accordingly become the natural and everyday understanding of how the human species is actually constituted.

Perhaps, then, the most shocking unspoken thing we have faced in the past 18 months is an idea that has to do not with Covid but with something far more fundamental and potentially unstoppable once it starts: the idea that there is nothing 'they' cannot do to us, or make us do to ourselves, unless we find ways of articulating coherently our situation and conveying this understanding to at least a significant majority of our fellows before it grows too late. For if the moment is allowed to slip by, and 'they' are allowed to succeed in what appears to be their mission, then the idea of an autonomous human being will afterwards — into the quasi-eternal future – make no more sense than the idea of a talking donkey does to us now. Perhaps there will be stories about such beings, but they will read as fantasies and fables. In this sense, then, those who have set themselves in opposition to the concept of 'groupthink' are opposing not merely an odd passing ideological quirk but the very core threat to the future of our species. And when we oppose it, we do so not merely on our own behalf but more so on behalf of those humans yet unborn, who, if we fail, will not know what they are missing, and, if we succeed, will take themselves as much for granted in their time as we have been blessed to do in ours.

GROUPTHINK CASE STUDY

The Witch Trials of Salem (1692)

This episode is an example of the second fundamental form of groupthink — 'enspelling' — the entrancement of a whole population with dangerous and mistaken ideas. It has many resonances with our present predicament, though, of course, it precedes the advent of mass media communications, and therefore presents the idea of 'spell' in undiluted and unmagnified form. It should be cautionary for us to consider what became possible even back then, long before television, the Internet and other hypnoidal instruments of modern culture.

It is also indicative of a minor kink in the somewhat artificial division we have created in this series between 'possession' and 'enspelled' forms of group-think, for clearly, the enspelled form is, in a quite literal sense, an example of the spiritual possession of a community by deranged emotions and ideas. This underlines a need for clarification, notwithstanding the usefulness of delineating various strands of groupthink: the two categories can leach into one another, as in the Covid cult.

In some respects, the Covid episode appears to have been timed to coincide with a moment in the culture of Western society that might be characterised as the speed-bump on the outer frontier of the spurt of freedom that had been in train since the 1960s. Among the symptoms is that this seemed deliberately to invoke some of the psycho-spiritual control mechanisms of religion, to tap into the residual religious imagination of humanity, in order to persuade people to 'willingly' incarcerate themselves and give up their claims to being truly free persons.

Act One of the published script of Arthur Miller's play, *The Crucible*, based on the witch trials of Salem, is punctuated with occasional notes by the author about the social and spiritual context in which those events occurred. 'When one rises above the individual villainy displayed,' Miller wrote in one of these notes, 'one can only pity them all, just as we will be pitied one day.'

The witch hunts were a perverse manifestation of the panic which set in among all classes when the balance began to turn to greater individual freedom. The community of pilgrims in which the witch trials unfolded in the dying days of the seventeenth century had changed from the people who had arrived on the Mayflower seven decades before. In the interim, Miller noted, they had developed a theocracy of their own, which had evolved from the necessary autocracy that had characterised their earlier existence in New England. This had been, however, an autocracy by consent, held together by a common ideology. Religious sentiment — a strong sense of the danger of evil forces — suffused this belief system. The earlier royal government had been replaced by a junta, which, despite its denotation, amounted to a relaxation of control. These conditions led both to a loosening and *a fear of loosening* — a sense that freedom might sweep away the security that had been established. 'Evidently,' Miller wrote, 'the time came in New England when the repressions of order were heavier than seemed warranted by the dangers against which the order was organised.'

Central to this process was the weaponisation of the Christian idea of Original Sin. As I have written elsewhere, the Covid manipulation programme sought to supplant the dying sense of that idea with an analogous one: that each human being is by dint of biological nature a danger to others, and that this defines our relationships in ways that, until March 2020, we had carelessly overlooked. The Covid cult reinvented the structure of this Christian concept, conjuring up a kind of pathogenic leper, stumbling about, a festering mess of microbes and viruses, spreading disease among his fellows and threatening them with imminent and miserable death.

A similar notion of contagion was a critical element of the witch hysteria of Salem more than four centuries before. The Pilgrims who had landed at Plymouth Rock in Massachusetts in 1620 and founded the first permanent settlement in New England were all Puritans, and none was permitted to exist outside their cult. Personal rights to, for example, property and 'freedom' were few and could be suspended at any time, being in particular contingent on continued membership and adherence to the religious rules. Pleasure of virtually any kind was regarded with suspicion. One description of the life of the Puritans related: 'There were no celebrations or holidays, no theaters or novels and no children's games or entertainments. Dancing was considered a serious sin.'

Not everyone is happy with increasing freedom. Some fear it, preferring the security blanket of — possibly — muted authoritarianism. Some are prepared to place any form of moral order, including medicine-based 'morality', above the call of freedom, welcoming the 'prohibitions' on themselves because these place even greater constraints on their more adventurous fellows. This may, in particular, be true of the old, who are fearful of the exuberance and excesses of the young. But it may also be true of the emerging young of Ireland 2020/21. There are signs, as I outlined in the April 13, 2021 Substack post titled 'No Future For You . . . th?' — that the millennial generation, raised in the debris left behind by 1960s hedonism — broken families, McDonald's parenting, crèche existence, general dysfunctionality — had grown with an unarticulated and perhaps mostly unconscious rage for order.

The Puritans of New England believed in the literal truth of every word in the Bible, which was their guide, their truth, their 'science'. Their obsession with

Original Sin, their belief that every human person is at birth already evil and at risk of eternal damnation — and that these congenital sins are incapable of being washed away — these were the mechanisms that stoked the frenzy that, in the end, turned spouse against spouse and had neighbour hunting down neighbour to purge sinfulness from the earth. Even if this sinfulness could never be purged, it was possible to stay its power sufficiently to enable the person to rejoin human society as a repentant sinner, to return, in conditional fashion, to the path of righteousness. This was done by public acts of confession, whereby the sinner admitted his or her sins to the community and carried out some ritualistic public act of penance.

The 'vaccine' is the instrument of the equivalent process in the Covid cult. As with the Puritans and conventional sin, the congenitally infectious nature of the human is impervious to investigation — due to the elusive nature of the 'virus', its invisibility and mutability, and the concept of 'asymptomatic infection', *et cetera*. Thus, only the public acceptance of the vaccine is sufficient to return the individual to the path of righteousness. In New England in 1692, those who declined to confess their sins publicly were banished from society, and some were hunted down and hanged. This, essentially, is the condition of culture the Covid cult is aiming for.

The witch-hunt was not, in Miller's words, 'a mere repression. It was also, and as importantly, a long overdue opportunity for everyone so inclined to express publicly his guilt and sins, under the cover of accusations against the victims. . . . Long held hatreds of neighbors could now be openly expressed, and vengeance taken, despite the Bible's charitable injunctions. Land-lust, which had been expressed before by constant bickering over boundaries and deeds, could now be elevated to the arena of morality: one could cry witch against one's neighbor and feel perfectly justified in the bargain. Old scores could be settled on a place of heavenly combat between Lucifer and the Lord; suspicions and the general envy of the miserable towards the happy could and did burst out in the general revenge.'

For the people of Salem in 1692, just as for the population of Ireland 2021, there was much beneath the surface sanctity, and much that emerged from this, that was other than it seemed. The fear of witches was emblematic of an ingrained, conditioned fear of Evil, the personified essence of the non-religious lifestyle. Satan was prowling the frontiers of their colony, waiting for a way in. Once the colony was perfected, they would be safe, acquiring conditional immunity to Evil, but in the meantime, it behoved them to be constantly vigilant and ruthless with those who remained casual about the danger. Witches were the handmaidens of Satan, having entered into pacts to infect their fellows with the spirit of Evil.

In the 1692 episode, the courts of Salem, Massachusetts, were, in effect, handed over to the witch-hunt hysteria, also called 'the delusion'. Between

March and September 1692, at least 20 accused people, and two dogs were put to death as witches, following extra-legal procedures. Many others were excommunicated, losing all their rights and property. It was well into the next century before the community came to its senses and began to realise what had occurred, belatedly awarding restitution to those who had survived its indictments.

CHAPTER 13
THE GROUPTHINK PSYCHODEMIC, PART III, SLOUCHING TOWARDS TOTALITARIA
29-08-2021

Never, before Covid, could a set of such radical and potentially subjugating ideas, and the programme for their implementation and enforcement, have become the occasion of such universal consensus.

'It is becoming more and more obvious that it is not starvation, it is not microbes, it is not cancer, but man himself who is his greatest danger: because he has no adequate protection against psychic epidemics, which are infinitely more devastating in their effect than the greatest natural catastrophes.'

— C.G. Jung, *Modern Man in Search of a Soul*

In his 2008 book, *Us and Them — Understanding Your Tribal Mind*, David Berreby explores the idea that tribalism is innate to humankind — that we are hardwired to band together with those who think like us, and oppose those who do not. Berreby conducts a careful study of how societies place imprints on the minds of their members, making connections in the individual brain between neurological programmes governing functions like language, sight and music, and the social requirements of conduct, law and morality. In one fascinating sequence, he looks at the role in history of what he calls stigma, exploring the possibility that many everyday tropes of modern fashion derive from past forms of marginalisation and scapegoating. To preserve necessary concepts of hierarchy and conformity, societies through history have created marks of exclusion to isolate individuals or groups deemed to be outside society's walls. In medieval Europe, groups like soldiers, criminals and wandering minstrels wore multicoloured clothes to distinguish them from 'normal' citizens.

Fashion and youth culture have long flirted with these signs of infamy and, since the 1960s, have majored in adapting and reinventing indicators of societal stigma, seeking to assert identity on the basis of the iconography of marginalisation. In the 1960s, long hair became fashionable for men because of its androgynous connotations, previously a big taboo. Similarly, shaved heads, because of the association with convicts, remained a symbol of exclusion until relatively recently. Berreby's fascinating thesis is that authority seeks to prevent the mainstreaming of such imagery not to protect young people from harmful associations but to prevent the iconography of societal rejection from devaluation. In other words, it is a fundamental impulse of societies — and by reduction of groups — that they reserve the capacity to expel malefactors and non-conformists. The countervailing idea of 'inclusiveness' is a relatively recent invention.

In times of doubt and controversy, a majority of people stick their dampened fingers in the air to see which way the wind is blowing, then replicate what the loudest and most 'authoritative' voices are saying. Such 'other-directed' categories tend to make up the 'hard centre' of the herd — those most difficult to sway with mere facts. Changes of mind generally start around the periphery, where the 'inner-directed' independent thinkers tend to gather, and it is there we find the dissenters and the banished, often in the same persons.

For a minority to convince the majority is not an arithmetic matter. The tipping point may actually be as low as 10 per cent. A decade ago at the Rensselaer Polytechnic Institute, New York — America's oldest technological research university — a study using computational and analytical methods found that when just 10 per cent of the population holds an unshakable belief, that belief is destined rapidly to be adopted by the majority.

Nevertheless, human beings behave as though built to herd rather than become heroes. Most people understand or sense that human beings are impressionable creatures — on account, perhaps, of their desiring to fit in, even at great cost, but also, in an associated way, in not wishing to appear obtuse or unintelligent, discounting their own perceptions and instincts as a result.

The Asch Conformity Test was a series of trials carried out at Swarthmore College, Pennsylvania, in the 1950s, aimed at discerning how susceptible people might be to peer pressure and how far this was likely to influence them in the things they believed or *claimed* to believe. It has often been noted that human beings fear nothing — not even hunger or thirst — more than being cast outside their own tribe, and these tests, also called the Asch Paradigm, comprised a series of studies directed by Solomon Asch to examine whether individuals would yield to or defy a majority group, and study the impact their responses had on their opinions, beliefs and actions. The results show a strong propensity in a minority of humans to follow the herd regardless of facts or even personal understandings. Asch found a strong pattern of yielding towards an erring majority opinion in more than a third of his test subjects, with three-quarters being prepared to concur with the majority's 'blunders' to some degree — in other words, consensus was more persuasive than truth. Doubt creeps in when we are outnumbered, pressing us to trust the majority.

Asch's verdict: 'That intelligent, well-meaning, young people are willing to call white black is a matter of concern.'

Some subjects, though suspecting something was wrong, lacked the confidence to go against the crowd. Some knew the others were wrong but went along so as not to seem 'out of step'. Further trials over subsequent years discovered that if one or more of the actors concurred with the subject's opinion, the number of instances where the subjects answered with the majority was reduced dramatically. The bigger the group, the more likelihood of conformity. The level of conformity was dramatically reduced in experiments in which the answers were written rather than spoken publicly.

This is why it has been so vital to the Covid deception that contrary views are excluded from public debates. Just one dissenting voice can liberate even a hesitant person to ignore the majority and speak the truth as he sees it. In a mass society, even a few dissenters can turn a general concordance around. That is why the authorities seek to blacken the reputations of dissenters, why journa-liars demonise truth-tellers as 'far-right conspiracy theorists', and so forth. It is also why PC ideas have proved so powerful in bullying the majority to remain silent on issues when certain perspectives are defined as taboo. All goes to demonstrate Irving Janis's third rule of groupthink: Its captives immediately move to marginalise 'wrongthinkers'.

All regimes, even tyrannies, depend on the acquiescence of the crowd. Those who dissent find they frequently incur the disapproval of other citizens, who prefer a quiet life in the early stages of despotism, when the threat is easier to ignore. By the time things escalate to a level intolerable to the majority, the price of confronting the regime is exponentially greater. If a significant number revolts at that stage, the gloves come off, and the society descends into outright and open tyranny.

'Groupthink' is not only nothing new — it is a reflex that has served the advance of humanity through the various stages of evolution. Only in recent times have we started to think of concepts like 'diversity' as good and concepts like 'marginalisation' as bad. Through much of the span of human history, instincts that divided were not merely considered virtues, but necessary ones. The problem enters in the context of several pronounced syndromes: the strange and potentially destructive behaviours of mobs in pursuit of unity; the damaging effects of like-mindedness in certain kinds of decision-making processes; and the effects of the behavioural 'sciences' in distorting human thinking in ways that, in turn, place instruments of disproportionate and dangerous power in the hands of manipulators. In his 1957 book, *The Hidden*

Persuaders, Vance Packard wrote about the then emerging 'depth' industry's discovery and leveraging of what were called 'subsurface desires, needs and drives' in human beings. Among the chief interconnected 'subsurface' levers found in most people's emotional profiles were 'the drive to conformity', the 'need for oral stimulation', and the 'yearning for security'.

Hence, although the declension of the groupthink concept may, at first sight, appear artificial, it is a necessary instrument for comprehending the history of what is a fairly clear-cut syndrome of human nature, as well as a pitfall of collective deliberation, and ultimately a lethal weapon of human enslavement. Acquiring a basic familiarity with the various techniques of persuasion and mind-control does not necessarily provide us with a more coherent schema for understanding human quirks and foibles under these headings, but it does serve to draw together a map of related aspects of human personality that may increasingly endanger the human species in general as techniques and technologies of manipulation become more sophisticated and exploitable.

These dangers have reached an unprecedented degree of rampancy in the 'Covid project'. Never before have near-total populations become so exposed and amenable to centralised forms of mind control; never before has a set of potentially controversial ideas and a programme for their implementation and enforcement become the occasion of such universal consensus. Never before have so many believed the same things on so little evidence or given up so much on such minor pretext. For example, the 'spontaneous' and universal belief in lockdown as a means of dealing with a respiratory ailment — never before proposed, never attempted — an idea imported whole from China that brought the West to its knees within weeks and became immediately an unquestionable dogma, turning inside out nearly 3,000 years of liberal democracy without as much as a shot being fired.

In this short series of three chapters, we have explored how the principles by which a group can succumb to dangerous like-mindedness were extracted and tabulated by Irving Lester Janis. We have looked also, in prior chapters and in a range of Substack articles over the past year, at a range of mechanisms whereby these same tendencies may be exploited in a broader population — techniques relating to propaganda, behavioural psychology, depth manipulation, surveillance, data accumulation and mass entrancement. We have examined the weapons of choice of multiple formerly democratic governments to impose their wills and subdue any potential for dissent or disquiet among their populations. We have examined the changing underfoot conditions that make it increasingly easier for governments and other powerful bodies to utilise such instruments to achieve an almost total compliance. Among the most important of these is control exercised over the failing legacy media — mainly by corruption through the use of advertising budgets, subvention and conditional subsidy — usually by governments, but also by public or private organisations with the means and motives to control public opinion. In effect, the media have ceased to be promulgators of understanding and have opted to become instead, under instruction from governmental and other clients, *manufacturers of consensus*, daily restoring the walls of lies they have built around their audience members.

We have also examined the manipulation of authority and deference in imposing and controlling a consensus of (mis)understanding and closing down or marginalising dissent. In these processes, we can observe the operation of the principles so brilliantly distilled by Irving Janis fifty years ago and outlined in the first chapter of this series. In effect, we have been trying to draw attention to the capacity that now exists for imposing one-dimensional thinking on whole populations, with the tendency of affected groups to automatically exclude, and even demonise, 'out-group' interests identified by Janis, serving to close down public discussion at moments when debate is most urgently required.

There was a reason why the philosopher John Stuart Mill, in treating the essentials of freedom in his 1859 treatise *On Liberty*, placed such emphasis on the importance of independence of thought, opinion and speech. Mill's main point was that since all freedom depends on the right of expression, a society desiring freedom needs to facilitate the maximum possible degree of free speech. 'If all mankind minus one were of one opinion,' he wrote, 'mankind would be no more justified in silencing that one person than he, if he had the power, would be justified in silencing mankind.' Mill's proposal might be called 'an antidote to groupthink'.

In the past year-and-a-half, we have observed the patterns of Irving Janis's diagnosis at work in multiple ways. It may not be that, in the overall imposition of the Covid tyranny, we are looking at a classic example of groupthink, for that would imply that the orders coming from on high were simply wrongheaded as opposed to malevolent, malicious and wicked. This may not be assumed. Where the issue of groupthink may enter in the first instance is with regard to the implementation of these diktats by secondary, tertiary or subsequent levels of officialdom or bureaucracy, and in the media who mirror these signals. Unsuspecting of utterly malign motives on the part of the uppermost manipulators, the inferior layers of executive actors may have been implementing a series of falsehoods in good faith based on ignorance, though sometimes with a degree of negligence amounting to criminality of itself.

But it cannot be assumed that what is happening arises in the first instance from error, incompetence or wrongheadedness: The signs and evidence indicate that it is a dastardly plot to destroy the human race in its present form, or at the very least, institute forms of control that will render its future existence unliveable by comparison with the past. The 'groupthink' problem may enter in by virtue of the mindlessness of implementation approaches, the failure to investigate from first principles, the neglect of due diligence exercises such as independent studies and cost-benefit analyses. Yet, another factor arises from the peculiarities of the hierarchy of command — what appears to be a system of compartmentalised authority, in which a few at the top may know what is actually happening, but the knowledge diminishes as instructions come down the chain, everyone being provided only with the information he or she 'needs' to know to implement the protocol.

The groupthink factor, then, arises chiefly from the failure of 'democratic' leaders to take seriously their roles as representatives of their electorates, their sudden resolve to see themselves not as custodians of their people's interests, protectors of the freedoms of their societies, and upholders of the integrity of the enabling institutions and instruments that exist to underpin those freedoms, but as *rulers in their own right*. Disregarding the fundamental nature of the power relationship at the heart of democracy, the political class — most lamentably of the countries formerly collectively recognised as 'Western civilisation' — have taken the opportunity afforded by what has long since emerged as a minor health scare, to usurp the authority and sovereignty of their peoples and, acting as proxies for undeclared, invisible outside interests, declared themselves the occasional gaolers of their own populations. In effect, those to whom We, the Peoples of innumerable countries have entrusted our most sacred liberties and delegated the accompanying powers — the implementation of legislative processes, the administration of justice, the application of state coercion — have almost without exception betrayed the sacred trust which this necessary assignment of power implies.

In this process, as we have seen, they have used the full panoply of manipulative instruments developed over the past century in marketing industrial products to willing consumers. In this process, additionally, they have employed mendacity, fear-mongering and the instruments provided under licence by parliament, laws, judicial process and policing to gain access to the most primal responses of their peoples and thereby subject them to a regime of incarceration, abuse, humiliation and dispossession. It has been clear for some time that these authorities have no intention of abandoning this course, at least until they have imposed some of the most radical alterations in human culture and behaviour ever seen outside the most grotesque and vicious despotisms, or the most fanciful dystopian tales. This has been comprehensively documented in prior chapters.

In the implementation of the plandemic, therefore, we can observe the playing out of Janis's three defining 'rules of groupthink': the mass promulgation of understandings based not on objective reality but on a distorted view of the world; the generation of 'in-groups' comprising intense believers in the unverified rightness of what they are imposing; and the labelling, marginalisation, discrediting and silencing of those outside the in-group — those conducting what the authorities of many countries have been referring to as the 'infodemic'. All this, in premeditated effect, renders stillborn the process of discussion and dissension which John Stuart Mill adjudged to be essential to democracy and freedom.

The programmes of mass manipulation and entrancement employed by the governments of the former Western democracies have been, more or less universally, in keeping with the descriptions provided by the English journalist Laura Dodsworth in her timely and comprehensive account of the use of these techniques and tactics in the UK, the 2021-published *A State of Fear*. It is, as Dodsworth says in her Introduction, 'a book about fear: Fear of a virus. Fear of death. Fear of change, fear of the unknown. Fear of ulterior motives agenda and conspiracy. Fear for the rule of law, democracy, the Western liberal way of life. Fear of loss: losing our jobs, our culture, our connections, our health, our minds.' But it's also, more precisely, about how the British government weaponised fear against its own people — 'supposedly', as Dodsworth says, in their best interests, 'until we were one of the most frightened countries in the world.'

At the heart of Dodsworth's book is an exploration of the strategy that appears to have begun with a resolution, determined at the outset by a key advisory group of behavioural scientists engaged in the formulation of government policy — the Scientific Pandemic Influenza Group on Behaviour (SPI-B), which stated in its March 22nd, 2020, report, *Options for increasing adherence to social distancing measures*, that 'a substantial number of people still do not feel sufficiently personally threatened.' SPI-B recommended that 'the perceived level of personal threat needed to be increased among those who are complacent, using hard-hitting emotional messaging.' As Dodsworth extrapolates, the British government was being advised, in 'one of the most extraordinary documents ever revealed to the British public' to 'encourage' adherence to the emergency lockdown regulations by means of cynically imposed fear.

This process, as we have previously explored, operates as a form of mass entrancement, employing standard techniques of the therapeutic and stage hypnotist, combined with understandings of the domestic narcissist/psychopath adapted to the public realm. This enabled the Covid operation to harness the dynamics of archetypal relationships between narcissists/psychopaths (politicians) and co-dependent submissives/empaths (citizens), in effect weaponising on a grand scale the dynamics of abusive domestic relationships. It is important to understand that this is not a literal expression of psychopathy, but a scripted protocol designed to induce in the targeted audience similar responses to those of the subjugated individual in an abusive intimate relationship, in this instance, to inculcate the necessary elements of the desired groupthink in one and in all. These techniques summon their victims to respond to the approved narrative, refraining from questioning its tenets or logic, and, in defence of it, joining in the demonisation of its out-group opponents, and their scapegoating if so instructed.

Of course, only the *cultivation* aspects of these conditions might be said to relate to forms of thought *per se*, since, in general, these tactics tend to bypass the rational mechanism of the human mind, and, by manipulating feeling and emotion, impose a degree of terrified certainty that exceeds in persuasion-power whole libraries of information and data in 'convincing' people as to the realness of the threat said to exist. This is what we have dubbed the 'enspelled' form of groupthink, though in its full-blown form it bears also the hallmarks of a very literal form of 'possession', the word we have used to describe the spontaneous capturing of a group of decision-makers by wrongthink arising from treacherous internal dynamics and undertows, and resulting in what Janis called 'fiascos'. In this, despite the protestations of the culprits, it bears more than a passing resemblance to the tactics operated by the Nazis in the expansion years of the Third Reich. How ironic, then, that almost universally, the culpable authorities of 2020/21 have resorted to seeking to demonise their critics by characterising them as 'far right'.

These tactics were replicated in virtually every country in the world, under the guidance — nay, insistence — of highly centralised authorities, most visibly the World Health Organisation, the European Union, the United Nations and the World Economic Forum. A centrally orchestrated groupthink was transmitted through the wires of bureaucracy and corrupted media to the minds of billions.

In the Covid context, the operation of groupthink can be observed under three main headings: (1.) in the operations of groups and bodies, including expert ones, which fell in with the narrative on the basis of a reduced view of science and medical understanding, eschewing the time-honoured means by which pathogens were absorbed and overcome within populations; (2.) in the manner in which media have represented these understandings; and (3.) in the responses of citizenries who decided that their governments knew best, regardless of what common sense and experience told them.

According to some of the world's leading scientists — Professor Sucharit Bhakdi, Dr Geert Vanden Boosche, Dr Michael Yeadon, and others — those who have orchestrated this disaster have generated a far worse problem than anticipated in even their most ludicrous initial computer-generated predictions. This apprehension arises both from the established lethality of the 'vaccines' and the weakening effect on the human immune system of the prior conditions imposed by lockdown, social distancing, hand-washing and mask-wearing; in other words, the danger has been exacerbated by their manipulation of structural elements of the human in ways that sought to distort and manipulate reality.

Covid is not — never was — a pandemic. It is, rather, what Carl Jung called a 'psychic' epidemic, a mass psychosis or, to be more precise as to how we arrived here, a generated dementia that grips the world and is now beyond the control even of its controllers. This occurs when a significant section of humanity loses touch with reality and descends into delusion. The Salem witch-hunt, and similar events in America and Europe of half a millennium ago, as well as the triptych of totalitarianisms that erupted in Germany, Russia and China in the twentieth century, are all examples of such madnesses. Jung wrote that, in such an episode, the affected individuals sink unconsciously to a lower level of intellectual engagement, becoming 'morally and spiritually inferior' to the civilisation they belong to, but without having any awareness of or insight into this. The causes of these madnesses are different to the triggers setting off madness in an individual. Generally, they arise from 'psychogenic stressors', for example, the flooding of a culture with negative emotions — anger, fear, anxiety, *et cetera* — which drive the collective into a state of mutualised panic. Whereas an individual may experience, for example, a 'psychotic break' — a combination of psychotic and non-psychotic responses which may have a paradoxically stabilising effect, enabling a processing of the various disturbances so as to allow the affected individual to emerge unscathed from the episode, the crowd, once stirred up, has no way back. It loses its grip on sanity, becoming, according to Jung, 'more unreasonable, irresponsible, emotional, erratic and unreliable.' Crimes which would be unthinkable for an individual are 'freely committed by the group smitten by madness.' There is no mechanism within the mob whereby it, or its constituent members, can become alerted to the psychosis, and no collective mechanism that might enable it to moderate its responses. In such a situation, the crowd becomes the instrument of either its own latent pathologies or external controllers seeking totalitarian power. There is, then, a degeneration leading to regression, the culmination state of mass delusion: *infantilisation*. The crowd places itself in the hands of its rulers, accepting everything they intimate or mandate. Since these delusions have almost invariably been initiated by the rulers, the result can be outright collective insanity, with the mob unthinkingly carrying our every wish and command of the rulers. This, really, is the nadir of the 'enspelled' form of groupthink. Other words for this are *brainwashing* and *menticide*, the latter coined by Dr Joost Meerloo, author of *The Rape of the Mind: The Psychology of Thought Control, Menticide and Brainwashing*, who defined it as 'an organized system of judicial perversion and psychological intervention, in which a powerful tyrant transfers his own thoughts and words into the minds and mouths of the victims he plans to destroy or to use for his own propaganda.'

Dr Meerloo, who experienced Nazi indoctrination methods first-hand in the Netherlands, systematically described the minute details of the indoctrination process in what he called 'Totalitaria': 'The masses must give up their freedom and cede control of all aspects of life to the ruling elite. They must relinquish their capacity to be self-reliant individuals who are responsible for their own lives, and become submissive and obedient subjects. The masses, in other words, must descend into the delusions of the totalitarian psychosis.' The population turns in on itself, seeking to root out the malefactors and crime-thinkers, whipped up and along by the ruling authorities. Common decency and reason are eradicated from the culture, replaced by terror and scapegoating of the imagined enemy within.

Merloo's writings, along with those of Hannah Arendt, offer among the richest understandings we have of the mechanics of the totalitarian impulse and the methods demagogues and totalitarians seek to capture the minds of their victims.

'The demagogue, like the totalitarian dictator,' he writes, 'knows well how to lay a mental spell on the people, how to create a kind of mass suggestion and mass hypnosis. There is no intrinsic difference between individual and mass hypnosis. In hypnosis — the most intensified form of suggestion — the individual becomes temporarily automatized, both physically and mentally. Such a clinical state of utter mental submission can be brought about quite easily in children and in primitive people, but it can be created in civilized adults, too.'

He peers into phenomena like the use of cliché in the generation of public opinion, the role of the human need for companionship, the application of psychological shock and regression (infantilisation), the manipulation of guilt feelings and the use of tendencies towards masochism in engendering strange pacts with tyranny. Totalitarianism is the sum of the personalities of its subjects, broken down and subjugated. It is also the tapping into the childlike fears and dependencies of the individual, which make him crave protection and security over freedom. Totalitaria is a mythical place in the imagination, 'a monolithic and absolute state in which doubt, confusion, and conflict are not permitted to be shown, for the dictator purports to solve all his subjects' problems for them,' enabling the uncivilised child in everyone to embrace a kind of liberation from responsibility and ethical frustration. 'Totalitaria — the Leviathan state — is the home of the political system we call, euphemistically, totalitarianism, of which systematized tyranny is a part.'

Our societies, he believed, are far more primitive than we like to imagine, and the more technologised the society, the truer this becomes. In *The Rape of the Mind*, he argues that humanity's love affair with machines and technology is gestating societies of robots, who seek the irrational as a form of escape from reality. 'Public opinion moulds our critical thoughts every day. Unknowingly, we may become opinionated robots. . . . We crave excitement, hair-raising stories, sensation. We search for situations that create superficial fear to cover up inner anxieties.'

No nation, he wrote, is immune from becoming a Totalitaria. 'Totalitaria is any country in which political ideas degenerate into senseless formulations made only for propaganda purposes. It is any country in which a single group left or right acquires absolute power and becomes omniscient and omnipotent, any country in which disagreement and differences of opinion are crimes, in which utter conformity is the price of life.'

He describes by happenstance life in PC Ireland of the past decade: 'The citizens of Totalitaria do not really converse with one another. When they speak, they whisper, first looking furtively over their shoulders for the inevitable spy. The inner silence is in sharp contrast to the official verbal bombardment. The citizens of Totalitaria may make noise and utter polite banalities, or they may repeat slogans one after another, but they say nothing.'

'In Totalitaria, there is no faith in fellow men, no "caritas", no love, because real relationships between men do not exist, just as they do not exist between schizophrenics. There is only faith in and subjection to the feeding system, and there is in every citizen a tremendous fear of being expelled from that system, a fear of being totally lost, comparable with the schizophrenic's feeling of rejection and fear of reality. In the midst of spiritual loneliness and isolation, there is the fear of still greater loneliness, of more painful isolation. Without protective regulations from the outside, internal hell may break loose. Strong mechanical external order must be used to cover the internal chaos and approaching breakdown.'

Menticide, or brainwashing, or cultivated groupthink, is the process by which a demented ruling class imposes on the collective mind of the population the programme for the achievement of its own aspirations to total power and control. Modern psychiatry offers several of the key tools required for this perversion. This starts out with a programme of fear-mongering, which is escalated to ramp up the state of delusion and derangement of the mob. For maximum effect, this is carried out in a series of waves, punctuated with quasi-normalising breaks, enabling fear levels to be increased by building them layer-upon-layer, like a lasagne, until the dish reaches boiling point. The breaks are just as important as the periods of fear-mongering. The processes of spreading disinformation, confusion generation and scapegoating are orchestrated to enflame the mob and provide it with a clear sense of an enemy. Confusion is a critical instrument, creating a sense of chaos among the crowd that prevents it putting things back together in a rational manner. Technology makes easy such a process of emotional 'jamming'. Separating, isolating people, interrupting the normal interactions of the population, are key instruments also, and it will not escape notice that these have been visible features of the Covid cult, causing the individual to become isolated from others, and increasingly mistrustful of his fellows. The media are central to this process — in a Totalitaria, it is their sole function. 'He who dictates and formulates the words and phrases we use, he who is master of the press and radio, is master of the mind. Repeat mechanically your assumptions and suggestions, diminish the opportunity for communicating dissent and opposition. This is the formula for political conditioning of the masses.'

Hannah Arendt, in *The Origins of Totalitarianism*, also identified constructed loneliness as a key tool of totalitarianism: 'What prepares men for totalitarian

THE ABOLITION OF REALITY 135

domination in the non-totalitarian world is the fact that loneliness, once a borderline experience usually suffered in certain marginal social conditions like old age, has become an everyday experience of the ever-growing masses of our century.'

Once isolated in their individuated states of loneliness, the members of a community or nation lose their place in the world, and, in doing so, become as fodder for the tyrants. Totalitarianism offers them coherence that is otherwise lacking: the coherence of terror. It removes complexity, replacing it with the simplest of concepts, and therefore eliminates also the confusion and chaos initially engendered by the totalitarians laying the groundwork for their schemes. Loneliness is a step beyond mere isolation, a sense of no longer belonging to the human community at all. This, above all, is what renders totalitarianism different to 'ordinary' tyranny. Rendering the world simple and negotiable, albeit at the price of a lost humanity, totalitarianism becomes seductive to those who are too fearful of reality to identify with other humans. The points of comparison between these descriptions and what has unfolded in the Covid cult need hardly be laboured.

Hannah Arendt believed that totalitarianism was not just another form of tyranny, but a unique and novel development — the total domination of a people through a combination of simplistic ideology and constant terror. It appealed to no traditional laws or forms of government, but rather to its own concocted Law of Nature (survival of the fittest, master race) or Law of History (a classless society with one class, the 'proletariat'). Its goal was the extension of that total domination to the entire world. In totalitarianism, she described all traditions, values, legalities and defences, all political institutions . . . *everything* is destroyed, and all behaviour, public and private, comes to be controlled by terror, which becomes the measure of all things.

It has seemed improbable to us, even to those of us who have been paying some measure of attention to history, that anything like this could happen in the here and now, that the world could descend into the cesspit of evil even within the living memory of previous episodes. But this is to see things the wrong way around, to regard profound evil as some kind of aberration in history, which is actually not at all what history tells us. Lulled into such a delusion, we believed that our time would be different — it being the most educated, enlightened, progressive democracy-loving era in the whole of history. But therein lay the trap: In truth, we lived through a period which had been imprinted with a consciousness of evil more radical and dramatic than perhaps anything that had happened before. We lived, therefore, through a 'cautionary period', which might be presumed to arise due to an enhanced mindfulness of man's potential for wickedness, a period when the consciousness of evil remained pronounced by proximity to it. But this rapidly gave way to complacency arising from the delusion of evil as aberration.

The lives of perhaps half of the people now alive jutted into the period 1945-1989, when one or more of the triptych of totalitarianisms was extant. But, for some time now — three decades, you might calculate — it has seemed that history had indeed ended, and humanity had advanced, progressed, evolved beyond such dark possibilities. It was as though our very *awareness* of the past acted as a kind of inoculation against a recurrence of the same patterns. It seemed unthinkable, right up to, say, 20 months ago, that Western humanity might ever again regress to such conditions. But now a different thought must surely occur: that the darkness is never safely to be regarded as aberrational; that increasing danger rises up in the soft soil of prosperity and complacency; that the greatest danger of all resides in imagining that we are out of danger.

And there are connected syndromes, applying both to those we might loosely call our 'leader class' and to ourselves, the 'led'. For a long time, we had looked to those to whom we delegated our sovereign power as citizens and human persons, and given them no thought in this regard other than contentedly to sigh ourselves back to sleep with the thought that, although they might be fools and minor knaves, they were at least incapable of evil; incapable, to say the least, of behaving like characters in some dystopian novel; incapable of seeking absolute power over us. Now, however, it must surely occur that the sole reason they may have given us this impression was that they lacked the opportunity to seize power, to behave like despots over us, and sell us, our children and our nations down the river. To be more precise, they lacked the power to do these things other than with extreme messiness: cries renting the air and blood on the streets. Now, however, technology, the behavioural 'sciences' and 'nudge theory' having put the means of controlling their populations — possibly absolutely and permanently — at their disposal, they emerge in their true colours. Now we see: They meant not a word of their prating about democracy and freedom. They meant, really, that they would pretend to govern democratically for as long as this was strictly unavoidable without getting the pavement all bloody, and not a day longer. And now, their hour come round at last, they slouch towards Gehenna to be reborn as killers of children and the old.

As for We, the People, well, the report card is not so auspicious either. We, especially in Western republics and democracies, thought ourselves proud liberals, libertarians, sovereign peoples, the freest the world had ever known — and democrats, of course, it went without saying. But now? What we can say of ourselves now is simply that we *seemed* to be like that. But, in truth, in the years of the 'cautionary period', we became as human beings had perhaps not allowed themselves to become for such a long period hitherto: We became complacent and stress-free. We stopped paying attention — to our leaders and to ourselves. We took both at face value: them in their shiny suits, ourselves in our mirrors. And, just as we looked to our leaders and fancied them self-evidently benign, little suspecting the imaginings that lay behind their fixed smiles, we looked in the mirror and read our own contentment as evidence of our own deep natures. We thought of ourselves as possessed of personalities forged in the ineradicable spirit of freedom. In reality, though, we were simply surveying our own stress-free dispositions and taking them for the naturalistic condition of the human being in history. It now emerges: Our freedom from historical stress was the *sole* aberrational syndrome, and, struck by this thought, we look around and see the actual truth of our natures and our times: We are cowards, collaborators, touts, snitches, scapegoaters and witchfinders; our leaders are monsters such as we have not met in our nightmares, and reality is exactly what might be expected from a collision of two such wayfarers — not a pretty vista by any stretch.

GROUPTHINK CASE STUDY

The Emperor's New Clothes

Perhaps it might be argued that the precise circumstances outlined in this Hans Christian Andersen fable strain credulity, but it cannot be said that the syndromes the story highlights are beyond the realms of the possible. Though a fable, therefore, it presents a real possibility, a 'case study'.

In Covid, the fear that makes people conform and see what is not there, is of sickness, death, and — possibly even ahead of these — the disfavour of the crowd. In the story of the Emperor's new clothes, the fears that make the crowd 'see' what isn't there are of the Emperor's displeasure, peer pressure and losing the favour of the crowd.

In calling out the Emperor's nakedness, there is nothing at stake for the boy but simply stating the truth. He speaks out of his guilelessness. He is not defending freedom, or his way of life. He is not trying to become a hero. And yet the anti-tyranny principle expressed in Václav Havel's essay *The Power of the Powerless* — one human being standing up and speaking the truth — is as honoured by his intervention as though he were defending all these things.

Democracy requires courage, sometimes disguised as recklessness, to defend it against the gibberish of would-be tyrants. To utter the truth at any time, even gratuitously, is an act of liberation. Who knows, if the Emperor's state of undress had not been called out, that he would not have seen in the episode ways to further his power over his subjects?

What is called for, then, is simply this: to speak out in public. The motive is less important. What matters is blurting out what is obvious or true, being seen, heard, refusing to accept the lie. It is important that the person is recognisable, identifiable. There is no point in blurting truth from behind a mask. Here I am — I, John Doe, of Liberty Street, Liesbury — the citizen, sovereign for once!

Freedom is only as strong as the availability of citizens willing to stand up and defend it. This is why, when the powerful seek to impose groupthink, they attack those who continue to dissent. No matter what the motivation for the control of free speech, it should never be permitted to silence a society, even in what is presented as a 'good cause'. A people governed by censorship, even of an apparently well-intentioned kind, is not free but already drifting towards tyranny.

The story of the Emperor's new clothes is overtly concerned with mass suggestibility and intellectual vanity — the idea that false ideas can put down roots by a process of contagion. It is, in short, a story of enchantment, and, therefore, an archetypal fable of the concept of collective enspelling, which we have identified both as a particular category of groupthink and a central tool of the Covid deception.

The story of the Emperor, his officials, the scoundrel tailors and the little boy — published 184 years ago, just four years before Charles Mackay's book and 58 years before Gustave le Bon's — is fanciful only if you have a constricted view of human nature. It tells of something central to the human structure that has only in recent times acquired the status of 'scientific' understanding.

In Andersen's story, the swindlers warn at the outset that their cloth has 'a wonderful way of becoming invisible to anyone who is unfit for his office, or unusually stupid.' Something like this was also a central element of the Covid confidence trick: the insinuation from the beginning that those who questioned the pandemic were *ipso facto* demonstrating ignorance of The Science. This conforms also to Irving Janis's third 'rule' of groupthink: The 'in-group' will try to smear and demonise the 'out-group'.

It is also interesting that, from the beginning, Covid acquired a quasi-ideological hue, with believers tending to be from the better-off, more 'educated' sectors, while sceptics almost exclusively emanated from the 'deplorable' classes. The inference being pedalled was that 'seeing Covid' was a matter of 'intelligence', but this divide has other keys to do with common sense, personal experience and real knowledge.

It is remarkable, too, how in Andersen's story, the characters offer an immediately recognisable correspondence with the characters of our domestic Covid narrative: the tailors, clearly equating to NPHET, the medical community, the HSE and purveyors of The Science; the Emperor and his officials corresponding to the politicians and media. The people, surveying the consensus of more intelligent beings, surrender to and continue to be captured by the narrative until the spell is broken by the boy. The boy represents the single, independent individual, celebrated in John Stuart Mill's treatise on freedom, *On Liberty*, who continues to adhere to his own unmediated, uncontaminated experience and perspective, even though the whole world is saying different.

The official actors in the Covid narrative behave, if anything, much more unthinkingly than those in Andersen's story, where there is actually a description of at least some attempt at verification. The Emperor, first alerted to the possibility of fraud, sends his Minister to inspect the looms. The old Minister finds them empty but, conscious that a failure to see the fabric would reveal him as a fool, decides to 'see' it. The swindlers proceed to name all the colours and to explain the intricate patterns of the weave. The Minister pays the closest attention to these descriptions so that he can report it all to the Emperor. The same happens with a second official. When the Emperor finally comes to see the 'weavers' at work, the two officials who have already 'seen' the fabric accompany him, and both exclaim: 'Just look, Your Majesty, what colours! What a design!' They point to the empty looms, each official supposing that the other can see something that he — each in his turn — is unable to. The Emperor, fearful of seeming unfit to rule his people, declares: 'Oh! It's very pretty! It has my highest approval!' Soon, to a man and woman, the citizens of the city, following the example of their leaders, conspire to ignore reality and cheer as the Emperor parades robeless through the streets.

Here we can observe the process that many centuries later was exposed and verified by the Ashe experiment: how the fear of being thought foolish causes people to make fools of themselves. It appears that the impulse to simply state a straightforward viewpoint is weak in many people, and this weakness is capable of being manipulated by unscrupulous actors. The little boy — the dissenter, sceptic, 'denier' — eventually breaks the spell, but not without incurring the wrath of the enspelled and those who, having compromised their integrity by going along with what they recognise to be a deception, are determined to keep the fiction going. Fulfilling Irving Janis's third rule of groupthink, some of those caught up in the 'consensus' angrily turn on the boy for pointing out the truth.

The Emperor, doubling down on his own hoodwinking, gives each of the swindlers a cross to wear in his buttonhole, and the title of 'Sir Weaver'. The officials, likewise, perpetuate the fiction for fear of incurring the Emperor's displeasure. The citizens of the city will not believe the evidence of their eyes because those around them are all saying something different. Each one is, in a sense, 'supported' in his continuing mystification by the gullibility or cunning of his fellows. But eventually, awakened by the little boy's cry of 'He is naked!', the crowd begins to shout as one:

'But he has nothing at all on!'

The Emperor, hearing this, is displeased, not because the people are wrong, but because he knows they are right. Now there is the added dimension in the likelihood of humiliation on account of having been duped by the tailors. The Emperor doubles down and down again, walking 'ever more proudly' in his nakedness. And the lords of the bedchamber take greater pains than ever to appear holding up a train, although there is no train to hold.

Hans Christian Andersen's story is a precise anticipation of the psychology of the Covid cult. The 'fable' of 2020 was first promulgated by 'global health officials' of the World Health Organisation, spreading rapidly to their equivalents in various countries, in Ireland to the now legendary NPHET, which passed the news of the tailors' splendiferous workmanship to the politicians, who in turn passed it to journaliars, who passed it on to the people. The people were unable to see anything, but were so cowed by the emphatic tones and injunctions of the politicians that they did not demur. On the contrary, they began to convince themselves, and each other, that there was something to see: a deadly disease that might strike them dead at any moment.

Step by step, the fiction was developed and expanded. The people, under instruction from their leaders, become convinced that they should wear face masks to protect themselves from the contagion, for which they had seen no direct evidence with their own eyes. Under instruction from the tailors of Covid, they moved away from one another, seeing no longer fellow citizens but walking biohazards who endangered human life just by walking around! Bit by bit, they became persuaded to let go of everything they once regarded as indispensable: their freedoms, livelihoods, privacy, the integrity of their homes, their children's education, the economic well-being of their communities. Surrounded by the evidence of the disproportionality and folly of all this, they failed to do what reason might have seemed to dictate — to initiate a comprehensive examination of all the evidence, insist upon the right to speak in defence of their way of life, call in the tailors and interrogate them — but instead joined all the more enthusiastically in with the schemes of those who seemed determined to disregard every last consideration as to the well-being of humanity, aside from the single fetish of 'saving lives', an objective for which no one could produce any evidence of success. In moments of doubt, each citizen upbraided himself into renewed silence: 'I am not a tailor, after all! What would I know?'

As the world fell apart all around, the people cheered its destroyers to the clouds, applauding those who incarcerated them and prevented them preserving the hard-won circumstances by which they have been able to provide for and offer hope to their own children. When, from time to time, a voice of questioning was urgently raised, it was just as rapidly stilled by ridicule or menaces. When occasionally presented with formal challenges, the courts, supposedly independent of other elements of the establishment, issued judgements of circular logic, declaring that if the government thought the situation was as serious as it did, then the situation must be as serious as the government declared. Even the children remained silent, but — just in case their bewildered hush might prompt one of their number to point to the general nakedness — plans were made to mask and 'jab' them before allowing them to return to join their friends in the schoolroom.

In this situation, the constant danger of the truth emerging became the factor that prevented it from doing so. The groupthink increased in proportion to the risk of its uncovering. With each passing day of the fiasco, the motivation of each participant to continue supporting the fiction grew and grew to the point where the more the outsider might expect the truth to spill out, the more the fiction became consolidated and embellished.

The politicians, knowing that they were doomed if the truth was finally exposed, doubled, trebled down. Likewise, the public, who, though wronged, suspected also that they had been complicit in their own hoodwinking. A mutualised 'contract' was entered into whereby everybody tacitly agreed not to squeal. The 'tailors' — the vaccine peddlers — were able to escape with an almost cast-iron immunity from prosecution. The procession marched on, ever more certain of its path.

The terror of being found out in such credulity, myopia, gullibility and/or stupidity is now too much to allow for a simple u-turn and individual fessing up, especially in circumstances whereby all involved others seem even more determined to keep the fiction going. The people become locked into their own destruction like a flock of sheep pushing against a gate from the wrong side, as the inferno from which they are fleeing encroaches from behind them, consuming everything in its path.

CHAPTER 14
THE TRUTH IS UNMISTAKABLE FOR ANYTHING ELSE

05-09-2021

Resisting totalitarianism demands not political revolution but personal refusal of history's usurping. The power of the powerless, defined by Václav Havel, is the power of each one to arise and say 'no'.

There are a few things we need to understand clearly about Václav Havel. Firstly, he was not, as is often suggested, merely an 'anti-communist' writer and intellectual whose work relates to one period of man, with diminishing significance now that the political conditions he wrote out of are no longer there. No: Havel's themes were universal ones, demonstrated in a specific political and ideological context. He distilled the particular from the general. His theme, really, was not Communism, but the soul of man under a system seeking to extinguish it. It might well be said that his ideas and observations have never been so crucial as they are now; certainly they have never been more crucial for the Western Europeans who have emerged from the complacency of post-WWII Europe, thinking themselves immune from the pathologies of their own and their neighbours' pasts.

Frequently in Havel's writings can be found references to the idea of Western democracy as representing merely a marginally preferential condition to Soviet Communism — which he called 'a convex-mirror image' of the democratic West. But he goes deeper, to talk always of 'freedom', which he understood, again, not as mere political freedom, but something more. He wrote and spoke always out of an awareness of the human desire to understand and describe reality, and a passion to define what it is to live truly — *absolutely* — within such a definition.

In speaking of the ideological configuration of this 'convex mirror image', Havel uses the word 'dictatorship', but in a particular way, taking pains, like Hannah Arendt and others, to emphasise that what we encounter here is quite different to the classical dictatorships of the past, which simply imposed their wills upon the people through naked terror and violence. At the core of the modern form of dictatorship — what he called the 'post-totalitarian' system — he identified the phenomenon of ideology, which he described as 'almost a secularised religion'.

'In an era when metaphysical and existential certainties are in a state of crisis,' he wrote in *The Power of the Powerless*, 'when people are being uprooted and alienated and are losing their sense of what this world means, this ideology inevitably has a certain hypnotic charm. To wandering humankind, it offers an immediately available home: all one has to do is accept it, and suddenly everything becomes clear once more, life takes on a new meaning, and all mysteries, unanswered questions, anxiety and loneliness vanish. Of course, one pays dearly for this low-rent home: the price is abdication of one's own reason, conscience and responsibility, for an essential aspect of this ideology is the consignment of reason and conscience to a higher authority. The principle involved here is that the centre of power is identical with the centre of truth.'

He provides a slightly more refined and precise definition of his sense of the meaning of totalitarianism in an essay, *Stories and Totalitarianism*, which he wrote in 1987, just two years before the Velvet Revolution.

Recalling merely in outline some of its central insights into the nature of totalitarianism, I reread it recently and was struck by something that had not — could not for reasons that will be obvious — have impacted me so greatly before. This time, it struck me that perhaps someone involved in formulating the Covid scam might have read the essay and been inspired by its introductory passage.

In those opening paragraphs, Havel relates a story involving a friend of his, heavily asthmatic, who had been in prison, where the authorities appeared indifferent to whether he lived or died. An American woman who heard about this contacted an editor in one of the leading US dailies, asking if they would cover the story. The editor responded: 'Call me when the man dies.'

Hável, though shocked, was also phlegmatic. Death is a story; asthma is not. He wrote, as though enviously, of Lebanon, where, at the time, many people were dying, and which was never out of the news. In Prague, there was totalitarianism but not so much death. As long as humans could remember, he wrote, 'death has been the point at which all the lines of every real story converge.' Like his friend, Czechoslovakia was unworthy of attention because it had no stories, and no death. He meant identifiably political deaths. There, he wrote, the war and killing took on a different form: 'they have been shifted from the daylight of observable public events to the twilight of unobservable inner destruction.' In these circumstances, Czechoslovak dissidents could not compete with the warriors of The Lebanon.

'We have only asthma. And why should anyone be interested in listening to our cough?

'One can't go on writing forever about how hard it is to breathe.'

This passage reads now like a prophecy of the present, not just of Prague but of London, Paris and Dublin. Under totalitarianism, everything is different, including death. But, in these countries which have yet to name their condition as such, death has become an infinitely malleable commodity, its meanings and even its definitions slipping in and out of focus. The 'story' in these places is about the avoidance of death, or the *purported* avoidance of death. Yet, death continues, being caused by its alleged cures — vaccines, ventilators — and allegedly by a virus that has never been isolated in natural conditions. And the story-tellers, as selective as ever, are not interested in just any category of death: in virus deaths, yes; in vaccine deaths, no. They are interested in those who have difficulty breathing, only if their difficulty is rooted in the correct ideological context. There must be no whiff of denialism, or anti-vaxxery. If they conform to these rules, their difficulty breathing remains a 'story'. Otherwise, they can just go to hell and die, or *vice versa*. If they die within 14 days of receiving a vaccine, then they qualify as 'unvaccinated', which means that, by implication, they died of their own negligence, even though the vaccine may have killed them. Still, the 'story' is clear: There is no story. The meanings of the deaths of countless thousands had shifted from the daylight of observable public events to the twilight of unobservable inner destruction.

Havels' plays and essays are in many respects prophetic, but I think that he would be surprised (he died in 2011) to discover that he had unconsciously presaged a central aspect of the Covid-19 episode: the weaponisation of respiratory illness as an instrument of warfare and death.

Every winter before 2020, in every country in the world, people died — sometimes very many people — without anyone, aside from their relatives and friends, taking more than polite or compassionate notice. They died of all kinds of things — essentially, the collapse of their vital organs as their immune systems guttered and gave out. In this, they were helped on their way by a number of factors depending on their whereabouts, in particular, the sometimes extremely harsh weather experienced in the northern hemisphere around the turn of the year, which gives succour to innumerable bugs and viruses which serve finally to overcome the immune systems of the old, pushing them over the edge of this dimension. In this twilight, devoid of media attention, many people died and had words like 'pneumonia' and 'influenza' scratched in bad handwriting on their death certificates. No one counted them. Few even noticed. That lacuna in public attention was to become the speck of grit around which the pearl of the Covid scamdemic was constructed. The 'story' had been scripted in advance and could not be deviated from. Suddenly, something like 'asthma' was 'news'.

As it happens, in *Stories and Totalitarianism* also, Havel helpfully explains the deep nature of totalitarianism, defining its central mechanism as the 'assassination of history' to achieve both 'nihilisation of the past' and mastery over the future. The instrument of this process he identified as the removal from history of the possibilities of human choice, mystery and autonomy. History becomes a fixed sequence of unfolding inevitabilities, and the role of human beings is merely to acquiesce and embrace what is pressed upon them. History, past and future, is appropriated in a manner that eliminates the human element — yes, the human *story*. All the unpredictability and possibility that arises from the human capacity for endless variety are removed and replaced with a sense that the future is simply an ideological continuum from the past, and that all that is required of the human person, citizen, is to move forward into a utopia that has been prepared according to the diktats of history. This process begins with the commandeering of *history past* by a single viewpoint, which is then made absolute, enabling *history present* to be reduced to that single aspect, thereby rendering *history future* amenable to total control. This, he wrote, occurs when the 'story' — that which gives human history its shape and meaning and structure — is eliminated from human culture. After that, he continued: 'Since the mystery in a story is the articulated mystery of man, his story began to lose its human content. The uniqueness of the human creature became a mere embellishment on the laws of history, and the tension and thrill in real events were dismissed as accidental, and therefore, unworthy of the attention of scholarship. History became boredom.'

To put this another way, what 'they' are calling 'the new normal' is a future into which we are 'invited' to enter as though into a city already constructed, along lines that have not been discussed with us, the putative future inhabitants waiting to be moved in. Everything is already decided — and not, we are archly informed, by some arbitrary human authority but by the mechanistic mind of time, which ordains the course of history according to immutable and unchallengeable laws in accordance with circumstances that are not open for discussion. This is totalitarianism at its essence. It is totalitarianism in any time or place.

The comparison is not too strong. What the dissident fights for, under Covid as under Communism (in as far as they are different), is the right of men and women to live lives by their own lights, according to their given natures and infinite desiring. But this, above all, is what the totalitarian seeks to plunder. The seemingly least offensive thing about the human person — her desire to be let alone, to live her life in accordance with the nudgings of intrinsic desires and impulses — is what the would-be tyrant seeks to quell. We, as previously noted, had thought ourselves immune from such impositions — after all, our leaders, like us, were raised in the acute consciousness of the dangers of totalitarianism. But this has emerged as having sedated rather than stimulated us. We have, therefore, blundered into renewedly ominous times for human beings seeking to adhere to the truth and the givenness of things. Few of us, even in our most dystopian nightmares, anticipated the craziness that has descended upon us in the past handful of years, and viciously in the past 18 months, and something tells me that the worst is yet to come. Or, perhaps, not 'something' — more like 'someone', a man called Václav Havel.

In another passage of the same essay, Havel refers to the nature of the shift that occurred in Czechoslovakia after the abortive Prague Spring of 1968, following which the mode of government changed from brute tyranny to totalitarianism. Before, things had been hard, with much misery, death and suffering, as well as idealism and heroism on the part of those who resisted Communist rule. There were stories, at least. But, after 1968 and the abortive Prague Spring of Alexander Dubček, things changed in ways that it takes a writer of Havel's capacities to describe. He refers to the infamous document, *Lessons from the Years of Crisis*, which set down the blueprint for life following the Soviet invasion of '68. The authorities had learned a lesson from the Prague Spring about 'how far things can go when the door to a plurality of opinions is opened' — the totalitarian system itself is jeopardised. His description of what happened next is of interest to the world in the era of Covid: 'In a process with its own, mindless dynamic, all the mechanisms of direct and indirect manipulation of life began to expand and assume unprecedented forms.' These words can be applied to the train of events in the world generally from the spring of 2020 to the rude and presumptive intrusion of supposedly democratic administrations into the most intimate areas of the lives of their citizens — into their homes, their relationships, their parenting, their most fundamental movements in the most private realms.

What results from such intrusions, Havel elaborates, is the expansion of the idea of just one central pillar of all truth and power, itself propelled by a singular rationale of history. The normative democratic exchange, whereby matters of concern to the society are discussed in public between voices from different perspectives, is no longer present. 'Mystery is dead, the story has disappeared from culture. Where everything is known ahead of time, the story has nothing to grow out of.'

This, under Communism, was followed by a 'cessation of history', which was replaced by 'pseudo-history', a succession of recurring anniversaries: celebrations, congresses, parades. Time blurs, stands still, goes in circles; one week, month, year morphing into the next, with few or no distinguishing features. Time becomes nationalised. Where once the country was led by fanatics, now it is led by bureaucrats who no longer believe in anything. Ideology reigns, but a dead version of a once-living belief system. History, left to its own devices, has the power to disprove ideological certitudes, and so, even under totalitarianism, history has to be marked but without the attribution of meanings. It is, therefore, flattened into something tiresome, trampled into its own dust, hammered into boredom.

The nihilisation of the past nihilises the future also. Just as the past is flattened, so also the future is rolled into a plain of tedium, its promise and openness no longer reachable. 'Society,' writes Havel, 'was petrified into a fiction of everlasting harmony, and man into a stone monument representing the permanent proprietor of happiness — these were the silent consummations of the intellectual assassination of history.' The boredom of the history books had leapt out into what remains of the life of the present. It is fairly clear that something a little like this trundled down the streets of Western nations in the flattened vistas of 2020.

In *Letters to Olga*, the volume of his letters written to his first wife from prison, Havel wrote that he had always rejected (for himself) the idea of a 'complete, unified, integrated and self-contained' belief system, because 'I simply don't have the internal capacity for it.' What he had, he told his wife, was *faith*: 'a state of persistent and productive openness, of persistent questioning, a need to "experience the world" again and again.' He elaborated that what he called 'the Order of Being' is multiform and elusive, and 'simply cannot be grasped and described by a consistent system of knowledge.' This is the key to understanding how the evil of totalitarianism may be overcome. That key is the deep personal response of the human being, not some idea or set of ideas that may be applied to the problem as though to an electrical or mechanical conundrum.

'The more slavishly and dogmatically a person falls for a ready-made ideological system or "worldview", the more certainly he will bury all chances of thinking, of freedom, of being clear about what he knows, the more certainly he will deaden the adventure of the mind and the more certainly — in practice — he will begin to serve the "order of death".'

In his most famous essay, *The Power of the Powerless*, he took this quest beyond the point of mere diagnosis, offering a method by which the human person — alone if necessary — might confront such a system and not merely reject its oppression but actively work, in a non-political, non-ideological way, to brings its power to an end.

At the centre of that essay is the image of the greengrocer in Prague who is required by the governing ideology to place a sign in his shop window bearing the slogan: 'Workers of the World Unite'. Havel takes us beneath the literal level of this episode, beneath the elements we might not notice because we are unobservant or unthinking or because what he describes seems to us to be obvious and, therefore, not worth dwelling on. He insists on naming things, on describing their meanings. But in the journey he guides us through, Havel enables us to enter into the mindset of the greengrocer, who places the sign, essentially, as a gesture of obedience. The sign might just as easily read: 'I am afraid and therefore unquestioningly compliant', but this would cause the greengrocer to lose face, and so the sign as it is serves both the needs of the greengrocer and the needs of the regime. The sign, therefore, becomes another kind of sign: of the operation in a culture of ideology, which Havel defines as 'a specious way of relating to the world' because it 'offers human beings the illusion of an identity, of dignity and of morality, while making it easier for them to part with them.'

Thus, he carefully elaborates, the social phenomenon of self-preservation exhibited by the greengrocer is subordinated to 'a blind automatism which drives the system.' By displaying the sign, the greengrocer has shown his willingness to enter into the prescribed ritual of pretence and has, therefore, colluded in his own enslavement. The sign contains a message relating to the ideology, which nobody really believes in, but its unquestioning promulgation becomes both an outward show of loyalty and a way of avoiding loss of face. An equivalent of the sign might be the face mask, known to have no beneficial effect, but nevertheless worn, and insisted upon, as a sign of compliance with official diktats, regardless of logic or benefit.

In a series of graphic images, Havel makes visible the process by which ideology operates upon the human person. Ideology enables the human being to be brought into harmony with the system, but this enslavement becomes invisible by virtue of being hidden behind high motives and ideals. It conceals the enslavement by creating a series of 'excuses' which allow both parties — system and enslaved — to deny, if not conceal, the true nature of their relationship. Ideology offers a pseudo-legitimacy, giving the relationship an external coating of morality. 'It pretends that the requirements of the system derive from the requirements of life. It is a world of appearances trying to pass for reality.'

Ideology is the quasi-metaphysical 'glue' that holds the totalitarian power system together, making complicit all those who are really its victims. The purpose is to dehumanise, to persuade people to surrender their human identities in favour of the corporate identity of the ideology.

Ideology provides the 'gloves' by which the system achieves its objective in a way that outwardly appears to eschew coercion. In such a system, everything is falsified, twisted, inverted and corrupted. Words, if they mean anything, mean the opposite of their dictionary definitions. In the human victims of the post-totalitarian system, anonymity and dehumanisation are key symptoms of the dictatorship of ritual and ideology.

In a further development of this process, ideology supplants reality precisely because, having corrupted what is real, the ritual becomes the only reality. In the end, ideology itself becomes the dictator — what Havel calls 'the dictatorship of the ritual'. And because the ideology is not human, it has a superhuman capacity to transcend the short lives of those who form the changing guard of power, providing the totalitarian caravan with a continuity which is difficult for mere humans to break. The ruling figures at any particular moment are mere puppets, 'blind executors of the system's internal laws.' Thus, those who aspire to power become, in the end, either casualties of their own insistence on continuing to be human — and therefore become cast out — or coterminous with the automatism of the system, in which case they are themselves dehumanised. Totalitarianism of this kind, therefore, becomes not something imposed on one group by another, but on everyone by everyone. Those who conform to the dictates of the regime, write Havel, become 'both victims of the system and its instruments.'

The syndromes just described, it will become obvious, have many parallels in Western culture, and not just recent ones. Havel speaks of the 'panorama' of slogans which litter the landscape of the Soviet-style dictatorship of ritual. In the West, as implausible as it may at first appear, the same function has long been supplied by advertising, a set of slogans-in-windows which have a more subtle existence than that of the placard in the greengrocer's window. But Havel is relentless in his clarity: 'A person who has been seduced by the consumer value system, whose identity is dissolved in an amalgam of the accoutrements of mass civilization, and who has no roots in the order of being, no sense of responsibility for anything higher than his or her own personal survival, is a demoralized person.' This demoralisation is what the ideological reduction seeks out and exploits for its own survival.

He writes: 'The post-totalitarian system is only one aspect — a particularly drastic aspect — of this general inability of modern humanity to be the master of its own situation. The automatism of the post-totalitarian system is merely an extreme version of the global automatism of technological civilization. The human failure that it mirrors is only one variant of the general failure of modern humanity.' Hence, the post-totalitarian system is merely a 'caricature' of modern life in general, a warning to the West of its own latent tendencies.

'There is no real evidence that Western democracy, that is, democracy of the traditional parliamentary type, can offer solutions that are any more profound. It may even be said that the more room there is in the Western democracies (compared to our world) for the genuine aims of life, the better the crisis is hidden from people and the more deeply do they become immersed in it.'

This, precisely, is a diagnosis of the reason why our supposed understanding of the lessons of history has all been for nothing, why our very awareness of the past has not merely failed to operate as a kind of inoculation against a recurrence of the patterns of our own pasts, but has served to delude us as to our own resilience against a recurrence. Possessed by the wrongthink of 'evil as aberration', we misinterpreted the meanings of the cautions history sought to convey. Taking our capacity to think and talk as indicative of something given and imprescriptible, we allowed ourselves to become deluded as to the source and continuity of these values. We took for granted what was 'given', failing to ask whence it came and how it was all done. The danger arose because we imagined we had, by our 'enlightenment' and 'progressiveness', placed ourselves beyond danger.

This, then, is our condition in what is left of Western democracy in the Year of Our Lord 2021, albeit described here from a different perspective by someone who has seen its exaggerated face up close to his. We, for our part, have persisted one day — maybe one week, one month — too long in misunderstanding what freedom is and in continuing to create, or enable the creation or acceptance of systems which institutionalised these misunderstandings in the manner of a slow-boiling pan under our feet.

Traditional parliamentary democracies, Havel insisted, offered no fundamental opposition to the automatism of technological civilization and the industrial-consumer society, for these niceties of liberal society, too, were being dragged helplessly along by these phenomena, which had become the enslavers of man by exploiting his weakness for comfort and ease. Thus, a new form of tyranny, which 'oppresses' man by cosseting him — Huxley rather than Orwell, or perhaps the Orwellian fist in the Huxlean glove. People are manipulated 'in ways that are infinitely more subtle and refined than the brutal methods used in the post-totalitarian societies,' but the processes of capitalism, materialism, advertising, commerce and consumer culture all combine to repress in the human being the questing for the 'something' that defines the human. In the communist system, fear of repercussions led to a quiescence that was usually enforced without external evidence of violence; in the West, the 'oppressor' is the human unwillingness to sacrifice material benefits so as to retain spiritual and moral integrity. And to seal the deal, Western man like to sneer at the very idea of spiritual or moral integrity, by way of showing off his sophistication.

In *The Power of the Powerless*, Havel makes many startling observations. 'People,' he states, 'live within lies as an alienated form of humanity, not because they have no choice, but because something about them makes it congenial to live this way. Human beings can accommodate themselves to the lie, including the lie that makes them less human. But the power of the lie, precisely because it is dependent on the collusion of the individual, can be broken by the individual choosing to refuse. To live within the truth requires just a short step, but its power is tremendous. Everyone who steps out of line with the lie 'denies it in principle and threatens it in its entirety.'

In this there is an answer to those who feel that the power of modern society, in whatever guise, is too overwhelming to be resisted by just one person. In truth, there is no other way of resisting but each person doing it for himself.

Havel reminds us that we, too, are complicit in our own enslavement. Deep in ourselves, we know that, in our reaching for freedom, coherence or security, we have left something vital behind. We become as refugees from our own misconception of what it means to be free, and, therefore, what it means to be human. We look wistfully backwards but cannot find a way of reintroducing ourselves to a total understanding of who we are.

Havel shows us that it is precisely in the single act of one person that the lie is exposed and undermined. 'Individuals can be alienated from themselves only because there is something in them to alienate. The terrain of this violation is their authentic existence.' The lie occurs, therefore, because the truth exists, is seductive and powerful; the lie is an attempt to suppress it. Hence, a sense of falseness should always alert us to the suppression of something real.

Havel shows us that to live in the truth, in the face of a powerful lie, is not as risky as it may sound. For truth finds harmony with itself and is unmistakable for anything but itself. The hidden sphere of truth is dangerous for the regime, but the ally of the slave. The truth does not require soldiers of its own but finds its strength in the repressed longing for authenticity, for human life as it ought to be lived. Hence, to live within the truth is to create a subversion that can only grow and grow. This is the 'power of the powerless'.

'This power does not participate in any direct struggle for power; rather, it makes its presence felt in the obscure arena of being itself,' is how Havel puts it. And the hidden movement it gives rise to there can suddenly erupt as a political or social phenomenon. This is why the regime will always prosecute even the smallest gesture that occurs as an attempt to live within the truth. The crust of lies needs to be broken just once, in one place, for the whole thing to split and disintegrate. In Havel's depiction, the truthful gesture does not have to be a grand political statement or initiative, but could be something far more prosaic, like attending a rock concert or a students' demonstration in defiance of the regime, both of which categories of gesture played momentous roles in the freeing of his own country. The simple act of insistence upon a truthful existence confronts the automatism of the system in a powerful way. The criterion is not the scale of the gesture, but its nature. It can take the form of an artist simply pursuing the truth in his work, or a citizen intent upon preserving her human dignity in a clear and uncompromising manner. It might be as simple as walking into a store without a face mask. It is not necessary for the ambition to be momentous, or the action earth-shattering of itself. Havel refers to such phenomena as 'pre-political events' or 'existential revolutions', which cause the virus of truth to seep through the tissue of lie, which eventually disintegrates — and no one can predict at what moment, or by what critical intervention, the moment of disintegration will occur. Havel writes: 'Most of these expressions remain elementary revolts against manipulation. You simply straighten your backbone and live in greater dignity as an individual.'

If we take Havel's analysis at its word, we begin to see that change in modern, post-democratic, and already subtly 'post-totalitarian' societies cannot come about by means of an alternative political vision, but will arise from the transformation of the moral and existential conditions of the society. We may knock down walls in order to meet the insistent demands of our deepest long-ings, but the answer we seek is not necessarily to be discovered in the concepts of freedom to be encountered on the other side, or in embracing the trappings of a rival system. Human desire is boundless and indefatigable, and freedom is not something a political or economic system can ultimately deliver, because the human appetite remains unsatisfied by physical conditions or resources. Polit-ical and economic solutions have their place, but at a certain point, something else needs to take over: an understanding that the things that suggest them-selves as the target of human desire are merely stepping stones to something else, and this always lies tantalisingly ahead, over the horizon. A freed human being is one who comes to know that what he desires cannot be bought any more than it is to be found on the other side of a guarded frontier.

   The locus of the necessary change, he tells us, converges on a parallel 'second culture', which builds itself underground, in secret, a layer of truthfulness growing underneath the tissue of lies. But this cannot, he stresses, amount to a separate reality, a retreat into a ghetto or an act of self-isolation by certain people for themselves. It would be wrong, he insists, to consider it an essentially group solution with nothing to do with the general situation. This risks becoming another lie to live within. Responsibility, he says, is something we must accept and grasp 'here, now, in this place in time and space where the Lord has set us down.'

   This phrase is typical of Havel's capacity for surprise. He was not, he often said, a particularly good Christian or Catholic, but he recognised his existence as occurring in a crucible of givenness, defined by horizons that had been placed there to orient his life. In his writings more generally — especially in his letters to his first wife, Olga, from prison — he places man in front of what he called 'the absolute horizon', establishing the total context and relationship which, by virtue of defining and describing man's natural circumstances becomes, precisely, the target of those seeking to enforce upon man some narrower form of self-understanding. Think, again, of Ireland in the past 18 months.

   Reviewing, in 1984, that volume, *Letters to Olga*, the collection of letters Havel wrote during the years he was imprisoned for refusing an ideological prescription, the German writer Heinrich Böll observed that Havel appeared to be the manifestation of a new form of religiousness, 'which out of courtesy no longer addresses God with the name which has been trampled underfoot by politicians.' Böll noted that Havel used careful constructions, such as 'the abso-lute horizon' and 'the spiritual order', rather than applying the name that is in general use, which is to say 'God' or 'Christ'.

   Indeed, Havel had wrestled with the subject in many of the letters. 'I have the feeling that something more than intellectualistic subterfuge is preventing me from admitting my belief in a personal God,' he wrote to his wife. 'Something deeper is concealed behind these subterfuges: what I am lacking is that extremely important "last drop" in the form of the mystical experience of the enigmatic address and revelation. There is no doubt that I could substitute the word "God" for my "something" or for the "absolute horizon", and yet this does not seem to be a very serious approach.' He acknowledged his closeness to Christian feelings, and was pleased whenever this was recognized by others; but still, he felt, one must choose one's words well. He baulked at the articulation of words that, though they might literally convey the reality of his belief, could also place him in a camp that would make him uncomfortable.

But although Havel avoided the intentional use of the word 'God', Böll concluded: 'I dare say that Christ is speaking in these letters, albeit a Christ who does not describe himself by that name and yet is still a Christ, and yet I must quickly erase this description again before those ever ready Christian drummer boys, representing their explosive version of Christianity, lay their hands on it.'

What Havel means, to the extent that there is any absence of clarity, is the very force or process by which we have been deposited here in this reality, the process by which we have been born, replete with rights and freedoms, to answer an invitation to live a life to be intuited as to its meanings and destination. That life, the journey it represents, is ultimately the meaning of our freedom, a freedom that belongs to each of us alone. It can be taken from us only if we agree to surrender it, or at least if we are unprepared to pay the sometimes exacting cost of keeping it. Defying such temptations, such short-changing of ourselves, such capitulation to the idea that there is something else — something that is not freedom — in which the meaning of life might be located, is ultimately what Havel was talking about: the power of the powerless, the dawning realisation that living in truth is the only coherent option, and that the truth is always easy to recognise because it is unmistakable for anything else.

CHAPTER 15
COVID TOTALITARIANISM: THE DEIFICATION OF ERROR
07-10-2021

Belgian psychologist Dr. Mattias Desmet may be the most articulate voice on the most clear and present danger facing us: the mob-baiting now being pursued by formerly democratic governments.

The most significant obstacle to our developing the necessary capacity to fight back against what is engulfing us is an imaginative block preventing us conceiving of the possibility that what seems to be happening could actually be happening. These things could not be happening here, now, for the very simple reason that they are the kind of thing that used to happen far away, in different times, to people who were not as 'intelligent' or 'educated' or 'advanced' as we are.

Dr. Mattias Desmet begs to differ with such perilous smugness. He is a professor of Clinical Psychology at Ghent University in Belgium. He lectures on Individual Psycho-analytics Psychotherapy and the psychology of the crowd. He holds a master's degree and PhD in clinical psychology, and a master's in statistics.

As the Covid subterfuge shifts from the manufacture of mass terror concerning a dubious virus — and a related indoctrination with spurious medical data — to the mass mobilisation of mesmerised populations in silencing voices threatening to expose these crimes, Dr Desmet has emerged as the clearest and most meticulous voice describing the dangers and intimating what we need to do to offset them. A selection of his remarkable video interviews can be found at the end of this chapter, which I have written by way of an introduction to his thoughts and interpretations, which I believe are among the most crucial things we might hear at this precise moment.

Dr Desmet's observations over the past 18 months have led him to conclude that the overwhelming majority of the world's population has indeed fallen under *a kind of* spell. It is not literally a spell, he stresses, but a 'mass formation', a term first used by Gustave Le Bon, the French philosopher who, 126 years ago in *The Psychology of Crowds*, was the first thinker systematically to outline how herd psychology differs from that of the individual. Le Bon it was who observed that the consciousness bestowed by membership of a crowd can be transformative, possessing individual members with 'a sort of collective mind which makes them feel, think and act in a manner quite differently from that in which each individual would feel, think and act were that person in a state of isolation.' In such a 'psychological crowd', individual personality disappears, brain activity is replaced by reflex activity: a lowering of intelligence, provoking a complete transformation of sentiments, which collectively may manifest as better and worse than those of the crowd's constituent members. A crowd may just as easily become heroic or criminal, but is generally disposed towards destruction.

'The ascendancy of crowds,' wrote Le Bon, 'indicates the death throes of a civilisation.' The upward climb to civilisation is an intellectual process driven by individuals; the descent is a herd in stampede. 'Crowds are only useful for destruction.'

These symptoms are manifesting now, perhaps as never before, in our once free Western world, in a process substantively resembling mass hypnosis, as a collective psychological response to the unrelenting, single-focus campaign of fear to which we have all been subjected for a year and a half. Indeed, we may now have reached a stage in this process that even Le Bon did not anticipate, for now the mesmerisers have available to them tech and techniques he could scarcely have envisaged. Using electronic means, it is infinitely easier to convert the individual to the collective mindset than if he were a member of an actual physical crowd. The advent of social media has made the present situation not merely possible, but possibly inevitable.

In his own time, approaching the end of the nineteenth century, Le Bon perceived a shifting in the nature of human reflection and attention. In an odd way, his words read to us now as quasi-contemporaneous: They might have been uttered just a handful of years ago.

'The present epoch is one of these critical moments in which the thought of mankind is undergoing a process of transformation. Two fundamental factors are at the base of this transformation. The first is the destruction of those religious, political, and social beliefs in which all the elements of our civilisation are rooted. The second is the creation of entirely new conditions of existence and thought as the result of modern scientific and industrial discoveries.'

What is called progress comes at a cost, sometimes a great cost, and that cost is rarely visible until considerably after the fact of its causation, which then becomes prone to the phenomena of historical disconnectedness and plausible deniability.

'Nature has recourse at times to radical measures, but never after our fashion, which explains how it is that nothing is more fatal to a people than the mania for great reforms, however excellent these reforms may appear theoretically. They would only be useful were it possible to change instantaneously the genius of nations.'

The effects of such changes, mediated via the psyches of human beings, may, in time, provoke consequences that not only were unforeseen to begin with but may perhaps undo and outweigh any beneficial aspects. Societies craving change for its own sake are especially vulnerable. A society in tumult is ripe for destruction. But the crowd always seek to justify that which it has been told is good, and demonise that which it has been warned to eschew.

'The masses have never thirsted after truth,' wrote Le Bon. 'They turn aside from evidence that is not to their taste, preferring to deify error, if error seduce them. Whoever can supply them with illusions is easily their master; whoever attempts to destroy their illusions is always their victim. An individual in a crowd is a grain of sand amid other grains of sand, which the wind stirs up at will.'

Facts are as nothing to crowds, which function via a kind of collectivised imagination, operating off images and the slogans which evoke them.

'A crowd,' Le Bon elaborates, 'thinks in images, and the image itself calls up a series of other images, having no logical connection with the first. . . . A crowd scarcely distinguishes between the subjective and the objective. It accepts as real the images invoked in its mind, though they most often have only a very distant relation with the observed facts.'

Le Bon's is one of the names most frequently dropped by Dr Mattias Desmet in the course of the interviews he has been giving in recent months, having spent some time reflecting on the situation facing the world in the light of what history and its sages has to tell it, and what he himself knows of the modern world. His interviews can be mixed in quality, but this is usually to do with the attunedness and interventions of interviewers, some of whom do not play to his remarkable strengths, which reside in exploring the granular nature of psychological processes as they play out in reality, and especially in collective reality. He is excellent on the way people's projection of their own free-floating personal anxieties, frustration and aggression on to the Covid/lockdown sagas enables the 'mass formation' process.

Mass formation, he explains, is a form of hypnosis imposed on a crowd, a factor which we have explored in previous chapters. He is in no doubt that we speak of a literal hypnosis, with all the potential effects and symptoms of the same.

He explains many aspects of what we have been witnessing, including the strange phenomenon of people's apparent indifference to their own deprivations, hurts and incurred damage arising from the lockdowns of the past 18 months: loss of freedoms, loss of work, income, education, human contact, leisure *et cetera*. During mass formation, he describes, there is 'a narrowing of the field of attention', which allows the crowd's constituent members to close out everything but that which the hypnotist tells them is important, which results in insensitivity to personal losses, and a willingness to sacrifice everything — education, jobs, homes, romance, health — and to disregard the losses and griefs of others. By offering a strategy to deal with the anxieties imposed by the crisis, the would-be totalitarians are able to create a bogus solidarity in a society that has destroyed true solidarity.

He is remarkably open about his own history of engagement with the Covid 'pandemic', acknowledging his early doubts about some of his own pronouncements. In the very early days, he briefly bought into the idea of a pandemic, but his suspicions were soon aroused by the disproportionality he observed between the measures being introduced and what he understood about the visible levels of risk from the virus. In those early weeks of the crisis, he wrote a paper titled *The Fear of the Virus is More Dangerous than the Virus Itself*.

Occasionally, in the early weeks (April/May 2020), he worried that he might have been wrong to publish this paper, but by the end of May was satisfied that his thesis was entirely correct. Looking at the data from a statistical perspective, he rapidly came to the conclusion that the danger was overestimated. He believed the psychological aspects were more threatening than any biological danger. Yet, he observes, 'the narrative continued as if the initial models were correct.'

'From the beginning I was afraid of the societal dynamics that were going on,' he says, and this fear appears to have been the prime motivation for his recent interventions.

By August 2020, he had come to see that he could describe how this process occurred. 'We were dealing with a massive phenomenon of mass formation.'

He also, interestingly, speaks of how, in December 2019, some weeks before the crisis erupted in China, he had some kind of premonition of impending menace. He went to his bank and paid back his mortgage — because he felt 'the society was moving towards a tipping point.'

'I wanted to be as free as possible,' he says. He remembers telling the bank manager: 'All the negative parameters of society have started to rise exponentially.' He believed that a major catastrophe was on the way, but is not entirely sure why he knew this.

He says there are four conditions that need to be in place to enable mass formation to occur in a society. The first is the presence of large numbers of socially isolated, atomised people. The social bonds between people need to have been weakened. This is the most important, and the other conditions follow from it. Secondly, there will be large numbers of people who experience a lack of sense-making in their lives and work — people who feel that their jobs are senseless, meaningless. Thirdly, there requires to be 'a lot of free-floating anxiety' — i.e. anxiety that is not connected to a mental representation so that the sufferer doesn't know why he is anxious and afraid. And fourthly, there needs to be a lot of 'free-floating psychological discontent' — anger and frustration at, again, apparently nothing in particular.

And you also need mass media — without which mass formation would be impossible. Desmet does not explicitly say so, but of course it is also essential that these media be biddable and readily prone to corruption.

hese conditions, he says, existed in Western societies long before the Covid crisis. There was, he says, 'an epidemic of burnout', as a consequence of something between 40 and 70 per cent of people in modern societies experiencing their jobs as senseless. He points also to the escalating use of psycho-pharmaceutical medicines to treat anxiety and depression.

As evidence of the presence of these conditions in Western society prior to the pandemic, he instances the consumption of anti-depressants in Belgium, his own country. There, a population of 11 million was using 300 million doses of anti-depressants *per annum*.

According to Desmet, the key root mechanism of mass formation, free-floating anxiety, is the most painful psychological phenomenon a human being can experience. It refers to anxieties that have no clear focus: The sufferer does not know why he feels anxious.

'Free-floating anxiety is very serious. It leads to panic. When a society is saturated with it, sufferers are desperate to connect it to a representation, and if someone presents a narrative in the mainstream media that offers an object of anxiety, and at the same time presents a strategy to deal with this anxiety, there is a good chance that all this free-floating anxiety in the society will connect to this object of anxiety indicated by this narrative presented by the mainstream media, and that there will be a huge willingness to go along with the strategy.'

The orchestrators of the mass formation are able to appropriate these variegated anxieties and direct them in their entirety at a single point of focus, in this case a virus. By then offering a strategy to deal with the virus crisis, the mass formation process also offers sufferers relief from their anxieties. The same happens with frustration and aggression, all of which were, in a sense, piled on to the Covid basket.

This is where the 'narrowing of the field of attention' enters in. The members of the hypnotised mass are enabled to close out everything, but that which the hypnotist tells them is important. They acquire not just an indifference to the losses of others but an insensitivity to losses of their own. They become willing to sacrifice everything under the attrition of the collective injunction — in this case, at least initially, the project of 'saving lives'. People do not see the consequences of the lockdown, nor feel empathy for the victims. Their relief at being relieved of their free-floating anxieties is enough to have them cleave to the newly-formed mob. It's similar, he says, to when a person is under hypnosis: It is possible to use the hypnosis as an anaesthetic to cut into the person's flesh, having thus made the patient completely insensitive to pain.

In these circumstances, the mesmerised acquire meaning and purpose they previously lacked. In a society in which solidarity has already been destroyed, a new bogus solidarity is formed. Once the solution/strategy is offered, he says, 'people start a collective and heroic battle with this object of anxiety.' This results in what he calls a 'mental intoxication', and it is this that makes mass formation indistinguishable from hypnosis.

Arising from this combination of factors, people acquire an intense interest in believing the dominant narrative. 'It doesn't matter whether the narrative is wrong. It's all about that they don't want to go back to this painful state of free-floating anxiety.'

'The more absurd a narrative is the better it functions as a ritual,' says Desmet. 'Whether the narrative is correct or incorrect doesn't make any difference.'

As part of the same process, he says, politicians who may have lost their grip on the people now have a way of becoming 'true leaders' again. There is, therefore, at this stage of the totalitarian process, a symbiosis of motivation between the leaders and the led; or, more correctly, the rulers and the ruled.

These circumstances combine to ensure that people don't want to go back to the 'old normal'. This is important: *Many among the mesmerised do not want their prior meaningless lives back.* 'We need to avoid giving people the impression that we want them to go back to the old normal,' cautions Desmet. We need instead to 'show them there are other ways to change this "old normal". We need to tell people that we don't need a crisis like this to create a new social bond.'

In such a crucible of explosive feeling and foreboding, some unsettling dynamics soon become visible. People begin to regard each other as either friends or foes. The 'friends' are to be cherished and cleaved to; the foes are to be excoriated and, where possible or necessary, banished or destroyed.

There are, in situations of mass formation, says Desmet, three distinct groups that manifest themselves. Only 30 per cent, he says, are really hypnotised and cannot be reached in any way. In addition, however, there are about 40 per cent who usually follow the crowd, and, from the outset, go along with that 30 per cent of total believers. There is another cohort of about 30 per cent who are not hypnotised, who try to speak out and resist. This group, he says, is extremely heterogeneous and disunited. If these people could unite, he says, they could bring the whole thing quickly to an end, but this seldom proves possible.

The reason some people appear to be immune to the hypnoidal power of the mass formation, he says, has to do with underlying ideological outlook. In this present situation, he says, the ultimate destination point of the totalitarianism is to effect the total acquiescence of the global population in a transhumanist project in which, in substance and effect, man will be absorbed into the world of the machine. He thinks that, essentially, the objectors are people with an aversion to this unnatural way of seeing the human person. This is an interesting theory and may help to explain why so many religious-minded people are opposed to the lockdown, vaccines, *et cetera*: Many of them, having had a deeper inculcation in fundamental anthropological understandings, instinctively or reasonably object to the unknowable and unnatural dimensions of what is proposed. Desmet may be on to something important here: that, although not yet explicit, the transhumanist agenda is already visible as the distant destination-point, with its meanings already saturating the playing area in the context of mandatory vaccines, biometric ID, social credit schemes and the accompanying surveillance regimes, restrictions, penalties, *et cetera*.

Intelligence, he says, is no guarantee of resistance to the hypnoidal attack. 'In mass formation, highly intelligent, highly educated people become exactly as intelligent as everybody else in the masses — everybody becomes equally intelligent, which usually means extremely stupid, in the masses.' At the start of the lockdown, many people said to him, 'Yes, it is terrible, but we can stop the rat race for a while.' This was mainly the well-off, who had less concerns about the economic destruction threatened by the lockdowns. The anxiety of the educated become fixated on different things, perhaps on the possibility of 'populists' taking advantage of the crisis. This is how the ludicrous 'far right' trope, stoked by cynical media, gained ground.

He speaks, too, about the dynamics of totalitarianism and what makes the present episode different to, for example, the totalitarianisms of the twentieth century. In this, and much else, he draws on the writings of the brilliant German philosopher Hannah Arendt, whose book *The Origins of Totalitarianism* remains the definitive deconstruction of the totalitarian process, which she characterises as an entirely new phenomenon of the twentieth century.

He reiterates Arendt's core point about the radical differences between totalitarianism and 'traditional' forms of dictatorship. Classical dictatorships are primitive and simple — a single dictator using uncomplicated fear. But in a totalitarian state, the psychological and societal basis of the tyranny is mass formation.

In a totalitarian state, a large part of the population believes in the narrative and is psychologically convinced that the proffered object of anxiety is the cause of all its concerns.

These beliefs, he says, are related to the penetrative effects of mass media but also the image of man as a machine — in part a consequence of industrialism, in part due to an 'obsession with science', another core theme of Arendt's, who emphasises also the key role of ideology as a nutrient of totalitarianism.

Desmet is not convinced of the 'psychopathy' thesis of totalitarianism, with particular reference to the Covid despotisms. The people who organise and impose this tyranny, he says, 'often do not believe in the things they say, but they do really believe in the ideology they promote, and they really believe that the best way to organise society is to treat people like cows on a large farm. They really do believe in this mechanistic, materialist, biological, reductionist ideology.'

Again, Desmet is citing Arendt, who did much to uncover and describe the ugly underbelly of Nazi machinations, in particular the propaganda and psychological elements. Totalitarianism, she believed, has specific characteristics that are constructed to appear random, arbitrary and senseless, when really they amount to a complex interworking of manipulations designed to break and isolate the human person, to lead him methodically out of his 'ordinary' life of hoping, working, thinking, loving, into a world where his every moment is dominated by the imposed irrationality that leads to a new, dehumanised existence for others and himself, and to a new, irrational form of 'sense-making'.

Arendt wrote: 'While the totalitarian regimes are thus resolutely and cynically emptying the world of the only thing that makes sense to the utilitarian expectations of common sense, they impose upon it at the same time a kind of supersense which the ideologies actually always meant when they pretended to have found the key to history or the solution to the riddles of the universe. Over and above, the senselessness of totalitarian society is enthroned by the ridiculous supersense of its ideological superstition. Ideologies are harmless, uncritical, and arbitrary opinions only as long as they are not believed in seriously. Once their claim to total validity is taken literally, they become the nuclei of logical systems in which, as in the systems of paranoiacs, everything follows comprehensibly and even compulsorily once the first premise is accepted. The insanity of such systems lies not only in their first premise but in the very logicality with which they are constructed. The curious logicality of all isms, their simple-minded trust in the salvation value of stubborn devotion without regard for specific, varying factors, already harbors the first germs of totalitarian contempt for reality and factuality.'

Ideologies are always dangerous reductions of reality, in many instances comprising pseudo-science masquerading as the real thing, rendering them exceptionally well-adapted to totalitarian rule. For the sake of justifying and validating the 'supersense' — the final triumph of the ideology — Arendt declared it is necessary for totalitarianism to completely destroy human dignity. This is because the recognition of their dignity implies an acceptance of our fellow men as co-builders of a world held in common on the basis of individual and consensual choice. This, to the totalitarian, is out of the question. An ideology which lays claim to interpreting all events of the past, and setting in train all events of the future, can have no place for the plans and choices of mere citizens. The danger lies in the very creativity of the human, which may seek to introduce something that is not foreseen in the ideology, and therefore likely to undermine it. Thus, totalitarianism requires the complete transformation of the individual and the collective so as to align the minds of men with the perspectives and objectives set down in the ideology. Once the supersense is installed, men will think only what the ideology allows.

Before Hitler and Stalin, wrote Arendt, such things were not imagined. Ideology is, literally, 'the logic of an idea', a schema of pseudo-thinking that creates a web of delusion. 'Its subject matter is history, to which the "idea" is applied; the result of this application is not a body of statements about something that is, but the unfolding of a process which is in constant change. The ideology treats the course of events as though it followed the same "law" as the logical exposition of its "idea". Ideologies pretend to know the mysteries of the whole historical process — the secrets of the past, the intricacies of the present, the uncertainties of the future — because of the logic inherent in their respective ideas.

'Ideologies are never interested in the miracle of being. They are historical, concerned with becoming and perishing, with the rise and fall of cultures, even if they try to explain history by some "law of nature".'

As Václav Havel has elaborated, ideology is an instrument for presenting time and history as immutable successions of events and 'progressions', indifferent to human longing or wishes.

The question at the heart of our exploration of the nature and meaning of totalitarianism, wrote Arendt, is: 'What kind of basic experience in the living-together of men permeates a form of government whose essence is terror and whose principle of action is the logicality of ideological thinking?'

This is the most chilling aspect: that totalitarianism finds its roots in some dislocated aspect of the human that is still human, that arises from actual human wants and needs — for peace, for serenity, for love.

'That such a combination was never used before in the varied forms of political domination is obvious,' she added. 'Still, the basic experience on which it rests must be human and known to men, insofar as even this most original of all political bodies has been devised by, and is somehow answering the needs of, men.'

Totalitarianism in its full-blown form, then, is something that comes *after*, but 'after' what? It comes after a lengthy 'preparation', not necessarily planned with malign intent, in which human beings become isolated, atomised, alienated and lonely — conditions for which the totalitarian has ready solutions in the promulgation of bogus community and imagined bonds of mutual hatreds. The negative undertones of these processes suggest some form of prior error, and this may well have been present, perhaps in the pursuit of greed or exploitation, but this is not any longer admissible. Totalitarianism is like a secondary condition that descends on a society that has, first of all, been subjected to certain processes of modernity: technologisation, industrialisation, individualisation, atomisation. It is, in a sense, like the lung cancer that ensues from a lifetime of smoking or the type 2 diabetes that results from an excessively sweet tooth. But it is not 'secondary' in the sense suggesting 'lesser' or 'minor' or 'subordinate': When it arrives, totalitarianism announces itself as the actual purpose and destination-point of the entire historical process, the discovery of the actual meaning of history. It follows, but is not collateral to, the events which preceded it. Indeed, its arrival announces a coherence to those previous events that had not hitherto been perceived: It 'makes sense' of the drifts and apparent randomness of the past, and in doing so, turns common sense on its head and compels man to admit his prior errors of understanding and accept that the true direction of history has now been revealed.

The totalitarian leader, unlike the classical kind, who becomes more benign as opposition falls away, becomes more vicious when unopposed, stoking up the masses to carry out atrocities long after he has suppressed all dissent. This is why every voice of dissent is so vital: to delay the moment when the totalitarian has free rein.

There is a distinction, Desmet emphasises, between 'totalitarian thinking' and 'totalitarian regime'. Totalitarian thinking, he says, is characterised by absurd argumentation and illogic, which seems extremely persuasive and 'drives a society across all ethical boundaries.' Eventually, by traversing the wastes of senselessness, the society evolves into a totalitarian regime that uses totalitarian thinking to rule. Right now, he believes, we are at an advanced stage in totalitarian thinking. 'They consider the human being to be a biological organism who should be manipulated and controlled through biological means. That's the ideology by which institutions like the WHO and individuals like Bill Gates start. It's tempting to say that these people are sociopaths or even psychopaths, but I don't think it is right. They are people who are ideologically blind. That is their main characteristic.' Gustave Le Bon, he points out, said that 'the hypnosis is even deeper in the leaders of the masses than in the masses themselves. They are more convinced of the ideology than the population. They have the feeling that in the end, when they have reshaped society according to their ideal image, they will end up in a technological transhumanistic paradise, almost without human suffering, and that is why they feel it is justified to inflict a lot of damage and a lot of suffering, because, in the end, the result of this revolution will be so marvellous that it justifies everything they do now.'

He also believes that we ought not to presume that every apparent phenomenon and effect of the tyrannical circumstances we endure is necessarily the outcome of a strategy or plan of the perpetrators. Totalitarianism metasta- sises. 'I think that once a society is grasped by one narrative, and once this mass formation emerges, I think that, more or less in a spontaneous way, it organises the entire dynamic of a society — very often without people being grasped by it, being aware that they actually reinforce and contribute to the dynamics. Things that seem to be intentional are often spontaneous outcomes of the processes.'

Now we may be at or approaching the most difficult phase of the totalitarian thinking process: when the mob, like an attack dog, awaits the instruction to go for its designated enemy. Dr. Desmet again cites Gustave le Bon: 'The masses only exist if they have an enemy.' In the beginning, the 'enemy' was the virus; now it is those who are not in thrall to or in fear of the virus, who question its severity and challenge the legitimacy of the official global response — those who refuse to go along with the official narrative. This causes the majority to bond together in a new way against the new object of anxiety, having formed a new 'social bond' against the dissenting group, providing itself with a new meaning in life. This, says Desmet, gives rise to a 'mental intoxication', providing a 'new deeply fundamental type of satisfaction for a human being.'

Under mass formation, people become 'radically intolerant of dissonant voices' while at the same time being 'radically tolerant' of their lying leaders.

Again, he cites Hannah Arendt on the 'atomised subjects' who have no connection with the larger whole — now, in fighting the new object of anxiety, their negative state becomes positive. Social isolation is replaced by an experi- ence of a strong social bond, 'which is the reason why people are continuing to believe in the mainstream narrative — even when it is blatantly wrong and utterly absurd. . . . They do not believe in the narrative because it is correct, but because it leads to this new solidarity, to this new kind of social bond, to this mental intoxication of feeling.'

'Usually this only stops after a lot of destruction,' he warns. Crowds are always 'intrinsically self-destructive,' as Le Bon repeatedly stated. 'The only positive way this comes to an end is if people can discover the real reasons for their dissatisfaction and [find] a new meaning. But once a mass emerges, it's hard to get people to search for the real reasons for their anxiety.'

Society, he says, was being prepared for such a narrative for a long time. For centuries, the dominant view of man has been a mechanistic-materialist view: Man is a machine, a little part of the larger machine of the universe — 'that is the ideology that has prepared the world for mass formation, and for connecting all our anxiety to a mechanistic-materialist organism such as a virus.'

The chief characteristics of modern masses, according to Hannah Arendt, is that they 'do not believe in anything visible, in the reality of their own experi- ence; they don't trust their eyes and ears but only their imaginations, which may be caught by anything that is at once universal and consistent in itself. What convinces the masses are not facts, and not even invented facts, but only the consistency of the system of which they are presumably part. Repetition, somewhat overrated in importance because of the common belief in the masses' inferior capacity to grasp and remember, is important only because it convinces them of consistency in time.'

Imagination, again, is the key — the process of engaging with reality through a gauze of fantasy. It is important that we grasp this: In the average victim of Covid propaganda, we are not dealing with the same person in the way we have known him or her hitherto. We encounter someone who has been fed with, and swallowed, a grotesquely distorted view of reality. She does not see what we see, or know what we know. And, on detecting this dissonance, she becomes, as she has been programmed to become, highly alert and intensely suspicious. Our disbelief in the things she cleaves to is connected in her mind with a danger to herself. We ought not to underestimate the dangers of this, or its potential for leading rapidly to confrontation and even violence. We are not dealing with people in control of themselves; we are not dealing even with people who remain themselves. The word 'hypnosis' must here be treated with the utmost respect and literalism.

We deal with extraordinarily powerful and largely unbridled forces. We ought not to approach our fellows in this condition with the mindset that we might change their minds. That is folly indeed. Instead, we must wait, watch, choose our moments, and strike delicately and precisely.

The most important thing, Desmet says, is to continue speaking out, to keep saying that we do not agree with the mainstream narrative, to interrupt the constant flow of lies (propaganda) with the truth. This unsettles the hypnosis, causing the mesmerised to turn in their sleep.

Desmet says we have to continue to share rational counterarguments in the hope of breaking the link of free-floating anxiety to the virus, which he describes as a kind of welded joint created at the highest level of anxiety. Warning people of the dangers of a totalitarian state — itself a possible new object of anxiety — might cause this joint to be broken and a new one formed.

The presence of alternative voices also serves to curb the viciousness of the rulers and constrains the mob in its excesses. 'Alternative voices, as Le Bon said, do not succeed in waking up the masses, but if the same group continues to talk and utter a different story, and ensure there is a different voice in the public space, then the masses might not become very cruel.

'We have to aim to keep a path for the small group that doesn't want to conform to the mainstream narrative. We have to continue to talk and to establish a parallel society that produces its own foods, its own clinics and hospitals and that can provide the means of surviving outside mainstream society.

'Mass formation gets deeper as the narrative is repeated and as other narratives disappear. The only way to prevent it becoming deeper and more intense is to make sure there is another narrative that leads to a certain cognitive dissonance that at least means that people will be a little confused while following the mainstream narrative.'

And, yes, he agrees, the short-to-medium-term outlook is bleak. When a society reaches the point of transgressing all ethical limits, there are no longer any guarantees. We must not be in any doubt as to the suggestibility of our neighbours. If we doubt that it could go much further, he warns, we should consider how far it has gone already. He ironically asks of people who are prepared to vaccinate children, to force pregnant women to wear face masks, to allow old people to die alone, 'Why don't we move to the next step and build concentration camps for people who test positive for Covid?' Their answer? — 'Why not?'

When he asks people how far they think the tyranny should go, they reply: 'Until the end of the [Covid] danger'.

'Do not believe that we could not end up with the same kind of measures that Hitler considered necessary to create his pure race. To be honest, I think it will be difficult to avoid ending up in some kind of new totalitarianism. But it will be a *new* totalitarianism. It will be, on the one hand, the same as the totalitarianism of the first half of the twentieth century, but it will also be radically different because it will be a worldwide totalitarian system. It won't have external enemies; it will only have internal enemies, and it will treat these internal enemies in a different way — as the external enemies were treated. This is something that is essential for the logic of totalitarian systems — totalitarian systems *need* an enemy; without an enemy, they collapse. So I think there is a good chance that the new totalitarian systems will tolerate the existence of the enemies, but it will marginalise them, push them outside of mainstream society.'

Which, up to a point, will suit the dissenters, who have never wanted much more than simply that they be let alone.

His dark prognostications notwithstanding, he is a little optimistic. We should remember, he says, that 'totalitarianism and mass formation always ends up destroying itself.' All we have to do is to make sure that our story survives and that we survive outside the system 'for a few years'.

How might it happen?

'If the masses wake up, they start to realise what has happened.'

Then what?

'Then they kill their leaders.'

'You will see that the small group will survive and, in one way or another, after the collapse, it will play an important role in the rebuilding of a society according to more human and more ethical principles.'

We may have some distance to travel, he says, but he believes this model of totalitarianism will destroy itself much more quickly than those of the twentieth century, because none of those systems intruded on the personal lives of the people to the extent that this one has 'in such a systematic and straightforward way'. He cites vaccines as a cardinal example of this form of intrusion and expresses the belief that the vaccination campaign may end up as 'the most spectacular disaster we've ever seen.'

There is, although it may not be obvious, something of an anomaly here in the phenomenon of a clinical psychologist offering a critique of materialist-mechanistic society, in the sense that the discipline of psychology is itself part of the mechanisation of man, part of the apparatus that seeks to break human behaviour and responses into a set of instrumental principles and patterns which, although they can often appear to have individual application, have not, in general, produced overall beneficial results. Indeed, as I've pointed out elsewhere, the discipline of psychology has all but destroyed the art of fiction. The reduction of understanding of the human to manmade scientific polarities has destroyed the mysteriousness that was once the *forte* of the novel and short story. In the realm of modern literature, the once revered novelist — the source of so much of our understandings of the human — has been demoted by psychology to the role of bumbling amateur who, to be taken 'seriously', has to immerse him/herself in Freud and adhere religiously to what he appeared to be saying.

Sigmund Freud was undoubtedly a genius — an artist, in fact, in his own right, who took us on epic journeys within our own minds. His ruminations on, for example, conscience and (though reductionist) happiness, have given us much food for self-scrutiny. But Freudianism, the pseudo-science that grew out of this remarkable corpus, has done untold damage, being absorbed into the societal machines of Western societies to impose itself on actually breathing humans as a form of Holy Writ. In the wrong hands, it can be lethal to human happiness, functioning and freedom. Psychoanalysis, too, has rendered instrumental everything about the human person, reducing the possibilities concerning human action to comprehensible, even simplistic pathologies and crypto-mechanical processes. This enabled the elevation of psychiatrists, psychoanalysts and psychologists to the status of engineers of human souls, capable of diagnosing patterns of behaviour in a stranger in much the way an old-style mechanic would detect the source of a rattle in the gearbox of a 1984 Volkswagen Mk2 GTI. Perhaps more than anything — yes, even more than the notion of chemical imbalances in the human brain — these developments caused the human person to think of himself as a sort of, well, Volkswagen.

So there is, as I say, this anomaly (even a *dangerous* anomaly) in people like Mattias Desmet (and, to give another example, Jordan Peterson) voyaging forth to diagnose the condition of the human person in these opening decades of the third millennium. A human person seeking self-understanding could, as quickly as becoming enlightened, feel hit over the head with Dr. Peterson's 25,000 hours of clinical practice. If anything, the problem with the modern world is a surfeit of experts telling us not just what is good for us, but what we are actually doing and thinking wrongly, and why — and what we supposedly need to do.

But there is also an upside. One could also note that all these practitioners have, in the era of YouTube, started to stray outside their disciplines, to commentate on macro, collective trends in human psychology, and this may actually be where they redeem themselves and their role. There is a *lacuna* in the conversation of modern society in relation to the actions and 'thought processes' of mobs. Most of the more interesting reflections on this aspect of human coexistence occurred in the last century or towards the end of the one before. For the past half-century, there have emerged no substantial practitioners in the precise area of crowd behaviour, perhaps because there are no 'patients' and few enough potential clients with a monied interest in exploring these matters. And it is hard to avoid thinking that there is nowadays something of an *omertà* concerning the differences and interactions between individual responses and those of the crowd. YouTube — probably unwittingly — has provided a generation of psychologists with a platform to begin filling in this *lacuna*.

In general, the new trend we perceive involves clinical psychologists co-opting the work of thinkers like Le Bon and Arendt and merging it with their own clinical experience in the individual context. This is not without value, but it is also beset by the contradiction already mentioned: that the interpretations of *engineers* of human souls must be taken with a soupcon of axle grease when it comes to arriving at any definitive understandings of flesh-and-blood beings. This discussion remains preliminary and tentative. There is a huge gap between the condition of (approximately) the first half of the twentieth century — dominated by Gustave Le Bon, Hannah Arendt, Jacques Ellul and Joost Meerloo — and the present, a span of time in which nothing radically innovative was added to our understanding of what we shall but loosely call collective psychology and its seemingly osmotic inclination towards totalitarian patterns — and this during a time of the most rapid growth in the promulgation of technologies lending themselves to the manipulation of collective psychology as never before. The great masters — Le Bon, Arendt, Ellul, Meerloo — are all gone and have had no significant successors to update or revise their thoughts in the light of an avalanche of tech diversion, tech addiction, tech toxicity, cyber-censorship, mass baiting and herding, and sundry other pathologies of this 'most modern' moment. It is to the end of updating these understandings, rather than the application of more elaborate or dubious schemas to the condition of the individual, that clinical psychology might today make itself most useful.

Desmet, Peterson and others — the British psychologist Richard Grannon, for example — are with us, have read their Le Bon and Arendt, and are capable of hypothesising us into some form of (albeit restricted) collective reflection on our plight. Desmet has so far emerged as the most interesting voice on the Covid totalitarian play, discoursing brilliantly on mass psychology and how it might be manipulated. Peterson has adhered to the continuing Combine-enforced *omertà*.

And none of these figures shows signs of having yet read their Jacques Ellul — another serious lacuna. For this and other reasons, I propose to devote the next chapter to the mid-twentieth century reflections of that remarkable Frenchman on the emergence and consequences of the *'technique* society' – (something more, and more ominous, than mere technology).

CHAPTER 16
ANTICIPATING THE TECHNOTARIAN (POST-COVID) NEW WORLD 'ORDER'

19-10-2021

French philosopher Jacques Ellul, writing 70 years ago, foresaw a world where human rights would be abolished and the population absorbed into a technical post-human utopia.

Where Jacques Ellul helps us with where we find ourselves now relates to two interlocking areas — propaganda and what we call 'technology', or he calls 'the technical fact' — demonstrating how these phenomena, unbeknownst to us, have for some considerable time been preparing the way for the most total form of totalitarianism the world has ever seen. He helps in pointing out things we do not see — for they are simply 'there', apparently part of reality — and explaining how, in fact, they have been elements of an entirely different reality, slowly constructing itself in our midst. He helps in showing how these apparently diverse elements come together into a single entity, which might be called the defining quality — or perhaps 'quantity' — of our modern societies. He calls it 'the civilisation of technique', or, as per the title of perhaps his most famous book, The Technological Society. This reality amounts to much more than technology, extending beyond the reach of mere machines. It is so ubiquitous and all-embracing that it appears to be no more than the organic nature of our reality. But it is not so. There were and are other possibilities — there have to be, for this model of reality has made us sitting ducks for control and subjugation by those who seek to set themselves above the human family, which, using, yes, techniques of propaganda, they first set out to convert into a mob primed to attack those who questioned their 'right' to do this.

The foremost problem may be that our cultures treat technologies as tools-with-plugs, mere addenda to the strength or scope or reach of the user. This is a dangerous fallacy, being possibly close to the opposite of the truth. But what, in this context, might be truth's 'opposite'? That, perhaps, since tools and men have always operated in symbiotic relationship, there is a point where technology ceases to be an adjunct of the human user, and the relationship enters a new dispensation, changing, inverting and reversing everything. A largely unnoticed example is the modern motor vehicle, which for a century or so continued to be something that, regardless of the centrality to its operation of the internal combustion engine, remained the servant of man. Latterly, however, in the age of the computer, a series of what at first sight appear to be 'improvements' have utterly changed that relationship. The primary issue, which has excited some comment, is the way the computer has turned the engine, for the typical user, into a sealed, opaque unit. Whereas in the past, the average mechanically savvy (perhaps we may add 'male') driver carried in his head a general sense of the functioning and inter-relationships of block, pistons, plugs, distributor, carburettor, gearbox, driveshaft, universal joint, he is now, in as far as being the ruler of his vehicle, in more or less the same situation as a retired matron driving — or being driven by — a 2021 Toyota Yaris hybrid at 35 kph in third gear. But there is worse: now, too, his progress along the highway is punctuated by a series of beeps, rings and curt instructions — he has forgotten to fasten his seatbelt, he has reached the speed limit, his tyre pressure needs seeing to — which cumulatively invert the prior master/servant relationship between the involved, competent driver and his vehicle. In somewhat disguised fashion, the vehicle has assumed control. The driver has become, in existential terms, little more than a passenger with some limited licence to direct the car where he wishes it to go. And, in a few more years, there will be no drivers, merely human bodies transported hither and thither by self-driving cars.

All this has been happening in the guise of comfort, safety and, above all, convenience. But in their murky depths, these processes have been subtly coaching the human passenger to regard himself in a new way: not as a human person seeking to subdue the earth and reign over it, but as an increasingly immobilised hunk of meat being ferried about the place to diminishing purpose.

Man becomes a tool — though not an especially useful one — in the hands of whom? In the hands of the 'few', the elite who, having convinced man that God was holding him back, have now stepped in to sit on the 'vacant' divine throne. Physically indistinguishable from the rest of mankind, the 'few' plan to maintain their dominion by the usurpation of earthbound power, having accumulated most of the earth's resources so as to leave the majority of men disempowered and to bribe enough of them to defend themselves from rebellion.

But man, as he stands, even at his best, is of limited use to the 'few'. When it comes to doing what is to be done, technology is more malleable, cheaper, more efficient, adaptable. And technology shows no inclination to rebel. Leaving aside, then, the messy business of the useless eaters, there is an urgent need to absorb the bulk of the human population into the mechanistic realm, to make them, in effect — and in no sense metaphorically — parts of the machine. This, in shorthand version, is the meaning of everything we have been experiencing for the past 20 months. It is also the theme of a book by Jacques Ellul, writing nearly 70 years ago — among the first, and certainly the most articulate, to spell out the hidden realities that long ago set us in train for this destination.

Ellul was a French philosopher, sociologist and Christian theologian, born in 1912, who wrote more than 60 books (roughly half of which have been translated into English) about religious questions, ethics, theology and the law, propaganda, freedom, the dangers of Marxism, and the potential for technological tyranny to overwhelm the freedom of humanity. His keynote work in this latter context is *The Technological Society*, published in French in 1954, and in English a decade later.*

Although his title contains the word 'technological', Ellul was not talking merely about machines and the industrial society that emerged from them. The book's title in French is *La technique ou l'enjeu du siècle*, which translates, more or less, as 'The technique, or the challenge of the century'. The English translation repeatedly employs the word 'technique' to convey something broader than technology or machines: the idea of a society founded on mechanistic thinking, technical processes, bureaucratic process, in which the human quotient has been educated as technicians and long since to 'think' and function mechanistically.

It is a mistake, Ellul writes, to confuse the 'technical problem' he alludes to with the machine itself. The machine is at the centre of the problem and yet a small part of it. Technique, he insists, has become almost completely independent of the machine, which has lagged far behind its offspring. 'It is the machine which is now entirely dependent upon technique, and the machine represents only a small part of technique,' he writes. It might seem that the closest word-concept available in English to what Ellul had in mind is offered by 'technocratic'/' technocracy', but these terms, leaning more towards the operatives, personnel of technique, do not capture what he intends. Perhaps the word he was rummaging for had not yet — *has* not yet — been invented? Perhaps something like 'technolotarian' or 'technotarian' might closer resemble his thoughts.

He uses 'technique' frequently as a poecilonym for 'science' and speaks of scientific work as synonymous with technique. He sees the two concepts as closely associated, hinting that he may be side-swiping also what nowadays is called 'scientism' — the tendency to elevate science to an all-encompassing

* Jacques Ellul's book can be found online for free.

system for understanding reality. 'The term technique, as I use it,' Ellul writes, 'does not mean machines, technology, or this or that procedure for attaining an end. In our technological society, technique is the totality of methods rationally arrived at and having absolute efficiency (for a given stage of development) in every field of human activity. Its characteristics are new; the technique of the present has no common measure with that of the past.'

The object of the 'technological society' is to utilise technique to maximum efficiency at the lowest possible cost, seeking the One Best Way in everything. 'Technique' is the parent of the technological society, the begetter of machines and technologies and the kinds of thinking that grow like fungi therefrom. It leaves no space for non-economistic concerns, like culture-for-its-own-sake, personal loyalty, patriotism, or romantic concepts of the past. In the 'technical society', production and consumption are the two ends of life's meaning. 'The only thing that matters technically,' Ellul writes, 'is yield, production. This is the law of technique; this yield can only be obtained by the total mobilization of human beings, body and soul, and this implies the exploitation of all human psychic forces.'

The pursuit of the One Best Way is the pursuit of optimal efficiency, cost-effectiveness and repeatability. To this end, everything, including man, must be measured and calculated mathematically so as to adhere to the demands of rationality. This he calls 'technical automatism', the chief characteristic of which is that it offers no element of personal choice to either the 'creator' or the consumer. 'Inside the technical circle, the choice among methods, mechanisms, organisations, and formulae is carried out automatically.' The One Best Way asserts itself, allowing no alternatives, and man, though stripped of his freedom, finds himself satisfied.

It is useless to rail against capitalism, Ellul says, for capitalism did not create our world: 'the machine did.' In the technical age, technology is the 'new God'. Technique saturates the modern state with its logic and demands: the calls for regulation, bureaucratisation, quantification, rationalisation, mechanisation, standardisation, materialism, scientism, procedures — all of which, separately and together, define and decide everything. In the technical society, there is no space for thoughts of nationhood or sovereignty. Results — enterprise, growth, performance, profit, efficiency, services — these are what matter.

In a society dominated by the logic of technique, all other considerations and logics become secondary, and yet the language of prior concepts of collective meaning and value continue to circulate as though they remain central. This is because the technical society cultivates a kind of cultural time-warp to conceal its true nature.

The technical society is not self-contained but part of a globalising power structure, which converges on the principles of technique. Technique amounts of itself to a form of dictatorship — ruling by logic and the coercion imposed by necessity. The technical society has long demanded an implicit submission. To succeed within it requires total acquiescence. Art and literature are 'escape valves' to release the pent-up energy that develops under the constant attrition of the technical. (Drugs, too, function as a cushion to absorb surfeit discontent.) These cultural forms are essential modes of release and relief, implying — and it was Ellul's view — that the technical society is Huxlean rather than Orwellian: The citizen can have everything except his freedom, but mostly, he does not miss this, having no clue what the word means.

The state is now utterly in the grip of the phenomenon of technique. The expansion of the state's power and influence into health, education and social welfare has made technique more central to its operation, and also pushed many private operators out of these sectors. This, together with the growing expense associated with technique, has provided the state with a near-monopoly of such instruments of technical power. Indeed, the state and the technical society have become, Ellul maintains, essentially synonymous. 'From the political, social, and human points of view, this conjunction of state and technique is by far the most important phenomenon of history,' he declares. 'It is astonishing to note that no one, to the best of my knowledge, has emphasized this fact. It is likewise astonishing that we still apply ourselves to the study of political theories or parties which no longer possess anything but episodic importance, yet we bypass the technical fact which explains the totality of modern political events.'

This ignorance, he suggests, springs from an obdurate traditionalism, 'which causes us always to live in the past and "explain" the present without understanding it.' Alternatively, he suggests, humankind may have unconsciously repressed knowledge of the danger represented by technique. This convergence of technical and state power, he argues, has enabled the state to reach into the private lives of individuals and families under the guise of assisting them to manage their own affairs. This has had numerous collateral effects, including the reorienting of ideology to become, in effect, a programme for lobbying state power in the interests of 'justice' and 'equality' — rendering political parties essentially indistinguishable, since they are all answerable to the same modes of technique.

Technique lends itself to an aristocratic society, implying an aristocratic government. Democracy is for show, present in theory, but nullified by the operation of propaganda and bogus political plurality. The aristocratic elite could not countenance the average citizen having a say in his own affairs. The most skilful — most technical — propaganda attracts the most votes, and everything is mathematicised to the extent that nothing is left to chance. These processes, he stresses, are politically invisible and only detectable at the psychological level.

His analysis, he insists, is not necessarily pessimistic. He is not a Luddite. He simply wishes to warn of general trends affecting the freedom of the social, political, and economic dimensions. 'In the modern world, the most dangerous form of determinism is the technological phenomenon. It is not a question of getting rid of it, but by an act of freedom, of transcending it.'

It may sometimes be possible for the individual to retain a degree of personal freedom around these collectivising mechanisms. Man, he concedes, has always had his existence determined by external factors — in the primitive past, by taboos, prohibitions, rites; in classical antiquity, by other social diktats. 'Heretofore, mankind did not bind up its fate with technical progress. Man regarded technical progress more as a relative instrument than as a god. He did not hope for very much from it.'

We have moved from one set of determinants to another, and then another. But the determinants he observes in the technical society, appear to him to be stronger and more oppressive than anything that existed before. 'The pressure of these mechanisms is today very great; they operate in increasingly wide areas and penetrate more and more deeply into human existence.'

The process of technical incursion on the human is fragmentary, multifaceted and ultimately dissociative, allowing plausible deniability to those who raise their eyebrows in response to accusations of manipulation or dehumanisation.

'A single technique and its guarded application to a limited sphere is the starting point of dissociation. No technician anywhere would say that he is submitting men, collectively or individually, to technique. The biogeneticist who experiments on the human embryo, or the film director who tries to affect his audience to the greatest possible degree, makes no claim that he is working on man. The individual is broken into a number of independent fragments, and no two techniques have the same dimensions or depth. Nor does any combination of techniques . . . correspond to any part of the human being. The result is that every technique can assert its innocence. Where, then, or by whom, is the human individual being attacked? Nowhere and by no one. Such is the reply of technique and technician. . . . According to them, the charge itself demonstrates an absence of comprehension and the presence of erroneous, not to say malicious, prejudices.'

Man's fate, he says, remains within his own gift. We are not helpless to preserve our own freedoms. '[I]f man — if each one of us — abdicates his responsibilities with regard to values; if each of us limits himself to leading a trivial existence in a technological civilization, with greater adaptation and increasing success as his sole objectives; if we do not even consider the possibility of making a stand against these determinants, then everything will happen as I have described it, and the determinants will be transformed into certain chains of events and sequences.'

'In my conception, freedom is not an immutable fact graven in nature and on the heart of man. It is not inherent in man or in society, and it is meaningless to write it into law. The mathematical, physical, biological, sociological, and psychological sciences reveal nothing but necessities and determinisms on all sides. As a matter of fact, reality is itself a combination of determinisms, and freedom consists in overcoming and transcending these determinisms. Freedom is completely without meaning unless it is related to necessity, unless it represents victory over necessity. To say that freedom is graven in the nature of man is to say that man is free because he obeys his nature, or, to put it another way, because he is conditioned by his nature. This is nonsense. We must not think of the problem in terms of a choice between being determined and being free. We must look at it dialectically, and say that man is indeed determined, but that it is open to him to overcome necessity, and that this act is freedom. Freedom is not static but dynamic; not a vested interest, but a prize continually to be won. The moment man stops and resigns himself, he becomes subject to determinism. He is most enslaved when he thinks he is comfortably settled in freedom.' If he surrenders to technique, or imagines himself immune from it, man is equally lost. 'However, by grasping the real nature of the technological phenomenon, and the extent to which it is robbing him of freedom, he confronts the blind mechanisms as a conscious being.'

The effect of technique is neither some gradual worsening nor improvement, but a radical redefinition of man in his environment. A significant part of the danger lies in the way technique is able to relieve man of the weight of responsibility for himself. 'Man is not adapted to a world of steel; technique adapts him to it. It changes the arrangement of this blind world so that man can be a part of it without colliding with its rough edges, without the anguish of being delivered up to the inhuman.'

The city is home to technique. We think of the city as being about human proximity, energy, sex, but before those, it was about efficiency, for which men were prepared to pay dearly in the coin of being. 'Men now live in conditions that are less than human. Consider the concentration of our great cities, the slums, the lack of space, of air, of time, the gloomy streets and the sallow lights that confuse night and day. Think of our dehumanized factories, our unsatisfied senses, our working women, our estrangement from nature. Life in such an environment has no meaning. Consider our public transportation, in which man is less important than a parcel; our hospitals, in which he is only a number. Yet we call this progress.'

The changes are both existential and aspirational. Man has acquired new habits rooted in his need for comfort, which in turn has altered his relationship with the facts of his existence. The man of the Middle Ages, he outlines, did not care if his rooms were badly heated or his chairs hard. Death was ever-present and taken for granted, and this consciousness defined man's sense of his own needs and limits. Technique was present, but undetectably. There was no sense of the future as a kind of destination, even — as it is now — a *place*, better and more virtuous than the present. Improvements were made for the sake of the moment, not the future. Society was not oriented toward the creation of new instruments in response to new needs. The emphasis was on the application of old means.

'The deficiency of the tool was to be compensated for by the skill of the worker,' Ellul explains. 'Professional know-how, the expert eye were what counted: man's talents could make his crude tools yield the maximum efficiency. This was a kind of technique, but it had none of the characteristics of instrumental technique. Everything varied from man to man according to his gifts, whereas technique in the modern sense seeks to eliminate such variability.'

'Instrumental' is a key word in understanding both Ellul and the sometimes subtle questions he seeks to elucidate. It means, in this context, something like 'a means to an end'. The skills were intrinsic to men; the tools were secondary. The end result was not the sole consideration: At play also were craftsmanship, skill, personality, human dignity, pride, honour. The 'technique' of the carpenter or the stonemason was intrinsic to his whole being, and created among the mass of men a spirit of fellow-feeling that nowadays survives only between, for example, poets or musicians. There was something that craftsmen held in common, something precious, which had to do with much more than the objects they brought into being.

A strong sense of this is conveyed in *L'Argent*, written in 1913 by Charles Péguy, evoking craft traditions steeped in honour and a desire for perfection. The leg of a chair had to be well made, not to ensure the craftsman get paid; not for the owner, nor the experts, but 'for itself, in itself, in its own way,' and this applied as much to the parts that were not visible as those likely to be in full view. This tradition dates from the beginnings of the race. More recently, this idea of man as a being rendered sovereign in his work was beautifully explored by Matthew Crawford in his book *Shop Class as Soulcraft*. To practice a craft, he postulated, is to enter into a relationship with a world that exists independently of oneself. A carpenter is bound by the evidence of his *spirit* level, an electrician by the irrefutable witness of the circuitry he has assembled. Do the lights work or not? The individuality of the tradesman is expressed in his engagement with a world shared with other similarly engaged beings, a world in which understandings are stored and exchanged. This, says Crawford, is the truest meaning of the word 'republican'. The defining spirit is a sociable individuality based on mutual passions. This is not the same as 'autonomy', a mechanistic, technical concept which denies that we are born into a world that pre-existed us. 'It posits,' insists Crawford, 'an essential aloneness: an autonomous being is free in the sense that a being severed from all others is free. To regard oneself in this way is to betray the natural debts we owe to the world and commit the moral error of ingratitude. For, in fact, we are basically dependent beings: one upon another, and each on a world that is not of our making.'

The modern citizen exists in a state of 'freedom' in which, like a calf in a gated field, he thinks he has the run of the whole world. In reality, he is penned in on all sides in his technical bubble, exploited for what labour he can contribute and what extravagances he can consume, dumbed down by 'education' and mass media and thrown scraps of diversion and provocation to distract him from the true nature of his situation. He has surrendered his sovereignty in return for a relatively comfortable existence, but without real meaning or the basis of a truly hopeful gaze on the future. The ideology of the technological society tells him that he was never more free, but he cannot escape the sense of limits the technology imposes. He *feels* autonomous, but, as Crawford illuminates, it is the autonomy of the automaton. Under these conditions, 'freedom' has already become a double-bind, for the freedom afforded by technology starves the user of the satisfaction of true freedom which flows from the capacity to make a real impression upon reality.

The human being in a technical society is situated not in relation to other human beings but to technique, which inevitably draws him away from himself into the crowd. This also destroys 'natural' collectivities — Crawford's 'republics' — which operated by principles and values long pre-dating the age of technique. Technique, being sociological of its essence, must be understood sociologically. 'Modern man,' Ellul writes, 'divines that there is only one reasonable way out: to submit and take what profit he can from what technique otherwise so richly bestows upon him. If he is of a mind to oppose it, he finds himself really alone.'

Left to himself, the man has no place, belongs nowhere, except perhaps his workplace, where he is in the constant grip of technique. Beyond that he is lost, a 'phantom', in Ellul's description. His personal destiny is fulfilled only by death, but between his adolescent adventuring and the moment of his checking-out, there is nothing he can claim as a decisive moment of action or change. 'Changes are the exclusive prerogative of organized technical society, which one day may have decked him out in khaki to defend it, and on another in stripes because he had sabotaged or betrayed it. There was no difference from one day to the next.'

Matthew Crawford talks about 'illiberal' work, by which he means trumped-up office jobs or treadmill clock-watching, jobs that make you feel more like a machine than the technologies you're supposed to be operating. This is the world Ellul anticipated, six decades before him. The worker does a job he hates, which bores him. He is moderately well paid, but doesn't feel he deserves even this level of remuneration. He carries out a single meaningless and dissociated function in a process he does not comprehend. Nothing of it belongs to his own spirit or imagination. His life, as experienced through his work, has no purpose other than to secure the wherewithal for his continuance, which has no meaning other than what is given to him by his necessity for material subsistence. Mostly, paid work exists in a crypto-totalitarian climate of dissociated authority, standardization of processes and mandatory guidelines. In a culture in which human skills and judgments have been siphoned out of all human context — patented, codified, tabulated and reduced to algorithms — there is a deep suspicion of human discretion.

This is the hard centre of modern human alienation and the crux of what is at stake in the unconscious hubris we nowadays indulge in as a consequence of toting, as unmitigated evidence of 'progression', technologies we imagine would have bamboozled our ancestors. Really, the joke is on ourselves. The drift of technology threatens to steal everything of us worth stealing: what remaining knowledge we may have of how to make or fix things, and the keys to all the doors this making and fixing once opened up into exhilaration — *freedoms*!, now lost and replaced by something called leisure, a different entity altogether.

The loss of these understandings has had profound consequences. Men have become reduced to, at best, supervisors of machines, many of them other humans reduced to the lowest level of technique. It is out of this disaster, Ellul postulates, that the concept of 'human rights' became necessary. The reduction of man rendered vital what might be called a 'redistribution of dignity' (my phrase, not Ellul's), of honour, of pride, all accompanied by their individual moral schemas. And, then, Ellul prophetically cautions: 'When these moral flourishes overly encumber technical progress, they are discarded — more or less speedily, with more or less ceremony, but with determination nonetheless. This is the state we are in today.' Their transitional functions fulfilled, the much-trumpeted charters, declarations and conventions of rights are quietly abolished. 'Rights mean nothing to a mankind surrounded by techniques,' writes Ellul. 'It is our responsibility to study man's situation *vis-à-vis* techniques and not *vis-à-vis* some no longer existent force. . . . Technique has rendered traditional democratic doctrines obsolete.'

Remember that these sentences were published in 1954 and, therefore, written perhaps a year or two earlier — seven decades ago. Our situation has worsened dramatically in the interim, and catastrophically over the past 20 months, but the foundational irritant was already present a lifetime ago, indeed had already taken several initial leaps towards the total domination that seems its automatic impulsion.

In the remote past, Ellul writes, it had been possible for the individual to step outside the sway of technique (which had always existed in one form or another) and control his own destiny. The individual could break away and lead, for example, a mystical or contemplative life. Tools were remote from man, and were only as advanced as necessary to assist or expedite his skills. Now, instead of the focus being on the perfection of the chair leg, it is the machines — the 'tools' — that stand to be perfected, upgraded. Technique, the pursuit of 'means without limit', has become unlimited, and evolves so rapidly that man, even the technician himself, is left behind. This technique-without-limit, Ellul says, is characterised by two features: the imposition of rationality on the impulsive and irrational, and a quality of artificiality. The first involves a reduction of process to mechanical systems, their logical dimension in particular — involving the division of labour, the pursuit of targets, and the use of systemic procedures that exclude creativity and spontaneity. The second, 'artificiality', removes the creation of things to the realm of the unnatural, and constructs a synthetic world, which suppresses the natural one. 'The two worlds,' writes Ellul, 'obey different imperatives, different directives, and different laws which have nothing in common. Just as hydroelectric installations take waterfalls and lead them into conduits, so the technical *milieu* absorbs the natural. We are rapidly approaching the time when there will be no longer any natural environment at all. When we succeed in producing artificial *aurorae boreales*, night will disappear, and perpetual day will reign over the planet.'

Technical activity, he writes, 'automatically eliminates every nontechnical activity or transforms it into technical activity.' This does not mean that there is any conscious effort or directive will. The process of technique is as though possessed of a mind of its own. It is not, he insists, Machiavellian. Everything happens as though spontaneously, in accordance with the 'laws of development of technique'. Both the puppet-master and his puppet are equally in thrall to the sway of technique, one exploiting the power it affords, the other already dulled and regimented by its effects. If this seems to display a naïveté concerning the influence of elites — now an axiomatic aspect of geo-events — it should be remembered that Ellul, in a different context, unpacked more completely than anyone else had done — or has done even to this day — the mechanism of propaganda and its capacity to access via the passions and instincts the malleable, crowd-directed aspect of man.

Ellul was an advocate of democracy, but believed that propaganda rendered its true exercise 'almost impossible'. Propaganda was, he believed, the Siamese twin of the technological society, which makes propaganda easy and thrives upon the effects. But, as he observes in *The Technological Society*, many of us regard propaganda as simply an amplifier of communication in, say, the defence of an idea or system. 'We hear constantly that it cannot, therefore, be of any harm to the democracies. After all, there is a plurality of political parties employing propaganda to maintain opposing or even contradictory ideas; the citizen has a free choice among them. Such a misapprehension comes from a frighteningly elementary conception of propaganda.' Propaganda, Ellul insists, is not mere communication but 'the manipulation of the mob's unconscious.' It operates not only, as is widely misapprehended, at the levels of factual elision and lies, but is capable of accessing also the reservoirs of religiosity, mythology and superstition. In *The Technological Society*, he cites a contemporary French philosopher and sociologist, Jules Monnerot: 'When an entire category of events, beings, and ideas is outside criticism, it constitutes a sacred realm, in contrast to the realm of the profane.' This, says Ellul, happens when something becomes the occasion of constant propaganda: 'As a result of the profound influence of the mechanisms of propaganda, a new zone of the forbidden is created in the heart of man, but it is artificially induced, in contrast to the taboos of primitive societies.' These processes render that matter, whatever it may be, subject to a kind of veneration that places it beyond question or criticism, rendering its deniers or opponents as heretics or blasphemers, and thus liable to sanction or punishment.

In another of his books, *Propagandes*, published in 1964, Ellul described propaganda as 'a direct attack against man' because it does not tolerate discussion and abhors contradiction. 'It must produce quasi-unanimity, and the opposing faction must become negligible, or in any case cease to be vocal.' This is why those who persist in thinking for themselves, or even in expressing unapproved views, invite such opprobrium in the technical society. It's not just that they threaten the reach or influence of the propagandists, for in truth, due to their inability to achieve total saturation through media, dissenters rarely do so. It is that, by their very presence, they put at risk the whole edifice. Their continuing dissent endangers the artifice that is essential for effective propaganda: the sense of naturalism, obviousness, factuality, that must accompany it. For this to work effectively, propaganda must be ubiquitous and universal, to appear to describe everything, from all sides, though in reality from one side only.

The problem, he writes, lies in the psychological situation of the individual assailed by a number of equally skilful propagandas acting upon his nervous system, 'probing and disturbing his unconscious, working over his intelligence, and exacerbating his reactions, the individual can no longer live except in a climate of tension and overexcitement. He can no longer be a smiling and skeptical spectator. He is indeed "engaged" but involuntarily so, since he has ceased to dominate his own thoughts and actions. Techniques have taught the organizers how to force him into the game. He has been stripped of his power of judgment.'

To submit to propaganda means to become alienated from oneself. 'Propaganda strips the individual, robs him of part of himself, and makes him live an alien and artificial life, to such an extent that he becomes another person and obeys impulses foreign to him.' This is achieved by suffusing the individual in the emotions and responses of the crowd, dissipating his individuality, freeing his ego of all confusion, unresolved contradiction and personal reservations. It pushes the individual into the mass 'until he disappears entirely'. What 'disappears', in fact, is the individual's capacity for personal reflection, independent thinking, critical judgment, these being replaced with ready-made thoughts, stereotypes, clichés, catchwords. 'Through propaganda,' writes Ellul in *The Technological Society*, 'we can train a man not to kill or not to drink alcohol; or we can train him to kill or to smoke opium.'

Propaganda operates by creating a kind of abstract universe involving a complete reconstruction of reality in the minds of those affected. This alternative world is built of words, which mutate into images that become realer than reality in something resembling hallucination. In this constructed 'sham universe', lies become truth, and the true seems far-fetched. 'Man will be led to act from real motives that are scientifically directed and increasingly irresistible; he will be brought to sacrifice himself in a real world, but for the sake of the verbal universe which has been fashioned for him. We must try to grasp the profundity of this upheaval. The human being has enormous means at his disposal, and he acts upon and in the real world. But he acts in a dream: he seeks other ends (those the incantational magic of propaganda proposes for him) than those he will really attain.' The ends he is moving towards are known only to the manipulators of the mass subconscious. What is being manipulated is a raft of predispositions, yielding a certain flexibility of response, a kind of ever-readiness and versatility of disposition that allows the propagandist, where necessary, to intervene to redirect the attention of the propagandised to a new purpose or task. '[T]he use of certain propaganda techniques is not meant to entail immediate and definitive adhesion to a given formula, but rather to bring about a kind of long-range vacuity of the individual. The individual, his soul massaged, emptied of his natural tendencies, and thoroughly assimilated to the group, is ready for anything. Propaganda's chief requirement is not so much to be rational, well-grounded, and powerful as to produce individuals especially open to suggestion, who can be easily set into motion.'

Propaganda leads to the atrophying of the capacities to judge, discern or think critically, and these faculties will not simply reappear when propaganda is discontinued or suppressed. Years of spiritual and intellectual reconstruction will be required to restore them. The victim of propaganda, deprived of one channel of opinion, will simply seek out another, like a junkie seeking a different kind of fix. This, says Ellul, will 'spare him the agony of finding himself *vis-à-vis* some event without a ready-made opinion and obliged to judge it for himself.' Once successfully propagandised, Ellul elaborated in *Propagandes*, the individual ceases to be a passive recipient of the propaganda and becomes an evangelist. He takes vigorous stances, starts to oppose others. 'He asserts himself,' observes Ellul, 'at the very moment that he denies his own self without realising it.'

In *The Technological Society*, Ellul describes in precise terms the process by which a mob is baited to attack a designated enemy — for example, the bourgeoisie or the Jews or, let's say, the unvaccinated in a 'pandemic' which people have been persuaded, through propaganda, represents an enormous threat to life and health. This insinuation of a scapegoat, again through propaganda, operates off what he calls the 'will to self-justification', latent in every individual, to which the propagandist can propose a ready enemy. Hate and resentment are tapped and harnessed. 'To exploit resentments, it is sufficient merely to send the individual on his way, equipped with a very simple set of "directions for use". . . . Suppose, for example, that the adversary has been designated as the author of all the individual's misfortunes and sufferings. (The bourgeoisie plays this role for the Communists, as the Jews played it for the Nazis.) After such suggestions have been launched, there is a surge of human resentment among the people. Like a flock of sheep, they stampede much further than they had actually been commanded to go, in obedience to another instinct which comes into play and which causes them to hurl themselves on the object of their resentment like a dog on a cat. Incidentally, this explains why there is no "criminal" in these cases. Pogroms are seldom ordered by the authorities. One need only manipulate popular resentments to bring them about.

'In exploiting the device of the scapegoat, propaganda leads people to transfer evil to the adversary. The adversary here becomes the generalized incarnation of evil, whereas, in the exploitation of resentment, the adversary appears as the cause of misfortune. This incarnation indicates that there is no rational basis for hate; it results solely from subconscious mechanisms. This explains a surprising statement made by Hitler in *Mein Kampf*: "It is necessary to suggest to the people that the most varied enemies all belong to the same category; and to lump all adversaries together so that it will appear to the mass of our own partisans that the struggle is being waged against a single enemy. This fortifies their faith in their rights and increases their exasperation against those who would assail them."'

Technique begets totalitarianism as a matter of course. Finally, technique causes the state to become totalitarian, to absorb the citizen's life completely. We have noted that this occurs as a result of the accumulation of techniques in the hands of the state. Techniques are mutually engendered and hence interconnected, forming a system that tightly encloses all our activities. When the state takes hold of a single thread of this network of techniques, little by little, it draws to itself all the matter and the method, whether or not it consciously wills to do so. 'Even when the state is resolutely liberal and democratic,' Ellul insists, 'it cannot do otherwise than become totalitarian.'

As though anticipating the huffing and puffing of politicians feigning outrage at the escalating 2021 use of such words against them, Ellul moved to explain: 'The words *the totalitarian state* inevitably evoke clichés and passionate opinions. But these no longer represent anything but historical reminiscences. The totalitarian state we are discussing here is not the brutal, immoderate thing which tortured, deformed, and broke everything in its path, the battleground of armed bullies and factions, a place of dungeons and the reign of the arbitrary. These things did certainly exist; but they represented transient traits, not real characteristics of the totalitarian state. It might even be said that they were the human aspects of the state in its inhumanity. Torture and excess are the acts of persons who use them as a means of releasing a suppressed need for power. This does not interest us here. It does not represent the true face of the completely technical, totalitarian state. In such a state, nothing useless exists; there is no torture; torture is a wasteful expenditure of psychic energy which destroys salvageable resources without producing useful results.'

The hallmark of totalitarianism remains, however, the 'camp' — sometimes the 'concentration' camp, but not necessarily in its caricature form. 'We must not be misled by differences in name. Work camps, re-education camps, refugee camps — all represent the same fact. [To Ellul's list, we might now add another: the quarantine 'hotel'.] We are speaking here of the concentration camp in its pure form, which has nothing to do with crematoria or hanging up the inmates by the thumbs. Such tortures are imputable to men, not to technique. The camp as an institution is making its appearance everywhere, under the most varied political regimes, as a result of the conjunction of social problems and police technique.'

The changing nature of society in the era of technique — the population explosion, mass migration, rising crime and terror attacks, the exigencies of supervision and surveillance — all these render essential the classification of individuals as *categories of individuals*, which in turn requires an uptick in menace and apprehension. Hence the centrality of the 'camp' and related phenomena such as 'preventive arrest, concentration of masses of innocent persons not for judging but for sorting, and so forth.' In the technical society, men require to be processed, treated, refined, pasteurised. What makes them different makes them dangerous, and should correctly be eliminated where possible.

Like many thinkers who have lived through totalitarianism, including Solzhenitsyn and Havel, Ellul insists on the moral proximity of totalitarianism to democracy. 'Sociologically, there is admittedly a world of difference between dictatorship and democracy. But in both the moral problem is suppressed; the individual is simply an animal broken in to obey certain conditioned reflexes. Indeed, there may be a difference between dictatorship and democracy on the plane of public health or statistics; but on the moral plane, there is a funda-mental identity when democracy achieves its ends through propaganda.'

The end result of the processes imposed in the technical society, he says, will be the creation of a new man: *L'homme-machine* — 'Man, a machine'. Man, even in Ellul's time, was being subjected to a prolonged time-and-motion study directed at observing, measuring, quantifying, evaluating his patterns of behaviour and response. Everything was already being systemised, schematised and tabulated. A theoretical control subject was being constructed to some future end — the ideal condition of man to enter his new 'incarnation'.

'In the coupling of man and machine, a genuinely new entity comes into being. Most writers still insist on the modem tendency, which they profess to discern, to adapt the machine to the man. Such adaptation doubtless exists and represents a great improvement; but it entails its counterpart, the complete adaptation of the man to the machine. This last does not lie in a remote future. Man's nature has already been modified; and it is to an already adapted individual that technique adapts mechanical apparatus. Such adaptation is becoming progressively easier, and even takes place spontaneously when the human techniques co-operate. The purpose of our human techniques is ostensibly to reintegrate and restore the lost unity of the human being. But the unity produced is the abstract unity of the ideal Man; in reality, the concrete application of techniques dissociates man into fragments.'

This pursuit of the 'ideal man', he says, is a form of the 'escapism' which led inexorably to the gas chambers of Auschwitz, the locus of the destruction of 'some millions of unimportant specimens.' He urges us to 'avoid the same mistake with respect to this all-virtuous ideal in the universal concentration camp we live in.'

A completely technologised world, he writes, will include whole categories of men incapable of adaptation, who will have no place at all. The remainder will be so rigorously adapted as to leave no scope for individuality. 'The complete joining of man and machine will have the advantage, however, of making the adaptation painless. And it will assure the technical efficiency of the individuals who survive it.' In preparation for this homogeneity of the species, mankind was being ushered with propaganda and advertising towards a mass society. The concentration of advertising messaging on the ideal image of man enables the process of preparation to happen more or less of its own accord.

Ellul was not hopeful concerning the capacity of some spiritual resilience of mankind to send this process into retreat. Literary, artistic and musical forms were often proposed, he noted, as evidence that such a spirit of resistance was available. While he did not believe that 'sources of vital energy', such as sexuality, spirituality, and capacity for feeling, had been impaired, neither did he think they could be relied upon in this context, having fallen from their former plinths of tribute to the mythologies of human nature and heroism and turned into mere amusements.

'All instincts seem more unbridled today than ever before — sex; passion for nature, the mountains, and the sea; passion for social and political action. There cannot have been many historical periods in which these forces were so evident or so authoritative. Again, I have no wish to deny whatever validity they possess. It is good for city dwellers to go to the country. It is good that a marked eroticism is wrecking the sclerotic traditional morality. It is well that poetry, thanks to such movements as surrealism, has become really expressive once more. But these phenomena, which express the deepest instinctive human passions, have also become totally innocuous. They question nothing, menace nobody.'

Technique already had the measure of such responses, he argued, enabling it to surround and localise them. 'Moreover, technique attacks man, impairs the sources of his vitality, and takes away his mystery.'

Jazz had been, he acknowledged, one of the most authentic of modern human protests. Deriving from the experiences of West African slaves who arrived in the port city of New Orleans in the late nineteenth century, the music leveraged the experiences of these lately liberated humans and seemed to offer both a healing and a kind of revolution. Ellul saw it differently. 'In their extremity, the Negroes discovered song, which likewise answered the needs of faith. Music expressed for them at once the despair of the present and the hope for salvation in Christ. Its culmination in delirium brought deliverance, but only as opium and alcohol did for others. . . . In jazz, they created a true art form. But with it, they also shut every door to freedom. Jazz imprisoned the Negroes more and more in their slavery; from then on, they drew a morose relish from it. It is highly significant that this slave music has become the music of the modem world.' Jazz was, in time, supplanted by rock' n' roll, of which the same might be said in spades. Literature and ideas, he argued, had also been castrated. Even the very best ideas had lost their spiritual efficacy by virtue of the complete separation of thought and action effected by technique. 'The very assimilation of ideas into the technical framework which renders them materially effective makes them spiritually worthless. This does not mean that ideas have no worthwhile effect on the public at all. They have a great effect, but not the effect their creators intended.'

Ellul did not specifically envisage the advent of the transhumanist society, though its foreshadow is to be detected all over his writing about technique. The idea — now a commonplace futuristic trope — that technology might create hermetically sealed chambers of crucial, instant decision-making, in which the outcomes will be decided by software that writes itself and algorithms that outgrow the intelligence of their creators, was beyond the sightlines of even the most fanciful sci-fi seers of his time. And yet, in substance and essence, he foresaw everything that confronts us now, simply by digging into the deep nature of what he calls 'technique'. His conclusion was that analogous processes would take place within human beings, radical shifts in the existential structure of mankind that would change out of all recognition the average person's engagement with reality.

'With the final integration of the instinctive and the spiritual by means of these human techniques, the edifice of the society will be completed. It will not be a universal concentration camp, for it will be guilty of no atrocity. It will not seem insane, for everything will be ordered, and the stains of human passion will be lost amid the chromium gleam. We shall have nothing more to lose, and nothing to win. Our deepest instincts and our most secret passions will be analyzed, published, and exploited. We shall be rewarded with everything our hearts ever desired.'

In summary, one might decide, 'We will own nothing, and will become convinced we are happy.'

YEAR THREE
2022

04 Jan - CDC recommends Pfizer booster at 5 months, and additional primary dose for some immunocompromised children

05 Jan - (Ch 17) *Inoculation Against Vigilance* ——

10 Jan - Record 23,909 daily cases, one million total. Chief medical officer estimates up to 10 per cent of the population contracted the virus in the previous week.

13 Jan - US Supreme Court upholds "vaccine" mandate for health care workers in federally funded facilities, puts vaccine-or-test mandate for large businesses on hold

13 Jan - US announces 500M tests for free distribution

21 Jan - Taoiseach announces nearly all restrictions lifted. "Today is a good day."

28 Jan - Department of Health no longer releasing daily Covid-19 figures.

31 Jan - FDA grants full approval to Moderna's "vaccine" for those 18+.

11 Feb - FDA authorizes bebtelovimab, a new monoclonal antibody, for emergency use

02 Mar - (Ch 18) *Whipnosis, Part I: Life as Trance* ——
06 Mar - (Ch 19) *Whipnosis, Part II: Narcissists in Lockstep* ——

07 Mar - Reported deaths globally pass 6M

📖 **20 Mar - (Ch 20)** *Whipnosis, Part III: Into the Womb of the Tyrant*
———

🌐 29 Mar - FDA and CDC authorize boosters for those 50+.

🌐 25 Apr - FDA approves drug remdesivir for patients as young as 28 days, weighing about seven pounds.

🌐 12 May - US reported deaths pass 1M; US flag flown at half-staff
📖 **14 May - (Ch 21)** *YOUR Government Hates YOU* ———
🌐 17 May - FDA authorizes booster for children ages 5-11 five+ months after "vaccination." CDC two days later.
📖 **30 May - (Ch 22)** *The Phony Sex War* ———

🌐 12 Jun - US rescinds requirement of negative Covid-19 test before boarding a flight to the US
🌐 18 Jun - CDC recommends vaccines for children 6 months+.

📖 **04 Jul - (Ch 23)** *The Liberal Ayatolliad and the Covid Coup* ———
🌐 13 Jul - FDA authorizes Novavax "vaccine" for emergency use

🌐 31 Aug - FDA authorizes updated vaccine booster shots from Moderna and Pfizer. CDC the next day.

🌐 19 Oct - CDC allows Novavax Monovalent boosters for those 18+

🌐 11 Nov - Number of Covid-19 "vaccine" adverse event reports shows 898,029 in the US VAERS system
🌐 30 Nov - FDA de-authorizes bebtelovimab for emergency use due to non-efficacy with Omicron subvariants

🌐 08 Dec - FDA authorizes bivalent "vaccines" for children 6+ months.

CHAPTER 17
INOCULATION AGAINST VIGILANCE
05-01-2022

Outrage greeting comparisons between current events and past instances of man's inhumanity to man may denote less respect for past victims than a desire to stop us speaking usefully about the present.

'The past is never dead. It's not even past.' — William Faulkner

---

The German philosopher Friedrich Hegel it was who said, 'The only thing we learn from history is that we learn nothing from history,' a charge that might bespeak amnesia or negligence or ignorance or, perhaps, inattention. But there is a sense in which it is even more true than Hegel may have intended: When the cultural context is constructed so that it is not merely difficult, or even impossible to learn from history, but actually *forbidden*, when certain events of the past, by virtue of being deemed unique, or uniquely sacred, or so definitively the experience of a particular nation, race or ethnicity as to be considered almost as the 'property' of that group, cannot be used for the purposes of contemporary comparison. In such situations, a tendency sometimes develops towards the rejection of all comparisons with the experience, even by way of speculation as to their possible repetition, on the grounds of inappropriateness, or 'disrespect, or even, in some sense, *sacrilege*.

This happens sometimes with colonialism, which is often claimed by racial activists as the experience only of certain 'minorities': black people, 'people of colour', and so forth. This is usually down to some mixture of ignorance and cynicism, and can usually be dealt with by advancing facts. But there is a more serious condition: when a particular experience has been genuinely unique up to the present but is barred from being cited by way of comparison, association or speculation in any context because the 'proprietors' of that experience exercise a veto on its interpretation and implications. The Jewish experience at the hands of the Nazis in the 1930s and 1940s presents the most obvious example.

The sheer horror of these deeds, paradoxically, makes them harder to believe. All of us have seen and read many things that have shocked us to the core, even making us doubt that human beings could be capable of such evil. Statistics do not convey it, even pictures of mass graves are an abstraction of sorts. In 2015, at the time of the 70th anniversary of the liberation of Auschwitz, a documentary titled *Night Will Fall*, a collaboration by British media mogul Sydney Bernstein and the legendary director Alfred Hitchcock — withdrawn in late 1945 because by then, the Allies had decided that rubbing the Germans' noses in the Holocaust might be bad for the post-war reconstruction — was aired on British TV. The documentary shows some of the harrowing scenes that confronted Allied forces when they arrived at Bergen-Belsen: the piled-up bodies of people executed by the Nazis just before the arrival of Allied forces, as well as warehouses filled with human hair, toys, spectacles and false teeth — all taken from the victims before their obliteration, all carefully packaged and labelled. It is a strange thing that these assembled appendages of accoutrements of human existence seemed more definitively to convey the horror of what had happened than the all too familiar pictures of piled-up corpses. Perhaps what breaks our hearts most effectively is not the sight of dead bodies but the evidence of life's traces remaining when it has been extinguished.

Part of the proffered rationale for the suppression of the documentary was an attempt to staunch the backlash against Germany arising from what, in the aftermath of the war, was emerging about the Nazi period. This suppression coincided with the start of a concerted attempt to transmit the idea that the Holocaust ought to be seen as a crime of the human species rather than of Germany *per se*, arising from a previously undetected pathology of humanity that just happened to materialise where and when it did. And yet, one of the consequences of this strategy was to unleash the countervailing idea that the Holocaust was some kind of insoluble mystery, that it was impossible to understand how human beings could behave like this, that the episode was some kind of one-off aberration involving one bad man, or bunch of bad men, and that, somehow or another, a recurrence of such evildoing, being inconceivable, was unlikely. This had a peculiar effect within Germany itself, solidifying the sense of national guilt while driving it underground, into the collective unconscious of the nation, incapable of being talked about and therefore immune from deeper understanding. The desire to relieve Germany of its shame in order to restart the world may therefore have rendered it impossible for a fuller cultural understanding of Nazism to emerge.

After Nazism, the world almost instantly reverted to thinking of evil as belonging to exceptional circumstances and unique categories of human being.

Today, we think of Hitler as a demon, and have some vague sense that he somehow hypnotised a whole nation to fall in or turn blind eyes. But there persists minimal cultural awareness of the dynamics by which Nazism operated. After the war, the imperative of 'peace-making' rapidly imposed another kind of wound: an injured memory proffering little clarity as to how the greatest crime in the history of the world came about. The world, including Germany, filed the Nazi era away as an anomaly of history, a Hollywood story of classic baddies with bad moustaches, but with nobody surviving on whom any significant burden of blame might be imposed.

A strange ricochet of these developments was that gradually there emerged a form of thinking whereby any attempt to extrapolate meanings and connections from the context of what had occurred in Germany — or in Russia and Eastern Europe in the decades immediately before and after — would be deemed improper, disproportionate and inappropriate. This meant, in effect, that it would become impossible to detect signs of similar phenomena emerging in the future, despite the very strong conviction that emerged in the 1950s that these totalitarian phenomena represented a new development with roots in the nature of modern society. In due course, these tendencies came to be augmented by another: the refusal of the victims and descendants of victims to permit the experience of, in particular, Nazism, to be drawn upon for the purpose of constructing hypotheses or comparisons concerning events in subsequent times.

Last year, speaking to the media outside Leinster House, the Tipperary TD, Mattie McGrath, made a comparison between the Jewish experience of Nazism and some aspects of Covid 'measures'. Speaking about the introduction of 'vaccine passports' in July, he asked: 'Is that where we've come to now, back to 1933 in Germany, we'll be all tagged in yellow with the mark of the beast on us, is that where we're going?' The Taoiseach, Micheál Martin, challenged McGrath in the Dáil about his comments, saying: 'I think you should refrain from your frequent use of language, and I've asked you to stop using terms Nazis and totalitarianism. You've made ridiculous assertions in this house that are offensive to people. You have repeatedly accused the government of being like Nazis, in this house.'

Mr McGrath asked to be spared the history lesson, not necessarily the best answer. What Martin had delivered was not a history lesson, but a demonstration of political bullying and evasion. McGrath may not be a debater of the first rank, but he was saying something brave and necessary. What Martin was saying *sounded* like a righteous response, but only because he followed the slipstream of a well-established truism. Minister of State, Thomas Byrne, joined him in kicking McGrath, saying: 'Nothing, absolutely nothing, compares to Nazi Germany. Every comparison made diminishes the memory of that unique evil, and the slaughter of millions of Jews.' This is the kind of thing that might get you a round of applause on the *Late Late Show*, but that does not qualify it as a *moral* response. Nazi Germany remains 'unique' only for as long as it remains unrepeated, and what McGrath was implicitly trying to do was postpone the moment of repetition indefinitely.

Interestingly, soon afterwards, to the chortling of journalists, Mr McGrath found himself the subject of a rebuke from the Auschwitz Museum, which tweeted: 'Instrumentalization of the tragedy of all people who between 1933-45 suffered, were humiliated, tortured & murdered by the hateful totalitarian regime of Nazi Germany to argue against vaccination that saves human lives is a sad symptom of moral and intellectual decline.' This, on its face, may have seemed to level a legitimate charge of disproportionality against McGrath. There are not, after all, six million corpses to be pointed to in evidence. 'Holocaust' is a word that ought to be used sparingly, not due to any etymological factor but because it has come to be used in a particular, sacred context and, therefore, ought not be trivialised.

But is that really the end of it? Mattie McGrath did not use the word 'Holocaust'. Nor did his point relate to a comparison between the Jewish experience and vaccination *per se*, but to the use of 'vaccine passports' — a recent and unprecedented instrument in supposedly free and democratic societies — to restrict the freedoms of people who exercise their right to make decisions about their own health. His argument might be said to have drawn a comparison not with 1933 but with September 1941, when the Nazis introduced the yellow Star of David to identify Jews in public, though interestingly, this moment almost precisely coincided with the building of the first Nazi gas chamber in Auschwitz. Perhaps more germanely, vaccine passports were introduced in Ireland in respect of a 'vaccine' that is not a vaccine (a gene therapy, actually), that is unnecessary, does not work in the manner claimed by its manufacturers and pusher-governments, and has already been shown to cause death and damage at levels far beyond which previous vaccines have been withdrawn.

Nor, in a climate of almost total censorship and suppression of critical voices, is it clear, even by the crudest interpretation of risks-benefits analysis, that there is any evidence that these 'vaccines' have 'saved human lives', as the Auschwitz Museum tweet asserted. This claim, devoid of evidence, is merely a tendentious repetition of government propaganda. It is well established that people are being killed by the Covid 'vaccines' — something in excess of 3,000 in Ireland alone, the equivalent of the death toll in 30 years of the Northern Ireland Troubles, *in just 12 months*. The global figure, calculated on a *pro-rata* basis, would be several million. In the US, even the conservative official statistics acknowledge some 21,000 deaths. In Europe, the European Medicines Agency — again, a conservative witness — had by late November 2021 admitted to 30,551 vaccine-related deaths, and 1,163,356 adverse reactions. That's a lot of human hair, spectacles and false teeth; and now they propose to start work on a depository of toys.

Mattie McGrath did not set out these facts, nor was he seeking to insinuate a comparison between the Holocaust and Covid vaccines. His point was a narrower one: that the requirement to produce documentary proof of vaccination in order to access basic services was analogous to the process that remains one of the dark hallmarks of the Nazi regime. As such, it was entirely valid and would have remained so even if it was incontrovertibly established that these 'vaccines' had saved lives, which is, as it happens, the contrary of the truth.

In rebuking him, fellow politicians and the Auschwitz Museum were trading off an established aura of reverence that surrounds the Jewish experience of Nazism. It is not necessary to question the validity of this reverence in order to establish that McGrath's commentary was valid in as far as it went, and that, although his remarks might well have sparked a heated debate (albeit one that was closed down peremptorily), his intervention was long overdue in circumstances where we had been labouring for 16 months at that point under the draconian laws imposed by the political system he is part of. McGrath ought not to have been subjected to reprimands grounded in the calamity of six million dead people. *That* was disproportionate.

When Minister Byrne said that 'nothing, absolutely nothing, compares to Nazi Germany,' he really meant that nothing in the present or future can compare to it. But is that valid? How can we know? Is it the case that 'every comparison made diminishes the memory of that unique evil, and the slaughter of millions of Jews.' Do we need to have millions of corpses to be entitled to warn against the possibility that totalitarianism might resurface? Must there be gas chambers too? Gulags? Quarantine camps clearly won't be sufficient, even while they provide an ominous echo. Are even these observations likely to be deemed 'offensive'? Isn't that just a little *convenient*?

Tyranny, torture, murder — these, surely, are the dangers we need to watch for? In the past two years we have had, undoubtedly, tyranny. Torture? Well, there are many kinds: torture of minds counts also, the torture of the elderly left to die alone in their beds. And murder? Read Denis Rancourt's devastating analysis of the death patterns of Covid. And are there not other things we might usefully be vigilant for also? The pursuit of Utopias, those 'Perfect Societies'? Life without death? Messianism? Building Back Better? The denial of the human person's right to decide his own level of risk, thereby depriving him of everything that makes his life worthwhile? The staking of human lives in medical experiments? The drift of politics towards power of dangerous kinds? Breaches of the Nuremberg Code?

Disrespect for humanity is always worrisome, as is the tendency to cover up inconvenient outcomes even as they grow more glaring and ominous. Our pogroms are so much more civilised now, what with Midazolam and ventilators and mRNA spike proteins, but still, they lack something in verity and transparency. No greater evils have ever been designed than the ones designed by those who imagine they are doing good. And there is, as Orwell observed, a tendency for stories of atrocity and cruelty to resemble one another.

The — until now — metaphysical singularity of the Jewish Holocaust experience does not need to be argued for: It is self-evident on the basis of the facts as historiographically established and handed down. Nothing of that is in dispute here. The question to be addressed relates to whether that singularity is absolute or contingent, and, in the event that it is *not* absolute — i.e. not incapable of repetition — whether there can be any entitlement of any individual, group or body to gatekeep its meaning in the manner that, for example, the Auschwitz Museum sought to do with Mattie McGrath.

Two years ago, the German journalist and editor-in-chief of *CATO* magazine, Andreas Lombard, wrote a remarkable essay, *The Vanity of Guilt*, for *First Things* magazine about the way his country had become haunted to the extent of self-abnegation by the deeds of the Nazis. His immediate context was post-2015 mass migration, but his theme was guilt: 'In the decades after 1945,' he wrote, 'the imperative of forgetting was succeeded by the imperative of remembering. Victims replaced heroes, and remorse and self-accusation superseded pride.'

Germans were required to remember their guilt and shame, and could no longer stand up for their nation or themselves. This was the tragedy of twentieth-century Germany: that to make it clear it did not wish to harm anyone, it had to harm itself.

He went on: 'This dynamic is pathological, viewed sociologically. But worse, it reflects a vanity of guilt that is dangerous and destructive in its theological arrogance. To a striking degree, the German political and cultural establishment has taken possession of the Holocaust. This terrible crime has become a precious asset to be deployed against anyone who dares to criticize the *status quo*.' Guilt can be employed as a weapon and used to bludgeon even the guiltless into silence.

In its aftermath, he elaborated, the Jewish Holocaust was treated as if it could prevent other crimes against humanity, if only it could be kept in the collective memory. 'By calling our evil constantly to mind, we would negate its power.'

But, instead, he said, the commemoration of the Holocaust has created 'a hubristic self-righteousness.' Germany had ordained itself a unique destiny of self-abnegation. And this, in turn, had been used — by Germany! — to accuse others by way of anticipating their tyrannies, their fascisms, their potential for Nazism. One of the obligations Germany seeks to impose on others in this way is the obligation to no longer protect their own borders. Because of Germany's prior treatment of the Jews, German leaders assume that 'negative nationalism should be obligatory for all of Europe and the world of tomorrow.'

Perhaps what he described here was an inevitable consequence of the particular kind of 'remembering' that was permitted in the wake of the Nazi period.

On the one hand, Germany had to remember; on the other, we should not rub its nose in the past. On the one hand, we needed to make sure that such things could never be repeated; on the other, we were not permitted to cite the Nazi period in any attempts to alert our fellows to any such particular danger except a *nationalist* one.

The energy for the insistence on 'negative nationalism', he said, derives precisely from the metaphysical singularity of the 1930s/1940s Jewish Holocaust. This principle states that this Holocaust is the greatest crime in history, and will always remain so. Its evil can never be surpassed. Or indeed equalled. But, strangely, he notes, it is usually non-Jewish Germans who make this claim.

'There is something suspicious about this,' Lombard expands. 'Germans claim singularity not as victims, but as perpetrators. The "perpetrator people" now exalt their own crime as the greatest in human history — a monstrous kind of negative pride. The accused steps up to become the supreme judge. The point is not what verdict he renders, whether it is acquittal or conviction. The point is his hubris, a hubris he conceals behind the verdict of maximum guilt.'

A metaphysically singular crime, Lombard says, can never be forgiven or forgotten. Reconciliation is impossible. But the twist in the tail is that it is the German refusal to ask for forgiveness that, most of all, makes this withholding of absolution inevitable. And as with Germans, so also with Gentiles.

The discussion of Nazism is managed, and not necessarily in a straightforward direction. We are permitted to speak of it if our objective is ideological opposition to nationalism. We may use it to condemn neo-Nazis, and 'far right' politicians, and, somehow or other, 'white supremacists', but not as a cautionary tale to place a check on the adventuring of mainstream, everyday politicians in the present.

The net semantic outcome of all this is that Nazism, in the context of its permitted leveraging, cannot be forgiven, but nor can it be repeated, other than in certain contexts. And nor can it be referenced by those seeking to issue warnings about the possibility of its repetition in other contexts or in a general fashion. The franchise of the crime is protected not just by its victims but by its perpetrators also. The idea that nothing compares to Nazi Germany, and that every attempted comparison diminishes the memory of 'that unique evil' is sufficient to prevent constructive lessons being adduced from that experience.

Perhaps the most comprehensive documenter of the totalitarian tendency has been the brilliant German Jewish philosopher, Hannah Arendt. In her definitive deconstruction, *The Origins of Totalitarianism*, she describes in forensic detail the operation of the Hitler and Stalin regimes, including the events and processes leading to the Jewish Holocaust, which she characterised as an entirely new phenomenon of the twentieth century. Arendt was not concerned with the particularities of German fascism or Russian communism in some general sense, but with the particular forms of government developed under

Stalin and Hitler. Her main focus is on Nazism — being herself German, with direct experience of the Nazi model, but also because, whereas Hitler was dead at the time of her writing, Stalin's reign of terror was to continue beyond her book's first publication in 1951.

In writing what became the first edition of her book between 1945 and 1949, Arendt was at pains to stress that totalitarianism was not simply another form of tyranny, but a unique and novel development — the total domination of a people through a combination of simplistic ideology and constant terror — and yet, with the dark paradox: totalitarianism ultimately rests on mass support. She set out seeking answers to three questions: *What happened? How did it happen? How could it have happened?* She had access to 'mountains of paper'— 'a super-abundance of documentary material on every aspect of the twelve years that Hitler's *Tausendjähriges Reich* had managed to last.'

Arendt, then, saw totalitarianism as a complex, subtle, unprecedented process, with a beginning, middle and a destination: total control. The destination could not be understood without the beginning or the middle, and the beginning was the foundation upon which the middle and destination phases were constructed. It is also clear that she saw herself as treating of a 'form of government' with clear indicators as to its emergence, which was responsible in the twentieth century for not only the deaths of six million Jews, but for upwards of 100 million deaths all told. Let us not forget that Hitler killed far fewer people than Stalin, and both of them together far fewer than Mao. But it seems that you need to reach Mao's level in our culture to have a restaurant named after you.

Our reaction to Nazism is more visceral than our reactions to the other totalitarianisms, but we ought to be cautious rather than smug on that account. Is it the numbers that offend us, or something else? That 'something else' certainly existed in Nazism: machines for killing, not just killing as a collateral consequence of some other inhumanity, but killing for killing's sake.

In the course of her forensic profile, Arendt details many of the arcane and unexpected aspects of the phenomena under her microscope. For example: the differences between fascism and totalitarianism; the totalitarian project of terrifying human beings 'from within'; the differences between 'the mob', 'the masses' and 'the elite'; the mob as 'caricature of the people', the 'masses' as an amalgam of 'neutral, politically indifferent people' who could not be incorporated into any form of organisation; the totalitarian leader as a functionary of the masses he leads; how totalitarianism uses threats of exclusion to terrorise people into line; the use of propaganda to convert prejudice from a mere opinion to a 'principle of self-definition'; 'the terrifying roster of distinguished men whom totalitarianism counts among its sympathizers, fellow travelers and inscribed party members.'

Arendt says that the Nazis inverted the commandment 'Thou shalt not kill' to 'Thou shalt kill'. She also notes that they remained observant of certain laws. They were not indiscriminately evil. They played 'fair' but within their own, self-made rules.

The central plank of totalitarianism is the pursuit of terror. What was 'attractive' in this for its adherents was 'a kind of philosophy through which to express frustration, resentment and blind hatred'. It was a way of forcing recognition of individual existence on the whole of society — by negating individual uniqueness.

The ideology of totalitarianism is directed at world domination, and its chief instruments are terror and the creation of a pseudo-reality in which to forge a cultlike mentality, embracing a majority but excluding a designated and delineated group. Surveillance is, therefore, central to the administration of the totalitarian system, and to the orchestration of terror and resentment among both elements of the divided population. Arendt identified three core elements in the totalitarian ideology: the claim to 'explain' the future as a fixed reality; the directing of the population as to the correct form of thinking and responding; and the freeing of human thought from experiential logic and spontaneous reason, which are supplanted by the singular idea on which the totalitarian movement is founded.

In the present case, if we may dare to observe so, the central 'totalitarian idea' is that of permanent emergency, which is to say the postulation of maximum imputed safety at the expense of freedom *qua freedom*.

The issue that Mattie McGrath touched upon — the requirement to carry, and produce on demand identification papers — is a mechanism for destroying individual autonomy, for it posits by implication that each individual is merely a singular quark, answerable to the whole via the state. It is a way of conveying an insult by the state to the very idea of the particular human person, never mind the sovereign human person. By conveying an implicit suspicion, it conveys also a dualism — state v. citizen — and a hierarchy of power that is primed with terror. Surveillance and monitoring of individual identity are also, in a totalitarian state, the preserve of the secret police, one of the chief instruments of state terror, whose job it is to monitor and eliminate the internal enemies of the totalitarian movement.

Surveillance exists not just for its own sake — for reasons of security or intelligence-gathering — but as an instrument of intimidation and levelling, of reducing each member of the mass to a state of terrified interchangeableness. The point of this, as Arendt outlines, is to 'make all men superfluous' — 'individuality, indeed anything that distinguishes one man from another, is intolerable.'

'Total power,' she adds, 'can be achieved and safeguarded only in a world of conditioned reflexes, of marionettes without the slightest trace of spontaneity. Precisely because man's resources are so great, he can be fully dominated only when he becomes a specimen of the animal-species man.' The purpose is to atomise the population, each citizen from each other — or, rather, to further atomise them, since our technical society, as so brilliantly illuminated by Jacque Ellul, has already done most of the heavy lifting for the pathocrats.

Isolation and atomisation are also the true purposes, in the present context, of face masks and 'social distancing': to convey to each citizen that he is alone except as an atom of the mob, and as such interchangeable with each other 'atom'.

Arendt eventually emerged with a detailed profile of a form of government that appealed to no traditional laws or existing forms but rather to its own concocted Law of Nature (survival of the fittest, master race) or Law of History. Its goal was the extension of that total domination to the entire world. In totalitarianism as she described it, all traditions, values, legalities and defences, all political institutions, are destroyed, and all behaviour, public and private, comes to be controlled by terror, which becomes the measure of all things. Her central thesis was that great evils are not carried out by individual monsters, but by 'ordinary' or 'regular' people, many of whom become convinced of being involved only in nondescript actions. In order to convince regular people to carry out atrocities, it is not necessary or useful to fill them with hate but simply to normalise and desensitise them to what would otherwise be considered unthinkable.

These fundamentals are of immense interest to us in our present situation, transcending any symptomatic differences between the then and the now. Must we wait for the evidence to pile up in the form of human corpses before we apply our minds to formulating meanings for things that strike us as peculiar or disturbing? If so, is there an acceptable level of carnage to be exceeded before we are permitted to note the early signs of a testing of the values of our civilisation? Must we seek permission from the descendants or alleged representatives of those who suffered previously from the conditions seeming to be incipient in our own time, before acquiring the right to render comparisons? Are we to avoid obvious similarities lest we cause offence? At what point, if any, would it become permissible to hazard a comparison? Is *politesse* more important than vigilance? How are we to be certain that such a culture of deference is not being constructed and manipulated by the same kinds of individuals who once manipulated the German or Russian peoples?

'Totalitarian regimes,' wrote Hannah Arendt, 'discovered without knowing it that there are crimes which men can neither punish nor forgive. When the impossible was made possible, it became the unpunishable, unforgivable absolute evil which could no longer be understood and explained by the evil motives of self-interest, greed, covetousness, resentment, lust for power, and cowardice; and which, therefore, anger could not revenge, love could not endure, friendship could not forgive. Just as the victims in the death factories or the holes of oblivion are no longer "human" in the eyes of their executioners, so this newest species of criminals is beyond the pale even of solidarity in human sinfulness.'

Must it come to this again before we are permitted to speak?

'It is inherent in our entire philosophical tradition,' she continues, 'that we cannot conceive of a "radical evil," and this is true both for Christian theology, which conceded even to the Devil himself a celestial origin, as well as for Kant, the only philosopher who, in coining that term for it, at least must have suspected the existence of this evil even though he immediately rationalized it in the concept of a "perverted ill will" that could be explained by comprehensible motives. Therefore, we actually have nothing to fall back on in order to understand a phenomenon that nevertheless confronts us with its overpowering reality and breaks down all standards we know. There is only one thing that seems to be discernible: we may say that radical evil has emerged in connection with a system in which all men have become equally superfluous. The manipulators of this system believe in their own superfluousness as much as in that of all others, and the totalitarian murderers are all the more dangerous because they do not care if they themselves are alive or dead, if they ever lived or never were born.'

It is clear from these quotations that Arendt believed that the 'radical evil' of Nazism was something new in human history, but that it was not going away again. She saw it as a matter of urgency that humanity should begin to comprehend this and to become watchful for its signs. She was not suggesting that the crimes of the Nazis were 'unique and unrepeatable' but something like the opposite: that their uniqueness at that moment offered humanity a warning that, if heeded, might serve to prevent a recurrence of those horrors. She resisted early attempts to 'generalise' the Holocaust out of its German context. In an exchange with the German writer Hans Magnus Enzensberger, she repudiated the suggestion that the mass killing of Jews was but one 'holocaust' among others. She had been dismayed when Enzensberger seemed to suggest that Nazism was not especially a German thing, but could happen anywhere — i.e. Nazism was a species-shaming phenomenon rather than a specifically German pathology. Arendt baulked at this, but chiefly, it seems, because it smacked of an attempt to exculpate the wrongdoers in her own country; had she not done so, she might herself have been open to charges of spreading the shame. In due course, she was to refine her argument into what has become one of the most penetrative phrases in all of philosophy's efforts to comprehend evil: *the banality of evil*.

In her magisterial 1964 book, *Eichmann in Jerusalem: A Report on the Banality of Evil* — her reportage and analysis of the trial of the Nazi bureaucrat Adolf Eichmann — Arendt profiled the archetypal functionary of the Nazi era. In writing it, she was at pains to stress that the pathology to be found in Eichmann arose in the specific setting of the totalitarian state established in Germany by the Nazis, and yet encapsulated the personality of the evildoer as an embodiment of every-dayness.

In her writings about Eichmann, Arendt delved deep into the question of evil as the potential reflex of 'normal' people. Although the world, including Germany, has managed to file the Nazi era as a kind of Hollywood-scripted conflict of bad guys and good guys, under Arendt's unremitting microscope it becomes something like an inevitability of a highly-developed post-Enlighten-ment, literate, self-referential, atheistic culture, in which there are only the laws created by the state. Nazism, we would prudently remember, unlike Bolshevism or Stalinism or Maoism, emerged in a 'modern', technocratic, democratic state.

Eichmann, as observed by Arendt, presented a new kind of problem. He was not 'evil' in the conventional sense, but in what seemed to be a novel way. He was evil, and yet he was also normal. His evildoing was of an everyday kind, yes, but more than that, his evil derived from his 'normality'. That meant that the kind of things he did might well be done by anyone. It might even mean that the more 'ordinary' the individual, the more likely he is to perpetrate such evils. Arendt noted, for example, that Eichmann seemed incapable of uttering a single sentence that wasn't a cliché. His evil arose from his denseness, his inability to think, which is to say, his inability to engage in a dialogue with himself. He uttered only words given to him by others. Another way of describing this might be to say that he was a man without a self, without an 'I'. He could only converse with himself in a language imported from outside, in a voice belonging to the world beyond himself. He had no internal sense of the absolute. His 'absolute' consisted in his duty to do what he was told.

'The sad truth.' Arendt wrote, 'is that most evil is done by people who never make up their minds to be good or evil.'

This is the great value of Arendt's work, and also the reason why we need to pay more rather than less attention to the particularities of the Nazi period: so that we may better understand them, so as to more easily spot them in other contexts, so as to turn 'never again' into a fact rather than a cliché. Perhaps one of the motivations behind the idea of sacralising the Holocaust is to conceal these possibilities from ourselves. Perhaps we fear that we cannot look squarely at Eichmann, the most 'ordinary' Nazi, because we fear that we might see ourselves. We shy away and leave the question as open or closed as it has always been. The 'banal' dimensions of evil remain distant, mysterious, because we became convinced that it remains unthinkable, which of course it does, though only because we choose not to think about it. This allows us to continue to believe that evil people are exceptional types of humanity, when, in fact, they may be almost the opposite: unexceptional to the point of dullness.

Is it not, then, to say the least, counterproductive to allow that experience and Arendt's insights into it to be fenced off from reality and stewarded by interests which, whatever their claim of entitlement to emphasise the Jewish wound, have no such right to block humanity from identifying early indicators of similar syndromes erupting in other contexts, and underscoring the parallels with prior events by way of alerting their fellows to the possibility of a looming recurrence?

Arendt's point was not as in the conventional response, at once exculpatory and hand-wringing: *We are all guilty.* If we are 'all guilty', then perhaps nobody is guilty? Is this the destination point of our courtesy towards the victims of past tyrannies? It is tempting to suspect so. Her point was that we are all *capable*, and therefore need to be on the lookout for early signs. It would, therefore, be foolish to allow ourselves to become blocked off — above all by ideological interests — from studying and rehearsing the lessons of history, or waylaid by dint of condescendingly imagining that our times have somehow (being too 'advanced', too 'modern', too 'enlightened') risen above such potentialities, entitling us to ignore the recurrence of signs and drifts that preceded the world's previous descending into the abyss.

Hannah Arendt was one of the great prophets of the twentieth century. She did not intend her books to be adornments on future smugness, or fossilised records of past barbarism. She intended them as warnings — as much to future peoples as future leaders. No one — *no one* — has the right to claim the history she excavated so brilliantly and claim to have the franchise on its exclusive interpretation. You might say that Mattie McGrath's comparison was . . . what? Lacking in proportion? Facile? Or perhaps *banal.* Perhaps that is precisely why we need to hear it.

Andreas Lombard, in his *First Things* article, cites Hannah Arendt: 'This guilt [of the Nazis], in contrast to all criminal guilt, oversteps and shatters any and all legal systems. . . . We are simply not equipped to deal on a human political level with a guilt that is beyond crime and an innocence that is beyond goodness and virtue.'

This was an understandable response in the moment that Hannah Arendt wrote those sentences. What had happened was radically different to anything that had happened before. But the very nature of Arendt's exploration, in particular with regard to Adolf Eichmann, opened up the very real possibility that such evil might henceforth become commonplace. There is a paradox here, then: She was alerting us to the nature of the unprecedented crime that, by virtue of occurring, could never again be regarded as unthinkable. What, now, might be the barrier, if barrier there might remain, to the Nazi crime being replicated or equalled or surpassed in its evildoing and consequences? One answer might be that the barrier or guarantee against recurrence resides in memory, in commemoration, in a determined refusal of amnesia. But if that remembering is constrained by an insistence that what is commemorated can never recur, then is this condition not counterproductive to the entire purpose of remembering?

What is it that validates the claim that the guilt of the Nazis will always remain 'beyond crime'? The methods of extermination? The number of the dead? Hitler's retroactively and tautologically repulsive moustache, which has become an exclamation mark in history? Is there a moral difference between a big moustache and a small one, or isn't that just a trick of looking through the wrong end of the telescope of Time? And can we not imagine a parallel reality in which that space-saver moustache might have become the height, if not the breadth, of fashion? (All it would have taken was for Germany to win the war and a few more years to have passed – if you doubt this, consider: Sinn Féin.)

Is it possible that the devil will contract only to manifest in forms that announce themselves as crude depictions of the evildoer? Do we think that all villains will laugh to announce themselves like the ones in spaghetti westerns? And if the evil of totalitarianism is deemed to be a peculiar eruption of the twentieth century, is there any reason to assume that its arc will not increase rather than the opposite?

Would it be necessary for our corrupted, power-crazed, sadistic leaders to parade in a row sporting Hitler-style moustaches before we could consider them capable of comparable crimes? Would mortality figures alone be insufficient? What about mass euthanasia? White coffins? What?

Yet, our culture now insists that it is so: We must not invoke the Nazi story, for to do so is by definition disproportionate and therefore disrespectful. It is, we are assured, unthinkable that anything remotely similar could be perpetrated by mild-mannered politicians in shiny grey suits, which opens up the odd circumstance that such politicians are about the only people who might nowadays, in present geopolitical conditions, attain the kind of power and opportunity to carry out such obscenities. But to seek by analogy with the conditions of 1930s Germany to warn of such a prospect is regarded as an improper appropriation of the Greatest Crime in History.

Can any of this be what Hannah Arendt intended to suggest? I think not.

In his 2019 *First Things* article, Andreas Lombard's central point was that the vanity of guilt leads to an inability to court forgiveness, either from your victims or from yourself, and this stymies the possibility of healing. This is important, and not irrelevant here. But more immediately vital is an understanding of how the power of the Metaphysically Singular Crime — perhaps 'crimes', since apartheid, colonialism, witch-hunting and slavery have, in certain (somewhat less fevered) ideological contexts, attained something like a comparable level of historical holiness — can be used to protect the perpetrators of potentially comparable crimes in the early days of their criminality. To deflect insinuations of similarity, and the attendant possibility of the alarm being successfully sounded, all the would-be tyrants need do is express outrage at the inappropriateness of the comparison and protest volubly at the implicit insult to those most grievously wronged by the prior crime insinuated as a comparator. Their accusers, who have sought to weaponise an unsurpassable crime, are instantly deemed far worse than those they accuse, irrespective of what facts may emerge to vindicate their concerns.

This creates not just a block on remembering but a kind of inoculation against vigilance. It means that the would-be criminals can turn the charge back on their accusers, who then become the true offenders, the sacrilegious opportunists who tried to misappropriate the Holocaust, apartheid, witch-hunts, the experience of slavery, *et cetera*, to a nefarious end. Thus, the putative (would-be?) perpetrators of comparable crimes are able to achieve immunity from criticism, or even general scrutiny, until late in the day — until, perhaps, it is too late to put a stop to their galloping. The only evils deemed to be capable of repetition are of the lesser-spotted type, and even these cannot be described or anticipated in the language that has already been used to describe the Metaphysically Singular Crime(s). Thus, the facts of Nazism, Communism, Imperialism, Neo-colonialism, become a kind of insurance policy against comparison. Rather than a guarantee against a recurrence, the greatest evils in history become prophecies of what has yet to befall us.

CHAPTER 18
WHIPNOSIS, PART I: LIFE AS TRANCE

22-03-2022

Something unprecedented — at least in scale — erupted in the world during the Covid ruse: the use by governments of behavioural psychology/mass entrancement as weapons of war against their own people.

As the first month of 2022 gathered pace as we moved towards the third calendar year of the fake pandemic, the determined stonewall of mainstream conversation was occasionally infringed upon by mutterings from the periphery of just about every Western country of a continuing die-off arising from the Covid vaccines. American insurance companies were talking of an unprecedented 40 per cent increase in life assurance claims; in Ireland, the national online death-notice site, RIP.ie, was showing an excess in mortality — in the Republic alone — equivalent to that suffered by the whole island in 30 years of the Troubles, and this for the single year of 2021. The same kind of pattern was whispered about by 'conspiracy theorists' in multiple European countries.

But nothing of this leached into the mainstream, where there was a continued push for mandatory vaccines, vaccination of children and penalties for citizens and parents who demurred.

A particular phenomenon was especially hard to ignore. All over the world, sporting events were being interrupted by the sudden collapse — sometimes fatal collapse — of athletes — footballers, tennis players, swimmers and so on — who had been at the top of their professional form. Yet, the mainstream contrived mainly to ignore this also, or sometimes to refer to it as something that had 'always happened every day'. This became an online meme: the everydayness of sudden death among athletes, the only advance warning for which was to be among the fittest of the fit.

The incidents continued and more and more people started to remark upon it. The former English top soccer player Matt Le Tissier made a number of passionate and articulate interventions in an attempt to draw public attention to the matter and was shunned and excoriated in equal measure.

Then, in early February this year, a crop of 'news' stories started to erupt in Western media about the growing risk of heart attacks, though not as a result of Covid vaccines. 'Energy bill price rise may cause heart attacks and strokes, says TV GP'; 'Rise in heart attacks attributed to pandemic-stress and poor diet'; 'Urgent Warning as 300,000 Brits living with stealth disease that could kill within 5 years'; 'More people are suffering stroke and heart disease after Covid, CT doctors say'; 'Heart disease: Reduce your child's risk'; 'Heart attack: The drink [alcoholic] that could trigger a "sudden" cardiac arrest'; 'Devoted football fans experience "dangerous" levels of stress'; 'How the weather is harming your health — from heart attacks to strokes and gout'; 'Does skipping breakfast increase your risk?'; 'Moving clocks forward an hour could be dangerous for millions of Brits with serious heart problems'.

To those on the outside of whatever is going on here, this is beyond bizarre. It seems to suggest that the media have started to treat their audiences as though at the intellectual level of children struggling to put their first thoughts into spoken sentences. It suggests a level of either condescension or insight that is startling, to say the least.

Why 'insight'? Because the media has, over the past 24 months, acquired a by now almost instinctual sense of how the public will react to different kinds of stimuli. They know that x happens when they do y. Three years ago, such a rash of stories would have provoked mystification and hilarity, but now they are likely to provoke — in a significant minority at least — credulity and even anxiety, as people who have fretted for two years about a virus with a 99.98 per cent survival rate now start to worry about their hearts and how they might be driving them too hard.

This cannot in any sense be described as normative, and yet, in some odd context, it now has the feel of something 'normal'. Somehow, seeing one of these headlines, you do not, as you might not so long ago, get the feeling that this is going too far, that now their scam will be rumbled, that no one could possibly believe that all these stories on a single theme, could suddenly erupt out of nowhere and be taken seriously. Somehow, though you may not register exactly why, you know that none of this is going to happen, that most people will either glaze over or make an appointment with their GP, understanding that they can expect to see more of this kind of story on the legacy media over the coming days and weeks.

This poses several separate but related questions: Why do so many people accept such nonsense without question?; Why does almost everyone else regard what is happening as unexceptional or at least unexceptionable?; Why have most of us become so defeatist about the chances of challenging this kind of irrationality?

All this is really symptomatic of the playing out of a particular kind of relationship between media and audience fostered over the past two years, in which the malleability of a significant number of viewers/readers/listeners came more and more to be relied upon absolutely, and a significant secondary quotient counted on to shrug and decide that this is just the way things are. It is as if the media are implicitly aware that, in order to conceal something that would appear to be obvious to any semi-sentient observer, they require only to insinuate an 'explanation' that is no more plausible than the storyline logic of a fairytale. Yet, this is not how things used to be. Some people were gullible, yes, but not *this* gullible, or at least not enough of them to make this kind of 'journalism' even marketable.

A change has entered in, some kind of factor that was not there before. It is as if journalists and editors are aware that they deal with a state or condition in at least a significant minority which somehow enables or facilitates such 'explanations' to pass muster without undue scepticism. What sort of state or condition might we be talking about?

Almost two years ago, I began having regular discussions with a hypnotherapist friend, John Anthony, about the possibility that what we might be dealing with in the Covid cult was a form of mass hypnosis. We exchanged many emails and spoke several times on the phone, and arising from those exchanges, I wrote an article titled 'On Viral Entrancement' that appeared in May 2020 on what was then the UK website *Lockdown Sceptics* (now *The Daily Sceptic*).

The conversations between John Anthony and me continued over the period of the Covid psyop, and I have more recently spoken to some other hypnotists on the topic with a view to deepening my own understanding. This three-part chapter series is the result. In it, I examine, with the help of John Anthony and others, the concepts of mass hypnosis/mass formation, the effects of narcissistic personality disorders on modern politics (as demonstrated over the past two years) and the use of these techniques to create a pseudo-reality which obliterates both actual reality and any possibility of successful truth-telling about it.

More than a few people I've spoken to on the subject over the past couple of years have themselves expressed scepticism at the idea that it is possible to hypnotise whole populations, or quasi-populations, all at once. They accept that something called 'mass formation' — as described by, for example, the Belgian psychologist Mattias Desmet, may exist as a real phenomenon, but think it fanciful to suggest that this might amount to hypnosis. They draw a line, therefore, before the notion that the 'lockstep' effect achieved by the creeps on behalf of the Combine in the course of the Covid scam might have been effected by mass entrancement. One correspondent observes that 'we don't need to seek out esoteric theories for how people moved into lockstep. Computerisation, and consequently globalisation, are a sufficient explanation for the destruction of intelligent communities.'

This observation resonated with my recollection of my own initial thoughts on the hypnosis connection. It did indeed seem unnecessarily esoteric, at best a metaphor of some kind, even a kind of rhetorical disparagement of the general intelligence. But, as I delved into the matter, it seemed to me that there was something of benefit here, something additional that cast some light on certain aspects of what had been happening — for example, the way the 'normie' population has seemed to become manipulable to the extent of coming to 'unknow' certain things, when the wind changed, that were already public knowledge. There are thousands of examples, but randomly you might think of the way alleged Covid deaths would be revised downwards (the 'with' and 'from' distinction), and yet, within days, the old, manipulated statistics would be back on the leader-board. There seemed in this to be the leveraging of some form of capacity for inculcated amnesia, which had no immediately apparent explanation. This, I learned, was a symptom of hypnosis.

Within weeks of the launching of the biggest political psyop in human history, John Anthony wrote to me: 'I would like to throw some light on exactly how one gaslights or attempts to gaslight an entire country into submission for whatever nebulous agenda may be the reason for the manipulation. One could use the words "psychopathy" and "narcissism" and the myriad associated language and phrases, but it is important here to understand that the intention is not to label or class any individual as such. Here, the whole emphasis should be upon the dynamic, the *modus operandi* used in these relationships, and hopefully, if I am able for this task, then anyone will be able to spot the emerging patterns of control and even be able to clearly forecast the next hand played by the manipulators or the architects of control.'

I started to probe around the edges of what is a vast and complex subject. My biggest questions centred on how it was possible, having established the circumstance for the creation of a trance, and having set it in train, to enable the hypnotist to communicate with the person in a manner that seemed to occur outside of conscious reality. I had seen hypnosis done on TV, and even was (I think) briefly hypnotised myself on one occasion, but I don't think I had any sense of being in an altered state at any stage. And I presume that most people who have had the experience would say the same. It certainly seemed, from what I had observed about the Covid rollout, that people received messages that appeared to become compartmentalised in their minds, and then pulled out under certain conditions — perhaps an argument with a sceptic, for example — but that otherwise this programming was subject most of the time to a form of suspension, perhaps even amnesia.

The most coherent and consistent public voice on these topics in the world in recent times has been the Belgian psychologist Dr Mattias Desmet, about whom I have written repeatedly over the past year. The earlier chapter, *Covid Totalitarianism: The Deification of Error,* provides a detailed account of his perspectives and analysis.

Desmet's analysis is not primarily focussed on the phenomenon of hypnosis as such, but rather on 'mass formation' — a rather larger context of manipulation into which hypnosis slots as a kind of SIM card. He has several times asserted that hypnosis is the same as mass formation, by which I think he means that hypnoidal techniques are central, though as he himself has been at pains to outline, mass formation involves much more than the creation of a trance state, and is rather more difficult to achieve.

As I understand his position, he is saying that mass hypnosis is used as part of a much larger programme of mind control in which the individual is rendered subject to the will of the collective. In the terms outlined by Gustave le Bon more than a century ago, this means that the individual has exited his own personal psychology and become part of the psychology of the mob, to which, once entranced, he is entirely subservient. Desmet says that people under this form of mass hypnosis will be prepared to sacrifice anything to the cause they have signed up to — 'even their own children.' People under the influence of mass/crowd formation, he says, 'are not aware of the egoistic disadvantages they suffer. Someone in this situation can have everything taken away from him — even his own life. He will not notice it.

'You can take his health away, his wealth away. You can take everything from him. He may lose his future, his freedom — he will not be aware of it.'

Asked if there is any link between this and intelligence (or lack thereof), he replies: 'Not at all,' continuing: 'And that's a strange thing: One of the major characteristics of a crowd or a mass is that everybody becomes as intelligent, or — maybe better — as *stupid.* And that applies to highly intelligent people as well as less intelligent people. That has been studied in the 19th century, very extensively. It was very clear that even the most intelligent people were completely blind and completely insensitive to rational argumentation, for instance. Masses are only sensitive to strong visual images and to repetition of, time and time again, the same message. And also to the presentation of numbers and graphs and statistics. If you present numbers in a visual way, it will have a huge impact on the masses.'

The willingness of people to sacrifice everything — *anything* — as though for some higher ideal, is something we have observed in certain unfathomable contexts in the past year. An especially disturbing feature of the 'vaccine' deaths phenomenon has been the way some parents, having lost one of their children to the mRNA 'therapy', have fallen in with the murderous objectives of medical and political authorities in dismissing any possibility of a connection between the 'vaccine' and the death. This has presented an objectively incomprehensible demeanour of resignation in the face of what, for most people, would be the unthinkable: the unnecessary death of a child in the pursuit of tenuous public health objectives.

Under the spell of mass/crowd formation, says Desmet, 'the field of attention gets really very narrow. People only see what the narrative indicates, and that's something typical for hypnosis as well. When somebody is hypnotised, he will only be aware of the part of reality the hypnotist focuses on, and that's exactly the same in mass formation . . . someone is only aware of the part of reality — both cognitively and emotionally — that is indicated by the hypnotising or by the mass narrative. And that's the reason why people don't seem to be aware of the collateral damage of the measures. In one way or another, people know somewhere that there is collateral damage of the measures, but it has no cognitive or emotional impact. That's the problem. There is no psychological energy attached to these representations, and that's why they have no impact at all.

'You see exactly the same thing in hypnosis. The attention is so focussed on one point, through a simple hypnotic procedure, that you can cut straight through people's flesh and bones — literally. You can make someone radically insensitive to pain to the extent that you can perform a surgical operation on this person — you can cut straight through the breastbone. The person will not notice it. That shows the power of hypnotic procedures — and also of mass formation.'

Historians and psychologists trying to get to grips with what happened in Nazi Germany and the Soviet Union had never encountered anything like it before. Mass formation, Desmet says, 'grasps people in the core of their being,' which is why totalitarianism can command such an extreme degree of power and influence over both crowds and individuals.

There are distinctions between hypnosis and mass formation, but the lines or commonalities are not clear, even in the interviews I have watched with Dr. Desmet. About 80 per cent of people, he says, are liable to become subject to hypnosis, but only about 30 per cent tend to succumb to mass formation. This seems to imply that mass formation is harder to implement, and yet requires to capture a relatively small fraction of the overall population in order to succeed. This makes sense in that, whereas hypnosis at the personal level is a reasonably straightforward procedure, a multiplicity of factors — susceptibility to propaganda, high emotional sensitivity, vivid imagination — must coincide to inculcate the individual into a mass formation.

French psychologist Gustave Le Bon was the first to talk about 'psychological crowds', which he diagnosed as forming a single being, responding always to unconscious thoughts, and conforming to laws of mental unity. The consciousness bestowed by membership of a crowd can be transformative of the person, according to Le Bon, putting individual members in possession of 'a sort of collective mind which makes them feel, think and act in a manner quite differently from that in which each individual would feel, think and act were that person in a state of isolation.' In a psychological crowd, individual personality disappears, brain activity is replaced by reflex activity, a lowering of intelligence, provoking a complete transformation of sentiments, which may be better or worse than those of the crowd's constituent members.

Le Bon elaborates: 'There are certain ideas and feelings which neither come into being, nor transform themselves into acts, except in the case of individuals forming a crowd. The psychological crowd is a provisional "being," formed of heterogeneous elements which for a moment are combined, exactly as the cells which constitute a living body form by reunion a new being which displays characteristics very different from each of the cells singularly.'

The relationship or interconnection of the hypnoidal world to 'reality' appears to be somewhat analogous to the relationship/interconnection of the dream to the waking state. Sometimes, I have noticed, I will emerge from a dream imagining that, for example, something significant in reality has suddenly been resolved. That is to say, among other things, that the resolution achieved in the dream seems, on first emergence, to be germane to my life in the actual world. Only with time — minutes, usually — does the dream come to seem alien.

We should remain mindful that those who have imposed the appalling conditions and circumstances of the past two years have had access, above all, to the very best of what behavioural psychology can offer. This, far more obviously than it has seemed to be a biological crisis, has been a psychological operation. The orchestrators of the public mood — the politicians, scientists, medical experts — have clearly been able to impose some kind of spell, if only in the first instance to be contemplated in metaphorical terms, in order to effect their will upon whole populations. It is not outlandish to suggest that they somehow managed to impose a trance, which — perhaps intermittently — transformed reality into a kind of dream world in which, as with actual dreams, nonsense comes to seem perfectly sensible and normal while it is happening.

There's a rather excellent video on the web called 'Mass Hypnosis Exposed (by a Hypnotist)', made by a Scottish hypnotist called Brian Halliday, in which he compares what the UK government and health experts have been doing for the past two years with his own stage show of a few years back when he was working as a professional hypnotist entertainer.

Halliday was a professional hypnotist for over 25 years, much of that time working as a fulltime stage hypnotist. He was astonished when the pandemic first kicked off to observe that the government were using almost the exact same techniques he had used while working in theatres.

In his relatively brief exposition, he zeroes in on the actual techniques hypnotists use and shows how they were adapted to the Covid scam, exposing some of the techniques used to psychologically manipulate people to follow governmental instructions and even programme people to get angry at those who didn't. For instance, he explains how he used hypnosis to create a sense of chaos in an audience before his performance, keeping everybody waiting 10 or 15 minutes after the time he was due to go on, maintaining the auditorium in total darkness before breaking the tension with strobe lighting just before walking onstage. In the same way, he claims, the drivers of the Covid scam have created chaos by inventing absurd regulations, constantly chopping and changing the restrictions and providing nonsensical explanations for various aspects of the 'measures'. If you subject people to a period of chaos and confusion, he says, they will do almost anything to relieve it. If you give them a 'way out', they will accept it. Hence, the unprecedented 'vaccine' take-up.

The London-based hypnotherapist Erkan Bilgi believes that, while hypnosis is somewhat different from mass formation, hypnoidal techniques can be adapted for the purpose of manipulating whole populations at once. It is, he says, the antithesis of therapeutic hypnosis, which seeks to achieve positive results by tapping into the individual unconscious. Mass formation, in his descriptions, appears to involve a kind of reverse-engineering of this therapeutic process. He agrees with Halliday that confusion-making is a central element of the hypnotist's art, though this can be used for both good and ill.

'Watch out for sentences that are intentionally made to cause confusion,' he says. 'These sometimes have a piece of information which the audience unwittingly accepts, as the conscious brain is too busy trying to make sense of what was just said. This technique is often used by conmen. For example, if I ask how much is that slice of cake and rather than say, "Three pounds fifty," the seller says, "Three hundred and fifty pennies and worth every penny!" — or, "Three pounds and worth every ounce!" — the message of "worth every penny/ounce" is less likely to be questioned.'

Hypnosis, under both the individual and collective headings, achieves an altered state, operating on the subconscious, which is where much of our unconscious 'thinking' takes place, adrift from logic and rationality. 'It is a kind of an altered state,' Erkan Bilgi says, 'but we go into a kind of trance state very often throughout the day anyway. Maybe the best way to explain it is if we think of it like an iceberg — the bit above the water is the conscious mind, and the submerged part is the subconscious. The subconscious is vastly bigger than the conscious mind, obviously, because a lot of our experiences are things that we pick up without really noticing. We often think of a trance as a sleep-like or zombie-like state, but actually, it's much more common than that. We experience it frequently throughout the day at varying levels. Sometimes, it can be a driving trance when we're going somewhere familiar, where the time seems to just vanish. Or the daydreaming moments when having a coffee or even, some would say, while hysterically reacting to a perceived threat. We go in and out of these trance-like states. For example, when we're daydreaming, we're thinking of a holiday we've had or something we're going to be doing later — our conscious mind dissolves. And hence, we can delve into our subconscious experience. So when we hypnotise people, what we're trying to do is just dissolve the conscious mind in the sense that we're trying to stop that rational thinking by making them relaxed or using some other techniques, like getting them to focus on one object for a long enough time, trying to get the unconscious mind to express itself. Hypnosis — in a therapeutic setting, or even on a stage setting, when it's done intentionally — if you have somebody's attention, you can lead them into a trance. It doesn't have to be a formal setting, like, "Please close your eyes and think of this, or relax and concentrate on this." It can happen in a conversational sense as well. It can be just a constant stream and I can jump from one topic to the next, and the speech pattern can sometimes trigger a light trance. And it can be done intentionally.'

'The other thing to note,' says Bilgi, 'is that the actual depth of trance isn't necessarily the most important thing for suggestions to take root. You can still do the same work by other methods. Getting someone into a trance-like state is useful, but on many occasions it's not essential in order for people to accept suggestions if you know how to structure those suggestions well. There is a model in hypnosis that states that a deeper trance state allows more direct suggestions to be accepted. However, if your suggestions are indirect, there's less need for a deep trance, and all you need is their attention.'

Bilgi's work as a hypnotherapist often involves confronting some dark association in the subconscious of a client — perhaps a phobia, some traumatic event from the past, a suppressed memory — and lightening it, creating new associations to drown out the old ones. With a spider phobia, for example, he would tackle it by trying to give the person more 'positive' ideas about spiders.

'When we do this, we have to involve as many of the senses as possible, so rather than just visual, we'll try to have some kind of kinaesthetic element — the emotional side of how you feel when you see this particular thing. It may be what you'd like to say to yourself, what you'd hear, and of course if it involves any sound or taste, we try to involve those too. We try to create memories that the subconscious mind will jump to when you've had any kind of trigger to that particular object or event. And if we can make that as powerful as possible, then that'll be the go-to thing.

'And another thing is we can actually change memories. Memories are a kind of plastic thing, a malleable thing. We tend to think of memories as quite solid, but they're not. If you think about witness statements — they try to take them as early as possible because over a period of time, details will change. Every time we recall a memory, we tend to change it, and it gets stored again in a new way, so it becomes slightly different from the original. It may be more intense or less intense. So, if you can recall an event, we try to get the subconscious mind to re-store that in a different way. So, if it was a negative event, we'll try to make it less colourful, more grey. It depends on how that person recalls that particular event.'

So perhaps one could say something along the lines that the 'trance' seems, from within, to be real. And externally, the person appears not to change. As in a dream, perhaps the 'material' experienced in the hypnoidal state is fundamentally as in reality: the logic and personnel of your life in the real world, albeit mixed up, though not in a way that generates an alert. Hypnosis, in much the same way, appears to open up a kind of parallel conduit of understanding and, in situations like a propaganda-generated hoax, renders palatable a series of imposed false understandings that manifest almost in the way of hallucinations, while seeming beyond question in terms of their factuality or meanings.

The hypnoidal subject remains himself and yet becomes, in a sense, a stranger who is already removed to a different plane. He is there and not there, present and absent. Seen like this, we begin to intuit why people we know have been acting so strangely for the past two years. Multiply the thought of one hypnotised person by a hundred or a thousand or a million — or 200 million — and it becomes quite terrifying. And that is approximately what we may be dealing with.

It also explains why it is impossible to reason or argue with someone in such a state. He or she is simply *not there*. He may argue, answer back, but will do so in the logic of the trance, a factor that is unlikely to betray itself fully as there will be fragments of real understandings mixed up with the hallucinatory material.

Emerging from a trance is a bit like coming out of a dream, says Bilgi. 'When you're in the dream, everything seems real, but once you've woken up, you realise that that was a dream. With the dream, however, because anything can happen basically, it's very easy to spot. However, when you're in a trance, even though you knew it was a trance, and it was a mainly pleasant experience, and you went through things, building a reality that you may want to work towards, the subconscious doesn't see it the same way. The subconscious mind treats it as real, to a certain point. The difference between real memories and imaginary memories is mostly the detail. So when we have a real memory, we have much more information. We know how we got there, we know what happened after, so there's a sequence, and it fits into our life somewhere, like a movie. Also the details that we see in the memory are very specific as well, so we'll notice much more detail in terms of what we see — the colours that we see. But when we try to create a memory — if I was to say, if you can just create a memory of going to

Disneyland yesterday, then, assuming you hadn't been to Disneyland yesterday, you can work on it and you can create an image in your mind, but it would be lacking in information. It doesn't have to be a whole series but it has to have consistency. It also has to have a level of depth. If we met every single day and I asked you to build on the "memory" in your mind over a period of time, it would come to seem real over time. And even though consciously you'll know that the memory doesn't exist, it will seem real enough, as if you'd actually been there. So you can build the memory and add as much detail to it as possible —so [it will include] how you felt, seeing the world through your own eyes, as a moving image rather than a static image, noticing the colours of things that you wouldn't normally notice, people's expressions *et cetera*. You really build this image up so it would seem very, very real. And you could almost convince the mind that it was real. You do the opposite with real memories: You take away information, you make things a bit more blurry, you'd make things a little bit more in the distance, black and white, *et cetera*. Take away the sound, replace it with something else. So that's the kind of thing we use in therapy.'

The mass formation manipulator does much the same thing, building up the 'memory' or understanding, piece by piece. A deadly virus. Airborne. Jumps up to two metres from nose to nose . . . *et cetera*. The picture is built up incrementally: 'If you get someone to agree to a small change in belief, it becomes much easier to get them to agree to a bigger belief change that they would not have agreed to at the outset. Agree to this small thing, and you've signed up to a belief system and identity without even realising it. So, if we agree to a three-week lockdown to flatten the curve, then obviously, we believe that lockdowns work. If we agree to "high-risk groups" being jabbed with an experimental drug, then we believe that the jabs are effective. So it becomes ever-increasing steps, and if a step doesn't work, then we just go back and start again.'

Words are crucial. 'The mind is always trying to make sense of the information coming in — if it regards it as relevant — and it does this by making associations and by using reference points. So, for example, when someone says, "I don't want to have the jab," a very powerful yet manipulative response might be to say, "You've had vaccines in the past, haven't you?" Words are hugely important, which is why it's not left to individual politicians or commentators to string sentences together. Rather, the best and most powerful sentences or descriptions are formulated and passed on to be repeated to the population. In fact, repetition is hugely powerful on its own. Again, a reason the mainstream media channels are so hypnotic. It's not hypnosis in a traditional sense. But it does create the same thing: powerful images, make the person become engrossed in a situation as much as possible.'

Paradoxically, even in the context of mass formation, he says, the trance is, by definition, individualised. 'I have done a group hypnosis session with actually quite a large number of people — in an auditorium with about 80 people, and we did a hypnotic induction. When we're doing hypnosis for a group, you want to be working towards positive memories. Once they've closed their eyes, they're not working as a group, you know; though, if the hypnotherapist is very skilled, then the suggestions can still seem very personal. So once you've got their eyes closed, they're now becoming detached from everyone around them, if you're successful. So it doesn't really matter that you're in a group — of five, ten or a thousand, it doesn't really matter. They would experience something as if in a room alone.'

Like any form of hypnosis, mass entrancement depends on the leveraging of several inter-related conditions in the subject(s): heightened emotion; focused attention; impairment of peripheral awareness; and an elevated imaginative state — all conditions contributing to vastly increased suggestibility. As we shall see in a subsequent chapter, the Covid-19 operation harnessed the dynamics of archetypal relationships between narcissists/psychopaths (politicians) and co-dependent submissives (citizens). Such processes, formulated with the assistance of highly practised psychologists and other experts in mind control, are capable of exploiting both individual psychological pathologies and complex understandings of dysfunctional family dynamics to expose and manipulate weaknesses in human persons and relationships so as to isolate citizens from one another.

'Imagination,' says Bilgi, 'is a major aspect of hypnosis and suggestion patterns. In fact, rather than tell people facts, it's better to get them absorbed in an alternate reality, and by creating a vision in the mind, the new reality can begin to take hold. It's the unconscious mind that makes more than 90 per cent of our decisions and we follow this up by finding conscious justifications to rationalise the decision we've already made. So the idea of a rational decision is ultimately an illusion.'

With an appropriate script and deliberate mimicry of well-remembered charismatic leaders of the past — *a touch of JFK, a soupcon of Churchill* — even the most pedestrian politician can affect a sufficiency of charisma or gravitas to seduce his audience into the zone wherein to weave word pictures and teleport his listeners to a place of collective imagining. A well-established mood of siege or crisis is sufficient to inveigle even stronger-minded middle-ground observers to join in. By affecting empathy, rapport, a sense of common purpose, the 'hypnotist' guides his subjects towards the desired frame of mind. He seeks access to the unconscious so as to remove each member of his audience to a common place: the herd mind, in which he knows they can all come to share approximately the same outlooks, so that henceforth they can be summoned there by signs and triggers while remaining in their armchairs.

TV creates an ideal medium via which to conduct this form of hypnosis, not least because the news comes sandwiched between movies and soap operas, which engage the imaginative and emotional elements of the mind. These, maintained by fictionalised versions of reality, provide the heightened state that renders the subject amenable to being lured into a kind of trance. Once achieved, the trance can be reactivated at will in anyone whose attention, primed on fictional narratives, remains in this state of focused imaginative attention, being highly prone to easy emotional arousal. The purpose is to tap into that part of the subconscious dealing with emotions. When in a self-induced trance, in the grip of rage, hatred, fear, anxiety, sadness, worry, envy, greed, self-ishness, humans tend to become cut off from their thinking brains and thereby susceptible to adopting a locked-in, limited view of reality. In the lockdown episode, fear was used as the chief emotional trigger to further the entrancement process.

'You have general fears, of course, that people experience,' Erkan Bilgi explains. 'In therapeutic settings, what you'd do to help someone dissociate from a bad memory, you would get them to see it from a distance in the third person, as an observer. A nice safe distance so that they can see without any threat to themselves. And that way, they can see what's going on in that traumatic event. But they're detached. Now, if you're a poor therapist, or you wanted to do something harmful, then you would ask them to go back as the first person to experience everything again through their own eyes. Now, that would be a very dangerous thing from the therapist's point of view because they could have what is called an abreaction. They could have a reaction that is the same as they had that particular time when the original event occurred, because what they're doing is they're re-living that memory again, and having the same reaction. So, if you were to do it maliciously, of course, you want to tap into those fears. If someone were to use hypnotherapy in this way — say in the media — you would go back to any events that were traumatic for the collective memory. You can use the virus, but you can also connect it to, say, Mad Cow's Disease, or any traumatic images from the past. You can build on the fear that people experience. So whether the thing is real or not, it doesn't matter, because the memory's still there. At the beginning of the coronavirus thing, there were images of Chinese people collapsing. Now everybody knows that that was made up. It wasn't real, but the memory's still there, so that impact will always be there. People not being able to breathe in hospitals — that's going to be a subconscious fear because nobody's going to address that.'

In a mass formation, presumably, the constant members need to come out of the 'trance' intermittently to go about their normal lives. Is there some trigger that takes them out and throws them back in again? Does it work off the emotion — when their ire is fired up again, they go back into the trance — is that it?

'In hypnotherapy, the more frequently you see a client, the more easily they go into trance, because of the turn of my voice, the surroundings — they know that they're almost in a hypnotic place anyway. They've experienced trance in that place many times, so once they step into that same environment, it becomes much easier for them. And those are the triggers to get into that state, an emotional state completely. This is why certain sentence patterns are used very frequently in statements. So, we've already accepted that we don't talk about "SARS-CoV-2," we talk about "Covid." Everything is "Covid"! So we don't talk about "infections," we talk about "cases." And of course, "cases" are emotionally connected to . . . we imagine somebody being in hospital, attached to a ventilator or whatever, because that's how they're being manipulated. So whether we're conscious of it or not, words trigger images, and if those images are very, very powerful, then without realising somehow, emotionally we have that response. In the media, that's what they do. They try to give us these images and connect them to sentences.

'The New Normal, to me, for example, instantly would have images of people walking around in masks, keeping their distance, empty trains, paying by card, never by cash. So I don't have to think about it, because they're the images that have been given to me. But it's important that these phrases are used very, very frequently, and prominently. So, any variations of this . . . they wouldn't be called something like a "New Reality" or something. It will always be called the New Normal. You can't break that pattern. So that's the trigger. If it's written down, it will always be written in the same way. So, Covid is always written in capital letters. That's how we're used to seeing it, and that's what fires it. If we see it in lower-case letters, it would not be the same kind of firing-off mechanism. So that's very, very useful from the media's viewpoint, and I'm sure they know that. We hear the same phrases coming from different people. That's very intentional.'

'The potential uses of Cognitive Hypnotherapy,' Erkan Bilgi maintains, 'go way beyond what many people associate it with. Ultimately, the aim is not just to help cure clients of their fears and addictions, but to empower them so that they can continue their life believing in greater possibilities and equipping them with the tools to fulfil their goals.' In the mass formation model, however, something like the same process appears to work using negative emotions — anger, fear *et cetera*.

Bilgi explains how the subconscious adopts stratagems to protect the person from experiencing memories or negative emotions that might cause upset or damage. One such is the fight-or-flight mechanism — essentially a protective mechanism activated by the unconscious, and which activates here to remove the person from potentially harmful emotions. Once engaged, the fight-or-flight mechanism exhibits vivid physical symptoms, all of them evolutionary in nature: narrowing of vision, quickening blood pressure, heart going into overdrive, digestive system closing down. These are self-protective responses, but prolonged they can cause intense damage to the person and the person's body. This provides an example of the reverse-engineering process: the use of fear tactics in mass formation propaganda can cause huge sections of a population to go into fight-or-flight mode, thus incurring the symptoms evolution has provided to protect and preserve, but here used in tandem with fear-mongering techniques to keep the population in an enhanced state of fear and stress. Erkan Bilgi says that a lot of his clients have, of late, been coming to him in a heightened state of anxiety — deeply injurious to their general health and immune functions — which he traces to this syndrome.

'The problem,' he says, 'is when we stay in that particular response for a very long time, it becomes very harmful to the body. The focussed attention on the danger makes everything around us invisible. If we're focussed on the danger of, for instance, the virus, then we're unable to appreciate everything else that's going on around us — the beauty of nature, the good relationships that we might have, anything positive in our life, because we're totally fixated on this perceived danger. So that's also quite an interesting thing that's going on at the moment — people that live in this harmful state, they're also having hormonal changes, there's more cortisol in their systems, so it's more harmful to them.

'To do this intentionally is very possible. Of course, from a therapeutic point of view you wouldn't want to do it. But if you had the opposite intention, it's very possible. If I were to do this in a trance, in a hypnotic state, what I would want to do really is fire up any fears that the client had, and you can tap into those just by asking, and you don't even have to ask.'

The Covid scamdemic was pulled off and maintained by a process of mass entrancement perpetrated largely by the media, leaving many people — a majority of most affected populations — terrified and unable to apply logic or reason to what they were able to see with their own eyes. Everyone who has been awake or has awakened knows a dozen people they regard as intelligent — good friends, in some instances — who have become deeply embedded in the deception, not alone unable to extricate themselves from the general terror but actually unwittingly behaving as marshals of Covid enforcement, scolding fellow citizens who are not wearing masks, engaging in bizarre public elbow dances on encountering acquaintances, and reacting with embarrassment and suspicion when they meet a dissenter, to whom they react as though to a knife-wielding maniac.

These conditions were achieved by months of persistent, repetitive messaging wrapped up in terror mantras and veiled threats. The scam was imposed through the use of subtle and not so subtle remote mesmerism, neuro-linguistic programming and saturation coverage of an almost entirely falsified narrative to effect a form of mass hypnosis that left only a small minority of Western populations — perhaps 10 per cent — completely unaffected. Mattias Desmet's analysis incorporates an additional 40 per cent middle-ground that 'goes along to get along' and whose constituent members are difficult to tell from the 30 per cent who are completely brainwashed. In Ireland, for certain, these figures are more likely to be 40 per cent and 50 per cent.

How that tiny few escaped indoctrination and entrancement is itself something of a mystery, not to say a miracle. Perhaps many of them had long since stopped reading, watching or listening to legacy media, thus acquiring immunity to what is actually the true 'virus': the industrial mendacity of mainstream 'journalism', which in effect constructed an alternative reality into which the propaganda that constituted virtually all of the scamdemic narrative was made to seem like iron fact, like the sky above and the solid ground below — as far beyond questioning as anything utterly false could possibly become.

CHAPTER 19
WHIPNOSIS, PART II: NARCISSISTS IN LOCKSTEP

06-03-2022

Covid exposed the pathological personalities of politicians. While pandering for electoral reasons to the concerns of 'normal' people, these actors harbour contempt for those who are not like them.

E veryone knows about the 'lone tyrannical psychopath' in history — your Stalin, your Hitler, your Pol Pot — whose apparently pathological personality draws an entire people to itself in the errand of destruction, and, in the process, destroys the people as well as himself. We are familiar also with the incidence of the psychopathic group — usually gravitating to and surrounding such a figure — the Party, the Brownshirts, the Khmer Rouge — to whom the psychopathic tendencies appear somehow to be transmitted intact in the interests and purpose of evildoing. The Covid Project, however, brought us a new concept: an entire generation of political leaders, most of whom had come to notice only for their mediocrity, transforming into — or *appearing* to transform into — psychopaths all at once, adopting the same threatening *mien*, using the same menacing language — indeed the same sentences and phrases — to bully their own peoples into accepting the deletion of freedom and the indefinite suspension of their lives, lying ceaselessly in the same way, constantly contradicting themselves and each other in the same ways, and, above all, appearing to take the same extreme degree of satisfaction, if not pleasure, from the sudden alterations in their personalities under the protection of their unity and the pretence of a good cause.

From April 2020, I was in touch with the Irish hypnotherapist John Anthony, who, from the outset, characterised what was happening as the use of hypnotic and NLP techniques by politicians who were either themselves narcissists or following a narcissistically-directed protocol. Narcissism, he assured me, might be the watchword and the common driving attribute of the implementation of the Covid agenda. As in the arena of romantic/sexual interplay, the narcissist in political life is a predator who sets out to deceive for his own gratification and gain. Anthony described how these traits translate from private to public sphere, to create what has since emerged as the signature political phenomenon of the Time of Covid. The people were subjected to the frog-boiling strategy: 'two weeks to flatten the curve,' followed by two years of fear-mongering, moral blackmail and plain tyranny.

Psychopathy, sociopathy and narcissism present on a graduating scale in reverse order of gravity, all three embracing similar conditions of solipsism, diminished or absence of empathy, shallow emotions, and lack of conscience. Though frequently used interchangeably, and exhibiting several common symptoms, they are clinically treated as different disorders. Of the three, narcissism is the most treatable because, unlike the psychopath or sociopath, the narcissist may develop a capacity to experience remorse or empathy. The narcissist is also less prone to violence than the other two types, which are sometimes jointly referred to under the heading 'Anti-Social Personality Disorder'. Sociopathy is environmentally transmitted, whereas psychopathy is innate, or at least hardwired following some traumatic episode.

In many psychopaths, sociopaths and narcissists, the tendency towards manipulating others is an almost essential recourse for a personality that, in all three instances, will be afflicted by pathological egotism. Compelling others to think and experience reality in like manner to themselves provides these people with a degree of relief which might otherwise be unavailable.

It is not always straightforward to place a line around narcissism that separates it cleanly from the other strains. In many instances, perhaps, the narcissist does not 'develop' to full psychopathy because of absence of opportunity or deficit of ambition. People are different. Many with non-violent antisocial personality disorders live their lives without damaging anyone outside their intimate circles.

Psychopaths and sociopaths account for about four per cent of the world's population — enough to deliver at least one or two such creatures into the relatively intimate circles of most 'normal' citizens. One of the peculiarities of these conditions is that, whereas they have been profoundly analysed by many experts, their nature remains culturally hermetic beyond the scope of direct experience. The ideological depiction of evil — from either side of various lines — clouds the true nature of the phenomenon when it manifests in the public sphere, so that people think in crude terms of political evildoing in a kind of spaghetti western frame of reference, in which the Bad Guys are the ones with the bad moustaches.

In his summer 2021 paper, *The Year of the Narcissistic Agenda, MAYHEM and MADNESS, March 2020 to June 2021 — Hysteria, Hypnosis, NLP and the Programming of a Nation,* John Anthony describes in exhaustive terms the outcome of this insidious campaign in Ireland: an entire population 'persuaded, enticed or influenced to lock up and isolate our elderly, close our businesses, restrict our movements, close our churches, neglect our dying, negate all our traditions including the shaking of hands and hugging, putting face masks on our children and isolating them from their families and friends, even closing down access to nature walks, beaches and forest parks for those who were privileged to be allowed outside their doors.' His objective was to sketch out a model put together from his own observations in the hope of conveying the strategies employed in the 'psychological war' waged to achieve this unprecedented set of outcomes.

The narcissist we speak of here is a chameleon — he (or she) changes colour to suit the environment, playing whatever role is appropriate to the person or persons he has decided to target. But all this occurs superficially: There is 'nobody home.' The narcissist is emotionally immature, but capable of hiding this. He is intelligent up to a point. He possesses characteristics of charisma and seeming confidence that others find enviable. He craves admiration, lacks empathy and is given to fantasy and grandiose gestures. He seeks, above all, control over others. The narcissist, writes Anthony, believes himself special and unique, capable of being understood by 'other special or high-status people or institutions.' He or she is motivated primarily by self-interest, but likes to be able to clothe this in spurious virtue and pseudo-morality.

These characteristics profile virtually every single political leader on the contemporary global scene. Indeed, one might observe that these appear to be essential qualifications, when one considers Boris Johnson, Leo Varadkar, Micheál Martin, Justin Trudeau, Jacinda Ardern, Emmanuel Macron, Daniel Andrews, Nicola Sturgeon, Gretchen Whitmer, and a hundred others.

'The weight of the evidence,' says Anthony, 'is that a horde of expertly picked, egocentric, easily manipulated, self-centred, narcissistic types were strategically placed in positions of power and trust in the medical, political and national media structures. It had to be a premeditated contrivance. How else could one have all political parties agree so uniformly while using almost identical rhetorical language across so many countries, accompanied by the same mass censorship and suppression of all contrary opinions and the blatant manipulation of statistical data? Their lack of empathy and low moral standing make for the ideal partners in crime. It's a crime for sure — one that has already been etched in our history.'

Hypnosis and neuro-linguistic programming (NLP) are among the tools the technocratic narcissist uses to achieve his objectives. John Anthony talks about the three sequential levels of manipulation: the 'love-bombing' or 'idealisation' phase; the devaluation process; and, finally, alienation. The controlling narcissistic first draws his victim in, then begins the process of belittlement, leading to a baring of fangs. Anthony demonstrates how the manipulative techniques of the narcissist can be adapted to the public realm, enabling the Covid operation to harness the dynamics of archetypal relationships between narcissists/psychopaths (politicians) and co-dependent submissives/empaths (citizens), in effect weaponising on a grand scale the dynamics of what was once reductively called 'wife-beating'.

The first phase in the creation of a hypnotic state, 'idealisation', is more familiar as 'love-bombing', whereby the controller/hypnotist strives to identify with and mirror the target individual or social group. He thanks the people for their stoicism thus far, praises them, reminds them they are 'saving lives', then spells out the next stage of the lockdown. The predator/perpetrator, in this case, is the state/government/president/governor, but also — and continuously — the media, exerting power to manipulate and control, using the weapons of fear, guilt and obligation, which impress the presence of constant danger on the reptilian lower 'brain', ensuring widespread compliance. This reptilian non-brain responds to repetition — of words and phrases, memes, catchwords, clichés, which embed the hypnotic suggestions to the extent that they become beliefs, thus immune to rational argumentation.

In the intimate zone of relationships, observes Anthony, 'the narcissist may target a suitable person who shows signs of compliance or low self-esteem,' though this is not the full story, as almost everybody can be manipulated depending on how domineering, assertive and skilful the predator. The 'love bombing' or 'identification' phase produces in the target a good feeling of having found the 'one', or 'soul mate', that many humans crave. The predator/narcissist sees this early stage as a fact-finding expedition to gather material for later use in bullying, gaslighting, moral blackmailing and guilt manipulation. Anthony places this alongside the initial speeches delivered by the politicians in the spring of 2020, promising that the necessary sacrifice would be brief, and declaring us 'all in this together.'

'Everything is terrific in the love bombing stage: the empathetic person feels they have found somebody that understands them, and listens to them, and the narcissistic person is listening to them and gathering information about this person, and begins to understand them and give sense to the information about them. In the second part of the process, the narcissistic person cannot maintain the persona; it's a false persona that they produce. They're massively insecure people. They need attention, and they need to get control, and they need this manipulation in order to validate who they are.'

The chief instruments of narcissistic manipulation involve the leveraging of guilt, obligation and fear, in variations on the nice cop/nasty cop routine. Language is the principal instrument of this process. In the Covid scam, John

Anthony outlines, the rollout of the programme of manipulation took the form of a rolling series of apparently mixed messages: 'The pandemic is coming and will cause millions of deaths'; 'We are with you!'; 'Stay at home, save lives!'; 'Clap/dance/light a candle for the front line workers!'; 'Being apart brings us together'; 'Let us leave no one behind'; *et cetera*. The language employed was top-heavy with negative phrases designed to instil fear and dread. Those who did not obey were told they were risking the lives of others and repeatedly urged to 'do the right thing.' These injunctions were accompanied by the use of embedded command phrases, apparently random and superfluous but always serving to emphasise the mandatory nature of what was being conveyed: 'There is no alternative!' 'All you have to do is follow the rules!' 'Experts' and celebrities were rolled out to supply further emphases, offering 'objective' confirmation of the scale of the crisis and the necessity for obedience, which further propelled the recruitment of citizens in the process of their own incarceration.

Anthony recalls listening to the then Taoiseach, Leo Varadkar, deliver his St Patrick's Day speech from Washington in 2020, in which he spoke to the Irish public for the first time about the impending Covid crisis. He recalls thinking straightaway that it was not a normal or fitting speech for the occasion. 'I heard Leo Varadkar's speech, and the speech was, "We are with you!" He was saying, "If you have lost loved ones, we are with you!" "If you have somebody sick in the family, we are with you!" And it just didn't sound right to me. I wasn't seeing it apparent in my own life. I was looking around at my family, my relations, and then I was looking at the society I lived in, my friends — and nobody knew anybody who had come down with this virus. Yet, "We are with you!" This was the phrase that he used when he spoke about the "coming calamity." And he said, "And it will come!" He seemed to know stuff that nobody else seemed to know precisely.'

First there is the 'honey period' when the prey is lured in. Then the boot goes in — and the denigration begins, subtly at first. As in: 'The surge will come!', the doubling down on the initial measures, the censorship of quizzical voices.

'The structure is the same whether it is the abusive partner, boss, government, CEO, church, state or doctor. It begins with identification or love-bombing. Then the denigration begins, and the abuse begins to be escalated slowly, and in a covert (mostly) way. This process I refer to as "death by a thousand cuts." The victims don't even realise [what is happening] because it is done incrementally and always with a public face that it is for the public good, or the victims' own good. Since that time,' he writes, 'we have been bombarded with hypnotic suggestion at every turn.'

The second phase, 'devaluation', is analogous to the live cooking of a frog. Words of praise and consolation are juxtaposed with house arrest in a form designed to provoke a kind of Stockholm Syndrome. Images and ideas of restriction, control, humiliation, are packaged in sentimental forms of manipulation:

nurses dancing amidst what we are led to presume are unremitting scenes of death; grandchildren waving to their heartbroken grandparents through a wound-up car window — the glass becoming a symbol of the invisible wall that may permanently separate them; the 'new normal' that quickly became part of the dread insinuated concerning an unknowable future. Generated confusion, mixed messages, are central elements: You must be sure to take care of old people — just don't go close lest you kill them; it is important to become infected to achieve immunity, but at all costs, avoid infecting other healthy people; wear a mask, even though 'experts' say they are ineffective (It's okay, 'the science' has changed!). This incoherence destabilises the sensibility of the subject, rendering him amenable to further manipulation. Since he cannot understand, he simply obeys.

Then comes the final phase of the hypnosis: 'abandonment', the iron fist. No more Mr Nice Guy. The police have been issued with more powers, more equipment, more vehicles, more guns, more batons, rottweiler-shaped robots to spy on the public. Reinforcements are brought in, including trainees, as part of the process of abasement. This is where the true motives may more readily be seen. The people's rights having been stripped away, we begin to awake to the folly of thinking of the controllers as our saviours or guardians. John Anthony explains that, in order to maintain control, a method known as 'intermittent reinforcement' is employed, whereby the tone of the controllers becomes more austere and threatening, establishing another layer of conditions in respect of the future. Unless compliance improves, we are warned, the ante may have to be increased. We should not expect a return to normal anytime soon — or at all. The 'second wave' is mentioned in tones of disappointed rebuke, setting up an expectation that failure to meet the contradictory requirements may result in further coercion. The 'variants' raise their multifarious heads. With each intermittent reinforcement, there will be a further erosion of civil liberties, and so the programme goes on.

'A stage hypnotist,' writes John Anthony, 'may bring a subject out of trance several times to induce a deeper trance each time. A malignant narcissist will give approval/aggression/disapproval, inducing a pattern of the very same type of addictive behaviour in a partner. Government propaganda uses the very same technique. This is accomplished in a variety of ways, all with a view to ultimate control: opening and closing business, lengthening and shortening permitted travelling distances, increasing and decreasing permitted numbers of contacts or the number of places you can have these contacts in, the length of time you can expect to be locked up for, the increase in how many can attend festivities, funerals or weddings and so the pellets of hope are turned off and on. We become entranced or fixated over everything except examining reality.'

Anthony speaks also of 'bread-crumbing', whereby the controller further undermines, devalues, and denigrates his targets. This concept derives from the idea of the subject of a romantic crush, who, though not reciprocating the feelings of the entranced person, nevertheless flirts a little, perhaps by sending occasional signs (breadcrumbs to hungry birds) so the attention does not dissipate. When the subject discerns the patterns of manipulation, control and abuse, his sense of the benign intent of the controller dissolves, and foul play becomes more apparent. If feedback indicates that the populace is beginning to wake up to the deception and manipulation, the controller must demonstrate that he is indeed working for everybody's good by intermittently appearing to be on their side. This registers in the entranced individual as a chemical rush of serotonin, oxytocin and other chemicals of relief, which facilitate the deepening of the stranglehold.

'The abandonment phase,' says Anthony, 'is where they can dole out abuse of all sorts. In the intimate context, the perpetrator may leave [home] — infidelity might be part of it. And this is where the compliant person begins to hit rock bottom. They have, in a way, abandoned their own experience and their own judgement, because each time they do something, they'll say to themselves, "Well, that's a very simple thing. I should have known that he doesn't eat steak for his dinner and I put on a steak — and I forgot, really," and that was the reason for the blow-up. And now the person is beginning to enter into a phase where they're so unsure of themselves, where the goalposts are constantly changing, and where the confusion is mounting in them, and they do not know because of this addiction, because of this ideal that they had about the person in the beginning — it's holding the map in place, if you like. But they are becoming less certain, and they are beginning to blame themselves. This method of levelling a constant barrage of both overt and covert suggestions is how any narcissistic abuser gaslights his victims, and that is no different in structure from the tyrant trying to impose a toxic regime on a population, designed for the benefit of the few.'

Gaslighting, he writes, 'can be done by malignant manipulation of the person's environment so that they begin to really doubt their own perceptions. They then turn to the manipulator for support or begin to rely on him to validate their reality.'

It is important to understand that, in this context, it is not necessary that the politician himself exhibit symptoms of personal narcissism — though this certainly 'helps': The instructions can be laid out in a protocol and implemented in a detached manner, here amounting not so much to narcissism as a kind of orchestrated psychopathy.

Lies are no mere collateral aspect, but an essential element. 'Narcissists are inveterate liars, and generally speaking, whatever they accuse others of is what they are guilty of themselves. Their lies are not always necessary but often are quite banal and trite. This can bestow a sense of power or control, albeit illusory, over their target. Like a cat playing with a mouse, the narcissist has a sense that he is somehow beginning to control the other's reality. It is the seedlings of "gaslighting." Later it develops into creating confusion by moving goalposts. It also feeds into intermittent re-enforcement. The other gets locked into thinking s/he will get it right the next time, not realising that there will never be a next time. The victim has taken a mental photo of the perpetrator at his best and forever blames him/herself, thinking that this person will return once conditions have been put right. They have just become the dedicated servant or slave.'

Trance depends on a bedding of emotion, ideally a strong one. The initial trance imposed in 2020 was grounded in fear, by far the best foundation. Fear is a powerful emotion. Few are immune to it, and generally, it grips people in an almost total fashion, especially when — as here — the emotion in question was essentially fear of death. On the pathways in the parks near my home, from mid-March 2020, it was hard to miss the intermittently placed chalk figures separated by arrows pointing at each figure, indicating the extent of two metres, designed to evoke the chalk marks investigators draw around the corpse of a murder victim. If you watched TV or listened to the radio, statistics of deaths, most of them invented or inflated — were rolled out by the hour. Terms like 'deadly virus' were used non-stop: The phrase 'new normal' had the effect of insinuating the loss of things long cherished, a state of bereavement characterised by sadness. The applauding by candlelight of 'front line' workers was transparently a way of compelling holdouts to throw themselves into the spell, an almost literal form of gaslighting in which we are required to celebrate our own loss of freedom.

Andrew Lobaczewski, a Polish psychologist who lived through Poland's suffering under both Nazi and Soviet occupation during and after World War Two, was the first person to describe the process through which a pathological minority can come to dominate a nation to the point of infecting its population with its pathologies. Lobaczewski was the intellectual executor of an assortment of psychologists, psychiatrists and other scientists who had come together to investigate the real nature and psychopathology of the macro-social phenomena of Nazism and Communism. The group worked underground in Poland during the Soviet occupation. Lobaczewski ended up as sole survivor, and it fell to him to collate and write up this material, losing two drafts — one hastily burned to avoid the attentions of the secret police, the other sent to the Vatican and lost without acknowledgement — before finally getting the research published under the title *Political Ponerology: a science on the nature of evil adjusted for political purposes*, in 2006. He died two years later.

'Ponerology,' from the Greek word *poneros*, is the name of a division of theology dealing with evil. But Lobaczewski is not concerned with theological definitions — his work relates to the formulation of a clinical classification and deconstruction of the concept of political wickedness. Before, evil was almost purely a 'moral' question, but he turned it into something like a scientific cate-gory. 'Experience,' he writes, 'has taught the author that evil is similar to disease in nature, although possibly more complex and elusive to our understanding.' 'Moral evil and psychobiological evil,' he claims, 'are interlinked via so many causal relationships and mutual influences that they can only be sepa-rated by means of abstraction.' In his work, he says, he acted like a physician confronting disease. He accepted 'the risks of close contact with evil and suffered the consequences.'

'Parallel to the traditional approach, problems commonly perceived to be moral may also be treated on the basis of data provided by biology, medicine, and psychology. . . . Experience teaches us that a comprehension of the essence and genesis of evil generally make use of data from these areas.' A new disci-pline thus arose: Ponerology. The genesis of evil was termed 'ponerogenesis'.

Lobaczewski's concept of the 'characteropathic personality' — a type that often rises to become a leader of what he calls the 'pathocratic' initiative — relates to a single acute condition involving all three elements: psychopathy, narcissism and paranoia. Stalin, he said, was a characteropath, and also suffered from a brain deformity — a common malady among psychopaths — indicated in the Soviet dictator in photographs by 'a typical deformation of his forehead,' probably from brain damage dating from birth or childhood. Drugs or child-hood disease can also be the cause of the onset of the condition, Lobaczewski says.

Lobaczewski demonstrated that, aside from destructive behaviours, the most reliable means of recognising someone with a dangerous personality disorder is through the detrimental effects they have on the ability of psychologically normal people to think. They do this by 'techniques' such as insisting on some-thing that is manifestly untrue, making illogical assertions, or stridently ques-tioning the most obvious facts. This leads to an erosion — eventually a deficit — of common sense, which in a group can have disastrous consequences, as Irving Janis has comprehensively demonstrated in his unpicking of the groupthink phenomenon. 'Normal' people in this situation,' Lobaczewski claims, 'find themselves in conflict with the newly dominant group and, being unable to assert common sense, tend to leave, to be replaced by more individuals with personality disorders.'

The internal dynamics of such a group are characterised by psychological bullying and, sometimes, physical violence, which have the effect of dividing the group into the manipulators and the subjugated.

Lobaczewski describes the 'spellbinder' — someone with the capacity to hold sway over others, sometimes to the point of messianism.

'The spellbinder places on a high moral plane anyone who succumbs to his influence, and will shower such people with attention and property and perks of all kinds. Critics are met with "moral" outrage, and it will be claimed by the spellbinder that the compliant minority is actually a majority. In a healthy society, the activities of spellbinders meet with criticism effective enough to stifle them quickly. However, when they are preceded by conditions operating destructively on common sense and social order — such as social injustice, cultural backwardness, or intellectually limited rulers manifesting pathological traits — spellbinders' activities have led entire societies into large-scale human tragedy. Such an individual fishes an environment or society for people amenable to his influence, deepening their psychological weaknesses until they finally become a ponerogenic union.

'On the other hand, people who have maintained their healthy critical faculties intact attempt to counteract the spellbinders' activities and their results, based on their own common sense and moral criteria. In the resulting polarization of social attitudes, each side justifies itself by means of moral categories. The awareness that a spellbinder is always a pathological individual should protect us from the known results of a moralizing interpretation of pathological phenomena, ensuring us of objective criteria for more effective action.'

Lobaczewski described a situation from his university days in Poland. A fake academic somehow got to become a scientific professor at the university and proceeded to deliver lectures comprising nothing but nonsense. Lobaczewski writes: 'He failed to distinguish between scientific and everyday concepts and treated borderline imaginings as though it were wisdom that could not be doubted. For ninety minutes each week, he flooded us with naïve, presumptuous paralogistics and a pathological view of human reality. We were treated with contempt and poorly controlled hatred. Since fun-poking could entail dreadful consequences, we had to listen attentively and with the utmost gravity.'

Most of the students, while pretending to absorb these 'lectures', were ignored by the professor. But that was the least of the difficulties. 'The world of psychological reality and moral values seemed suspended like in a chilly fog. Our human feeling and student solidarity lost their meaning, as did patriotism and our old established criteria. So we asked each other: "Are you going through this too?" Each of us experienced this worry about his own personality and future in his own way.'

They noticed that some of their fellow students — of the order of six per cent — started to alter their worldviews. Moreover, their speech patterns started also to mimic the fake professor's chatter. They became less friendly to their colleagues. Eventually, these former colleagues, who came from every social group in Poland, all joined the Communist Party. 'Benevolent or critical student arguments bounced right off of them. They gave the impression of possessing some secret knowledge; we were only their former colleagues, still believing what those professors of old had taught us. We had to be careful of what we said to them.'

Lobaczewski calls this process of personality-demolition by the name 'transpersonification'. Some of those affected became zealots of the ideology; others withdrew from the context and gradually returned to normal. But here is the most astonishing part: Each one who left was replaced by someone else. The 'magic number' of six per cent was maintained, no matter what. In evaluating those who had succumbed in order to analyse the phenomenon, they concluded that the six per cent were generally marginally less 'talented' than the average of the students, which appears to be a polite code for 'less intelligent'. These events had a profound effect also on the ostensibly untouched majority, the 94 per cent, who 'suffered varying degrees of personality disintegration which gave rise to individual efforts in searching for the values necessary to find ourselves again.'

'Approximately 6 per cent of the population,' he says, 'constitute the active structure of the pathocracy, which carries its own peculiar consciousness of its own goals. Twice as many people constitute a second group: those who have managed to warp their personalities to meet the demands of the new reality. This second group consists of individuals who are, on average, weaker, more sickly, and less vital. The frequency of known mental diseases in this group is at twice the rate of the national average.'

The core issue here, as it emerged, is not the machinations of the narcissist/psychopath *per se*, but the fact that there exists — and he senses that there exists — susceptible individuals who can be 'worked on' for malign purposes and recruited in the service of wickedness. This is the key 'secret' of the totalitarian project: the psycho and his victim in partnership.

'Something mysterious gnaws into the personality of an individual at the mercy of the psychopath,' writes Lobaczewski, 'and it is fought like a demon. His emotions become chilled, his sense of psychological reality is stifled. This leads to decriterialization of thought and a feeling of helplessness culminating in depressive reactions, which can be so severe that psychiatrists sometimes misdiagnose them as a manic-depressive psychosis.

'When the human mind comes into contact with this new reality so different from any experiences encountered by a person raised in a society dominated by normal people, it releases psychophysiological shock symptoms in the human brain with a higher tonus of cortex inhibition and a stifling of feelings, which then sometimes gush forth uncontrollably. Human minds work more slowly and less keenly, since the associative mechanisms have become inefficient. Especially when a person has direct contact with psychopathic representatives of the new rule, who use their specific experience so as to traumatize the minds of the "others" with their own personalities, his mind succumbs to a state of short-term catatonia. Their humiliating and arrogant techniques, brutal paramoralizations, deaden his thought processes and his self-defense capabilities, and their divergent experiential method anchors in his mind. This is followed by a shock which appears as tragic as it is frightening. Some people from every social group —

whether abused paupers, aristocrats, officials, literati, students, scientists, priests, atheists, or nobodies known to no one — suddenly start changing their personality and worldview. Decent Christians and patriots just yesterday, they now espouse the new ideology and behave contemptuously to anyone still adhering to the old values.'

Lobaczewski identified Germany in the 1930s as a society captured by these pathological conditions, which in that context, he argued, had their roots in World War One, following which a pathologically-rooted absence of German guilt made inevitable some kind of sequel. 'The Germans inflicted and suffered enormous damage and pain during the First World War; they thus felt no substantial guilt and even thought that they were the ones who had been wronged. This is not surprising as they were behaving in accordance with their customary habit without being aware of its pathological causes. The need for this pathological state to be concealed in heroic garb after a war in order to avoid bitter disintegration became all too common. A mysterious craving arose, as if the social organism had managed to become addicted to some drug. The hunger was for more pathologically modified psychological material, a phenomenon known to psychotherapeutic experience. This hunger could only be satisfied by another similarly pathological personality and system of government.'

Those thus afflicted learn to recognize each other, even in childhood, and in a crowd acquire an almost instinctual awareness of the proximity of individuals similar to themselves. Having seized or attained power, this pathological rump will assert control over the most intimate areas of human existence — through propaganda, indoctrination, terror, scapegoating and extermination. These 'pathocrats' will encounter surprisingly little resistance, but in any event, will peremptorily extinguish any opposition with extreme prejudice. Lobaczewski outlines how societies afflicted by this syndrome — what he called 'Macro-social Evil', i.e. large-scale evil that overtakes whole societies and nations — break down into two stratifications: the normal and the psychologically abnormal, with the latter representing a tiny but all-powerful element, with the capacity to hold sway over the majority and the propensity to spread its psychopathy by a contagion of ideology and mesmerism.

The trickle-down effect of pathocracy, says Lobaczewski, can 'affect an entire society, starting with the leaders and infiltrating every town, business, and institution. The pathological social structure gradually covers the entire country, creating a "new class" within that nation. This privileged class feels permanently threatened by the "others," i.e. by the majority of normal people. Neither do the pathocrats entertain any illusions about their personal fate should there be a return to the system of normal man.

'After a typical pathocratic structure has been formed, the population is effectively divided according to completely different lines from what someone raised outside the purview of this phenomenon might imagine, and in a manner whose actual conditions are also impossible to comprehend. Pathocracy corrodes the entire social organism, wasting its skills and power. Typical pathocrats take over all the managerial functions in a totally destroyed structure of a nation. Such a state must be short-term, since no ideology can vivify it.'

'In any society in this world,' writes Lobaczewski, 'psychopathic individuals and some of the other deviants create a ponerogenically active network of common collusions, partially estranged from the community of normal people. . . . Their world is forever divided into "us and them" — their world with its own laws and customs, and that other foreign world full of presumptuous ideas and customs in light of which they are condemned morally. Their "sense of honor" bids them cheat and revile that other human world and its values. In contradiction to the customs of normal people, they feel non-fulfillment of their promises or obligations is customary behavior. They also learn how their personalities can have traumatizing effects on the personalities of those normal people, and how to take advantage of this root of terror for purposes of reaching their goals. This dichotomy of worlds is permanent and does not disappear even if they succeed in realizing their dreams of gaining power over the society of normal people. This proves that the separation is biologically conditioned. In such people a dream emerges like some youthful Utopia of a "happy" world and a social system which would not reject them or force them to submit to laws and customs whose meaning is incomprehensible to them. They dream of a world in which their simple and radical way of experiencing and perceiving reality [i.e. lying, cheating, destroying, using others, etc] would dominate, where they would, of course, be assured safety and prosperity.

'Those "others" — different, but also more technically skillful — should be put to work to achieve this goal. "We," after all, will create a new government, one of justice [for psychopaths]. They are prepared to fight and suffer for the sake of such a brave new world, and also, of course, to inflict suffering upon others. Such a vision justifies killing people whose suffering does not move them to compassion because "they" are not quite conspecific.' The pathocrats, belonging to a different species, are not concerned with the feelings and concerns of 'normal' people.

Later, he elaborates: 'A normal person deprived of privilege or high position goes about performing some work which would earn him a living; but pathocrats never possessed any practical talent, and the time frame of their rule has eliminated any residual possibilities of adapting to the demands of normal work. If the law of normal man were to be reinstalled, they and their kind could be subjected to judgments, including a moralizing interpretation of their psychological deviations; they would be threatened by a loss of freedom and life, not merely a loss of position and privilege. Since they are incapable of this kind of sacrifice, the survival of a system which is best for them becomes a moral idea.

Such a threat must be battled by means of psychological and political cunning and a lack of scruples with regard to those other "inferior-quality" people.'

There is, then, this intellectual inversion: the mediocre declare themselves all-knowing and condemn the others as inferior, thus breeding a true mediocrity that proclaims itself otherwise. This may be why mediocre societies in which a lot of people are promoted beyond their abilities tend to favour whip-cracking totalitarianism. You're all but certain to find this in societies where 'gender balance' and other forms of tokenism have taken hold. Inadequate people require visible authoritarianism to defend them from the threat posed by the talents, abilities and ambitions of others. Societies run by cadres of the psychotic mediocre are driven by fear, most of all by the fear of those clinging to power of the people they wield it over. For this obvious reason, societies that set equality-of-outcome as a mandatory social policy goal are at a high risk of descending into tyranny. This is also the inevitable fate of societies in which the political 'leadership' has slid to the lower reaches of mediocrity by virtue of the outsourcing of meaningful power and authority. You cannot expect to attract into politics the 'brightest and best' when all the job requires is the implementation of instructions. Hence, in a globalist world, all our societies have become totalitarian 'accidents'-waiting-to-happen. Such factors, Lobaczewski says, decide whether a society will experience evolution or revolution.

To summarise: Having gained a foothold in a society, a psychopathic group becomes irresistible, using indoctrination, intimidation and fear-tactics to subdue dissent. The group acts like a magnet for like-minded narcissists and others afflicted with anti-social personality disorders. With such a group in control, the society as a whole rapidly becomes pathologised, with a tiny majority able to control and dictate to the entire population. Ideology is a core instrument of this operation, and the ideology-of-choice is all but invariably of a pathological character, being usually camouflaged with good intentions towards the majority's well-being, a consideration that evaporates as the boot comes in. The sole objective is power, and after a time this becomes clear, as all pretence of benevolent motivation is abandoned. And yet, it is important too that some semblance of the initial masquerade remains even after total power has been claimed, for this causes the victim class to cling to the hope that the brutality and abuse are but temporary 'necessities', which will disappear one day to be replaced by the former mood of benevolence.

Here, as elsewhere, there is a cycle. In hard times, men learn to think carefully, truthfully and creatively, because this is necessary for survival. In good times, they succumb to loose, indulgent thinking, so hastening the return of hard times. Too much contentment, says Lobaczewski, is bad for a society. Catastrophe waits in the wings. The good habits of reasoning and moral reflection formed in the hard times grow weaker. At such moments, Evil rears its ambiguous head, and the cycle starts over. Paradoxically, it is the hard times, not the good, that lead to genuine progress because that's when people are forced to think straight and sensibly.

These patterns may have become accentuated in the modern era because men, in general, have become less attentive to the fragility of peace and culture in the human world. TV has rotted out the brains of whole generations. The World Wide Web has filled the gaps with vile nonsense and spite. As a result, the hard times become harder, and the good times spike into the hedonistic red. Again, these patterns suggest that something like what's happening now was not merely inevitable but actually planned.

Lobaczewski's descriptions of the 'psychopathic group' bring to mind the raft of vaguely-defined supranational bodies, highly secretive and seemingly intent upon bypassing democracy, which have sprung up in the Western world since the middle of the twentieth century: the Bilderberg Group, the Trilateral Commission, and especially the World Economic Forum (WEF), a kind of international 'club', and grooming/brainwashing clinic for emerging political figures, which seems to have nurtured some of the most manifestly pathological political figures of recent times, including former German Chancellor Angela Merkel, current Canadian prime minister Justin Trudeau, Jacinda Arden, prime minister of New Zealand, and Leo Varadkar, formerly Taoiseach (PM) of Ireland and currently — while awaiting his re-ascension to that position next December — treading water as Tánaiste (deputy prime minister). One of the most striking things about the WEF (also known, disaffectionately, as 'the Party of Davos') is that it seems to inculcate in most of its members a supra-national loyalty to the objectives and values (anti-values?) of the group rather than to their own nations and peoples.

There is no objective necessity for, or benefit to, ordinary humans of a group like the WEF. Not unlike the Trilateralists and Bilderbergers, it claims to be 'improving the state of the world by engaging business, political, academic and other leaders of society to shape global, regional and industry agendas'. In reality, it is a school for psychopaths, in which the nascent pseudo-leaders of the former Free World are trained in the manner of climbing plants to assume the ideological demeanour of the club, disregard all previous loyalties to country, people, electorate or posterity, and implement the agenda of the puppet-masters. The WEF is as the 'support' that allows the would-be future 'leaders' to grow independently of democratic concerns, which in many instances results in the cultivation of what Andrew Lobaczewski described as 'pathocracy' — a system of government wherein a small pathological minority takes control over a society of normal people.

The narcissist/psychopath does not necessarily think of himself as doing ill. On the contrary, his sense that he knows best and is unassailable in his good intentions allows him to give rein to his deepest power cravings in a manner that provides him, at least, with plausible deniability. He has the benefit also that the vast majority of people tend to believe that most of their fellow humans are disposed towards good, and to be 'puzzled' when people behave in a manner that appears to be wilfully wicked. In such circumstances, most of us are inclined to look for underlying factors to 'explain' such behaviour: a difficult childhood; some kind of encroaching mental illness; something we may have said or done to hurt or offend; or some kind of necessarily secret danger that requires them to act harshly in order to 'save' everybody.

These conditions, Lobaczewski claims, have, through history, contributed to the cultural suppression of a functional consciousness of evil. 'The character and genesis of evil thus remained hidden in discreet shadows, leaving it to play-wrights to deal with the subject in their highly expressive language, but that did not reach the primeval source of the phenomena. A certain cognitive space thus remains uninvestigated, a thicket of moral questions which resists under-standing and philosophical generalizations.

'The pathocratic world — the world of pathological egotism and terror — is so difficult to understand for people raised outside the scope of this phenomenon that they often manifest childlike *naïveté*, even if they studied psychopathology and are psychologists by profession. If a person with a normal instinctive substratum and basic intelligence has already heard and read about such a system of ruthless autocratic rule based on fanatical ideology, he feels he has already formed an opinion on the subject. However, direct confrontation with the phenomenon causes him to feel intellectually helpless. All his prior imaginings prove to be virtually useless; they explain next to nothing. This provokes a nagging sensation that he and the society in which he was educated were quite *naïve*.'

This helps in understanding some aspects of the Covid episode. For exam-ple, although the playbook in use clearly replicates almost verbatim the language and logic of Orwell's *1984*, many of those who have ingested that book with alarm and alertness were unable to identify the same symptoms playing out under their noses.

'The facts,' write Lobaczewski, 'are that "good times" for one group of people have been historically rooted in some injustice to other groups of people. In such a society, where all the hidden truths lurk below the surface like an iceberg, disaster is just around the corner.' Good times also result in a depletion of psychological skills and moral criticism. When things turn bad, these condi-tions can be exploited by the pathocrats. Such a society is ripe for what Lobaczewski calls 'pathogenic bacteria' — cultural infections of contagious psychopathy.

'The psychological features of each such crisis are unique to the culture and the time, but one common denominator that exists at the beginning of all such "bad times" is an exacerbation of society's hysterical condition. The emotion-alism dominating in individual, collective, and political life, combined with the subconscious selection and substitution of data in reasoning, lead to individual and national egotism. The mania for taking offense at the drop of a hat provokes constant retaliation, taking advantage of hyperirritability and hypercriticality on the part of others. It is this feature, this hystericization of society, that enables pathological plotters, snake charmers, and other primitive deviants to act as essential factors in the processes of the origination of evil on a macro-social scale.'

Lobaczewski suggests that such a shift occurred in America and the world after 9/11. But he holds, too, that such times provide a vital rebalancing of civilisational evolution, serving to regenerate positive values like empathy and reason.

'When bad times arrive and people are overwhelmed by an excess of evil, they must gather all their physical and mental strength to fight for existence and protect human reason. The search for some way out of difficulties and dangers rekindles long-buried powers of discretion. Such people have the initial tendency to rely on force in order to counteract the threat; they may, for instance, become "trigger happy" or dependent upon armies. Slowly and laboriously, however, they discover the advantages conferred by mental effort: improved understanding of psychological situations in particular, better differentiation of human characters and personalities, and finally, comprehension of one's adversaries. During such times, virtues which former generations relegated to literary motifs regain their real and useful substance and become prized for their value.'

The good news is that, because a pathocratic society fills the upper layers of leadership and authority systems with people who generally suffer from the same pathologies as the rulers, mediocrity is an unavoidable by-product, which renders all but certain that such a society will be short-lived, because all areas of public life — economy, science, technology, culture, *et cetera* will go into radical decline. Gradually, even those who approved of the regime's actions at the beginning, will tire of it and start to withdraw their affection. This may, in the early stages, result in an uptick of terror tactics — the vindication of Orwell's observation that all tyrannies rule by fraud and force, and eventually by force alone. Eventually, however, history has shown that even terror and force will be insufficient to insulate the regime. This happens when the 'normal' people begin to reclaim their balance and reason and gradually start restoring the damaged social bonds and structures.

'During the initial shock,' writes Lobaczewski, 'the feeling of social links are fading; after that has been survived, however, the overwhelming majority of [a] people manifests its own phenomenon of psychological immunization. Society simultaneously starts collecting practical knowledge on the subject of this new reality and its psychological properties. Normal people slowly learn to perceive the weak spots of such a system and utilize the possibilities of more expedient arrangement of their lives. They begin to give each other advice in these matters, thus slowly regenerating the feelings of social links and reciprocal trust. A new phenomenon occurs: separation between the pathocrats and the society of normal people. The latter have an advantage as regards talent, professional skills, and healthy common sense. The pathocracy finally realizes that it must find some "*modus vivendi*" or relations with the majority of society: "After all, somebody's got to do the work for us."' At this stage, he claims, things begin to improve as the pathocracy seeks to insinuate itself as a 'normal sociopolitical system' — what he calls the 'dissimulative phase.' The 'normal' people tend to go along with this, taking advantages of the relaxations and other benefits. This bears some resemblance to the phase we have entered into in Ireland in recent weeks, with the 'relaxation' of 'measures' and the general sense that Covid is 'over'.

Lobaczewski's book, then, is ultimately hopeful. The gradual wearing off of the trance can enable 'normal' people to realize that the pathocrats are infinitely less smart than they had led everyone to believe: 'One of the first discoveries made by a society of normal people is that it is superior to the new rulers in intelligence and practical skills, no matter what geniuses they appear to be. The knots stultifying reason are gradually loosened, and fascination with the new rulership's secret knowledge and plan of action begins to diminish, followed by familiarization with the knowledge about this new reality.' Gradually, the knowledge spreads, and the society acquires a 'resourcefulness of action which enables it to take ever better advantage of the weak spots of the rulership system.'

In the end, walls come down, and the pathocrats either surrender or run for the hills.

CHAPTER 20
WHIPNOSIS, PART III: INTO THE WOMB OF THE TYRANT
20-03-2022

Mass psychosis is real. Its purpose: to facilitate the creation of a pseudo-reality, supplanting the actual world and drawing humanity into its fictions, to unleash mass demoralisation and compliance.

The Covid ruse is, without doubt, the most extravagant confidence trick ever perpetrated on human society. It has been astonishing to watch — how easily the politicians were able to sell their message, how relentless the media in promulgating it, how effectively all dissenting voices were suppressed, marginalised or cancelled. It has been truly astonishing — and also terrifying — coming to understand that Covid was no more than a smokescreen to cover the overnight transformation of the economies, societies and legal systems of the hitherto free world into something akin to a neo-Bolshevik totalitarianism. Only when you consider the events of the past 24 months beyond the reach of their pretext do you come to understand that we in the West have arrived at a real problem moment.

The most critical factors were the acquiescence of the people and the connivance of the media. Our skunkish politicians would have been powerless had they not succeeded in corrupting beyond redemption what had been our Fourth Estate. But this, in turn would have been impossible without the malleability of entire peoples in the face of a 'threat' that a ten-year-old child, left to her own devices, would have seen through in an hour of study and reflection. As, back in April 2020, the former judge of the UK Supreme Court, Lord Jonathan Sumption, said in a BBC interview: 'The real problem is that when human societies lose their freedom, it's not usually because tyrants have taken it away. It's usually because people willingly surrender their freedom in return for protection against some external threat. And the threat is usually a real threat but usually exaggerated.'

Covid provoked such conditions, he added, and the people demanded action of some kind. Anyone who has studied history, said Sumption, will recognise in this the classic symptoms of a collective, infectious hysteria, where the need for action exceeds the appetite for reason. This, he warned, is 'how societies become despotisms.'

At the beginning of January this year, Joe Rogan interviewed on his podcast the scientist Dr Robert Malone, the inventor of the nine original mRNA vaccine patents, which were initially filed in 1989 — including the idea of mRNA vaccines, which in 2021 emerged as the basis for Covid vaccines proffered by Pfizer and Moderna, which Dr Malone then warned about in the strongest imaginable terms, demanding in a July 2021 interview with Del Bigtree that they be removed from the market.[*]

Many lies have been told about Dr Malone, but the most controversial aspect of his Joe Rogan interview had to do, not with his areas of specialisation, but a more general commentary he had offered on the conditions of hysteria which had been visited on the public in order to impose this lethal programme. Back in November 2021, he had had a conversation with the Belgian psychologist, Professor Mattias Desmet, who had been dissecting for some time the bizarre phenomenon whereby it appeared to be possible to, in effect, mesmerise entire populations in such a way as to persuade them to accept even self-destruction.

'Now what Matthias Desmet has shared with us — brilliant insight!' Malone told Rogan, 'is another one of those, "Aha! — now that part makes sense!" [moments] — which is that this comes from basically European intellectual inquiry into what the heck happened in Germany in the '20s and '30s, you know — very intelligent, highly educated population, and they went barking mad. And how did that happen? The answer is mass formation psychosis. When you have a society that has become decoupled from each other and has free-floating anxiety in a sense that things don't make sense . . . we can't understand it, and then their attention gets focussed by a leader or series of events on one small point, just like hypnosis. They literally become hypnotised and can be led anywhere.'

It was alleged by 'fact checkers' that Dr Malone's characterisation of a 'mass formation psychosis' was not a scientific concept. Strictly speaking, this is true, but it is also disingenuous to the extent that it seeks to deny, in the same stroke, the existence of 'mass formation', a long established concept, and also — similarly — 'mass psychosis'. This became, too, an interesting exposition of the

---

[*] A video of this interview on *The HighWire* can be found by searching for 'mRNA pioneer raises covid vaccine concerns'.

machinations of 'fact-checkers' — essentially paid pedants seeking to highlight any minor flaw or weakness in the argument of anyone deemed to be unfriendly to the Covid agenda.

Dr. Malone made no secret of the fact that he had gleaned his understanding of crowd psychology from Professor Desmet, who had emerged as the most compelling voice on these subjects. Malone is a non-specialist in this area, in effect a layman, and understandably extrapolated from Professor Desmet's explications an understanding that, whatever its clinical basis, is in harmony with the interventions of both Professor Desmet and Lord Sumption. This would perhaps not be such a serious matter had it not led to the intervention of rock 'n' roll veteran Neil Young, who tried to have Rogan cancelled from Spotify on account of 'misinformation' he alleged had been peddled in the Malone interview.

Desmet has for some time, in analysing the Covid context, been applying some very cogent reinterpretations of the work of the French philosopher Gustave Le Bon, and the German/Jewish philosopher Hannah Arendt, to the matter of the condition of the public mind under saturation propaganda. The phrase Desmet has repeatedly used is 'mass formation' (Le Bon's term) which he plausibly linked to hypnosis, and from there to propaganda. By the time Malone got to the Joe Rogan podcast, however, he had added the word 'psychosis' to the mix, implying some kind of mass pathology, rather than mass indoctrination. Desmet, in a subsequent interview with Gemma O'Doherty, clarified that he would never seek to extrapolate an individual pathology to a mass context, as the two are entirely different. He correctly pointed out that he had never used the term 'mass formation psychosis' — in effect a layman's extrapolation, which works at a certain level of analogy, but is also loose and confusing and, in that sense, unhelpful. But, in fact, Professor Desmet may be mistaken, and Dr Malone actually — if purely by accident — correct. The concept of collective psychosis is a long-established clinical definition, having been comprehensively studied and written up by the Dutch psychiatrist Dr Joost A. M. Meerloo, and greatly elaborated in his 1956 book *The Rape of the Mind: The Psychology of Thought Control, Menticide, and Brainwashing*

'Menticide' — the killing of the spirit — is a long-accepted term for what happens to a population under a process of manipulation in which a powerful tyrant transfers his own thoughts and words into the minds and mouths of the 'masses'. Dr Meerloo, who coined the word 'menticide', was born in the Netherlands and remained there until the Nazi occupation forced him to flee in 1942. His focus was on the techniques used in interrogation — mental torture, brainwashing, what he called 'verbocracy' and the use of fear as a tool of mass submission. He focussed also on the questions of loyalty and treason — the possibility that, through studied manipulation, anyone can be turned into a 'traitor'. This he calls 'the rape of the mind', or 'menticide'. It might also be categorised as brainwashing, or cultivated groupthink — the process by which a psychotic ruling class imposes on the collective mind of the population a programme for the achievement of its own aspirations to total power and control. Modern psychiatry and the behavioural 'sciences' offer several of the key tools required for this perversion.

The process begins, invariably, with a programme of fear-mongering, which is gradually escalated to ramp up the state of delusion and derangement of the mob. For maximum effect, this is carried out in a series of waves, punctuated with quasi-normalising breaks, enabling fear-levels to be increased by building them layer-upon-layer like a lasagne, until the dish reaches boiling point. The breaks are just as important as the periods of fear-mongering. The processes of disinforming, bewildering, confusing and scapegoating are orchestrated to enflame the mob, providing it with a clear sense of an enemy. Confusion is a critical instrument, creating an atmosphere of chaos among the crowd that prevents it constructing things in a rational manner. Technology makes easy such a process of emotional 'jamming'. Separating, isolating people, interrupting the normal interactions of the population, are key instruments also, causing the individual, even in the midst of the mob, to become isolated from others and increasingly mistrustful of his fellows.

In *The Rape of the Mind*, Meerloo describes the transformation of the free human mind into a machine by the use of cultural undercurrents and techniques of mental coercion and manipulation — 'among the oldest crimes of mankind.' The word 'rape' comes from the Latin *rapere*, to *snatch*, but it also relates to *rave* and *raven*, intimating *overwhelm, enrapture, usurp, pillage, steal*. 'The danger of destruction of the spirit may be compared to the threat of total physical destruction through atomic warfare,' he writes. 'Indeed, the two are related and intertwined.' Menticide can turn a man into a 'mechanical imitator of his tormentors. "Menticide" is a word coined by me and derived from *"mens,"* the mind, and *"caedere,"* to kill [and] "genocide," meaning the systematic destruction of racial groups. (NOTE: Here I followed the etymology used by the United Nations to form the word.) Both words ["genocide" and "menticide"] indicate the same perverted refinement of the rack, putting it on what appears to be a more acceptable level. But ["menticide"] is a thousand times worse and a thousand times more useful to the inquisitor.'

The first aim of the Gestapo, Meerloo outlines, was to force prisoners under torture to betray their friends and provide new victims for torture. He and his colleagues in the Resistance experimented with narcotics in the hope of hardening themselves against pain. What they gained in physical results was lost in the mental realm, as the narcotics made them more vulnerable to mental pressure. He describes the responses to torture as a form of trance: 'Fear, and continual pressure are known to create a menticidal hypnosis. The conscious part of the personality no longer takes part in the automatic confessions. The brainwashee lives in a trance, repeating the record grooved into him by some-body else.

'The demagogue, like the totalitarian dictator, knows well how to lay a mental spell on the people, how to create a kind of mass suggestion and mass hypnosis. There is no intrinsic difference between individual and mass hypno-sis. In hypnosis — the most intensified form of suggestion — the individual becomes temporarily automatized, both physically and mentally. Such a clinical state of utter mental submission can be brought about quite easily in children and in primitive people, but it can be created in civilized adults, too.' Crowds are easier to manipulate than individuals, because each individual tends to go with the group's shifts and drifts.

In these ways, he writes, the tyrant can construct what he calls a 'Totalitaria', which he characterises as a kind of 'cold war' occupation of the mass mind. 'Totalitaria' is a mythical place capable of being recreated in the imaginations of the majority of humans, 'a monolithic and absolute state in which doubt, confu-sion, and conflict are not permitted to be shown, for the dictator purports to solve all his subjects' problems for them, allowing the uncivilised child in everyone to embrace a kind of liberation from responsibility and ethical frus-tration.'

The media are central to this process — in a Totalitaria it is their sole func-tion. 'He who dictates and formulates the words and phrases we use, he who is master of the press and radio, is master of the mind. Repeat mechanically your assumptions and suggestions, diminish the opportunity for communicating dissent and opposition. This is the formula for political conditioning of the masses.'

TV, he writes, is central. Whereas 'every step in personal growth needs isola-tion, needs inner conversation and deliberation and a reviewing with the self,' this is hampered by television, which 'prepares the mind more easily for collec-tivization and cliché thinking,' persuading onlookers 'to think in terms of mass values,' intruding into family life and cutting off 'the more subtle interfamilial communication.' Television, because it leads to mental apathy, has hypnoidal powers over human beings by virtue of closing down the necessary inner conversation. Totalitarianism, Meerloo argues, is nothing other than the domi-nance of technology over humanity, the mechanisation of our lives and our minds.

'The continual intrusion into our minds of the hammering noises of argu-ments and propaganda can lead to two kinds of reactions,' he claims. 'It may lead to apathy and indifference, the I-don't-care reaction, or to a more intensified desire to study and to understand. Unfortunately, the first reaction is the more popular one.

'Readymade opinions can be distributed day by day through the press, radio, and so on, again and again, till they reach the nerve cell and implant a fixed pattern in the brain. Consequently, guided public opinion is the result, according to Pavlovian theoreticians, of good propaganda technique, and the polls [are] a verification of the temporary successful action of the Pavlovian machinations on the mind.'

Demoralization of the target audience is yet another step in successful mind control. This and numbing the senses by repeated assertion are key elements in utilising mind control techniques. 'The big lie and monotonously repeated nonsense have more emotional appeal in a cold war than logic and reason.' He examines also public opinion, the role of the human need for companionship, psychological shock, regression (infantilisation), the manipulation of guilt feelings and the growing modern tendency towards masochism and the strange pact it engenders with tyranny. 'The bulk of the totalitarian-minded in the democratic societies are men and women who are attracted to this destructive way of life for inner emotional reasons unknown to themselves.'

Man, he stresses, requires to be constantly on the look-out for verification of his impressions and perceptions of the world, lest he develop delusion, and most of the causes of delusions are not purely organic: The same effect could be produced by hypnosis and mass hypnosis, which, by dislocating the person from the higher forms of alert consciousness, reduce him to the primitive stage of collective participation, creating an experience of oneness with the crowd.

Totalitarianism is the sum of the personalities of its subjects' minds, broken down and subjugated. It is the tapping into the childlike fears and dependencies of the individual, which make him crave protection and security over freedom. The leaders of Totalitaria employ catchwords instead of philosophies. Words like 'communism' and 'democracy' are merely instruments in the hands of the would-be tyrants, what Meerloo calls the 'labelomania' of 'verbocracy'.

'We can say that verbocracy turns [citizens] into what psychology calls symbol agnostics, people capable only of imitation, incapable of inquisitive sense of objectivity and perspective that leads to questioning and understanding and to the formation of individual ideas and ideals. In other words, the individual citizen becomes a parrot, repeating ready-made slogans and propaganda catchwords without understanding what they really mean, or what forces stand behind them.' Thus, 'a common delusion is created: people are incited to think what other people think, and thus public opinion may mushroom out into a mass prejudice.'

In such a culture, rhetoric increases in inverse proportion to sense. 'Many speakers use verbal showing off to cover an emptiness of thought, to stir up emotions and to create admiration and adoration of what is essentially empty and valueless. Loud-mouthed phoniness threatens to become the ideal of our time.'

Our societies, he believed, are far more primitive than we like to imagine, and the more technologised they become, the more true this is. Humanity's love affair with technology has gestated a society of 'opinionated robots' who seek the irrational as a form of escape from reality. 'Public opinion moulds our critical thoughts every day. . . . We crave excitement, hair-raising stories, sensation. We search for situations that create superficial fear to cover up inner anxieties.'

'The mechanization of modern life has already influenced man to become more passive and to adjust himself to ready-made conformity. No longer does man think in personal values, following more his own conscience and ethical evaluations; he thinks more and more in the values brought to him by mass media. Headlines in the morning paper give him his temporary political outlook, the radio blasts suggestions into his ears, television keeps him in continual awe and passive fixation. Consciously, he may protest against these anonymous voices, but nevertheless, their suggestions ooze into his system.'

These undercurrents, running wild in human society, turn everyone into a potential controller and a prospective victim. 'If one reasons with a totalitarian who has been impregnated with official clichés,' Meerloo writes, 'he will sooner or later withdraw into his fortress of collective totalitarian thinking. The mass delusion that gives him his feelings of belonging, of greatness, omnipotence, is dearer to him than his personal awareness and understanding. What is perhaps most shocking about these influences is that many of them have developed not out of man's destructiveness, but out of his hope to improve his world and to make life richer and deeper. The very institutions man has created to help himself, the very tools he has invented to enhance his life, the very progress he has made toward mastery of himself and his environment — all can become weapons of destruction.'

This process of robot-construction reduces each one 'to the mechanical precision of an insect-like state.' The subject 'cannot develop any warm friendships, loyalties, or allegiances because they may be too dangerous for him. Today's friend may be, after all, tomorrow's enemy. Living in an atmosphere of constant suspicion not only of strangers, but even of his family — he is afraid to express himself lest the concentration camp or prison swallow him up.'

No nation, he wrote, is immune from becoming a Totalitaria, a country in which political ideas degenerate into senseless formulations made only for propaganda purposes. 'Totalitaria' is, to a high degree, a synonym for Andrew Lobaczewski's characterisation of the 'pathocracy'. It is any country in which — in Meerloo's words — 'a single group, left or right, acquires absolute power and becomes omniscient and omnipotent, any country in which disagreement and differences of opinion are crimes, in which utter conformity is the price of life.

'The citizens of Totalitaria do not really converse with one another. When they speak, they whisper, first looking furtively over their shoulders for the inevitable spy. The inner silence is in sharp contrast to the official verbal bombardment. The citizens of Totalitaria may make noise, and utter polite banalities, or they may repeat slogans one after another, but they say nothing.

'Totalitaria makes the thinking man a criminal, for in our mythical country, the citizen can be punished as much for wrong thinking as for wrongdoing. Because the watchful eyes of the secret police are everywhere, the critic of the regime is driven to conspiratorial methods if he wants to have even a safe conversation with those he wants to trust. What we used to call the "Nazi gesture" was a careful looking around before starting to talk to a friend.' In these conditions, dissent equals criminality. From one day to the next, a citizen can become a hero or a villain, a scapegoat or a statesman, depending on strategic party needs. 'The ordinary, law-abiding citizen of Totalitaria, far from being a hero, is potentially guilty of hundreds of crimes. He is a criminal if he is stubborn in defense of his own point of view. He is a criminal if he refuses to become confused.'

Moral inversion rules. 'Nearly all of the mature ideals of mankind are crimes in Totalitaria. Freedom and independence, compromise and objectivity, all of these are treasonable. In Totalitaria there is a new crime, the apostatic crime, which may be described as the obstinate refusal to admit imputed guilt.

'In Totalitaria, there is no faith in fellow men, no "caritas," no love, because real relationships between men do not exist, just as they do not exist between schizophrenics. There is only faith in and subjection to the feeding system, and there is in every citizen a tremendous fear of being expelled from that system, a fear of being totally lost, comparable with the schizophrenic's feeling of rejection and fear of reality. In the midst of spiritual loneliness and isolation, there is the fear of still greater loneliness, of more painful isolation. Without protective regulations from the outside, internal hell may break loose. Strong mechanical external order must be used to cover the internal chaos and approaching breakdown.'

As with schizophrenia, he writes, a Totalitaria prevents a manoeuvrable and individual ego from emerging. 'In schizophrenia, the ego shrinks as a result of withdrawal; in Totalitaria, [it shrinks] as a result of constant merging in mass feelings. If such a shrunken ego should grow up, with its own critical attitude, its needs for verification of facts and for understanding, it would then be beaten down as being treacherous and nonconforming.'

All this, says Meerloo, leads inexorably to a collective psychosis, a delusional thinking that begins with the leaders but soon infects their subjects, unleashing all kinds of demons and leading the society towards self-destruction. Each human surrenders his individuality to the collective, subjecting himself to integration and standardisation, which in turn escalates the emptiness of the robot, fuelling the collective desire for destruction. By isolating individuals within the mass, allowing no free thinking or exchange, no external corrections of the drift of public thinking, it becomes easy to 'hypnotize the group daily with noises, with press and radio and television.' Through the use of fear and pseudo-enthusiasms, any delusion can be instilled. 'People will begin to accept the most primitive and inappropriate acts. Outside occurrences are usually the triggers that unleash hidden hysterical and delusional complexes in people.'

Meerloo's words, perhaps more clearly than those of any other analyst of these conditions, resonate with the agonies we have experienced over the past two years, perhaps most of all the growing sense of an imposed loneliness that seems to envelop us and spread as though a virus preying on human souls. Isolation, claims Meerloo, is the most essential implement in the totalitarian's kit.

'Pavlov formulated his findings into a general rule in which the speed of learning positively correlated with quiet isolation. The totalitarians have followed this rule. They know they can condition their political victims most quickly if they are kept in isolation. In the totalitarian technique of thought control, the same isolation applied to the individual is applied also to groups of people. This is the reason the civilian populations of the totalitarian countries are not permitted to travel freely and are kept away from mental and political contamination. It is the reason, too, for the solitary confinement cell and the prison camp.'

Fundamentally, says Meerloo, man fears his own liberty. 'Above all, to live is to love. And many people are afraid to take the responsibility of loving, of having an emotional investment in their fellow beings. They want only to be loved and to be protected; they are afraid of being hurt and rejected. Totalitarianism is man's escape from the fearful realities of life into the virtual womb of the leader. The individual's actions are directed from this womb — from the inner sanctum. The mystic center is in control of everything; man need no longer assume responsibility for his own life. The order and logic of the prenatal world reign. There is peace and silence, the peace of utter submission. The members of the womb state do not really communicate; between them, there is silence, the silence of possible betrayal, not the mature silence of reticence and reservedness.'

It is frequently observed that totalitarianism differs from tyrannies involving an individual dictator, being really a form of 'conspiracy' between the oppressors and the oppressed — indeed, a form of sadomasochistic conspiracy in which both participants crave that which they experience. But a further difference that reveals itself in this present situation of the world is that totalitarianism, instead of emerging from a singular nation and spreading outwards, has this time emanated from the centre, in a top-down manner, seeking to conquer the whole world from above. The 'Great Reset' and 'New Normal' are expressions of this new form of tyrannical imposition — deeply pathological programmes of control and coercion that suddenly, in early 2020, manifested throughout the hitherto Free World from a deceptively auspicious sky. The purpose has already revealed itself as totally total. It is no longer local or distant, but ubiquitous. It seeks total power over not just behaviours and actions but over thoughts themselves.

This new form of totalitarianism has all the hallmarks of the twentieth-century model, but also several important new dimensions. We have experienced, at the hands of our own 'democratic' leaders, the abrogation of 'inviolable', 'inalienable', 'indefeasible', and 'fundamental' human rights and freedoms, receiving in 'return' rule by decree, propaganda, the marginalisation of opposition, the scapegoating of a demonised *Untermenschen*, censorship, social segregation, *et cetera*.

And yet, paradoxically, this new form of totalitarianism remains, in a sense, invisible. Such is the nature of the 'training' being administered to the populace that, for most people, it does not seem to be there — the very suggestion of it appears preposterous. This new totalitarianism, having camouflaged itself in the white-coat uniform of the medic, presents itself as a benevolent and caring phenomenon. It suggests itself not merely as reality, but as benign reality. At first sight, even at second and third sight, it does not appear to be a political or ideological phenomenon. Who could question the project of 'saving lives'? Its pathological nature, in other words, has folded itself into the phenomenon of its own claimed good intentions. It is a pseudo-reality, but more convincing than the real one. No matter how preposterously implausible its governing narrative and impositions, it is much more credible than the idea that it is not real. This totalitarianism appropriates to its purposes the coercive licence of the state, but mostly subtly, generally delegating the use of menace and implied violence to citizens themselves, who voluntarily elect to police their fellows. It has all the outward appearances of democracy, an illusion greatly assisted by the maintenance of the 'free' market, and the consumerist diversionism it begets. As Larry Fink, CEO of investment behemoth BlackRock, lip-smackingly declared, this totalitarianism is a much better match for capitalism than democracy has ever been: 'Markets don't like uncertainty. Markets like actually . . . totalitarian governments, where you have an understanding of what's out there. . . . And democracies are very messy. As we know, in the United States, we have opinions changing back and forth.'

In such a society is embedded the violence that is essential to its continuance. The 'measures' and 'restrictions' appear to be consensual, in the sense that they are insinuated as a response to a public demand for increased safety, but that is a trick. They are 'justified' by industrial lying and enforced, ultimately, by state coercion: The people's right to protect themselves by forming police forces and armies has been turned against them, this civic authority delegated to waiters, bouncers, robocops, security personnel, who assume the right to deny citizens their most basic entitlements with the insinuation of compulsion, even violence, which remains an ever-present implication. This represents the refinement of totalitarianism into a model that acquires a degree of plausible deniability even as it becomes more powerful, pervasive — and *invisible* — as it stretches into every nook and crevice of the intimate lives of the citizenry.

Of course, the difference between the present totalitarianism and the twentieth-century kind is a difference in method rather than a difference in principle. Lies and covert coercion — the iron fist in the velvet glove — have long been part of the early phases of totalitarian creep. Pseudo-reality — a planned parallel reality — is always the foundational layer of the pathocracy. Many of the greatest horrors of the history of humanity owe their occurrence solely to the establishment and social enforcement of a false actuality. The pseudo-reality is constructed in the public mind in the way a cult constructs a version of reality to draw in its devotees. It is also, in a way, analogous to the suspension of disbelief entered into in a cinema or theatre, in which the participant participates on the basis of trust and agrees to go where he or she is led. This is very close to, if not synonymous with, a hypnoidal trance, being dependent on the leveraging of repose, imagination, suggestibility and emotion. The dominant emotion is usually a negative one — fear or anger. Of course, this trance, like the movie or play, has a finite life; in the end, the participant must get out of his seat, blink, and walk back into the real world, with a sense of emerging from a kind of dream state. Some commentators have suggested that this is more or less what confronts us here, implying that in due course, we can all simply stand up and walk away. This is a questionable theory, as we shall see.

The purpose of the pseudo-reality is to create a path towards the utopian future that is the destination of all totalitarian projects. But there are differences of gravity and scale. Here — in this 'play', this 'movie' — the set has supplanted reality; the movie 'location' is where you live, where you work, in the pub (when it's open) and the café (when you're allowed in), in the actual cinema or theatre. The pseudo-reality is not the alternative world, but, for all intents and purposes, the 'real' one. You are in it almost all the time, so that, occasionally, when the 'real' world attempts to break through, it is like watching a snatch of a movie on a big screen in a darkened theatre through a swinging door as you cycle past at speed.

The ultimate purpose of propaganda is to construct at the centre of reality something akin to a kaleidoscopic projector casting lies on to the vacant space in the public imagination, which expands exponentially under that influence, persuading or compelling the population to live inside its projections and agree that these add up to reality. The endlessly repeated reflections and refractions of the same untruths render the overall effect misleadingly coherent and seemingly unassailable. Here, the functions of inclined mirrors of the kaleidoscope are carried out by multiple media screens and platforms, which reflect and deflect, refract and diffract back the same images and thoughts, so that, without some external point of reference, it becomes impossible to perceive the total effect as other than actuality. Just as the kaleidoscope can create infinite patterns of the same image, a corrupted media sector can create countless versions of the same lie.

The pseudo-reality is constructed linguistically with the objective of convincing/recruiting a significant minority of — generally — pathologised individuals, and sufficiently terrifying another quotient of the population that they do not question the imposed fictions. Often, too, the pseudo-reality requires a lens of expertise, demanding that matters pertaining to technical questions and categories be described by 'specialists' — a kind of priesthood — whose functions include 'educating' the public in the language of correct description, much as the tailors in the fairytale 'described' to the emperor and his courtiers the non-existent clothes they were weaving for his Excellency. For these reasons, the manipulators tend to concentrate their attentions at first on the 'educated' classes, which is to say heavily schooled, moderately intelligent and 'informed' people in the fields of politics, media, academia and the broader 'educational' sector. This addresses an apparent paradox of the mass formation phenomenon: that it affects the more 'intelligent' at least as much as the less so. In fact, it is better adapted to minds that depend largely on rote learning in a discrete area among a narrow range of disciplines. Totalitarianism also holds greater attraction for such people because their 'intelligence' depends on having an existing structure to fit into. Generally, too, such people tend to be afflicted by a vanity that exaggerates their own level of intelligence, and so are easily flattered into acquiescence in a schema with the external appearance of complexity — thus requiring something like their 'exalted cognitive abilities' to comprehend. This syndrome is subject to convenient disincentives: Should they cling to notions suggested by objective reality rather than, for example, 'the science', they render their 'intelligence' open to question, a risky embarkation in a nascent totalitarian context. Fearing being shunned or cast out by their peers, and thereby coming to the unfavourable notice of the Regime, they will prefer to acquiesce in the pseudo-reality. Here, then, a moderate degree of intelligence can become an impediment, causing some to construct complex fabrications to rationalise the pseudo-reality and thereby becoming its more enthusiastic adherents. In such manifold ways, sovereign human beings hand their power up to the Regime.

The thinly disguised mediocrity that tends to flourish in such conditions provokes a constant insecurity which pushes the subject into a central role in purveying the false narrative, and this is where the downright nastiness arising from scapegoating and demonisation campaigns initially takes root. But, for related reasons, the 'intelligent' subjects of these processes are also prone to hubris — born of continuously trying to pretend that they are smarter than they are — and this tends to be the cause not just of their own undoing but of the undermining of pseudo-reality projects, including narrative-building, in which they have a vital function.

It is a hallmark of totalitarian thought processes that they generate a phenomenon that in the former 'Eastern Bloc' was termed 'Absurdistan' — a satirical appellation for a country with absurdity as its central cultural hallmark. The only logic to such jurisdictions and their internal systems is a certain internal coherence of the ubiquitous illogic. Thus, for example, someone who dies within 14 days of receiving a vaccine is deemed to be unvaccinated, nominally because the 'effects' of the vaccine do not fully kick in for two weeks, but really because this is an ideal way of laundering the mortality figures, since about half of vaccine deaths occur within a few days. If this seems confusing, it can be only because of an inability to enter into the logic of the pseudo-reality — a clinging to the 'real' even though this has been declared morally suspect. Thus, 'intelligent' people tend to be quicker at creating an adequate rationalisation, this being how the technical brain tends to work. Combined with the techniques of demonisation directed at outright critics, these factors help to drive the middle-ground into the arms of the Regime, at first by causing waverers to distance themselves from outright unbelievers, and then incrementally by absorption into the herd. Thus, we can observe the configuration of the three-part compartmentalisation outlined by Mattias Desmet: 30 per cent utterly bought in; 30 per cent resistant; and 40 per cent in the middle who go along with whichever side seems to be winning. Fear of ridicule by peers is a strong force in compelling those in the middle ground to deny their own sense of what is true.

Words, phrases, sentences, provide the building blocks of the pseudo-reality. This involves a conscious use of the language emanating from power centres as something other than a tool of communication and understanding. The purpose is, essentially, mendacious. Its objective is to deceive, but not in minor ways. It is directed at the construction of an alternative version of reality that becomes so persuasive as to obscure what is real. It constructs in words and images a kind of imaginative stage-set, before which an entirely fictional version of reality can be enacted. The more people come to accept the pseudo-reality, the closer they move to the mentality of the governing narcissists/psychopaths. This is why it is foolish for 'normal' people to try to 'understand' why their neighbours accept the pseudo-reality, imagining them to be misinformed or simply emotionally overwrought. In fact, according to Andrew Lobaczewski in *Political Ponerology*, they have become functionally pathologised, which is to say that they have come to find the false reality more tolerable than the real one, because the false reality relieves them, at least temporarily, of the pathologies they had developed within normal society. This may be a relatively small sector of the population — 6 per cent in Lobaczewski's direct experience in Poland — but its influence is infectious upon a segment of the 'normal' population, which will adapt to its thinking so as to rationalise the pseudo-reality sufficiently to be able to exist within it. Normal people don't think like psychopaths or schizoids but, presented with the double-binds of the constructed reality, may engage in mental gymnastics of accommodation so as to make their sense of reality approximately fit the imposed everyday understandings.

As the process develops, the grey areas in the middle tend to disappear, and a clear polarisation develops between those who believe in the pseudo-reality and those who continue to dissent. This renders real violence inevitable. Gulags, show trials, zero tolerance towards even minor dissenters, and other extreme symptoms of the twentieth-century model inevitably follow, though bearing different names, like 'mandatory hotel quarantine', 'naming and shaming', and 'emergency measures'.

This process of creating a pseudo-reality is very similar to certain forms of religious adherence, and, therefore, works very well in societies in which a once ubiquitous religiosity is on the wane. It is remarkable that this process involves the constant insinuation of a *moral system*, overturning the normative rational process by which reality is objectively described, and inverting also the cultural context, placing pressure on the 'normal' people to justify their understandings of reality, while elevating the pseudo-reality to the level of fact. The 'morality' thereby generated, because it is pathological, feels infinitely more powerful — and therefore more 'moral' — than any normative moral system. The rhetoric of the totalitarian drive incorporates elements of moralism, sanctimony, pietism and authoritarianism.

Over the long run, a process of incessant gaslighting pressurises dissenters to accept the pseudo-reality, if only for a quiet life, which works in many instances, since believing the lie is socially much more advantageous than insisting upon objective reality. The suspected 'denier' will always be presumed guilty, the onus of proof residing with him or her to demonstrate compliance and good faith; failing to do so is deemed to be the basis of self-exclusion. The rules are always blurred, so that everyone is always on the back foot, always open to a charge of non-compliance coming from an unexpected quarter. A strange dissonance enters in: Those who continue to see reality in objective terms, and to that extent to deny the pseudo-reality, are deemed to be the ignorant ones. Societies that are culturally inclined towards 'agreeableness' can be the most susceptible to this syndrome, placing their members under extreme pseudo-moral pressure from their pathologised neighbours/compatriots and conniving regimes, until they succumb to the lie. This process recruits ordinary people as its agents of enforcement, not just as spies and snitches, but as actual enforcers who accuse their fellows of immorality on the grounds of their non-acceptance of the pseudo-reality.

Clearly, these conditions are not acceptable to the kind of people who, in the everyday course of events in 'normality', might themselves be deemed 'normal', or to the logic of what is called 'common sense'. In these conditions, such 'normal' people either eventually conform or enter a long process of dissent. But, as things develop, the society thus afflicted becomes increasingly psychopathic as more and more people are absorbed into acceptance of the pseudo-reality. Many do so because they lack the fibre to resist, or find it congenial to be on the side of Power. Many normally sane and reasonable people will become 'infected', coming more and more to resemble the tyrants they initially looked askance at. From the inside, this appears to be 'normal', for there is nothing to alert the sufferer to the distortions he has entered into. He sees only the pseudo-reality, which is by now the only reality he knows. Those who remain outside are the strange ones, the ones to be regarded with suspicion and caution, and perhaps removed from society for the good of everyone, as in Justin Trudeau's infamous question: 'Do we tolerate these people?' In this, we can detect an answer to the perennial question as to how 'good' people become complicit in genocide.

In the description of these conditions, we can more readily see how 'the unvaccinated' become 'the *Untermenschen*', how face masks function as Swastika lapel pins, how 'green passes' become as Aryan ID papers. Objectively senseless social restrictions and mandatory public-obedience rituals — 'lockdowns', 'social distancing', 'sanitisation' — are directed at the familiar smear of the human person as biohazard, an offence to hygiene. In this pseudo-reality, the world is united in a total war, not against an external enemy but against an internal, biological one.

The intensity of such pressures drives the 'normal' person, even despite his own rational understanding, towards acceptance of the lie. The total nature of their neighbours' acquiescence, together with the effects of being constantly gaslighted, make even reasonable people acquiesce in the broader cultural conditions, growing convinced that their own intuitions are wrong or that they ought to at least appear to be of the same mind with their neighbours for the sake of social harmony.

The pseudo-reality is almost impossible to describe in sentences owing any allegiance to factuality, logic or moral order. It is constructed precisely to bypass such phenomena, albeit in a way that augments its own appearance of internal coherence for those disposed or motivated to examine it. It must, by definition, remain partly mysterious to those who remain within the normal human world, and indeed, it may seem not merely improbable but impossible to someone who has had no previous direct experience or opportunity for observation of its like, or is not in a state of delusion. And because it is completely concocted, it cannot be checked or even coherently critiqued. It operates at the level of pure sentiment, by the most literal interpretations of words and responses, almost at the level of parody.

This process serves at once to 'evangelise' further compliance with the lie and to demoralise those who knowingly acquiesce in it. Thus, the ultimate objective is the insinuation of *pseudo-reality as sole reality* while at the same time permitting an unspoken awareness that it is utterly false. The resulting total demoralisation is, in fact, the destination-state. By all accounts, because such edifices of pseudo-reality lead to unrestrained amorality and illogic, they eventually collapse under their own weight, though not without bringing down the affected society also. It is self-evident that a utopia based on such foundations is impossible, so that all that endures for long is raw power and brute force. This means that many people will die before the turnaround occurs, and entire countries may be brought to their knees.

The seizure of the nation's media is a *sine qua non* for a Totalitaria/pathocracy. The conditions of modern society — mass media, personal computers, smartphones, tech surveillance and data processing — render most people susceptible to the insinuation of a pseudo-reality. In the nature of things, we must, of necessity live in a bubble in which a fog of lies is being constantly generated and renewed by propaganda. Such a fog became almost omnipresent in the Time of Covid.

The fog does not tell of the virus: It *is* the virus — in the sense that its constant presence informs everyone that the virus remains and is deadly and, therefore, to be feared. We have learned that people do not use the media as a source of information, but as a kind of mediator between themselves and the truth. It is like the way passengers on an airplane immediately look to the trolley-attendants when there is a sudden outbreak of turbulence. They do not ask the stewardesses if it is serious, or what might be the cause, or how long it is likely to last, but instead simply watch the stewardesses for signs of panic. If the stewardesses are continuing to serve drinks and talk to one another, most of the passengers (apart from those with bad nerves or serious hangovers) go back to reading their magazines. In the same way, people no longer read newspapers or even listen to the TV news; instead, they assess the general content and the manner of its delivery with one question uppermost in mind: *Should I be worried?* They do not apprehend facts or data, but simply *signals*.

Editors and journalists have learned that this new tendency can be manipulated. For example, they know that to cover themselves, they can actually publish information that, of itself — in the old days — would have been sufficient to bring the whole thing to an end (for example, the truth about the PCR test or the trick of counting all deaths of people 'with Covid' — according to a PCR test! — as if they had died 'of Covid'). Many people may read such a report and at first ask themselves if it might be true and, if so, why this revelation has not brought the whole thing to a halt. But then, watching the 9 o'clock news and seeing nothing about it, they assume that they must have misunderstood. Thus, a Big Lie is not so much retold as simply *maintained*, much as a bouquet of flowers might be maintained in a vase for a fortnight by topping up the water every day. A Big Lie is easier to 'maintain' than a little lie because the little lie has, by virtue of being little, not yet gotten off the ground, and, by virtue of its unfamiliarity, attracts more scrutiny and scepticism. With the Big Lie, which of necessity must become ubiquitous, it is simply a matter of *looking* — perhaps just looking at, for example, the masked face of a neighbour — to be assured that the virus is still 'in the news', and therefore still 'deadly'.

Most people by now require to know almost nothing factual about the virus, the vaccines or the reasons behind the suspension of human life for two years. Today, they may catch a headline on the front of a newspaper, and that is the sum total of their intelligence-gathering. The text underneath might be total gibberish (it would be an interesting experiment) and no one will notice. All that is important is that their neighbours remain convinced — or at least *appear to* remain convinced — that there is a serious crisis and that it shows no signs of abating. That is enough for them. They cannot be bothered with facts, for what difference could knowledge make? Moreover, the lie is not passive, but incessantly proactive. It issues constant information and instructions concerning itself. In a sense, the acquiescent do not have to be 'believers' as long as they obey these instructions, which many of those within the middle ground may do just for a quiet life. In this miasma, then, it does not matter that the lie is a lie: it has consequences as if it were the truth, and soon its adherents begin to think not in terms of truth or falsity but of what its power over them amounts to. They do not necessarily wear a mask because they are afraid of becoming ill, but because they fear even more the disapprobation of their neighbours. And this may happen at an unconscious level, so they would deny it, if confronted, and thereafter continue denying it to themselves.

The modern 'newspaper' (especially online) is designed to assist this process. In the online 'paper', many of the articles are behind paywalls, which means that most readers see only the headline and the first couple of paragraphs. This is, in most cases, enough to 'inform' them, in the sense of topping up their certainty that an enormous threat to their safety lies just six feet away, and conveying some — implicit or explicit — call-to-action on the basis of this fear. We need a new word for this, since it no longer has anything to do with journalism or publishing the news, but is really an adjunct to the process of mass formation/hypnosis. Perhaps we might borrow a word from the masters of the three-card-trick, in which the process of 'showing' the 'money card' to the 'mark' who has already been set up by the card shark's 'shills' is an intrinsic part of the deceit. 'Money rag' would be a better term than 'newspaper', though it lacks something.

Perhaps never before has humanity witnessed such a split in human society where one side cannot see what the other sees, or thinks it sees, to the point where those who see what isn't there demand that those who see what is there be silenced lest the blindsided have to listen to descriptions of what the cast-out insist is reality. We deal, then, with not so much a plague as a *play* — an 'interesting' play, engaging even. The problem is that we are not members of the audience, but characters on the stage, unwitting 'actors' in a drama scripted by others, with eclipsed motives, who are not part of the apparent action. And we cannot escape from the theatre, until we find a way of resolving the plot in our favour.

CHAPTER 21
YOUR GOVERNMENT HATES YOU

14-05-2022

The world's governments have waged a two-year war on behalf of rich, powerful interests seeking to destroy the sovereignty and futures of their own peoples. This war now enters its most lethal phase.

A crime is being committed on an ongoing basis, all across the world, free and unfree. It is a crime of commission and omission, and arguably the most serious in either category that has ever been perpetrated. We are facing multiple crises, but our governments tell us only about crises that are not crises, or at least not crises that *involve* us, as opposed to *affecting* us. Effusing moral blackmail in all directions, they shruggingly point towards the war that they started with the precise intention of creating an alibi for themselves so as to avoid the wrath of their peoples and the punishment that ought properly to await them.

In Ireland, three months ago, the 'crisis' that had allegedly assailed us for two years — the 'crisis' of a 'deadly' disease — evaporated overnight to be replaced by the 'crisis' of a war in a country nearly 2,500 miles away. At first sight, it seemed unlikely that such a conflict might affect us in any substantial way, but immediately, our Government announced that it would be taking an unlimited number of refugees from the affected country, guesstimated at 200,000 — into a country whose government has for the past decade declared itself perplexed and powerless in the face of a housing shortage affecting 10,000 of its own citizens. Instantly, those who thought that a war in Ukraine was none of our business were 'proved wrong'.

We who have been seeking to confront the attempted destruction of our lives and societies occurring over the past two years have many times speculated as to whether the dominant note of the political responses might more correctly be ascribed to stupidity or to wickedness. The jury remains out. Stupidity, as we have noted, is no excuse, especially considering that these politicians have been proactive in pushing potentially lethal poison serums and preventing people exercising fundamental freedoms on foot of a refusal to accept them. These are not victimless inanities. There must, we have ruminated, be some legal limit on the stupidity of people who exercise public power, especially when that stupidity leads to loss of life or serious injury, which in this case is most certainly the case: a dramatic uptick in working-age mortality in multiple countries of 40 per cent and more.

Many times, we have noted prosecutions and convictions — sometimes followed by lengthy prison sentences — of such as train drivers and ship captains who have been in charge of vehicles which became involved in accidents that resulted in death or injury; generally, they are charged with something like negligence or reckless injury. Regardless of the intelligence of those implicated, or their provable scale of knowledge of what they have been involved in, analogous charges are surely relevant to the actions of multiple politicians, scientists, doctors, judges, journalists and police officers, whose actions have prolonged and exacerbated the criminality, cruelty and misery of the past two years.

Whether people are aware of this or not — and many, due to the criminality of the legacy media, are not so aware — we now face perhaps the greatest calamity faced by the world for three-quarters of a century, at least. Within a year — probably much sooner — our economies, monetary systems and currencies will experience outright collapse; hyperinflation (already in train) will reach Zimbabwean levels throughout the formerly civilised world, which will be followed by unprecedented levels of stagflation (a combination of inflation and recession, soon sliding into outright depression), which will be accompanied by shortages of the most essential provisions for human survival, i.e. food and fuel, resulting in famine and other extreme hardships, which in turn will lead to chaos and societal breakdown, which we can expect to be met by a ramping up of the totalitarian responses which the morally bankrupt 'authorities' of our countries have been road-testing for precisely this purpose over the past 25 months.

It is exceedingly likely that, in addition to the risks of hyperinflation, within a few months, the chief currencies of the free world will, without exception, become subject to outright collapse, which means that the savings of citizens will become worthless. This will affect virtually all existing currencies, including the dollar, the pound sterling and the euro. In the unlikely event that anything remains in the wake of this meltdown, this is likely to be subject to governmental 'bail-ins,' which is to say that any remaining financial assets will be liable to partial or total confiscation. A global digital currency is planned, but leaving aside the myriad other problems and dangers arising from this, the chances of any future compensation of citizens under such a system are unpromising.

Right now, it is as though nothing like this could possibly be imminent, since it is receiving either negligible or extremely opaque or misleading coverage in the legacy media. Throughout our lives, we have become accustomed to a more or less honest press, which we have felt able to rely upon to alert us in times of danger. This press was by no means perfect — it was afflicted by manifold financial compromises and ideological corruptions. But never in the history of Western civilisation have we before been threatened by anything remotely like what is coming without as much as a murmur from the Fourth Estates of our nations and societies, to prepare us to defend our own and our families' lives.

The absence of a warning, as we must surely know by now, offers no reassurance whatsoever. The dog-not-barking has been sedated and muzzled. Though expected to continue paying for these corrupted platforms, we must look elsewhere to discover and confirm the truth. Moreover, we need to be watchful for the new role of the old 'Fourth Estate', which resides in deflecting us from any kind of certainty or even awareness of what is really happening. We most certainly need to take notice of and override the insinuated scorn that is one of the modern media's core products: the rejection as 'conspiracy theory' of everything and anything that does not fit the prescribed Narrative. For the past two years, these tendencies have destroyed innumerable businesses and cost millions of lives. To be waylaid by the same voices now will almost certainly prove fatal to the very civilisation we have hitherto felt able to take for granted.

The world, including the former 'free world', faces a calamity of existential proportions, and it will accelerate rapidly in the very near future. To describe this in factual terms is to invite the incredulity of most of those who may hear or read it described. It does not seem possible that those upon whom we have depended to protect our societies, our economic welfare, our lives and our well-being, could possibly not be warning us in the event that some such catastrophe is now imminent. That, after all, is the very definition of their function, and arguably the whole of their necessary purpose. But that is precisely what is occurring.

Let us state things straightforwardly: The world, including the former 'civilised' world, now faces shortages of essential products that are likely to lead to widespread hunger, hardship, and very possibly starvation and death. The flashpoints are the most critical conceivable: food and fuel. Moreover, there is every reason to believe that these shortages are being deliberately engineered to achieve something akin to that outcome.

A number of inter-related phenomena are feeding into the escalating difficulties: hyperinflation; commodity shortages arising from organic and imposed (orchestrated) factors; supply chain issues; an orchestrated fake war; globalism-inflicted problems such as container shortages and shipping hold-ups; weather wars that target farmers in their capacity to sow their crops. As things currently appear, the crop yields this year will, if they are harvestable at all, be among the lowest ever, in part due to a bizarre run of cold and rainy spring weather in both the US and Europe. Even those farmers who have managed to plant their usual quotas expect lower yields.

All this was entirely predictable. More than two years ago — as early as late April 2020 — economist friends of mine were telling me that enormous, perhaps irreparable, damage had already been done to the economies of the West. One such close observer told me of his contacts with the advisors to various governments — including the government in Dublin — which had revealed a total ignorance on the part of such actors of the consequences of what they were imposing on their societies.

By the coming autumn, the damage looks set to become clear, as a result of a worldwide dearth of fertilizer (the consequence of hyperinflation, factory closures and resulting supply chain issues arising from the Time of Covid), as well as a rash of 'unexplained' fires and 'explosions', escalating from mid-2020 at food processing plants and warehouses across America and Europe. In addition, a host of alleged disease outbreaks among farm animals worldwide — bird flu in chickens worldwide, Japanese encephalitis in Australian pigs; wasting disease in deer herds in Texas; and sheep culling in Northern Ireland due to CO_2 emissions — have resulted in massive destruction of livestock on the basis of a tiny number of infections mostly 'detected' by the infamous PCR test.

The astonishing thing about the emerging food crisis, which can be acutely observed in a country like Ireland — a heartbeat ago a predominantly agricultural economy — is that the mainstream of our societies is, or appears to be, utterly oblivious of the disaster that is unfolding, never mind understanding its actual nature. The steep uptick in mysterious fires and explosions at food factories since the turn of the year — and a couple of planes crashing into other plants for good measure — were at first met with indifference and avoidance from so-called journalists. More recently, this indifference morphed into scorn, as media that could no longer continue ignoring these incidents began reporting various instances of this unprecedented contagion of destruction as, yes, 'conspiracy theory'. A couple of weeks ago, within hours of one another, hundreds of virtually identical media reports emerged dismissing the idea that the fires might have been started deliberately, all using the same boilerplate text. Typical was the headline on the *Daily Beast*'s 'report' of April 29th: 'The Right's New Conspiracy Theory: Kamikaze planes and Food fires.'

Now, however, possibly as the slow-burn result of an April 22nd report on *Tucker Carlson Tonight* on Fox News, the media have more or less universally condescended to drop the 'conspiracy theory' trope. As Tucker put it to a guest who reported on the phenomenon: 'An hour ago, a plane crashed into a General

Mills [US-based food company] facility. We had already planned this segment. I mean, I'm sorry, I'm sorry, the onus is on people who think that's a "conspiracy theory" to explain what is going on. What are the odds of that? I have no idea.'

*The kind of journalistic stupidity and corruption that Carlson was alluding to might be greeted with the usual 'What's new?' if the world was not, after all, on the cusp of a worldwide food famine. But the facts have become too overwhelming of late for the familiar nonsense to pass muster any longer, as it becomes more and more clear that the world now faces what may be the gravest crisis of human survival in many centuries. How the criminal failure of reporting will be explained away when the worst happens remains to be seen.

The sole issue being conceded by the political class is that the Ukraine conflict has created some 'supply chain issues'. Political 'leaders', such as US president Biden, Canadian premier Trudeau and German chancellor Scholtz, have recently been warning about an imminent global 'hunger crisis' — arising (of course) from the Ukraine war, the alibi which was skilfully engineered from the start of 2022, as the 'pandemic' narrative was scaled back. That everything that is now happening is the doing of Putin is what most of those who even appreciate that there is a looming problem have now come to believe. The shocking thing is that the war has, so far, had a minimal effect on most Western economies, and where it has, it is because of the ludicrous 'circular firing-squad' sanctions, which have done infinitely more damage to the sanctioning countries than to Russia, the alleged target. To the extent that the European Union is at present being hit by shortages of oil and gas, this, too, is because of the effects of the sanctions boomeranging back to strike at the duped and deluded peoples of Europe. Where the war will certainly have an effect within a few months is when the shutdown of huge swathes of the Ukrainian agricultural economy adds its quota to the shrivelling of wheat and vegetable supplies throughout Europe and America.

A 'shortage of food' is not the same thing as 'food shortages'. We are not talking about a shortage of items in the shops — perhaps of cornflakes or lentils or flour. We are talking — in the first instance — of shortages of just about everything that human beings eat to stay alive: bread, meat, vegetables, fruit, dairy products, rice, pasta . . . And within a short time of these shortages becoming manifest, they will amount to a total absence of fresh foods, to be followed in short order by an escalating scarcity of pre-packed foods — in tins, cartons, bottles — as the effects of panic-buying and rationing kick in. This means that many people will have *little or no food*, which implies that, within a couple of weeks, people, including children, will begin starving to death — and not just in the 'developing world'; this will occur also in the parts of the world

---

* This video report can be found on the web by searching for 'Tucker Carlson reporting on the fires at food processing plants'.

that, up until 25 months ago, constituted part of the 'modern', 'industrial', 'civilised' West.

In addition, the already food-deprived countries of Europe will come under pressure from mass evacuations of refugees from Africa and the Middle East, arriving in the 'democratic capitalist West' with high hopes of what they will presume to be the continuing supply chains of the European Union. Little will they know that the EU is now run by individuals whose deficiencies include psychopathy and incompetence in equal measures.

As Christian Westbrook — otherwise 'Ice Age Farmer' — said recently:

'If we pretend that we're some alien species in a faraway space, watching humanity, we would be scratching our heads right now and asking ourselves, and rightly so, understandably so, "What the Hell is going on down there right now? It seems that they've given up all hope of continuing as a species! They're just stopping their food production! They're not planting their crops in many cases, or they're changing to different things at the last second! They're not fertilizing the crops they do have! The greenhouses that they spent tons of money and years building are empty now!"'

Were this all simply due to bad luck or even gross incompetence, it would be terrifying enough. Far more shocking is that it is clearly all part of a carefully prepared programme — the 2030 agenda, or Fourth Industrial Revolution — planned to ensure that control of all food supplies becomes centralised and subject to hyper-regulation and conformity, including the elimination of live-stock products from the human diet. This is likely to be accompanied by a licensing system for food production that will, in all likelihood, put an end to home producers growing vegetables in back gardens and allotments. Self-sufficiency will be declared a reactionary activity as the powers-that-shouldn't-be ramp up their attacks on food sovereignty of all kinds. The bogus alibi for this is 'climate change', but the real purpose is the securing of total control over the food chain so that the Combine of 'secret unknowns' can retain life-or-death leverage over every citizen: *Do what you're told if you want to go on eating.*

The Covid Project, then, had three triggers: the plateaued peak of the world's oil resources; the related collapse of the world's money systems; and the advent of artificial intelligence, the Technological Singularity and the transhuman-ist/posthumanist revolution. The first provided the Combine with motivation, the second with urgency, and the third with opportunity. Everything converges on the transhumanist agenda, the ultimate objective being the total subjugation of the human person, so we cease all nonsense about being autonomous beings. And all this in turn confides that, just as the leaders of the former Free World have for the past three months been in bed with actual literal Nazis in Ukraine — while seeking to smear anyone who calls them out as 'far right' — they are soon to emerge as having been in league not merely with psychotic murderers, but actual genocidists, over the span of the 'Covid Project'.

In truth, the portents of our current undoing have been visible for years in the objectively bizarre phenomenon of so-called public representatives from multiple supposed democracies heading off to the annual WEF shindig in Davos to hobnob with other wannabe tyrants seeking to sell out their own peoples. The idea of a 'club' of international political leaders ought to be regarded as unthinkable in any democratic country, where politicians represent their electorates/citizens, and no one else. It is clear from the images that emanate from these occasions — the strutting and preening of these toxic traitors — that they see themselves as existing somehow separately from those who elected them. We have fallen a long way from the democratic and republican ideals when Klaus Schwab, the nominal head of the WEF, is able to boast that he has 'penetrated' cabinets around the world to force his economic philosophies upon multiple former nations, thereby circumventing the inconvenience of the ballot box and in effect abducting the duly elected representatives of sundry peoples, who bask in his approval and pseudo-affection.

It has been reported in Ireland in recent days that the leader of our Government, the Taoiseach Micheál Martin, is shortly to travel to Davos, Switzerland, for the postponed annual conference of the World Economic Forum (WEF), which has been orchestrating this catastrophe over the past several years. Under the theme/title, *Working Together, Restoring Trust*, the Annual Meeting 2022, running from Sunday 22nd to Thursday 26th May, will be the first global in-person leadership event since the start of the pandemic. It is appropriate that Martin will attend this historic meeting of murderous psychopaths, since he, like other Western political leaders, has for the past two years been centrally involved in contriving the conditions for the coming cull and planned final subjugation of the global population.

Over the course of the 'Covid Project', the political actors responsible for the constrictions, cruelties and unasked-for changes inflicted on our lives and societies have presided over the transfer of something in excess of $3 trillion from small and medium-sized businesses to the richest oligarchs in the world. This, when it is mentioned at all in public discussion, is treated as some odd collateral element of the 'battle' against the 'pandemic'. Of course it is nothing of the kind. It is germane to the central meaning and end-purpose of the lockdowns, and the reason, for example, why the World Bank has, since the outset, referred on its website to the 'Covid Project'.

This represents more than a straightforward upward transfer of wealth, which would be momentous enough in its own right since it is something that has allegedly preoccupied the left-liberals of the world for generations, all of whom have now lapsed into a surreal silence. It also implies a shift in the nature of the meaning of words like 'capitalism' and 'democracy' — from terms denoting systems broadly designed to mechanistically deliver benefits to whole populations, to words that have miraculously been renovated to describe an entirely new kind of world.

The key to understanding what has happened is to perceive that the electorates of the world have been deprived of their sovereignty, which has been snatched from them under cover of a pseudo-emergency, and handed — along with the $3 trillion dollars — to the richest men (they are all male, and almost entirely Caucasian) in the world.

In this new world, 'democracy' will be driven not by the will of electorates / sovereign people, but by the requirements of the oligarchs who, as a consequence of the past two years, have successfully demanded the disabling and removal of the leverage previously exercised by voters, and its replacement with a 'franchise' amounting, in effect, to the naked power of money. The oligarchs are now, in a very real sense, the only 'voters', at least the only ones that matter — voting in the secret 'election' to which the masses of the world's former democracies are not even alerted. The oligarchs agree to fund the political systems, and the political systems agree to continue providing the oligarchs with whatever they need in order to continue growing richer and richer so they can abundantly cater for all the financial needs of the political system, while incrementally gaining control over the whole world and everyone in it. It is said that this project of transformation operates on a need-to-know basis, that each operative in the chain of command knows only as much as his or her role requires, implying that politicians, in general, are far denser than we ever imagined. There is another school of thought in which the politicians of the world have been signed up to Faustian pacts by which they have agreed to become the deliverers of their fellow humans to slavery and perdition in return for favourable treatment in the coming dispensation.

Of course, what the politicians fail to grasp is that their own usefulness provides them with merely a shade more longevity than the rest of humanity. They are, in this equation, the equivalents of the *Judenräte*, the councils set up within Jewish ghettos in 1933 by the Nazis to enforce their desires and demands. The functions of these bodies included weakening resistance, ensuring that orders and regulations were implemented, and spying on and identifying Jews for eventual 'deportation'.

Where the Combine of 2022 plans to take us has the appearance, superficially at least, of something like a neo-feudal world, but is more complex than that. The lockdowns were, in a sense, predictive of the future in the context of the enforced idleness they imposed upon the human race by virtue of the insinuated fear of death arising from a deadly virus. This was, in part, a rehearsal for a world without conventional work. In the early stages of the post-'pandemic' world, this model will become part of a trial in which the world's populations will be invited to consume without producing, to see if it is possible, in practice, to create an economy that operates on a more or less totally mechanised process of production, with a consumer base comprising idle, unproductive consumers who simply spend the money which is skimmed off the top of the transactional wealth accumulation process so that it may serve this manufactured economic model, while ensuring that the totality of the world's wealth and tokens gravitates to, and remains within, the control of the oligarchs. The objective is not power for the purposes of enrichment, but the other way around: money as the instrument of total power.

Their plan is that the many must submit themselves as instruments of the few — the 'elite' which has finally stepped up to sit on the throne recently presumed to have been vacated by the deity. Physically indistinguishable from the rest of mankind, the 'few' plan to maintain their dominion by the usurpation of earthbound power, having accumulated most of the earth's resources so as to leave the majority of men disempowered and bereft, while bribing a sufficiency of willing collaborators and traitors to defend them from any possible rebellion.

The super-rich have never wanted to share the planet with those who merely struggled to get by and wished for nothing other than the means to do so and be let alone to do it. They most certainly do not want to share the planet with those they have made poor, and might — some of them anyway — be inclined to seek revenge.

We had displeased our 'betters', who now become our new 'creators' — both by our unclean natures and our desire selfishly to exploit the resources of the earth, as we claimed God had permitted us to do. The escalating numbers of the human race as a whole had, in the estimation of the elites, threatened to leave an insufficiency for themselves. The self-proclaimed gods had become alien and hostile to man, desiring all things to be theirs. More precisely, we had outlived our usefulness, for very soon, technology would deliver the few of the need to have the many around them. The harmony between the people and the hidden elites had suddenly revealed itself as fictional. Man, as he stands, even at his best, is of limited use to the 'few'. When it comes to doing what is to be done, technology is more malleable, cheaper, more efficient, adaptable. And technology shows no inclination to rebel. In these circumstances, there has arisen a clear and urgent need to absorb the bulk of the human population into the mechanistic realm, to make them, in effect — and in no sense metaphorically — parts of the machine.

In this emerging world, the delusions and pretences of politics and ideology have all been exposed. Money talks; nothing else does — and no one but the monied may. It emerges that the only reason we were permitted for so long to indulge our fantasies about rights and freedoms was because the means did not exist to corral us in ways that were not too messy for people with delicate stomachs. Now that the means are available, it is a different matter.

Hitler's Third Reich, Stalin's Soviet Union, Mao's Cultural Revolution were all ideological projects devoted to abolishing contradiction from the human subject and reconstituting him as the less problematic posthuman. But the means in those times were inadequate to the ambition. Fundamentally, the elaborate ideologies of the last century sought to abolish the human soul, to eliminate the individual will, and to switch off the subjective consciousness of men. That was a beginning, a practice run. Now it is possible to intervene in the biological and cognitive levels of the human construction, changing these fundamentally. The remarkable finding of the present age, satisfactorily confirmed in the Covid Project, has been that man is programmable by the technologies already on hand. Moreover, by a certain enforceable logic, human beings and technology had already begun to converge, becoming so close that they already formed a unit in virtually every sense except the physical. The smartphone, for example, had become as much a body-part as the hearing-aid, and without a smartphone/computer, the human person would be helpless in the modern street or building. It was surely time to move on to the next phase: the abolition of the human soul.

The few who have no souls, seek to abolish the souls of the many out of jealousy, being unable to live with the idea that something so beautiful and so uncontainable could at the same time remain to them both vital and obscure. They insist on total control, to which the human soul represents the chief impediment. A world without soul would be a world of lies, a world which denies that which is hidden and mysterious, a world that insists on filling the vacant spaces with made-up stuff that has no life and therefore rings persistently false. The world of the lie is a world strung upon a false framework, a pseudo-reality that passes for the real thing. This is the world we were introduced to during the 'Covid Project'.

The tech savants inform us that a total fusion of man and tech is now on the cards and that this will be an unremittingly good thing. The young in particular, being trained to love their smartphones more than themselves, are disposed to believe this. Technological enhancement will remove pain and grief, inferior thinking and fear, and render each of us smarter than the whole human race of 2022 put together. Every day, in every way, man becomes not merely more capable but more ethically perfect, because 'progress' itself implies a process of moral refinement. So the theory goes.

This is, in a sense, then, the 'final' part of the Plan — although in reality, there will be no 'final' part that is not the 'final solution', and we are, more or less, arriving there now. It does not take a genius to work out what will happen, sooner or later — and probably sooner. The oligarchs who constitute the Combine will grow tired of the contrived game and lose interest in providing and subsidising the diversion of the vast majority of useless eaters, previously known to themselves — laughably now — as citizens, and sovereign peoples. The model and method are already tried and tested. There are all kinds of ways of getting rid of people who have become superfluous to requirements: bloat them with poisoned foods; drive them to opioids, suck the meaning from their existences, drop by drop; euthanise them with fear and, failing that, with sedatives purporting to be for calming the fears. Trialling these methods was, again, a central function of the 'Covid Project'. Now that all the boxes have been tried and ticked, it is purely a matter of re-mobilising the machine that worked so well before.

So, the 'posthumanist' phase is planned — in as far as it affects the generality of the present human populations — as a mere staging post, a little temporary diversion on the way to the condition of literal post-humanity. The secret unknowns will operate the available technologies to upgrade themselves, to create the means for transcendence here on earth, but that is not their plan for the generality of the species. In the short term, they will need other humans as guinea pigs in the occasionally risky experiments that may be involved. After that? 'God' knows. All we can say for certain is that nothing will remain of the world we know.

'Too bad,' as Baudrillard declared: 'It's Utopia.' If human ingenuity alone were the measure of progress, then we might well, at this moment of possibility, be moving towards some kind of fantasmagorical paradise. But such an aspiration now reveals itself as excluding consideration of the fallen nature of man, overlooking the fact that, through history, man's ingenuity has outpaced his moral growth, a banana skin that lies there waiting to trip the Law of Unintended Consequences. This, perhaps, is humanity's best hope in the coming phase.

To believe that this wicked madness can work at any level in practice is to misunderstand humanity, as well as the workings of money, production and consumption. For reasons that are self-evidently intrinsic to the nature of the human edifice and the structure of reality, this plan is destined to fail spectacularly. The Combine of secret unknowns, possessing fabulous but mainly inherited wealth, has not the faintest idea how a world actually works. But the last two years have surely taught us that the incoherence at the heart of their plans will not protect us from the stupidity of those who have become drunk on the challenge of pushing their programme of demands, willy-nilly. In a short while, it will become obvious that the project is doomed to failure, and by then, they will have completely dismantled the world as it was.

I have for some time been continuously wondering — perhaps naïvely in view of the possibility of Faustian pacts — if there would come a time when the political and journalying small-fry would begin to wake up to what they have been involved in. How much longer could they continue to yell 'far right' and 'conspiracy theory' at every attempt to articulate what was actually occurring? Did they really not know? Is that even possible? Tragically, broadly speaking, *it is*: Looking back, I would have to say that most of the journalists I met over the years were as thick as pig dung, but there used to be the odd intelligent one, so where they got to during the 'pandemic' is a mystery that leads to all kinds of unproductive speculation.

For the past two years, the media faithfully reported the 'analyses' of central banks predicting that the reopening of society, when it occurred, would be followed by an unprecedented boom. They did not say which kind of boom, but now it emerges that, with fingers crossed behind their backs, they most likely meant 'akin to the explosion of a bomb capable of destroying the human quotient of civilisation while leaving everything else untouched'.

The 'surprise' of politicians and journalists confronted by the escalating signs of general collapse is informative of either a grotesque ignorance or profound cynicism bordering on bloodthirstiness and/or psychopathic derangement. Economists, too, not merely failed to foresee what is now happening, but predicted the precise opposite. What a shocker: that forcing people to remain economically idle for two years in a locked-down world and dropping helicopter money into every backyard, could result in an economic crash!

And, even yet, this unfolding nightmare is buried under a mess of propaganda with governments acting on behalf of their external puppeteers, functioning to rigidly control the dominant consciousness of the world and its channels of communication and conversation.

Our politicians, for whatever reason, have delivered us, in the manner of a battalion of Judases, to the antechamber of Hell. It is not, given the constructed drifts of culture, as if we were certain of avoiding blundering in here of our own accord, but they made it all but unavoidable, above all by denying us the opportunity of a conversation in which we might have alerted one another to the possibilities and the dangers.

Our governments hate us. The government of the United States has thus far spent $54 billion sending arms to Ukraine but nothing on trying to relieve an acute shortage of baby formula throughout America.

The decision of the Irish Government to accept unlimited numbers of Ukrainian 'refugees' was taken without reference to the Irish people who stand to be profoundly affected by it. By the middle of May, Ireland had already taken in 27,000 'refugees' under this heading. In late April, the Irish Minister for Justice, Helen McEntee — who had herself recently withdrawn an offer to accept a Ukrainian family into her home on the ground that her residence's remote location might cause such a family to become 'isolated' — was to be heard musing in public about her hopes that the government might not be required to 'force' people to accept refugees into their homes. 'Obviously we want to make sure,' she said, 'that we don't find ourselves in a situation where we don't have space and accommodation because we've been very clear we're not going to turn people away. We're not going to put a cap on the number of people. We want to encourage people to come forward, not to force anybody to have to give up their property or accommodation.'

Our governments hate us. Affecting to protect our health and lives, they extinguish our freedoms and use our own sovereign capacity for self-protection, entrusted to them under franchise to be exercised for our benefit only, as a means of suppressing our questions and objections. They lie incessantly, apparently oblivious or indifferent to the transparency of these lies. They use our money — given into their charge for the betterment of our lives — to buy off our media so that they may further conceal their own mendacity and maintain the constructed pseudo-reality as a level of unassailability to general deconstruction. They abandon, cancel and delete the inheritance of rights and freedoms deriving from a process of evolution stretching back several millennia, and then speak as if such concepts had become the preoccupations of reactionary forces.

Perhaps there is here an element of revenge. When I was a child, politicians, generally speaking, were exalted figures, respected by the people as though a class of royalty. An MP, TD, Senator or Congressman — was something to be. In recent decades, however, the stock of politicians has fallen — to some extent due to the deterioration in the ability and characters of many of those entering the field, and this, in turn, arising from the handing upwards to supranational bodies of the true power of decision- and law-making. But another factor, without doubt, has been the growing trivialisation of politics by a relentless form of journalism that is interested mainly in smut and tittle-tattle, the red-top tabloid incursions of the past half-century, initially appearing to offer an earnestly populist account of serious matters of public interest but rapidly descending into the sewer, its fodder becoming the venalities, indulgences and weaknesses of flawed humans as a brand of entertainment. Nowadays, it is rare for a politician to negotiate the full span of a career without some whiff of scandal, either personal or financial — sleaze or graft. As a result, the stock of the average politician has dropped alarmingly, so that, up to the start of the Covid period, most people had become irredeemably cynical about politics and its pursuers, dismissing politicians as 'all the same' and 'in it for themselves'. Strangely, in the Covid period, all such sentiments went underground and politicians rose again in the estimation of the public, presumably as an expression of gratitude to them for having saved everyone from certain death.

But this turnaround was too little too late, and the worm of resentment had already entered the soul of the average politician, who now recognised an opportunity to avenge himself on the public for its growing and unconcealed contempt. Perhaps unconsciously, the political class took to the protocols handed to it from on high with more zealousness than might, if we were paying attention, have seemed decent, to retaliate for the slights and humiliations of recent decades.

And perhaps, too, none of this was accidental. Perhaps the tabloid press, which had majored in the exposure of political scandals, was not, after all, an organic phenomenon. Perhaps the minds that dreamed up Covid and the lockdowns foresaw also a future requirement to create conditions in which politicians might become more than willing to stick it to their electorates. Perhaps the proposal was to provoke several decades of debasing politics and politicians so that, when the opportunity arose, and those in power were required to put the boot in, they would do so more in anger than in sorrow.

Whatever, we are where we are now, with the political class having crossed the ethical line into the dark territories of betrayal, treason, tyranny and deathdealing — with no possibility of return or redemption.

It is tempting to insinuate an *unless*, but at this moment, it seems, we have passed all possibility of *unlesses*. But let it not be said that the full implications of what is happening were not signalled in advance, that the implicit predictions of the intentions underlying what has been happening and what is about to happen, were not recorded in full. To the extent that any of this still remains avoidable, the latitude of mitigation available to each or any of the participants/perpetrators of this unprecedented holocaust must depend on their blowing the whistle now — today, tomorrow, within a few weeks at the very outset — turning themselves in to the relevant authorities, and placing their countries in the temporary hands of ethical and competent people who will seek to manage the world back to sanity and safety.

If there is a single ethical public agency remaining in the world, May 23rd (affording time for latecomers to arrive and settle into their Davos accommodation) would be a good day for a valiant band of such worthies to descend on Davos and arrest all present on various charges ranging from genocide to collusion. And if such a band of White Hats was to experience any initial doubt or confusion as regards its capacity to tell one criminal and his record from another, the generic indictment of 'conspiracy to plunder and murder' might be a good place to begin.

CHAPTER 22
THE PHONY SEX WAR
30-05-2022

Feminism's real purpose was to lead the state into the most intimate realms of human existence and, far from liberating women, to render men, children and women to new forms of tyranny.

OMNIPOTENT VICTIMS AS WEAPONS OF WAR

In a euphemism-laden statement in mid-March 2022, a coalition of 20 'civil society organisations and healthcare providers', led by the National Women's Council of Ireland, demanded the removal of the 12-week gestational limit to enable abortion on request up to 'viability', to ensure 'people' do not have to travel abroad for the 'procedure'. This group also demanded an end to the three-day wait period enshrined in Irish legislation to provide mothers time to reconsider.

In a related event at the end of April, Orla O'Connor, Director of the National Women's Council of Ireland (NWCI), a body claiming to be 'mandated to represent the views of our members across Ireland to achieve true equality for women and girls,' similarly reprimanded the Oireachtas (Irish parliament) Joint Committee on Health that it was 'completely unacceptable' that 'just over half of maternity hospitals' were providing abortion 'services'. Abortion, she said, should be available on request up to 'viability', to ensure that no woman or 'pregnant person' is forced to travel abroad for essential reproductive healthcare.

So, not just a misspeak, a slip of the tongue, an accidental formulation. Delivered from a carefully constructed script: i.e. premeditated, probably funding-related, and non-negotiable.

No woman or pregnant person: While they butcher the future of Western civilisation, the angels of the abattoir engage in a macabre burlesque of words, which is also, of course, part of the death protocol: the belittling of life in every conceivable way.

I had a personal as well as an ethical and linguistic interest in this statement, having many years ago strayed unwittingly into the NWCI's crosshairs. More than 20 years ago now, I wrote intermittently about the reality of what is called 'domestic violence', pointing out that all the reliable independent research on the subject indicated that women were just as violent as men. The NWCI participated in a press conference in which I was denounced for 'endangering the lives of women and children.' *The Irish Times*, the newspaper for which I had written the articles, published a defamatory account of this press conference without seeking a response from me in accordance with its own ethical guidelines.

Now, it seems, the NWCI no longer represents just women with or without children, but also 'pregnant persons', whom these two statements appear to suggest constitute a separate category to women, which reason suggests must therefore be . . . *men*. In fact, what the NWCI and other 'feminist' bodies have in mind, in using terms like 'pregnant persons' and 'pregnant people', are women pretending or claiming to be men, or, in the argot of transgenderism, 'identifying as men'.

Many of the same feminist bodies justifiably object to the converse phenomenon of men identifying as women and claiming Olympic medals and the like by virtue of their all but inevitable superior strength. But, in this instance, they appear to have either accepted that women identifying as men are no longer women, or have slipped into some twilight zone between the sexes. Alternatively — the NWCI may have unilaterally decided that the NWCI is no longer a 'women's council', or indeed a women's anything, and now represents also certain categories of 'men', for the moment to be filed under the evasive heading, 'people'. How, if this is the explanation, can the NWCI still be seen as representing 'the views of our members across Ireland to achieve true equality for women and girls'? Is it conceding defeat and admitting that the best way for women to achieve 'equality' with men is to act like and pretend to be . . . *men*? That would be an odd kind of 'feminist' manoeuvre.

Happily, there is a much less head-wrecking explanation as to the meaning of the NWCI and its Director's statements: It is that the NWCI is not, and never has been, a 'feminist' body in the sense that its ultimate objective was to make the world a better place for women; it is now, and always has been a Cultural Marxist organisation, the chief aim and purpose of which was and is to destroy the anthropological basis of human civilisation and replace it with chaos. The purpose of the 'pregnant people' trope, as we have seen with other forms of confusion-making, is to demoralise whole populations by forcing them to accept and adopt dissonant and mutually contradictory concepts. This revolution has, in recent times, crossed a line beyond which 'feminism' is no longer to be regarded as a useful 'product', and, as with other 'feminist' organisations, much of the NWCI's funding now depends on it abandoning its previous masquerade.

The 'feminist' phase of the 'women's movement' mission was simply that — a phase. The NWCI Director's reference to 'pregnant persons' signals that this phase is now over. Adult males of a certain 'category', i.e. women pretending to be men, can now — at least according to the National Women's Council of Ireland — become pregnant and have abortions, albeit for the moment in their capacity as 'persons' rather than 'women', on indeed 'men'. And the NWCI also caters for another category of (men pretending to be) 'women', but it is unclear whether such 'persons' qualify to be included in the ranks of 'pregnant persons'.

This is an important development in many ways, not least in that it announces that the charade of feminist activism is now coming to an end, and that the 'women's libber' is now to take her/his/their/its place in the chorus line of radical Marxist saboteurs for the final number.

What was called 'feminism' was actually the first wave — the advance guard — of Cultural Marxism, the late 20th-century reset of the communist agenda designed to convert the ideology of Karl Marx from the economic to the personal realm of human existence. The context of this nomenclature was the urgency— arising from the failure of the working classes of capitalist societies to embrace their historical destinies by following the call of communism — that a Marxist revolution confined to economics would not succeed. Rather than exhibiting a passion for the victory of the proletariat, the working class wanted merely to gain a higher standard of living, and showed little interest in tearing down the system and taking control of the means of production in accordance with Karl Marx's formulation of their historical role. Hence, 'Cultural Marxism', which begat what we now recognise as modern feminism, multiculturalism, the 'gay rights' movement and, latterly, the initiatives seeking to legitimise a multiplicity of gender types and cast doubts on the very validity of the concepts of masculinity and femininity.

Cultural Marxism, then, a mutated version of the original, is directed at changing fundamentally the way Western societies conduct their everyday operation in the most private areas of their domestic and community lives. Adopting and co-opting 'minorities' — blacks, gays, women (although not exactly a *minority!*) — it seeks to tap the cultural power of these respective victimologies to bludgeon down the edifices of Western civilisation, in particular marriage, parenthood, family, nationhood and religion. When you rinse it right down, the Cultural Marxist/PC political correctness/Woke revolution has as its objective the emasculation of the white male and the eradication of all values and power systems which are laid at his door, including religion, tradition and the 'hetero-normative' nuclear family.

It is strange how, in seeking to raise issues concerning the suppression of the truth, you almost invariably end up discovering what the truth is, even though, at the time, you may have started out with only the foggiest idea of what you are dealing with. An example is what happened to me in the 1990s when I first started to write about fatherhood, parenthood, the systemic and systematic brutalisation of fathers and father-children relationships in family law courts, and also the tangential issues like domestic violence law, suicide patterns, the social and political indifference to men's health, and eventually the precise nature of feminism and its strange responses to what I was attempting to articulate.

The central issue — the one I returned to again and again — was family law and family courts, which had already insinuated themselves as the Inquisitions of the modern era. The 'crimes' unearthed in these courts can include a father contacting his own children without permission of the mother or the court, or visiting a house he built with his own hands, or failing to meet a child support order that is far beyond his ability to pay, or disagreeing with the policies of mother or school concerning sex education, or one of a thousand other contrived misdemeanours that, in the hidden realm of the family court system, invite punishments capable of destroying the very existence of the 'accused'.

The word 'Kafkaesque' has been so overused, misused and abused that its meaning has become both clichéd and confused. Varying definitions refer to menacing complexity, the bureaucratic labyrinth of illogical authority, the unnecessary complication of what ought to be straightforward, the terrors of endless interrogation, forms of quasi-omnipotence slightly out of emotional focus, the surrealism of senseless power, a persistent nightmare of (un)reason, the collapse into hopelessness of trust in justice or systems, the actualisation of paranoia, and so forth.

But almost all definitions of the Kafkaesque overlook what is probably its most potent and emblematic characteristic: the state's arrogation to itself of a right to intrude impertinently into the most personal and private realms of the human without evidence of actual wrongdoing. The most disturbing moments of the opening section of Kafka's best-known novel, *The Trial*, relate not to the official mission or intentions of the warders who come to arrest K., but the way they deliberate over the quality of his nightshirt — telling him that he will have to wear 'a less fancy one now' — and going on to devour his breakfast.

This is a precise and resonant encapsulation of the totalitarian impulse. Total-itarianism is not political; it is always personal, a thought that may present an appropriate moment to remember an early feminist slogan: 'The personal is political,' a central plank of the Cultural Marxist platform. In this phrase, we can perceive, too, an early iteration of the value system that became ubiquitous in the Covid period, whereby the state assumed the right to intervene in the inner-most havens of human existence, turning the family home into a makeshift prison and assuming an entitlement to count and regulate the number of persons present at any given moment in our living rooms. The word 'arbitrary' is inadequate to describe this, just as it is inadequate to describing the subter-ranean nature of family law in modern Western societies, in which the husband/father has been all but invariably the target of the emerging *nouveau* tyranny.

It is no accident that family law courts have become forums for the plunder and criminalisation of fathers, and unsurprising that men are increasingly wary of a concept of marriage that could mean that, one fine morning, they could awake to find that they have been arrested, lost their homes, wealth, property and children and face a battle to stay out of jail.

When I first tackled this topic as a journalist, I thought that what I was writing about was simply a neglected element of the kind of justice deficit that journalism existed to ventilate. I was simply trying to give voice to questions that almost no one else appeared to be asking — certainly no one in Ireland, the country where I had grown up with no sense at all that it might one day present as one of the most loathsome tyrannies in the former free world. I had no idea that I had stumbled into the future — that the grotesque injustices I was describing were not random or accidental, but part of a malign agenda to destroy families, parenthood, marriage and even romance, undermine manhood and so eliminate chivalry, heroism and other great virtues of the human, claim children for the state as the overarching societal super-parent, and sow seeds of antagonism between men and women that would one day lead to a harvest of sexual alienation and incomprehension that could be weaponised to imprison the human race.

When I began this mission to understand and explicate, I was essentially a soft-leftist, which is to say I liked the idea of being kind and generous to people who had less opportunities than I had. Before that, I was, by inclination, a rock 'n' roller. That's where I started my life in journalism: writing about U2 and Elvis, Dylan, Hendrix and Lennon, all the icons of a liberal youth culture faith that assumed its own righteousness and irrefutability and was implicitly on the side of all kinds of emerging freedoms. Where my generation came in, back in the 1960s (actually the 1970s, which was when the Sixties arrived in Ireland), it all seemed easy: we just overturned the stalls of the grey-bearded patriarchs and denounced them. The headline issues were clear-cut and objectively irrefutable: universal civil rights, ending apartheid, nuclear disarmament, and, of course, gaining 'equality' for women.

My interest and involvement in the territory signposted 'Feminism' came about because, aside from the fact that I was, many years ago, involved in a rela-tively public struggle to defend my own parental rights in respect of my daughter (now in her mid-twenties), I had, as a writer and journalist, been addressing the situation of the father in culture and law in my work going back to the early 1990s. In 1994, a play of mine, *Long Black Coat*, which dealt with the cultural marginalisation of fatherhood, was staged in the Irish cities of Kilkenny and Dublin, receiving some awards and reasonably intelligent press coverage. Oddly, it was set in the future — in 2020, as it happens — and overlaid the apocalypse of fatherhood on the metaphor of a nuclear crisis.

For a long time, I saw the pattern of discrimination against fathers as an expression of deep prejudice and bias. I analysed the extensive brutalisation and ostracisation of fathers as problematic on grounds of injustice, and was mystified as to why I was the only one who had noticed these drifts. I have more recently come to realise that I was observing the early stages of a sinister wave of social engineering, now rapidly moving up through the gears. Gradually, over the past 30 years, I've come to the conclusion that the attacks on fatherhood were really not down to simple prejudice, but represented the advance march of an ideology we can now observe entering its full stride. The point was not hatred of fathers but the early stages of a concerted attack on normative ideas of family, parenting and marriage.

By marginalising fathers, the system was creating a culture of vulnerable mothers, highly dependent on state largesse, women who, with their children, would be more likely to become vulnerable to the reconstructive designs of the regime. The last thing the ideologues wanted was the emergence of a cooperative post-divorce version of the fractured family: fathers and mothers, albeit living separately, raising their children in relative harmony. That is why governments almost everywhere have resisted introducing a serious, legally recognised mediation option for family disputes, and refused point blank to permit any enhanced rights for unmarried fathers while promoting infinitely more tenuous 'family rights' claims from other quarters. Thus, when the push came on from the powerful LGBT lobby to have gay marriage installed in the Irish Constitution as a body of 'rights' equivalent to those conferred on heterosexual couples, the feminists and feminists' groups who had two decades earlier opposed parental equality with all their might and main, were all on the front line clamouring for equal parenting rights to be accorded to homosexuals of both sexes.

What was really going on was a reconstruction of cultural understandings, not to favour either women or men but to promote new and radical models of family as remote as may be imagined from the normative, natural model. The biases I noted with growing incredulity and consternation back in the 1990s were just an early symptom of a dispensation that would before long contrive to speak of and treat gay couples (male or female) as being better parents than lone mothers or lone fathers, with biology an irrelevant factor. What I was recording was never simply an attack on fathers; it was always directed at the endgame of so-called 'marriage equality' — with the ultimate destination being the state's assumption of the right to decide the conditions and fates of all children and all families.

The final objective was the redefinition of parenthood from biological to political concept, with the state enabling a variety of eccentric 'family' types while continuing to demolish the core kind. This means that, in substance and effect, the state becomes the ultimate 'parent' of every child. Susan Shell, in her book *The Liberal Case Against Gay Marriage,* writes: 'The right to one's own children . . . is perhaps the most basic individual right — so basic we hardly think of it.' But Shell, like me, was aware that, under the terms of the emerging dispensation, we would very soon find ourselves in our liberal democracies in a generalised context whereby children would become something akin to commodities to be redistributed at the whim of judges and officials. A parent would be someone appointed or rubber-stamped by the state, his or her 'parenthood' the diktat not of biological fact but of legal definitions. Shell writes: 'No known government, however brutal or tyrannical, has ever denied . . . the fundamental claims of parents to their children. . . . A government that distributed children randomly . . . could not be other than tyrannical. . . . A government that paid no regard to the claims of biological parenthood would be unacceptable to all but the most fanatical of egalitarian or communitarian zealots.' This, however, was the endgame of the 'feminist' revolution, funded by taxpayers' money and protected by state institutions funded by the same mechanism.

There was a time when most people reacted to such pronouncements with dismissiveness and scorn. Why would the state contrive to do such a thing? At first, I too resisted the idea that such a monumental inversion of public understanding of nature could ever become possible. It has taken me most of the past three decades to comprehend that this is possible — not as a naturalistic phenomenon, but precisely as the outcome of fantastically effective propaganda, educational capture and covert coercion. Bulwarked by the utterances of celebrities, the acquiescence of cowardly politicians, the push of vested interests and, latterly, the intimidatory spleneticism of cyberanonymous 'social-justice warriors', these industrialised lies have consolidated themselves as the core of the official belief systems of our societies. Now, with the onset of phases q to z — queer fascism, transgenderism, 'Parents 1 & 2', and Drag Queen Story Hour — to be followed hard by polyamory and even the attempted legitimisation of previously taboo matters like ephebophilia, hebephilia, and eventually paedophilia — the totalitarian ambition of these destructive ideologies enters its late phases.

For a long time, delving into this morass of toxicity and venom, I had no idea. When I first came into conflict with what was called feminism in the mid-1990s, part of me was very confused by the apparent hypocrisy of the responses I was getting, and part of me was reacting with a form of what I can only describe as an inchoate and irrational *guilt*, because the area towards which I was being drawn was increasingly at odds with what I had hitherto regarded as my natural way of thinking.

And yet, all the time, there were these incongruencies, hypocrisies and contradictions. On the one hand, feminists claimed they wanted men to take a larger share of childrearing; on the other, when I proposed that we formalise this by placing it on a legal footing, they attacked me and tried to have me cancelled. I wrote and published thousands of words in the course of my attempts to get my head around this, much of them in an attempt to enter the minds of those who were attacking me. Was there some area of legitimate offence-taking that I was missing? I could not identify any. After all, if the goals and ideals of first-generation feminism were genuine expressions of its ambitions for humanity, feminists ought to be finding common cause with me. Surely, by enabling men to share the role of child-minding, feminists could accelerate their own ambitions for 'equality'?

When I stumbled across some of these seemingly contradictory tendencies, close on 30 years ago, my first thought was that I had run into some kind of overlooked vein of the human rights agenda that my fellow enthusiasts for freedom and justice had simply not gotten around to pointing out. But then, as I began writing tentatively out of my observations of family law injustice and the overwhelming preponderance of males among suicides, I couldn't help noticing that those advocating rights for women, gays and other minorities, far from seeking to join my campaigns, seemed anxious to shut my mouth, regularly denouncing me publicly and forming delegations to demand that my editor relieve me of my position. I had, it appeared, made the naïve error of assuming that concepts like 'justice' and 'human rights' were indivisible and continued to have more or less the same meanings as in the dictionary. Something else was at play, but I could not put my finger on what it was. It took me a long time to find a frame capable of containing anything like the full picture. Sometimes, in the early days, driven by anger, I made statements that, subsequently, I felt had been over the top. But as time passed and I discovered more of the connections between various phenomena, it became clear to me that nothing I had said before had been in the least disproportionate: This ideology was far more poisonous than any capacity of mine to describe it.

The feminist writer Mary Daly, in her 1973 book *Beyond God the Father*, wrote that men are 'an ontological evil in the universe.' To write such a thing today about any sub-group of human society, other than adult male Caucasians, would be to court a jail sentence. Hate-speech by feminists has no such consequences. Indeed, this mode of expression is co-opted by authority figures and celebrities as an instrument of virtue-signalling, with men often the worst offenders. At the core of the propaganda is that any act of any man is the responsibility of all males, even the sons of the accusers, from the moment they are old enough to be no longer protected by the designation 'children'.

Vacillating between my inherited assumptions and my lived experience in reality, I was almost equally shocked when first I started to come across critical evaluations of feminism like that of the Harvard Professor of Yiddish literature, Ruth Wisse: 'Women's liberation, if not the most extreme then certainly the most influential neo-Marxist movement in America, has done to the American home what communism did to the Russian economy, and most of the ruin is irreversible. By defining relations between men and women in terms of power and competition instead of reciprocity and cooperation, the movement tore apart the most basic and fragile contract in human society, the unit from which all other social institutions draw their strength.' Likewise, the verdicts of men like Robert Bork in his book *Slouching Towards Gomorrah*: 'Radical feminism is the most destructive and fanatical movement to come down to us from the sixties. This is a revolutionary, not a reformist, movement. . . . Totalitarian in spirit, it is deeply antagonistic to traditional Western culture and proposes the complete restructuring of society, morality and human nature.'

Gradually, I came to understand that feminists had functioned as one half of a pincer-movement honey-trap that had weaponised the Sexual Revolution to draw men into their web with the promise of uncomplicated and inconsequential sex, to be followed by a stiff invoice in the currencies of pain and dispossession. In tandem with the orchestrated Sixties revolution and its Flower Children, feminism helped to weaponise sexual desire, particularly male sexual desire, in the manner of a judo foot sweep, yielding to the opponent's energy so as to use his own force against him. But each short ejaculation contributed its share to the growth of feminist power, and in the end, the consequences of free sex became very complicated indeed. By buying into the promise of free love, men left themselves open to losing their reputations, wealth, property, jobs, and even their freedom, creating the greatest threat to civil liberties to occur in Western societies up to two years ago, when, as I say, the methodologies road-tested in the domestic arena were catapulted into the total public realm.

Among the things I was forced to accept was that virtually everything about the relations between the sexes that the vast majority of men and women had been led by constant propaganda to lazily accept — that women are in grave danger of violence by men at all times; that fathers are at best secondary parents; that the most dangerous place for a child is the nuclear family — is completely, monstrously wrong. That so many people have come to believe these assertions is a tribute to the strategic disbursement of vast amounts of public money, most of it diverted from taxation of the citizens of all Western countries.

Back at the beginning of this 'interesting' voyage, I rather prematurely announced that we had arrived to the Age of the Omnipotent Victim. Kafka, in *The Trial*, (I wrote a quarter of a century ago), had made visible the phenomenon of absolute and arbitrary power exercised anonymously, perhaps the great tyranny of the age then just departed. In the age about to unfold, I postulated, the greatest tyranny would be the spectre of absolute power in the hands of the apparently defenceless victim: 'We stand on the threshold of an era when, by virtue of being black, female, or the claimed sufferer of abuse or deprivation, the Omnipotent Victim will be set beyond justice, morality, fairness and the law, and anyone she accuses will be automatically convicted. In this future, if you come into conflict with someone whom our various ideologies designate as victim, by virtue of sex, race or origin, you had better have your affairs in order in advance of the hearing. Victims are never guilty of anything, and those they accuse never innocent.'

I have but relatively recently come to realise that, way back then, I had stumbled across perhaps the most rapidly metastasising and insidious of the terminal cancers by then radically afflicting modern society: the stripping out of the rights of ordinary citizens, without presumption of innocence, without due process, often without evidence, sometimes without the accused being told what he is accused of, with the intention and effect of invading that person's life to the very core, stripping him of dignity and protections, reducing him to the status of latter-day serf — all under cover of secret courts claiming to protect mothers and children from the bogeyman called Father. I had tripped across something that led me inexorably to a conclusion that, however implausible it seemed even to me, the greatest impositions on human rights in our societies were bearing down not upon any of the trumpeted minorities of quotidian media insinuation, but against the very category implicitly indicted by these propagandas: *men.* As the Soviet system targeted the political and economic structures, these latter-day tyrants wanted control of intimate and family relationships; and this was occurring under pressure of the attrition of feminist propaganda in culture. The alleged cause of female equality was being used to dismantle human civilisation as it stood.

For what may not be immediately obvious reasons, the modern family court has come to represent the most telling and irrefutable microcosm of this destructive initiative. The explanation is actually straightforward: This is the arena in which the truth about power relations in the modern world emerges most starkly — in which the interests of women predominate, not merely at the behest of feminism, but also, by dint of the female hold over men, because one of the last remaining essentially 'male-dominated' systems sees this as a 'correct' state of affairs that holds no threat of loss to themselves. It is also the frontier of the civil war feminism has fomented between the sexes, being the locus where female domination of the intimate sphere is policed, even while, inch by inch, women are incrementally facilitated in moving towards domination of the public sphere also. Here, women are permitted to have it both ways, if only, in each individual case, as a token concession by — in the majority of instances — the most powerful men.

Divorce, the chief sanction of the family law system — which largely came about as a result of feminist agitation — resulted in the opening of the family home to the full and secretly exercised powers of the state. The mechanisms that developed out of 'no-fault' divorce — secret hearings, summary justice, the suspension of normal evidential requirements and the introduction of pseudo principles like 'the best interests of the child' — created a contagious mentality among legislators, administrators of justice, and law enforcement, whereby it becomes increasingly acceptable to suspend due process in favour of vague, subjective and selective criteria, invariably enforced with extreme prejudice by ideologically-motivated activists posing as neutral administrators — what the great American scholar and writer Stephen Baskerville calls the 'feminist gendarmerie' of social workers, psychologists and psychiatrists, child protection experts and enforcers, counsellors, mediators, divorce planners, forensic accountants, and so forth. From the persistent agitation of feminists, and, more recently, homosexualists piggy-backing on the feminist revolution, the legal procedures relating to family life have been cut apart from the mainstream of law and justice, and enabled to expand exponentially without significant political objection. The list of areas into which the new culture of quasi-legality has spread includes domestic violence, rape and sexual assault, sexual harassment, stalking, child abuse, bullying, hate crimes, hate speech and sundry others. In each of these areas, guilt is established on the basis of accusation only: the subjective feelings of the accuser are the principal determining factor. If the accused pleads innocence, well, he would, wouldn't he?

What happens in a family court is not so much that the system straightforwardly crushes the father/man, but that the system conspires to persuade all those with power to decide that it is the duty of the man to acquiesce in the idea of his being crushed (because the alternative seems to be the unthinkable crushing of a woman), with the two sets of lawyers (essentially — or at least usually) operating apparently to a chivalrous male notion of 'gender' roles rather than to an expressly feminist agenda. Thus, in the very engine rooms of the social reconstruction project, feminism conceals even its own existence behind a subterfuge of protecting the interests of children and 'vulnerable' women, having ultimately subverted the man-created culture of justice to drape a cloak of justification on the ultimate subversion of human reality at the most intimate level of human existence. All this is grounded in a foundational bed of anti-male, anti-father propaganda that has been pouring into the trenches of our culture for decades.

An 'interesting' aspect that has manifested in the past two years is the manner in which the methodologies first tested in the family law system — the arbitrary breaching of fundamental family rights, the effective suspension of due process, the brutalisation of the human person in the most private realms of existence and being — have now, in the Covid cult, been extended to entire populations. Little did we know that we fathers were lab rats for the New World

THE ABOLITION OF REALITY 283

Order's designs to destroy not merely fatherhood, but also family, parenting, motherhood, marriage, the economic lives of the able classes, and finally, the very humanity of the core populations of Western civilisation, thus destroying the civilisation itself. With Covid, Cultural Marxism entered its most 'inclusive' and possibly final phase — a new epoch in which all humans would be invited to volunteer to be victims, albeit a sub-category of such constructed to be relatively devoid of omnipotence, since it aspired to include everyone but the 'elites' in a new slave class. Covid enabled state regimes, on behalf of higher authorities, to issue an open invitation to all: agree to your own absolute vulnerability, and we shall protect you, while also removing your freedoms, which only get you into trouble. Convinced that life as it stood was far too risky to be approached in the reckless manner of the past, the vast majority of the world's population agreed to this Faustian pact. Like many a beleaguered, hopeless father in the long night before a family court hearing, the human being, worn down by conflict and anxiety, agreed to surrender his soul and become a vassal of the Regime. In the future, there would no longer be men nor women, nor children, but merely slaves — the many slaves of the few, on whose bountiful mercy everyone would henceforth depend.

To understand what has happened in the past half-century or so, and how all this has converged and entered a new orbit since April 2020, we need — each of us in our own memories of our lives — to go back in time and reconsider many things we took for granted as they happened. If we do so, we may find that phenomena we had taken at face value have now acquired entirely different shapes and meanings — meanings that are, on deeper examination, nothing like as organic or innocent as we may have imagined.

For example, we might begin to examine the nature of the 'freedoms' that have been rolled out — or shoved down the throats of the majorities of our populations — over the past 50 years or so: the 'freedom' to kill nascent human beings as a means of securing immunity from sexual consequences; the 'freedom' to burlesque the idea of marriage; the 'freedom' to surrender fundamental rights and freedoms in the name of 'solidarity'; the 'freedom' to engage in Pavlovian attacks on dissenters from the dominant narratives and ideologies. Soon — perhaps too late — we may begin to consider the connections between these 'freedoms' and the loosing of restraint and self-control they have engendered throughout our societies, a symbiosis that has now enabled the political class to ramp up political coercion and control on the grounds that the world's appetite for 'freedom' has gotten out of hand.

We have been grievously misled. For most of all of our lives we imagined we were aboard some kind of freedom-and-progress project potentially implicating the entirety of the human species. At its core, this project appeared to be directed at persuading each and all of us that, by being kinder to our 'minorities', we might participate in the elevation of the human species to a new level of civilisation. By rescuing women from the kitchen sink and the maternity ward, by giving homosexuals whatever they demanded in recompense for past slights and injuries, by opening our borders — and our wallets — to the denizens of less 'privileged' economies, we would make our world gentler, kinder and therefore better. 'Equality' would be the watchword of this revolution of improvement — albeit, as we could hardly help noticing, a strangely distorted equality, from which one party — the Omnipotent Victim — would always stand to gain and the other — the sucker at the table — always to lose.

In reality, we have been engaged not in a kind of velvet revolution but an undeclared war. A superficial reading of this war might conclude that it was a war by the world's governments on their own peoples, and in a sense, that is what it amounts to. But, deeper down, it is — like all wars — a war about resources. For now, the point is to dispossess those among the world's population who fall into the middle range of economic existence, transferring their wealth in an upward direction, an exotic variation on the family law practice of asset-stripping men in the interests of 'equality'.

The beneficiaries of this mammoth global heist are largely anonymous and out of sight. They are the richest of the rich; they already own more between them than the rest of the world's population put together, but the focus of their concern is that they do not yet own *everything*. There are many names used to summon up this collective spectre of greed and viciousness; some people call them the 'Illuminati'; others talk about a 'cult' or 'cabal'; others refer to the 'secret unknowns' or the 'predator class'. I call them The Combine, a term I have borrowed from Chief Bromden, the protagonist of Ken Kesey's novel *One Flew Over the Cuckoo's Nest*, subsequently made into a movie by Michael Cimino, featuring a different protagonist, R.P. McMurphy, played by Jack Nicholson. The Combine is the term Chief Bromden used to describe the body, agency or force — a kind of evil syndicate, is how he characterised it — bearing down upon humanity, seeking to oppress it and re-set its behaviour. The Combine runs everything using technological and human agents like Nurse Ratched and her vicious orderlies, rendering that half-century-old book and movie among the most prophetic works in the history of popular culture.

Over the last thirty or forty years, we have invested an enormous amount of thought, resources, feeling, passion, sweat and blood in what we might call the superstructure of human dignity — human values, rights, freedoms, the defence of human dignity and individual autonomy. And it is perhaps not coincidental that, over the same period as the human race was constructing this edifice of rights and freedoms, its scientists and philosophers were working overtime to dismantle our most fundamental understanding of the limits of the human edifice, preparing for a time when human beings would in effect declare themselves deities by acquiring the capacity to generate new human life by artificial means, terminate human life at the point just beyond initiation or before its natural end, and put in place the detailed plans for a posthumanist future when human beings would be absorbed into the machine, leaving their souls and their free wills behind.

Most of the political battles of the past half century have — ostensibly, at least — been waged around questions of extending human rights to previously disenfranchised groups, such as women, gays, minorities, the disabled, and so on, theoretically adding to (though in reality aspiring to supplant) the pre-existing universal rights entitlements arising under the headings of Fundamental and Personal. The 'new rights' were the Cultural Marxist-sponsored rights, the additional entitlements extended to 'minorities', though, as we have seen, not as cost-free as they were presented. These campaigns, though appearing to pursue various agendas — 'women's liberation', 'gay rights', 'anti-racism', *et cetera* — had really just one purpose: to sow the seeds of the chaos and demoralisation which would make it easier to effect these purposes. This chaos has been rampant now for close on a decade, and is approaching its apogee — the moment when the secret unknowns/predator class/Combine will finally have its way with the world, or else the world will awaken as one man and face the tyrants and their messengers down.

In the Time of Covid, we shredded pretty much all of this catalogue of rights, apart from the Cultural Marxist elements — to the total silence and apparent indifference of the normatively understood primary defenders of freedom. April 2020 may yet go down in history — if there is a history — as the month that liberalism died.

It was, shall we say, *interesting* to observe that, in the Time of Covid, abortions continued uninterrupted, even though most other 'medical procedures' were suspended, and anti-racism demonstrators were given the run of streets from which the everyday populace had been as though surgically removed. This provided the merest flash of the deeper-down nature of the Cultural Marxist agenda, which all the time had not been about extending rights, but taking them away. By creating discrete sets of rights for defined groups and entities, the attendant ideological process implicitly opened up the possibility that 'rights' might exist for named categories and not for the unnamed, which is to say any category listed by the Cultural Marxists as bearing responsibility for indictable historical wrongs. Broadly, as we have noted, these beneficiaries fell into three categories: gay, black and female. And yet, individuals in these categories were as radically circumscribed as anyone in the general context by virtue of the withdrawal of fundamental rights. Thus, a homosexual man could adopt someone else's child and speak therefore of his 'family', but his entitlement to go into a shop without a humiliating face covering was just as circumscribed as that of the most devout Christian grey-bearded Caucasian. A black lesbian had every protection for her homosexuality, 'gender' and colour, but had no greater right to travel more than two kilometres from her home than the straight, 'white' Christian father of a nuclear family with three children.

There were multiple reasons for the liberal silence about what was emerging from the spring of 2020, but the primary one was that liberals, having become convinced that the most important freedoms were the more recently-minted ones — for abortion, homosexual rights and open borders — and that the old varieties,, being in conflict, as was suggested, with 'the common good', were henceforth to be regarded as suspect. This syndrome played out during the Covid subterfuge to the great benefit of the orchestrators, who became spectacularly richer in the two years of Covid's First Act.

Some conservatives, because of their almost universal immersion in religious ideas — some due to a profound grounding in Christian anthropology, others simply recalling the church doctrines on sodomy, the right to life and the Thomist treatise on migration — had automatically recoiled from these claimed new rights. Now, they rose to defend the more fundamental kind, as these came under severe threat to the apparent indifference of the 'liberal' left. Liberals, observing this reaction, doubled down on their defence of the Cultural Marxist-sponsored rights, but reacted against the conservative defence of fundamental liberties. This, and a little judicious state and corporate nudging and tweaking, ensured that defending the most fundamental rights of human beings came in short order to be seen as a reactionary activity.

This established a precedent by which the very definition of 'rights' underwent the final stage of a phased rewriting. By this redefinition, rights are no longer rights, but concessions by the Regime on the basis of victim-points, though these are to be regarded not as automatic entitlements but ideological gifts that may be withdrawn or amended for any reason or none. In this staged procedure, without a word being spoken to say what was actually happening, the age-old guarantor-words of fundamental/personal rights — 'inalienable', 'imprescriptible', 'indefeasible', 'antecedent', 'anterior', and 'inviolable' — were silently dissolved. It was no longer forbidden to extend or withhold 'rights' on a selective basis — for what had the 'majority' been doing for 'minorities' for dozens of years? It was no longer reasonable to say that individual rights might be absolute, for the 'common good' (seen, in this context, as the surrendering of each individual's rights to a community whole that was by definition incapable of exercising them) so demands. The moment when the collective rights of robots might be invoked to justify the total withdrawal of rights from humans seemed to take a few jerky steps forward.

These objectives had been in the works for decades, and were always the endgame purpose of those troubling and anomalous phenomena to which we ascribed entirely different meanings. So it was with feminism. There was no women's revolution, but rather a paid-for colour revolution purchased by rich oligarchs with sinister agendas.

Feminism has been the Trojan horse of Cultural Marxism. It was also the first wave of what we have experienced for the past two years, for all this is of a piece. 'Women's liberation' was only marginally about 'equality of the sexes' — a sweetener/camouflage to obscure its true nature. It was really about the destruction of the normative world and its core institutions, including family, nation and faith, as well as the even more fundamental understanding of the structure of the edifice of human civilisation itself. The family was first attacked via the father (though this was to be a preliminary manoeuvre, to be followed up in due course by the undermining of the mother). The nation was, similarly, destabilised by the emasculation of males, so that ultimately there would be no one left to defend it. Abortion was the central plank of the attacks on faith, religion and spirituality, as it forced people to choose between the understandings of their religious upbringing and the call for 'compassion' for women wishing to rid themselves of unwanted children. Feminist crusading, with its mixture of ingenuous complaint and breezy menace, made for a well-adapted battering ram — under all three headings.

What made feminism so adaptable for this purpose was its initial surface unexceptionability, its appeals to justice and equality; its attraction to 'enlightened' men as a means of signalling their 'virtue'. The symbiotic dynamics of sexuality and chivalry ensured that the 'revolution' would not be resisted no matter how ugly its methodologies or the price it inflicted on innumerable men. Such men were treated as casualties in a war that had already been decided as to its outcome. For these and other reasons, it appealed, superficially at least, to a working majority of women.

Academia and the media were the nurseries in which the ideologies designed to push and disseminate the cultural changes necessary for this revolution were developed. It was important that these institutions were almost entirely sedentary in their cultures, allowing for little or no distinction as between the functioning or operation of men as against women. Many of the men who worked in these institutions would have been the first in the male lines of their families to do non-physical work, or 'women's work' as it had once been designated in more robust circles. In order to justify this and abide with it, they needed to create a sense among themselves that they were, in fact, superior to men who worked and existed by sweat and muscle. For such 'transitioning' men, it created a distorted sense of identification with women, as well as an enmity towards men who, by virtue of their muscularity and loud voices, seemed to be refugees from a pre-modern age and, therefore, at once threatening and a little repulsive. Of course, all this was contorted by the fact that, sexually speaking, women often made no distinction between the two categories, or, when they did, tended to go for the sub-modern model. This effect was counterbalanced by the influence of rock 'n' roll, which, through the promotion of androgynous images and ideas, created a new sexual currency which served to devalue the older, muscle-based model and allowed the emasculated weaklings to inherit the Earth. And all this seemed to go swimmingly for most men until the moment when the reality of feminist power loomed suddenly large in their lives — perhaps by the loss of their homes and children — and in the unassailable nature of the emerging new facts: women now 'shared' power in the exterior world, but had surrendered none of their power in the domestic realm, and were therefore at least three-quarters of the way to the feminist goal of total female supremacy. If this seems a stretch, the truth is perhaps a little more extreme: When you consider the various statistics to do with male health and mortality, the rates of suicide by young men, the escalating educational evisceration of boys and young men, and latterly the #MeToo movement, which threatened the final emasculating of sexually active men, it becomes clear that, in the war against men, it is already much later than even the more alert among us have been thinking.

Now that the velvet gloves have been removed, we are beginning to see the final destination a little more clearly. Among the many feminist canards that have been rumbled in the recent months is the idea that a world run by women would be a gentler, kinder place. The authoritarian behaviours of such as Jacinda Ardern, Nicola Sturgeon and Ursula von der Leyen — as well as the bloodthirstiness of Victoria Nuland and Liz Truss in the context of the conflict in Ukraine — have surely put paid to such ideas for whatever remains of human history.

Female leaders have been at least as zealous in their implementation of Covid tyranny as almost any of the male figures on the geopolitical stage. In fact, by dint of sheer literalism in their presentation of the 'facts' and 'measures', the women leaders have mostly far outstripped their male counterparts, combining nannyish scoldings with a kind of take-it-or-lose-everything shrug of indifference to the suffering and consternation of those they had rapidly come to see as their 'subjects'. It is as though their former feminine diffidence had concealed a monarchical fantasising that can now be given free rein — the sham of their female tenderness evaporating like dew in the sun when the cosh was placed in their manicured hands.

CHAPTER 23
THE LIBERAL AYATOLLIAD AND THE COVID COUP
04-07-2022

The eclipse of 'liberalism' in the Covid assault was no accidental effect of transient confusion, but the inevitable outcome of the paradox that liberals desire to change man more than to free him.

A question asked surprisingly rarely over the past two years of trampling on the inheritance of classical European liberalism is: *Why no outcry*? If we were to judge purely on the degree of emphasis on these values over the course of our conscious lifetimes — be they long or short — from, say, the end of the Second World War to April Fool's Day 2020, a matter of 75 years — we must surely think it strange, if not disquieting, that so much that was taken for granted could be abandoned with so little commotion. In such an inventory, it would become clear that almost nothing but the basic needs of physical survival have seemed more important than individual freedom under various headings. Some of those headings — it is true — have been occasionally controversial, but only because they have touched on areas where one freedom of one person has encroached ominously upon freedoms of another. But even these disputes have been waged around the premise that the maximisation of freedom is to be qualified only in the reconciliation of such conflicts, and then only minimally and in a manner that is clearly delineated.

As the world took off again after its brief cardiac arrest in the spring of 2020, it seemed that all such scruples had been jettisoned in favour of a new dispensation that seemed worrisomely familiar. In this suddenly erupting regimen, it was as though the emphasis on personal freedom had been some kind of radical mistake, that — valourised unto the day before yesterday — it had overnight revealed itself as some kind of treacherous folly. Without warning, the world seemed to reach an imperceptible philosophical crossroads and abruptly deviate from the path it had been certain of for nearly 3,000 years. As it continued, the general thrust of its conversations appeared to intimate that it had been decided, after all, that a course long regarded as unthinkable had suddenly been subject to a brief re-evaluation, followed by almost instantaneous and near total adoption. At the core of this new way of seeing was an idea that, on first examination — being presented in terms like 'solidarity' and 'the common good' — seemed to be merely a retreading of the long-applied convention of applying qualifiers in respect of the individual rights of one actor when they rubbed up too abrasively against rights of another or others. But on closer scrutiny, it became clear to any shrewd observer that what was afoot was not some minor process of circumscription or recalibration, but a radical rewriting of fundamentals. The 'common good' being spoken of here was not some refinement of prior understandings but a redefinition of civilisational reality to co-opt ideas associated with an ideological outlook hitherto regarded as failed, extreme, detrimental and deadly — a form of collectivised understanding that elevated the security of the group above the liberty of the individual — indeed, as rapidly became clear, in which individual rights were to be regarded as dangerous.

In the Preamble of the Constitution of Ireland — by way of an example that may help to tease out the scale of the deviation we seek to capture here — the aim of promoting the 'common good' is not defined as any kind of collectivist purpose, but the guaranteeing of 'the dignity and freedom of the individual' so that 'true social order' may be achieved. In this — the classical liberal, common-law model — the purpose of the political community — the *polis*, in Grecian terms — is not collectivisation, but social cooperation under headings like 'the material', 'cultural' and 'moral', in the interests of the maximised development of each individual person. In this model there is no collective, at least not one deemed deserving of legal protection, and this for the very good reason that such a dispensation would be a fast train to totalitarianism. In a liberal democracy, the purpose of a *polis* — political community — is, in principle, to cultivate the 'common good' not for the benefit of some abstract collective — the 'greatest good of the greatest number' — but so each individual member of that association might prosper to the highest degree possible. In this model, as expressed in the words of the great Irish jurist Declan Costello, whenever the exigencies of the common good are called to justify restrictions on the exercise of basic rights, 'it has to be borne in mind that the protection of basic rights is one of the objects which the common good is intended to assure.' Hence, the *polis*, as such, is not nurtured for its own sake — or at least its cultivation is always predicated on the enhancement of the lives of its individual members. Indeed, in this model, the preference of the collective has no meaning capable of being detached from the fundamental, personal rights of individual citizens. To argue for the 'common good' in collective terms is, therefore, a negation of the very concept of human rights and dignity.

This may seem a subtle distinction, but it is, so to speak, illuminated by means of an analogy between the common good and the concept of street lighting. The system may be collectively owned but its benefits are individually conferred. Each citizen, with the help of the streetlights, sees with his own eyes, and is thus enabled to pursue his life in the public space after dark. There is no everyday context in which the lighting is used for collectivised purpose. Even a 'public' event, such as a carnival, is enjoyed individually rather than collectively, and it is this the public lighting enables rather than some shared experience of enjoyment.

We know, further, from history and the writings of astute observers, that the idea of collectivised benefit as some category separate from the individual benefit, exists only as a form of hazard — the crowd, or mob, under manipulation or direction of collectivist demagogues. Only under such conditions does anything identifiable as a 'collective psychology' materialise, and this 'group soul', in as far as it suggests some collective experience capable of being balanced against the rights and dignities of individuals, is both illusory and dangerous.

The key to understanding the democratic implications of what occurred in March/April 2020 is to see the 'pandemic' as a subterfuge for a radical assault on freedom predicated on a bogus or exaggerated claim of a potentially lethal contagion — a global coup. The 'virus' narrative was used to demolish the edifice of individual rights that had hitherto constituted the core of Western freedom, and to supplant it with an imperative to protect an abstract collective from harm deemed to threaten the group via the individual. This served overnight to annul a raft of rights and freedoms hard won over multiple centuries, and this with the ostensible support of a majority of the individuals affected. Accordingly, for over two years, a minority of befuddled observers in the former Free World has been pondering how it could be that people who have been steeped in the stories of Soviet totalitarianism, the works of survivors and heroes like Solzhenitsyn and Havel, as well as the fictional works of Orwell and Huxley, could so casually embark upon the treacherous path these witnesses and writers had so thoroughly signposted and cautioned of. How this came to pass is the conundrum we face at this possible terminal moment for Western freedoms.

In a May 2022 article for *Unherd*, *Covid was liberalism's endgame*, the great contemporary American philosopher, Matthew B. Crawford, asks whether it might be the case that liberalism always had an 'innate tendency towards authoritarianism' and decides that the answer is yes.

Crawford sets out the conundrum within the topography of philosophical historiography. He is himself much more than an academic — a great practical philosopher of the present moment, who normally grounds his thinking in both personal experience and the inheritance of Western thought. Here, however, his edifice wobbles slightly due to the shortcoming of many efforts to explain some elusive phenomenon of the present in purely philosophical terms: it treats the discrete theories of the masters he has selected to illuminate the conditions under analysis as though together they might add up to an understanding unavailable in their separate parts — in other words, he approaches the thoughts of philosophical icons as building blocks rather than raw lumber to be adapted and reconstituted to the particularities of the conundrum under examination.

Crawford, I would say, from observing his work and contributions over the past two years, has been a thoughtful Covid sceptic, taking for granted that the lockdowns were unnecessary and unhealthy. Sketching a comparison between the Spanish Flu of 1918 and the Covid episode, he observes: 'There is an inverse relationship between the severity of these pandemics and the severity of measures to control them.' Two whole years ago, he published an article on *UnHerd* asserting that 'Grasping bureaucracies are using lockdown as an excuse to choke the human spirit.'

His most recent book, *Why We Drive*, published in early 2020, 'accidentally' relates to some of the central Covid questions, one of its chief themes being the dangers of 'safetyism' in the context of the ominous imminence of the self-driving car. Safetyism, he argues, has supplanted all other moral sensibilities, creating a downward spiral of life-enhancing risk, which ultimately delivers us not to zero-Covid, but zero-adventure, moving us ever closer to max unfreedom.

In this latest *Unherd* article, he examines the use of 'states of exception', which suspend the normative charter of self-government and install processes of government-by-decree by politicians unmandated to this end. This, Crawford attests, now threatens to become the norm rather than the exception.

The access key to such a transformation is the use of emergency to trip the democratic circuitry, defaulting to an allegedly unavoidable despotism that rapidly courts totalitarianism. The language of war is used to create one after another 'emergency', so that we arrive willy-nilly at a state of quasi-permanent crisis, requiring the state to intervene to secure public safety, *et cetera*. Crawford interestingly relates this concept to that of a contemporary incarnation of the 'moral panic,' in which some victim category stands to be protected over and above the norm, leading to an upsurge in bureaucratic supervision, to the detriment of egalitarianism and normative 'liberal' expectation. He rightly draws a line connecting these developments in recent political life to the manifestation of the accelerator of Covid in the spring of 2020. By Crawford's illuminating account, the totalising effect of these syndromes serves to steal the essence of liberalism, dragging society backwards while affecting virtue. These tendencies, already implicit in the modern liberal model, he writes, became rampant in the Covid episode. The 'pandemic' both 'accelerated what had previously been a slow-motion desertion of liberal principles of government,' and 'brought to the surface the usually subterranean core of the liberal project, which is not merely political but anthropological: to remake man.'

Here, he has put his finger on the central contradiction of liberalism: that it conflates 'freedom' with human 'improvability' — a belief in radical human progress; the unfettered transformation of social values; antipathy towards the 'old order' and its guardians; and the drive to radically change the real, existing man to recreate him as a quasi-perfect hybrid being. This concept of human-improvability is sometimes known as 'anthropological palingenesis' — a drive towards 'rebirthing' man as a radically new phenomenon, born out of the desire that man himself be the sole and overarching 'creator', capable of generating or recreating anything within his sphere of influence, including — especially — himself. Crawford at first sets down as mutually contradictory the ideas of freedom and anthropological palingenesis, and proceeds to show how their combination under Covid resulted in a seismic shift in the nature of political freedom. The 'remaking' of man, though ostensibly a 'liberal' project, requires an illiberal form of government to advance it. But the virtuous aura of collective 'self-improvement' renders it ostensibly compatible with the liberal desire for 'progress'. This is why the lockdown measures met with such little liberal resistance: 'It seems the anthropological project is a more powerful commitment for us than allegiance to the forms and procedures of liberal government.'

In a philosophical deep-dive, he weighs up the competing metaphysics of John Locke and Thomas Hobbes, plumping for the former's benign, common-sensical notions of self-government over the latter's claim that our 'irrational pride' makes it essential that we be *ruled over* for our own good and protection. This — now ascendant — Hobbesian notion is at the root of the 'technocratic, progressive' model of politics, which we nowadays identify with the periodic shiny-suited manifestations in Davos, and unmandated manifestos like the 2030 Agenda and the Great Reset. This model has spawned also the behavioural model of politics that assails us now from all directions, apparently requiring that we be 'nudged' by our 'rulers' in our own interests. In this model, Crawford outlines, we are regarded 'not as citizens whose considered consent must be secured, but as particles to be steered through a science of behaviour management that relies on our pre-reflective cognitive biases.' This, indeed, is a post-citizenry form of 'democracy', in which the individual mutates into a 'client' of the state, carrying our duties and paying tribute in return for protection. This model delivers us to compulsory measures by mandate of 'the science', to the cult of the expert, and ultimately, the algorithm, by which all visible human agency is bypassed. A once free people wakes up one day to be ruled by shy, 'self-effacing' actors whose names and faces have never appeared on an election poster. This process of mystification breaks the chain of democratic accountability and renders inscrutable the systems and process by which a society is governed. 'Technocratic progressivism,' writes Crawford, 'in fact requires the disqualification of experience and common sense as a guide to reality, and installs in their place a priestly form of authority, closer to the Enlightenment's caricature of medieval society than to [the Enlightenment's] own self-image.' It also spawns a fearful, credulous type of non-citizen who behaves in society like a timid child on his first day in a new school.

This raises an obvious question: Was Thomas Hobbes even a liberal? His philosophy, says Crawford, is 'liberal in the sense that it is founded on consent. But it turns out this consent depends on a re-education program that reaches quite deep, and is never finished.' Hobbes believed that each human person, predatory and insatiable, is the enemy of each of the others, thus necessitating a strong state, which he named Leviathan, after the biblical sea creature that only God could tame.

The Hobbesian view of the human is as much a metaphysics — albeit a negative one — as a political philosophy, and tends towards darkness. It is mistrustful and sceptical of the claimed human capacity for discerning and choosing the good. It disputes the reliability of conscience, but then delivers the self-mistrusting humans over to the consciences of 'higher' — presumably because more knowing and trustworthy — humans. And here we can observe the centrally oxymoronic quality of the term 'liberal democracy': in the logic of the Leviathan, the liberal instinct tends incessantly towards a willed tyranny, since the selfishness and greed of 'illiberal' man requires no less. Hobbes, seeing his species as constantly on the brink of civil strife, requiring strict state supervision to guard against its own dark instincts, leaned towards benign monarchism. 'Ordinary' humans are weak, vain and egotistical, and thus their own worst enemies, their pride leading them always into trouble, from which only more elevated forms of consciousness can save them.

An obvious problem with this conception relates to whom might be deemed — and by whom? — a worthy supervisor of these unreliable tendencies. Meet Hobbes's 'Leviathan' — the 'King of the proud,' to whose will the people must submit in their own interests. The 'liberalism' factor enters into this exactly how? By virtue, it seems, of tacit consent: human weakness, pride and victimhood requires a surrendering of individual power, removing the right of dissent until the danger has passed. 'Men,' Crawford observes with precise acuity, 'will submit to Leviathan only if they inhabit a moral universe that has been emptied of transcendent referents.' God — the sole threat to Leviathan — must be eliminated.

We know, of course, that grotesque propaganda and media censorship of alternative voices magnified the fear about Covid way out of proportion to any risk, and these conditions resulted in a relieved handing-over of personal and collective sovereignty and the most fundamental rights and freedoms into state 'safekeeping'. This resulted in a toxic circularity, whereby control within the escalatingly technocratic political process was amenable to purchase by the state, using propaganda to maintain its massed population in quiescent demeanour. In this contrived climate, alternative interpretations of the unfolding reality were designated 'disinformation', pulling the ladder up on the possibility of escape.

The temptation for the modern Leviathan is that the condition of permanent emergency offers the possibility also of unending power. And here, absent the monarch of old, the ruler is someone who has acquired the authority to suspend the normative checks and balances by dint of a claimed democratic consent that is rarely, if ever, formalised. Modern 'democratic' politicians are not supposed to be 'rulers' but public representatives, delegates, at most 'firsts among equals'. The spectacle of the entire panoply of state powers of coercion being summoned up in such a situation, against the very people these mechanisms are supposed to belong to and serve, is ugly beyond description, and yet, in the Covid episode, this aspect attracted minimal adverse criticism. This effect, says Crawford, is achieved by 'cultivating the vulnerable self' — using fearmongering to maintain the individual in a state of trembling so he never thinks to recall his power. The technocratic-progressive state has advanced means of nurturing the vulnerability of the citizen-who-has-ceased-to-be-a-citizen, so as to forestall any such reawakening.

Crawford postulates that, in part, the general acquiescence in Covid excess bespoke a hidden 'desire to *belong*' after the long decades of liberal individualism, a felt need to be required to discharge duties rather than simply claiming 'rights' and entitlements. In this context, he posits, the 'war against Covid' evinced some positive aspects, including a welcome shifting back to public-spiritedness. But this was itself a reaction to conditions created by the very ideologies that found their culmination in the Covid episode: high levels of social fragmentation and atomisation — arising from secularism and family breakdown and spawning anxieties and aggressions that provided ripe conditions for mass formation. The paradoxical solidarity of social distancing dramatised the nature of atomised society, while providing a common cause that drew people temporarily together. This, as Hannah Arendt observed, provides ideal conditions for totalitarianism, drawing people into the mass — mob — as a form of over-correction where no other means of achieving togetherness is available.

Like the psychologist and analyst of modern mass formation, Mattias Desmet, Crawford argues that it is unnecessary to adduce a conspiracy of elites to explain an operation like this, since the 'shared public morality of the sacralised victim' is sufficient to create the necessary cohesion and iron out any contradictions. For example, the apparent 'unfairness' of permitting BLM protests in honour of George Floyd, without social distancing, while batoning anti-lockdown protestors for the same alleged liberty: 'explained' by underlining the righteous heroism of 'mainly peaceful protestors', as against the selfishness of the anti-lockdown campaigners — elevating the victim/martyr above the 'self-interested' urge to freedom.

Crawford is chiefly interested in liberals' 'lack of curiosity' concerning the many contradictions of Covid and the remedies brought forward allegedly to counteract it. He points out that there have been no great moves to, for instance, calculate the costs of the lockdown in lives and health, which might indeed be deemed odd given that this was supposed to be the point of the whole thing. 'The real attachment,' he decides, 'seems to be, not to actual health, but to a source of collective meaning that floats free of the empirical: the Covid emergency itself.' But this collective purpose, he writes, 'was of a peculiar, negative sort.' It was also blinkered — shutting out its own limitations and contradictions so as to claim the singular and ultimately unattainable outcomes posited at the beginning. Thus, what he identifies and names is almost what might be described as an object within a game — a precise outcome within defined rules, ignoring and discounting everything that does not fit the regulatory definitions. A ball ending up in the net directly from an indirect free kick is not a 'score' within the meaning of the rules — just as a death caused by lockdown cannot be counted against the 'gains' achieved against Covid. The 'game' of 'pandemic meaning' evolved around a singular set of objectives, excluding all other considerations: *The good that was latched onto as a source of collective meaning during the pandemic was that of minimising deaths attributable to a single cause, never mind the wider field of harms done by the lockdowns outside this tunnel vision.'

And this also, he observes, caused us to discount losses and damage that might, at another time, have generated outrage: masked children, abandoned grandparents, stalled human interaction — together amounting to 'a kind of enforced nihilism.' The narrow metrics of the 'game' permitted the ignoring and discounting of manifold wrongs, including the coercive sanctioning of attempts to seek meaning under different rubrics, and appeals to constitutional guarantees to be trod underfoot.

In these broad strokes, Crawford illustrates how the Covid Leviathan insinuated itself as a necessary corrective to human weakness — not, in this case, moral weaknesses, but biological ones: the human susceptibility to infection and capacity for transmission. This, he writes with implacable precision, resulted in 'the consummation of a project that puts the flight from death, rather than attraction to the good' at the centre of our political metaphysics. Human life was reduced to survival at all costs, including the cost of jettisoning the possibility of living while alive.

The nature of our recent culture — the 'technical society' as anticipated by Jacques Ellul, which blocks human beings from their own humanity, renders inevitable the Faustian choice of palingenesis over freedom. As a result, we have arrived, says Crawford, in an age of 'spiritlessness', consumed in equal measure by rage and depression, both arising from forms of relativism that lead us to mistrust our own capacity to know what is right and what is good. The liberal prohibition on imposing our judgements and values on the world has reduced us to an entirely subjective method of apprehension, which we mistrust, and which now prompts us to reject liberalism itself in favour of an uneasy safetyism rather than a confident culture dominated by reason, passion and self-belief. The instilled fear of our own dark natures has turned us into our own gaolers.

Crawford's logic here is as though an elaboration on the theme of R.R. Reno's 2019 book, *Return of the Strong Gods*, which describes the period of 'disenchantment' in Western culture from the end of WWII, initiating a retreat into the woolly, therapeutic safetyism that followed — a contrived device to, you might say, render the West too small for its jackboots (That part hasn't worked out so well). In what has been designated 'the authoritarian society', humanity looked upwards: to the flag atop the flagpole, to the horizon, to the heavens. Nazism was a macabre pantomime of these constructs, the darkest of slapsticks arising from the collision of chaos, vanity, propaganda and human hearts unburdened of the fear of God by man's deluded ambition to become God. Clowns became tyrants and then mass murderers. But its legacy meant *inter alia* that the strong gods — the great human passions of patriarchy, patriotism and piety — must be banished, forgotten. Unable to understand what had just happened, the cultural leaders of the West scapegoated the very qualities that, if purified and isolated, offered the only chance of salvation. Reno outlines how Western society rewrote its own programmes in the wake of World War II to prevent a return to authoritarian rule. Citing a cross-sample of such contributions — Karl Popper, Albert Camus, Friedreich Hayek, Milton Friedman, and others — he demonstrates how their writings dismantled a culture rooted in strong loyalties — to God, fatherland, nobility, heroism, Being, justice, home — and supplanted them with weak, therapeutic ideals like 'diversity', 'tolerance', 'equality', and 'openness' — all constructs that inspire nothing but self-interest. According to this post-war consensus, stable convictions and strong passions had to be avoided. The West's leadership class insisted that we be metaphysically homeless, even as it sheltered itself, and so, as though together, we took the Hobbesian path.

In something of the same spirit, Matthew Crawford writes: 'Hobbes wanted an education that emphasises that human nature (especially that of the "noble") is selfish and base. Why? Because any appeal to a higher good threatens to return us to the horrors of civil strife and must be debunked.'

Rather than aiming for the highest good, man should instead concentrate on avoiding death. 'Lowering the sights of political life in this way helps tame the pride that leads to conflict.' Men will submit to Leviathan only if they inhabit a moral universe from which God and other transcendent intimations have been banished. Man cannot be trusted to desire the good, and so his desires must be curbed and rendered suspect to himself. Foremost among these desires is what the Greeks called *thumos* — spiritedness — the part of the soul that craves recognition and holds to great passions and values, like patriotism or heroism — a 'fire in the belly'. Ideally, Crawford observes, the process of divining 'the good' properly happens in dialectic with *logos*, the voices of the gods speaking from within — in Christianity, the voice of Christ expressed in conscience — which, in a well-ordered soul, functions as the reasoning element and, in combination with *thumos*, leads to correct action. This process has fallen under extreme suspicion in the modern era, being condemned by the therapeutic culture as overly prone to subjectivism and prejudice. Modernity requires responses to be 'rational', value-free and, ideally, disengaged. Man's spiritedness, therefore, must be conditioned by the pedagogic programming of the regime, and moderated by the obedience of the subject.

But, Crawford asks: 'What happens when the regime is one in which this spirited, evaluative activity is short-circuited altogether, subordinating the (various) distinctions that make for (competing visions of) the good life to mere biological life, bare existence? That is, "health" as conceived by "public health"? This is aggression against our nature as evaluative beings. It would seem to be the consummation of a project that puts the flight from death, rather than attraction to the good, at the center of our political metaphysics.'

In such a culture, man's *thumos* — spiritedness — becomes frustrated, disordered and involuted. Eventually, according to Crawford, it simply dies:

'An older term used for melancholy in psychiatry is *athumia* — a failure of *thumos*. To be *athumos* is to be disheartened; lose heart; suffer a want of heart.' That, he says, 'seems to be where we are, collectively: rage and depression.'

He draws also a line back to what he calls the 'ambient political crisis dating from 2016' — the shock-waves from such as the Trump and Brexit phenomena — which put the (liberal) establishment on a war footing. Essentially, he is saying that the Covid Project seemed almost instantly to ignite something in Western liberalism that had long been there: a desire to compel humanity into a 'better' way of seeing and acting in the world.

In October 2020, as it happens, I wrote an article on a related line of thought for Front Page Magazine called 'The Ideological Stripe of Covid-19' (see Chapter 2), exploring possible reasons why responses to a biological condition might have broken down so cleanly on ideological lines in the Covid episode.

One of the points I made had to do with the priming of the Covid artillery with ideological fuse wire, provoking liberals to support government actions, and conservatives to reject them. Less clear is how this was achieved, though it appears that the 'signalling system' employed within the logic of the Covid exercise facilitated a leveraging of mutualised ideological antipathies to provoke a division that was not itself implicit in the pure facts of the 'pandemic'. Thus, although Trump — US president at the time — was not especially sceptical of the virus narrative, it was successfully implied that he had been slow to respond, or was incompetent and / or sceptical in his handling of the crisis. Thus,

Trump came to be seen, rather implausibly, as an icon for sentiment hostile to the truth or gravity of Covid:

Even though it makes just a limited amount of sense, it does at this stage appear that, in some odd and irrational way, Covid is actually a left-wing phenomenon. This undoubtedly has to do with authority, indeed with the authoritarian tic that seems to afflict many leftists. . . . Covid, as has been seen everywhere, is an intensely authoritarian phenomenon. The first measures introduced by governments practically everywhere were directed not at protecting public health but at awarding powers to themselves to restrict and coerce their citizens and impose draconian penalties for breaches or dissent. This kind of thing suits leftists just fine and dandy. Not only do they enjoy seeing the boots of the regime on the faces of fellow citizens, but they themselves seem to enjoy, like masochists under the whip of the master, the lick of leather on their own hides.

The logic of postmodernism and Cultural Marxism suggest that 'liberal' understanding of history was of a series of fixes designed to stitch things up on behalf of, first and foremost, the Christian, white male. The only conceivable remedy is to remake the world as the antithesis of this.

I noted, too, an element that has been uppermost in the work of Matthew Crawford: the centrality of a workplace divide between muscularity and what Mattias Desmet calls 'bullshit jobs', now ubiquitous in the era of Big Tech globalism:

At a basic human level, the kinds of people who gravitate to left or right tend to divide also, generally speaking, in terms of physique, occupation, and mentality. Leftists, shall we say, tend less towards muscularity, work generally in offices, salons or cubicles, and think the world owes them a living, an expectation the world generally speaking appears to honour and come up, as it were, trumps on. They also consider themselves better educated, but in reality this means that they spent more time than others being indoctrinated with the virus that now afflicts their brains. I find it interesting that working class/blue collar people seem to see through Covid in a flash, whereas the average college graduate goes around in what appears a terrified trance, thinking he's going to meet his death around every corner.

Covid has emerged . . . as an accelerant on all things the average Cultural Marxist holds dear: restrictions on practice of religion and public assembly, cycle lanes and other green stuff, compulsory face masks which make everyone as unattractive as the average blue-tinted Cultural Marxist, disincentives to voting in person, and so forth. It emphasises the 'common good', which somehow reveals itself (who knew?) as extending to the state the right to restrict citizens as though self-evidently some kind of criminals on the mere possibility that they might be 'infected' with a non-lethal disease. It has no regard for charter, proclamation or constitution. It does not care for family, nation or God — is, in fact, the enemy of all three.

What is called 'liberalism' nowadays has long exhibited a tyrannical/moralistic element, a desire to compulsorily 'educate' people concerning flaws in their anthropological outlooks and understandings. Having taken total hold of the media, this liberalism became not so much a movement or a philosophy as a Jeremiad — a non-stop harangue directed at the nature of reality and the way it had been regarded in human culture for thousands of years. Failures to comply with liberal diktats were invariably presented in liberal proselytising as *moral* failures. It was a short hop from there to the notion of the human person as a walking biohazard, endangering his fellows due to fecklessness and ideologically-founded scepticism.

This form of liberalism — if such it ever was — had always seemed somewhat remote from the classical kind, which in the main favoured free markets and *laissez-faire* economics, limited government and civil liberties under the rule of law. Classical liberalism was about people doing as they pleased, as long as they did no harm to others — living and letting live. The modern 'liberal' mutant, by contrast, is a ragbag of nice-sounding sentiments that present up close as not especially wholesome, and, on closer examination, as destructive. Unlike the classical forms of liberalism also, this more recent form had always seemed to be of a slightly unstable disposition, exhibiting various forms of incoherence that its adherents were unable or unwilling to explain. An earlier incarnation was accompanied by a set of economic prescriptions, tellingly not akin to economic liberalism conventionally understood — a strange mix of market values combined with a soft leftism that favoured a kind of condescending *noblesse oblige*-style regime of patronage over the poor by the well-to-do. This element gave rise also to the 'anti-racist' element of this mutant liberalism: a profound condescension towards the 'Third World' masquerading as compassion and solidarity.

People calling themselves 'liberals' since the 1960s have never really believed in freedom broadly defined, but have had in mind mainly things to do with sex: contraception, abortion, homosexuality, *et cetera*, as well as drug-taking and other recreational obsessions — for all of which they sought to bully everyone else into sharing their singular enthusiasm. For half a century, their sex-obsessed concept of 'liberalism' dominated the cultures of Western societies, steamrolling over everything and everyone with the help of corporate money and devious propaganda, its incoherencies protected from scrutiny by corrupted media and the force-field of political correctness. This pseudo-liberalism sought to turn upside down the value-system of the civilisation that once was Christendom, attacking its most central civilisational mechanisms — love of God, nation and family — in favour of an empty and faithless materialism, and has long justified genocide in the form of abortion, facilitating a short leap to other forms of population limitation. It has self-evidently been intent upon engineering the cultural demolition of the West by dint of orchestrated mass migration, the destruction of the nuclear family and, as though by way of a 'booster' to all these programmes, the genocidal Covid coup of the past two years. As is now clear, 'liberals' certainly never had in mind the basic liberty to live your everyday life in ways that do not involve encroachment on others.

A phrase which found brief favour among sentient writers in the heyday of Irish press commentary of the 1990s was 'liberal ayatollahs', which I believe was coined by the great Irish literary analyst Declan Kiberd — or, if not, by his brother Damien, the most visionary Irish newspaper editor of the pre-millennium period. The term perfectly encapsulates the deep nature of latter-day 'liberalism', which has no capacity for compromise or negotiation, but survives by its own fanatical energy.

And yet, though undoubtedly incoherent, toxic, nasty and even violently hate-filled, most modern 'liberals' are not especially power-hungry. They crave only the means to impose their views and prescriptions — their Jeremiad — on others, and will avail of any means, no matter how contradictory, to achieve this. To see things in clear focus, therefore, we need to think not of a group or sector, but a kind of ceaseless tirade, not so much of liberal 'ayatollahs' as a 'liberal *ayatolliad*'.

Liberalism seeks not absolute power but the power to dictate those matters of ideological concern to it that are likely to be resisted by people of a different outlook. Liberals are, therefore, happy to attach themselves to more powerful interests, pursuing different objectives that do not clash with the primary elements of the liberal agenda. In recent times, liberals have sought common cause with the corporate sector, indifferent to the prospect that this alliance would, self-evidently, be in conflict with the economic dimensions of their 'liberal agenda'. Nor did that agenda, aside its wettish economic aspects, offend the more prosaic objectives of the corporates. A tacit partnership was set in train, in which the economic elements of liberalism were put on the back burner. Thus, while liberals like to daub their opponents as 'fascists', the Covid coup, in effect, delivered them to a partnership that invited a condition objectively indistinguishable from that conveyed by the original meaning of the word 'fascism': an alliance with corporate power.

Drawing together the threads of his thesis, Matthew Crawford cites another Irish writer, C.S. Lewis, in his exposition, in *The Abolition of Man*, of what he called 'the spirited man'. Is there, Crawford wonders, a way of counteracting the Hobbesian drift, and diverting man back on to a path defined by self-love and love of freedom?

C.S. Lewis may have more to offer us on this question, which Matthew Crawford forbears to delve deeply into — in deference, perhaps, to the 'liberal' readers of the platform he is writing in. Lewis's chief preoccupation in the essay cited by Crawford — *Men Without Chests* — was that, in the name of progress and human supremacy, humanity was at risk of inviting the enslavement of the many by the few. In abolishing God, we do not elevate all humans into the imaginative spaces once occupied by God, but only those who have climbed to the higher floors of the human space. In that essay, Lewis rinses down divergent but universal understandings of the Eternal, Infinite and Absolute — Platonic, Aristotelian, Stoic, Christian, Oriental — to a single code, co-opted from the Chinese concept of 'the Tao', which he calls 'the greatest thing'. The Tao is the thing out of which even gods are born. 'It is the reality beyond all predicates,' writes Lewis, 'the abyss that was before the Creator Himself. It is Nature, it is the Way, the Road. It is the Way in which the universe goes on, the Way in which things everlasting emerge, stilly and tranquilly, into space and time.' The Tao, he says, is 'the doctrine of objective value, the belief that certain attitudes are really true and others really false, to the kind of thing the universe is and the kind of things we are.'

Rejecting Hobbesianism, Lewis insists that we either submit our wills to a higher being, or we surrender both our wills and our hearts to the reduction implicit in the idea of man becoming his own master. Once man reduces himself to the material element, he sees himself as at one with all other matter, which rescues him from subservience to a Creator — sure — but immediately re-enslaves him to one, or some, among his fellows. In doing so, man-in-general succumbs to something he would be well advised to avoid: returning himself to Nature. Under the law of the Tao, human beings remained outside Nature. They and their edifices once existed, alongside the Supernatural and the Spirit World, in opposition to it. Our 'modern' 'rationalism' has denied us this facility, thereby returning us to Nature, where we are but one more animal. Man rightly belongs to the other dimension: of consciousness, freedom, values, self-awareness. Nature recognises no values, being red in tooth and claw. And, if man has returned himself to Nature, then, in continuing with his mission of conquering Nature, he seeks dominion over *himself*, which is really dominion of one man over another, or of the few who acquire the means of control over the many who are *ipso facto* deprived of such access.

Lewis says: 'Either we are rational spirits obliged for ever to obey the absolute values of the Tao, or else we are mere nature to be kneaded and cut into new shapes for the pleasure of masters who must, by hypothesis, have no motive but their own "natural" impulses. Only the Tao provides a common human law of action which can overarch rules and rulers alike. A dogmatic belief in objective value is necessary to the very idea of a rule which is not tyranny or is an obedience which is not slavery.'

As we look upon Nature, name its component elements, and work out the 'mechanics' of each one, we 'conquer' it and also destroy the taboos that kept us separate from it. By claiming dominion over it, we paradoxically bring ourselves back into its clammy embrace. Similarly, by developing mechanistic understandings of our own workings, we return ourselves to Nature, where we consider ourselves as some separated, objectified entities, no longer subjects but third-person quantities. In reducing our social existence to rules and moralisms and received wisdoms, we nudge ourselves towards this objectified state, where we stand with the rest of Nature to be examined, naked, by the Camp Commandant.

The debunking of the Tao, of tradition, and 'traditional values', comes at a high price, leading us to what Lewis — three-quarters of a century ago — called 'the world of post-humanity', which 'some knowingly, some unknowingly, nearly all men in all nations are at present labouring to produce.'

Man, devoid of God, Who is replaced by mere men, self-chosen and elected, seeks to place the flags of his colonialism on the summits of the future, and corral posterity within templates of his design. Any implicit sense of having dominion over the future is, by definition, delusional, since by going forward in error, man moves inexorably closer to the obliteration of his own species. As Lewis observes, each new power of man is also a power *over* men. Each advance leaves us weaker as well as stronger. This is the condition to which the liberal ayatollah has delivered the world.

And this process of delusional colonialism reaches through history, seeking to claim all time, past and future, to the dominion of (some of) those who live now. This is the 'liberal' project, exposing the idea that humankind seeks to improve the human situation on behalf of society as a piety that seeks to hide a bad motive behind a good one. In reality, mankind seeks dominion over the future, to set the stamp of the present on all of the projected humanity as yet unborn, while also cutting the lines of communication that run underneath our feet into the past. Just as we have become proportionately impoverished by the technologies and reductive understandings we have received from our immediate predecessors, so our descendants will be reduced in their potential by the instruments, edifices, paradigms and modes of understanding we bequeath them.

Lewis postulates that when we consider something analytically — i.e. positivistically — and then adapt it to our own convenience, we reduce it to the level of Nature — 'in the sense that we suspend our judgements of value about it, ignore its final cause (if any), and treat it in terms of quantity' — precisely what humanity in general has done in relation to Covid, its orchestrators and the lockdowns they have wrought, all of which remain beyond generalised critique or censure.

Man, then, has marooned his present incarnation in a moment he has not himself, individually or collectively speaking, exactly *chosen*. Having snipped the wires to the past and strived to disable the freedom and autonomy of future generations, he is caught in a moment he can't get out of, and doesn't know where he might choose to go if he could. It becomes increasingly unclear what is the point of it all. What propels the vehicle of progress is actually not the desiring of men-in-general, nor the energy of humanity's own ambition — recognisable as a stated objective in historical time — but a residual dynamism that has survived the wanton destruction of vital inherited quantities, now rapidly losing speed. Man moves forward under the momentum of that which he had sought to obliterate. The more he succeeds in his objectives, the closer he brings his own extinction. He speeds up history by striving to become its master, thereby pushing it out of his reach. Ultimately history controls him, because, in the totalitarian viewfinder, its *denouement* is already written. By striving for mastery over Nature, man becomes the victim of that which he imagines himself capable of vanquishing.

The totalitarian project, as Hannah Arendt made clear seven decades ago, comprises a form of symbiosis of the 'leaders' and the masses — without either element, it could not function. Thus, when man colludes in his own de-absoluti- sation, he hands himself over to the lynch mob, whose personnel he hopes to appease by concurring with their outlooks and attitudes, provided he is sharp enough to anticipate their caprices. Thus, by acquiescing in the abolition of God, many colluded in advance with what Lewis calls 'the abolition of man' — man as the ally of his own gravediggers, who turn out to be men very much like himself.

Ultimately, all these disastrous developments arise from a failure of imagina- tion. No longer able to conceive of God's existence — a failure laughably depicted as a gain of increasing 'rationalism' — man has condemned himself to the Hobbesian misanthropy directed at himself, which leaves the field open for every form of tyrant and tyranny to enslave him, including totalitarianism, in which he essentially enslaves himself, albeit to external agents — his undemoc- ratically nominated representatives imposing upon him sanctions and restric- tions that he accepts as his due on account of his own poor image of himself. Man has 'thought' himself into the ante-chamber of his own extinction, because he forgot that imagination, a higher form of thought, is the only true key to accessing the gateways to the future.

CHAPTER 24
TRANSCENDING 'THE SCIENCE'
26-09-2022 (AN INTERVIEW WITH DR MATTIAS DESMET)

The Belgian psychologist who has cut the key to unlocking the Covid tyranny is hopeful about a positive outcome and the chances that freeing ourselves will change our world for the better.

The recent green-eyed monster attacks on Dr Mattias Desmet from within the anti-Covid Cult Resistance have been as dismaying as they have been fatuous, for, in their sheer indifference to plausibility and reason, they have cast far more doubts on his frequently eminent accusers than on Desmet himself. In fact, it requires just a few minutes' conversation with Mattias Desmet in person to feel certain that the accusations against him are manifestly baseless, for he is a man of such striking straightforwardness that almost anyone might be a more legitimate target for suspicion of double-dealing. For anyone who has watched even one or two of his dozens of video conversations on the web over the past year and a half, this would already have been apparent. For anyone who has read his latest book, *The Psychology of Totalitarianism*, the particularities of the accusations will have read as absurdity upon absurdity — until, that is, it becomes clear that none of his critics shows any evidence of having read it.

I don't propose to go too deeply into the details of these accusations, not for fear of giving them legs — for as arguments, they are as invertebrate gastropods compared to the elegance and poetic grace of Desmet's own propositions: they neither walk nor fly. Rather, my fear is that dwelling too long upon them might bring disfavour upon several people whom I have admired in their own crusading against the current and continuing tyranny. Their interventions have done them no credit at all, and, unfortunately, have been all too obvious in their feebleness, as illustrated by one laughable accusation to the effect that Desmet is wrong about there being a Covid mass formation, because there could have been no mob during the Covid period since we were all locked down. Such a simplistic concept of what a mob is ought to attract nothing other than pity, as so also do the accusations that Desmet is a shill of the (presumably American) Deep State, has plucked the concept of mass formation out of thin air, and is seeking to 'blame the victims' for the tyranny of the past two and a half years.

Mattias Desmet has responded to the accusations in a typically coherent and good-humoured fashion. In a Substack post, he responds to two of his critics, the husband and wife team, Peter R. Breggin and Ginger Ross Breggin, who accuse him of asserting that Covid totalitarianism arises not from violent evil leaders (the global predators) but from the people themselves 'whose emotional needs create the dictator'.

There have been other critics also, and I expect there will be more to follow. Either they do not understand what Desmet is saying, or they are deliberately twisting it. One of the accusers — Peter Breggin again — has even accused Desmet of alleging that people like himself, who have awoken to the scam, are as culpable as the perpetrators and the sleeping sheep. It is clear from everything Desmet has been saying that Peter Breggin — or anyone who has been awake to the Covid subterfuge — is not included in the 'mass' as defined by Desmet, who allows that perhaps 30 per cent are unaffected by the trance.

Mattias Desmet is not 'blaming the victims', but seeking to describe the symbiotic process by which the manipulators succeed in killing their spirits. He is certainly not 'blinding us to the identity of the true culprits'. Rather, he is trying to convey a more complex, less binary point: that the contemporary kind of totalitarianism (because of mass media penetration, primarily) differs radically not merely from classical dictatorship but also from the twentieth-century forms of totalitarianism. Being fuelled by an all-pervasive ideology, this form of totalitarianism co-opts the mass in what can seem an almost 'voluntary' collaboration with the tyrants. Desmet does not deny the existence of tyrants or their nefarious agendas, but makes the point that they are, as individuals, dispensable and interchangeable within the structure of the trance. The underfoot conditions in the society — mass alienation, free-floating anxiety, anomie, bullshit jobs — create an amenable 'mass' which readily embraces the ideology that seems to offer its constituent members some strange kind of relief, including a bogus form of solidarity, which makes it easier for the manipulators to exercise control. He does not rule out an orchestration, but simply emphasises that this 'top-down' understanding is inadequate to grasping the nature of the total phenomenon.

There are a lot of misstatements in the Breggins' analysis. They seem, quite shockingly, in view of their venturing into the territory at all, to be unfamiliar with the work of people like Hannah Arendt, Gustave Le Bon and Joost Meerloo. There is a clear and solid line of scientific development for the thesis Desmet is postulating, which they show no signs of being aware of. Insofar as the mass formation idea is concerned, Desmet brings together various threads that have long existed in the field, but in a very convincing way that has long been regarded as axiomatic.

I believe there is a great deal of substance in Desmet's thesis that the totalitarianism we face is more of a symbiosis than a simple dictatorship — at least to the extent that many people are being suckered into going along with it, thus policing their fellows and making it possible for the authorities to use only a minimum of coercion (often, no more than the threat of coercion, a kind of feint that but rarely comes to total actuality) and in which the dissenter is essentially put under more or less constant pressure by his neighbours. His descriptions resemble very much what dissenters have experienced in encountering forms of 'policing' that erupted from their neighbours more often than from formal police forces. Desmet's point about the symbiotic nature of totalitarianism is a variation on Václav Havel's idea that each person is 'both a victim and a supporter of the system': 'Each person somehow succumbs to a profane trivialisation of his inherent humanity and to utilitarianism. In everyone there is some willingness to merge with the anonymous crowd and to flow comfortably along with it down the river of pseudo-life.'

Mattias Desmet, likewise, is not seeking to reallocate blame in any exculpatory sense, but actually to show how the conditions of the mechanistic society make it easier for tyrants to operate without necessarily being seen as such by the vast majority of the people.

Envy will always be with us. But I have noticed that it has become almost obligatory for almost anyone who stands up against the tyranny and manages to gain a significant profile to be denounced as a 'shill' or a 'plant' — by their own supposed side. The 'Shill!' slur has become a kind of suicidal secret weapon of the Resistance, with some people on 'our' side of the argument persistently accusing others of being 'controlled opposition' as an alternative to mounting any kind of coherent opposition of their own. The result is that they play into the hands of the enemy by damaging the morale of their own side. It really amounts to a kind of Catch-22: in order to avoid being 'outed' as a fraud, it is necessary to remain totally ineffective; the moment you begin to make an impact, the smearing begins. The 'shill-finders' remain on constant high alert, recognising as a symptom of falsity any sign of someone breaking through to the consciousness of the public, and immediately they pounce. To insulate oneself against this risk, one has to remain under the radar, being spectacularly unsuccessful. And proof of guilt is provided by denial.

I met Mattias Desmet in person for the first time last Wednesday, prior to his public appearance at the Button Factory in Dublin's Temple Bar, where I was to be one of the evening's brace of interviewers. We had encountered each other remotely earlier in the year, when I interviewed him via Zoom about his recently published book, *The Psychology of Totalitarianism*, having been a champion of his work for more than a year since I first came across him on YouTube. I brought along to lunch a gift of a book of essays by the aforementioned Václav Havel, the late Czech dissident, playwright, philosopher and poet-politician, whom I had mentioned to him in the course of our Zoom conversation. I suspected he would already have read one of the essays, *The Power of the Powerless*, as I had seen him writing furiously as we spoke about it, and so it proved. But, flicking through the book, his eyes lit upon a pulled quote at the opening of the Preface, extracted from one of the essays in the book, titled *Thriller*:

'I am unwilling to believe that this whole civilization is no more than a blind alley of history and a fatal error of the human spirit. More probably it represents a necessary phase that man and humanity must go through, one that man — if he survives — will ultimately, and on some higher level (unthinkable, of course, without the present phase), transcend.'

Desmet nods furiously at this, affirming that Havel is correct: History throws us these curve balls so that we may play them and grow as a species — as I understand both men to mean. Havel is speaking in *Thriller* of the recent shift in human history from societies rooted in myth and reason to societies clinging to ideology and pseudoscience — the 'necessary phase' to which he refers there. But the word 'transcend' also crops up frequently in Desmet's diagnostics and reflections, usually in the context of his exposition of the pathway of rationality petering out, to require a leap of transcendence into the realms of mystery, poetry, intuition, empathy, and even irrationality.

Interestingly, Havel proceeds as follows from the above:

'Whatever the case may be, it is certain that the whole rationalistic bent of the new age, having given up on the authority of myths, has succumbed to a large and dangerous illusion: it believes that no higher and darker powers — which these myths in some ways touched, bore witness to, and whose relative "control" they guaranteed — ever existed, either in the human unconscious or in the mysterious universe. Today, the opinion prevails that everything can be "rationally explained," as they say, by alert reason. Nothing is obscure — and if it is, then we need only cast a ray of scientific light on it, and it will cease to be so.'

And this, if his critics could but take the trouble to listen and read, is what Mattias Desmet is really on about. A central theme of the Czech resistance to which Havel belonged was the idea that a rationalistic totalitarianism derives, in the first instance, from a mechanistic automatism, by which rule-based social and political processes driven by a 'technoscientific' worldview serve to eclipse the general capacity for critical thinking, giving life to an 'absolutism' that inevitably leads to amoral decision-making and despotic rule. This, really, is

Desmet's theme also, though he approaches it via the psychological route of studying the phenomenon of Covid mass formation and its effects on human beings.

In his book, he writes:

'The discourse surrounding the coronavirus crisis shows characteristics that are typical of the type of discourse that led to the emergence of the totalitarian regimes of the twentieth century: the excessive use of numbers and statistics that show a radical contempt for the facts, the blurring of the line between fact and fiction, and a fanatical ideological belief that justifies deception and manipulation and ultimately transgresses all ethical boundaries.'

His book, as I have written in reviewing it, offers a description of modern society in the drifts of an escalating mechanistic culture, of which totalitarianism is the ineluctable destination. Gummed up in a congealing mechanistic ideology, man is reduced to a biological organism and subjected to the positivist logic whereby every aspect of thought must be eminently demonstrable. The resulting destruction of the symbolic and ethical elements of human culture, he writes, results in the devastation of relationships and the isolation of the individual, turning the human person into an atomised subject whose entire existence is as though reduced to elementary particles that interact according to the laws of mechanics. This provides the building block of the modern type of totalitarian state.

'This epistemological point of departure,' Desmet elaborates, 'has bearing on the ideology's conception of the ideal society. Ideally, society is led by expert technocrats who make decisions based on objective, numerical data. With the coronavirus crisis, this utopian goal seemed very close at hand. For this reason, the coronavirus crisis is a case study *par excellence* in subjecting the trust in measurements and numbers to critical analysis.'

He frequently cites the great Jewish-German intellectual, Hannah Arendt, more than once highlighting her assertion that totalitarianism is ultimately the belief in an artificially created paradise: 'Science [has become] an idol that will magically cure the evils of existence and transform the nature of man.'

The destination-point of this process, Desmet describes with a wave towards Silicon Valley, is transhumanist man — the merging of the human being with the machine: We have arrived, he seems to be certain, at a studied attempt to unravel both our civilisation and our human nature.

'Yes,' he confirms, 'I think that it's a process of radical dehumanisation that's happening right now. And that's difficult when there is a certain ideology which really imposes itself without limit on a society, and there is no other option — then that ideology dehumanises the entire society because it leaves no space for . . . Yes, it's immense, and at the same time — and that's where I maybe differ from my father — my father had a rather pessimistic view on what would happen, and in the end, I'm very optimistic. I think that it will be difficult, but I think that if we make the right choices, at the strategic and the ethical, and even at the intellectual level — you have to start from the right analysis, and if you construct a correct analysis, you will automatically choose the right strategy. Well, perhaps not automatically, but there is a good chance that you will choose the right strategy and also make the right ethical decisions. But I think that if we do so — and I'm convinced that we will do so — that there will be a group of people who will really make the right choice in the situation; and, in the end, we will see what a beautiful process it actually is, and how necessary this process is. The old ideology —this delusional belief in human rationality — will be exactly what we need to bring to the fore exactly the opposite, namely that it will give birth to that which transcends mere rationality.'

When I interviewed him in June, I sought to get at something that seemed to me to be obvious about Desmet but which I had not heard him called upon to address: that he was possessed of, or by, some quirk of history or personality that had enabled him to see deeply into the Covid scam from the beginning, when most of his contemporaries in both psychology and science more generally were falling into their place in the mass formation. I somewhat puzzled him, I think, by asking if his 'secret' might have had something to do with the fact that he is qualified in two relevant disciplines — psychology and statistics — thereby giving him an edge over mono-focus colleagues, much in the way that someone who has learned two languages in childhood can figure out other languages much more quickly when older.

It was a clumsy and rather unlikely concept, but in my defence, I submit that I was working off an intuition that now emerges as correct. Desmet *does* have a 'secret' inheritance from his childhood that has perhaps, more than any other single factor, enabled him to step up at this moment and see what is there more rapidly and coherently than others. I was on the right track but following the wrong trail. The 'secret weapon' of his insightfulness relates to his childhood, and in particular to his father, an autodidact small business-owner with an unusual suspicion of education.

'My father was someone who studied a lot. He was someone who was interested in all kinds of things. But he didn't want his children to go to university, or to go to school even. Because he thought that, if you go to school, you try to gather knowledge not because you have a passion to know but rather because you want a certain degree, or a certain societal status or something. Well, I didn't listen to him, and I went to university. And, after one year, I came back home and I showed him that I had passed my exams in an excellent way, and he said, "I knew you could do that, but I have no respect for it!" At first, I was angry, but now . . . I went through my academic training, and I was offered a PhD project, a grant, and I got my PhD after four years, and then I could stay at university for a post-doc, and that's how I became a professor. And actually, I learned a lot at university, but at the same time, in one way or another, I could understand my father better and better because, when I started to do my PhD, I was first doing a classical research project in psychology, but I immediately had a feeling that all these research methods that are used in psychology, they are not really valid and they will never lead — all these psychological tests questionnaires and so on, that are used to quantify psychological phenomena — in my opinion, they don't really teach you a lot about the object that you are studying. In the first place, they are used, I think, because they make your research *look* scientific, and it makes your research *appear* to be objective, but I really doubt if that is the case. A really objective research project does not really have to express things in numbers or figures — it has to bring you in close contact with the object. That's what objectivity is for me. It allows you to approach your object, to bring you in close contact with it, and most research methods in psychology absolutely don't being you closer to your object. If you ask someone to fill out a questionnaire, I don't think that the questionnaire will tell you more about the person than if you just *ask* him and *talk with him,* have a conversation with him, and as open-minded a conversation as possible.

'So I was very disappointed in the research methods in psychology. And then I decided to change the focus of my PhD and to investigate the research methods themselves, and after a while, I published a small book, *The Pursuit of Objectivity in Psychology,* and, well, most academic researchers got really angry with me, because it exposed, in my opinion, the weaknesses, and the problems, and the limitations of classical research. I don't say that all psychological research is bullshit. But a great deal of it is.'

What kind of man was his father? Was he politically minded, religious?

'He was not a political soul. He didn't identify with one or another political party. He was religious, but he refused to identify with any dogmatic or institutionalised religion. He was a very strong-minded person, someone who never hesitated to go against the group, and who tried to speak out in his own way. It was something that was characteristic of the family on my father's side. He was fanatic in many respects. Too fanatic.'

About what?

'Hmmm. About what? About his aversion for schools!' *(He laughs.)* 'Because I went to university against his will, but I learned a lot at university. I don't think that everything is bad at university.'

Mattias Desmet is perhaps coming more and more to see how his direction was formed, even if sometimes in the form of reaction, by his father's personality and its unconscious influence on his approach to thinking. In a way, his relationship with his father (who died a decade ago) mirrors his own historical thought process, in which, at the age of 35, he went on a journey upon the highway of rationality and found that, after a time, it deviated into a coherent irrationality, for which the language of scientific methodology was no longer any use. He followed the path with diligence and attention until its rational surface began to disintegrate, and then he started to better understand his father's position. Without either element — the exploitation of scientific ratio-nalism or his father's scepticism — he would not have grasped things as he has. Without one or other element he would not be the scientist he is. Never has this been clearer to him than in the past couple of years of his entanglement in the Covid saga.

'Yes, I think that you have to walk the path of rationality. You have to walk it until the end, and then you have to transcend it, I think. I'm not against ratio-nality — not at all — but I think that a lot of people think it is the *goal* of our human existence, whereas it is only a means toward the real goal, which is to transcend rationality. Yes! Well, I'm happy that I didn't listen to my father, actu-ally, and at the same time, I really discovered the value of . . . [what he was saying]. I have been working at university now for 19 years, I think, and I — well! — in one way or another, I don't think that a university really represents the true spirit of science. They really say that I can speak in my own way and so on — that I have freedom of speech — but at the same time, I feel that there is a huge pressure at university, and that many colleagues take a distance from me, that many colleagues just take for granted what is published in the newspapers about me. I always think that that is a very weak position as an academic.'

At the Button Factory last week, he said something to the effect that he had come to realise, after the spring of 2020, that his life up to that point had not been completely real, that he had been living a kind of artificial life, that only now does he see the point of his journey into psychology and scientific inves-tigation.

In December 2019, he was on holiday with some friends at a chalet in the Ardennes, in Belgium, when he heard about 'the virus'. He knew immediately that this life was about to change.

'I had this feeling, this intuition that, one of these days — and I told it to my friends — that we would wake up in a different society. And it was very real, that feeling. And when I came back from that holiday, I went to the bank and paid back my mortgage, and I didn't know exactly why I did that because, from an economical or a tax perspective, it was probably not interesting to pay back my mortgage. But I wanted to be as independent as possible, to be free as possi-ble. I wanted to liberate myself from the banking system which I believe to be responsible for many of the problems in the world. And two months later, the coronavirus crisis started and I immediately had the intuition: this was the crisis that I had been anticipating.'

Yet, having in one sense foreseen what was happening, he was nevertheless shocked at aspects of what unfolded.

'You know, I was also surprised when it all started, although I had been anticipating it in a certain sense. I couldn't believe what was happening around me. When it all started back in February of 2020, I just expected that all my colleagues at the university would all object and say, "Look! This is unbelievable! We have to make a proper cost/benefit analysis! Don't you see that there will be more victims claimed by the measures than possibly can be by the virus?" So I was very surprised myself. But very soon, I started to understand that what we were dealing with was a very dangerous phenomenon, which was the beginning of the emergence of a totalitarian system, and at the same time, it wasn't that something came true that I hadn't been expecting my entire life.'

Almost immediately, he published an opinion paper, *The Fear of the Virus is More Dangerous than the Virus Itself.* The die was cast, his future mapped out at this moment of coalescing between the emerging landscape of control and his intuition of such a calamity long before it happened — some understanding that these dark and dangerous forces were always right there in the hallway beyond his lecture room, on the next seat of the tram.

'Yes, definitely. I often said that when the corona crisis started, it was as if my entire intellectual training prepared me for it, because I had been studying science, scientific ideologies, and the way in which science ended up in a deplorable state just before the corona crisis started. We often forget the reputation crisis in 2005 reveals the terrible, deplorable state of academic research. I had always had an avid interest in the limits of materialism, because I believed that this idea that the natural universe is a mechanistic phenomenon is the real problem we are dealing with here. And even more, the idea that we can understand life, the universe, reality, and the human being, completely in a rational way — that's the real problem — it's the hubris of the human being that believes they will grasp the essence of life, crack the code of life, that it will show a rational understanding. That's the real problem: people who are incapable of tolerating uncertainty and who don't see that the answers to the big questions of life will never be rational in nature, but will always be of a different nature.

'For me the essence of the human being is humane as long as it can be a little bit uncertain, as long as it can really listen to someone and believe that maybe this other person also has something valuable to say. And if a human being becomes radically certain, so certain of its own perspective, then it inevitably will destroy each and every other human being that thinks differently. And that's exactly what happens in a mass formation: people become completely certain of their own perspective, so certain that they think that anyone who is not thinking like them is not a human being anymore, and consequently can be destroyed. Mass formation is dehumanisation of everything that goes against the masses, and consequently people in the masses become radically convinced that it is justified to destroy everyone who doesn't go along with it.'

For related and other reasons, he has avoided political pathways. 'Just like my father,' he says, 'I am not a very political being. I don't identify with one or other political ideology or orientation.'

'Who am I? At that level, I'm a very rational person in a certain way. I always try to understand — *stubbornly* try to understand rationally, at all levels. But I'm also a very poetic person, I think, someone with a strong mystical sensitivity, and for me, it was just so liberating when I suddenly started to understand that science itself shows us that the essence of life is not rational. It was as if, suddenly, the doors opened, and I could walk out of the prison that rationality always is, I think. We need to be rational, and we need to go through all the tunnels of rationality, but I think that, in the end, the really profound experience of our existence as human beings happens first when we transcend rationality, I'm sure of that. And I refused to do so before I could understand — rationally — why rationality was limited.'

Knowledge — of perhaps every kind — is contingent, not least because the language we use to acquire and explore it is itself a tool that traps us in its wires of logic. We use the least inadequate words when we speak of the unknowable.

'Yes, I distinguish always between, on the one hand, rational language in which you try to convey a certain meaning, in as precise and systematic way as possible, and then the more evocative, or resonating type of language, such as poetry or mystical context — that's something different. And in poetry you're no longer imprisoned in language because you touch something, you make something resonate in the other, without fixating it on a certain meaning. I think that's the drama of the human being, that it constantly tries to fixate on the meanings of the words in an attempt to grasp the essence of life, when the essence of life always escapes the meaning of words. And that's why Niels Bohr [Danish physicist who received the Nobel Prize in Physics in 1922] said that, when it comes to atoms, language can only be used as poetry. I started really to understand that when I was 35 years old. I suddenly understood that what he was saying, literally, was that, really, logical language cannot grasp the essence of atoms — they behave irrationally. You can only evoke. You can just, through poetry, get in touch with, resonate with, this mysterious and sublime behaviour of atoms.'

I tell him about the beautiful definition by Peter, brother of the great Irish poet, Patrick Kavanagh, of the relationships between a poem and its words:

'In a poem, the words are the least important part. In a poem, the words burn up in a tremendous thread of something unusual.'

'That's wonderful,' Desmet responds. 'That's what I'm saying. And if you want to destroy a poetic experience, you have to try to rationally understand the poem. It's immediately destroyed. It's as if there is a string that is vibrating and you try to fix it. You try to take the vibration. But in the act of trying to grasp the string you actually destroy the sound of the string.'

I tell him that, although he does not come across as 'left' or 'right', he does, however, suggest himself as some class of a liberal, who clearly belongs to those post-60s generations who believed in people's right to be let alone to live their lives more or less as they chose. He does not demur. He has been shocked by the responses of his fellow scientists and academics, and of the intellectual community in general, in the face of the greatest rights-grab in modern history.

'It's extremely strange. You know, Joost Meerloo coined the term "mental surrender". He said that if a totalitarian system emerges suddenly — he doesn't use the term "mass formation", but he refers to the emergence of the masses in totalitarian systems — and [he says] that this emergence of the masses is such a tremendously powerful phenomenon at a psychological level — such that even those intellectuals who really opposed the totalitarian ideology before the mass emerges might suddenly change their opinion, and suddenly begin to talk as if they support the totalitarian ideology.'

(Dr Joost Meerloo, who coined the word 'menticide', was forced to flee the Netherlands in 1942, following the Nazi occupation. The focus of his work is on the techniques used in interrogation — mental torture, brainwashing, and the use of fear as a tool of mass submission. He focussed also on questions of loyalty and treason — the possibility that, through studied manipulation, anyone can be turned into a 'traitor'. Meerloo's phrases — 'the rape of the mind' and 'menticide' — relate to what he characterised as the process by which a psychotic ruling class imposes on the collective mind of the population a programme for the achievement of its own aspirations to total power and control.)

Desmet continues: 'That's what he calls the "mental surrender" of many intellectuals and many politicians, and so on. No matter how critical they were of the totalitarian ideology before the mass emerged, they might suddenly change their opinion *without even realising it themselves!* Suddenly, starting to talk in the opposite way. I've seen this with many intellectuals in Belgium — people who wrote books about the dangers of conformism, about bio-fascism, and so on. And suddenly, the corona crisis started, this mass emerged, and they suddenly took a completely different position, and they started to attack in a very vehement way, a very avid way, the people who went against the totalitarian system.'

How does it work?

'It depends a little bit. It depends on whether these intellectuals, these politicians, really fall prey to the mass formation, whether they are in this hypnotic state that is the real state of mass formation. In that case, it just means that, psychologically, they bought into the narrative because it leads to all these psychological advantages, such as that the narrative allows the individual to control his anxiety, to let out all his aggression on someone, that it leads to this new social bond that is typical of mass formation. So, if these intellectuals really fall prey to the mass formation, it is because there are all sorts of psychological advantages situated at the more effective anti-personal . . . the social level. So there's an instrumental, tactical choice not to go against the masses, who are such a powerful voice in the society at this moment.'

Isn't this really a new kind of stupidity, possibly arising from too narrow a focus?

'Yes, that is one of the mechanisms behind it. Like, a mass formation really makes the focus extremely narrow — that's why it is identical to hypnosis. In hypnosis, someone's attention is focussed on one small aspect of reality, and the rest of reality disappears. But, in mass formation, exactly the same happens. All these emotions are withdrawn from reality, and they are freely floating in the mind of the person, and then suddenly, all the anxieties and frustrations and aggressions are focussed on one small aspect of reality — like a virus — and that's when all the rest disappears. And that's why people were really not capable anymore of making a proper costs/benefits analysis. It was just impossible even to simply tell them, "Okay, there will be victims claimed by the virus, but there will also be victims claimed by the corona measures". Even highly intelligent people were simply not capable anymore of seeing that there would be two types of victims. And that has everything to do with this narrow, hypnotic focus of attention.'

Giving the lie to critics who allege that he is a (by definition) carefully cultivated *agent provocateur* who spills out pat analyses of complex topics, Desmet is an extraordinarily open and honest interlocutor even on matters relating to his own areas of expertise, frequently hesitant before an unfamiliar question and pondering it openly for several minutes. This happens when I ask him if he can identify any of the clues he may have noticed previous to what he calls 'the corona crisis' in people that alerted him, even if unconsciously, to the potential dangers inherent in a mass of mono-minded people. For several minutes, speculates about various aspects of the question as though racking his memory for connections and testing them with some unseen spirit level.

'Ahh!'

'Hmm.'

'I think . . .'

'Maybe . . .'

'Wow! In a certain way . . .'

'There's a . . .'

He begins one possible explanation and then rejects it as peripheral. Then he returns to his father:

'You know . . . [long pause] Maybe it also has to do with a certain religious . . . As I said, my father did not belong to any dogmatic or institutionalised religion, but he spoke Hebrew, he analysed many of the Jewish religious literature in the original language, and he explained to me the meaning of the religious metaphors and so on. And while I rediscovered that in my own way, he also mentioned to me, from when I was a small child, that in Jewish mystical literature, everything went through a cycle of seven steps. The first six steps were the rational steps, and the seventh step was the step to God, and that was the step that transcends rationality. He frequently told me that, in these times we are living in now, that we are dealing with a system that went through the first six steps, but refused to take the seventh step.'

I tell him that this is almost exactly what Aleksandr Solzhenitsyn said when accepting the Templeton Prize at the London Guildhall in 1983, about the reasons for the destruction of his country, Russia, by Bolshevism. Solzhenitsyn recalled that, when he was still a child, he would hear the old people saying that all the disasters befalling Russia were happening because God had been forgotten:

'Over a half century ago, while I was still a child, I recall hearing a number of old people offer the following explanation for the great disasters that had befallen Russia: "Men have forgotten God; that's why all this has happened." Since then, I have spent well-nigh 50 years working on the history of our revolution; in the process, I have read hundreds of books, collected hundreds of personal testimonies, and have already contributed eight volumes of my own towards the effort of clearing away the rubble left by that upheaval. But if I were asked today to formulate as concisely as possible the main cause of the ruinous revolution that swallowed up some 60 million of our people, I could not put it more accurately than to repeat: "Men have forgotten God; that's why all this has happened."'

Mattias has not heard the quotation before. He nods vigorously. 'Yes. Yes! It's strange how certain things you heard when you were a child . . . that your entire life seems to lead back to these simple things you heard when you were small.'

How, I wonder, is he so hopeful that our societies, under the attrition of this horror show, will become 'educated' — ideally not in the way his father was suspicious of, but in a different way — about what human existence is really about, and what the natural human responses ought to be, or were, or would be if we didn't interfere with them mechanistically all the time. How has he become too hopeful about that — that we can learn together?

'Yes, I am very hopeful. And I have this feeling that it is happening already, this feeling that there is this new connections between people. I often feel that — as if people connect in a more direct way to each other. Like we are talking now. I would have never met you without this crisis, and I feel this connection with a new network, a new group of people. And I think that what needs to happen will happen spontaneously. We won't have to do it ourselves. The only thing we will have to do is just stay true to these principles. We have to try to find the eternal principles of humanity. And from time to time, I discover such a principle for myself. Like, *talk with everyone*. You know, there are all these people who have been stigmatised as "far right", as "conspiracy theorists", as "anti-vaxxers", as "climate deniers", and so on. And I think: *Just forget about all these things and be willing to talk, to share words with everyone*. That's what we have to rediscover, and we have to follow these ethical principles — that's crucial, no matter what we lose by following them. We have to be prepared to sacrifice a lot just to stay in touch with these ethical principles, and then all the rest will be done for us.'

For Václav Havel, and his mentor, the older dissident Jan Patočka, who died following an episode of police brutality in 1977, morality was its own objective and not something to be seen as a means to an end. You lived in the truth for its own sake, not to attain victory. The point of humane action was to remain human. Morality was not a construct of man's need to create order, but — on the contrary — what defined the human being. The true dissident disposition is not instrumental, but carried out for the intrinsic value of doing it, as Patočka put it, 'for the sake of nothing' so as to achieve something 'for the sake of everything'. Such action has, as its end, some sense of liberation, yet along the way is focussed solely on the moral power it is capable of generating, which is itself the key to its non-violent character. Mahatma Gandhi, too, insisted that the dissident must set for man a path independent of ends, centred on the raising up of his own consciousness to embrace a higher set of values, including personal responsibility and a willingness to live within the truth.

'Exactly,' Mattias responds. 'And that's exactly the opposite to a rationalist approach to life, because if you think rationally, you begin to think, "If I follow that principle, I might lose my job. I might lose this or that!" If you think rationally, in the end you always become a coward. I think rationality can help you a little bit to discover these principles, but these principles are always born from an experience that transcends rationality — sometimes an experience of the heart. It is this resonating knowledge which is so important, and which I will try to write about in my next book. Just the crucial experience: What is the kind of knowledge that transcends this rational knowledge, and that's what can bring us in touch with the principles of life. And, if we are then prepared — and that's crucial — to follow those principles, to live up to these principles no matter what the cost, then that is all we have to do. It's extremely simple and, at the same time, something extremely difficult. If you read the autobiography of Mahatma Gandhi, for instance, that's exactly what he says. Gandhi was not a big intellectual, not at all. He was constantly thinking about what the nature of truth is. And every time he discovered something about truth, he tried to change his life and to revert to his new discovery about the nature of truth. He was not smart; he was not handsome; he was not a good speaker; he was not a good writer. But he was very loyal to truth, and that gave him the power to do something that nobody else could do: to get the English out of India. So that's what we should realise — that, as Havel said, the power of the powerless, that even if you lose your power, you still have your full power as a human being, if you have the courage to live up to your principles as a human being.'

His optimism is contagious, oddly, because its delivery is devoid of bombast. He speaks evenly and without affectation. His demeanour is serious, and yet warm, an unusual combination in a practitioner of science. His personality perfectly matches the philosophy he adumbrates.

In our conversation over lunch the previous day, he had linked from Havel's view of the necessary lessons of twentieth-century mechanistic rationalism, via the early incarnations of totalitarianism, to the idea that we have now entered into some kind of final stage of the learning phase. The twenty-first-century brand of totalitarianism, he suggests, will be the culmination of that adventure, though not necessarily in a dark or fatal way. Again, he is hopeful:

'All totalitarianism starts from the belief in human rationality. Whether we are talking about Communist totalitarianism in Russia, or fascist totalitarianism in Nazi Germany, in both cases, there is a certain pseudo-scientific theory, which is the historical materialism of Marx, or a certain neo-Darwinism race theory, as in Nazi Germany. There's a certain pseudoscientific theory that is used to reshape society, and that is relentlessly imposed on society, a certain absurd logic [based on] this utopian pseudoscientific theory. So, in both cases, we see that totalitarianism always testifies to the delusional belief in human rationality. But this time, we are dealing with a worldwide system, which is completely different. There is no hope that an external enemy will save us. We will have to solve it from within, from inside the system. When there are external enemies, they can destroy the system with aggression. This time, there is no higher authority — not on this earth. And that makes a huge difference, because in the kind of totalitarianism in the first half of the twentieth century, people could still hope that an external enemy could still destroy the system. Now, forget about that — that option simply doesn't exist, so it will have to be solved from within. And from within, aggression is not an option. Aggression is always so destructive for any internal resistance to a totalitarian system. People like Hannah Arendt, and so on, described that. Non-violent resistance is by far the most effective resistance from inside the totalitarian system. So, we will have to walk that way. That is the only solution. And that makes a huge difference: There will be no other option than to go through that tunnel, the tunnel of non-violent resistance, no matter how difficult it is. And it's in that tunnels I think, that people will truly change, will go through an enormous evolution as human beings. That's exactly what Solzhenitsyn describes in *The Gulag Archipelago*. People in the concentration camps also couldn't rely on aggression to defend themselves against the totalitarian regime, and the people who chose, in the concentration camps, to stay loyal to their ethical principles, they were the ones who came through this enormous transformation as human beings. And this might happen now, on a much larger scale, with all the people that choose to resist in a non-violent way. So that's one major difference with the process of totalitarianisation in the first half of the twentieth century. And another major difference, I think, is just the ideology itself. Like, the fascist ideology had this cult of the hero, which was not very rationalist in nature, was very romantic in nature, and so on. So the typical totalitarian rationalism was merged with all kinds of non-rationalist elements. We don't see that now. This transhumanism is a completely rationalist ideology. It's more pure. What is surfacing now is like a pure mechanistic rationalist ideology, much purer than in the first half of the twentieth century.

'The transhumanist ideology is just the contemporary and pure manifestation of the idea that the human being is just a machine — that it is a material machine, which is part of the larger material machine of the universe. That's actually the basic ideology that slowly became more and more prominent throughout the last four or five-hundred years — this idea that the human being can be analysed as a machine, that it can be explained as a machine, that you can control it as a machine, that you can optimise it as a machine, and so on. That's what transhumanism is: the manifestation in public space of this mechanist view on the human being.'

I note, superfluously, that the previous totalitarianisms lasted, respectively, seven decades and roughly a dozen years. The Nazi manifestation was accompanied by a war, which may have abbreviated what might otherwise have lasted decades as well. This suggests, doesn't it, that the final Act could be a long battle, especially if pursued from our side in non-aggression fashion?

'Maybe. It could also be a rather short battle — we don't know — because this totalitarianism might be extremely self-destructive. We don't know. Sometimes, the more means the totalitarian system has at its disposal, the faster it destroys itself. And in the end, it *always* destroys itself. But how long it takes, nobody knows.'

He thinks that, already, the plotters have made some fundamental mistakes which may rebound against them. 'Here in this situation, I have never known of a totalitarian system injecting its population at such a scale with experimental vaccines. It's an extremely dangerous thing. It might quite quickly resolve the situation.

'And that is also a strange thing: The leaders of the contemporary totalitarian system are not people like Stalin and Hitler. Not at all. They are, as Hannah Arendt predicted, these dull bureaucrats and technocrats. That's what she said: The ultimate totalitarianism will be led by dull bureaucrats and technocrats, people who function as a kind of robot.'

But nonetheless vicious . . .

''Yes! Nonetheless, very vicious. Yes!' *

---

* Two additional interviews with Dr Mattias Desmet are included at the end of this book.

YEAR FOUR
2023

CHAPTER 25
THE LAW OF THE LAND & THE LIE OF THE FREE LUNCH
20-02-2023

A corrupted economics provides us with a false model of human reality. Its incubation as a proposal for collective living rendered inevitable what has happened to our freedoms and our futures.

Although its meaning has in modern times eclipsed the Greek, Kantian and even Christian concepts of the phrase 'the good life', I had not until recently truly grasped the precise resonance of the 'good' part in the phrase as commonly used nowadays — the 'Good Life', as in 'escaping the rat race', seeking to create a worthwhile, honest and meaningful existence in proximity to nature, generating the means of one's own existence, *et cetera*, i.e. the meaning implied by the eponymous title of the 1970s BBC comedy series starring Richard Briers, Felicity Kendal, Paul Eddington and Penelope Keith. But, now I think I get it, after reading Roy Sebag's short (no more than 15,000 words) new book called *The Natural Order of Money*, which got me thinking anew about where we humans are now, after three years under assault on our spirits from the global elites and the 'leaders' we naïvely trusted with our countries.

Back in the 1990s and 2000s, at the height of Ireland's Celtic Tiger boom, I used to get myself into trouble with 'progressives' and 'modernists' by talking ('nostalgically') about my widowed grandmother's farm when I was a child, in Cloonyquin, six decades ago, in the flatlands of County Roscommon, in the West of Ireland, where she used to produce about 80 per cent of her family's needs — meat, vegetables, bread, milk, butter, jam, eggs — and then, when the travelling shop came around on Saturday evening, would carry out her two trays of surplus eggs and barter them for the things she couldn't generate herself. This invariably sparked great hilarity in bystanders — provoked, they implied, by the quaintness of my reminiscence — but it has always seemed to me to offer a clearcut model for a healthily functioning economy: producing as much as possible of your own needs, with sufficient surplus to barter for whatever you lack. It has also seemed obvious to me that most of the problems of the modern world emanate from our deviation from this model. So, I thought I would try to write something about 'The Good Life' that might help to rescue the concept from its ghetto of oddity and eccentricity, where it attracts only the nostalgia of the old and the condescension of those not yet old enough to know that nostalgia is the memory of stability and sense.

Sebag's book is very taut and beautiful: his central thesis is to explain and demonstrate why gold became the 'natural money' of humanity (its adaptability and usefulness as both a measure and a reward, plus the fact that it is itself literally rooted in the natural order). He succinctly explains why gold became, and remained, and is — in efficiency and effectiveness and symbolism — irreplaceable as the natural money-substance of our species and its transactions. In presenting his argument, he constructs a model of reality that describes also the natural and stripped-down state of a functional economy, cutting through the verbiage and theorising of the academic and purchased economists that have bedevilled attempts at fundamental perception through modern times. Essentially, his model conforms to the impulse expressed in my recollections of my grandmother's farm, being based on the production of essentials, first for the producers, and then a surplus for those across the borders of the real economy in a different land.

Sebag draws in words a circle subdivided by another, inscribing in the inner one the words 'the real economy', the entity that, at the centre of human self-sustaining activity, produces the essential needs of mankind — food, fuel and primary materials, all in compliance with the laws of nature, i.e. operating in coherence with the natural world. This 'real economy' comprises — is manned by — such as farmers, fishermen, hunters, lumberjacks, coalminers, oil drillers, turf cutters. The outer circle comprises the 'service economy', a secondary entity governed by the same rules. His purpose is to remind the modern reader that economic activity is governed, willy-nilly, by basic natural laws. Maintaining a 'natural' money to anchor economic systems has been the default practice in most societies until the relatively recent past.

Nature, he argues, not man himself, makes the ultimate judgement on human behaviour in this context. Food is the bone marrow of human cooperation. Without it, humanity perishes. Next, and similarly, comes fuel. After that, the roots in nature become weaker, yet they are there. Every economic actor along the chain to the outer circumference of the circle remains accountable to the source, via the farmer and the other primary producers. Central to this is the role of money. Gold has long been the optimal substance for use as what Sebag calls 'natural money', which, in mirroring nature's limitations, acts as a brake and safeguard against attempts to cheat the system.

In telling this story, he strips down and makes visible a model of the functioning economy that places centrally the 'productive' sector (farming, fishing, hunting, fuel-harvesting and the recovery of base materials) — subject to the iron laws of nature and necessity, but incorporating also the secondary, outer-layer economy, also highly functional for as long as it adheres to and respects the same set of natural laws that the farmer and the fisherman must obey. For example, he writes, 'a bad harvest may cause the farmer to fail to produce a crop, or geological scarcity of ore may prevent a miner from carrying out further operations.' These rules also govern the outer economy, which produces not essentials but secondary products and services.

The 'primary cooperators' in the real — i.e. productive —economy are the farmers, hunters, *et cetera*, who 'mediate energy sources in the form of foods from the natural world into the greater economy.' What he calls 'the chain of temporal and energetic succession in any economy' begins with the food producers, who act as the generators of the basics of survival and surplus. Next in this chain come the fuel producers of the economic system, such as the lumberjack and coal miner, who work 'to harvest non-nutritive energy sources from nature which provide heat and motion.' The tertiary members within this primary network are the elemental producers, such as the miner for metals: 'The product of their activity is a tangible good which is employed as a necessary input in the preceding types of primary activity. In a simple or subsistence economy, it is conceivable that the three roles may be intertwined to such a degree that they can be carried out by one and the same person.'

All actors in an economy, either individuals or members of a cooperative system, are accountable to natural standards of measure and reward, a set of iron laws that must be respected on pain of disaster. 'Ecological accountability', i.e. direct answerability to the limits of nature and the natural standards of measure and reward, renders the real economy and its custodians amenable to the laws of nature. But the service economy is also answerable to these principles, albeit indirectly, because it is ultimately dependent on the harmonious operation of the real economy. Without food and fuel, the policeman becomes weak and dies; without fundamental elements, our electronic systems will not operate, and the computer programmer will be unable to function. 'Ecological accountability,' Sebag explains, 'expresses the fact that the cooperative system is always and everywhere tethered to the natural order and to our necessity of negotiating with it in order to produce the energy embodiments that we need. When we eat breakfast, when we start up our cars to drive to work, when we open our laptops and begin to type, we are implicitly involving ourselves in the natural order and its standard of measure and reward. We are taking in the maintenance of the land, the tilling of the soil, the sowing of the seeds, the days of rain and sun, and the long hours of harvest. The farmer is told by nature how and when his crops can be grown. We participate in this edict each time we partake of this harvest for our own purposes of activity. No service economy is self-sufficient, just as no man is an island. We cannot live without nature's reward, just as our bodies cannot survive without breathing in the oxygen that surrounds us.'

This, then, is 'economics', which becomes complicated in its theoretical forms by 'virtue' of deviation from or corruption of this fundamental model by innovations created essentially to cheat nature and usurp the means of human survival and action. These are always, he says — *always* — doomed to fail. And all this remains true, no matter how complex our human societies appear. Any deviation from economic accountability can only ever be temporary. Although it is often subject to amnesia within the remoter elements of the service economy, ecological accountability remains an iron law, as though written on the land.

'This forgetting of accountability,' he writes, 'is only possible because the service economy possesses the ability to temporarily decouple itself from the natural order for the very reason that it lies at the periphery of its generative and degenerative cycles. The real economy, on the other hand, enjoys no such luxury, for it is directly dependent upon nature's commandments. What follows from ignoring this reality is an unnatural view of prosperity as something which can be mastered, determined, and distributed according to the personal desires and subjective ideals of the service economy. It is then that the relationship between the real and service economies becomes *parasitic*.' In a parasitic system, he writes, the service economy demands energy embodiments (the products of human activity resulting from negotiation with the natural world) from the real economy 'irrespective of nature's limits and cycles, thereby attempting to circumvent or transcend the natural standard which governs the success and failure of the real economy.' Once mankind deviates from an understanding of nature's cycles of generation and degeneration, it begins to stray into danger. The result of such attempted divorcing from ecological accountability 'threatens the sustainable relationship between humanity and nature, and the symbiotic relationship between the real and service economies.'

It is obvious that what has 'gone awry' in our 'modern' economies is that we have, first of all, reversed the hierarchy of the productive and service economies, placing 'services' at the centre, then multiplying these far beyond the scope of our needs, and thereafter creating false moneys which have institutionalised these follies as something unexceptionable, and from there enabled spurious notions of wealth to promulgate themselves, spawning all kinds of incoherencies and absurdities that cockeyed forms of economic thinking have fooled us into taking for normalcy. False moneys — the instrument of this hubris — enable mankind to sidestep the laws of nature, chiefly because, as Sebag explains, they 'fail to meet the most basic requirements which the natural order of money exacts from us: that money itself be an energy embodiment. If our money fails to constantly remind us of the natural order and what it requires of us, then we simply forget about ecological accountability and our collective dependence upon the farmer and upon nature.'

By reflecting the imperatives of ecological accountability at all points within the economic system, a true system of money becomes an earthing entity in a three-way process connecting it via the human to the land, and back again, and around and around. It is a carrier of the values that underpin the entire enterprise — the law of the land and the sea and the air — extending the natural imperatives from the potato field and the riverbank to the restaurant and the bank, imposing its logic on all those who handle it. 'In this way,' Sebag explains, 'money anchors notions and ideals of prosperity to the objective accountability of the real economy, to the natural pulse of energy embodiments, by ensuring that the whole society measures and rewards activity relative to these dynamic cycles of generation and degeneration. A money which reflects ecological accountability ensures that when the real economy does well by cooperating with nature, the greater economy also prospers; and when the real economy does poorly, so, too, does the greater economy suffer.'

Gold, being the longest-lasting, the most energy efficient, and the rarest of the possible energy embodiments that nature bequeaths us, was through millennia the money of choice of human societies. Gold is sublimely capable of measuring and rewarding the production of energy embodiments without clashing or competing with them, enduring through time while maintaining the same weight and correspondence to larger reality. 'Gold,' Sebag elaborates, 'is a pure element that nature dispenses by weight in exchange for the more abundant, ephemeral, and even more necessary energy embodiments that we require for vitality and movement. The farmer and the gold miner thus share much in common, insofar as they must answer to the natural standard and to the brute facts of nature. While the gold miner is energetically dependent upon the farmer, in a society that has moved beyond subsistence, the gold which the miner harvests serves as the best measure and reward for the food which the farmer harvests.' The software engineer can assume that he will receive food from the farmer only if he is constantly reminded of the natural order by their shared money.

In the modern economy, a contrived form of money — paper money issued by fiat, generally as debt, promotes unsustainable forms of cooperation. The modern economist fails to appreciate the dependence of human societies on the natural world, and on the farmers, miners, and other energy producers, seeing nature, as Sebag puts it, 'as a machine to be tinkered with in order to obtain efficiencies and nominal growth.' When money becomes thus perverted, he says, the peripheral actors thrive, and the farmer is compensated as if he were an afterthought. 'So farmers and shepherds are persuaded into leaving their familial land to attend university and work in the City; the new generation would rather work menial office jobs than get their hands dirty in nature.' The land, 'which once was tilled and worked for the greater benefit of society,' is rezoned for housing, i.e. maximised profitability in the 'service' economy.

The Covid episode, as I have explained in several articles on my Substack page, 'John Waters Unchained', emanated from precisely these contorted conditions, having been triggered by international governments in response to an August 2019 appeal from the world's largest asset management agency, BlackRock, to the effect that the global economy was about to come down and required to be put on life-support. It is obvious that, in order to rescue ourselves from our present predicament, then, we need to demolish the present model and reconstruct the economy along the lines of the original prototype, placing the production of essential needs at the centre, and working outwards only in as far as each cycle of growth or expansion can be justified by its coherence and adherence to the laws governing outwards from the centre.

The central error that humanity has allowed to occur in its societies and communities, then, is to permit money to slip from forms in which it has maintained an intrinsic reflection of the limits of the natural world to one in which it provides merely a token representation of this former state. Thus, paper tokens and digital iterations of monetary amounts have rendered widespread the illusion that money has value in and of itself, and out of this has been generated whole global industries in the shifting and sifting of such tokens to the point where what are no more than glorified casinos have come to seem like the real economy.

The only true purpose of money remains: as a means of measure and reward, a convenient commodity/instrument to facilitate the exchange of products and services, which also offers an intrinsic reflection of the values being exchanged. Without the necessities of human existence — the foodstuffs and fuels and primary substances — gold would be an unexceptional and meaningless material. Its 'value' derives from its 'affinity' with other forms of 'energy embodiments', among which it is, you might say, first among equals. Once established as the natural money of humanity, of course, this purity of purpose stood to become corrupted, which indeed it was, with gold coins being 'shaved' to multiply the transactional value of the gold. And this procedure has been mimicked and itself multiplied in fiat money systems since the abolition of the gold standard, to the extent that an 'economy' today is primarily a poker table upon which what passes for 'wealth' is generated or destroyed in a series of three-card-tricks. To believe that money itself is the valuable thing is not merely to lose the economic plot, but to misunderstand human existence. To 'trade' not in things that humans need and desire, but in the tokens by which they have arranged to exchange these quantities, is to make inevitable the enormous distortions that now cripple our nations and embolden the corrupt bodies now claiming to govern them.

Debt, in economic terms, is the expression of human desire exceeding human capacity to immediately generate human needs. In a certain light, it is a kind of 'negative image' of the natural process whereby the service economy is born of the surpluses produced within the real economy. The 'spurious surplus' represented by debt is nowadays at the core of the inversion that has taken over our economic systems, whereby debt is an 'asset' of the lender by virtue of being a liability of the borrower. We live, then, in a minus world, where indebtedness is the measure of 'prosperity'. Humans have natural inclinations to seek more than we need or can afford, but in a localised, truly rational economy, subject to the laws of the land and ecological accountability, these tendencies are rigorously policed. If any Saturday evening, my grandmother had only one tray of eggs, she would have had to do without sugar or salt for the coming week. She accepted this and lived with it. Unless this principle is reflected in the money system, it is only a matter of time before disaster strikes.

I have observed before that the process of modern 'money creation' might be deemed a form of priestcraft — the manipulation of money systems by designated, ordained bankers, who generate power and wealth for themselves and their accomplices, often at the expense of optimum social functioning and human security. The chief mechanism of this process is a kind of *ex nihilo* ('out of nothing') *de*substantiation of the symbols of exchange and wealth retention, a perversion of the human means of measuring its produce and rewarding its producers. The money system is owned and controlled by private banks, which create money/debt, thus tying each worker to a different, parallel process of enslavement, which by default becomes the 'purpose' of his working. The virtual economy's apparent sustainability, like that of the virtual world more generally, is illusory because its roots are in the immeasurable debt that has accumulated in the world in the course of our recent economic evolution.

These developments have been driven fundamentally by the spurious notion — much trumpeted nowadays by politicians — that 'services (and/or information/knowledge) are the future', as though an economy without productive elements could ever be sustainable by other means. Another trite idea — that the future will be technological, and that working people are 'on the wrong side of history' — a fiction based on the incoherence of fiat moneys, is supported chiefly by the strength of the numbers of those who have bought into it. Ultimately, the bills will come through the digital letterbox and plop on the virtual doormat.

The biggest problem in our economic world now is that almost all those who explain what is happening have, by definition, a vested interest in the delusional system that places false money at the centre of everything. Thus, we are rarely permitted to see events in essential terms. By definition, economists are experts in money, but know nothing about keeping hens or making country butter. So, when they talk about 'the markets', they add to both the confusion and the problem: mesmerising us with jargon, but also distracting our attention from the basic connections that need to pertain between what we produce and what we expect. Journalists, bedazzled by anything smacking of 'science', treat these constructions as holy writ.

But economics is not a science, and never was. Nor is it an ethical programme. It is merely a lurching system of half-understanding that, to avoid disaster, needs to remain aware always of the unpredictable behaviours, uncontainable needs, irrational impulses and unquantifiable freedom of humanity. Money, properly understood, is merely a collection of counters and tokens which fulfil a mechanical function in society, as already described. The debt problem of the contemporary West is a technocratic distortion arising from a malfunctioning of a system that was at best only crudely adapted to human needs, and far more directed at enabling a tiny self-styled 'elite' to cheat reality.

An 'economic' system plugged into a gambling casino is at the whim of the most volatile and ruthless of human emotions: fear and greed. Speculation, borrowing, lending — but also, on the other side of the line, rampant consumerism — are largely virtual activities, divorced from everyday human necessity. They have real effects in the real world, but are not themselves real in the same way. They are games played around the necessities of human existence, using the security and welfare of the entire community of real people as collateral for bets. In many ways, it is quite mad, although very little of the commentary draws attention to its insane aspects. On the contrary, the great 'hope' underlying much present commentary is that we will soon be able to reboot the mechanism for one more spin around the block, this time with the 'consumers' contained in a digital prison.

Those of us who operate in the — outer, secondary — service economy, tend to live in cities and thereby judge ourselves superior to those who get their hands dirty out in the sticks. Really, though, we are already slaves of a new kind: indentured to technologies which steal our time, creativity and imagination, and moneys that mislead us as to our security. Technology is the 'new religion', we hear people say, and imagine they mean in the sense that it compels us to believe in things we do not understand. But, really, it is the 'new religion' in that it invites us to hand our lives over to it and place our trust blindly in the outcome. The revolution of the 1960s, aside from the 'liberal utopia' it unleashed into Western culture, also proposed a New Beginning based on the creation of a technologically-achieved utopia, which allowed us to look upon all previous efforts at achieving freedom with condescension and pity. In parallel, the emphases of our economies moved from effort-and-reward to a process not unlike gambling, with workers offered, when the omens were good, cheap loans instead of wage-rises and money — paper or digital money, usually — treated as the ultimate commodity and repository of real value. Now, in this 'modern' world, the information and communication society has supplanted production as the central logic of economy and the dominant form of society, and virtually every action carried out under this dispensation seems ontologically pointless to the one performing it. In the new 'workplace', the worker is no longer what he was: a pivotal figure who creates something essential and leaves his mark. He is but an ant trapped in the present, without past or future. But the ultimate folly is that he is brought to believe that this condition somehow supplants that which preceded it, that in which the natural money of humanity — gold — served to 'police' the economic processes to ensure that they were approximately and cumulatively in harmony with the order of nature.

Every so often, in a café or restaurant in one of the great cities of the world, I have that same sensation I had on the first day in my first job — pushing paper in a railway goods office in Co Mayo nearly 50 years ago: I look around and realise that all those present, male and female, make their livings from secondary or tertiary economic activities, unproductive in any fundamental sense — you might even say parasitical on the main business of wealth creation. Yet, invariably, these people — young, well-to-do, fashionably dressed — convey an air of felt indispensability to the cultures and economies of their societies. If I were to drive 50 or 100 miles from one of these establishments and visit a roadside diner, I know I would be instantly struck by the fact that the very different clientele to be seen there — labourers, farmers, tradesmen, factory workers — have about them an air of humility, if not defeat. This is the endgame (un)reality that flows inexorably from humanity's deviation from the iron laws of nature, and the pre-hubris replication of those laws in an organic system of money that was built to ensure fealty to reality. Those who continue to, yes, *man* the real world, on the wrong side of history, are the ones facing obsolescence in a world in which the real is no longer what it says in the dictionary. The 'parasites' are inheriting the Earth. It is important to stress that the political divides manifesting from these circumstances are not really between old and young, traditionalists and progressives, left and right, or even, in the old sense, between metropolitans and rednecks. The divide can be tracked in terms of wealth and privilege, but the wealth is largely spurious and the privilege, therefore transient. Deeper down, the divide is between those who are tied or committed to the concrete and those who have grown up thinking that the virtual is the only true kind of reality. And it is a measure of the intellectual disintegration of our cultures that it is the concrete that is being left behind, that the thinking elements of our societies appear to hold that a virtual world based on debt and babble is sustainable in the long term.

A useful division I have occasionally defined here is between the Able Men of Greek legend and the Virtual Men of the postmodern metropolis. Ostensibly, the two groups are separated by 'education', style and accent, but in reality, they are divided by a trivial mutual resentment based on spurious notions of class and sophistication, weaponised by unseen actors into a full-blown culture war, which in reality is utterly delusional in the sense that it fails to recognise any distinctions between 'essential' and 'inessential' work — or, worse, gets these concepts back to front. In recent times, this war has crystallised linguistically to suggest it as being a political quarrel between Populism and Progressivism, but these, like their ancestors, 'conservative' and 'liberal', are increasingly meaningless concepts, especially when considered against the partly occluded backdrop of what is actually unfolding in the world. In a sense, there is the basis for conflict in the fact that the Able Men are the ones who make and mend human reality on a day-to-day basis, whereas the Virtual Men are essentially, or for the most part, leeches upon this process, and indeed, in many instances, on any given day, work assiduously to undo the good that the Able Men did yesterday. Yet, almost nowhere in our culture is this reality recognised for what it means. In fact, it is the Virtual Men — those whose roles are secondary or tertiary to those of the Able Men, who are generally regarded — especially by themselves and each other — as the vital and invaluable ones.

In his 2016 book, *Men Without Work: America's Invisible Crisis*, Nicholas Eberstadt shows that, although unemployment in the US had been falling in what he calls the 'gilded era' (post WWII), there had been, simultaneously, a 'flight from work' by men in their prime. Even while manufacturers were finding it difficult to fill vacancies, the number of working men aged between 25 and 54 was at that stage fewer than at the end of the Great Depression of the 1930s. Approximately one in eight men in their prime had left the workforce altogether, and about one in six were without paid work, a trend that had been visible since the mid-1960s (and which has now recommenced after a brief period of remission in the short period of the [first] Trump presidency). The graph of this male exodus from the workplace manifests an almost straight 45-degree upward line, disregarding recorded booms or recessions, indicating that market demand is not the critical factor. Roughly seven million American men had — it seems of their own volition — left behind not just the idea of trading their skills and talents in the marketplace, but in many instances, turned their backs on all forms of commitment and responsibility. The greater part comprised single men without parental responsibilities and boasting limited formal education, a majority of them African Americans. For every man in his prime deemed unemployed, there were three others who were neither working nor looking for work. Almost three in five were receiving at least one disability benefit, a factor that, as Eberstadt observed, though not the driver of the phenomenon, was certainly financing it.

What Eberstadt exposed was an existential rather than an economic crisis, with most of these men wasting away for an average of 2,100 hours a year in front of screens, bingeing on TV, pornography, sugar and painkillers, no longer feeling that America had a place for their humanity. These men didn't 'do' civic society, religious activity or volunteerism. If 1965 work rates pertained in the US at the time of his writing, Eberstadt maintained, there would have been approximately 10 million more men with paid work than there were. He confessed to finding this baffling in view of the fact that national wealth had, he noted, doubled since the turn of the millennium. He expressed similar incomprehension about the fact that, globalisation and deindustrialization notwithstanding, these American patterns had not afflicted other Western societies to anything like the same extent. He called it the 'silent catastrophe', expressing surprise and dismay at its ignoring by politicians and commentators. In the wake of the Covid episode, and in the continuing conditions wrought by sanctions against Russia arising from the Ukraine war, the malaise that Eberstadt described is now spreading throughout the West, most markedly in highly industrialised societies — Germany, for example — which are now in rapid decline.

Perhaps there is no enigma. One theory is that the root of the crisis is in a culturally constructed obsolescence of American men, ostensibly in retribution for the alleged sins of patriarchs past. America, aside from being at the cutting edge of human progress, is also at the vanguard of its downsides. In a review of *Men Without Work* for *National Review*, George Gilder, author of *Sexual Suicide and Men and Marriage*, observed that the situation described by Eberstadt is no more nor less than the 'supreme triumph' of 20th-century democratic-liberalism, the outcome of a 'massive plague of affirmative action' and gender tokenism. This 'strange withdrawal of men,' Gilder wrote, 'merely reflects a massive campaign waged on every American campus, where women now account for some 60 percent of students; in every government department where gender rights enforcers lurk litigiously; in every civil rights crusade twisted into a unisex jamboree; in every judicial process from family court to the Supreme Court; and stretching from every local fire department on into the military, from Abu Ghraib to Camp Pendleton, from West Point to Annapolis, where women are pushed ahead at every opportunity in defiance of differences in physical prowess and mechanical aptitude. The prevailing idea is that male success is somehow illegitimate, a product of bias and conspiracy, and that in a gender-neutral environment, women would equal men in all elevated or conventionally male roles.' Not only has the culture built by feminists conspired to insinuate that women are, aside from being women, also the 'new men', but the workplace has been remade by affirmative action criteria to relegate the kinds of activities that men were good at. Gilder writes of the 'triumphant regulatory revolution that endows federal bureaucrats with the prowess to suppress any fundamental innovations and entrepreneurial disruptions that incidentally might disproportionately employ men. Better to expand the epicene bureaucracies and docile nonprofits with jobs allocated by quota. Better to teach new generations how to stop nuclear plants, carbon nanotubes, weapons, pipelines, and factories than how to use or build them.' This culture has become entrenched as the result of a withdrawal of women from marriage and mother-hood, and of men into short-term and feral sexual behaviours. 'The chief motive for male work is the approval of women and children and a successful role as father and breadwinner,' Gilder noted. 'Men enjoy jobs that are distinctly male and affirm them as men. Take these away, and you have Eberstadt's invisible catastrophe.'

The catastrophe might be called the loss of a mythology of manhood, or — even more fundamentally — identified as a collapse of ecological accountability, and a repudiation of the essential laws of human functioning, once read from the land where men worked to provide the essentials of human existence. While the men Eberstadt writes about are not all or even mostly white, the loss as it afflicts white men is more hopeless precisely because men, unlike other classifi-cations, do not constitute a recognised victim category, and do not have a cultural right to complain. If we look past its superficial aspects of manipulation and destructiveness, we see in this unfolding the faint trace of green — green for envy, envy of the Able Men who built human civilisations, envy of the physique built without benefit of gyms or dumbbells, envy of the one who can make two blades of green grass grow where only one grew before. Look again, then, at the way Woke grew out of a perverted version of women's liberation, which did its best to destroy manhood and fatherhood; look at the LGBT trivialisation of marriage, parenthood and family. Look at the phenomenon of Drag Queen Story Hour, a satire of men aimed at stealing the hearts and minds of their children.

On February 16, 2023, the Biden administration in the United States intro-duced the *Executive Order on Further Advancing Racial Equity and Support for Underserved Communities Through The Federal Government*, which permits racial and other forms of discrimination on the basis of identified characteristics. The new law, in effect, permits the entire edifice of the US government to exercise discrimination on the grounds of protected characteristics of 'underserved communities' — i.e. the listed identifying characteristics first weaponised by Cultural Marxism. By St Patrick's Day, every federal agency must have created an 'agency equity team' to 'coordinate the implementation of equity initiatives' and report progress to the 'gender policy counsel' and the White House 'envi-ronmental justice officer'. This initiative, to be overseen by former US President Barack Obama, is essentially a mechanism to confer benefits and privileges on everyone apart from straight, white men, who are, by virtue of being cast outside the protection of the order, the body of humanity implicitly identified as 'the enemy'. Superficially, what we seem to be witnessing is an advanced femi-nisation, queering and colouring — or perhaps, more succinctly, an advanced emasculation — of the economy and public space. But this, as is clear, is misdi-rective. The purpose is no kind of equality, but the nurturing of mendicancy and dependency, with plunder in mind.

It is by no means coincidental that those working at the heart of the real economy are the ones with the muscles and guns. In these trends, we can see moving shadows of the rationale for the attacks in 2020 by such as the Dutch government on its farmers and the Canadian government on its protesting truckers. The key factor here is not sex, 'gender' or orientation, but something else. Something is being targeted here, just as it has been targeted for half a century, but now with lethal intent. Straight white men are not being done down because they have testicles, any more than the women and blacks are being elevated because they are female and/or dark of aspect. At play here is the first question of economic philosophy: Who owns the means of production? The qualities being targeted are strength, stamina, knowledge, autonomy and, above all, the power that derives from centrality to the real economy. What is being undermined is human sovereignty of productivity in the fundamental context of food, fuel and primary materials. The colour and sex elements serve to disguise what is really happening, implying — depending on your perspective — either some facile prejudice against white men, or a desire to impose 'equality' or 'justice' on the economic affairs of humankind. But really, what is happening is an ultimate plundering of human agency and dignity, which promises the permanent disabling of the real economy, or what is left of it, and its supplanting with a managed, technologised, subsistence economy for the majority, and a First Class economy, manned essentially by slaves, for the benefit of the 'elites'.

In an interview with Jordan Peterson in late 2022, former Republican Speaker of the US House of Representatives, Newt Gingrich, made an intriguing observation that seemed to provide a new and perhaps more appropriate nomenclature for what I call the Virtual classes. He referred to 'the world's first mass aristocracy', a phrase of Thomas Wolfe's in an essay on 'radical chic' in which he deconstructs a 1970s cocktail party at the penthouse home of the 'composer and humanitarian', Leonard Bernstein, held to raise money 'for the poor'. 'Wolfe,' Gingrich describes, 'focuses on the Filipina maids who are serving the champagne to the rich people who are there out of *noblesse oblige*, [and it] is one of the most devastating insights, and this, of course, was written in the '70s. But what you've had is the emergence of the world's first mass aristocracy: people so well off they don't have to do anything, they don't have to know anything, so what they know is trivial, shallow and has no relationship to wisdom. In a sense, it's the perfect postmodern world; it's a world in which no fact matters, no taste matters, there is no standard, and you can pretend to be something by having read three totally irrelevant books and seen five totally irrelevant movies, and therefore you're clever, and cleverness has replaced wisdom and you, of course, are superior to all of these [poor, uneducated] people. You know, one of the reasons that the elites dislike Trump so much is that Trump talks like a blue-collar worker.'

Wolfe's concept of 'the world's first mass aristocracy' proposes a fascinating hypothesis of a world dichotomising into those who work meaningfully and those who leech off that work for the sake of doing something rather than nothing. The emergence of this new 'aristocracy' — self-imagined and coronated, of course — presumes the emergence of a society in which technology and artificial intelligence will unseat the Able Man as the asserted moral author of American/Western life and reality. It looks as though the machines have levelled the moral credentials of the population, placing the white-collar class in final control, eliminating the claims not only of muscularity and sweat, but of the auto-didacticism that elevated these qualities into a mythology of *manhood*. The first hammer-blow to this was delivered by feminism, but the gay revolution finished it off, suggesting effeminate men as morally superior to he-men, finally denigrating the virtue of muscular work. The new mass aristocracy is hostile to the traditional people and culture of America, having declared a war that is, in effect, against itself, since it is primarily directed at the White population of the West. It does this, of course — unwittingly — at the prompting of the Combine/secret unknowns, who oversee human activity from the shadows up in the gods.

The 'progressivism' we have tended to think of as the unavoidable outcrop of modernity, has never been the point or purpose of its own unfolding, and actually is of its nature regressive, since it seeks an authoritarianism that will supervise the destruction of the values and attitudes that have enabled the West to become what it is. Its unstated purpose was to unleash a destructive ragbag of ideologies on society, with a view to the total destruction of those perceived as its enemies. The unspoken part is that what is being purveyed will, in the end, destroy everything and everyone. Ultimately, then, the 'mass aristocracy' will be as redundant as virtually everyone and everything else. In a world that no longer requires human work, the secret unknowns will tolerate no aristocracy but themselves. The Virtual classes, having been useful in the process of marginalising the Able man, feel they have a legitimate expectation of being granted 'seats on the ark' when the moment of outright calamity (otherwise, 'The Great Reset') is unleashed. Alas, legitimacy has nothing to do with it, and these useful idiots will, in time, discover that, having dislodged the incumbent occupiers of the previous moral platform, they have already outlived their usefulness and will vanish down the same trapdoor as their erstwhile 'enemies'. The 'mass aristocracy' is shortly to discover that the secret unknowns don't care about gays or blacks or women pretending to be men or men pretending to be women — they care only about stripping out the bothersome rights and freedoms of the human population of the West, and this chore now nears completion.

What has happened can be addressed in varying ways. You might say, for example, that the problem overall resides in the generation of excessive levels of debt, but that, though accurate, is not a precise articulation. One iteration of the true difficulty, in accordance with the scenarios outlined by Roy Sebag, might be that the outer service economy has long ceased to obey the laws of nature and reality, and has started to steal from reality in order to continue making quick and easy profits. But something similar can be said to have occurred within the central, 'real' economy, which has ceased to hold to the absolute line of nature's limits, and developed other ways of seeking to cheat reality and the future. Examples of this cheating might be listed as the use of chemical fertilisers and pesticides, the rearing of non-indigenous crops for a quick turnaround, the artificial subsidisation of unviable or damaging practices, and so forth. Something the delinquencies of both the real and service economies have in common is that their excesses and abuses have arisen mostly from obedience to diktats from above. In other words, the real, deep issue is adherence to a tech-bureaucratic globalism that refuses to recognise the natural law.

What we find is that everything under the headings of economics and finance has been affected by a process of inversion — what was once first is now last and what was abhorred — the fetishisation of tokens — is now first. Roy Sebag's equation of utility and reason has been turned inside out, so that the type of entity nowadays regarded as the epitome of success, power, advancement and sophistication, such as the WEF, Twitter/X, and indeed Big Tech more generally — are in practice the most useless if not harmful, to say nothing of unproductive, of all economic operators. These, though hogging the top of the pyramid, might well be deemed among the governing delinquencies and fundamental drivers of modern economics' most dismal tendencies — parasites on the backside of a gangrenous body. And this image is most likely both accurate and instructive. It is certainly the case that the WEF is a parasitical instrument that seeks now to draw power to itself, and thereby impose on the world the ultimate consequences of drifts that have been in train for a long time. It is also true that the WEF, dating from the early 1970s, has been in existence more or less from the beginning of this process. But it is also the case that it did not begin to exercise real power until relatively recently in the deterioration of human economic interaction. Now, most certainly, though unelected and without mandate of any kind, it seeks to impose itself as some kind of absolute authority, leveraging the general deterioration of man's circumstances to consolidate its illegitimate authority. Twitter, by the same token, though highly 'effective' as an instrument of intimidation and censorship, and thereby capable (at least until the arrival of Mr Musk) of providing air cover to the insurgency of the WEF, is merely piggybacking on a state of cultural and moral dilapidation that long pre-existed it. These institutions, which seem to bespeak the malaise in a highly resonant way, are merely downstream manifestations of a condition that began, not with some top-down ordinance, but in the piecemeal liberty-taking of regular people seeking to obtain a quick and lucrative result from processes that, of their nature, will remain subject to such manipulation only on a short-term basis. In short, the problem is an old one: the pursuit of the free lunch. To put it more succinctly: phenomena like Big Tech and Big Technoc are excretions of human weakness left unchecked: the capitulation to temptation when presented with a short-cut that seems to involve only a venial breach of the law, but which, over time, results in the destruction of human husbandry and its natural order. In saying this, I seek not to exculpate the emerging instruments of top-down tyranny, but to suggest that what arises from a more general failing of humanity may prove amenable to a radical reversal of the same trends. Big Tech and Big Technoc are, in a sense, merely extreme manifestations of human grasping and underhandedness. Yes, these bodies have become not merely parasitical, but actively predatory, and that is certainly a new and bigger problem. But the deep issue has to do with surrendered sovereignty over the trade in human energy and endeavour: having ceased to value it, we awoke to discover it stolen.

Although many of the controllers who emerged from the service economy hide behind concepts of environmental harmony and ethicality in order to press their destructive agendas, they are utterly out of sync and tune — often to the extent of outright hypocrisy — with the concept of ecological accountability. We see this in the ways the motherWEFfers fly into Davos in hundreds of private jets, to preach green probity to the world, demanding that the people 'eat ze bugs' while struggling to speak through mouthfuls of prime steak. Though they affect to promote a planet-friendly philosophy, their personal behaviour (which they claim is offset by the gains of their deliberations and interventions!) bespeaks their true disposition, which is precisely demonstrated in their attitude to farmers and farming: they want to destroy them and acquire their land for a steal.

There is something stark and fundamental here that we may miss because of the effects of the corruption and chaos-making wrought by the very circumstances we ought, long ago, to have tumbled to. It is that almost everything bad that is happening in the world has to do with this urge or tendency to cheat, to skim off, this incessant pulling towards grift and graft that infects our culture now. This is true of economics, but also of inter-racial relationships, intimate relationships, relationships between the powerful and disempowered, and so forth (though not by the perverted descriptions of Cultural Marxism). We might, without incurring undue controversy, pronounce that these drifts are at the heart of the events that have transfixed and traumatised us for the past three years: the hubristic assumptions of the 'elites' that they had the right to place our lives on ice; the attendant sequestration of freedoms; the suspension of democracy; the attacks on sovereignty of innumerable kinds; the democide of the old for the part purpose of terror propaganda; the corruption of the public conversation; the warping of the visages and demeanours of public 'servants', transforming overnight into tyrants; the mobilisation of former police forces into stormtroopers on behalf of the paper money hoarders; the faces of judges implacable before entreaty, their robes inflated by bulges of fake money; *et cetera*.

In the lead-up to these events we can, with hindsight, observe the drifts that led inexorably to the present moment: the fatuous belief in gratuitous expansion at both the economic and political levels — bigger stores, farms and political 'communities'; the denigration and consequent demotion of manual work, the elevation of the service economy to the status of exalted virtue, encapsulated in the term 'white collar'; the consequent unleashing and apprehension of consumerist frenzy as though it were something valuable in itself (Lotto, the January sales fever, Black Friday *et cetera)*; globalism with all its attendant evils; secular-atheism and its denial of the sacred; the toleration of secret societies; the bureaucratisation of societies to the point of cultural and economic sclerosis; the gratuitous generation by social welfare of mendicant underclasses living far from conditions of poverty but in unearned comfort and expectation; the unleashing of untrammelled mass movements of people in search of an illusory prosperity — an imported underclass to match the indigenous one; the prioritising of the needs of corporations (as for example in the use of water and electricity by data centres) over those of human beings; the bogus coherence attributed to global outcomes such as Irish supermarket shelves being daily crammed with German briquettes and Polish potatoes, while our bogs sprout tumbleweed and our farms are colonised by nettles and ragwort; and so forth.

All this is falsity, not merely in ethical terms, but in the offence it offers to practicality and logic. Not every element of our economics is wholly bogus, but, contemplated cumulatively, it amounts to a false model of human reality. Its incubation as a proposal for collective living rendered inevitable what has been happening to us, to our freedom and our futures. It has raised up, as though a boil on the arse of the world, the WEF, with its incarnation of every form of ugliness imaginable: ugly thinking, ugly faces, ugly accents and sentences, grotesque hypocrisy, avarice, power-greed and hubris.

The natural order places the production of essentials at the centre of human endeavour, and facilitates the generation of ancillary functions and transactions on the basis of created surplus of such essentials. It is obvious that what has 'gone awry' is that we have, first of all, reversed these entities, placing 'services' at the centre, multiplying these far beyond the scope of our needs, and thereafter creating false moneys which have institutionalised these follies as something unexceptionable, and enabled spurious notions of wealth to promulgate themselves, spawning all kinds of incoherencies and absurdities that completely cockeyed forms of economic thinking have enabled us to take for normalcy, and from there delivered us to our present state of kakocracy — government by the worst among us. We ought not be so surprised.

CHAPTER 26
COVID, THE LAW, AND THE DRUMS OF WAR!
19-03-2023

Three years ago today, Ireland, following a US lead and in lockstep with the entire democratic West, took down its Constitution, which remains, in effect, suspended, as though the world were at war.

S ince the day of my mother's funeral, in the middle of September 2012, I have been involved in what has seemed a continuous political battle. At first, this battle appeared to be loosely related to issues concerning family and children, albeit invariably converging on the Irish Constitution. First, there was the so-called 'Children Referendum' of November 2012 — really designed to transfer rights from parents to the State; then there was the 'Marriage Referendum' of 2015, which inserted in the Constitution a wording that permitted same-sex couples to be married, thereby redefining constitutionally not just the word 'marriage' but also the words 'parent' and 'family'; in 2018, came the attack on the right to life of the most vulnerable human person of all: the child in the womb, which 'broke the duck' on the Constitution's capacity to protect human life, with possible consequences into the future that we can now merely shudder at. All three amendments were passed, the 2012 referendum being the closest contest. In that referendum, just half a dozen activists fought the combined forces of the State and corrupt media, and ended up getting 42 per cent of the vote. The other votes were lost by approximately two to one.

My resistance to these onslaughts on the bedrock of Irish freedoms has had a consistent basis sometimes mistaken for Catholic zealotry, though in fact less a matter of Catholic doctrine than a determination to preserve particular fundamental understandings of law, having their roots in the *givenness* of everything, now under terminal sentence in Ireland and elsewhere. Of course, many of these understandings are part of Christian teaching also, but I make the distinction because I find that, nowadays, people have become oblivious to the fact that they would be necessary and true even if Christ had never come.

In my 'campaign folder' for the first two referendums — the plastic envelope I carried around from studio to campus to parish hall — were the remnants of an ancient, yellowing booklet, a copy of the *Dreacht Bhunreacht*, the draft constitution sent out to households prior to the plebiscite of July 1st, 1937, in which the text of the Constitution was passed by the electorate, by 56.5 per cent to 43.5 per cent. It has the draft text in Irish and English — the Irish in the old Gaelic script, complete with those fondly-remembered overdots or *buailtes*, and those exquisite capitals that, as schoolchildren, we learned to etch on blue and red-lined paper with nib and ink. This copy had been my father's and bore the signs of being carried in his pocket for many months, even years. The cover was missing and the back page all but detached. The pages were dog-eared, fraying and as though singed in the fires of history.

In more recent times, escalatingly since the third referendum in May 2018, I have come to understand that I was, in fighting these amendments, failing to see the wood for the trees. The 'trees' were, respectively, the instant issues of each referendum: the interference with parental rights; the redefinition of marriage, parenthood and family; and the right to life. The 'wood' was the Constitution itself, and in particular what is sometimes called the 'Irish Bill of Rights', the enumeration of Fundamental Rights and Personal Rights in Articles 40 to 44 inclusive. The purpose of each of the referendums had been to fell, or at least destabilise, some of the most critical of these rights, with special attention to those pertaining to families, probably with a view to disabling or removing this institution as a rival source of authority to the State, and ultimately to total global power.

This is the true terrain of these recent battles. In the referendums of 2012 and 2015, a few of us diagnosed a plundering of the fundamental rights of families in a manner that was actually unlawful, unconstitutional, and profoundly dangerous. In all three referendums, the Irish government, by sleights-of-hand and unadorned lies, convinced the public that it had a right to vote on matters that were actually beyond the remit of either Government or People. The targeted articles (Article 42 in 2012, Article 41 in 2015 and Article 40 in 2018) made clear that the rights set out in their texts were not extended or generated by the State, but were 'antecedent' and simply 'recognised' by and within these constitutional texts. The assault of 2020 (the Covid coup) was a wholesale undermining on the very core of constitutional protections, sometimes referred to as 'the Irish Bill of Rights'. The rights inherent in Articles 40-44 include the right to life, to equality before the law, to reputation, property, to the inviolability of one's home, to practice one's religion, to *habeas corpus* procedures, to freedom of expression, public assembly, to form associations and unions, to the protection of family life, to education, and also a number of unenumerated rights, including the right to bodily integrity and recognition for the dignity of the person, the rights to earn a livelihood, to privacy, to communicate, to have access to justice and fair procedures, to travel within and beyond the State, and many others, some as yet unidentified. All these rights were ostensibly suspended in 2020, but, in reality, confiscated, for by granting themselves the entitlement even to suspend them, the relevant authorities-without-authority were already acting *ultra vires* the Constitution, and so could not be trusted to restore the natural order or forswear to disturb it again.

The Irish Constitution and most of our laws are rooted in natural law and English common law concepts of freedom: We are free people under God unless, for exceptional and proportionate reasons, our Government is compelled to curtail those freedoms in the interests of the common good, and such interventions are bound by an ethic of minimalist proportionalism. We, the people, grant the government any powers it may have. The idea, therefore, of the people being imprisoned in their own homes, on the basis of a crisis that had already begun to reveal itself as grossly exaggerated by spurious and discredited projection models, was deeply repugnant to the sovereign status of the Irish people.

On March 19th 2020, three years ago today, the Irish Parliament (Dáil) enacted a set of laws ostensibly related to Covid, reversing 800 years of Irish struggle for freedom and independence. The laws remain. It is now clear, in the wake of that assault, that the purpose went much further than combatting a 'pandemic' now widely understood as, at best, a hoax to facilitate the stripping of every fundamental right, under multiple categories, from future generations of human beings, in Ireland as elsewhere. These events occurred more or less in perfect lockstep. In this, the respective 'authorities' of sundry onetime democracies appeared to feel assured of the acquiescence and cooperation of the personnel of virtually the entirety of their political systems, significant elements of their judiciaries, as well as the implicit collusion, or at least obedience, of the vast majority of State operatives, plus a media sector subject to financial inducement for the purpose of its corruption.

On the Wednesday after Easter, April 15th 2020, another former mainstream journalist, Gemma O'Doherty, and I launched a constitutional challenge to the Covid-19-related lockdown measures introduced three weeks earlier by the Irish government. We were seeking a judicial review of the enabling legislation and regulations and an injunction or declaration to bring it all to an end.

We submitted our initial papers, therefore, midway through Easter Week, the most potent week in Irish history, the occasion of the Easter Rising of 1916, when Easter had fallen approximately a fortnight later.

It was already striking how similar were the legislative packages introduced around the world. For the first time in history, and contrary to all existing laws, an infectious disease was combatted not by quarantining the infected, but by radically restricting the freedoms of the healthy and unaffected. People were ordered to remain at home other than for 'essential' journeys and daily exercise, which was restricted with specific limits and without permitted periods of rest. The police force, An Garda Siochána (Guardians of the Peace!), was given sweeping new powers to question, fine, or detain those who do not comply when given orders to return home. Citizens were summarily denied the right to mix freely, go to pubs, cafes, and restaurants, hold or attend sporting events, travel to earn their daily bread, enter beauty spots and wilderness areas to be alone with themselves and their maker, even pause mid-stroll on a park bench to read a book or gaze at the sea. Garda officers even stopped people just walking or cycling down a street, quizzing them concerning their most routine and unexceptionable movements, in some instances resulting in people having their shopping trolleys searched for 'non-essential' items.

In the manner the tyranny evolved — without meaningful debate or noticeable dissent, with a widespread instantaneous decline into levels of spying and snitching that had taken the GDR Stasi many years to perfect — it became one in which the population was invited to become complicit, and many were happy to fall in. Ireland, in lockstep with other Western countries, experienced a multiple organ failure on the part of its major institutions, the great pillars — estates — of Irish democracy. The Oireachtas (parliament) failed to debate these momentous impositions; the President failed to exercise his prerogative to refer them to the Supreme Court. The media failed to ask even the most rudimentary questions. No significant member of the legal profession emerged to warn against the implications — no former Minister for Justice or Attorney General, no Senior Counsel or academic lawyer. It fell to two laypersons — who had worked many years in journalism while it was still a decent and honourable profession — to raise these most fundamental matters relating to freedom and the rule of law, to have the Covid laws scrutinised by the courts so that the people might be reassured that at least some of the organs of State were still functioning as they should, and that there existed some means of protection to ensure that such a calamity as this could not routinely be repeated.

It has for some time been established that Covid was an economic and military operation, not a health-related one. What the World Bank subsequently called the 'Covid project' flowed directly from an alert issued to the US Federal Reserve, the G20 and several supranational bodies on August 15th 2019, by BlackRock, the world's biggest asset-management agency, warning that the world's economies and currencies were on the brink, and that an extreme intervention would be required to deal with the coming downturn by placing the world's economy on life-support.

In recent times, persuasive evidence has emerged to indicate that the Covid 'project' was controlled from the outset by the US Department of Defense

(DOD), and everything we were told was political theatre to cover up the fact that it was constructed, not as a health initiative, but as a military operation. In January this year [2023], documents confirming this were obtained by the independent researcher/journalist Alexandria (Sasha) Latypova, an artist and former executive of a pharmaceutical Contract Research Organization. *

Other research into this murky area has been conducted by Katherine Watt, an American paralegal and journalist, and extensively reported in recent months by Patrick Delaney on LifeSiteNews, and by Redacted and other 'alternative' platforms. According to Watt, many of the preparatory laws and measures were rolled out during the second Obama administration, 2014-2017, when a number of emergency measures were introduced, including Executive Order 13674 (2014), which authorised the US Health and Human Services (HHS) to exercise control of civilian apprehension and indefinite detention power, on the basis of suspected asymptomatic SARS-like respiratory illness. †

Sasha Latypova's research uncovered enormous variability among batches (or lots) of biological injections marketed as 'Covid vaccines'. While 70 to 80 per cent of these batches had shown just one or two reported serious adverse reactions on public reporting websites such as VAERS, 4 to 5 per cent revealed thousands of injuries. Latypova told LifeSiteNews that 'we have a chaotic mess of everything from sham injections that may be mostly just saline, all the way to extremely dangerous/deadly shots, all of which are being distributed under the same product brands and labels.' In email correspondence with LifeSite, she wrote that the US government owned the ('vaccines') product through each step of its production 'until it is injected into a person,' which means any American who obtained the vials in order to study the contents could be prosecuted for stealing government property. It also remained a contractual violation for governments outside the US to test these products.

'So, there is no tracing of any of the ingredients, their real origin, etc., and the product is wide open to adulteration (accidental or intentional) and falsification,' she wrote. Therefore, 'if the U.S. Government wanted to insert anything that has been on the shelves and unused from the strategic stockpile of biological agents, they can do that and [there is] no way to check. Or, any foreign governments can do this in their countries. The possibilities are endless.'

Latypova also claims that, in early 2020, when President Donald Trump declared a Public Health Emergency under the authority of the Stafford Act, this meant that 'medical countermeasures' (mRNA 'vaccines') would not be regulated or safeguarded as normal pharmaceutical products. They were fully produced, controlled, and distributed by the DOD, which classified them not as

---

* Sasha Latypova's research articles on this and related subjects can be found at her 'Due Diligence and Art' Substack.
† Katherine Watt's work can be found on her 'Bailiwick News' Substack.

medicines or pharmaceuticals, but as 'Covid countermeasures' under the authority of the military. She also claims that supposed health regulators, like the FDA and CDC, orchestrated a 'fake theatrical' public relations performance to give the impression to an unsuspecting population that standard safeguards were in place.

The Stafford Act was disaster preparedness legislation introduced in 1988 to enable an orderly and systematic means of providing federal natural disaster assistance for state and local governments in carrying out their responsibilities to aid citizens, being an amended version of the Disaster Relief Act of 1974.

Latypova has put forward the hypothesis that the 'pandemic' was the doing of a cabal of central bank private owners — not, she stressed, the same as banks themselves. This aspect remains 'fuzzy', she says, whereas the structure of the Covid crime itself 'is not fuzzy at all'.

She described the 'crime scene' as follows:

'We have a mass murder/mass injury event ongoing, and bodies are piling up. The deaths and injuries are the result of the forced injections of 'health products' that do not comply with any regulations for pharmaceuticals nor the required lists of ingredients or advertised chemical composition. Thus, they should be deemed de facto poison. Even if the manufacturers managed to produce these substances with fidelity to the label and the law, the products would be still extremely dangerous to administer on a mass scale due to numerous toxicities built into their design, which is perfectly well known to the regulators and manufacturers. Albeit, the latter got rid of employees with expertise and conscience to know this in the years immediately preceding 'covid success', and replaced them with diversity hires and software. The needles are in the hands of 'nice people from healthcare' who are doing their jobs as commanded by their superiors. I am tracing this organization back, starting from the weapon of murder and assault — the needle.'

She believes that the mass injuries and deaths by the mRNA/DNA injections are intentional and should be investigated as 'a crime of mass murder and attempted mass murder by poisoning.' She also says that the lack of any enforcement action by the US Department of Health & Human Services (HHS) on the injuries and deaths is also intentional, as demonstrated 'by the now very obvious refusal of the officialdom to stop them or limit in any way, despite clear evidence of their harm.' She says HHS is following the orders of the National Security Council and the US Department of Defence (DOD) as the Chief Operating Officer of Operation Warp Speed — i.e. the HHS is operating under the military command structure. She says the command structure of the crime in the US context is as follows: POTUS=>NSC=>DOD=>HHS=>state and local health authorities => owners/administrators of health delivery settings=>local vaccinators.

Katherine Watt has documented the extensive 'pseudo-legal' structures put in place over decades, which allowed the DOD to execute its 'Covid-19 vaccine' bioterrorism attack upon its own citizens, killing and maiming many thousands with complete impunity. She uses the term 'pseudo-legal', she says, 'because you cannot legalise a crime.' What has been effected is 'legal' on paper, but this legality is vitiated by virtue of the criminality involved.

Watt states without equivocation, based on her research:

'The interlocking corruption of federal emergency management, public health and drug safety laws, for the purpose of mounting a covert biological attack by the US Government on the American people under the fraudulent characterization of biological weapons as "Covid-19 vaccines," was deployed fully starting Jan. 27, 2020 and continues to be fully operational at the present time [three years later].

'These and related HHS Secretary declarations, Presidential Executive Orders and Congressional appropriations, suspended ordinary federal product procurement contracting laws and ordinary federal drug safety regulation and informed consent laws, apparently authorizing pharmaceutical corporations, the Department of Defense and the Department of Health and Human Services, in conjunction with several other federal agencies, to develop, produce, fraudulently market, and distribute biological weapon prototypes to American doctors, nurses, pharmacists, medical students and other medical personnel.

'These actors were apparently authorized to injure and murder patients with legal impunity using procedures and products (including withholding of effective non-EUA products as treatments; restraints, starvation, dehydration, isolation, sedatives, Remdesivir/Veklury, ventilators), to drive public panic and acceptance of the lethal injections colloquially known as "Covid-19 vaccines".

'The products are bioagents deployed by actors within the US Government and pharmaceutical/bioweapons industry manufacturing contractors, intended to injure and kill American people as targets, and exported to other countries' governments to injure and kill their people.'

'In a nutshell,' she says, 'the government's purpose is to commit mass murder/depopulate the world, without public knowledge and without legal consequence, and enslave survivors for wealth and power centralization through digitized "vaccine" passports and digital currencies, without public knowledge and without public resistance.'

'The basic goal of the architects, which has been achieved,' she writes, 'was to set up legal conditions in which all governing power in the United States could be automatically transferred from the citizens and the three Constitutional branches into the two hands of the Health and Human Services Secretary, effective at the moment the HHS Secretary himself declared a public health emergency, legally transforming free citizens into enslaved subjects.'

Watt has compiled a detailed account of the legal history of the American domestic bioterrorism programme, which dates from 1969 and culminated in the Covid operation. In respect of Covid, she states that Jan. 27, 2020 was the effective date of US Secretary of Health and Human Services Alex Azar's Determination that a Public Health Emergency Exists, signed Jan. 31, 2020, retroactive to Jan. 27, 2020. This has been extended continuously since, most recently on Oct. 13, 2022. Effective Feb. 04, 2020, HHS Secretary Azar issued Notice of Declaration Under the Public Readiness and Emergency Preparedness Act for Medical Countermeasures Against Covid-19.

Arising from these instruments, she states: 'Investigators, researchers, physicians, nurses, pharmacists and other individuals involved in product dispensing, use, or administration to human beings apparently have had, and today have no legal obligations to comply with laws and regulations that applied previously to use of experimental, investigational, unapproved or approved biological products or devices, including compliance with informed consent laws, medical monitoring of recipients during product use and post-administration monitoring and reporting of adverse effects.

'Recipients of such products are not legally recognized as experimental subjects or patients receiving experimental, authorized or approved products, because "use" of the products "shall not constitute clinical investigation." There is no stopping condition, because there is no legally-relevant "clinical investigation" to be stopped.

'On the basis of a self-declared "public health emergency" and self-declared classification of products as "emergency use medical countermeasures," including an unreviewable determination as to the relative risks posed by a communicable pathogen as compared to "medical countermeasure" products, the Secretary of Health and Human Services can suspend informed consent obligations and rights, on behalf of the entire American population.'

There are some remarkable and strange resonances between this account of events and some of the subtexts of the early months of Covid in 2020 and into 2021. It is almost dreamlike to recall that many of the political leaders of Western countries became fond of referring then to the situation in wartime vocabulary, speaking about the 'war against the virus' and the battle to 'flatten the curve'. The then US President, Donald Trump, in one of his daily briefings from the White House, actually used the word 'wartime' to describe what was happening, but with what may have been an intentional hint of a *double entendre*. 'I'm a wartime president,' he said. 'It's a war, a different kind of war than we've ever had.' About halfway through the second sentence, he appeared to become conscious of perhaps saying something he was not supposed to, resulting in a slight hesitation before his part-clarification or fudge at the end.

There may be quite a story to be told one day about Trump and the Covid 'war'. In some respects, his behaviour has seemed erratic — pushing to begin and advance Operation Warp Speed, and then afterwards appearing to endorse and defend the 'vaccines' at what seemed every opportunity. Clif High, a man I am inclined to listen to very closely, says you have to listen carefully to Trump: He may not always be saying what he appears to be saying.*

By Clif's analysis, Trump pushed to launch the 'vaccines' to forestall a Deep State/motherWEFfers plan to lock down the world for a decade until it succumbed to the plan for a global digital currency, with attendant bells and whistles. In this way, Trump may have saved up to half a billion lives — the kind of casualties to be expected from that kind of prolonged lockdown. If, on the other hand, he had done the predictable thing by opposing the vaccine, he would have been buried by the corrupt media and probably abandoned by a fearful public. It's a war, Clif says, and in wars, it is often a question of pursuing the lesser among evils.

There is another odd resonance here with a theme that surfaced almost immediately on the ramping up of fear in March 2020. I wrote about this disturbing aspect at the time for the American magazine *First Things*, in an article titled *Covid-19 and the New Death Calculus* — published on March 18th 2020, just one day before the enactment in the Irish parliament of the Covid laws.

A central point of the article was to draw attention to comparisons being made with 'military triage' in wartime, then a common media trope. An article in the financial pages of the UK's *Daily Telegraph* on March 3rd 2020 had raised the possibility that, unlike the Spanish flu pandemic of 1918, which had 'dispro-portionately affected' younger 'breadwinners,' the coronavirus crisis might have the benefit of primarily killing the elderly. 'Not to put too fine a point on it,' wrote Jeremy Warner, 'from an entirely disinterested economic perspective, the Covid-19 might even prove mildly beneficial in the long term by disproportion-ately culling elderly dependents.'

Warner was not an outlier. Many European authorities and medics were already speaking in rather blithe terms about triaging in favour of younger, more 'productive' virus victims. The context was usually the 'hard choices' that had to be made when resources and staff became overstretched. I wrote:

'Those who talk blithely about "combat triage" appear to imply that the modern workplace is the equivalent of a combat zone and the primary issue is therefore prioritizing those who can be trussed up to get back into "battle." What they appear to be saying is that if someone has passed a particular number on the dial of chronological age — retirement age, more or less — that person should be left to die.'

This 'war triage' logic has not gone away, and some observers have noticed a similar note in the response of authorities and media to the escalating damage and death arising from the 'vaccines', which we recall were treated as 'counter-

---

* For more on this search for the Bitchute video: 'Clif High explains the linguistic strategy of Donald Trump's Vaxxx comments'.

measures' — i.e. a military response, with all laws concerning vaccination testing suspended. Dr Pierre Kory, a former critical-care specialist at the University of Wisconsin Medical Center, and one of the principals of Front Line Covid-19 Critical Care Alliance, a nonprofit organisation founded by dissident doctors, has observed, most acutely: 'If you look at a lot of the policies, it has military all over it — right down to ignoring the massive amounts of vaccine injuries and deaths. I think that's a very militaristic view. It's like sacrificing people for the greater good of this vaccine campaign. And it's quite terrifying.'

And all this chimes with a response — or, perhaps, *feeling* — we had at the time we took our constitutional action in April 2020. War was on our minds also, but in a different way: We were asking ourselves, albeit in a manner somewhat disbelieving of our own question: *Are we at war?*

The reason for our asking this question of ourselves was not that we had tumbled to the scenarios subsequently revealed by Katherine Watt and Sasha Latypova, but because a war was the only thing that might have been used to 'justify' the measures that had been introduced in Ireland — which were more or less indistinguishable from those implemented in every former Western democracy.

I have more recently been told, on reliable authority, that a top-level meeting including politicians, judges and other key members of the Constitutional Government took place in Dublin in December 2019, at which it was 'agreed' to suspend the Constitution when the Covid 'pandemic' began to be rolled out. This, amounting to a State of Emergency, would have been illegal — unconstitutional — there being no lawful context in which authorities in Ireland — *of any kind* — could even begin such a discussion unless there was an imminent war or armed rebellion, a matter that would ordinarily have to be placed before the Oireachtas (parliament) in full public view.

This principle is set down in Article 28.3.3° of the Irish Constitution, *Bunreacht na hÉireann*, which insists that no declaration of any kind of emergency, and therefore no wholesale suspension of fundamental rights, is possible other than in circumstances described as 'war or armed rebellion'. This was one of the initial factors influencing Gemma and me to take our case, as it seemed to us to be illegitimate for the government to introduce such a broad range of measures impinging on the most personal rights, freedoms and dignity of citizens when no context existed remotely equivalent to these conditions. When we placed the impediment represented by Article 28.3.3° at the centre of our submissions, the responding State authority, the Department of Health, claimed that it had not sought to use this article, had not declared a State of Emergency, and had not, in fact, suspended the Constitution. The State lawyers came up with a cock-and-bull story to the effect that the language of the Constitution had always permitted incursions on individual rights, and it had merely implemented a number of these, which together did not amount to a suspension.

Unsurprisingly, this passed muster before the purchased judges in the lower courts, but we had some residual hopes — for reasons that will become clear — in the event that we could take our case to the Supreme Court.

In our submissions, we said that Article 28.3.3° amounted to a definitive bar — a 'backstop' — on a government imposing what was, in effect, a State of Emergency (while asserting not to be availing of the provisions of Article 28.3.3°, and not having declared an emergency). We argued that the government did not have any right, given that it intended such a wide, indeed exhaustive and comprehensive range of incursions on the personal and fundamental freedoms of citizens, to ignore the existence of Article 28.3.3°. Such an incursion might be appropriate in some narrower measure or set of minor measures, or in a context involving, say, an individual or family, a small portion of whose rights might conceivably be set aside in particular circumstances in pursuit of some greater good — this being subject to court challenge which would place a stop on the roll-out of the measures proposed — but not when the entire population stood to be affected. We submitted that the extent of the lockdown restrictions was such as to dictate that the terms of Article 28.3.3° made a referendum essential before such measures could be deemed constitutional.

The State, while continuing to claim in court that it had not sought to avail of the blanket capacity to suspend fundamental rights available via Article 28.3.3°, was less clear-cut as to what alternative option it imagined to be available. It would seem that it decided to employ a form of piecemeal abrogation of rights, relying upon the accumulation of these abrogations to provide it with an outcome similar or comparable to that which might have been achieved had the wording of Article 28.3.3° been better adapted to its purpose. We submitted that the reason this was not an option is that, when the Article was drafted, scenarios such as those being pursued by the government were expressly considered for inclusion in the amended article, but were comprehensively ruled out. The various historical texts of Article 28, together with the account of the circumstances surrounding the amendment of the Constitutional text in 1938, as comprehensively outlined in *The Origins of the Irish Constitution, 1928 – 1941* (author G. Hogan, and *mark that name*), make it abundantly clear that the option of extending the provisions whereby a comprehensive State of Emergency, or anything equivalent to such, might be declared beyond the permitted context of 'war or armed rebellion' was deliberated upon at length before that option was passed over. In that exercise, the Constitution was amended (by vote of the Oireachtas, the Constitution still being in its bedding-down period) in the most minimal fashion as to achieve the necessary clarity and cover considered to meet the exigencies of the international situation then manifesting — what the world nowadays refers to as 'World War II', but has always been referred to in Ireland as 'The Emergency'. Much discussion ensued about broadening the concept of 'emergency' to include other eventualities, but this was described by the then

Taoiseach (prime minister), Eamon de Valera, at the end of the process, as 'unnecessary'.

We achieved a preliminary hearing of the High Court to adjudicate on the question of whether a judicial review of the Covid legislation should be conducted on the basis of our submissions, which took place in May 2020. Our application was rejected, with extreme prejudice, by the judge. The following January, our appeal reached the Court of Appeal, where three judges again rejected our application. Then something extraordinary happened: While our appeal to the Supreme Court was being processed, a new appointment was made to that court: Mr Justice Gerard Hogan, then working in one of the European courts, who was to return to Ireland to join the highest court in the land. What was remarkable about this was that Hogan J was the author of *The Origins of the Irish Constitution, 1928 – 1941*, which we had been citing *inter alia* in our submissions in support of our contention that what the government had done was unlawful because in blatant disregard of Article 28.3.3°.

When the date of our Supreme Court hearing came around in March 2022, though not optimistic — given the general condition of establishmentarianism permeating the Irish judiciary — we had at least a rather exciting point of interest with regard to what Mr Justice Hogan might have to say about an argument that was largely, though not entirely, based on his own legal text.

The outcome was even weirder than we could possibly have anticipated. Six of the seven judges on the Supreme Court panel followed the lead given by the lower courts, rejecting our application for judicial review. One judge dissented and found in our favour — Mr Justice Gerard Hogan; but he did so on a series of general points, while rejecting our argument in respect of Article 28.3.3°. This was not merely bizarre; it seemed legally impossible.

In his dissenting opinion, Hogan J stated the general situation as follows: 'The applicants contend, however, that there is no power to declare an emergency other than that specified in Article 28.3.3. I agree that the only circumstances in which the operation of the Constitution can be overridden in certain circumstances is when the legislation in question has been enacted under cover of Article 28.3.3. But this does not mean that there is no other power on the part of the Oireachtas to recognise the existence of an emergency, the only difference is that in the case of these other emergencies, the legislation does not enjoy the immunity from constitutional challenge contemplated by Article 28.3.3°.'

Hogan J went on to state that a government could declare anything to be an emergency if it is required 'to act with great urgency'. The caveat, he said, is that such emergency legislation is open to challenge on account of falling outside the narrow definition in Article 28.3.3°. That is partly true, but there is another caveat: that any such restrictions, in such a notional 'emergency' — none of which had arisen in the 83-year life of the Constitution — can be imposed on only an extremely short-term basis.

The 'existence of a wider emergency power is clear,' Hogan J insisted — something he had not alluded to in his book — 'albeit indirectly — from the text of other articles, in particular Article 24, which makes a general provision for situations deemed to be "urgent" and "immediately necessary for the preservation of public peace and security, or by reason of a public emergency, whether domestic or international." The language of Article 24.1,' he elaborated, 'which is clearly different from that of Article 28.3.3° — contemplates the existence of a public emergency (other than one prompted by war or armed rebellion) in which the Oireachtas may have to act with great urgency. There would seem to be no reason why the threat posed by an epidemic would not fall into this category.'

But such situations as Judge Hogan hypothesised about in these observations are nowhere specified, or delineated, within the Constitution, and the circumstances that arose at the time of the framing of Article 28.3.3° — as, again, set out in Mr Justice Hogan's own book — would seem to make clear that the framers of the Constitution considered the possibility of providing for categories of emergency other than 'war or armed rebellion' — epidemics included — and decided not to. There can be little doubt that what occurred in March 2020 — when we experienced, in effect, a total suspension of constitutional rights — was many orders of magnitude more restrictive and severe than what had occurred during the 'Emergency' otherwise known as WWII, for which the original wording of Article 28.3.3° was amended by vote of the Oireachtas. In Ireland, as in the UK context he was referring to, the words of the former UK Supreme Court judge, Lord Jonathan Sumption, speaking in April 2020, could be applied without amendment: 'This is the largest interference with personal liberty in our history. People sometimes say that this is the worst thing that's happened, the largest scale interference with liberty since the war, but actually it's worse than that — even in wartime, we did not lock down large parts of the population. We did not assume the powers of direction that the government has assumed.'

There is a difference, perhaps paradoxically, between an infringement on the personal right of an individual and one bearing down on the aggregate of the personal rights of all citizens, which is at issue in this case. The first may infringe upon one person (or a small number of persons) and yet be justified in the 'common good', perhaps by virtue of some peril to the community, including the individual rights of other citizens (which is what the 'common good' actually means). But in the encroachment on the rights of all citizens, all at once, though at first sight appearing merely to be the aggregation of individual instances of such infringement — and therefore to be subject to the same logic — there is both a qualitative difference and a question of balance that renders almost any such incursion unthinkable on the basis of self-evident disproportionality.

The framers of the Constitution had deliberately and with aforethought side-stepped the option of providing for any such situation as the government in 2020 was claiming the right to create.

It would seem perverse if, in the absence of any clear provision to cater for situations other than 'war or armed rebellion', a government was able to impose far stricter restrictions outside of Article 28.3.3° than those applied at the time the wording of that article was revised (because its terms did not seem to fit the emergency then threatening: viz. a war in which Ireland was not directly involved). It is surely unimaginable that, retreating from expanding the article further at that time, the framers would have been tolerant of far more draconian measures being introduced without any solid constitutional foundation, having themselves chosen the path of caution for fear of extending precisely such liberties to future administrations.

Mr Justice Hogan went on: 'As Mr Waters correctly noted in his oral submissions, this general issue was addressed by Gavan Duffy J in The State (Burke) v. Lennon [1940] IR 136 at 145. Referring to Article 24, Article 28 and Article 38, Gavan Duffy J said: "The need to provide for times of emergency was clearly foreseen and the emergencies in contemplation where defined. . . . There is no provision enabling the Oireachtas or the Government to disregard the Constitution in any emergency short of war or armed rebellion."'

Far from following Duffy J's logic, however, Hogan J turned it on its head, asserting that this 1940 reference to an 'emergency' amounted to recognition of 'an emergency other than one which invokes Article 28.3.3', a possibility that he had failed to raise in his own 2012 book. Here, one might have expected the judge to refer to the 2011 case of *Dellway Investments Ltd & Ors v NAMA & Ors* — also extensively cited in our submissions — in which his late colleague, Mr Justice Adrian Hardiman, dealing with precisely this question, had stated:

'A property owner [for example] has a clear right to have his property respected by the State and safeguarded from trespass or seizure by others; but there may be imperatives arising from a state of war or armed rebellion, an accident, or an acute emergency created by fire, natural disaster or other sudden and extreme circumstances which justify transient trespass upon his property without his consent or without taking the time to see if he, as owner, wishes to urge any reason against it. Thus, the placing of a fireman's ladder in one's garden, to save imperilled life and property does not require audi alteram partem if the garden's owner is absent.

'But it is the business of the law to identify such circumstances; otherwise, the cry of "emergency" would be sufficient to set all rights aside at the whim of the Executive. Our Constitution makes specific provision for "war or armed rebellion". It is not for the Courts to extend those provisions to a situation which is not one of war or armed rebellion. That would require a decision of the people in a referendum, if they thought it necessary or prudent to confer such unreviewable powers on the State. The cry of "emergency" is an intoxicating one, producing an exhilarating freedom from the need to consider the rights of others and productive of a desire to repeat it again and again.

'It is abundantly clear, therefore, that only under the provisions of Article 28.3.3° is the State freed from constitutional restraint by virtue of declaring a State of Emergency under its existing provision or, in the event that a situation requires as much, by amending them to the needs of the situation at the time obtaining.'

This, in fact, is what occurred in 1938/39, when the then government faced a situation that it believed was not covered by the Constitution as enacted. Hence, the amendment referred to above. And if a government in the past was so punctilious in guarding against any danger of extending excessive powers to future governments, it may certainly be said that, confronted with the circumstances of March 2020, Mr de Valera's government would have forsworn to act as the government led by Leo Varadkar — who had lately lost whatever mandate he might be deemed to have possessed — and would have told the supranational authorities to take a running jump at themselves, or immediately called a referendum.

The extra-Article 28 entitlement of the Government to suspend constitutional rights and freedoms must be measured against the concept, in Mr Justice Hardiman's analogy, of 'transient trespass'. And whatever might be decided as to the permissible extent or duration of such measures, it cannot be in doubt — again, using Mr Justice Hardiman's example and language — that the citizen must very expeditiously become entitled to question the extent and duration of those restrictions, in the only place in which he or she can usefully do so: in a court of law, which we were seeking to do, but being repeatedly rebuffed. Hardiman J's analogy of the 'ladder on the lawn' also implies that, whatever might be the consensus view of how long or short, how rough or tender such 'transient trespass' measures are entitled to be, there can be no doubt about the proposition that the justification for transient trespass upon the freedoms and rights of the citizen 'without his consent or without taking the time to see if he, as citizen, wishes to urge any reason against it', must be extremely abbreviated.

Neither Hogan J nor any of the other 10 judges who deliberated on our substantive application for judicial review addressed this judgement of Hardiman J, which quite clearly rules out the declaration of an emergency, even when it is not described as such, other than in accordance with Article 28. In the Covid context, the word 'emergency' was all over the legislation enacted on March 19th 2020. A marginal entitlement of the State or Government to encroach briefly upon the fundamental rights of some or even — perhaps conceivably, at a stretch — all citizens, had been expanded into an *ad hoc* provision for the almost total suspension of the Constitution, which at the time of the Supreme Court hearing had continued for two years, and might, even now, at any time be resurrected on any pretext or none. And this is the fundamentally disastrous consequence of what occurred in our case: that Mr Justice Hogan's sanguine sense that, denied the protection of Article 28.3.3°, the State remains answerable to the people for its actions through the courts, is only valid if the courts agree to permit the citizens to call the State to account before them. If they do not, the notional idea of an alternative route to declaring an open-ended emergency offers a charter for despotism. In a certain light, retrospectively reading Judge Hogan's exploration of the issues raised in our submission, it almost seemed that, in finding in our favour on other points, he was constructing a round-the-houses justification for upholding our case rather than accepting the most clear-cut one, which is that, under no circumstances could the blanket derogation of fundamental rights imposed in March 2020 have been justified outside of the terms of Article 28. 3.3°, and most certainly beyond a few weeks at most — unless . . . unless? — *unless a war had been declared and he was aware of this declaration and of some necessity or injunction to take it most seriously, but either wished to cover his tracks or, perhaps — to put the same thing rather differently — wished to do a decent thing in the course of doing what he knew to be wrong.*

If, to hypothesise, the Irish government had knowledge that the 'virus' threatening Ireland was actually a bioweapon of some kind, thus justifying the invocation of Article 28.3.3°, the situation might be radically different — legally as much as otherwise — to how it appeared. And perhaps this notion more than hints at a possible device-of-choice of those wishing to avoid the legalisms of peacetime. If so, it is likely that something similar to the events that rolled out in Dublin arose also in practically every other Western country. As to why this did not emerge, then or afterwards — it is likely that such a scenario, if canvassed in public by any such government, might have sparked a panic that would have brought forward the threatened extremes of horror.

Many thoughts and questions form a scrummage for attention, arising from this litany of facts, truths, observations, experiences, speculations and feelings.

Is all, or the brunt of the above even possible? — that is the uppermost, the loudest question. Is it possible that the 'war' that was used to close down humanity in 2020 had not yet happened at the time of that closure, but existed only as a future hypothesis that was, nonetheless, impressed upon the world's political and legal authorities as a probable sequel to — or, indeed, an intrinsic element of — the Covid project? Perhaps, then, the world was 'on a promise' of war? Perhaps that war was baked into the Covid cake by those who had made it? And, perhaps, its intimation to the legal authorities of sundry nations was baited by the sanctimony that, only by doing what they were told could the world's wigs and shiny-suits have any chance of averting that eventuality. Was the bizarre and unseemly behaviour of the Irish judiciary, in bastardising the Constitution they were enjoined to serve, the outcome of some kind of mental reservation enabled by the promise or threat that, if they did not do what was required in the first instance, they would have to do it in the last? For now we know that we have indeed an actual war on our hands — and on our hearts and minds — that we have had one, in truth, for more than a year — and that this war has had the potential, at any moment, to explode into the deadliest the world has ever seen. Perhaps that, from the outset, was the intent and purpose behind the militarisation — in advance — of the Covid project. Was it thus that all obstacles were removed, all objections, all talk of proportionality, all preciousness about freedoms? Was that the fiendish logic behind the militarisation of the enabling legislation in the US, going back half a human lifetime? So that those who stood on their principles could be presented with a Hobson's Choice: *By all means, stand by your constitutions and their freedoms today, but tomorrow you will not have the choice. Stick with the letter of the law, and, before long, you will find that your options are narrowing and your laws powerless to prevent what is coming.*

And perhaps: *Do it this way and you may mitigate the loss of human life, for what is coming is not negotiable.*

Since the beginning, we who have, yes, fought these events and fought those ostensibly responsible for them, have regarded ourselves as participating in a spiritual war. By that, we did not mean a war of religions, or even a war between the religious/spiritual and the atheist/heathen. This was a war between Good and Evil, between the most primal and fundamental forces existing in reality, with at stake the entirety of human futures, hopes, lives, loves and being. This is the only context in which we can hope to make any sense of the scenarios, hypotheses, connections, verities and realities outlined in the above.

The plan — the Covid scheme or scam, together with or incorporating all the ancillary 'projects' (Ukraine, climate, BLM, mass migration, trans, *et cetera*) — has not yet succeeded. The truth comes dropping slow. The wheels of Revelation turn slowly, but grind exceedingly fine, and, in the end, expose the transparency and lucidity that governs all earthly existence: that it is finite, but precious, and that the demands of Truth cannot long be ignored. All the above passes now into history, and where we go next, we go with nothing to lose but our souls.

CHAPTER 27
THE ABDICATION OF LIBERALISM
22-05-2023

---

* A **plutocracy** (from Ancient Greek πλοῦτος (ploûtos) 'wealth', and κράτος (krátos) 'power') or plutarchy is a society that is ruled or controlled by people of great wealth or income. Unlike most political systems, plutocracy is not rooted in any established political philosophy. Throughout history, political thinkers and philosophers have condemned plutocrats for ignoring their social responsibilities, using their power to serve their own purposes and, thereby increasing poverty, nurturing class conflict and corrupting societies with greed and hedonism. – from Wikipedia

---

For three years, maybe unknowingly a little more, we have struggled with questions that seemed to lack conceivable answers. Nothing made sense. Our questions bounced off the problem(s) and boomeranged back to floor us. Were our 'leaders' being blackmailed or merely bought? How did they sleep at night, given the things they spent their days doing? Where were the liberals? Where were the civil libertarians? The model we had worked with until roughly the end of the month before it all began seemed overnight to have become derelict, and yet it was standing still, if only in our minds. It remained as though a ghost, speaking a version of the world that had gone. We could not shake it off as it manifested from our mouths in blurted rhetorical statements like, 'You can't do this in a democracy!' That such a model of civic existence might be gone forever was something we allowed to crystalise but slowly in our thoughts. Better to see this as some kind of aberration. It had started, after all, as an 'emergency', and even though we knew in our hearts that this was bogus, it gave us some kind of comfort to cling to. The unthinkable could be received some other day.

So we built our edifices of thoughts and theories, adding to them all the while as though rocks and slabs and slivers to a drystone wall. Sometimes, like a jigsaw, the picture seemed to enter a sudden new phase of self-understanding, filling us out with expectation as it filled itself in. A whole new corner might erupt, all but completed, and leave us as dazzled as saddened by what it seemed to suggest. But still, the overall picture remained elusive, so we flirted and dabbled with what the Kafkian dung-beetles who were implementing all this were calling 'conspiracy theories', seeking to push towards some kind of Big Bang moment when it might all become clear.

Sometimes, we momentarily forgot parts of what we have already understood, fixing on some adjacent detail at the expense of the big picture, focussing — to mix in another metaphor in keeping with the spirit of the condition and the times — on a tree rather than the wood. Sometimes, we forgot that what confronted us was a forest of thoughts and possibilities rather than a group of unconnected trees. Then, in the midst of staring at a particular interesting oak, we caught sight of the shadows behind it, and took to describing anew the forest we had already observed but strangely mislaid from our purview — its depths and murk, its windy paths and briar patches. How had we forgotten all this again? Suddenly the wood seemed all important, and the trees somehow passé, beside the point.

In considering the meanings and mechanics of what has happened in these past three years to our democracies and our hearts, there appear to be at least two layers requiring to come under equal degrees of consideration. The first is what might be called the 'invasion' — the indisputable assault upon our nations from outside; the sudden, passive-aggressive usurping of our countries and the ways of being of their native peoples; the apparently overnight capturing of those we still laughably called our 'representatives'; the dramatic shift in the demeanour of our neighbours, who now seemed to have forgotten everything they had ever claimed to believe until the day before yesterday. The questions in this context abound: Who, really, were these invaders? What were they seeking? From where or what did they derive their authority? How did they achieve what they achieved so easily, meeting almost no significant resistance?

There have been many attempts to answer these questions among others, many of them partial, others merely speculative. Although the edifice of lies that accompanied the invasion is beginning to show cracks, we do not have any clear answers as to the overall nature of what is happening. We know a little more than at the beginning about the external would-be colonising force. At the level immediately beyond our national boundaries, there was, for certain, the layer of supranational bodies — the World Health Organisation (WHO); the World Economic Forum (WEF); the United Nations (UN); the European Commission

(EC), and some others — clearly issuing orders and mandates, but all the while conveying a sense that they were also merely implementing a set of protocols issued from above. There was something determined about their behaviour, an imperviousness to actual facts or events, a lockstep pattern that conveyed some element of non-negotiability that sometimes seemed to disconcert them almost as much as it disconcerted us.

Then, there was the odd figure of Bill Gates, travelling under the banner of his infamous eponymous foundation, seeming to be acting as some kind of sweeper behind the supranational backline. He it was who acted as a kind of dogsbody of the global coup, issuing bulletins and clarifications, responding to developments, 'speculating' about future possibilities, as though all-knowing, as though he amounted to more than a mere interested observer, and yet lacking any visible qualification in a contest where 'expertise' was vaunted as the quintessential element of someone's right to be heard. If any of us ventured an opinion, we were likely to be asked: 'Oh, and where did you do your degree in microbiology?', but no one asked Bill this question.

All this seemed to suggest some even higher 'authority' — clearly neither expertise-empowered nor elected, to which all the other bodies and their respective spokespersons — national and supranational, and Bill Gates, too — appeared to be beholden and subservient. The nature of this entity has been but vaguely defined. It is commonly referred to as an 'elite', by which is generally meant not an intellectual or moral elite, but a financial or supra-political power, perhaps an alliance of trillionaires, perhaps a constellation of asset-management organisations or banking moguls, perhaps some kind of arcane secret society, maybe a religious sect of some kind — a Satanic mafia? — or even a coalition of several or all of these elements. This aspect of the discussion lacked clear delineation or illumination, and therefore remains murky. It is much speculated about, under multiple headings: the Cult, the Cabal, the Illuminati, the Predator Class, the Khazarian Mafia. I call it 'The Combine', a phrase I borrowed from Chief Bromden, the protagonist in Ken Kesey's 1962 novel, *One Flew Over the Cuckoo's Nest*. The Chief saw The Combine as a force directed at taming human nature, grinding mankind down to the level of mere brute animal, rendering humanity compliant to its will. 'Combine' is a good word — it gives expression to a confederacy of anonymous plutocrats seeking to thresh, break, grind, strip, disconnect, winnow, reap and gather humanity and put it to use in service of its newly declared masters. The Combine represents, too, the increasingly mechanised structure of all nature and human society in this 'modern' moment — an immense, invisible force that grips mankind almost without touching, a process set in train a long time ago with the objective of repressing mankind and re-setting its behaviours so as to achieve greater utility for the machinators. The Chief's conception of the Combine arises in part from his personal story, in which the land upon which his people worked and lived was seized from his family to build a hydroelectric dam in service of the palefaced man. In my country, Ireland, we suffered a comparable assault, though this featured one palefaced man grinding down another. Here, now, in my country and yours, it's déjà vu all over again.

All this movement and blur occurs above a line that, unlike what is above, and most of what is underneath, is itself clearly defined. This is the line between the puppet masters and the puppets, connected only by the gossamer-like threads by which control is maintained over the marionettes below. Beneath that line are our former constitutional republics, liberal democracies, free societies, civilisations — with their supposed leaderships and political classes, academics, journalists, artists, philosophers and peoples — all of whom, once free and independent actors, have been reinvented as puppets. The leaders no longer lead, but issue orders as though by rote. Those whose job it was to question things — the scribes and investigators of the press or media — seemed, at an early stage, to intuit that questioning things was no longer permitted, and became propagandists as a tolerable second option.

The liberals had all flown. Like a murder of crows, they had sat in assembly upon the grass in their thousands, facing south. A hush descended as they observed what was happening. Then it became quieter and stiller, as though someone was expected to speak, and then even quieter, stiller, until — suddenly, as though to an unseen, unheard, sub-reality signal — there was a whoosh! unpreceded by any instruction or sign, and thus began the piecemeal ascent of the crows in noisy unison, as they headed for their homes in the heavens. We watched as the cloud of blackness that had, until that moment, been the voicebox of our freedom move ever closer to the ultimately decisive horizon. A numbness entered into those who remained on the ground. They appeared to have been muted, lockjawed, by some contagion of hopelessness. Our 'leaders' went into motion, flexing their puppet limbs, evincing unfamiliar smirks, uttering new and ominous phrases.

What had happened? Had there been, after all, a virus, a pandemic — a pandemic of unhope? A pandemic of fear? A pandemic of our worst fears? Is this why so many people — almost everyone — succumbed in the very first moments? And not only succumbed but immediately turned in rage upon those very few who had not? Is it possible that, deep within themselves, they had long been expecting this moment of annunciation? Had they known all their lives that their freedoms were too good to be true, that it was all happening on borrowed time? Why else did they submit when they might have refused? Leaving aside the question of a secret dimension of compulsion, undoubtedly present from the outset in the menacing tone of the chief puppets, they could have said no. Each could have assessed the evidence from his own perspective and weighed it in the balance. They might have ripped the masks from their faces, and thrown them on the ground, as gauntlets cast before evil. They need not have looked around to see what all the others were doing, and fallen into lockstep. They could have shaken their heads. They could have said, 'We're grand as we are, thanks, but no thanks!'

This is the territory of *Die Illusion der res publica* — 'the Illusion of the republic/commonwealth' — the ominous title of a recently published essay by the German philosopher, Michael Esfeld. In this essay, he directs his attention chiefly to the meaning of events below the line referenced above. He is concerned with events and phenomena among the puppets rather than the notional string-pullers. His questions relate to the condition of our 'democracies', our 'open societies', our 'constitutional republics', and why these appeared to fold at the first firing of an inaudible starter pistol: How could this happen? And what happened anyway — really? How could the world's great democracies, the products of nearly 3,000 years of civic evolution, collapse overnight because of an unglorified head-cold? Is this capable of being understood?

Michael Esfeld is a specialist in the philosophy of physics and the philosophy of mind who, in 2020, being a member of the once highly prestigious German National Academy of Sciences Leopoldina, took issue with the leadership of that organisation because of its pro-establishment stance in the Covid scam. The sudden realisations that led to this moment of initiative also caused him to conclude that the West's political establishments were never sincere in their espousing of liberty, rule of law, division of powers, inalienable rights and all the other much vaunted 'democratic values'. Pondering what had just taken effect, he came to the conclusion that all these concepts had long been part of a gigantic sham with its roots in the Cold War. For very much longer than we have imagined, he says, Western political classes had had deep hankerings after authoritarianism and merely contingently allowed their populations to believe in 'liberal' concepts that had — for them — already transmogrified into fictions even as they helped to galvanise Western society in a condition of order and cohesion during the Soviet era. As soon as the circumstances changed, they began to put these childish things away.

The lockstep nature of what occurred in the spring of 2020 has already been exhaustively discussed among the Resistance, and is hardly a matter of controversy, even among those who refuse to hear or see. The same scare, the same remedies, the same diktats, the same measures, were rolled out everywhere — certainly in all Western countries — and all at once. In these matters, it has become increasingly important to emphasise that we speak chiefly of the West, which is self-evidently the immediate target of the coup now in train, with other regions and territories included chiefly as a process of misdirection to bolster the fiction of a global pandemic.

From the start, the conceptual centre of the assault appeared to be situated some considerable distance left of some notional ideological mid-point. Before long, there emerged a pattern of events that seemed to link what was happening with things that had gone before, in which negative elements of the past histories of particular countries were leveraged in events that appeared to emerge spontaneously from the conditions created by the 'pandemic'. A signal example was the George Floyd episode of the summer of 2020, when BLM activists were allowed to run riot with impunity, first around American cities, then around the cities of the entire West, while the majority of the populations of these cities were locked down. Very soon, what was happening began to demonstrate, in each territory, a dedicated, particularised form of attack upon the past, upon values, upon long-consensual ways of being. Race was employed as the primary front in the US, the object of assault being the historical experience of slavery; in certain European countries, the focus was on colonial/imperial histories, and the wrongs perpetrated thereby — histories now being revivified by the orchestrated arrival of hordes of outwardly indifferent, but actually highly programmed, aliens seeking to claim (what it was implied was) their entitlement. In my country, Ireland — which had no history of imperialism to account for — the normative light skin tone of the indigenous race was sufficient basis for an assault not dissimilar to that occurring at the southern border of the United States. In a broader sense, the 'crimes' being adduced had in common that they placed each nation's alleged past in the dock, and then moved directly to the implacable implementation of sentence.

It was not that the perpetrators of the escalating assaults on democracy and freedom — either those above or below the line — cared one continental for whatever suffering particular categories of human being might have endured in the past. What mattered was that these grievances could now be weaponised to alter fundamentally the configuration of power in Western countries. What the conspirators were interested in, chiefly, was a new form of subjugation, which would, in the first instance, bear down on the alleged former 'oppressors' (or, more correctly, their descendants) and, from there, on everyone. To summarise in a manner emblematic of the prevailing logic: a new oppression had been launched in the name of avenging an old one. But the forces behind it, whomsoever they might call themselves, were the inheritors of the forces who had instigated the old oppressions.

Esfeld avoids, even dismisses, the idea of examining matters in the context of what is called 'conspiracy'. This approach tends to invite a nodding of heads in some sections of the audience, while getting backs up in others. This is not greatly vital in the context of comprehending his thesis, which, in the main, relates to the pre-existing conditions of Western democracies which enabled the current descent into tyranny to occur. His project is not so much to explain the entire workings of the Covid tyranny, but to discover why so many supposedly liberal institutions and individuals failed to provide any resistance. Although many objections might be raised to his dismissals of the conspiracy hypothesis, his paper offers a vital exercise in focus on the conditions that served to render the coup so easy.

He pays a great deal of attention to what had been happening to the 'liberal' mind to cause it to succumb so readily to despotism of this particular kind, and to the conditions that caused it to evolve in this manner. His fundamental explanation is that we never lived in liberal republics in the first place, but merely jurisdictions so depicted in order to differentiate them from Soviet Communism during the Cold War. Once the war ended, they began to revert to nature. He also emphasises how the seemingly vital role of reason in these liberal democracies has latterly been usurped by 'The Science' — which is to say, by scientism.

His compressed explanation is stark:

'It was an illusion to believe that until spring 2020, we lived in a stable, open society and a republican constitutional state. This was only because the anticommunist narrative that prevailed until 1989 required a relatively open society and a relatively well-functioning rule of law. Thus, with the demise of this narrative following the collapse of the Soviet empire, it was to be expected that a new collectivist narrative would take its place, sweeping away the pillars of open society and the rule of law that existed as a demarcation from Soviet communism.'

Part of Esfeld's thesis is that collectivist narratives have a natural primacy over open societies, with which they are incompatible. He also seems to imply that collectivism — the absolutist rule of the common good — is the default demeanour of human societies. By this, I infer him to mean that, as the allure of certain civilisational values wanes, the potential for fear-induced tyranny increases. He says that we must 'bid farewell to the illusion that a republican constitutional state, characterized by the monopoly of violence and of law-making and judiciary in the hands of central state institutions, is the tried and tested means to guarantee the basic rights of the people and to realize an open society.'

The phrase 'open society' — by the way — does not refer to open borders, but to the maintenance of cultural and legal conditions which recognise the right of everyone to self-determination in a manner that is non-judgemental and non-intrusive — essentially what we speak of as 'liberal democracy'. This may be an important point due to the misuse of the term 'Open Society' in the name of a certain organisation which frequently gets a mention in the context of what is currently happening to the West and the world: The Open Society Foundation under the leadership of George Soros, which really directs itself at razing targeted societies and their cultures by forcing them to open their borders to indifferent or hostile alien elements.

Esfeld parses:

'The open society, in the sense of Karl Popper (1945), is characterized by the fact that different ways of life, religions, worldviews, etc., live together peacefully and enrich each other both economically (division of labour) and culturally through mutual exchange. The open society is held together by no shared notion of a common good. In this sense, it is value-neutral. The only thing that applies is that everyone is obliged to respect everyone else's right to freedom of life. There are no specifications as to how this way of life turns out. There is no corresponding narrative that shapes society.'

He conducts a thorough post-mortem on the concept of constitutional republicanism as an instrument of the open society, and finds it remarkably wanting, identifying multiple symptoms that might have alerted us had we been paying more attention.

At the heart of the liberal democracy is a contradiction, a fatal flaw that may well be deemed the central cause of why we have fetched up where we have: The liberal state, because it requires state oversight and tacit coercion to maintain the fragile balance required by openness to a multiplicity of different views, ethnicities, creeds, cultures and opinions, is constantly in a condition of expansion.

Paradoxically, the abundance of power in the hands of the state with its monopoly of legislation and adjudication is a consequence of the open society, namely the consequence of the fact that in this society, no doctrine of a substantive, general good prevails.

There is a further issue: that liberal democracies generally operate on the basis of a simple majority, leaving even very significant minorities perpetually alienated. This becomes even more confounding in the contemporary Cultural Marxist state, in which the State 'adopts' certain minorities as ideological protectorates, while ignoring or oppressing others.

In this context, Esfeld cites a rather more archaic concept — that of the 'notional state treaty', which establishes the monarch/ruler, who cannot thereafter be deposed by the same mechanism:

'There can be no legitimacy within the republican constitutional state to take action against the state authority because one would then place one's own judgment about what is law against the judgment of the state authority. However, the power of the state appears precisely to prevent everyone from using force to impose their view of what is right. The fact that such state power is necessary is, in turn, the consequence of the fact that society does not have a shared conception of a substantive general good. The unlimited power of state authority in legislation and judiciary is the consequence of the value neutrality of the open society. The fact that the republican constitutional state has developed into liberal democracies does not change this. In a democracy, decisions are made by majority vote. Whatever a majority decides to be right, that is considered right and is enforced against the respective minority under threat and, if necessary, also with the use of coercion.'

Accordingly, in a constitutional republic, the state, by virtue of the system whereby the law is made on the say-so of a simple majority — and not being itself a party to the social contract — acquires a form of near absolute power, in the fashion of a monarch of old. To adapt Esfeld's construction by way of summarising his point: 'The [state authority] is charged with making and enforcing law in the territory. But the [state authority] is not a party to the contract. Contracting parties are exclusively the inhabitants of the area concerned. It follows that when the [state authority] makes and enforces law, [it] does not act as a party to the notional state treaty, but as an organ empowered by this notional treaty to legislate. This means that state power is not limited by the state treaty.'

The confidence trick the state pulls in enacting and enforcing laws is it pretends to be impartial as between potentially conflicting citizens, and, therefore, to be implementing the democratic desires (in each case) of a majority of its citizens. In reality, the state imposes its own agenda, which, in this instance, was the implementation in its jurisdiction of the desires/demands of financially or otherwise powerfully influential outsiders who may never have set foot in the territory affected. The extent to which the administration is meeting or addressing any democratic impulse within its own borders is, accordingly, purely theoretical.

This is precisely what most of us who tried to resist observed during the early stages of the Covid episode: the summary suspension of constitutions and the rights and freedoms they were presumed to protect, all on the basis of an opaque and — as it emerged — grossly exaggerated threat, without any real possibility of democratic or judicial oversight. Moreover, as though instinctually, the checks and balances purportedly built into the system to ensure its continued answerability to the people were closed down in what seemed to be another lockstep initiative. The acquiescence of people was achieved largely by propaganda, censorship and the promulgation of baseless fear. Those of us who raised questions were immediately treated as enemies of the State, which, by Esfeld's explication, is exactly what we were.

It gets even worse. In any given instance of the resolution of a controversial issue by majority vote, the defeated minority has no recourse short of violent insurrection, which, due to the State's monopoly on legal violence, is nigh on impossible. Indeed, as we have been observing, the mechanics of Cultural Marxism, which have now been installed in the operating systems of most Western democracies, enable such a government to create a quasi-permanent majority by 'adopting' a multiplicity of disgruntled minorities — victimologies, essentially — which, by dint of welfare and ideological patronage, can be leveraged to ensure that the munificent state is always able to impose its will. This supporting coalition of Cultural Marxism victimologies is fluid and adaptive, so that, even if some of its constituent elements become disgruntled by a particular proposal, these can be outvoted by the co-option of others, so that the government is never left without an adequate margin. Indeed, a seductive aspect of mass migration is that the majority-of-minorities can be continually augmented with new arrivals, who become reliable voting fodder by virtue of the State's capacity to treat them 'generously' from the public purse.

The modern 'liberal' society, therefore, reveals itself as functioning off a kind of trick. It posits 'democracy', but then, often through the manipulation of public opinion, marginalises a sector of itself so that the 'democracy' becomes an instrument of subjugation as much as of freedom — subjugation for one, freedom for another.

Moreover, the presumed responsibilities of the constitutional republic enable the already powerful State forces to expand state-power in the name of protecting each citizen from every conceivable form of risk or danger. The citizens are not empowered or entitled to take the law into their own hands, so that, as Esfeld goes on to elaborate, every grievance, every instance of alienation, every excluded citizen, every potential risk, becomes an instrument of further state power:

'The problem is this: once there is a state authority that has the power of monopoly of force and law-making and adjudication in an area, the officials of that authority tend to expand their power under the pretext of protecting every person in their area from being attacked by other people. In other words, this abundance of power attracts precisely those people who want to exercise power and, therefore, embark on a career as a functionary of this state authority — such as politicians, in particular, who try to win elections with ever more far-reaching promises of protection. In this way, the so-called "welfare state" emerges, which exercises a monopoly of protection against all possible life risks (illness, poverty, inability to work in old age, etc.) and thus crowds out voluntary associations that can provide such protection. The 'welfare state' binds the people in its field technocratically to itself by protecting them from life risks, which its organs claim to guarantee as a monopoly.'

This is the destination point of Esfeld's thesis: that what we have been experiencing is merely the beginning of a multi-faceted onslaught that is planned to continue into the distant future, changing form as deemed necessary, but without let-up. His thinking parallels that of Fabio Vighi, expressed in my January 2022 Substack post, 'The Economy of Permanent Emergency'.

What makes Esfeld's thesis different is his emphasis on the capacity of what he deems a 'postmodern totalitarianism' to ignore reality, as it imposes a false reality to supplant it:

'That's what makes postmodern totalitarianism so dangerous: it's a hydra. When a head has been cut off — like debunking the staging of the Corona crisis — a new head immediately appears, such as staging the challenges associated with climate change as a life-threatening climate crisis. The purpose of the small narratives, each of which is a partial good, is precisely that they can be used to continue totalitarian rule at will: as soon as a narrative breaks down because the catastrophic consequences of its implementation become apparent, one is able to pull another narrative out of the bag to maintain the totalitarian rule of sweeping social control. To this extent, postmodern totalitarianism has understood the lesson of the *bon mot* attributed to the American writer Ayn Rand: one can ignore reality, but one cannot ignore the consequences of having ignored reality (see Rand 1964, Chapter 1). The Corona regime ignored the reality in which there were no virus waves dangerous for the general public. However, this regime could not ignore the consequences of ignoring reality, as is evident, among other things, from the immense damage to health that this regime has caused. But the postmodern regime does not end there. It can quickly conjure up another equally factless regime that ignores reality. Again, you can let that regime run until the consequences of ignoring reality can no longer be ignored — then move on to the next narrative.'

In this model, everything that arises provides fodder for the tyranny and the implementation of total social control. Money, climate, virus, orchestrated inward mass migration, social unrest, dissent, unwanted commentary — all these can be converted into instruments of coercion and control. Each element is, in its way, contingent, but the underlying logic is not. There will always be some instrument or another by which the tyranny can be advanced and deepened. Even when things go wrong, they will go wrong in a localised manner, and the problem can be isolated and resolved, spun or memory-holed without terminal consequences for the overall project.

These tendencies are fuelled, Esfeld outlines, by several factors, of which he emphasises these four: Political Scientism, Cultural Marxism, the Welfare State, and State Capitalism.

Political Scientism: When demands for central state control of people's actions through political coercive measures are derived from the claim that knowledge developed by modern science and its methods can grasp everything, including human thought and action, and therefore can be used to trample human rights and freedoms — 'Follow the science'.

Cultural Marxism: Esfeld calls this 'post-Marxism', though it might be altogether better described as 'post-Marxian Marxism' — the Frankfurt School reinterpretation of Marx for the intimate arenas of sex and race. This is what, for 25 years, I have called 'the culture of the Omnipotent Victim' — the leveraging of the latent pseudo-moral power of 'minorities' as an instrument to attack the prevailing cultural forms of the West, such as Christianity, 'patriarchy', what is called 'heteronormality', and the moral claims of Caucasians. The emerging post-Marxian Marxist State essentially reverses the order of the administrative power in order to favour history's alleged victims, and punish their alleged victimisers — or, rather, the descendants of these. At the core of the logic is the idea that it was only by cheating humanity more generally that Western civilisation came into being and endured for nigh on three millennia. Interestingly, this claim originates, exclusively, from within Western civilisation itself.

The Welfare State: Esfeld essentially sees what is happening under the headings of Covid, Woke, Climate, et cetera, as unwarranted extensions of the State's traditional remit. What is happening (for example, during the Covid episode) amounts to a radical extension of the welfare state to intrude on the private lives of individual citizens, to enforce (purportedly) good behaviour in non-criminal contexts and to implement a form of historically-situated redistributive justice — all by way of acquiring additional and unwarranted powers for the state and political establishments, spuriously legitimated by pseudo-science and an arbitrary assumption of moral grounding. In a sense, then, the welfare state was a baby step along the way to the Covid tyranny. This, and related mechanisms designed to nurture individual groups of voter-citizens, results in a Balkanisation of the population. The welfare state thus develops, according to Esfeld, into a 'warfare state', which in turn enables the State to licence itself to assert greater control, which leads inexorably to collectivism dominated by a perverted notion of the 'common good'.

State Capitalism: This is really fascism by the dictionary definition: a coalescing of the energies of the political state and corporations, to their mutual benefit. The corporations/entrepreneurial classes provide financial, propaganda and demagogic support for the political system and its offshoots and, in return is underwritten from the public purse. The current transition to a specifically postmodern totalitarianism feeds off the alliance of the forces of the welfare state and state capitalism, the forces of political scientism in science, and the ideology of post-Marxian Marxist intellectual postmodernism.

Then we come to the nexus of Esfeld's explication: Why, in the face of these developments, did liberalism instantly collapse, and so many who might have been expected to resist immediately bend over to accept their 'punishment'? How did the institutions of state and of democracy, from the supreme courts to parliaments, fall victim to moral collapse?

I believe that, in this analysis and otherwise, Michael Esfeld is breaking through to something very important, starting with his tweaking of the concept of totalitarianism, already canvassed in this context by many commentators, most notably Mattias Desmet. Esfeld introduces a new element, speaking of 'actually existing post-modern totalitarianism', which suggests that it is not some ominous cloud on the horizon but something that has already arrived and bedded itself down. The 'postmodern' element arises chiefly from the evisceration of reason, as he explains:

'Postmodernism is primarily an intellectual current that has gained importance since the 1970s and which opposes the claim of universality of the use of reason. [By its logic] the use of reason is not universal, but bound to a specific culture, religion, ethnic group, gender, sexual orientation, etc.'

Thus, the story goes, it is only by the imposition of a purely subjective — and in that sense 'random' — interpretation of facts and reality, that a particular cohort or group may impose itself on a much broader section of humanity, or even on the whole. What has been presented as an objective interpretation of reality is, in reality, a set of pretexts for the claiming of power. By this logic, universal knowledge is impossible, and its assertion a fraud. In its stead, the postmodernists have succeeded in insinuating a fractured version or reality in which there is no core claim to logic, reason or even fact.

Esfeld continues:

'The result of this relativization is that, in society and in the state, the same law no longer applies to everyone, but that certain groups are to be given preference. Likewise, in science, it is no longer just what someone says, but also who says it, what the culture, religion, ethnicity, gender, sexual orientation, etc., of the person in question is. The consequence is that reason as a means to limit the exercise of power is no longer available. Reason as an instrument for limiting power stands and falls with the universal claim of the use of reason to be the same for all people. The result is that a subjective point of view is imposed on everyone, namely the point of view of the most influential group (which may well be a minority, even a small minority, numerically).'

Esfeld claims that what we are observing amounts to the emergence of a new and discrete form of totalitarianism — a postmodern form — different not only from the violent forms of the twentieth century, but different from the softer forms we have intuited in various contexts in more recent times. He speaks of a postmodern, hydra-headed totalitarianism, a leviathan flitting between faces, each one capable of retreating or being defeated and decapitated, and yet returning later to the fray, with another of the monster's many heads having taken up the prosecution of the tyranny in the meantime.

What is specifically postmodern here, he outlines, is that, 'in contrast to the old socialist totalitarianism of communist or national socialist stamp, we are no longer dealing with a grand narrative that postulates an absolute good: the ultimate goal of history in the classless or the purebred society that is predetermined by supposedly scientific knowledge (materialistic or biological laws of nature). In place of the one big narrative with the one absolute good, there are a number of small narratives, each of which postulates a partial good, such as health protection, climate protection, and the protection of minorities.'

In the engine room of this hydra-headed leviathan is the politburo of an understanding of science in which 'experts' assume a role of not merely scientific knowledge, but also moral wisdom and authority, a mindset accompanied by a view of humanity that sees mere citizens — lacking this expertise and moral wisdom, and therefore requiring to be guided and, if necessary coerced — as 'physical objects whose life paths can and should be steered towards the general good by scientific knowledge.' This in itself is not especially new, being a feature of colonisation throughout the history of recent centuries. Esfeld's characterisations perhaps unknowingly echo Padraic Pearse's analysis in his essay, 'The Murder Machine', in which he describes a significant element of the Irish population in his time as behaving in the manner of 'mere Things'. What is striking is that this state of thingness seems now to have been willingly acceded to on a quasi-universal basis.

Esfeld tellingly emphasises that, in the context in which Western civilisation had seemed to prevail for centuries, the Covid episode, the climate 'crisis', the Woke assault, all struck as events that were, at the same time, 'amazing and unexpected'. It is as though the preparation had all been at a subconscious level, so that, when the moment struck, the typical response was of recognition, albeit accompanied by a slight sense of fleeting shock.

It may be important to remind ourselves here that the spectre of Soviet totalitarianism was by no means greeted with universal disapproval in the West. Indeed, right up to the collapse of the Berlin Wall, elements within the 'intellectual' crucible of the West continued to nurture a 'sneaking regard' for actually existing socialist regimes, as though a twitching of some atavistic hankering for collectivism. The student revolutions of 1968 offered an example of this aspect of the collective instinct, a movement ostensibly driven by individualism that spawned or inspired a whole new wave of Western collectivist organisms, before petering out in libertine excess. Although left-wing politics remained a strong feature within the political systems of most Western countries — with the exception, nominally at least, of the United States — this remained a restrained and somewhat underwhelming phenomenon until the 1990s. Aside from a period of radicalism in the 1970s, the general sense within the political mainstream was of 'socialism' as little more than an ameliorating and harmless kindheartedness. In general, leftist parties entered power as junior coalition parties of centrist or, less frequently, right-wing parties, and rarely otherwise. In the few exceptions — the UK Labour Party in the 1970s and Francois Mitterrand's ascent to power in France in the 1980s — the outcomes were decidedly inauspicious, with labour issues or recessions tending to bring things to a rather septic head. The late-Cold War period was characterised by right-wing retrenchments in America and Britain — with Reagan and Thatcher emerging as the colossi of the age, and the general hangover impression from that was that the failure of the Mitterrand experiment had scuppered the chances of the Left coming to power elsewhere in Western Europe for a very long time. Thereafter, only by camouflaging itself in the clothes of its opponents could the Left gain access to power. After the fall of the Berlin Wall, the more successful episodes of leftists in power were characterised by radical shifts in the ideological character of such parties as New Labour in 1997, when the party of Wilson and Callaghan, after two decades of floundering, reinvented itself as a heady mix of neo-liberalism and Cultural Marxism under Tony Blair. Having been a clandestine Trotskyist as a student, Blair, as leader of the Labour Party, positioned himself somewhere between Thatcher and Clinton, playing the field of ideology and possibility. New Labour, as he reinvented it, was socialist in name only, and yet was secretly driven by an entirely new set of leftist ideas, which related to the possibilities of leveraging minority grievances to build and maintain power under an ambiguous and constantly shifting banner, possibly the earliest above-ground manifestation of the new dispensation.

Throughout the Cold War, counter to the overarching climate of Western chariness about socialists, and despite the well-documented atrocities of the actually existing socialist regimes, Western media worked hard to water down the accounts of Stalinist tyranny, with most journalists continuing to be broadly leftist in outlook. This parallel-reality brand of 'actually unexisting socialism' persisted chiefly by dint of evasiveness and denial. This, together with the stealthy advances of such as Blair, acquired for the new ideologies an ambiguous camouflage, ostensibly suggesting that socialism was being watered down and absorbed into a centrist mix of common sense policies characterised by a judicious blend of left and right. In reality, the seeds of an even more radical form of Marxist-Trotskyism were being smuggled into the centre of the City, and in the time-honoured fashion: a Trojan horse dressed up in compassion, generosity and tolerance — more 'gifts' from the Greeks.

When the Covid craft landed, it was as though those 'actually unexisting socialists', having waited so long for their hour to come around, having sniffed in vain after every breeze in ideological history in search of a path to power, having surrendered every principle of their philosophies except the craving to control — to change human behaviour by fair means or foul — recognised in the Covid moment the signal for the initiation of their longed-for denouement, and instantly adopted an almost instinctual demeanour of acceptance and collaboration. They took off as though in fulfilment of the description by Mark Cocker, in his book, *Crow Country*, of the assembly of crows ascending in unison, albeit 'scattered like patterns of iron filings across the metallic sky of winter' — yes, yes, yes, and drawn as though by a magnetic force to an intuited ideological nesting place.

It had been a cardinal principle of Western civilisation that human beings are self-determining entities, and this is to be respected by every other human being: Human beings are not a means to an end, but the end in itself, and therefore not bound by concepts such as 'the common good'. While they lasted, these values were — technically — 'enforced' on one and on all by a legal system and a police force, but only to the extent of preserving basic order and core values, always on the basis of consent. A republic, Michael Esfeld points out, is supposed to be characterised by citizen participation in the process of governing, and a separation of powers as between the three arms of government — executive, legislative and judicial. These conditions, ringed around with checks and balances, offer no explanation for what has been happening in recent times. Notwithstanding Esfeld's analysis of the four factors to be observed in the runes of the present imbroglio, if we had truly been living in constitutional republics, these understandings would fall short of an adequate explanation for what is occurring — why these recent phenomena (Covid, climate, Woke) could 'sweep away the open society into one closed under a collectivist narrative, and the institutions of what previously appeared to be a constitutional state subordinate themselves to this narrative.'

Esfeld claims that neither the concept of a panic-driven emergency, nor that of an overarching conspiracy, help to provide an adequate understanding of what has happened. We must, therefore, question the premise that we had lived in open societies or constitutional republics in the first place.

Why, he asks, were the 1957-58 Asian flu and the 1968-70 Hong Kong flu not met with responses like those we saw in 2020? In those episodes — as, indeed, in the Irish 'Emergency' of 1939-45 and beyond (otherwise WWII)— the measures adopted were nothing like those implemented in 2020 on the basis of a radically lesser crisis. There were no bans on major events, and normal social and economic life continued, including dancing, sporting encounters and travel, which was circumscribed only by shortages of petrol.

The answer is obvious, he observes: [in those earlier instances] 'the open societies and constitutional states of the West had to distance themselves from the communist regimes in Eastern Europe. The contrast between West and East Berlin was obvious to everyone. Responding to a virus wave with coercive political measures would have been incompatible with what the West stood for.'

Esfeld here summons up Francis Fukuyama's 1992 thesis that humanity had, with the fall of the Berlin Wall, attained the 'end of history'. Liberal democracy, founded on science, the rule of law and human endeavour, had attained victory. Esfeld interprets Fukuyama as meaning that the collectivist experiment had ended in failure, and therefore collectivism was dead. Liberal democracy, with its openness and high degrees of tolerance for different belief systems, worldviews and lifestyles, had no need for 'a collectivist narrative of a substantive common good that holds society together.' Moreover, in these societies, the use of reason had operated to place limits on the exercise of power. In science the facts ruled supreme — authority was not a factor. The rule of law ensured equal rights for everyone, and the electoral system and separation of powers provided the necessary checks and balances to guarantee that abuses or excesses would very rapidly be curbed.

During the Cold War, the anti-communist narrative in democratic Western countries had served to ward off any threat from the Soviet bloc, as well as deterring internal drifts towards radical collectivism. With the fall of the Berlin Wall, an end was brought not merely to Soviet Communism, but also — though less manifestly — to the contingent, reactive nature of Western liberal democracy. The open society had prevailed, and therefore — paradoxically — was no longer essential.

Fukuyama missed a trick, Esfeld argues, in failing to see this possibility. The key to understanding what happened, he claims, is that liberal democracy was not cherished for itself, but because it represented a clear and opposite alternative to Communism. It was this, rather than some innate enlightenment or liberalism that created the conditions obtaining until the 1990s. Liberal democracy was not the preference of Western leaders for its own sake, but because it allowed for a clear demarcation with the Soviet bloc. This narrative did not permit Western leaders to act too repressively or interfere in the intimate lives of the people. When the Soviet enemy disappeared, this era quietly, osmotically, came to a close. Unbeknownst to the surface culture, new collectivist narratives started to edge forward in the West. The genuine advocates of the open society were unprepared for this, 'clinging to the illusion that open society had prevailed qua open society.' (Fukuyama may have rendered them even more complacent on this point.)

'Of course,' Esfeld continues, 'the masterminds of this new, collectivist narrative did not come forward as what they are, namely enemies of the open society (as political scientists, intellectual postmodernists, and postcommunists are). The new postmodern, collectivist narratives tie superficially to the open society: they are globalist instead of nationalist (separating a society as a people or nation from other societies), pluralistic and inclusive — though not for the unvaccinated, oil-fired users, internal combustion engine drivers, meat eaters, non-gender language users, etc., in short, all those who cling to their previous way of life and their property rights, including the power to dispose of their bodies. In essence, pluralism and inclusion here do not go any further than the pluralism and inclusion of the bloc parties of the time in the states of the Soviet empire.'

Globalism benefits only the super-rich and privileged, who possess the means, motive, power and opportunity to transcend all restrictions. On everyone else, the collectivist narrative implicit in the globalist project bears down in a radically adverse way. Yet, many of the devices of the new totalitarianism enable its sponsors to clothe themselves in a semblance of virtue. This, Esfeld insists, is a recipe for wholesale self-delusion:

'Nevertheless, this connection to the open society has the consequence that many friends of the open society have not yet realized that we are on the way to a society that is closed under a new, specifically postmodern totalitarianism. Denial of what is now unfortunately obvious is still widespread. They simply hold on to the fact that what prevailed in 1989 was the open society and the principles of the republican rule of law. But we must take seriously the idea that this assumption is wrong. Because with this assumption one cannot only not understand what has happened in the meantime, but is also tempted not to even perceive what is happening.'

Esfeld maintains that, if we give way to the possibility that our assumption about the basis of liberal democracy was wrong, we arrive at a cogent explanation for what is happening now. From there, it flows inexorably that liberal democracy was simply a 'narrative that is [now] superfluous'.

A different narrative is now filling this gap, he says, 'which superficially ties in with its rhetoric to the existing open society in order to conquer its institutions, but actually does what narratives that are supposed to hold society together — and people who are supposed to hold such narratives together, pushing forward to exercise power in the name of 'the general good' — tend to do: establish a collectivism to which people must submit in their ways of life.'

This, again, suggests something to the effect that some form of tyrannical collectivism is the default condition of human society — that 'society' and 'collective' are actually synonyms, something Margaret Thatcher was anxious to remind us of ('There is no such thing as society' — *Woman's Own*, 1987). Esfeld believes the population of the West was fortunate to experience freedom and openness until 1989. Political scientism, he says, always leads to totalitarianism if not stopped in time within the science or civic community:

'I would feel happier if I could dismiss this hypothesis as false. But you should take it seriously. Because it explains why the institutions of the republican constitutional state, right down to the constitutional courts, are failing, why so many people are not only running along, but why especially the members of the leadership classes of what appears to be an open society, with full zeal, are moving in the direction of a new single-minded totalitarianism, why do the liberal and conservative parties and their supporters also participate?, etc.'

All this, he says, was inevitable once the narrative that had developed to differentiate the West from the Soviet empire expired. The narrative that has replaced it is essentially collectivist, founded in scientific, earthbound concepts of the 'common good', which is essentially understood as a coercive utilitarianism, the greatest good of the greatest number, in other words, totalitarianism.

What is most interesting about Esfeld's thesis is not so much its novelty (although some of his insights are sharply original) as the achievement of the most succinct expression of something that is, in reality, extremely complex and difficult to encapsulate in all its moving elements.

What I gather from his essay is that the totalitarianism we now face exists for its own sake, rather than for the sake of any particular ideology. Designed less as an initiative to push humanity in particular ideological directions than as a descent into tyranny for its own sake, it reveals itself as inspired by the occurrence and failures of past forms of totalitarianism. In some ways, it is an attempt to replicate the 'workable' elements of Nazism, Fascism and Communism, which fell apart because of their single-minded natures, while avoiding their 'mistakes'. The chief distinction, he argues, is that whereas these forms were the pursuit of means to achieve particular ends, the totalitarianism currently emerging in the West simply employs forms of what might be called 'ideological software' to propel the project, but without limiting itself to any particular dogma. This is quite true. Various voices on our side over the past few years have posited communism or fascism as the dominant notes of what is happening, but in truth, what confronts us has shades of both categories of horror, and also intimations of novel ones.

This provides an ominous verbal understanding that confirms what our guts have been telling us. As a mutual friend, summarising Esfeld, puts it: 'All the ideologies which are plaguing us at present involve ignoring reality and will inevitably lead to a collapse that cannot be ignored. The new totalitarianism takes this unavoidable collapse into account and has refashioned itself as the vessel that contains the "ideology du jour". Once the Covid narrative collapses, you replace it with the climate narrative. The climate narrative collapses? No problem, just replace it with the woke narrative, and so on. Thus, what we have on our hands is a kind of totalitarian totalitarianism. It is not enough simply to oppose the ideology du jour; the attack needs to be directed at the underlying intellectual structure.'

This is a succinct and accurate summary, which I shall modify only by replacing the phrase 'totalitarian totalitarianism' (a bit of a headwreck as well as a mouthful) with 'whatever totalitarianism' — or, precisely, '"Whatever!" Totalitarianism' — my own extrapolation from Esfeld's thesis. I think it a rather good name for what we now face. At the centre of its mechanical operation is a leveraging of apathy, cynicism, indifference, listlessness, alienation, defeatism, nihilism and ennui, as well as a coddled complacency born of extended prosperity, peace and security, and a consequential culture of self-indulgence that has obtained for more than six decades. The virtually universal capitulation in 2020 of the young and the liberal classes — the ones whom the rest might have expected to be first out of the traps screaming blue murder — was, in many respects, the most disenchanting part. In truth, the authoritarians-without-authority were able to tap into a mindset that, riddled with anxiety born of an unacknowledged self-imposed loneliness, and presumptive of their own capacity to defend anything worth defending if needs be, the liberal classes sat back and 'trusted the government', 'trusted the science', trusted, in sum, the endurability of their own value-systems on the slim basis of their having survived hitherto. A complicating factor was that many of those we might ordinarily have looked to were technically or instinctually left-liberal inclined, which meant that they were actually the first to fall before the march of an apparently benign state advance. In a certain light, too, it becomes clear that multiple categories of the human — left, right and centre — had become lulled into a false complacency by the apparent recent obsession of the political mainstream with the rights of minorities. After all, how could politicians who insisted on the rights of gays and migrants in the teeth of 'conservative' and even 'far-right' resistance, not be punctilious in protecting the more fundamental rights and freedoms of all persons?

The nub of Esfeld's thesis gravitates towards the Covid project's perverted definition of the common good, the conversion of an overwhelmingly personally-directed dispensation of freedom-forging into a quasi-totalitarian one. This form of totalitarianism, as our mutual friend says, has no end but itself, and has one ultimate identifying characteristic: brute force. Yet, Esfeld does not detour to point out that the 'common good' is here an invention, a perversion of the concept that exists in English common law, and therefore in most of the constitutions of the anglophone world, whereby the common good is seen as the aggregate of individual potentialities and freedoms. The postulation of the common good in response to lab-made viruses, the grotesque hoax about climate, and the contrived sensitivities of Woke hysterics, are bogus invocations, by any sane or reasonable definition. Esfeld rightly traces this perversion back to a misappropriation of science, but does not deal with the sleight-of-hand that occurred at an early stage in the Covid episode, when the 'common good' was presumed in all contexts to refer to something along the lines of 'in the interests of the collective, even if to the detriment of all or any individuals'. By this interpretation, any loss, privation or damage incurred by the individual was to be regarded as inconsequential as compared to the necessity to pursue the largely theoretically-backed objective of 'saving lives', corralling the population into a collective state of OCD-by-proxy — governed and enforced by experts. No one afterwards was able to say how many lives — if any — had been saved, or whether one of them might be his own.

In the course of preparing our appeal to the Irish Supreme Court in the challenge taken by Gemma O'Doherty and me (ultimately rebuffed), I came across an essay written some three decades earlier by the eminent Irish judge and onetime attorney general, Declan Costello, in which he both anticipated and forensically rejected such an interpretation:

The notion of the common good is derived from the concept that a political community exists to provide a whole range of conditions (material, social, moral, cultural) so that each of its members can realise his or her development as a human person. Thus the common good is the whole ensemble of conditions which collaboration in a political community brings about for the benefit of every member of it. This point is made clear in the preamble [to the Irish Constitution, which expands on the common good as follows: '. . . with due observance of Prudence, Justice and Charity, so that the dignity and freedom of the individual may be assured, true social order attained, the unity of our country restored, and concord established with other nations.'], for the common good is not the good of the political community as such (which is a concept inherent in the totalitarian

State and inimical to the protection of human rights) but is an end to be promoted for specific purposes, which include the furtherance of the dignity and freedom of every individual in society. The concept of the common good in the Constitution is one derived from scholastic philosophy and differs fundamentally from the utilitarian concept of the greatest good of the greatest number. This concept is seriously flawed in that it attempts to measure happiness and compare it with pain, and also because it provides a theoretical justification for the restriction on the rights of members of minorities. When, therefore, the exigencies of the common good are called in aid to justify restrictions on the exercise of basic rights, it has to be borne in mind that the protection of basic rights is one of the objects which the common good is intended to assure.

This perversion had become all but an inevitability in societies with an engorging State head, in which power may be jealously hived off and sequestered for use against those from whom it derives, all in the name of spurious concepts of 'openness', 'democratic values', the 'public interest' and 'the common good'. These tendencies, too, Esfeld claims, derive from the 'end of history' moment that flowed from the fall of the Berlin Wall:

'The anti-communist narrative . . . necessitated that "welfare" could not encroach too much on privacy, i.e. the outlined development into a surveillance state, with extensive state social control under the pretext of protection by the dominant narrative because of the demarcation from the communism of the Soviet empire, was slowed down. But that doesn't change anything about the following: The republican constitutional state needs the full power of the monopoly of violence and legislation and judiciary, because, in the open society, there is no prevailing doctrine of a substantive general good. However, this abundance of power sets in motion a development in which the holders of state power continue to expand their legislation, and thus their regulation of people's lives, in order to provide ever better protection against all possible risks in life. In this way, society is welded together in a technocratic manner. Since this cohesion is not technocratically bearable and justifiable alone, it calls a collectivist narrative back on to the scene.'

Thus, almost seamlessly, with the aid of a strong external cohering threat, the open society transmogrifies into its opposite: a system for total social control. With political scientism as the chief instrument, this new narrative is able to pass its tyrannies off as necessary incursions on human freedom because they are rooted in 'facts' and 'reason', though neither concept very often stands up to scrutiny. The Covid coup, says Esfeld, was a tyranny waiting to happen:

'This is the explanation for the development that has become apparent since spring 2020: this development is quite simply what was to be expected. Those who, like me, did not expect it succumbed to the illusion of the *res publica*, the illusion of the republican constitutional state as an organ that protects people's basic rights and implements an open society.'

Esfeld enables the beginnings of a crystallisation of the meanings attending our own state of absolute shock in observing the total indifference of liberal establishments to the dismantling of the edifices they had inhabited — and in a sense, curated and protected — for decades if not centuries. He also provides a framework for understanding the willingness of liberals to bury, under instruction, the value systems about which they have prated all their adult lives, and the total silence of the liberal commentariat in the face of all these obscenities. The basic implement of this operation was 'The Science' — the citing of alleged scientific principles where no absolute scientific consensus existed.

At the heart of these subterfuges, as Esfeld observes, is the constant absurd insinuation that these rights and freedoms can be 'won back' by good behaviour: By complying with lockdowns, or injection mandates, or carbon targets, or caving in to the intimidation of rainbow flags, the citizen can — it is implied — return to where he was before. Thus, the 'emergency' is constructed to strip the citizen of his 'inalienable' (hah!) rights, and the new dispensation is insinuated as a necessary path of recovery in which the citizen becomes convinced that only his own 'original sin' or personal misbehaviour has delivered him to, and maintains him in, this state of unfreedom.

This, he observes, is obviously not about freedom or rights, but about privilege as a reward for conforming to the injunctions of an unjust regime.

Esfeld also notes that, although the patterns of the assault are similar, the personnel driving each individual tyranny — Covid, climate, trans, et cetera — are broadly different. He refers here, I am sure, to the non-political contexts of 'expertise', administration and propaganda, since the political orchestrators tend to have their fingers in all the pies, which all emerge from the same oven.

It is strange, is it not?: We have lived our lives to this point for 30, 40, 50, 60, 70, or whatever number of years, without any of these things — pandemics, climate crises, existential revolutions — happening at all, and now, like buses to a bus stop that has seemed invisible for an eternity, they descend in veritable fleets and bevies. Yet, few remark on there being anything strange or unusual about this coincidence of disruptive activity, as though it is the deliverance of an unusual but natural confluence of ill-fortune, sent by the gods in whom we no longer admit to believing.

Professor Esfeld cuts to the chase:

'Eventually, this claim to knowledge, and this view of people, are taken up in politics and the media with the aim of building a regime of comprehensive social control that does not recognize privacy.'

This is the heartless heart of what is happening. The emerging reinvented State fears and hates the privacy of the individual because the private space — a sanctuary of home or head, hearth or heart — is where and how autonomy is exercised, and the sovereign individual is liberated from, and achieves superiority over, the machinations of State actors. To attack privacy is to attack thinking and reasoning and, therefore, questioning. The hate speech laws and other such instruments which have been floated in multiple Western former societies amount to a form of public imprisonment of the democratic impulse — an internment of the heart to prevent it yielding up its feelings. This process is merely the culmination of one that has been in train for many decades, surging in an exponential way in the recent period of technological revolution, featuring the internet, social media, smartphones, data harvesting, surveillance, et cetera, and entering its final phase with the Covid scam. We have arrived at the culmination and convergence of several simultaneous initiatives against the privacy of the individual, which is to say the slamming of the totalitarian (trap)door on a past of relative freedom, qualified democracy, rule of law, and the solitary mind. As Esfeld observes, the lockdowns enabled the State to intrude not merely on the intimate family space, but also on the very body of the former individual, now to be subject on a constant basis to 'the common good':

'Not even one's own body is in one's own possession anymore: Due to the vaccination orders, it is subject to the state's power of disposal. In the climate regime, it can be regulated down to the last detail how one is allowed to live, how one is allowed to move around and what one is allowed to eat. In the wokeness regime, they can regulate what you can say (and think) down to the last detail.'

What we have been experiencing is merely the beginning of a multi-faceted onslaught that is planned to continue into the distant future, changing form as deemed necessary, but without let-up.

This is war by other means. It is not something else. We are under attack, and our own representatives have been recruited as mercenaries against us. We are already well advanced into the process of our conquering.

Human beings, Michael Esfeld stresses, are naturally free. They can exercise choice. They are free in their thoughts and actions. The discoveries and diktats of scientists do not take away our free will. Knowledge liberates, freeing us from things that might, without it, influence our thoughts and actions in a negative way, curtailing our freedom, as though voluntarily. We are free to choose, and therefore the future is not closed — it remains open.

The mistake we have made was in allowing the open society to be combined with constitutional republicanism, with all its flaws and dangers — in trying to encapsulate the open society in a republican constitutional state characterised by the monopoly on the use of force and the monopoly on law-making and the administration of justice. What we need to do, he says, is sever the link between the open society and the republican concept of the rule of law, because this is what has supplied the power to the abusers who now seek to destroy our freedom for all future time.

The way to achieve this, he says, is already available. Natural law and the Anglo-Saxon tradition of common law offer a way of finding and enforcing justice that does not depend on a central state authority with a monopoly of power and of law-making and enforcement in a territory. It is primarily a matter of recognising the law instead of enacting the law: recognising when a person or group of people lives his/their life in such a way that it encroaches on the right to free life of other people.

As in any case of knowledge, he elaborates, this knowledge is best achieved 'through a pluralism that allows for trial and error or correction, rather than a monopoly in the hands of one force. Freedom rights based on natural law can be clearly defined as property rights, including ownership of one's own body, and can thus be made operational without the need for legislation by a central state authority to resolve the conflict. Likewise, the literature on libertarianism sets out how security services can also be provided and enforced through voluntary interaction and association, rather than requiring a central state monopoly on the use of force, provided that a common-law regime is effectively implemented.'

Liberalism was never about freedom, but always nurtured a profound desire to change humanity above all other aspects. This rendered it a willing ally of tyrants promising to do the dirty work of such a project as a means of obtaining an approach-road to power.

There is an additional factor, which is the liberal's disdain for any form of criticism of his philosophy — from what is called 'conservatism', for instance — which it tends to see and dismiss as rooted in backwardness and reactionism, seeking to encroach upon and stymie the virtue-propelled liberal's 'right' to do as he pleases. Our societies have long lost sight of the idea that 'conservatism' does not call for killjoyism, that its true foundation is a longing for a restoration of the virtuous order of work and duty and courage and sacrifice and loyalty and heroism, long since uprooted by transgression and degeneracy and comfort and security and mass culture. Very often, the opponents of liberalism were expressing something absolutely vital to human functioning, but in our emerging culture capable of being heard only as a plea for a return to the past. The bipolar notion that what was not fully 'open' must ipso facto be 'closed' has been destroying the very fabric of human society and culture, but liberals would concede nothing of this for fear of unleashing a slide back to the hypothetical dark ages. Only the utter perversion of truth and reason could enable a society to arrive at the idea of the defence of the claims or 'rights' of drag queens being placed ahead of those of poets or priests or philosophers in the instruction of children, but when such a notion becomes an issue of conflict, it very rapidly turns into a matter of ideological principle. As Leo Strauss observed: 'the sublime is unknown to the open society.'

Such a society rapidly becomes one in which there is no one willing to lay down his life — literally or metaphorically — to retain or defend it, and that is the beginning of the end, for that way lies cowardice and mutism, which are essentially invitations to tyranny, which sits patiently awaiting its chance. Safetyism is a key symptom of liberal degeneracy, because it fears death more than it fears filth or disgrace. These are the conditions which we observed unfolding from the Ides of March 2020: the abdication of liberalism.

And herein lies the ultimate irony. By following the logic of its own course, liberalism has evolved past its own optimal point, into a dark tunnel in which the antithetical values of coercion and terror and oppression will undoubtedly be unleashed to play their part in restarting the cycle, giving birth to a new generation of heroes, who will come to believe in old ideas and virtues, because, having studied the nature of humanity's descent, they will realise that there are worse things in reality than being old-fashioned.

---

* *The content of Michael Esfeld's essay has been expanded into a book which addresses all of these issues and questions in greater philosophical depth. The book,* Restoring Science and the Rule of Law, *is co-written by Esfeld and Christian Lopez, is a philosophical deep-dive into the questions arising from Esfeld's essay,* Die Illusion der res publica. *These include: the explosion of scientism; the collapse of reason arising from relativism; the new dominion of 'experts'; the demolition of the presumption of liberty; the 'illusion' of the constitutional republic, and, with it, the rule of law; the shift from the welfare state to 'welfare totalitarianism' — as well as proposal for the restoration of authentic science and the rule of law, which essentially amounts to the generation of a new Enlightenment based on reason and voluntary social engagement.*

CHAPTER 28
FAKE MONEY AS CLUSTER BOMB
29-05-2023

Western civilisation has suffered a moral inversion achieved by an inverted form of money, flipped from rewarding work and creativity to remunerating filth, ruin and genocide in disguise.

Jesus Drives Money Changers from the Temple.
Then they came to Jerusalem. And He entered the temple area and began to drive out those who were selling and buying on the temple grounds, and He overturned the tables of the money changers and the seats of those who were selling doves; and He would not allow anyone to carry merchandise through the temple grounds. And He began to teach and say to them, 'Is it not written: "My house will be called a house of prayer for all the nations"? But you have made it a den of robbers.'
— The Gospel of Mark, 11:15-17

Money is — clearly — not what it used to seem to be. Once it was the measure of human work, and genius, and produce, by virtue of being the token of reward for all these. Now it is as though the measure of the threat to our civilisation.

Once, not long ago, there was no money for anything. It was sometimes called 'austerity', but more often 'tight budgetary policy'. Now, it seems, there is no scarcity of money. In Ireland, for example, whereas for more than a decade, there has been a visible and much-debated 'housing crisis', with thousands of Irish families languishing on the housing lists, there was nothing to be done because there was 'no money'. Now, there is an abundance of money to house migrants from all over the world in five-star hotels and stately homes, to kit them out in the latest Nikes, and Levi's with the pocket padded with bill rolls, and passports paid for out of petty cash, but still those thousands of Irish families languish on the housing lists. There is 'no money' to help them, and anyone who says that this is unjust is instantly recognisable as a racist.

The love of money is the root of all evil. In a day or two, a month of compulsory celebration of LGBT power and menace will kick off right across the globe, mostly financed from the pockets of people who have no right to speak against what is, in truth, a massive exercise in bullying and intimidation, and, even more fundamentally, an attack on the values and morals of Western civilisation, and — far less abstractly — upon its children. Money is no object when it comes to sexual perversion, cultural railroading and camouflaged noncery. Here in Ireland, last Friday night, the final episode of the long-running talk show, *The Late Late Show,* involved a charity fundraiser which resulted in a €58k donation to BeLonGTo (LGBT+ youth organisation) and a rather more modest €20k to a children's cancer charity.

A tweet from Women, Children and Family Advocate captured the secret thoughts of many watching:

'There's no € to be made from terminally ill children but a lot to be made from confused, vulnerable children with mental health issues. Karma won't be kind to these evil people.'

Money is no longer money. It is a weapon of war, used by those who are charged with its custody against those to whom it is supposed to belong.

False money destroys economies, nations and communities.

Earlier this month, the UK *Spectator* reported on a strange syndrome afflicting the British economy: mass unemployment combined with a shortage of workers.

The economy of Manchester, in the north, is floundering for want of workers. With more than 40,000 jobs currently advertised in the city, almost nobody is prepared to work for the rates on offer: £10.75 per hour as a stockroom assistant in Ann Summers, £14 an hour as an exam invigilator, £75,000 a year as a sales manager with a chemical company, or as a trainee army officer at £34,000 for the first year. Even though 18 per cent of Mancunians are claiming unemployment or sick benefits, nobody wants these jobs. Birmingham, Liverpool and Glasgow tell the same story. In Blackpool, close to a quarter of the population is out of work. Nationwide, claims for sick benefits have doubled since the lockdowns, with most of the increase spoken for by mental health conditions.

It is obvious that this has to do mainly with the fallout from the Covid subterfuge, though not even the *Spectator* is willing to spell this out — its main point being that the government has simply upped levels of immigration to take up the slack: 'While the first wave of mass immigration in recent decades was an unforeseen consequence of expanding the European Union, this one is planned.

The Tories have taken back control and used it to ramp up immigration to a level that New Labour would never have dared attempt.'

This is newsworthy, but beside the point. During the fake pandemic, the UK government paid workers 80 per cent of their incomes to stay home. Now it expresses puzzlement because a worker who earned £344 per week for not stacking shelves in Ann Summers is disinclined to go back to stacking shelves in Ann Summers for a differential of £2.15 per hour. The *Spectator* article puts it mostly down to Brexit, but you don't need to be a conspiracist to detect that the situation now facing the UK is due to something more like a pincer movement of Covid insanity and problem-reaction-solution scenario.

Fake money changes everything. There is nothing that is safe from it or immune to it. Fiat money is fake money: tokens of exchange that really represent nothing except civilisational destruction.

In that retroactively spectral period of early 2020, just before the 'pandemic', an odd phenomenon erupted around Ireland, for which no explanation was yet available to fit the facts of the moment. This was the emergence of a sudden rash of charging posts for electric cars — all for use free of charge — in odd sections of filling stations, opposite drive-thru McDonalds, in the corners of vast carparks. Even stranger was that, here and there throughout the country, for no apparent reason, among the standard charging points for generic electric cars, there would be a batch of dedicated charging-points — greater in number — for one particular type of electric car, a car named for a Serbian-American inventor of the late 19th and early 20th century, Nikola Tesla, who had reputedly invented a wireless system for generating electricity that had been suppressed because it was feared it would destroy the oil business. The puzzle in this was, or seemed to be, that there were almost no Teslas on the road, and these charging-points were accordingly almost totally unused. They stood as though the graveyards of a lost civilisation, some miracle of Norman democratic impulse or desiring, standing there like Megalith monuments, seeming to have forgotten their function or not yet having been allocated one. Very, very occasionally, when you had gotten used to seeing them, you would, in passing with the usual reluctant curiosity, take a second or third glance to find that a vehicle of some kind was actually charging there, and you and others would ramble over to kick its tyres — in spite, or envy, or muted admiration. They were cars alright, but not as we had known them. Their odd, somewhat clumsy but beautiful shapes drew ambiguous glances, as might a beautiful girl in a tutu and Doc Martens. *Who might own such a car?* was, more or less, the unspoken question still hovering in the ante-chamber of everyone's larynx. *Did they know something we didn't?*

A few months into the 'pandemic' — by late summer, certainly — something even stranger started to manifest. More and more of these Teslas became visible on the roads and at the charging points, seeming not so much to make sense but as though to provide at last some kind of justification for something that had before seemed like a strange constellation of art installations, monuments to a future that seemed unlikely. More and more Teslas were to be seen charging at these post-historic sites. Some were beautiful, though always in a way that seemed flawed, as though to humanise them. Others were almost ordinary, nondescript, but with a hint of the same gawky grace. For the first time in history, it seemed that it had become possible to live horse and get grass.

Prices of the Teslas ranged between 50 grand and approximately three times that, but more models, some costing in excess of 200 grand, were promised to be in the works. As more and more became known about what might be happening to the world, it was as though the Tesla had been invented to become the receptacle for money that had no other place to go, as well as being a state-ment about the owner's position in a future that would become more and more inhospitable for most people who had no money left to go anywhere (but would be 'happy' in their immobility). As the 'pandemic' rolled on, with the world's businesses largely in hibernation, people who had already been rich seemed to be getting richer, while those who hadn't became decidedly poorer, but invisi-bly, at least to themselves, as an engineered inflation crept up behind and picked their pockets.

Once, one of the chief virtues of money was that it was scarce. This was what caused its value to track the greatest effort and virtue and enterprise of men. Now, it is plentiful — if only for certain things – we must surely know that something has gone badly wrong.

Little more than a decade or so in the past, it was as though money had all but become extinct. Now, our governments splash it around the place on things we did not ask for: cycle lanes that turn our public thoroughfares into Olympic stadia; street furniture that no one ever sits upon; the purchase of farms for the purpose of closing them down; modular homes for unvetted migrants while native citizens sleep in tents; roadworks that never end.

The present calamity is the culmination of a process of an unravelling of Western civilisation that has been in train for some time, perhaps a century or even more, when, all the while without our suspecting, all the conventions and protections we had allowed ourselves to believe existed as our guarantees of freedom and opportunity were being broken apart and carted away to the scrap-yard, under our very noses. The issue arising, then, is not that, unless we defeat the evils now confronting us, 'we shall not have a civilisation'. The issue is that we do not have a civilisation, and have not had one for a long time. If we had, then the people now in charge of our countries would never have risen above the roles of nightclub doormen, or traffic wardens. They would certainly not be in positions where they could help to dismantle the millennia-old understand-ings that served to create the greatest civilisation the world has ever witnessed. Nowadays, we hear nothing but talk of the excesses and extravagances of that civilisation, and nothing of the great principles and ideals — for the greater part of heroism, sacrifice and postponement — that brought it into being. Now, too, we hear only words of contempt for the founders of that civilisation, those men of steel and iron, grey of hair and suit, who placed a restraining hand on zealotry and exuberance when it came to matters of public interest or concern, knowing that this would unleash the pent-up energies of their people in the direction of a better future. These now quaint-seeming individuals, who spoke in resonating sentences evoking great passions and visions, who seemed to hold the public interest as the dearest thing, and whose private lives and deeds, where visible, found the purest harmony with their words, are spoken of by knaves and imbeciles as though their efforts had caused nothing but grief and destruction. Now, their places are taken by smirking scoundrels, for whose venality, fecklessness and ignorance no words have yet been invented — insipid creatures of ambiguous sexuality, puffed up with a power corruptly acquired, drunk on a cheap pseudo-passion for the rights of degenerates to trample over every institution of man, working from morning until night to dismantle the very walls of their nations and civilisation — and enabled in all this by the avail-ability of fake money, a commodity that trumps all others precisely because it is worthless.

We must conclude that this was not an accident, but an orchestrated imposi-tion of the most vapid mediocrity upon the institutions of state and culture. If we look back, we can see the signs: the handing upwards of the people's power, generally under false pretences, the quiet, disillusioned withdrawal of good men and true, the weeding out of discordant voices, the elevation of a new kind of 'hero' — one who came to notice because he seemed to be the very antithesis of the good and the true.

All this was enabled by money, but here we stumble upon an extraordinary truth: Money of the old kind could not have facilitated such an insurgency of mediocrity, for it was hard to come by, and there were better uses for it. The new dispensation became possible as the direct and inevitable consequence of the explosion in the political life of Toytown money, in a process sometimes referred to as 'quantitative easing' (QE), itself a by-product of the aforementioned inco-herence of fiat currencies and the associated phenomenon of fractional reserve banking.

The effects of false money sloshing around our economies can hardly be over-emphasised, and yet it is rarely, if ever, talked about. This fake money is as though a cancer that has metastasised and ripped through the entire corpora of multiple nations, infecting everything and everyone, directly or indirectly, until all human hopes and morale have begun to unravel and disintegrate. It is what motivates the doctor who lines up his patients for an injection he already knows may injure or kill them, while assuring himself and all within earshot that he is 'saving lives'. It is the impetus and conscience-salver of the nurse who, with apparent equanimity, could turn people away from the ward in which their beloved, having been brought to death's door on a ventilator, cling to life in the vain hope of saying goodbye to those they have loved — and, afterwards, having despatched the body to the mortuary, lets off steam by executing complex dance moves for a TikTok video. It is the fuel that propels the twisted journaliar to launch attacks on 'far righters' whom he knows to be the kind of people he once, a long time ago, had been educated to emulate or even become. Fake money is a dissolver of principle and an antidote to tribal solidarity. It is ultimately what causes the formerly drum-beating nationalist politician to dispense sneers and menaces in the direction of people who are pleading to know why their country is being thrown to wolves, a plausible pre-echo of being told by their children's rapists to shut up and enjoy the show.

The evils that have been unleashed in the past three years — albeit with their roots in a prior, preparatory putrescence of indeterminate duration — can chiefly be seen as arising from the availability of a form of money which exists solely for the execution of evil. False money is at the root of every one of the unholy things we have witnessed for the past three years, and which continue in the face of pleading by decent, honourable people, while the majority stands silently, idly by, waiting for a slice of the action. Fake money results in terrible and otherwise incomprehensible outcomes that contradict every principle ever uttered in the time when money was a scarce token of exchange in respect of necessities and of reward for doing good things. Once money ceased to be seen as a tool, and became itself the coveted substance, immorality was inevitable. Fake money begets societies comprising nothing but lies. It is the bastard offspring of materialism at its extremes.

Fake money eats into everything and is ultimately what produces the sense of strangeness we have experienced in the past 40 months. We gave too much credence, in 2020, to the idea that the strange behaviour of politicians and doctors and pseudo-scientists and journaliars had to do with fear, or (even more naïvely of us) with a genuine desire to save people from death or illness or suffering. They were all the time following the instructions of the false money, which held for them a mesmerising power far superior to hypnosis. And, while it has been important to examine some of the more arcane contributors to our calamitous situation — propaganda, mass formation, groupthink, the slow death of the constitutional republic, *et cetera* — there is a much more immediate and obvious factor that we tend to misread: the power of a perverted money system to corrupt every and any institution, individual or group. Perhaps, then, it was nothing like as complicated as we have been imagining. Perhaps there was no need for us to ponder whether they were being threatened or blackmailed: maybe inducement provided the single-word explanation for everything that was happening. They were as whores, inured and indifferent to morals or scruples.

Money always held out the possibility of corrupting our civilisation. Ten years ago, a study by researchers from the universities of Harvard and Utah, published in the journal *Organizational Behavior and Human Decision Processes,* suggested that people are more likely to lie or make immoral decisions after being exposed to money-related words. The findings showed that 'even if we are well-intentioned, even if we think we know right from wrong, there may be factors influencing our decisions and behaviours that we're not aware of,' one of the co-authors said.

The study asked college students studying business to make sentences out of various word clusters before answering questions and playing several games. Some of the phrases contained a financial focus, such as 'She spends money liberally,' and others that were neutral, such as 'She walked on grass.' Researchers found that people who were exposed to the financial phrases lied more often in subsequent activities if they knew doing so would earn them more money. Subjects shown the money-related words were also more likely to make an unethical decision even when there was no direct financial reward, such as hiring someone who promises to share insider information concerning a competitor. Even the word 'dollar', they discovered, had the power to quiet an individual conscience.

In another study by a group at UC Berkeley, a fake game of Monopoly was secretly filmed in which players were unevenly endowed with 'money'. The hidden cameras exposed the 'rich' players moving their pieces more loudly around the board, and celebrating their 'wins' with whoops and jeers and becoming increasingly rude to their opponents who'd drawn the short straws. At the end, the 'rich' players talked as though they had earned their success, even though the game was manifestly rigged, and their win should have been seen as inevitable. This tells us that, in general, our concepts of reward have become perverted by cultures in which money has, for some, become easier to come by, and confers benefits regardless of effort or integrity.

We know also that rich people are proportionately less generous than poor people: They give away significantly smaller shares of their wealth. In California, where drivers are legally required to stop for pedestrians, a study showed that half of expensive cars would fail to stop for pedestrians, whereas none of the cheaper cars did so.

A study by the University of San Francisco found that poor people were much better than rich people at reading the emotions of the faces of other people in photographs and mock interviews. But, when the wealthy were instructed to imagine themselves in the situation of the people they were looking at, their scores improved. This tells us what we already intuit: that as someone's personal wealth increases, his capacity to feel compassion and empathy reduces, to be supplanted by feelings of ever-mounting entitlement and self-interest. We had a warning of this in the 1987 movie, *Wall Street:* we laughed when its anti-hero Gordon Gekko declared that 'Greed is good!' This, too, is a perversion — of the natural urge to provide, to go forth and multiply.

Another way of describing what has been happening in our societies in the past three years and counting would be to say that such anti-ethics have wormed their way into the hearts of our power-centres, and the convergence of the resulting forces of amorality are now rapidly accelerating the inequality in a culture that had, until what seems like the day before yesterday, claimed to repudiate that phenomenon as no other.

Money, on becoming an addiction, overrides the conscience and wipes out all virtue.

A psychologist, Dr Tian Dayton, explained that a compulsive need to acquire money is often considered part of a class of behaviours known as 'process addictions' or 'behavioural addictions,' which are distinct from substance abuse.

'Process addictions are addictions that involve a compulsive and/or an out-of-control relationship with certain behaviors such as gambling, sex, eating, and, yes, even money. . . . There is a change in brain chemistry with a process addiction that's similar to the mood-altering effects of alcohol or drugs. With process addictions, engaging in a certain activity — say viewing pornography, compulsive eating, or an obsessive relationship with money — can kickstart the release of brain/body chemicals, like dopamine, that actually produce a "high" that's similar to the chemical high of a drug. The person who is addicted to some form of behavior has learned, albeit unconsciously, to manipulate his own brain chemistry.'

He was talking here about the 'normative' effect of money on individuals in controlled societal circumstances. He possibly never envisaged that whole societies could be rendered rapt before the power of false money, when all restraint — of individuals, institutions, systems, governments and corporations — may be suppressed by the immediacy of easy opportunity.

These evils arise, it is important to remember, not from money, but from its corruption and corrupted forms. An epidemic of fake money is just about the worst thing that can happen to a society because it embraces the possibility of just about every other bad thing you can imagine. It facilitates invasion and plunder. It suppresses principle and conscience. It overrules the effects of education and tradition. It dissolves scruples and renders guilt be quiet.

Fake money, once liberated into a society, unleashes a wholesale anarchic attack on the underpinning values of that society, placing at nought the power of restraint, postponement, balance, moderation, discretion, ecological accountability and all concepts of fair dealing. Fake money unravels everything: patriotism, reason, the effects of historical rhetoric, ideology, common sense, religiosity — all these phenomena fall before it.

Fake money has, in the past three years, made it possible and worthwhile for whole battalions of pseudo-liberals to agree to the complete transformation of their cultures and the obliteration of most of their formerly professed values. It makes possible the now rampant internal racism against the Caucasian populations of multiple Western countries and the prejudice of the well-off towards the working class, and allows respectable middle-class parents to create choruses of approval at the prospect of other people's children mutilating their bodies in the name of progressivism. It persuades schools, colleges and universities to impose these ideologies on their students in a non-negotiable way. It enables those who consider themselves aloof from the consequences of policies like coercive mass inward migration to 'welcome' the newcomers they have no intention of helping, and daubing as racists those who honestly declare their fears and doubts about what is happening. It allows newspapers, radio and TV stations and online platforms to provoke and conduct pile-ons against anyone coming to notice for dissenting from these agendas.

But, possibly the worst thing about fake money is that it is not entirely fake. It has the capacity to be real only when the powerful so decide, because the chits and receipts and IOUs survive, even when the safes and bank vaults and wallets are empty. In this regard, though we may have nothing to show for it, we are incurring debts that will eat up the inheritance of our children's children's children.

Fake money has costs, but no value. The extent of the effects of false money, because it is false, and therefore quasi-infinite, is incalculable, invisible. But we can observe a qualified measure of it in the excess deaths currently imposing on humanity a new, real and unannounced — and officially ignored — pandemic, for this is a context in which its reality becomes visible and palpable, measurable only in grief and pain.

Wikipedia tells us that 'Counterfeit money is currency produced without the legal sanction of a state or government, usually in a deliberate attempt to imitate that currency so as to deceive its recipient. Producing or using counterfeit money is a form of fraud or forgery, and is illegal. The business of counterfeiting money is nearly as old as money itself.' This summary is accurate enough in respect to situations where small amounts of counterfeit money are introduced by petty criminals or fraudsters, but it does nothing to describe or alert us to the dangers of counterfeit money entering an economy under the supervision of the government. In this context, the devastation can only be total, for it twists all natural understandings in their seating and places an irrational greed at the centre of everything. This greed replaces normative desires and ambitions for such as livelihood, advancement, security, comfort, land, property, and even affection, with a frenzied hunger to take advantage of the avalanche while it is in train. It is as if an overhead helicopter has started to rain down one-hundred Euro notes, and a voice announces via a klaxon that everyone may keep whatsoever he claims. This, in truth, is precisely what is happening:

Helicopter money: '*A phrase coined by the American economist Milton Friedman in 1969, when he wrote a parable of dropping money from a helicopter to illustrate the effects of monetary expansion. A helicopter drop is an expansionary fiscal or monetary policy that is financed by an increase in an economy's money supply. It could be an increase in spending or a tax cut, but it involves printing large sums of money and distributing it to the public in order to stimulate the economy. Mostly, the term "helicopter drop" is largely a metaphor for unconventional measures to jump-start the economy during deflationary periods, which consist of falling prices.*'

Friedman elaborated: 'Let us suppose now that one day a helicopter flies over this community and drops an additional $1,000 in bills from the sky, which is, of course, hastily collected by members of the community. Let us suppose further that everyone is convinced that this is a unique event which will never be repeated.'

$1,000 may seem an inadequate sum with which to dramatise such a thesis in 2023, but today's equivalent of $8,360 might certainly have an arousing effect on a populace.

We can imagine the effect of a helicopter flying over a small village and letting loose such a sum in large and small denomination bills. It is likely that the populace would emerge, at first sneakily, from their homes and rapidly descend into a kind of mania as they competed to pick up as much as possible of the spoils from the sky. One would not anticipate hearing them say things like, 'After you!' and 'No, you first!' What one could expect would be mayhem, as people vied to fill their pockets and shopping bags with as many notes as they could get, with all niceties abandoned in the ensuing scrummage.

Something analogous has obtained in our culture for the past three years, as people acquiesced in behaviours that would normally be alien to them, in order to access some of the false money made available for those willing to implement an agenda directed not at building or maintaining human society, but pulling it apart for reasons they neither understood nor cared to understand, at least for as long as the money continued to fall from the sky. These people, not coincidentally, also happened to be the most powerful in terms of the recognition accorded on a hierarchical basis by the society: politicians, doctors, judges, law enforcers, scientists, journalists (so-called), civil servants, *et cetera*. The 'victims' of these phenomena were chiefly those who had been accustomed to generating their means of survival from their own ingenuity and effort: farmers, shopkeepers, tradesmen, *et cetera*. As time moved on, however, as already noted, the munificent attentions of the authorities shifted from the indigenous population to the State-invited outsiders, whose pampering appeared to be a form of tease or gaslighting directed at the indigenous population, in particular those who were already impecunious.

What we have been observing, however, resembles more an air raid than a helicopter drop: False money, flipped from its original meaning and purpose and directed only at evildoing, has functioned more in the manner of cluster bombs aimed at the vulnerable points of the remaining morale of society. In a certain light, the Ukraine war is simply a metaphor for what is happening to the world in general, and the West in particular.

This campaign of supposed plenitude amounts, in the final analysis, to a colossal assault on the laws that govern economic activity, the hardwired connection between work and productivity and measure and rewards, as outlined by Roy Sebag in his slim volume, *The Natural Order of Money (see Chapter 29)*. It amounts to an attempted terminal assault on the concept of ecological accountability, described also by Sebag, whereby each actor in the economy, no matter how far removed from fundamental processes of production, is bound by the same laws of adherence to reality and its balances, requirements and limits. It amounts to the final unmooring of money from human activity in the matter of producing and providing essential human needs, and after that, non-essentials and luxuries, replacing all this with a formula that dispenses tokens of nothing but untruth, as a burlesquing 'reward' for obedience to criminality and the criminals conducting it.

In the Celtic Tiger, the constructed 'boom' set in train in late-1990s Ireland as the initiation-point of the current wealth coup, the power of cheap money had driven people insane with a desire for property and other tokens of a success that had eluded them in all normative contexts. Now, three decades later, a similar process has been operating on the capacities of those who already have more than the means of self-sustenance to leverage the resources available through the money system — the circulatory system of society — to accumulate further wealth in a way they imagine will change their lives for ever. Yes, they may have to do hard and unpleasant things, but when it is over, they will drive around in their Teslas and convince themselves that looking to secure their children's futures has been a worthy and moral exercise.

But all this is a mirage. The money is not real. In a sense, and rather uniquely, the 'transactions' have been — secretly, invisibly — karmic and just, for they offer mere time-limited tokens for evil deeds. Nobody knows precisely when the tokens will run out, but those ultimately in charge of their disbursement know that they will eventually become worthless, and that there will therefore be nothing lost to their dispensers arising from their apparent reckless munificence.

Milton Friedman did not anticipate, or at least did not explore, the likely social and moral consequences of helicopter drops. He saw the matter in purely technical terms, a mechanism for effecting a permanent once-off expansion of the amount of money in circulation, which would stimulate spending, expand economic activity and provoke helpful levels of inflation. He did not foresee that it would stimulate also irrational greed, jealousy, rage, viciousness, violence and hatred, that it would provoke politicians to destroy their countries and dismantle their cultures, prompt regular people to sell out their neighbours and the values that had enabled the construction of their nations. He did not appear to understand that it might, in a short time, contribute to the overturning of 2,500 years of conditioning in patriotism, democracy, liberalism, tolerance, freedom-reverence, reason and justice-love, in bringing forward the death-knell of the civilisation once called Christendom.

This may, even by now, be irreversible. To combat and set in reverse what has been occurring, a political movement would need access to the same levels of pseudo-money as the incumbent establishments, and to maintain access to it after gaining power, and use it in a reverse fashion — for the achievement of good — for as long as this was necessary to rebuild Western civilisation. This is next to inconceivable, and so we appear to have painted ourselves into a corner that there is no obvious way of escaping.

Now, we begin to comprehend the meaning of all those Teslas. They were the visible evidence of reward for participation in evildoing, the manifestation of the false money in concrete — i.e. alloyed and plastic — form. The Teslas announced themselves as prizes for believing that gravity could be defied. The rejection of economic fundamentals — and the abuse of the natural law of the land, sea and air implicit in the entire exercise of helicoptering economics — was culminating in the strange shapes of clunky but beautiful cars that seemed to represent the foreshortening of effort by dint of its supplanting by grasping, greed and shamelessness. And there was another factor: Though not greed-free, the Tesla offered a kind of cut-price reassurance of conscience, for it had — had it not? — a virtuous aspect, that of 'saving the planet'. Between saving lives and saving the planet, how could greed not be good?

Thus, by Sebag's definitions, the 'pandemic' was a once-off opportunity to cheat nature, to abbreviate the period of effort and pain involved in accumulating enough f**k off money to f**k off with. The problem is that there may be nowhere to go.

CHAPTER 29
THE ABOLITION OF REALITY, PART I: THE VIRTUAL THINKS US
24-07-2023

In grasping the meaning of this moment, the most compelling theory may be that of French philosopher, Jean Baudrillard: We have moved into a copy of reality bearing scant resemblance to the original.

The exhaustion of language in the face of the calamities of the past 40 months is the consequence not so much of a linguistic deficit of humanity, but a shocked response of humans to a sudden and gratuitous caprice of reality for reasons that no process of logic or reason seems quite able to explain. Words glance and skate off the surface of this new reality, unable to acquire the traction of meaning, or even the quality of gravity (both senses) to remain apropos. People say that everything has 'gone crazy', seeming to forget that they said the same thing many times when it wasn't true, or not so true. Now that it is truer than true, the word 'crazy' is pathetically inadequate, as is 'deranged', or 'bonkers', or 'lunatic', or 'mental', or 'cracked', or 'insane', or 'unhinged', or 'berserk', or 'batshit crazy'.

We hear ourselves saying that things have become 'surreal', but unconvincingly, because surreal is something we associated with molten clocks or dislocated toilet bowls, but now we are using it in everyday sentences in contexts it barely scratches the surface of.

Taking another tack, words that belonged in books and movies — like 'dystopia' and 'gaslighting' — have started to turn up in reality, like the booking agent has sent the wrong band to a children's party.

For the past 40 months, drowning in seas of speculation, and what sometimes sounded — even to ourselves — like hyperbolising, we have struggled to form sentences to describe what has been happening to us. It often seemed like we had run out of words, so that even when we felt we had communicated something clear and cogent as a description of our situation, it fell some distance short of lassoing the matters we contemplated, or provoking the anticipated sudden start of recognition in whatever bystanders might be within earshot. It was not just that everything was unprecedented and 'weird', but that attempts at the articulation of descriptions of 'reality' seemed, all the time, to convey something else, something parallel or adjacent, but never quite synonymous or coterminous or correspondent.

There was something in the conduct of public agents — I mean not just politicians and civil servants, medical experts, scientists, *et cetera*, but also journalists, or whatever we might call them now — the established interpreters and mediators of reality, journaliars — that suggested an advance knowingness of everything they were telling us, accompanied by a sense of normalcy that grated with our experience and yet was strangely plausible. It was like we had entered some kind of nightmare vista, in which everything was being presented as though some kind of elaborate, pre-planned prank, perhaps for a birthday party or a retirement do, in which everyone was playing a scripted part, and, any minute now, someone would lose his straight face, give way to giggles, and admit that it was a ruse and a hoax — just for a laugh — and didn't they have us all going there for a while, *haha haha haha ha ha*?

Of course, this characterisation of things, though resonant in some respects, is cast, we might at first sight say, in entirely the wrong colours. It conjures up mischief in its mild forms, steeped in good humour, playfulness, affection, suppressed hilarity, whereas the forces and phenomena we deal with here are nothing like any of that. What we deal with here is mischief at the most malevolent level — the fixed grin of the intimate assassin; a mask of compassion upon a visage of pure evil; dark, grinning clownery that threatens to erupt into catastrophe, the deepest darkness that human beings can evince. Here we have encountered a ceaseless stream of deception of the most devious kind, an industrialised unleashing of the most systemic wickedness, a terror and a thieving of everything we had hitherto been able to take for granted in the modes of our security in, and familiarity with, and our feeling of being at home and at peace in, the world. And all this at the hands of people whom we had nominated, elected and ordained as our representatives, trusting them with the keys of our sacred institutions and homelands and civilisations.

Here was, for certain, tyranny, though cast in the light of 'saving lives' and 'the public interest' and 'the common good'. And here was death, both in the form of a constantly menaced prospect for which we were required to forfeit everything conceivable as life-enhancing, and, simultaneously, in the shape of a profoundly suspected, unmentionable and barely conceivable menace that seemed to be shadowing certain categories of people in certain types of situations — old people in nursing homes, for example, or those of any age who placed their full trust in doctors, scientists and their government to tell them what was true and what was not. In the beginning, they spoke ceaselessly about the prospect that many people would die, and there was no evidence of it; and yet many people were soon dying in unprecedented numbers for reasons that were not permitted to be discussed or even mentioned.

A change came over people that caused them to go along rather than question. It was as though their brains had fallen out and splattered all over the ground, causing them no more than a moment's pause before they continued as if nothing had happened. It was, in some way, like our nearest and dearest had suddenly started to act like villains from the scariest and most blood-curdling horror movie. What we were observing bore almost no relationship to what we had grown accustomed to in lives of whatever duration to date — except that the personnel who seemed to be in charge of events were familiar to us, and their manner only so slightly detectable as different: the merest uptick in menace, and yet such as to be unmistakable for anything else.

As it went on, it grew more and more sinister and yet seemed at the same time to retain some element of continuity with the reality we had left behind. Figures whom we seemed certain in our recollection of their having spoken all their lives upon the value of liberty and justice and free speech were suddenly speaking as though such ideas could no longer be contemplated — in 'the public interest' and for 'the common good'. More and more, in innumerable sets of circumstances, the people we had appointed to represent our interests seemed to behave in the manner of a spouse seeking an alibi for a breach of trust and loyalty, turning upon us as though the fault for whatever was happening lay with ourselves.

We flirted with unfamiliar concepts: Mass formation, pseudo-reality, psychopathy, ponerology, groupthink, brainwashing, mass hypnosis, gaslighting . . . And yet none of these terms or concepts seemed to take us but part of the way to comprehension, or even to fit the circumstances or touch the meanings of events in a way that animated or vivified or activated things, or enabled us to describe more successfully to one another exactly what was happening and how we were feeling about it.

'Gaslighting', to take one example, was a word that seemed somehow to erupt into a previously unthinkable level of usage. A word that, in 2020, was already 82 years old but had yet to enter the popular lexicon, it had lain there, as though waiting for almost a century, practically unnoticed, minimally comprehended and under-utilised, and suddenly it was on everyone's lips and fingertips, emerging to occupy a semantic space that nothing else seemed to fit or fill, which in turn had to mean that new or sharply unusual conditions had suddenly manifested underfoot. Suddenly, it was everywhere. People would utter it with conviction and apparent confidence of its being instantly understood, and yet, at first, at least half of every gathering had to stop and ask one another what it meant. Within a few weeks, almost everyone was not merely aware of its meaning, but using it in every second sentence.

Its origin had been peculiar, to say the least. In 1938 there was this play called *Gas Light*, and in 1940, and again in 1944, two films, from which the word had emerged in its semantic wholeness, but still lacking a general context. Up to the spring of 2020, it conveyed — or could be used as a space-filler for — a condition of human interaction that required a brief seminar of explication on the occasion of its every usage.

Hearing the word 'gaslighting' for the first time, a sharp bystander might deduce from the instant circumstances that it meant something like 'taking someone for a fool', or 'driving the fool farther', or perhaps 'compelling someone to doubt his own sanity'. But what had any of this to do with gas or the lighting thereof? In the play and the movies, the word alludes to the actions of an abusive husband, who gradually dims the gas lights in the family home while pretending to his wife that nothing has changed, with the objective of causing her to doubt her own sanity, so he can commit her to an institution. The wife repeatedly asks her husband to confirm her perceptions about the dimming lights and other symptoms of his underhand chicanery, but he insists on the version of reality he is manufacturing.

Unless you had seen the play or one of the movies, you had no way of 'feeling the meaning' of the word, or using it without feeling a fraud. Almost nobody, as it turned out, had seen the play, and few had seen anything other than a short clip from one of the movies. It was the strangest word ever, and yet, in its strangeness, seemed to become more meaningful and piquant and appropriate, as though its impenetrability somehow assisted in describing things that had no rational description. By the middle of 2020, everyone, whether they had seen or even heard of the play or movies called *Gas Light*, knew exactly what gaslighting felt like. By that time, it had for weeks become the quasi-universal manner of describing the standard mode of communicating utilised by every politician, health spokesperson, officially accredited scientist, TV presenter and purchased journalist in the world. The word acquired a life of its own, remote from its cinematic context, with connotations of a kind of slow murder of the human spirit, and ultimately of the body, by something like lacerating and ultimately lethal lies. By then, we had the impression of being surrounded by walls of lies, as though the world had turned into the stage-set of a horror drama and we were children for the first time encountering such a phenomenon as theatre, but without prior warning that what we would experience would not really be real, so that it entered our souls as nothing had before, or perhaps in a manner in which, quite unprepared, like when we had attended our first 'fit up' play by a travelling theatre company that had inveigled its way into our junior school to perform on the day before the summer holidays were due to begin, and suddenly we found ourselves as the dumb witnesses to menaces and slyness and violence and murder, and other experiences we had never even dreamed of in the innocent lives we had lived hitherto. Each of us, in turn, looked to the others, hoping for signs of a mischievous fabrication, a deliberately concocted drama, a jape, a prank, a joke. But the faces of others gave us no comfort in our sense of the unreality and impossibility of what was afoot, and by their seriousness caused us to gradually drop our guileless smiles as we waited in confusion for some moment of clarity or revelation.

And so, more or less, things remain. For the past 40 months, we have struggled with words in our attempts to describe what has been happening to us and our world, mostly with so little success that we simply repeat the word 'gaslighting' as though it has become a kind of verbal pacifier. Such has been the unprecedented and shocking nature of events, almost on a daily basis, that we have struggled to find words adequate to describing our feelings, and more and more have opted for a bemused silence, which is slowly killing those who adopt it. Many among us have been unable even to diagnose the necessity for new ways of thinking about what is happening to us, or for new words to conduct that thinking in. We have been thinking, perhaps, that the words need to come first, but perhaps this is a mistake. Perhaps the constructs need to be sketched, so that new words volunteer themselves? Or perhaps it is time to address the possibility that the problem is not linguistic, but conceptual — not to do with the function of description, but with identifying the deep nature of some fundamental change that has taken place in the depths and folds of our societies and cultures. Perhaps this shift had been in place for a long time but escaped our notice because the circumstances thrown up by reality did not sufficiently engage the changed conditions to convey that things had ceased to be as they once were.

Nothing we have come up with yet seems quite adequate to the task of explication. Some explanations — the end of times, collective possession, mass hypnosis or brainwashing, a wave function collapse or some similar kind of disintegration and rebuilding of our temporal grid — seem for a time to be functional as metaphors, but become implausible when placed against our subjective experiences and the habit we have formed of applying historical facts and logic to the comprehension of change. We have known nothing of these phenomena before — other than in plays or movies — so why should they invade our actual lived existences now? There is no explanation that seems completely to fit the narrative course our lives have followed through our childhoods, into adulthood and on to wherever we may find ourselves; and yet, the symptoms of radical change are everywhere, and most of all — as we are rapidly discovering — between our ears.

Something utterly new is occurring, something that, if it happened before, happened in remote places or different epochs, so that no one is able to recall any point of reference to say that, 'Oh, this is just like how it was way back when . . .' And, because there is no such point of precedent, many of us feel obliged to take events at face value, to believe that a pandemic could happen without evidence in anything other than constant assertion; that a senile man could be elected president of the largest democracy in the world; that athletes have always died in great numbers but no one in authority had ever noticed before; that, after 150,000 years of human evolution, women and men are suddenly morphing seamlessly into one another; that a world which for several decades had fretted about the evils of child molestation has suddenly decided that children were not getting enough sex, and hurries accordingly to ensure that ugly old men dressed as female prostitutes are facilitated in waving their privates at five year-olds as part of their *seducation* — there, now, is a new word that fits — and that any incoherencies of any of this can be satisfactorily accounted for by accusing those giving voice to their bemusement of wearing (invisible) 'tinfoil hats' and making a nuisance of themselves for the sake of vexatiousness.

After 40 months of struggling with everything, committing more than two million words to the ether, I am only now beginning to develop a viewfinder through which to look at what has been happening. It has to do, I now believe, with a fundamental shift in the nature of reality, amounting to the abolition of reality as we have known it. After nearly three years of writing on Substack, I now believe I have a sense of the theme and tone of the book I have felt I was writing from the beginning, which I now propose to proceed with under the working title: *The Abolition of Reality.*

'Oh yeah, very original!' I hear the retort, 'It's The Matrix!'

Not really. In a recent Twitter conversation between Andrew Tate and Tucker Carlson, Tucker boasted that he had never seen the movie called *The Matrix*. Tate couldn't believe it. I can go one better: I've seen half the first movie, at least twice, but couldn't stay the course. I don't like sci-fi, not because I'm not interested in the future, but because I am, and because I need the future to seem naturalistic, organic, not makey-uppy, like those essays we used to write in school back in the twentieth century about 'Life in 2000 AD', in which everybody would drive around in hovercraft and, for lunch, eat one speckled pill at the centre of a large plate. I never feel that sci-fi in books or movies reflect adequately the way reality morphs and weaves through time, because it always misses the most striking aspects of those processes observed across the span of a life. A strange quirk of time in this sense is that it seems not to change anything much at all, day to day, year to year, or even decade to decade, in the continuous warp and weave of itself, and yet, whenever elements of the past manifest in the present, they — observed as though from a temporal distance — look improbably unlike how you remember them. If you look at a Mark One 1970 Ford Escort from behind on a 2023 streetscape, it looks unsafe and highly sprung, like a wobbly anorexic in a miniskirt, at once futuristic and impossibly antiquated, and you wonder if anyone could possibly have designed a car like that and what were they thinking of. And yet, you have the clearest memory of envying your friend because, one day in 1971, his father drove one of these contraptions, replete with sports wheels and sheepskin seat covers, and a doggy in the rear window that nodded at the traffic coming behind.

If I look at the photograph of a streetscape from the 1980s, I don't feel like it's a place I came through, even when it's of my hometown, and there are signs of constancy, like the church or the bridge near the dancehall, which make it unmistakable. I have no memories of being in such places, or seeing such strangely-shaped motor vehicles or such unspeakably unfashionably dressed people. Everything in it seems to be some kind of reaction to something that isn't visible, as though it is some kind of fancy-dress demonstration born of perverseness, a form of burlesque of spite against a past that cannot be imagined but is obviously repudiated.

This appears to be a continuous feature of the evolution of human history. The past has come to look like something mad, as though it has yet to come; the present gives the impression that we stopped being able to imagine the future sufficiently even to write one of those essays, because the future is already invading the present at a pace that makes our imagined vistas look old-fashioned before they've come into focus. And yet, our experience of the present is as a condition unhinged and revolting. Time has seemed to bolt, to go to seed, like a field of cabbages, so that nothing remains useful, or meaningful, or hopeful.

The roots of these tricks of time and chronology seem to begin with the increasing technologisation of everyday reality, a relatively new concept in the sense that the devices now available appear to confer greater and faster evolutionary possibilities on the quotidian life of the average human being. The difficulty here is not about the complexity or unknowability of technology, but the capacity of the imagination to grasp things that are not yet, as it were, 'discovered' — in the sense that we are still experimenting with the last generation of technology by the time the next one comes along. We have time — if even this — only to figure out the operational functioning of our devices before they become obsolete, but all the while, their cumulative effect is time-consuming, mind-changing, epoch-remaking, and existentially radicalising in ways that we have no time or capacity to imagine. Our present is constantly undermined by the contingency of waiting for inventions that have not yet happened but cannot be avoided, which will change everything . . . *again*. Like, say, if in the 1970s, a group of myself and my contemporaries had been shown a piece of film of a streetscape from 2023 with people walking around, with this indecipherable object glued to their ears, or held out in front of them like a prayerbook — how long would it have taken us to figure out what it was?

The other day I asked my four-year-old step-grandson, Kojak, what Twitter is, and he said: 'It's a place people go to send messages to people they don't know.'

Perfect, especially the part about it being a *place* and, even more so, the part about sending messages to 'people they don't know'. Such concepts would have been unthinkable when I was his age. (Elon Musk needs to talk to our Kojak!) But to most users, Twitter is just Twitter, a tautology. We spit out words as though we know what they mean when, at best we have only the flimsiest of understandings of their implications other than what we've gleaned from repeated hearings and our own repetitions of whatever we make of these.

Can you actually imagine what cyberspace is actually *like*? I mean, we know what it means — more or less: a kind of placeless place where words and images pass one another in something akin to space on their way between two people who have never met each other, or perhaps they have, but it doesn't change anything. All these memos and essays and prose poems and poetic poems and love letters and sexts and selfies and memes and immunology papers, all lightly bumping off one another — if they do — *en route* to an unimaginable number of destinations from an incomprehensible number of points of origin. But could you explain it to your grandmother? We comprehend cyberspace without understanding it. We imagine it, but in a fuzzy way that has no root or origin in, or relationship to, three-dimensional, concrete reality. Our imaginations are capable of assimilating this at least sufficiently for us to operate the relevant mechanisms, though probably no more. And yet, we cannot describe it, not in everyday sentences that provide the concepts that are necessary to comprehend it with the same level of concreteness as telling someone: 'I fell off my bicycle at the bad bend before the red bridge on the hill between the church and the post office.'

In a similar way, we talk impressively and blithely about transhumanism and the singularity and having our heads chipped by Elon and the forthcoming new utopia of non-sacred transcendence, but in truth, we literally do not know what we are talking about. We may use all the correct words and phrases, but we cannot imagine what this will be like, because it will not be 'like' anything we can currently imagine.

Consider this definition:

Transhumanism preaches the possibility of a technological enhancement of the human body, both through the use of technological prosthesis and by means of a life extension made possible by the use of genetics, biomedical engineering and nanotechnology. The ultimate goal of transhumanism is to completely overcome the need of a biological hardware through the integral fusion between man and machine made possible by mind-uploading, a technique that would pour out on a digital infrastructure the entire contents of the human mind.

The first sentence is relatively comprehensible. The second reads like nonsense.

But then, try thinking about trying to explain to your grandmother, even a decade ago, what transgenderism is. Yet, here it is, right up your street, and even your grandparents have to deal with it. I know, because I'm one of them, but at least I still have the capacity to know it is nonsense, whereas the ones who just have words to vaguely grasp its implications have other words with which to rationalise and accommodate to it: *'You have to move with the times.'*

The truth is that many things we take for granted in technological, technocratic reality are such that we feel compelled to accept and, in a sense, 'comprehend' them without actually understanding them or knowing how they work. Or, even if we do know how they work — in the sense that, perhaps as scientists or technologists, or just nerds or consumers, we know the lingo and the concepts and how they fit together, but how far into that reality does the understanding of all but a tiny few extend before they have to say something like, 'Nanotechnology wasn't part of my degree!'? Very often, when we delve into these areas, we employ metaphors and analogies to aid the process of explaining ourselves, or even explaining *to* ourselves. Perhaps we have always lived in worlds that are over our heads, but — over time — managed to arrive at conceptual accommodation with them, blithely trotting out words and phrases that communicate our sense of their general meaning, even though we may be unable to penetrate them beyond the first layer of their actual nature and configuration and implications, and in reality merely re-generating the object in the form of words that 'stand-in' for it without capturing or describing its essence.

The late French philosopher Jean Baudrillard was both a poet and a prophet, though — appropriately — in different senses to those normally conjured up by those words. He was a prophet not in that he predicted the future, but that he predicted the future of the future, so that he was able to move ahead of it and coin sentences to describe not just what he saw but what it might signify. He is often described as a 'postmodernist sociologist', but this he denied vociferously, just as he rejected the idea that he remained in later life a Marxist. He was, in fact, more of a poet than he was any of those things, although I do not believe he wrote a poem in his life, despite inspiring more than a few of them.

I think of Jean Baudrillard as a post-postmodernist in that he seeks to think his way to the very end of the nothingness that postmodernism presents, and perhaps build a new city on the other side. He seeks to draw our attention to the fact that everything is no longer how it seems — which is almost the same as saying that nothing is as it seems, though not quite: nothingness has moved closer to man.

The topography of reality is relatively unchanged, but its deep nature is utterly different to how we 'remember' and sense it. As a result of our preoccupation with the material — as in physical — world, the 'world as it is', we overlook that most of what frames our reality exists in the abstract, the fictional, the imaginative and the virtual.

His theory of the 'simulacrum' relates to his wider analysis that the capacity of mass media to scrutinise every event as it happens has frozen history in its tracks, creating a bad copy of reality, which we have moved into, lock, stock and wheelbarrow. The continuity of instant information has removed the temporal element by which history used to resolve matters as they unfolded, so that all sense of solidity has evaporated. There is no longer a past, present and future in which meaning can become visible, or appear to.

His style is superficially playful yet deeply serious underneath. His games are richly entertaining, but the enjoyment is tempered by the idea that these games are actually ways of seeing reality for what it actually is, or is now. Baudrillard rummages through culture in an attempt to discover elements which will make clear what has happened, attributing to them unexpected definitions which jolt us into a different way of looking or listening. Making music, for example, is 'eavesdropping on myself'. Poetry is a revealing 'trick' with language; it 'gives you more' but by means of what seems a sleight of hand as between the substance of language and the substance of the world, which actually bespeaks something real. The 'rules' of poetry are not arbitrary linguistics, but phonemic reflections of reality, creating 'harmonies of meaning'.

But he also distinguished between searching for meaning and finding it. He says that if we find meaning then we must have lost our heads completely, and must avoid being drawn into such follies, as if there was never such a thing as 'base reality' in the first instance arising from the metaphysical.

I suspect he is really seeking to justify an interpretation of reality in which he sees a metaphysical dimension, but only also as a simulacrum, a constructed metaphysics to meet the needs of an inadequate achievement of evolution. But this strikes me as an unfinished hypothesis, for it overlooks the necessity to define a point of origin. Yet, Baudrillard must, I believe, be placed in a different category to other deconstructionists, because although an 'atheist' himself he insists on the indispensability of metaphysics, albeit what he calls the 'bourgeois metaphysics of totality' — in other words a concept of language that includes the unknown and unknowable and aspires to capturing at least the sense of the human need for and 'fantasies' of such. He takes us a fair distance in the search for meaning before shrugging his shoulders as if to say, 'That's it!', but still we imagine he might have had more to say had he not died when he did (in 2007).

It is as a 'prophet' that we come to him here. He predicted the condition of the *now*, i.e. this moment in which you are reading this, but less in its specifics as in its general condition. Through the second half of the twentieth century, he recognised that the very essence of reality was about to change, or had already changed, under the attrition of technology, so that nothing we would henceforth encounter would be anything like what we had been used to, or what we might expect on that basis. By his own admission, he knew nothing of technology, but managed to see beyond the trees to the wood. His observations are, therefore, not really a function of foretelling, but of observational logic and poetic witnessing of the changes in culture and life that have accompanied the technological revolution.

He wrote in prose, but not in a manner suggested by the reductive implications of that word. Like all great poets, he never actually said what he was saying, but trusted the words to resonate with the time that would come after, which they did and continue to do. It is not possible to find a single sentence or paragraph in his work in response to which one might say, 'Ah! This is what he meant!', but the sense of what he means is to be harvested cumulatively through immersion in his words. Really, he is not talking about events or developments in the world so much as a relocation of the centre of gravity of the world, culturally speaking, so that it can no longer be regarded as the same world depicted by history, and literature, and even science, with the further implication that its denizens can no longer be comprehended sociologically, or psychologically, or even intuitively.

What he suggests, reduced to a sketch, is that, as a result of the operation of tech, networks, laptops, smartphones, the internet and, by implication, social media (though he died just as this was getting off the ground), reality as we knew it had ceased to be and had been replaced by a 'copy' of itself, which was nothing like the original. It is strange that, in writing this chapter, something similar happened to the text containing my descriptions of reality and of Baudrillardism. I am writing it on a laptop, which provides me with a running word count. For no particular reason, through no inclination or instruction of mine, the file on which I was working offered me the option of making a copy of itself. This might have been an alarming moment, because I had no way of knowing — other than reading the 7,000+ words I had written in both the copy and the original — which was the most complete of the two. I found the original and noted that it had 7,567 words; I checked the copy and saw that it had 7,633. I chose to continue with the copy, abandoning the original to the condition of fossil. Now, this chapter is a copy of itself, but larger than in the original, and this is something like what Baudrillard suggests has happened with reality and the state of my being within it.

We have entered, he says, a 'simulacrum' of reality. Because of the fracturing of reality by technology and technological communications, it has become impossible to restore coherent patterns to events that had been 'atomised' by virtue of being processed, circulated and re-broadcast to the point of timelessness.

Outside of certain postmodern circles, it is commonplace for public commentary to assume that reality is something fixed in particular foundations, and, therefore, a phenomenon that media simply describe or analyse in the form it takes standing there. Baudrillard (though not only him) takes a different view: that the object standing there is as much the creation of the descriptions and representations as it is of any concrete process of production, and Baudrillard would correct me: 'Much more'. The difficulty we have in comprehending this has to do with the relative slowness of the evolution from one form of reality to the other. Once upon a time, the object was indeed all there was; now, the object is merely a starting point, a fleeting entity that immediately becomes an image, and may no longer be there, or may have been, in the first place, an instrument of misdirection or a figment born of and reproduced by propaganda. Now, the image is all, and the imagination, therefore, is the best instrument for comprehending reality.

Such is the strength of irony soaking Baudrillard's prose that it is not possible to divine the precise location of his thinking in the spectrum stretching between metaphor and literalism. It seems clear that he is speaking metaphorically — but then again, perhaps not. He never states nor acknowledges that he is dealing in metaphor. Yet, nor does he fully explain the process by which such concepts as he depicts might have entered into reality as though material things, something that remains objectively unimaginable, if not impossible. But one thing we can say for certain is that his hypothesis, for all its fanciful aspects, offers an approximation of an explanation, or at least a contextualisation, for most of what is happening now, for what has been happening to us, for instance, in the past 40 months. The things occurring in 2023 that take our breath away if contemplated from the perspective of, say, 1989, are gradually becoming as though naturalistic. To elaborate on this sociologically, or psychologically, or politically, seems to get us nowhere except spinning around in the same circle. If we think that we have slipped out of time, then no other explanation is required. And, yet, our clocks still work as they did.

It is worth repeating for the sake of emphasis: It is hard to glean from Baudrillard's sentences how literally he intended his characterisation to be taken, or to grasp precisely the extent to which he may have meant them metaphorically, or even metaphysically — but the sense is that he is at least glancing off literalism. For someone who did not 'know much about the subject', he writes dazzlingly about the impact of technology on human consciousness and culture.

For Baudrillard, as a function of the forces he focused on, history had already ended. Picking a fight with the Italian writer, Elia Canetti, who in 1945, in the wake of the bombing of Hiroshima and Nagasaki, claimed that mankind had vacated history having rendered it unreal, but would one day return, Baudrillard declared such a restoration impossible. Canetti's view was that the bombings had eclipsed the Sun as the source of earthly human power: 'Light is dethroned, the atomic bomb has become the measure of all things. The tiniest thing has won: a paradox of power.' And yet, Canetti remained optimistic: Balance would again be restored.

Baudrillard thought differently. Because of the fracturing of reality by technology and technological communications, he insisted, it had become impossible to restore coherent patterns to events that had been 'atomised' by virtue of being processed, circulated and re-broadcast to the point of an unstable timelessness. The indifference of the majority of humanity to either meaning or content as other than distraction, had caused history to slow down and fall even further behind. Again, it is difficult to grasp precisely the extent to which he may have meant this metaphorically, but the sense is that, as always, he is at least glancing off literalism, because the imaginary is all that remains of the real. If only in some respects, reality is an imaginative construct. If you are able to persuade the majority that what is real is the way you describe it, you are halfway there. If you can furthermore construct the semblance of that reality, like a stage set, across the line of vision of the population, what is left to contradict your account of what reality is?

Under the attrition of the conditions Baudrillard intuited in the world as he read it, everything turns into a movie. Because everyone is nowadays conditioned to think of unfolding reality in this way, it is not difficult for would-be manipulators to impose themselves and their plans for the world. Accustomed to following three-act narratives, the people respond as though naturally to scripted versions of 'reality' — pseudo-realities, the new commodity of media.

Moreover, the tenor of events conveyed via technologies has become such as to create doubts concerning whether this content is even remotely credible, since the technical possibilities, and the quasi-perfection of the delivery, are such as to bring into question the existence of a source event — something humanly-generated behind the commodity that plops fully formed into my Inbox, for example — just as the perfection of stereophonic sound casts doubt that the music could have originated from an organic orchestra or performer. Since we cannot return to verify the source, we are cast into a netherworld between doubt and certitude, neither believing nor disbelieving, lacking either faith or scepticism. Baudrillard described this phenomenon decades before the onset of deepfakes.

'Oh right!' you may pipe up again, 'It's the Matrix.' Yes, but be careful! Baudrillard also precedes the Matrix in all its incarnations. He is the father and Godfather of The Matrix. His work it was that inspired the movies of that name, but, although involved at an early stage as an adviser, he later disowned the project as having departed from his intentions.

He did not foresee the total implications, however. As a metaphysical anarchist (though not a nihilist or an amoralist), he did not see any of this as necessarily representing a catastrophe. In a passage about the modern 'subject' in his book *Impossible Exchange*, he speaks — ironically, one hopes, but perhaps not — of the 'liberation' of the subject through technologies, networks, screens, causing him to become fractured, 'both subdivisible to infinity and indivisible, closed on himself and doomed to endless identity.'

If one wished to be prosaic and old-fashioned — i.e. working by the logic and methods of the departed world of 'reality' — one might plunge in and divine a series of 'sociological' explanations for the things he claims for the simulacrum and how things have played out since his death. You might say, for example, that among the effects of the past and future waves of technologisation is indeed, as he says, a form of 'liberation', but that the 'liberation' in question is one that tends towards chaos and disorder, and therefore may be the opposite of freedom. But why, how? Perhaps because that is the nature of power, of whatever form; perhaps because the nature of culture is to abhor a vacuum; perhaps because, in removing the children earlier from the supervision of their parents, popular technology renders them culturally feral — in a certain sense 'smarter' than their parents about things that matter only in the simulacrum, but which in time become the only things that matter to them — and therefore prone to manifesting de-civilising tendencies.

This sense of 'liberation' transmits itself through the culture, licensing changed behaviour by everyone implicated, so that soon only the hermit is left unaffected. At its core, the 'liberation' spoken of by Baudrillard had to do with the insinuated notion that the past had ended, history had ended, and therefore virtually — so to speak — everything that had mattered before no longer did, or mattered a great deal less than it had. The effect on the young afflicts the thinking and behaviour of parents, who also happen to be the lawmakers, judges, police officers, doctors and TV presenters. In general, these — though still recognisable as figures of authority — had long since sought the elusive quality of 'cool' on account of the inward pressure of the post-1960s culture, and so were rather easily persuaded. In as far as what has occurred can be communicated sociologically, this is about as much as needs to be said. Baudrillard barely, if ever, addressed these circumstances in sociological terms, but spoke always as though of a form of magic, probably because he knew that this was the way the effects and consequences were going to manifest in the world. What he did not so much predict was that it was going to be overwhelmingly a *black* magic, at least as it proceeded. Up to the time of his death the effects seemed to be precisely as he had predicted them; it is only in the past decade or so that the toxic, destructive nature of these phenomena has become clear.

So: At some uncertain point of rupture in the not-too-distant past, man ceased to live in reality but moved unknowingly, as though sucked into a black hole, a 'simulacrum' of the real — and yet lacking all but the most superficial similarities to it — a virtual world made of circuits and networks and pixels and memes, in which it was necessary for man to virtualise himself so as to cease to be a subject in the old sense with an 'I' and a soul, and become as a unit of the crowd. The 'perfect' subject of the simulacrum, Baudrillard writes, is an individual who has also a mass status — as a particle of the mob outside his window. He is 'the dispersal of the mass effect into each individual parcel . . . Or, alternatively, the individual himself forms a mass — the mass structure being present, as in a hologram, in each individual fragment. In the virtual and media worlds, the mass and the individual are merely electronic extensions of one another.'

Again, we may try to translate: 'Ah, The crowd! Mass formation.' Yes, of course — but . . .

Man fragments into many and becomes a crowd, which in turn becomes as though an individual mind. This is somewhat close to the characterisations of Gustave Le Bon, almost a full century before Baudrillard. But Baudrillard proposes an additional possibility: Technology creates a fragmentation that (simultaneously?) afflicts both the crowd and the individual, as though the quantum structure — which previously defined the individual only — has somehow become an equally functional description of the crowd. The individual no longer exists, though the presumption of his existence persists, because he leaves footprints and seems to be standing there. But in 'reality', according to Baudrillard, there is no one there. Now there are only crowds, but for the moment, the constituent 'elements' (humans) presume themselves to be as they were: separate and independent.

All this happens at the level of apprehension by the imagination, which is really the only reality we can know. What is real is what is capable of being imagined, and this is more concrete than what is true, or concrete. Baudrillard draws distinctions between 'reality' (what has disappeared) and 'the real', which replaces it.

A simulacrum is not the same as a fake. The simulacrum is hyper-real, which is to say it is realer than reality, which is abolished in the process of the simulacrum's creation. It is, says Baudrillard, 'the generation by models of a real without origin or reality.' It is the map without a territory; the map is all there is, the territory may as well never have existed before the map, and probably didn't — 'and nor does it survive it'. The map precedes the territory, which is abolished. We live in the map, imagining it is reality, whereas there is no longer a reality and only the map is real. The simulacrum is a space in which there is no difference between 'true' and 'false', or between 'the real' and 'the imaginary'. There is no difference between a person simulating insanity and an insane person, and, by the same token, no difference between a politician stating something he claims to be true and a politician telling the truth, for once he has stated it, it becomes true.

The real has been replaced by the *signs* of the real, which are more convincing than the real, on account of there no longer being any distinction between the real and the imaginary. This presents a strange involution of thinking: It is implicit in everything Baudrillard writes on this subject that he is addressing the condition of culture, and it is in this sense that he seeks to parse the meanings of 'reality', 'the real', the 'fake' and 'the simulacrum'. Culture is the only real phenomenon, because what we believe becomes what we know, which becomes the only truth that counts. Whatever emerges from this cultural schemozzle will be all the reality we can know. Thus, when Baudrillard speaks of the conflation of 'the real' and 'the imaginary', he is defining the precise nature of the role of the imagination — collective and individual (insofar as this remains relevant) — of humanity, and in doing so saying that what we imagine, or are brought to imagining, will be the reality that imprisons us. Just as there is no difference in 'reality' between 'the real' and 'the imaginary', so too with Baudrillard's hypothesis, which concerns the imagination but, in doing so, defines the (new) 'real'. The only evidence of 'the real' is in what we imagine for ourselves about what reality is, which has *ipso facto* become the sole actually existing reality.

This (new) 'reality' emerges, as though spontaneously, from the viscera of postmodernity. The 'real', says Baudrillard, is produced 'from miniaturized cells, matrices, and memory banks, models of control — and it can be produced an indefinite number of times from these. It no longer needs to be rational because it no longer measures itself against either an ideal or negative instance. It is no longer anything but operational.'

This observation contains enormous resonances for what has happened to politics, government and the rule of law in our countries in recent years, but especially in the past 40 months.

Baudrillard's essential thesis centres on the idea that the effects of technological and communicational developments had been such as to move the function of mass media from tracking, or — more often — concealing reality, to actually generating reality. This is what he refers to as 'simulation', a process of constant reproducing of reality out of the signs, codes and models of media, filtering in turn the signs, codes and models of politics, ideology, science, medicine, et cetera. This has been achieved mainly through the use of digital technologies, whose binary nature serves to subdivide the world (i.e., mostly its population) into two essential elements (my speculation: originals and copies, thinkers and repeaters, purebloods and cyborgs, et cetera). These processes he saw as forms of forgery, mirroring those of medieval monks copying texts from ancient manuscripts, the mass production processes that followed from Frederick Taylor's streamlining of the production line, Andy Warhol's work with repetitive multiples of iconic images, and modern devices like the camera, the photocopier and the scanner — and, of course, the internet.

Baudrillard's chief preoccupation is with considering the effects of these processes on the subjectivity of the individual. The shift from object to image (i.e. a visual recording of an object or person) changed the human perception of reality. This, he argued, was moving us out of reality, in which everything was

as it appeared, into hyperreality, in which everything was whatever we imagined it to be. Hyperreality is the world of the viral, the fractal, the exponential
and the metastatic, an infinitely dividable reality in which reason and comprehension depend on managing the speed at which the material of reality shifts —
i.e. a coping with constant chaos and change, with an endlessly repeated reissuing of images and facts, in which instability is the natural order and for which
the generation of cancerous cells within the human body presents the most
appropriate metaphor. In this, writing up to half a century ago, Baudrillard
anticipated the algorithm and the neural network, which today evince the
impression of being no more than the vindication of his theory: programmed
mechanisms capable of simulating intelligence, cognition and even sentience,
but which remake reality moment-to-moment according to formulae that even
those human agents that create them are unable to predict as to their logics,
actions or effects.

Here we come to Baudrillard's insistence that all this can alter not merely
facts but ethics and reason as well. The problem here is that, although the
machine may be designed by a human intelligence, the 'magic' of the algorithm
may confer capacities greater than the sum of the inputs. If the programmer
primes the machine with an 'ethical' programme, and adds in a number of
layers of additional coding, ascribing weightings to various moral and ethical
factors, the programme enables the machine, on the basis of an instantaneous
scrutiny of comparative data, to 'think' about situations that had not occurred to
the programmer, perhaps because they were not yet even possibilities at the
time of installing the programme. The impenetrable, indivisible algorithm has
already ushered in an undeclared era of hermetically-sealed, instant decision-
making, in which the outcomes of life-changing human decisions may be
decided by software that writes itself and algorithms with the capacity to
outgrow the intelligence of their creators. These processes can only take forms
that are arbitrary and summary, which means that the future cannot possibly be
otherwise. The even stranger thing is that, even in advance of the algorithm
gaining a total hold on human culture in this way, many of the human actors
governing our societies and their cultures appeared to ape these tendencies
without ever having observed them in action. Hence, the lying automaton of the
Covid era who claims to be 'saving lives' while ordering the mass slaughter of
the elderly to maintain an adequate level of scare porn; the pathocratic politician
who evinces 'compassion' for fraudulent migrants while destroying the hopes of
his own people; the journaliar who had misled his audience for 40 months
appearing at a public demonstration about media salaries with a placard
declaring that 'Truth matters'.

Baudrillard says: 'The universe of simulation is transreal and transfinite: no
test of reality will come to put an end to it — except the total collapse and slip-
page of the terrain, which remains our most foolish hope.'

In the hyper-real world, all shade and subtlety are lost, because the binary is the sole measure of distinction and definition. The 'real' is merely a series of ones and zeros. Even God can be simulated, and this means that the world is no longer a world created by God, but by those capable of simulating God. This involution is the core of what is happening to us now. In a world after God, all things are permissible.

Baudrillard is sometimes dismissed as a fake philosopher who creates webs of words that mean little or nothing. But the test is whether what he says makes us feel a correspondence with what we experience more compelling than any of the 'rational' explanations, and he passes this test every time — and with colours that fly better with every passing day. Perhaps he is not really a philosopher at all — but rather a seer into the meanings of things. But what's the difference, since most 'real' philosophers have already vacated both the territory and the map?

I would say that Baudrillard is the first and most comprehensive prophet of totally secularised reality, in the sense that he has announced the core meaning of a world not created by God. This is not to suggest that God did not create the world — for the purposes of this analysis, that question remains an open one — but Baudrillard announces a world in which God's intentions, laws, even His materials, have been usurped and superseded by a world in which man has become . . . not the god he imagines, but a highly proficient forger of reality, whose reign must be acknowledged and accepted until it comes to triumph or, more likely, grief.

In a 1995 essay, *The Double Extermination* (about the WWII Holocaust, but this is not the immediate resonance that interests me), Baudrillard spoke of the delusional nature of mankind's sense of its own relationships with the virtual, which is presumed to be some kind of tool to extend human power over reality, but (in reality) is something altogether else.

'Today, we do not think the virtual, the virtual thinks us. And to us this elusive transparency, which separates us definitively from the real, is as unintelligible as is the windowpane to the fly which bangs against it without understanding what separates it from the outside world. The fly cannot even imagine what is setting this limit on its space. Similarly, we cannot even imagine how much the virtual — as though running ahead of us — has already transformed all the representations we have of the world. We cannot imagine this, for it is the particularity of the virtual that it puts an end not just to reality, but to the imagining of the real, the political and the social; not just to the reality of time, but to the imagining of the past and the future (this is what is known, in a kind of black humour, as "real time"). So we are far from having understood that information's entry on the scene spelt an end to the unfolding of history, that the coming of artificial intelligence spelt an end to thought, etc. The illusion we still harbour about all these traditional categories — including our illusion of

"opening ourselves up to the virtual", as if it were a real extension of all potentialities — is the illusion of the fly unflaggingly banging up against the windowpane. For we still believe in the reality of the virtual, whereas the virtual has
already virtually scrambled all the pathways of thought.'

Later in the same essay, he re-emphasises the extent to which everything —
politics, sociology, history, thought — has become virtualised:

'The social, the political, the historical — even the moral and psychological
— there are no longer any but virtual events within all these categories. This
means it is useless searching for a politics of the virtual, an ethics of the virtual,
etc., since it is politics itself which is becoming virtual, ethics itself which has
become virtual, in the sense that both politics and ethics are losing the principles
governing their action, losing their force of reality. And this even applies where
technology is concerned: we speak of "technologies of the virtual", but the truth
is that there are now only — or there will soon only be — virtual technologies.
Now, there can no longer be any notion of artifice in a world in which thought
itself, intelligence, is becoming artificial. It is in this sense that we can say that it
is the Virtual which thinks us, not the other way around.'

This implies that such as politics and ethics are things of a past that becomes
a receding and beguiling memory, which would go some way to 'explaining'
some of the things we have been witnessing for the past 40-odd months: the
sudden break into amorality by politicians, the silent abolition of nations and
laws, the tyrannification of police forces, the outright corruption of judiciaries,
the flipping of media models from approximate truth-telling to outright and
ceaseless lying. And, here in what passes for a present, just as the 1970 Ford
Escort seems simultaneously to resemble both a spaceship and a gangling jalopy
when parked in a contemporary streetscape, and looks like it was designed as
some kind of defiant response to a 1960s Ford Prefect or Popular, so the value
system of the emerging reality is being formulated as the antithesis of what
came before. In this dispensation, good becomes bad; bad, good; pervert,
paragon; up, down; in, out; truth, lie; liar, fact-checker. This is why things feel so
weird, why words have run out of road. We move in a new world, while imagining we live in a continuum from the old.

Such insight into reality may remain elusive for many because the new
constructs sprout, as though organically, from older, more stable ones, inheriting
and adopting the modes and codes of these to an extent that enables them to
pass for naturalistic continuations into a new era that promises only good
things. The habits of existence in linear time have insinuated a continuous plausibility that survives the most radical alterations of direction and character, and
somehow, in the imagination of a majority, the transition is unnoticed. Standing
on the foundations of the old model, the present edifices appear as simply a
modernised version of the same basic idea as before, whereas they are, in fact,
something utterly novel, without precedent, good or bad. Edifices of trust

constructed multiple generations ago, and handed down with joy and pride, have been inherited by inhabitants of an entirely different world, in which the operational 'ethic' is to bleed everything for instant profit and to regard human beings as a superfluous irritant, unless they are immediately useful, which mostly they are not. Moreover, our habit of associating concepts, by way of analogy, with the material world continues to beguile us into waiting for this (new) world to stabilise itself according to the old (immutable?) rules.

There is also, Baudrillard warns, something dangerously therapeutic about this new world. Andy Warhol remarked that 'the more you look at the same exact thing . . . the better and emptier you feel.' He was referring to the repetitious nature of popular culture, which he leveraged for the purposes of both commentary and exploitation. His belief about the emotional benefits of repeated viewing led him to repeat images in his own artworks. We look upon his Marilyn Monroes and instantly feel that they are 'iconic' of a time when repetition was a virtue, perhaps the only one. Now, we live in an incomprehensible world in which the familiarity bred by repetition of half-remembered sensations is the only thing that gives us peace.

CHAPTER 30
THE ABOLITION OF REALITY, PART II: KINKY TOTALITARIANISM
31-07-2023

'Through an unforeseen turn of events . . . it is from the death of the social that socialism will emerge, as it is from the death of God that religions emerge.'
— Jean Baudrillard

T he 'liberation of the networks' to which Jean Baudrillard referred is not a technical freedom. The technological aspects are not disputed, but are a given, baked (or fried) into the combination of capacitors, microchips, motherboard, processing unit, hard disk, pendrive, software, and random access memory, otherwise RAM, that constitute the 'computer'. An equally critical element of computer systems, all the gearheads seem to agree, is the 'liveware', which includes the programmers and systems analysts, but also the 'end users', who engage and interact with the computer to give it its life and content. It is the end-user liveware who experience the 'freedom' offered by the networks.

It is not, by definition, an analogue freedom, and this may offer us a clue as to how the meaning of freedom became distorted to the extent that people calling themselves 'liberals' no longer regard it as a vital quantity, while the words to describe it remain unmodified and in use. The 'liberation of the networks' is neither existential nor metaphysical, at least not in the old senses. It is not a freedom of the spirit, but of the emotions and the instincts. It is the freedom of the addict, not of the questioner or investigator. It is the freedom to be free, on the terms of a ring-fenced ideology, rather than the freedom to simply *be*. In other words, it is a freedom of concepts and sensations, rather than of the imagination — of the gut and below, rather than the heart and above. Its

THE ABOLITION OF REALITY   415

cardinal quality is of a particular category that might be defined as 'freedom to enjoy', or 'freedom of the flesh', 'freedom of the impermissible', freedom to fulminate, to pontificate, to trumpet, to rant. It is a freedom that trashes commandments as the arbitrary impositions of the bearded old, destroys taboos without asking why they arose, and removes the intimate from the private realm and places it in the public square. In this liberation, the pubic becomes public, and becomes amplified beyond prudery or shame by the networks, which neither exhibit nor tolerate either quality, and announce this disavowal with pride.

What this artfully excludes is the core of freedom, previously understood, albeit implicitly — unspokenly — as the freedom to proceed through reality unimpeded — by one's own lights, but also on the path suggested by the facts and circumstances. This is the freedom to 'be' in 'the world', to move, to explore, to advance, to aspire, to attain, to yearn — and yet to hold all these impulses in abeyance in the knowledge that no such trajectory is capable of achieving total correspondence with the propelling drive or desire. What the liberation of the networks is *not* is freedom to proceed, in any direction, towards the horizon, as the intuited destination-point of the human journey, this being the most fundamental, nomadic instinct of the human person — to walk purposefully towards the skyline with a light regard for wherever one passes through, always conscious that the driving disposition of the human is to move through this dimension on the way to some indeterminate place, which may be named or unnamed, but is either way unknowable. This is, at its core, the meaning of religious experience: the creation of an imaginative accompaniment to the journeying of the subject in 'moving through' reality in a manner that defines the optimal demeanour of the human, on the way to another, intuited, imagined, place.

It is striking that, in the lockdown of 2020, what was targeted was not the freedom to, for example, fornicate, even though that might have been deemed a likely source of transmission, or the right to abort an inconvenient child, or even the right to riot (provided that the rioting was directed at targets other than the Regime), but the right to proceed more than a specific distance. It was as though each citizen had been shackled to a particular point in the world — usually his home — by a chain of, depending on the jurisdiction, 2 kilometres in length, or 5, so as to — as though precisely — prevent him from advancing towards the horizon.

If there is a single factor that defines and explains the shift that has occurred in the world, it is the adoption of network freedom as the only true kind, and the downgrading of the 'freedom to advance across reality' to the point where mention of it provokes only puzzlement. And, in the absence of this understanding of human existence, reality itself has disappeared and is being replaced by a counterfeit. This, essentially, is what I take from Baudrillard's 'simulacrum'.

The liberation of the networks is crude, indulgent, unrestrained, grotesque, gross, lewd. It bears no resemblance to technology, and yet, as Baudrillard comprehended, is indissolubly married to it. It is a purging of everything inherited, a colossal incontinence that takes the greatest pride in its dissoluteness. It represents the inversion of transcendence and the obliteration of the metaphysical. It is the embracing of chaos to the point where the New World Order that it signifies ought properly be called the New World Disorder.

Perhaps, if he were still with us, Baudrillard might, at this stage, as was his wont, inform me that what I describe is not synonymous with his thesis. Not only would I have to accept this correction, but would do so gladly, for I am not sure that even Baudrillard understood his own hypothesis, and being permitted to 'borrow' his hypothesis for these chapters, regardless of their grasp of his ideas, is extremely invaluable in communicating the otherwise inexplicable. Even if I misunderstand him, that misunderstanding is transcended by the fact that what I divine from his words appears to provide a map for the present in ways that I do not believe he anticipated.

As I said in the last chapter, I don't take Baudrillard literally, in that I do not imagine that he is talking about some kind of deliberately constructed — silicon brick by silicon brick — digital prison. I think he is talking in parables, in which he is saying that the effects that he appears to describe us as experiencing are 'like' this or 'like' that. I believe he is silently saying, almost before every sentence, 'It is as though . . .'

In a sense, then, his concept of the simulacrum is more of a simile than a metaphor. He is not talking about the conventional idea of a 'simulation' — a computer-generated illusory universe in which we exist only as holograms. I shy away from the idea that he is talking about a world resulting from an alien experiment, or a teleported construction of future humanoids, sent spinning backwards through time; or some kind of quantum coup driven from CERN, or someplace; or some cosmic silicon-heavy giant sitting in dark space in his underpants, trying to decide if he'll wipe me out with a spot of quantum retro causality magic, or just have me run over by a bus. I believe, as I said in the last chapter, that Baudrillard, a poet above all else, is talking about culture in the only way he can manage to explain its behaviours as he sees them. In a way, I believe his hypothesis is akin to the way that I have come to see the possibility that what I fear will become indistinguishable from 'intelligent' or 'sensate' algorithms: I do not literally believe that it is possible for a computer to become sensate or conscious or 'more intelligent than humans', but I do believe an algorithm or neural network is capable of being programmed with behavioural intelligence and multiple-layered data to render it capable of replicating the condition of an intelligent or sensate being in a manner that might be impossible to distinguish from an actual such human. As with this hypothesis, Baudrillard's simulacrum evolves not in the manner of a biological organism, but in the processing of information in such a way that the computational outcomes look cannily organic. I don't see this as a 'simulation'. I think I am closer to Thomas Sheridan's idea of the Vedic concept of the 'Maya' — a 'consensus illusion' that we all share, except that I would say we do not so much create the phenomenal world as an illusion but that we render it 'real' by virtue of our consensual observation and description of what we 'perceive'. I think there may be some elements of this in Baudrillard's thinking, although he strikes me as an implacable atheistic sceptic of supernatural notions of transcendence. In this context, his 'simulacrum' is an altered perception of reality, and accordingly, a de facto altered reality, which (I'm guessing) most likely erupted out of 1960s notions of freedom and was amplified and accelerated by the explosion of popular tech from the late 1990s onwards. There is, therefore, in the simulacrum, an insinuation of cultural forces meeting technological forces to create something not self-evidently implicit in either. Humanity has control of the simulacrum in a cultural sense only, which is to say that it can adjust the simulacrum through cultural initiatives and modifications or reinventions of tech forms. There are no 'controls' other than the process of human existence and being, and those governing amplification and acceleration. We can 're-simulate' by acts of cultural intervention, psychic overtures, and possibly even some forms of spells. But mostly, our interventions take the more modest, prosaic forms of the kinds of attacks on human consciousness represented by a novel, a movie, a poem, an essay, or even an article or interview.

In this sense, the conditions I seek to nail in this essay are not especially esoteric, and certainly not in the realm of woo. I seek to forge sentences that might resonate with the way others may be experiencing the things I see and feel. What confronts us is a culture that has altered radically under the attrition of ideological clamouring and wholesale misuses of power — including celebrity power, banking power, judicial power, media power, with political power merely following what appeared to be a winning programme. To a high degree, what we seem to be talking about here is the expedited construction or reconstruction, in a matter of weeks or months, of cultural edifices that might normally take decades or even centuries to build or remodel. In some respects, the simulacrum is useful only up to a point in explicating this phenomenon, which, as I keep saying, is overwhelmingly cultural in the manner in which it makes landfall on our awareness. What I seek to articulate is really a way of obtaining emotional traction in reality at the level of imagination, rather than engagement with concrete, physical, material reality, which is how we have mostly been prone to think about questions of changing reality hitherto.

An equally useful but limited metaphor might be that of 'The Longhouse', a concept I confess I first encountered in a *First Things* article titled 'What Is the Longhouse?' from last February, written by Jonathan Keeperman, under an alias of L0m3z.

The article has been among the online edition of the magazine's 'most read' for the past six months, something that, as far as I know, is unprecedented, as articles normally fade away in a couple of weeks. I can see why: The article, though it leaves much unexplained or unelaborated, is fascinating. Rereading it again recently, I was struck by the idea that, from another angle, it contains many of the elements arising from the current 'Situation' that I am identifying in Baudrillard's simulacrum.

ChatGPT tells me that The Longhouse is:

A traditional style of dwelling historically used by various indigenous peoples, particularly those of the Haudenosaunee (Iroquois) and other Native American tribes in North America. It is a long and narrow building made of wood and covered with bark or thatch. Longhouses were communal living spaces, accommodating extended families or multiple families within the same structure. These structures played a significant role in their culture and social life, serving as homes, meeting places, and centers for community activities.

Keeperman asserts that The Longhouse was not a dwelling place, but more of a gathering space for a tribe in which it ventilates matters of concern and tries to resolve disputes by consensus. It seems to have functioned a little like a church — a linear, long, narrow building — and yet was not a religious building, more a town hall or a substitute for what, in modern society, became the role of the café. To an extent, the concept appears to collapse the distinction we have had in Western societies, whereby the temple / church was the sole building in the village / city you might enter without 'permission', and yet was a separate and quite different place to the home. Each Longhouse was different to all others, reflecting the unique sensibilities and characteristics of a particular tribe, family or community. It represented a worldview and way of life, a spirituality, a connectedness with nature and the infinite / eternal, but also a way of seeing the world outside the family, community or tribe. The Longhouse was the focal point of the pre-colonial tribal world, and was to be found in cultures as diverse as those of the American Indians and in countries including Afghanistan, Japan, India, Burma, Thailand, and Cambodia. The most notable examples are those built by cultures such as the Iban in Borneo, the Gogodala in New Guinea, the Vikings in Norway and Denmark and the Iroquois in North America's lower Great Lakes region.

I am open to the idea that what I seek to pursue in these chapters is at least partially accessible by this avenue also. Perhaps what I have in mind, though triggered by Baudrillard's characterisations of the atmosphere of his simulacrum, is an ideological simulacrum, a governing programme of ideas or thoughts that might furnish the 'Longhouse' of a society in a manner that suggests continuity while representing rupture.

Keeperman, adapting the concept to the modern moment, elaborates:

'Maybe this term means nothing to you. Even for those of us who use it, the

Longhouse evades easy summary. Ambivalent to its core, the term is at once politically earnest and the punchline to an elaborate in-joke; its definition must remain elastic, lest it lose its power to lampoon the vast constellation of social forces it reviles. It refers at once to our increasingly degraded mode of techno-cratic governance; but also to wokeness, to the "progressive", "liberal", and "secular" values that pervade all major institutions. More fundamentally, the Longhouse is a metonym for the disequilibrium afflicting the contemporary social imaginary.'

The author sees the concept historically in a frame much wider than that supplied by ChatGPT — as a building only in a metaphorical sense, but moreso as a cultural storehouse of values of 'peoples throughout the world that were typically more sedentary and agrarian.' The household was a corporate group, and the Longhouse was a home, a kind of parliament, a court and an office of social organisation. It was here that the tribe resolved disputes in which indi-vidual autonomy came in conflict with collective identity.

Really, the term 'Longhouse' refers to the locus of a community possessed of common ideals and objectives, seeking to live together on the basis of consen-sus. In a 'modern' society, the term might be used — and Keeperman uses it — to describe a nation being carried along by a virtually coercive 'belief' system imposed by majority rule or propaganda or tacit state diktats. In the old Long-house, members could 'vote with their feet' — i.e. leave to join another commu-nity. Thus, while the article is interesting, it is by no means a perfect analogy. Although I am not sure how much of Keeperman's thesis is original to him, or whether this concept has already been adapted to the modern context, the hypothesis offered by the *First Things* article, though intriguing and compelling, seems also somewhat stretched, though perhaps no more than my own use of Baudrillard's simulacrum. And yet, it is extremely interesting and relevant.

In our 'modern' context, the author asserts:

'More than anything, the Longhouse refers to the remarkable overcorrection of the last two generations toward social norms centering feminine needs and feminine methods for controlling, directing, and modeling behavior. Many from left, right, and center have made note of this shift. In 2010, Hanna Rosin announced "The End of Men." Hillary Clinton made it a slogan of her 2016 campaign: "The future is female." She was correct.'

It is clear already that the Jonathan Keeperman thesis is a great deal removed from that of Baudrillard, and yet it outlines some elements that might be inserted without difficulty into the simulacrum hypothesis. The modern Amer-ican Longhouse (contrary to the incessant discourse implying continuing discrimination and inequality) is dominated by women and female thinking. The same is true for all European societies, certainly the Western parts. This implies a profound, unacknowledged change of culture and values. It means that, for example, principles of justice have been altered in their very fundamentals, and not in the ways that were comprehensively anticipated. From this new culture has emerged concepts like political correctness, victimology, affirmative action, trigger warnings, 'protected characteristics', cancel culture, the shift from reason to feelings, Safetyism, the 'Karen' phenomenon, and so forth. The modern Longhouse is ruled by The Omnipotent Victim, and this has made all but inevitable the 'success' of, for example, the Covid coup, which pivoted on the notion of risk avoidance, a maternal quality and preoccupation.

Keeperman continues:

'The implications of the Longhouse reach yet further across the social landscape. The Longhouse distrusts overt ambition. It censures the drive to assert oneself on the world, to strike out for conquest and expansion. Male competition and the hierarchies that drive it are unwelcome. Even constructive expressions of these instincts are deemed toxic, patriarchal, or even racist. . . . It is the same for the arts. Woke obsession with diversity and inclusion, the rise of "sensitivity readers", and racial quotas in film, overshadows the equally insidious fact that so much of what passes for "high" culture has devolved into dreary, toothless portrayals of static lives. There is a failure of imagination on all sides. The right's retreat into the classics, while edifying, will not supply the modern symbols and narratives necessary to guide us out of the Longhouse.'

Keeperman concludes:

'We must resist the soft authoritarianism of the Longhouse's weepy moralism. We must not succumb to hysterical pleas for more safety, more consensus, more sensitivity. Ennobling work awaits us. But we must first recognize the Longhouse for what it is and be willing to leave its false comforts behind.'

Something highly germane to all this that Keeperman does not consider is that these may not be organic processes, but orchestrated initiatives calculated to exert immense and radical pressures upon the world and its population, and achieve unprecedented changes that together are as far from liberation and the associated ideals of democracy, that can be imagined. In other words, what confronts us is not at all — at least not in its conception — the fruits of agitation for equality, but of hidden expressions of power that most of the human population have never countenanced as even existing. For that matter, neither did Baudrillard appear to detect the presence of a watchful, conspiratorial force in the world, a force that, for perhaps decades if not centuries, had been feeding certain stimuli into the cultures of the more advanced societies, which, in the increasingly mass media-saturated world, was by the change of the millennium amounting to almost the entire globe. It is understandable: He did not want either to enter into the world of the prosaic, to become embroiled in facts that, by their nature, would make his hypothesis an ugly or convoluted one. Yet, for us it is important to understanding: From this malevolent source of manipulation came the material out of which the new world would be forged — sexual freedom, rights specific to minorities, climate change, critical race theory, *et cetera*. As the manifestations of these phenomena began to ramp themselves up, the political class, having already forfeited all power, jumped immediately to cling to the back of the bandwagon.

The Longhouse, no more than the simulacrum, is not a perfect instrument or motif, but, in considering the forces that have overcome our nations in the past 40 months, it is helpful to have in mind some definite location in which 'culture happens', even, as here, a quasi-metaphorical place functioning as both temple and house, where the public and the private might happen as though inextricable, one from the other. Though the traditional longhouse was spiritual (not religious per se), the modern one is predominantly sensual/sexual in that it leverages physical desire as the ultimate human satisfaction and destination.

Now, in our societies, in the place where 'culture happens' — no matter how we may seek to describe or define it — very strange and unprecedented things are happening. One could start almost anywhere, but let's start with politics, the organising system of our cultures, and consider what has happened to the process of representation.

Baudrillard, writing in 2001, spoke of a 'silent insurrection' in modern society, among the symptoms of which he identified 'a refusal to be represented' (he meant politically). He had in mind a refusal arising from the technologisation of modern life and the consequent alienation of the human person from a sociological reality that, in the simulacrum, rings ever falser. Some two decades later, his analysis reveals itself as prophecy. Caught between the real and the virtual, the modern inhabitant of cyberspace is no longer representable in the old way. Politics and the freedom offered by democracy have revealed themselves, in this diagnosis, as 'bit-part playing and a shabby hoax', for many cyber-savvy young people a 'doltish activity' in which they have no interest. The liberation of the networks is a better bet.

More alarmingly, Baudrillard talked about a strain of humanity that had moved beyond freedom, meaning and even identity, to a 'place' where human beings become as subjects of a new order, continuing to use the language of politics but no longer recognising its purpose or usefulness in their lives. Ideas like 'running the country' or 'envisioning the future' are alien to them because they believe that, like their iPhones and laptops, 'the country' is somehow looked after, or looks after itself, and the future will be there waiting for them when they get there. They seem to envisage a democracy run along the same lines as a Google search: a random series of benefits tailormade to their needs and delivered like baguettes hanging on their door knockers when they awake from their dreams or nightmares. 'What interest,' asks Baudrillard, 'does the modern individual have in being represented — the individual of the networks and the virtual, the multifocal individual of the operational sphere? He does his business, and that is that.'

Sure enough, the young as we encounter them in our families and neighbourhoods seem to be unreachable, mainly because they no longer live in the 'real' world, but as though in a form of Baudrillardian simulacrum, in which technological values rule and the main obsession is creating and defending your 'identity' so you can keep on killing rather than getting killed.

Once, teenage boys collected election leaflets in the manner of football cards, but nowadays most people under 40 could scarcely tell you the name of their Minister for Justice. They don't care. And yet, as though paradoxically, they will acquiesce in some particular abuse or injustice conducted by the same Minister for Justice, provided that her reasoning is rooted not in history or legal jargon, but in the ideological sci-fi world they imagine themselves to inhabit in the present, and so long as she delivers her diktats while dressed in rainbow colours and appropriately-sculpted shades.

There is something strange here, something that erupted in plain sight in the middle of 2020 in the demeanour of many young people towards the tyranny of lockdown and its sundry associated 'mandates': Not only did they not seem to object, but they even seemed to like it. Further observation of the responses of the young to the machinations and demeanours of such as Macron, Trudeau, Varadkar, Ardern and Sturgeon suggested something new and freaky: Today's voters might be open to entering into a kind of sadomasochistic relationship with their rulers provided they are allowed to think of it as just a game and are never bored. The pain they 'enjoy' is not of the physical kind, but relates to the idea of being dominated by a figure evincing some form of perverted sexual energy, a form of punitive domination combined with what was almost a form of 'cuckolding' in respect of their hitherto inalienable right to freedom.

Things that seem to bore the young include: historical facts, economic theories, arcane explanations for why things are as they are, and justifications for action rooted in constitutional jargon rather than 'compassionate' ideological language. Constitutions mean about as much to such beings as rolls of kitchen towels. History is too complex and complicated and . . . boring. Economics is incomprehensible, and pointless. Immunology might as well be Double Dutch. If it seems weird to be leaving these subjects to the kinds of people who generally tend to 'go into' politics, then consider the question as to whom else, in the modern world, might they be 'left to'. In a world where 'expertise' is increasingly fragmented between ever-shrinking and unconnected disciplines, only the politician is 'qualified' (by being there, occupying an ancient, elevated position that no longer has power) to speak across the disciplines, make a definitive statement and announce a remedy by way of decision which becomes mandatory by default. A strange paradox of the modern disposition towards politicians is that, in a time when they have been stripped of all authority and power, and are loathed and despised in a manner never before experienced, they have become more and more like a secular, if not an occult, priesthood of science. Paradoxically, the young dislike their politicians while finding it easy to 'love' them (in the 'loving Big Brother' sense), to submit to them, to be their slaves and bitches. This is due to a little-remarked element in the ether of public culture today that was not there before: a latent frisson of only slightly repressed sexual perversion, mainly arising from the sexual fixation of modern ideologies, the levels of pornography that have been just a click away from 'reality' for more than two decades, and the absence, since the abolition of God, of a more fundamental focus of desire. This aspect has been amplified by the presence of more and more women in positions of power— often quite unpleasant women, like Jacinda Ardern and Nicola Sturgeon and Ursula von der Leyen. Today's electorates may not admire or respect their politicians, but they relish them almost in the roles of kinky gaolers, who implement their ideological choices while simultaneously exercising the whip hand. Totalitarianism, couched in the demeanour of BDSM, reveals itself as an acceptable mode of tyranny because it has the appearance of consensual role-playing while being driven by a deeply resolute purpose, which in turn accentuates the 'appeal'. That it is, in almost every conceivable sense, a playing of roles does nothing to mitigate the risk of misadventure, since in the 'game' being played there are no limits or safe-words. In truth, the function of the media as destroyers of meaning (see below) ensures that the absence of reality or realism makes this circumstance even more fraught than either a genuine tyranny or a 'genuine' role-play.

Back in the spring of 2020, the politicians — it goes without saying — did not think in terms of culture or Longhouse or simulacrum, but picked up stray signs of a change in the wind, to which their trade, by nature and necessity, has always been alert. They did not waste time pondering upon the old — who could be relied upon to remain tribal or so marooned in their out-of-touchness as not to notice or react to a shift in the direction of party or policy. It was with the young — the future — that the urgency lay. What emerged was not a shift rooted in any deep understanding — by virtually anybody — of what was occurring. The politicians followed the young, who followed the propaganda; the technologically-illiterate old, having lost all sense of authority over the nature of reality, followed the young and the politicians. Again, what began to unfold can be crudely described in these mechanistic terms, at least sufficiently to indicate that it had some form of rational basis — but in reality, it manifested as a form of alchemy, some strange, unprecedented shifting of the Earth on its axis, some magical transformation born of chronological time, some melting and regrouping of the quantum structure of reality, which, I would say, is how, even now, it best yields itself to apprehension.

We take it for granted that politicians want power, but nowadays, with power belonging mainly to the extra-political domain — the multinational corpo-colonisers, the acronymed supra-nationals, the motherWEFfers, the bureaucrats who slide invisibly on the greased rails of totalitarian ambition — a new kind of politician has emerged who fits this new era precisely: one who wants position rather than power, prestige rather than influence, a State car rather than a licence to change reality, a career rather than a legacy, but who, nonetheless, 'gets off' on the idea of power, even though he has none. Power has slipped through political fingers, not just to the multinationals, stock-jobbers and bureaucrats, but into a process little short of miraculous in its stochastic, algorithmic nature, and this too dovetails beautifully with the mentality of the unrepresentable as described by Baudrillard. The minds of the young have been hollowed out and are primed with various forms of distraction as fits the need of the moment, when they may be filled with details of the latest psyop or mass formation.

Politics, as a result of these trends, has arrived at an unscheduled midlife crisis. Sheathed in skintight jeans and driving a red hairdresser's Ferrari, the politician has turned his back on his natural constituency: those who know about the past and its meanings, and the role of proclamations and constitutions, and how these phenomena matter in the present. Their heads turned by the scorn of the young, our alleged leaders play the part of medallion-chested lounge lizards who court the mini-skirted, stilettoed bimbos who huddle in groups at the disco giggling into their cocktails at the ludicrousness of their suitors, the pursuit of the unrepresentable by the reprehensible. This mode of operation is perfect for the mission of those behind the New World Disorder.

The onetime Mayor of New York, Mario Cuomo, in an interview with *The New Republic* in April 1985, said: 'Parties campaign in poetry, but they govern in prose.' He meant that electioneering politicians need to leave the greatest possible room for different interpretations of what they are promising, whereas, in the cabinet room, there is a need for specificity and restraint. It is a neat and smile-inducing reduction, though probably superfluous nowadays in the context to which Cuomo was referring, a time when politicians are so unprecedentedly despised and yet depended upon and looked to as never before. Their efforts to campaign in poetry provoke nothing but derision, and yet their prosaic efforts at dominion are remarkably effective. Nowadays, they campaign in promises and govern — nay, rule — in psychopathy. Conversely, the public has become incapable of understanding reality when described prosaically; it requires a hyper-imaginative, esoteric explanation to capture their attention and animate them and if it feels like a movie, no matter how nightmarish, so much the better. The tendency of modern electorates is to accept almost anything at face value provided it is not prosaic, so long as it may be couched in tangled explanations with their toes in elaborate post-structural theory and their fingers, ears, nose and tongue in the postmodern.

The issues no longer have to do with electioneering and governing, but with the means by which an electorate may be subdued to the extent of being ruled over. For this, Cuomo's haikuesque formulation must be reversed: Now it is better to act prosaically and explain poetically. By this method, a modern 'ruler' may attain a postmodern level of Machiavellian sophistry, adequate to ruling over his people in a manner that pleases them without any element of affection.

The 'real life' simulacrum, then, is a pathocracy. We are, all of us, now the put-upon spouses of shiny-suited creeps with the aura of having dark secrets who threaten and menace us at every turn, as though suddenly rendered volatile and unstable, striking out at us without warning, uttering profane epithets which imply that all the fault for whatever it is that has suddenly gone awry lies with us, the battered ones. It is clear that they are answerable not to the logic of their own 'households' but to outsiders in some remote location — or multiple locations — who issue instructions and protocols of action and behaviour that result in a ubiquity of virtually indistinguishable conditions in multiple countries all at once. These functionaries and their behaviours are not simply eruptions of authoritarianism, nor even expressions of a novel totalitarianism, but simply actors who believe in nothing and can be filled out with any beliefs those who control them (through money or fear or blackmail) wish to impose. But it is worse than that: They are imbeciles whose stupidity looks like naïveté, who evince a bland innocence in the face of the pleas and protestations of their own people: 'It's not us, it's the virus! It's not us; it's the climate! It's not us; it's Putler!'

Our political establishments have become emotionally unstable, pathological, twisted, biased, desperate and reckless with, for example, their labelling of persons and groups who question them as 'extremists', which is both a received protocol and an act of desperate flailing at an imagined threat, with a view to subduing their subjects with the notion of an internal enemy. They are captured, seemingly compromised, and far more obviously beholden to external forces than to indigenous pleading. They are not simply authoritarian; but approach in their demeanours, statements and actions a murderous, witch-hunting pitch of vitriol for anyone they perceive as threatening their dogmatic utopian vision for the world. But it is worse than that: They have accepted at face value the indifference to human life evinced by their genocidal puppet masters. They preach the virtue of preserving life, but their every action indicates that they cross their fingers while uttering such platitudes. They no longer care. Their moral calculus, such as it is, has no place for consideration or caring as to whether people die early, soon or now.

Right now, no sane person could decide anything that did not somewhat incorporate the idea that life would be much better for virtually everyone if the political class in its totality resigned and went away, leaving the nations of the world ungoverned and unruled. The trouble, as we have seen, is that words like 'sane' and 'insane' have drifted away from meaning like carnival balloons slipping from the grip of excited children and floating up, up, up above the wires, and off into the ether.

Baudrillard anticipated not merely the abolition of the real, but also that of political power, which ineluctably followed, and, after that, the loss of the social, which, he said, would give rise to socialism.

In *The Procession of Simulacra* in his 1981 book, *Simulacra and Simulation*, he wrote:

'Through an unforeseen turn of events and via an irony that is no longer that of history, it is from the death of the social that socialism will emerge, as it is from the death of God that religions emerge. A twisted advent, a perverse event, an unintelligible reversion to the logic of reason. As is the fact that power is, in essence, no longer present except to conceal that there is no more power. A simulation that can last indefinitely, because, as distinct from "true" power — which is, or was, a structure, a strategy, a relation of force, a stake — it is nothing but the object of a social demand, and thus as the object of the law of supply and demand, it is no longer subject to violence and death. Completely purged of a political dimension, it, like any other commodity, is dependent on mass production and consumption. Its spark has disappeared; only the fiction of a political universe remains.'

All this is enabled and concealed by the media, whose purpose he foresaw would change from dispensing information and meaning to destroying both. Because we had moved into a world of more and more information, there would be less and less meaning, for the reason that a constant spew of information negates the possibility of any finality of understanding. 'Information is directly destructive of meaning and signification,' he wrote in *Simulacra and Simulation*. 'The loss of meaning is directly linked to the dissolving, dissuasive action of information, the media, and the mass media.'

It is the media and the promulgation of information, he writes, that causes the 'destructuration of the social', dissolving both meaning and the social, 'in a sort of nebulous state dedicated not to a surplus of innovation, but, on the contrary, to total entropy.' Beyond this, there are only 'the masses', which result from the neutralisation and implosion of the social. Hence, predicted this former Marxist, *on to socialism*.

The media, as we have been experiencing acutely in the past 40 months, carries out the functions of destroying meaning and social reality in multiple ways, including:

- telling lies;
- telling the truth on the following day and, on the third day, reverting to the lie;
- telling the truth in the bottom left-hand corner of Page 34, so that, when a protest is raised, it can indignantly be pointed to;
- simultaneously, in the same report, conveying that a story is both true and false;
- attacking those who tell the truth that contradicts all this.

A factor in the growing chaos of the world, indubitably, is the fracturing of reality by virtue of the ready availability of instant accounts of events from else-where, something that attacks our sense of the significance of the hereness and nowness of our own moment-to-moment experience of 'reality'. In the past, news of events in the distant world was conveyed after the fact, at 6 o'clock or 9 o'clock, or in the next morning's newspaper. When something shocking occurred that somehow broke into our personal realm, we would respond to it afterwards by trying to calculate 'where we were' at the moment the event in question occurred. What was I doing at the instant John Lennon was shot? Perhaps I caught a glimpse of Lennon's face on a bank of TV screens in an elec-trical shop as I passed on a bus, and was left wondering, as the bus proceeded to the next stop: *Has he released another album?* The effect of this was not to split reality but to suggest a vast multitudinous world in which events happened randomly and were conveyed to me, because they had happened and by virtue of my interest as a citizen in knowing what was happening. This exalted not merely the individual citizen as someone who required to be informed of events, but also the reality which he inhabited. It was sense-making, and also partic-ipatory.

What happens now is different. The news comes instantly, and, in doing so, suggests itself as more urgent and important than anything I might be doing. It arrives in a manner that suggests my very purpose in being here, existing now, is to await the arrival of this news, to receive it and react. We are all simply audi-ence members of a News-day. The bulkiness of the smartphone in my pocket is a constant reminder that I am in this mode of waiting. Life is elsewhere, and I merely sit in suspended animation, anticipating or awaiting some new calamity or sensation to have occurred in some distant place. I live, therefore, not in the place I happen to be, but in all the other places in the world that might poten-tially be the occasions or locations of reports pinging through on my smart-phone, which is to say virtually everywhere, with emphasis on the virtual. I am everywhere; where I am is nowhere, the hole in the doughnut. At the same time, there is a suppression of any sense that the events being relayed to me are even occurring at whatever distance is implied. They are the only 'here', and the only 'now'. We are cast into them, and, therefore, removed from the actual world. We experience momentary faux emotions as each event — each air raid, each tornado, each celebrity death — comes and passes. In the future, our 'memories' will reflect only these 'stories', and all vestiges of our actual experiences will have evaporated. I live in the entire world, except the part of it where I sit or stand or lie, which means that I too am abolished, disappeared, unless I can make myself visible by becoming the subject of a news report, a remote possibil-ity. Reality is fractured, but not cleaved in two; for actually existing reality is no longer capable of competing with the virtual kind, which is always there, always brimming with happenings, which fill the emptiness of my presence in the 'here' and the 'now' in a manner that destroys both the *hereness* and *nowness* of things. Not only is there no reality, but humanity itself begins to doubt its own existence.

In this new model, news programmes on television, for example, are no longer, actually, news programmes, but performances of prepared scripts that are written to create crafted impressions of what is 'happening'. Since I do not watch television, I have only recently begun to understand this syndrome — mainly as a result of occasionally finding myself in a room with a switched-on TV set, which I am not in a position to turn off. The change from even when I stopped watching television just short of a decade ago, is instantly palpable. Some items, relating to inconsequential stories, are more or less unchanged, but anything in which the manufacture of the simulacrum is at issue, such as (of late times) Covid, Ukraine, climate, transgenderism, homosexuals, coercive mass migration, and suchlike topics, is packaged more or less as a short piece of theatre, in which all but literal 'actors' (and sometimes those too), who have been vetted as to what they might say, and most likely coached to refine their contributions so they function adequately to convey the pseudo-reality, are used to fill in various parts of the script. People who watch television a lot may be unable to perceive the falsity of this, whereas those who abstain from watching assume that what is happening on television is merely the promulgation of directed, controlling, always slightly twisted information so as to 'influence' their thinking. In fact, what is happening is beyond mere lies: It is constructed falsity. It is the material of an alternative reality reproduced to replace the actual real, and to conceal the 'genuine' reality's prior abolition.

This 'scripted journalism' has many other manifestations, which artfully mimic the patterns of what we once may have trusted as 'true' reporting, but are actually designed to confuse, confound, to spark false hopes, to have people doubt their own eyes, ears and memories, to provoke people to secrete hostility towards certain others, and ultimately to instil submissiveness and despair. Among the many important aspects of this kind of 'news' management and presentation are the techniques of compartmentalisation, coordination and constant repetition. The repetitiveness bears a resemblance to the manner of the play-listing of pop music on the radio, which enables the hooks of favoured songs to be hammered into the heads of the audience.

Among the many techniques used in this kind of programming are devices that enable occasional minor — but more often major — untruths to be inserted in the programming, controlled explosions of truth which, not being reiterated multiple times, may as well not be mentioned at all. An example might be the way that, in late March of 2022, Boris Johnson flew from London to Kiev with the purpose of scuppering the peace talks then taking place between Russia and Ukraine. This was reported at the time, but soon 'forgotten' by virtue of not being constantly reiterated. This provides deniability in the event that someone subsequently accuses the broadcaster or newspaper of failing to report something, and yet the absence of emphasis ensures that it never reaches the point of arousing the curiosity or doubts of the audience, which never gets to actually 'know' the information in its true context and meaning.

The 'far right' narrative, much in favour among journaliars in the Time of Covid, is another salutary example of scripted journalism. It is actually a device to galvanise the 'in-group' of the groupthink, by constantly referencing the (largely fictional) 'out-group' — this sinister and blurry manufactured spectre on the outside, that somehow — it's unclear how — threatens to invade the group and subject it to Hitlerian methods of manipulation and Maoist techniques of terror. That the 'far right' does not exist does nothing to deter those engaged in spreading the lie. On the contrary, the lack of evidence for the existence of the 'far right' tends, in the climate being created, to heighten the public sense of the danger. The 'far right', like Covid, can be asymptomatic. The evidence for its existence is its absence. That it is nowhere to be found 'proves' that it is everywhere; that it says and does nothing implies a menacing, brooding presence that might strike at any moment.

The reason such abuses of truth are possible is because of an unannounced contract of *omertà* that pertains between the media and political and official entities and bodies, in which the business model of media is flipped from truth to lies — all this being made possible and permissible by the conditions of the simulacrum. The deal is that the media will do or say nothing to draw attention to the perpetration of fraud, or the institutionalisation of mendacity, but will report deadpan whatever is issued by way of a formal script, no matter how ludicrous, spurious or contradictory, by the Regime. This means that the Regime is at all times guaranteed that none of its nefarious acts or statements will be highlighted sufficiently for the 'coverage' to have any meaningful impact. This means also that there is never, as in the past, a *'Gotcha!'* moment, a calling to account, a delivery of judgment on political stewardship or behaviour, which in effect means the abolition of the Law of Consequences in the execution of the media's traditional role of calling power to account. Since there is no longer any real power (none accruing to the politicians as such, having all been devolved upwards out of visibility and accountability), the exercise of covering political life has become a kind of game in which, even as the stakes grow higher and higher, the conscience of journalism has been set so low as to render these behaviours as though victimless and harmless.

Real journalism used to enforce real consequences — it was the cultural equivalent of policing. This used to mean that a 'story' was not simply a space-filler or a piece of entertainment — it had meaning in the real world. Just as, watching a movie, a play or a TV crime series, you could expect events within the story to result in consequences towards the end, so it was in real life, largely thanks to honest journalism. This is partly why journalists came to refer to their material as 'stories'. As the story unfolded, it would become the subject of public discussion: *'Heads will roll!' 'Is so 'n' so toast?' 'Will she have to go?' 'She's a goner!' 'Will the government fall?'* Et cetera.

Tony Blair's spin maestro, Alastair Campbell, used to say that if a politician who becomes the subject of a negative media story cannot get that story off the front pages within a week, he or she is *ipso facto* toast. This observation bespeaks a naturalistic process, within the operation of news, that ensures a real-time dynamic of consequences arising from the public ventilation of a particular issue.

All this was abolished in the Covid episode. The 'purchased' nature of media ensured that 'stories' would no longer have consequences — or would have consequences only for those who sought to question the 'authorities'. In this model of 'media', the management of every 'story' ensures that meanings are all the time within the control of the 'authorities'. All news content is released or eked out in a process of constant collaboration between governments and 'health authorities' on the one hand, and media managers on the other, to ensure that it achieves its intended purpose, which no longer has anything to do with informing the public as to what is happening in the world. The purpose is to manage public perceptions to the extent of imposing a false version of reality on the public imagination. This model has now endured with barely a stumble for the past three years, a period in which the Covid fiction, and related inventions, would continue to be believed, and anything with the potential to damage that objective disposed of or minimised. In this netherworld of pseudo-reality, the authorities are never 'guilty' of anything — blame is a condition accruing solely to those who criticise the authorities. Because what is on the news today appears to contradict what was on the news yesterday — without any accompanying corrective or clarifying narrative — does not mean that either or both versions are wrong, or that there is any necessary contradiction between them. The authorities will explain all this in due course, and meanwhile, we should continue to believe in their good intentions.

This is an entirely new phenomenon in the public and political life of our nations. All our lives, we have lived with an approximately reliable expectation that when things of significance happen, they will be reported in the media, and that when the story changes, it will be subject to updating or correction. Furthermore, if the authorities err or do wrong, it is the journalist's job to expose this. These became almost reflex assumptions of viewers, listeners and readers, implicit promises that were accompanied by the constant tacit assurance that, if something was reported, that report was the most accurate and truthful account of events that journalists could assemble at a particular deadline moment or hour, and would be followed through in all its implications until the public interest was entirely discharged.

The problem is not just that this is now changed utterly. The even more radical effect is that most people, being unaware of any change having occurred, continue to trust the media as though it were some kind of 3D photocopier of total reality. The citizens, fearful or merely watchful, look to the sentry posts, see that they are manned, and breathe sighs of relief. But the figures at the posts are men of straw.

Most people have no idea that the information they are being fed on a number of key topics is constantly subject to manipulation and spin. This has the effect not so much of splitting reality as obliterating it and replacing it with a remote, virtualised simulacrum in which, though the environment appears to remain unaltered, the 'content' of the culture is utterly different. There is, at the same time, this ghostly impression of actual journalism. The nature and presentation of the article or report seem to suggest something like the same context as would once have resulted in a dramatic playing out of consequences, but here there is simply this faint jaded sense of another stroke being pulled. It is like trying to light a fire with wet sticks: The ingredients all look more or less the same, the match lights, the firelighter takes, the rolled-up newspaper ignites and burns energetically; but a few minutes later, there is nothing but a smoking mess of blackness.

This, I find, is an aspect of what has been happening that almost no one has noticed or understood to its depths. Even when people perceive the wrongdoing of the 'authorities' and the venality of the journaliars, they seem to regard these behaviours as though aberrational malfunctions within a normative system of naturalistic call-and-response. In fact, what is happening is a complete travesty, not merely of the news but of the process by which news has long been apprehended. As a result of absorbing such 'stories' over three-and-a-half years, the public has become 'trained' to suspend its sense of expectation concerning any particular story, unless a process of repetition and coordination conveys that it is 'reasonable' to do so.

What this means, in sum, is that the authorities, through their corruption of the media, have built a glass, bulletproof cage for themselves to operate in, where they are, in effect, impervious to criticism and consequence. This process has not even begun to be understood, and has no discernible prospect of termination. Each new development, no matter how potentially harmful to the perpetrators of the Most Heinous Crime in History, can be 'explained' away in what appear to be logical and reasonable terms, always presenting the motives and intentions of the authorities in the most auspicious light possible. The outright compromising of journalism in this period ensures also that journaliars have no motivation to expose this process, or own up to their own part in it. This wicked symbiosis, therefore, persists at the centres of our public squares, pumping out a pseudo-reality that is impenetrable even by those who are able to perceive something unusual, because the vast majority, even when something rings strangely, assume the discordant note to be simply a necessary and logical side-effect of the process of emergency truth-telling. But it is important to stress that the appearance of this pseudo-reality is such as to be quite the antithesis of mendacious. Its veracity is beyond question because it is not simply a version of reality — it is, or appears unquestionably to be, a description of reality such that any attempt to tell the truth will itself seem to be mendacious and/or paranoid. It does not conceal the truth to conceal reality — it supplants both.

Spending a few hours, days or weeks immersed in Jean Baudrillard's challenging but vital description of the undertows of our culture in time, it is impossible to shake off the thought that his analysis, though complex, sometimes improbable and sometimes seeming to be no more than ironic wordplay, contains more than a sense of providing some kind of sketch, at least, for what has been happening to us in the 'real' world more than a decade after his death.

In late spring this year, I emerged from such a period of immersion in his works, to be confronted by two potted rhubarb crowns gone to seed in my greenhouse after I placed them there to protect them against a promised late frost, and went away for a few days. They had, in the exquisite horticultural term, 'bolted' — both crowns having sent up tall shoots — more than six foot high — with pods of seeds at the business ends. Such an event can amount to a quite radical setback: the seeds are rarely very useful, and the plant has expended all its energy in this vain gesture — all arising from the sudden change in conditions, which confuse the plant's 'hormones' as to the actual time of year. The only remedy is to cut the errant shoots back and, in the case of rhubarb, plant the crowns outdoors and hope that they will settle down to a normal existence.

It dawned on me that this might be a close to perfect metaphor for what we are undergoing in the socio-political realm. Western civilisation is in the throes of a process not dissimilar to 'bolting'. Having 'evolved' beyond the subsistence and prosperity stages, we have entered a phase in which — to borrow my mother's persistent admonition to us as children: *We don't know what to do with ourselves.*

As a result, under a process of malevolent manipulation by nefarious forces, we have succumbed to a condition that civilisation had hitherto strived to sublimate, but which is as though baked into our biological structure: the impulse to ignore our limitations in the hope of discovering new vistas and perhaps the beginnings of perfection. Western civilisation, which seems to be in a death spiral of demographic collapse, despair, nihilism and self-absorption, is, in reality, seeking a new way of being, having appeared to exhaust the old one, but really has arrived at a state of unprecedented confusion, having been misled as to the causes of its confusion, and confused all the more by the sly interventions of malevolent actors.

'Bolting', also called 'running to seed' or 'going to seed', redistributes a plant's energy away from the leaves and roots to instead produce seeds and a flowering stem that wastes the plant's energy to no good purpose. Bolting usually signals the end of new leaf growth and indicates that the plant has passed its optimal state. The phrase 'going to seed' means 'to deteriorate'. It is derived from the natural act of annual and bi-annual plants going to seed at the end of their lives, and is provoked by the plant's intimation that it ought to reproduce itself. When it happens at an earlier stage, it can amount to disaster, even for a perennial plant like a rhubarb crown.

The 'bolting' metaphor can be replanted in the technological, the political, and the cultural arenas, in all of which the surge occurs as a process of human alteration, distension, and intensification, as we struggle to achieve continuity in alarming new conditions that we can but remotely and clumsily comprehend. In the human context, the syndrome manifests as various forms of behaviour indistinguishable from madness. Under the attrition of propaganda, we are convinced that what is happening amounts to 'progress', when in reality, it is a sign that we need to go back to the ABCs.

Outside of certain postmodern circles, it is commonplace for public commentary to assume that reality is something fixed in particular foundations, and, therefore, an objective phenomenon exhibiting a constant shape and character. Baudrillard and others take a different view: that reality, standing there, is as much the creation of the descriptions and representations as it is of any scheduled process of production — a reapplication of the 'observer effect' in physics. It would be understandable if we experienced difficulty in accepting such a theory as having any applicability to events in, for example, the geopolitical or social contexts — after all, we have observed such events all our lives and have been able, approximately, to comprehend them; and yet, we cannot dispute that, more and more, only the utterly esoteric seems to gain traction in attempts to explicate or understand where we have fetched up now. We should remember that we have lived through times of exceptional technological and cultural change — at least at the level of consumer devices — and that, in our apprehension of this, we are more than likely working with tools of reasoning that have been developed and utilised in utterly different — more prosaic — conditions. Thus, the difficulty we have in comprehending the leaps that are necessary in order to achieve sense may have to do with the suddenness of the changes, accompanied by — paradoxically — the relative slowness of the evolution from one form of reality to the other. Things are changing — 'suddenly', 'dramatically', yes — but not so fast as to alert us to the necessity to change our viewfinders. Despite the turmoil, we are still reading the transformation as an organic shifting, and are relaxing into a kind of complacency when really we ought to be on red alert.

The problem may be that what we are looking at may be a kind of ghostly after-image of an old reality, already supplanted by something that fits the vacated place and bears a passable resemblance, but is ('in reality' — hah!)

something entirely other. Baudrillard assists us with this in his reflections on the 'image'. Once, he warned, the object was indeed all there was; now, the object is merely a starting point, a fleeting entity that immediately becomes an image, and may no longer be there, or may have been, in the first place, an instrument of misdirection or a figment born of and reproduced by propaganda.

For him, the catastrophe had already happened. We had entered a kind of paradise, or at least crossed the line into the future, in which the past — history — no longer had the meanings it had before. Man's construction of history, he argued, had long been a form of simulation, since it ordered events in such a manner as to destroy their randomness and imbue them with meaning. For this and other reasons (victory bias, for example), history was neither credible nor convincing. Only by creating a simulation of reality could history be managed as a kind of backstory of humanity, trundling forward towards some kind of culmination, a necessary backdrop for ideological salesmanship. This meant, in effect, that the ideology of progress always demanded the falsification of history, and, therefore, also of the present, an interference that occurs even while the event under consideration is happening. Contrary to our assumption of naturalism, this tendency to deliver meaningful stories by way of history and current affairs is a quirk of our culture, in which randomness and unpredictability have been 'managed' before they arise. The obituaries of public figures are written long before they die, and pandemics and other 'acts of God' may be subject to rehearsals just months before they occur.

We have crossed the road to move into the simulacrum, carrying all our clutter and kit, sleepwalking through the night to find our new homes in the virtual and waking up in the morning with just the vaguest sense of having moved from someplace else. We enter the simulacrum and become its citizens, taking it for the real. We are as avatars, facsimiles of ourselves, standing outside our selves and moving our beings about as though pieces on an electronic chessboard, or symbols on a handheld video game.

Technology of the sort we are speaking of here, collapses time, eliminates the process of maturation, and delivers a passable imitation of maturity, which is really just a shell, inside of which is emptiness. This is especially visible in young males, who have always been the ones who must come to grips with the external world at a moment when they remain inexperienced, unrefined, immature, naïve, but nevertheless required to shoulder the physical cost of 'progress', sometimes by offering up their lives.

As we have observed again recently in the proxy war in Ukraine, it is young men who must pay the ultimate cost of the follies and conceits of politicians and ideologies. Here we go back to The Longhouse and Keeperman's description of its contemporary state as, I would say, a matriarchy disguised as a patriarchy, ruled over by the Den Mother. In this sense of its camouflaged reality, it provides a metaphor also for the simulacrum.

Robert Bly warned in *Iron John* that the elimination from our culture of the teaching, benign-authoritarian father had left us with generations of young men who were 'numb in the region of the heart'. Because young men are never allowed to come away from their mothers, they stand on the threshold of manhood but cannot enter. The umbilical cord had been severed, but little more. Still tied to their mothers' apron strings, young men struggle to find ways to announce their manhood. With their fathers cast into silence, they are starved of the wisdoms and mythologies that might sustain a healthy male existence. They have no experience or sense of what male emotions might be like, and are therefore presented with a choice between having female emotions or no emotions. Often, they choose to have no emotions, in which case their options are reduced to nihilism or self-destruction. Today, as Keeperman reminds us, we have elevated this condition to that of, yes, pandemic. Adrift in the numbness that engulfs them, many of our young men now walk with an outward appearance of normalcy but inwardly lurching uncontrollably — lurching from, for example, a learned piety to intense rage — all the time seeking something to provide some illusion of feeling while simultaneously keeping the numbness at bay.

We need to get our Longhouse in order. But this needs to be preceded by a conversation in which the truth is permitted to be heard.

The 'liberation of the networks' has caused the truth to be buried deeper than ever before. The technology delivers articulateness, cleverness, sophistication, knowingness, jadedness, wryness, exhaustion. It delivers these even to a terrified 12-year-old boy who has seen nothing, known nothing, experienced nothing, felt very little but fear and anxiety and, when he is lucky, a little hope that all the troubling, confusing things that seem to be true will one day dissolve and be replaced by order and guidance and — whisper it — values. He has searched in himself and in the world for the ideals that he intuited from the stories his mother or older sister read to him as a boy, but cannot find anything to begin from. Reality is disappointing — slow and unresponsive, incapable of delivering anything like the feelings he has intuited from screens since before he could read. He has delved into the depths of his fantasies and known everything that human sexuality is capable of delivering, but without the human element. He wants to feel something but experiences only victimhood and loathing and a flimsy kind of hoping that seems to have no evidential basis in anything he encounters. He subsists in something akin to the ghost of a chemical addiction, which has frozen his heart in terror and chilled his soul into hiding. He has sequestered himself away in his room with his Gameboy and taken this for life. He has discovered the World Wide Web, which seems to be a place where you can live without being alive, a place where you can send messages to people you don't know, and keep things like that. His body has grown, his vocabulary too, his penis is hungry and prone to an iron hardness, but his heart has shrivelled for want of sustenance, and his emotional life exists purely as virtual reality. Because the world is something that comes to him through the thing in his hand, he has no reference points besides. He cannot touch or hold or seize or dismantle something in an attempt to understand how things work, what things mean. This, tentatively, is the beginning of what we are talking about, for without knowledge of the true nature of manhood, the boy is doomed to self-destruction or worse, and by virtue of this, our societies are doomed to the haemorrhaging of spirit and fight that might, in other circumstances, have served to defeat the forces that now threaten us all. This was the first and most fundamental of the attacks mounted by the arch-manipulators, intensified now by the flooding of our societies with military-aged men from cultures unaffected by the emasculation process. We are on a hiding to nothing.

To establish the roots of this catastrophe in what remains of the 'real' world, we need to look to any technological development as such, but to the condition of The Longhouse, not just the symptoms described above, but in particular the corruption of education, its replacement by what I call 'seducation' — a deliberate process of instilling the anti-values of noncery in the heads of children who, having made their approach through the already twisted culture, rarely have the wherewithal to question it, and — looking up to see if their elders are as agitated as they — note the lack of perturbation all around.

Preceding or coterminous with all this was the destruction of Christianity, which removed from the culture not merely morality and empathy and hope, but also the capacity to walk upright through reality towards some indefinite but constant point, and the sense of why this was essential. More or less simultaneously, science was replaced by scientism, an ideology of certainty that dismisses and destroys democratic opinion (and ultimately democracy), as well as all lived human experience. This was accompanied by a pseudo-democratising of communications, whereby the most idiotic voices took over the square of public conversation — or, the 'town hall' — replacing wisdom and actual experience with vitriolic opinion based on nothing but repetition of what was already overstated.

The nature of the way we apprehend knowledge paints us into the totalitarian corner. Once, regular people knew a little about a broad range of matters, from politics to fashion, and intelligence resided in reconciling these various elements and comprehending their connections. But today, we live in an era of compartmentalisation, whereby each person is 'educated' to know more and more about less and less: each discipline is fragmenting into ever more numerous sub-categories, and each individual is more and more driven into some particularised zone of 'expertise', in which proficiency offers the path to income and respect, which is to say dignity, but not to wisdom or reason or common sense. Thus, unless one is disposed to become a politician — which almost nobody is — becoming interested in the minutiae of politics is not merely boring, but also potentially impoverishing. Politics and politicians are permitted to crack their whips so long as they agree to remain at a personal distance and speak in the strangled languages of pop culture. But they are not respected, and no longer even liked.

In much the way that he describes the world as having passed a point of rupture, Baudrillard himself, in his work, crosses an invisible line between sociology and philosophy into art and metaphysics. His insights can sometimes seem close to impenetrable, but they are worth pursuing, if only because they sketch out the territory in which we must all henceforth consider ourselves. He takes a perverse view of human nature, deciding on something close to masochism as a remedy for man's postmodern condition. Where I part absolutely with him is when he insists that reality can have no meaning and that this is something we ought to embrace, that affirming meaninglessness is actually liberating: 'If we could accept this meaninglessness of the world,' he wrote in *Impossible Exchange* (2001) 'then we could play with forms, appearances and our impulses, without worrying about their ultimate destination . . .' Citing the Romanian philosopher Emil Cioran, he declared: 'we are not failures until we believe life has a meaning — and from that point on we are failures, because it hasn't.' Instead of fighting the world of images and objects, he insisted, we should simply embrace its rule as a quasi-metaphysical absolutism, seek out its essences and mysteries and become conversant with it. We should surrender to the object and the screen because we have no future independently of them.

This, in turn, means acceptance of the default sadomasochistic dominion of the New World Disorder — the hidden puppet-masters and their localised proxies who crack the whip and call the shots. But this would be to kick the ladder from under ourselves, leaving no way back to 'reality', on the presumed basis that humanity itself is unwilling to go there. By taking this avenue, man would be turning his back on the option of imagining a divine master, or fearing His wrath or punishment. In these circumstances, humanity would become its own gaoler, and only those with long memories remain sentient enough to resist this. The eradication of the transcendent would be a 'perfect crime', imprisoning us in a manufactured 'metaphysics'. This, above all, is wrong, not merely because it is false, but because, even if it were true, its logic would destroy the sole surface upon which experience tells us man is capable of achieving traction in reality, which is the only locus of his hopes of a meaningful existence.

Right now, we need belatedly to bring our young men together and gather them around the campfire at the edge of the forest to talk to them about manhood and pain and wounds and history and story and love and death, and explain to them why they were allowed to grow without faith or hope, as though they were unworthy on account of having committed some unnamed crime, and how all of the things they have come to fret about and fear were not their doing but the sins of our culture gone to seed.

And then we shall have to ask them to forgive the wrongs that were done to them.

And then we must ask them to stand in the breach for the battle that is coming.

Have we the right to ask this of them? I do not know. But neither do I know of any other option for saving Western civilisation.

CHAPTER 31
'TRUST THE EXPERTS' IS THE VIRUS
07-08-2023

A radical shift in political culture in the Covid coup put centre-stage in public affairs a long-gestating tendency towards the fragmentation of knowledge and the elimination of synthesising voices.

Here is an infallible rule: a prince who is not himself wise cannot be well advised, unless he happens to put himself in the hands of one individual who looks after all his affairs and is an extremely shrewd man. In this case, he may well be given good advice, but he would not last long because the man who governs for him would soon deprive him of his state. But when seeking advice of more than one person, a prince who is not himself wise will never get unanimity in his councils or be able to reconcile their views. Each councillor will consult his own interests; and the prince will not know how to correct or understand them. Things cannot be otherwise, since men will always do badly by you unless they are forced to be virtuous. So the conclusion is that good advice, whomever it comes from, depends on the shrewdness of the prince who seeks it, and not the shrewdness of a prince on good advice.
— Niccoló Machiavelli, The Prince

'WHAT ARE YOU — *HENRY FORD*?'

'The weird thing that happened around Covid, and I had never noticed this before, at any other time of my life:' says the American comedian and YouTuber, Jimmy Dore, '[is that] you weren't allowed to ask questions at any point during this. You just had to do what The Man on the TV said

— right? — you had to do what the man on the TV said, without questions, and then you were a good person. But if you question it, then you're a white supremacist Trumper Naz . . . woah, no, no, no! No! "No, I didn't vote for Trump. I just have *questions!*"

'"*Jim-mee*, only dumb people ask questions!"

'Isn't that weird? It was the weirdest thing I'd ever seen. Even comedians would get on stage and try to shame people for trying to get informed about a medical treatment that was experimental, that they had to take, and if they didn't take it, they would lose their jobs, and they wouldn't be able to travel. And when people tried to get informed about it, other people shamed them. They would say, "Please tell me you're not going to, [air quotes] 'Do your own research.'" You've heard people say, that: "Please don't 'do your own research . . .'"

'You know, before Covid, "doing your own research" used to be called "reading"! Now you're shaming me for reading, at the behest of Big Pharma? It's like I woke up in the middle of a Bill Hicks bit: *"Wall, it looks like we got ourselves a reader!"* — that's how much people internalised the propaganda from Big Pharma, which was that they would be anti-intellectual enough to shame people for reading, while they were wagging their finger at them for doing it! You would never shame people for doing that, no matter what other subject it was, no matter how unimportant. Like if I was to say, "Hey, I'm going to go buy a car!" . . . *"Don't look into it!"* . . . "Well, how will I know which car to get?" . . . *"Ask the salesman — he's the expert! What are you — Henry Ford?"'*

It's so true, so clear. In this short rap, we can almost glimpse the total meaning of comedy as a serious endeavour.

Put like that, it's funny, laughable, ludicrous. But it *happened*, and it was our neighbours and brothers and sisters and sons and daughters and parents and grandparents saying these things to us and treating us as retards when we refused to buy it. The tropes Jimmy Dore is mocking were to begin worded only slightly differently to his satire, and they became as though instant verities on social media and on the other governing platforms of our cultures. Suddenly, a majority of the human race seemed to surrender all autonomy, all discretion, all initiative, placing their lives and existences in the control of men in shiny suits and, sometimes, white coats supplied for a photo op, as though by Central Casting.

Dore's 'translation', encapsulation and metaphorisation tickles our funny bones because he so clearly sketches a parallel that releases a years-long tension created by a cultural belief system that contradicted everything that same culture had held to for as long as we could remember before that. Suddenly, in the name of science — nay, '*The* Science' — obscurantism was not merely fashionable again, but actually mandatory. Suddenly, ignorance was in. And, even more ridiculously, this new dispensation was being pushed by people who would diss without thought, for example, an interest in the transcendent, as a fetish for sky-pixies. Overnight, after 335 years of alleged progress and post-Enlightenment enlightenment, philistinism was fashionable, cluelessness was classy, benightedness was the new Big Idea , and empty-headedness the happening thing. Those insisting on the values of the Enlightenment were condemned as barbarians by those rejecting them, and the culture as a whole, and all its high priests and priestesses, got to its feet in toxic applause. Objectively speaking, it seems impossible, but still — we know — it *happened*, just three years ago, delivered out of the blue by a process of cultural railroading generated in an improbable and overnight rearrangement of cultural furniture ordained by a convocation of vested interests, and funded by administrations with access to the deepest pockets in the whole of history. The idea of it happening now is as dizzying as, four years ago, it would have been unimaginable.

Just think: this is funny because *it actually took place*. But, right now, seen against the backdrop of an entire life lived in the Free West — is it even *possible*? Was it a dark dream? Yet, how dark must be our laughter to be able to find humour in something so recent and so scarifying that we are even yet unsure whether we mightn't have dreamed the whole thing.

We come back to the hypothesis of the French philosopher Henri Bergson. In his book, *Laughter — An Essay on the Meaning of the Comic,* in which he proposes that humour derives fundamentally from rigidity in human behaviours and affairs. We find funny, he says, anything that breaks away from the natural patterns of human life, by becoming mechanistic and predictable. Hence, what makes people laugh is the absence of alertness and elasticity in the object of ridicule, i.e. forms of sclerosis arising from the culture of the group, things that deviate from the law of life, which abjures rigidity and mechanisation. But, here, the rigidities are not simply those of sclerotic authority, or bureaucracy, or power, but of our friends and neighbours, our brothers and sisters, our parents and children, the man behind the cash desk in the supermarket who used to be so friendly and, well, *funny* — all these and many more, who for a full two years at least, became the attack dogs from the Valley of the Squinting Windows where the Stasi live.

And the dark heart of our laughter says something else that defies or elides words: *If they could do this, what else might they do?*

The Man on the TV: the same shadowy, jerky figure we could observe move as though silently behind the lace curtains of every window we passed after dusk in that darkling spring of 2020; the Man in the White Coat; the Scientist; the Specialist; the Sage; the Expert — all these figures whose words were no longer just opinions or advice, but the hard stuff of dogma, dictum, doctrine, directive, edict — stood as public prosecutors of We, The People, who stood before them, the Accused, who, by virtue of a deficiency of the correct letters after our names, had no defence against those who had, who knew, who under-stood 'The Science' and, moreover, were ordained to chant it in our direction as a signal to stop and bow down. The Covid Cult of the Expert prosecuted and leveraged human infectiousness, the very mechanism whereby hitherto the human body had contrived, when it did, to remain strong and healthy. The experts, the medics, the scientists-on-message, all lined up to convey the verdict that man was deadly to his fellow, an infectious host of innumerable pests and parasites, a festering mess of pathogens rather than a creature comprising an embodied soul made in the image of his Creator, the equivalent of a suicide bomber with 40 lbs of explosives strapped to his waist with the pin out of the activating grenade.

If you were to identify a single avoidable pathology of collective humanity that led to and enabled the horrific events of 2020 and continuing — events that have brought to a shuddering halt the freedom, the democratic culture, the value-systems (and, imminently, the prosperity) of what we call 'The West', this would have to be it: the Cult of the Expert As Super-wicked Step-parent to the Whole Human Race, and the way a generalised acquiescence in this arrange-ment contrived to seep into and take hold of human minds and sensibilities to the point where slavery, destruction and even death were preferable to disobedience.

Now, it is slowly dawning on the human race that the step-parent was a gargoyle in disguise: The 'experts' promised to ward off the evil spirit of disease, but in reality — calculating, cunning, malevolent in the extreme — all the time delivering into the respiratory ducts of our societies an unprecedented chaotic evil, in the name of curing and saving — in reality dispensing death and disease and injury at a level previously unseen, while still wearing the white coats of benevolent ministration and smiling as if nothing at all were amiss.

The booby trap at work here was, in part at least, the eruption in public culture of a phenomenon in human affairs that for the longest time had existed as a matter of respect for learning and healing powers at the level of personal interaction. Most of us, all our lives, had been aware of and compliant with the quality of deference on display in our cultures to doctors, nurses, surgeons, biologists, and the like, the men and women of great learning whom we could trust to looking into the inscrutabilities of our bodies, or advise us concerning arcane matters to do with the structure of real-ity. In childhood, the sound of the doctor's voice on the stairs was calming, soothing, all but absolutely reassuring. His hurried step as he entered the sick room caused the crowd around the bed to pull back into the corners, making clear his path to the patient. A stethoscope was produced, in the style of a conjuring trick, from a slightly smudged and over-burdened white pocket. A brief period of listening was followed by a moment of reflection; then, a diag-nosis — nay, a *verdict*. The watchers relaxed. The child in the bed smiled as

though modestly accepting applause, her illness being the cause of this necessary miracle.

How this familiar tableau metamorphosed and metastasised to the point where it was able to undo a civilisation is perhaps the most important reflection or study that our societies need — and soon — to undertake, if Western civilisa-tion is to be restored to anything like its prior condition of liberty and reason. Something wholesome, well-intentioned and good became something dark and destructive and downright malevolent in a time when the act of thinking became a kind of crime, and the desire to know what is true, what is reasonable — what *is* — became an occasion of accusations of error and sin. *What are you — Henry Ford?*

On television and radio, in the newspapers, the 'expert' was featured and feted all the time. He or she told us what was true, what we should concern ourselves with, and what — and whom — we should put out of our minds, what was significant, what that significance was, and how it affected us or was none of our beeswax. This counsel became the popular understanding of things. The subjectivity which had defined the human mind for centuries was pushed to the side in favour of a more 'objective' way of understanding. And this form of understanding was applied not merely to things outside our own experience, but even to our own experience of ourselves, our bodies and their functioning, our sense of freedom, our spirits. Psychologists and psychiatrists explained to us why we do things or think things, and these explanations came to rank higher than our own understandings of what we knew and believed, and how we had acted all our livelong lives.

Above all, the non-expert was required to fall silent. *Where did YOU do your microbiology degree?*

Hiding behind the pseudo-authority of 'The Science', the new religion of public life, which attributed all knowing to 'experts' on the basis of the letters inscribed after their names, decreed that the unlettered should wait in silence for The Science to speak through its anointed priests. This was beyond respect or even deference: By fiat of the sponsored convocation, the 'experts' acquired a power that trumped that of the people or the institutions they had constructed to manifest and sublimate their power. Those with fewer letters were advised, then enjoined, then instructed, to maintain a proportionate silence; those with competing qualifications who disagreed with the narrative were smeared and vilified into the margins and inaudibility.

If this had simply amounted to a bamboozling of the public on a passing, incidental issue — a long con flimflam operation designed perhaps to defraud the public of money or seduce its political loyalty, it would have been merely reprehensible. But what happened in the Covid episode was much, much worse than that. What occurred amounted to a coup against the autonomy of the people, not just politically, but in the most intimate realms of their existence. It amounted to a seizing of the right of human beings to decide for themselves in respect of their own bodies — bodies they had inhabited for 20, 35, 47, 59, 68 or 93 years — under the insinuated, imposed injunction that they were not 'qualified' to make decisions concerning those bodies, or even know in any meaningful way if anything were amiss with them, or how that was likely to play out. The normal doctor-patient relationship, whereby the would-be patient sends for, visits or 'reaches out' to the doctor, who in turn responds to whatever queries his patient may have, and proposes a course of action on this basis, was reversed: Here, the doctor became, in effect, a weaponised cultural instrument and underhanded psychological device, confronting the individual person with the 'facts' of his own alleged lethal infectiousness, and demanding, as an 'expert', that he deliver himself to whatever remedies were proposed by the omniscient authorities.

In this period, too, journalists, their employers having been bought and paid for by the orchestrators of the coup, more or less surrendered one of their central traditional functions — that of translators and mediators of 'expert witness', harking to the specialists in various disciplines and putting their thoughts into comprehensible language, interrogating each assertion until its rational basis became clear. Among the many baleful outcomes is that the pseudo-realities constructed by 'experts' became more and more impervious to lay deconstruction, which meant that the laity, under multiple headings that increasingly threatened their freedoms, jobs, businesses, wealth, and even their very voices for speaking truth, became more and more trapped in innumerable categories of imputed 'ignorance', while the 'literate' experts droned on in incomprehensible sentences that brooked of no response except capitulation. As the months gave way to years, the Covid coup consolidated in the minds of a majority that anything declared or decreed by a certified 'expert' could not be questioned, other than by another accredited expert, and then only if his qualification was exactly the same as the first speaker, and he was not of the 'far-right'. Unsurprisingly, after a while, almost no one, it seemed — and certainly no outright lawman — was willing to challenge anything, even on the basis of common sense. More and more, we were being shunted towards an outrightly materialist way of seeing everything, or — perhaps more correctly — accepting everything, without question, that Big Pharma wished us to believe.

This, far more than it was a biological crisis, was a psychological operation — 'psyop'. We should remain mindful that those who imposed the appalling conditions and circumstances of the past nearly four years have had access, above all, to the very best — or worst — of what behavioural psychology can offer. It is not outlandish to suggest that the orchestrators of the public mood — politicians, scientists, medical experts — somehow managed to impose a trance, which transformed reality into a kind of dream world, in which, as with actual dreams, nonsense came to seem perfectly sensible and the utterly preposterous as though the stuff of the clearest familiarity.

The American philosopher, Richard M. Weaver, in his 1948 book, *Ideas Have Consequences*, described humanity as already, even then, having given up all its other freedoms in return for the economic kind. This comes as a bit of a shock to the present-day reader, who might think of 1948 as a prehistoric era of pre-technocratic freedom. One of the more interesting chapters in a fascinating book is titled 'Fragmentation and Obsession', in which he analyses the cult of specialisation, which immediately struck me as remarkably germane to what's been happening to our world in the recent years and months. He had in mind the — at the time of his writing — a then relatively incipient era of specialisation, by which the 'expert' was soon to become elevated to the level of godhead, but only on the narrow terms, and with the thin remits of his particular specialisation.

His account of these matters begins in the Middle Ages, with the 'philosophic doctor', who 'stood at the center of things, because he had mastered principles.' This figure was the integrator and moderator of all disciples and arguments, a fount of supreme intellectual wisdom and explication.

'On a level far lower were those who had acquired only facts and skills,' writes Weaver, and all these fell silent when the philosophic doctor rose to speak. He, the philosophic doctor, was in charge of 'the general synthesis', and his learning was grounded in the master disciplines of metaphysics and theology. His knowledge of ultimate matters entitled him to answer ultimate questions. 'This is why, for example, the faculty of theology at the Sorbonne could be appealed to on matters of financial operation, which in our era of fragmentation, would be regarded as exclusively the province of the banker.'

The ultimate purpose of the system of education and administration out of which the philosophic doctor emerged, was 'to perfect the spiritual being and prepare for immortality.' Materialism, however, made this objective incomprehensible to the majority, and so it was, in time, replaced by a system that prepared the person for 'living successfully in the world.' This may, to modern ears, seem imminently sensible, but that is because of a misunderstanding that has developed concerning the metaphysical: because immortality is no longer universally believed in, it is presumed that preparing for it is, or may be, a waste of time that might be put to better use learning about how to make money. Obtaining a metaphysical education, however, was not simply to do with the next world; it also offered the student an enhanced capability of achieving greatness in this world — greatness in thought and deed and achievement — because of the ability it conferred to discern between ideas, and integrate any conclusions that might emerge. The metaphysician was not confined to a bounded knowledge of the metaphysical, but understood too how this impacted the

physical world, and could tell where the consequential trajectories of interventions and actions might lead, and calculate the interaction of interventions and
actions under different headings, and how they might serve to exacerbate or
ameliorate one another.

Education, Weaver claimed, is ultimately about comprehending a hierarchy
of values, which implies a sufficiency of knowledge of multiple disciplines to
establish priorities between them. This does not imply or necessitate a total
knowledge of everything, or even anything, which is in any event impossible,
but it does impose a facility to sort and parse the concepts relating to multiple
disciples in a way that enables them to cohere in the culture inhabited by the
people.

In the modern era, by Weaver's analysis, the ramping up of materialist
notions caused the philosophic doctor to be replaced by what he called the 'gentleman', a secular version of his predecessor, who substituted for a depth of
knowledge of metaphysics with a grounding in humanities and the liberal arts.
'The most important thing about the gentleman,' Weaver observed, 'was that he
was an idealist, though his idealism lacked the deepest foundations.' He was a
'man of broad views', characterised by self-restraint and a necessary degree of
sentimentality, and was broadly unsympathetic to materialism and self-aggran-
disement. He was courteous and apparently lacking in ego. He was a man of his
word, magnanimous in victory and gracious in defeat. The gentleman's role was
to establish hierarchies of thought, priorities of action, and above all ideals, and
to deliver judgements on the general relationships between things. 'On one
thing was he deficient:' wrote Weaver, 'he had lost sight of the spiritual origins
of self-discipline.'

Although this lack had grave consequences, Weaver suggested, 'it did not
prevent the gentleman from standing in for the philosophic doctor: He will
serve as an exemplar to a humanist, secularized society as the other did to a
religious.'

Weaver believed that, for as long as it could maintain a gentleman class, by
hereditary succession or recruitment generation to generation, Western society
would be able to maintain a measure of protection against certain congenital
tendencies of human societies.

At the time of his writing, 75 years ago, Weaver was of the view that the
concept of the ideal had continued to endure, but by then, the gentleman had
been obliterated from virtually every Western country. Nevertheless, even in our
own times, we can recall that a special veneration was often shown to the poet,
the philosopher, the playwright, the statesmen, the patriotic hero, even the
sportsman under certain headings — all of whom carried on elements of the
personality of Weaver's 'gentleman'. All this appears to have dissipated now,
under the attrition of liberal ideologies and state sponsorship of 'the arts'.

Weaver says that the gentleman was 'ousted' by modernism — in practice by politicians and entrepreneurs, 'as materialism has given its rewards to the sort of cunning incompatible with any kind of idealism.' The once revered gentleman was to become an impecunious eccentric, 'protected by a certain sentimentality, but no longer understood.' After World War One, he said, Europe turned for leadership to 'gangsters' (he had in mind such as Mussolini and Hitler) who 'though they are often good entrepreneurs, are without codes and without inhibitions. Such leaders in Europe have given us a preview of what the collapse of values and the reign of specialization will produce.' And here we stumble across perhaps the first and most prevailing problem with specialism: that it enables the 'experts' to believe that, such is their knowledge of their own area that it amounts to a form of total knowledge.

Weaver's exposition of this phenomenon is so astounding in its seeming prediction of the present state of affairs that one's first response is to doubt that it could possibly have been far enough advanced by the late 1940s for him to write such an account as he did.

I shall attempt as comprehensive an account of his general position as it is possible to provide in a terse summary.

Specialism, he argued, is a new development in human culture, and not an especially auspicious one. Going back to classical antiquity, specialisation was thought of as illiberal. Great proficiency in any particular domain was regarded with suspicion by those who sought to understand things in the larger frames of philosophy and metaphysics. Too much focus was detrimental to broader understanding. The 'men of letters' of the eighteenth and nineteenth centuries wished to be known as gentlemen first and writers merely incidentally. To regard such sentiments as 'exhibitions of priggishness,' he writes, is 'to miss the point entirely; they are expressions of contempt for the degradation of specialization and pedantry.' This is because specialisation of any kind limits the growth of a man to a fully developed capacity to comprehend reality, a quality essential in a leader of men. This is why science was not thought a proper pursuit for a ruler: because the necessary attention to particularities is inimical to the possibility of synthesis. The philosophic doctor and his 'secular heir', the gentleman, were concerned with 'the relation of men to God and the relation of men to men.' By concentrating on the minutiae of any subject, they risked losing sight of the higher purpose of thought, which involves maintaining a broad view of connections and syntheses.

Weaver perceived here a shift in the societal understanding of concepts of knowledge and wisdom. The modern thinker, he believed, was like a drunk seeking to maintain equilibrium, evading the growing sense of relativism in the culture by focussing on details and seeking conclusions that may be 'objectively' verified. These tendencies had become accompanied in culture by a fixation with facts, which had come to replace truth as the touchstone of philosophical inquiry. He noted the pervasiveness of games and quizzes designed to test the individual's store of facts, which he saw as hand-in-glove with these new trends in thought. Knowledge had ceased to be wisdom and had become the mere acquisition of disconnected facts. 'Where fact is made the criterion, knowledge has been rendered unattainable,' he writes. 'And the public is being taught systematically to make this fatal confusion of actual particulars with wisdom.'

Plato, Weaver reminded us, observed that, at any stage of a process of inquiry, we are moving either towards or away from first principles. Now, he said — by 1948 — the previous distrust of specialisation had been supplanted by a new distrust of generalisation. 'Not only has man become a specialist in practice, he is being taught that special facts represent the highest form of knowledge.'

The growing suspicion of general concepts and ideas — both in its nominalist and mathematical manifestations — had provoked a widespread phobia of inherited forms of logic. Because general arguments necessitated some insinuation of truth — which was itself suspect — we were striking back towards asserting only particulars.

Even then, he was connecting these incipient developments to what can only have been the most fleeting traces of emerging ideological tendencies. Values, he noted, had become suspect also. Liberalism, as the dominant ideological creed, was urging against categorical statements about such as race, religion or nationality, because these risked attribution of value, which in turn prompted division.

'We must not define, subsume, or judge,' he writes, 'we must rather rest on the periphery and display "sensibility toward the cultural expression of all lands and peoples".'

This, he declared 'a process of emasculation.'

Thus, humanity was on the road to increasing fragmentation of the general picture, and a consequent obsession with each of its constituent elements, all of this carved up between men who lacked for no element of knowledge except what it all meant. And all this 'knowledge' promising, as Weaver foresaw, nothing but collapse.

These tendencies he diagnosed as evasions of responsibility and pain. By escaping into the details, the 'modern egotist' could avoid both by insisting on the fallacy that the bigger picture can be constructed out of an array of smaller conclusions. The result was that judgements were never made. This, he anticipated, would be disastrous as the technological age continued to unfold.

'Such obsession with fragments has grave consequences for the individual psychology, not the least of which is fanaticism. Now, fanaticism has been properly described as redoubling one's effort after one's aim has been forgotten, and this definition will serve as a good introduction to the fallacy of technology, which is the conclusion that because a thing can be done, it must be done. The means absorb completely, and man becomes blind to the very concept of ends; indeed, even among those who make an effort at reflection, an idea grows that ends must wait upon the discovery of means. Hence proceeds a fanatical interest in the properties of matter which is psychopathic because it involves escape, substitution, and the undercurrent of anxiety which comes of knowing that the real issue has not been met.'

For this reason, he continues, science and technology placed the soul of man in grave danger. The substitution of means for ends had provoked a disproportion concerning purpose, which he defined as a form of insanity. By knuckling down to study the facts and details, the greater risks and consequences could be elided. 'Let us not question the genuineness of the sigh of relief when people are allowed to go back to their test tubes and their facts.'

Weaver's analysis, written three-quarters of a century ago, seems to me to describe precisely the general nature of our contemporary societal pathologies, as well as underlining the particularities of what we encountered in the Covid scam, offering an almost total diagnosis of the core of the cultural problems now confronting us. Weaver pointed to the growing emotional instability and volatility of temperament already to be observed in inhabitants of urban settings in 1948, accounting these as symptoms of fixation upon small tasks — the industrial world invading the very mind of man. 'It shows itself in fits of fickle admiration,' he observed, 'in excitation over slight causes, in hyper-suggestibility and proneness to panic, all of which render most unlikely that sober estimate of men and things characterizing the philosopher.' By contrast, the man standing close to nature remained stable and balanced, sustained by his broader view of reality and its essence.

Is this not all too familiar to us, we who labour under the yoke of Woke and write, as though for some form of time capsule, under the shadows of the boots that, as Orwell predicted, threaten to come down at any instant upon our faces and writing fingers?

Yet, superficially, this culture of specialism, its attention to detail, its obsession with fact, is impressive and seductive. It seems to look deeply into things, a plumbing of reality that seems to be more penetrative and capturing than the broad stroke of the generalist.

An observer, coming into some modern metropolis from a province where traditional values are yet rooted, is impressed by the way in which judgments are made without reference. He encounters arguments which are brilliant, perhaps, within a narrow scope, but which, when pushed a step in the direction of first principles, collapse for want of basic relevance. He finds movements, propagated with all the cleverness of sophisticated techniques, which appear absurd as soon as their presuppositions about human nature and human destiny are laid bare. The fragmentary character of such thinking permits contradictions and sudden reversals, and these prevent emotional composure in the face of choice.

The nub of the issue, Weaver divines, is that the specialist is 'psychically inferior' to both the gentleman and the philosophic doctor who preceded him. It is clear that this is not some marginal commentary, some nibbling at the edges of what men seem to have the potential to become culturally problematic, but a profound, essential analysis of the already malfunctioning core. The specialist who thinks of himself as part of the self-perfecting mission of 'progress' is, in truth, immensely inferior to his predecessors — the gentleman and the philosophic doctor — in the most vital conceivable respects.

'He is like some parvenu striving to cover up with self-assertion the guilty feeling that he is not qualified. For the truth is that fanaticism and emotional instability, tension and flightiness, are incompatible with that seasoned maturity which we expect in a leader. The man who understands has reason to be sure of himself; he has the repose of mastery. He is the sane man who carries his center of gravity in himself; he has not succumbed to obsession which binds him to a fragment of reality. People tend to trust the judgments of an integrated personality and will prefer them even to the official opinions of experts. They rightly suspect that expertise conceals some abnormality of viewpoint.'

The specialist, he says, 'stands ever at the borderline of psychosis,' which inevitably leads to the thought that a society grounded in such 'expertise' could not but become unstable, unhinged, deranged, and, not to put a tooth in it, mad. Men obsessed with fragments can be no more reasoned with than psychotics, he declared. This amounts to a vanity rooted in obsession with minutiae. The qualities required to preserve a civilisation were incalculably subtler, which meant that it would have to be saved 'from some who profess to be its chief lights and glories.'

In 1937, just months before the beginning of the Second World War, the novelist Robert Musil delivered a lecture in Vienna titled 'On Stupidity', in which he tried to separate everyday stupidity — which is of a type where insight occurs infrequently but nevertheless is always a possibility — from a higher stupidity: the stupidity of the elites, a phenomenon almost impossible to describe, it being 'a dangerous disease of the mind that endangers life itself.' Musil was critiquing the stupidity of the regime then in control of Austria, which would dress up stupidity 'in all the clothes of truth.'

We now find ourselves at a comparable moment, but this time, the conditions that Richard M. Weaver was to diagnose a decade later are now achieving their full-blown manifestation. In the spring of 2020, all around the world, but markedly throughout what we call 'The West', the 'expert' elites, using ideology as a kind of talisman, launched a sustained attack on human existence aimed at destroying everything it had been up to the day before. With their smooth bedside manners and their pristine white coats, the experts imposed themselves as heroic life-savers, carrying out selfless acts of public ministration and compassion. They did not, of course, reveal the extent of the financial recompense they were receiving for these endeavours and benevolences from the corporations who stood to gain if the lies being sold were believed and absorbed.

In our modern world, its moment-to-moment public discourse characterised by statistical analysis, cybernetic opinion polling, scientific data and sociological positivism, we have reached a situation in which the very future of our civilisation is threatened because there is no over-arching wisdom. There are no philosophic doctors and the 'gentleman' is a figure of fun. The poets and minstrels have gone over to the dark side, and the higher thinking of the metaphysicians, theologians and philosophers is not considered relevant unless it comes grounded in some form of pseudo-scientific research. Opinion polls and focus groups are the oracles of our time. Higher truths cannot be mentioned without being dismissed as religious mumbo-jumbo or superstitious nonsense. The dogma of scientism which allows for no consideration of anything that is not objectively demonstrable according to a narrow schema of methodology, is the Gospel of the Day.

Communism, as a Marxist experiment, was built on the dogmas of positivism and scientism. Positivist socialism continues to believe that somehow society can be controlled by man armed with 'The Science', that a utopian society can be formed and enforced by man, through a sense of supposedly higher knowledge and understanding, even though this, as Weaver describes, is akin to the fixed gaze upon the middle-distance of the drunk who fears losing his balance and collapsing. Ardent socialists continue to repeat the disgraced shibboleths of the failed socialist experiment. No matter how many times this experiment is shown not merely to have failed but to have delivered outright disaster, the world keeps returning to it as to a beguiling ex-lover who claims not to have been given a fair chance to prove her affection.

Modern education encourages specialisation as a virtue, and dismisses grounding in the humanities as a kind of indulgence in irrelevancies. The more 'educated' people become in our cultures now, the less able they are to see what is under their noses. One of the chief reasons people from a manual work background were better able to see through the Covid ruse was that they were not compartmentally 'educated' but generally better able to integrate their thinking with the evidence of their senses by virtue of using, for example, their hands in the course of their quotidian actions and activities. Manual labour is much derided in 'educated' circles, but many forms of such work allow for a much more integrated, holistic view of the world. Every human being, in the earliest stage of life, discovers the world via the senses: sight, touch, smell, sound and taste. In the world up to a couple of generations ago, this, augmented with a sprinkling of the 'three 'r's', was the whole of an education, and afterwards, the individual had to investigate the world on his own, using the methods and skills he had acquired from the cradle. What we call 'education' today cuts off the sensual aspects of learning at a relatively early stage, and switches to an exclusive mix of abstractions and concepts, all acquired by dint of committing to memory the selected contents of a narrow range of books, all of them ideologically chosen. Among the consequences of this is that the automatic use of the senses, and the memory of previous sensual experience, to confirm or rebut the validity or veracity of a received 'fact', is abandoned in favour of rote learning and the construction of a version of the world that is 'rational' in the sense that all its parts are designed to relate to and connect with all the others. The problem enters in when, as the pupil ascends through the system, he is more and more required to specialise, to acquire a detailed 'expertise' within a narrow section of overall knowledge, and only a very sketchy impression of all the rest, and all of this is removed from his sensual grasp of the world. This is one of the things that Richard M. Weaver saw coming.

And there is, furthermore, a collective problem related to this: that, whereas each pupil, each graduate, each qualified 'expert' has, at the end of this process acquired a profound and detailed knowledge of his own specialisation, and all the specialisations, taken together, amount — theoretically — to the totality of all possible knowledge, there is no over-arching discipline by which the implications of each area of expertise may be seen in relation to all the others, and accordingly have its judgements and verdicts adjudicated within a total scheme of things. Instead, what we have is a babble of specialisms, each one discrete and, in a sense, absolute, but by no means capable of reconciliation as to their overall meaning in culture or social discourse. Expert A knows everything about subject Z; expert B knows everything about subject Y; expert C knows everything about subject X, and so on. But expert A knows nothing about subjects X and Y; expert B knows nothing about subjects X and Z; and expert C knows nothing about subjects Y and Z. And, when conflicts occur across boundaries between the disciplines, there is no expert — no philosophic doctor or 'gentleman' — capable of reconciling or resolving them. Such is the tragedy of the modern culture of experts. In the 'babble of expertise', each 'expert' speaks over the shoulders, or to the shaking heads, or the raised hands of the others suppressing their yawns, each one waiting his chance to speak his only truth, neither listening nor synthesising. And, while each one speaks, each of the others is as though a layperson, more often than not just as baffled by the arcane argot in use, and unable to say whether what he hears is true or false. And, in the same fashion as the total layman, he is told he has no right to an opinion about any of it, and so when asked, responds that it is 'not my area of expertise'. Thus, each 'expert' is not merely qualified only in a single subject, but he, no more than the total layman, is not permitted to challenge or question any of the other 'experts', or he too will face the equivalent of the question: *What are you — Henry Ford?*

This is why the experts of the present day almost always seem like comical figures. In truth, though speaking with great authority on a single subject, they know almost nothing about anything else. Indeed, their concentration of energies into a single discipline has starved their imaginations of insight into other matters, and so they are as though dunces in about 99 per cent of reality. The humble binman who reads the *New Scientist* or *Popular Science* may know a great deal more about a greater number of topics, and yet is utterly without authority, whereas the specialist has the power to bring whole civilisations to a standstill by recommending that citizens be locked in their homes or injected with what, being untested, may turn out, for all anyone can predict, to be a lethal poison.

In this world, there is no reconciliation of risks with remedies, no balancing of precautions based on an overarching calculus, no overall authority 'qualified' to demand such measures or responses. The politician nods at everything; the journalist is silent before it all; the cleric shrugs and suggests a prayer. None of the books from which all this alleged learning emanated in the first place are available to be scrutinised, and their contents independently verified. There are no independent verifiers, no fact-checkers of the factoid experts. The sole recourse of the layman listener is to carry out, to the highest degree possible, the letter of what every single expert says should be done, even if these actions and courses are mutually contradictory to the point of inviting more or less instant chaos. Hence, our culture has become a kind of parody along the lines that Machiavelli warned his prince against, with politicians incapable of mediating between contradictory advice from a range of autonomous and discrete 'experts' whose opinions and advices appear to be irreconcilable as far as the politician is able to say. And this is before we take account of the hidden material interests at play from the perspective of each of the sundry experts who throw their tuppenceworth into the mixture. The result being a distorted jabber of unchecked and uncheckable theories and opinions, it ought not be a surprise to encounter, in reality, a few years down the line, a pervasive and metastasising chaos.

As to whether it might be possible to reverse these tendencies, Weaver was pessimistic. The restoration of a genuinely liberal system of education, he thought, would be a start, but it is implicit in the other sections of his book that he did not imagine this to be a possibility. At the heart of his thesis was that democracy was itself damaging the chances of retaining a functional civilisation. The most important general event of his time, he argued, was the steady eradication of the necessary distinctions and hierarchies that create society. If society is something that can be understood, it must have structure and hierarchy. Without these elements, there can be no integration of variegated human beings, and as a result, the centre is unable to hold, and chaos inevitably follows.

It was clear from the outset that the 'Covid project' was a coup: in each territory, an *autogolpe* — self-coup — in which the prior value systems were being torched and demolished. Such was the official contempt for freedoms, rights, constitutions and the rule of law that any half-intelligent person must have been able to intuit that there could be no going back under the prevailing systems of politics and administration. The willing or coerced participation in the coup of multiple layers of disparate establishments, and their willingness to act in a tyrannical lockstep, ought to have conveyed to the populations of the West that all bets were off and the bookie had cashed up and gone awol.

One of the key giveaways was the placid willingness of political establishments, and the governments they administered, to publicly delegate authority to 'expert' agents, agencies and entities beyond the political realm. In the past, it had been a principle of political leadership that, whereas all governments had always had advisors, these were generally kept in the background — indeed, in some instances, maintained quite separately from the governmental chambers, and consulted only when a particularly arcane difficulty required to be approached on the basis of specialist knowledge. The legendary Irish Taoiseach, Charles J. Haughey, for example, famously declared that economists ought never be allowed into the same room as government ministers, but should be maintained in a separate room at a fair distance and, when required, have messages brought to and from them on pieces of paper. The point, obviously, was that political authority was a matter of sacred delegation by the people, and ought not be sub-franchised to unelected agents or entities.

All this went out the window from the outset of the Covid scam. Politicians, ministers, prime ministers, presidents, all suddenly demonstrated their preparedness to share the stage with grey-looking, slightly clownish figures who spouted figures and statistics and formulae in a manner that exhibited no sense of responsibility to explain itself. The politicians, standing in the shadows, merely nodded their heads or shrugged their shoulders. Thus did they make a mistake analogous to that described by Machiavelli, of handing their authority to a dissonant chorus of babblers, who gradually altered the tone of their announcement so as to exclude the spectre of the politicians from what became their unmediated issuing of diktats and prohibitions. The political establishments of the West were, in effect, cuckolding themselves, facilitating the 'expert' proxies of the external colonising overlords, and all the while pretending to be still in charge. One possibility here is that, mistaking their own cowardice for cleverness, the politicians failed to see that they were publicly handing over the authority entrusted to them by their peoples. Another — even more ominous — is that they already knew that the death hymn of democracy was being sung, and that part of what was happening was a kind of dramatisation of contempt for the democratic process, a ritual of slash-and-burn being conducted in plain sight so as to place beyond doubt that there would be no going back to old assumptions or the old order. Thus, on the orders of the predator overlords, our political establishments were collaborating with their own symbolic public castration, possibly on a promise of reward via the medium of fake money or the prospect of seats on the ark, but either way having already abandoned their oaths and their promises, and most of all the people to whom these oaths and promises were made. They understood that the New World Disorder was coming, but knew of no 'expert' capable of turning it back in its tracks.

YEAR FIVE
2024

CHAPTER 32
THE EMPTY RAINCOAT, PART I: WORLD WITHOUT EMPATHY
14-01-2024

An old magazine or book functions as a kind of time capsule, which, by virtue of its particularities, eccentricities and eclecticism, can yield up three-dimensional emotional bromide-prints of the past.

WHAT IT IS LIKE NOW

Maybe we sometimes become unnecessarily inventive in our attempts to understand what is happening to the world — though especially to the West. Maybe it is simpler than it seems, even though its simplicity can sometimes be the most shocking, the most incomprehensible thing.

Beep-beep! The human race is being tooted to the effect that it must go into reverse. But the 'elites' will go forward into what they assume will be a bright future. The world will become not merely two-speed, but duo-directional — forwards and backwards.

This is astounding. That the entirety of our democratic institutions has been dismantled as though under cover of darkness. Last night, they were there; today we got up, and they are gone, and without any discussion, that we can recall, having occurred.

It was decided.

Just not by us.

It was decided that, since democracy was a failed system from the viewpoint of wealth accumulation, important decisions should no longer be referred to the people. The 'elites' made the decision themselves, by way of starting as they intended to go on.

The representatives of the people were present, after a fashion, but they were no longer — other than nominally — the representatives of the people. They looked now not outwards to their putative fellows, but upwards to the emperors in the gods. It was as if someone had reached down and unplugged the sovereign and authoritative energy of the people, and plugged in the stout cable emanating from above.

The 'above' is interesting, for it is a vantage point achieved not by democratic means but ordained on the basis of wealth — and therefore power — and self-election. But it should be acknowledged, in the interests of factuality, that the representatives of the people did not demur from this arrangement, and, indeed, undertook to ensure that the people would come to accept it also, marshalling all the instruments that had been put in place for the protection of the people, *against the people*.

It was the matter-of-fact manner in which all this was effected that made it, in a sense, mysterious. It was not a coup conducted with tanks and guns and armoured cars trundling into towns in the middle of the night. It occurred without sound or activity, so that it remained unclear exactly when it had been effected, or even if anything had happened at all. Hence the word 'coup' seemed inappropriate, and lent itself to disputation, if not derision. But the signs were there, not just in the diktats being issued by the former democratic leaders of the people, but in their altered demeanours, expressions and utterances. Now they spoke not as leaders of a government or a people, but as though the representatives, proxies, of an occupying power, which is, in fact, what — as though overnight — they had become.

For 46 months and counting, we have parsed, diced and spliced the possible explanations for the inexplicable: Why did our 'liberal' world collapse under the swat of the first rolled-up newspaper carrying the threat of an untested bug wrapped in a tissue of lies? Before this blow, everything collapsed: the conventions, the charters, the treaties, the constitutions, the rules of law, the laws of the earth, the sea and the skies. Nothing remained standing in those sunny days of April 2020, in the wake of the Ides of March, when all this seemed to happen as though on just another day at the office.

We have laid down, time and time again, the questions: Was it the slow disintegration of liberalism under the contamination of Marxism? Was it, purely and simply, the return of the repressed ghost of colonialism, seeking another chance to subdue and claim the world? Was it something to do with the relentless assault of the jackhammer of propaganda? Was it the slow insinuation in the human heart of a technical instinct of apprehension? Was it some long-hidden craving for authority that had somehow survived the attrition of the consumer society, the hedonism of the post-1960s West, the babble of modern pop culture, the constant talk of liberation, egalitarianism, equity, equality, diversity, plurality and rights? Was it some secret, undetected collapse of our constitutional repub-lic(s) that became visible only when, as though with a rotten oak tree, someone passing thought to touch it with a finger and, the finger meeting no residual resistance, the Republic, like the tree, was toppled?

And did it not seem — if only for the sake of a coherent metaphor — that the undertones and undertows of all this suggested the brooding presence of some alien watchers, swaying to some different beat, tapping into invisible channels to effect their will via the venality of the morally lesser humans?

Or ought we just, as usual, recall and follow the advice of Deep Throat to Bob Woodward in that underground carpark, more than half a century ago: *Follow the money?*

Or, was it something set deep in human nature, some craving for authority mating with and wedding a long-suppressed lechery after power, the two finding common cause and mutual, consensual satisfaction?

Or all of the above, simultaneously and together, with the possible exception (for the sake of rationality) of the brooding alien watchers?

We pondered all these conundrums, and more. We tore out the remnants of our hair, and shredded the licences for our TVs. We made bonfires of our news-papers and magazines, which now seemed to take us for fools. But the mystery seemed to remain. All of these 'explanations' were in one way or another satis-factory in themselves, without appearing to crack open the puzzle, which remained more or less intact, even after we had pondered each one in turn.

What melted the resolve of the West?

Was it money? As simple as that? Something as old as, if not the hills, then certainly as old on the oak trees on the hills and the deep roots with which they plumbed the ground in which we imagined our civilisation to be abundantly founded?

Was it power chasing money or money chasing power, or a three-legged race between the two that overcame, surpassed, eclipsed and defeated everything we had taken for granted about the nature and structure of said civilisation?

We remember, or think we do, a mist of wistful yearning for a perfection of the crude freedoms we had carved out for ourselves — the non-stop talk of liberty and future that had accompanied our childhood playing, our teenage rebellion, our adult plans and schemes — but yet we had awoken one March morning to find it wrapped up and stamped and ready to be collected, having been sold by men in shiny suits that seemed to think themselves our owners and masters.

Those of us of a certain age were strikingly divided into those who were champing at the bit and foaming from the ears, and those who seemed barely to notice that anything had happened at all. This difference seemed to arise from what we had in common: that, at one stage or another, we had been crypto-lefties, to whom freedom meant more than something. Few of us had been to any significant degree ideological, but just thought left was kinder than right. Somewhere along the way, we had divided into those who regarded these sentiments as tickets to a seat at the table of power and influence, and those who, disenchanted, had drifted to what their erstwhile comrades called The Right and we — for I was one such — deemed simply The Middle Ground of Common Sense.

But, *oh!*, what fun we had, in those halcyon days of the Sixties/Seventies/Eighties, when we were young and innocent and free! Yes, *free*. We were all lefties then, all raging against 'The Man', even though we were but vaguely aware of who 'The Man' might be. We raged against Thatcher also, and sometimes said she was a man too, and exalted Red Ken and Arthur Scargill. We lapped up *Boys From the Blackstuff* and, for a month in the autumn of '82, were, all of us, Yosser Hughes. But that was not all we were. We were rebels and freedom-lovers, and liberals and luvvies (though not self-confessed). In June 1984, I travelled to Galway with the sole intention of shaking my fist at Ronald Reagan, on account of the US's interference in Nicaragua and El Salvador. It was a highly successful trip. On Eyre Square, the President saw me from his passing car and, at first making to wave in my direction, seeing my clenched fist, turned sharply and waved to the far side of the street. I came home, tired but happy.

We did not just *believe* in freedom: freedom was the meaning of our existence, the freedom we enjoyed and the freedom we wished for ourselves and people we would never meet.

Though few have much to say on the matter, there is an imaginative difficulty in accessing the meaning, significance, even the reality of all this. It seems to be happening and yet could not possibly be happening. It is implausible, and yet it seems to be real. Plumbing its depths of strangeness and injustice is not easy, not least because this necessity is hardly ever or anywhere recognised. People who understand what has happened know that this is utterly unprecedented in the whole of human history; people who do not are oblivious to there being anything amiss at all. There are therefore, in a sense, two different ways of describing reality — one as something like the end of the world as we have known it; the other as just another day at the office.

We depend on the surrounding conversation to affirm what we understand as reality. When that is not present, or is radically corrupted, or is internally contradictory, the effect is to make us doubt at some non-specific level what we 'know'. We are cast adrift in a no-man's-land of disbelief and confusion. We do not fall into the arms of the propagandists — we know to hate them because we know they are lying because we know what is true. But we also know that there is sometimes a difference between what is true and what is *real*, and that this is one of those times. Beliefs, even if clearly mistaken or wrong, acquire a certain weight by virtue of being stated by large numbers of people. And, no matter how strong your conviction concerning what you 'know', it becomes something different to reality when it is contradicted by the perspectives, the demeanours and the silences of large numbers of the adjacent population.

All the things we ever said, all the things we claimed to believe, all the things we thought and taught — everything, from the whole of our lives and for a distance before them, stretching back into history — all has turned to dust. We are as though children on our first day at school, if not our first day on God's Earth.

WHAT IT USED TO BE LIKE

The issue here is memory as a path to truth. In the miasma of a pseudo-reality, it becomes not merely harder to know what is true, but also, arising from the operation of certain escalatory mechanisms of that process of befuddlement, impossible to remember what the past was like as a measure of comparison with the present, so that one cannot any longer be certain that one's sense of alienation is not simply being distorted by subjectivity. As we have been observing for the past 47 months, it is remarkable how easily people can be persuaded that things they took for granted in the past never actually happened, and that things that seem disturbing about the present arise from their own misperceptions and misrememberings. Manipulation of the news about the present can assist in creating this effect, as can a cessation or curtailment of talk about the past which, by virtue of being repeatedly denied, may increasingly seem to amount to muddled recollections, or just still more misapprehensions.

Memory is a vital tool in keeping straight and sane in such circumstances. It would be easy to fall into a mode of thinking in which it had strayed beyond question that, for example, the menace and venom of the political class was a normal and habitual state of affairs. Given the unanimity of those holding official megaphones in conveying a singular perspective, it might even be easy to think that the hostility was in some way deserved, that we, the people (small 'p' now, in keeping with the overall temper) had deserved no less or no more. This, more or less, is what George Orwell meant when he cautioned that 'who controls the past controls the future; who controls the present controls the past.'

The difficulty is in retaining contact with the past so that its deep nature may be retained in a state of relatively intact recovery, in the event that some issue of dissonance arises as between past and present. It is a question of imagination, but even more so of *feeling*. What matters is not so much 'the facts', though a grasp of facts may be highly germane, but of the capacity to reach and access the elusive feeling that derives from the incongruences between what is happening now and what experience and memory tell about what happened before. Something vital may be missing, causing a break in connection, so that I appear to be adrift in a dream (for which read 'nightmare') world, where all the physical topography is as it always appeared, but almost nothing that is happening within it makes any sense. It is as if there has been a rupture of logic, or human personality, or behavioural patterns, or . . . *something*. It is by no means clear what that 'something' is. People have changed, most of all those who hold the stage. They speak differently, using different forms of reasoning, different tonality, a novel edge of menace. They seem to have forgotten how things used to be, the way we used to take certain things as given, such as the sovereignty of the people, and the necessity to bear the next election in mind at all times. But the changes are so integrated into the personalities of the newly empowered despots that they remain elusive to scrutiny. It is only in the overall feeling it evokes that the change manifests itself, and this is beyond description.

In seeking to plumb and parse these circumstances, I find my old stacks of political and cultural and (even) music magazines from the 1970s and 1980s to be an invaluable tool of comparison, providing a yardstick by which the deviations can be measured and verified. There is something about an old magazine that is a little like looking through a window into a past time and feeling the life that is there in all its clarity and authenticity. These magazines that I had almost begun to agree with my wife were a pointless waste of space, have now revealed themselves as a vital instrument of combatting the pseudo-reality of 2024.

An old magazine functions as a kind of time capsule, which by virtue of its particularities, eccentricities and eclecticism, can yield up three-dimensional emotional bromide-prints of the past. To scan or read an article from 40 or 60 years ago, and to derive from it a flavour of the sentiment and demeanour of its moment in time, and then to compare this — imaginatively, emotionally — with what the present feels like, is a strangely powerful thing. The sensations that result, with their dissonances and tensions and jarring ironies — can lead to new ways of understanding what has happened to make the present and its happenings what they are.

Books, too, of course, though they are less consistently reliable, since so many books are 'timeless', especially novels, which is to say that, by virtue of being self-enclosed worlds, they tend to focus on longitudinal perspectives of the human condition, and do not vibrate in the same way with the official or political lives of nations. Old magazines, especially ones dealing with current affairs or cultural matters, are by far the most reliable hedge against the imposed amnesia of the present and the coming time.

Occasionally, though, one comes across a book that carries within it an unusual capacity for exploding capsules of truthful memory concerning what it was like before. Towards the end of last year, I came across, in a secondhand shop, a copy of a book I first read when it came out many years ago, and which I remember as having a profound impact on the thinking of that time — a time of growing uncertainty and discussion concerning the already shifting and heaving nature of the approaching future, chiefly in the realms of work, income, meaning and human dignity, as a consequence of the coming technological revolution. This book was published exactly 30 years ago, in 1994, a moment in history that has been mentioned by more than one observer as representing some kind of milestone at the end of the 1960s period of uncomplicated freedom, and the beginning of the era that preceded and laid the groundwork for the one that ended in or around the Ides of March 2020, when things started to get *really serious*.

The book in question is *The Empty Raincoat*, by Charles Handy, a seminal cultural intervention that erupted into the world just at the moment when the dilemmas of the future world, economically and behaviourally, were beginning to be faced and considered, a handful of years before the dawn of the third millennium, which was to see shifts in human reality that were to make his book possibly far more vital to the future than it seemed at its moment of publication. The title refers to a figure Handy came across in an open-air sculpture in Minneapolis, USA, called 'Without Words', by Judith Shea. It depicts a raincoat in bronze, upright but empty, representing the absent person, the disappearance of the human. Handy described it as the 'symbol of our most pressing problem.'

Published in 1994, *The Empty Raincoat* — subtitled 'New Thinking For a New World' — is a book that, in large part because of its title, contrived to spark a moment of democratic wondering between the economic crises of the 1980s and the unknowable future lying mysteriously ahead. It is one of those books that you 'remember' in a certain way — in one sense as banal, almost, as a textbook of management theory, but which withal catered to the everyday public imagination in its time — and which now surprises you when you revisit it at a 30-year remove because it reveals itself as having spoken, in its moment of exploding, to more than was actually known at the time of its publication. It fingered a pulse in Western society that had become alert to the possibility of human obsolescence arising from technological advancement and the problems accruing therefrom, but later was to become seduced out of this wakefulness. In this sense, it acts as a useful mnemonic of the moments before we entered the present phase, with the escalation of 'prosperity' from the mid-1990s, culminating in the crash of 2008, and then the rapid slide down the totalitarian hill to 2020.

Handy wrote:

'What is happening in our mature societies is much more fundamental, confusing and distressing than I had expected. It is that confusion which I am addressing in this book. Part of the confusion stems from our pursuit of efficiency and economic growth, in the conviction that these are the necessary ingredients of progress. In the pursuit of these goals we can be tempted to forget that it is we, we individual men and women, who should be the measure of all things, not made to measure for something else. It is easy to lose ourselves in efficiency, to treat that efficiency as an end in itself and not a means to other ends.'

In that brief paragraph, we see captured a snapshot of both the optimism and *naïveté* that characterised human culture up until a few short years ago, in which the assumption of human centrality to human-constructed civilisation and its value-systems — including democracy and constitutional republicanism — was implicit in everything within the public realm that was not concerned with transcendence, a time when politicians were axiomatically understood as the servants of their electorates, when the purpose of politics was to support and exalt human endeavour and happiness, and when the point of economics — the 'science' of economy — was to serve, first, foremost and last, the needs and desires of human beings.

It is mildly shocking to read it now and to think that he might have written the above paragraph in the expectation that it would meet with approval not just from those who might read it, but even the society as a whole, from top to bottom. Reading it in a moment so far removed from such thinking, it is necessary to adjust focus, to twiddle the tuning knob, to crouch down in the undergrowth and watch this strange creature of human thinking mooch about in its territory, oblivious that it is being observed from a temporal distance of three decades.

It is quite shocking to contemplate these words in the very cold light of 2024, at a time when control of previously undreamt-of technology has fallen into the hands of a tiny elite of ruthless men; when the World Economic Forum), having claimed authority over humanity without accruing a single vote, has ordained that, in the near future, we will own nothing and be happy; and when the political establishments of all the Western 'democracies' have folded before all such demands, and the agencies and resources of states are being marshalled to enforce the operational diktats that have been formulated to make all these things happen.

If you were to conduct, using Charles Handy's book, one of those imaginative exercises in comparison — as between the period in which he wrote his book and the present — you might find yourself at the end of the experiment with two words battling for space in your head — one from 1994, the other from the present.

The word I might choose to describe the sentiment and demeanour of *The Empty Raincoat* is elusive in its particularity, but approximately accessible in its intonation: 'Compassion'? 'Ministration'? 'Kindness'? 'Love' (in its broadest senses)? 'Humanity'?

The 'empty raincoat' motif was not so much a warning of human obsolescence in the obvious sense of a decline into practical uselessness by virtue of technological replacement, but more a warning about the loss of creative human agency to the organisational behemoth.

But something attracts me about the book's title that I do not wholly understand. It is mysteriously evocative, especially for a book ostensibly about biz org, and remains a little odd even when you see it explained. I 'get', more or less, the idea of the 'empty raincoat' — a foretelling of something like the threat of a disappearance of the qualities that brought our civilisation to the pitch it was at in 1994. But then I detect a resonance in his title that I am unsure as to whether Handy intended it.

Why did a book about business organisation (though not only that) come to have such widespread appeal? I wonder if it may be because people, at first sight, misread the title as 'The Empathy Raincoat' — for that, though meaningless, would have been closer to capturing the book's tone, mood, demeanour and sensibility. With the addition to the word 'Empty' of an 'a' and a 'h' (*ah!*), the title seems to achieve a capturing of the total disposition of Handy's time capsule.

The Empathy Raincoat is closer to what the book seems to say now, in 2024.

Empathy. Once this word came close to describing the general thrust and intonation of the vast majority of public contributions, whether in the form of books, articles, speeches, interviews, poems or songs. Sometimes this stream of good intentions could set off the tolerance alarms, but in general it was something that we mostly took for granted as the necessary soundtrack of a coexistence that we sensed to be precarious, volatile, and precious. The point, always, was to suggest ways in which this or that might be made better. The tone was such as to honour the common dignity of humanity and its striving for a more harmonious and auspicious coexistence.

In a pretty emblematic passage, Handy writes as though *The Empathy Raincoat* were indeed his title:

'We misinterpreted Adam Smith's ideas to mean that if we each looked after our own interests, some "invisible hand" would mysteriously arrange things so that it all worked out for the best for all. We therefore promulgated the rights of the individual and freedom of choice for all. But without the accompanying requirements of self-restraint; without thought for one's neighbour, and one's grandchildren, such freedom becomes licence and then mere selfishness. Adam Smith, who was a professor of moral philosophy not of economics, built his theories on the basis of a moral community. Before he wrote *A Theory of the Wealth of Nations*, he had written his definitive work — *A Theory of Moral Sentiments* — arguing that a stable society was based on "sympathy," a moral duty to have regard for your fellow human beings. The market is a mechanism for sorting the efficient from the inefficient, it is not a substitute for responsibility.'

The one-word signal reaching us from 1994, then, might be something like 'sympathy'/ 'empathy' — some 'bottom-line' sense that, when Handy was writing his book, he was trying to ensure the future would be better for human beings, above all that he was taking it for granted that caring about the condition of the human race into the future was a worthy and proper disposition for an author to adopt.

Nothing could be further from the kind of words we might arrive at now, by way of capturing the essence of where, just 30 years later, our societies have fetched up. I'm almost reluctant to say it, but there can surely be no controversy at this stage about the suggestion that any meditation upon the present would be bound to yield a word such as 'control', or 'enforcement', or 'menace', or 'malevolence', as a means of naming the dominant note of the culture we inhabit.

The idea of public officials, politicians or health tsars lining up to issue diktats to the people about their presumptions concerning rights, entitlements and freedoms; about the requirement for radical amendments in their behaviours and expectations; about the imminent threats of diseases (how would they know?) and wars (ditto); about the requirement to moderate their opinions and arrest their thoughts well short of utterance — such things would in 1994 have generated shock waves throughout our societies, to be interpreted instinctively as announcing the onset of some kind of mock dystopia, some contrived hoax calculated to test the alarm systems or rehearse the fire drills, to be followed by bursts of raucous laughter and exclamations of 'Had you going there for awhile!'

The point of politics then was certainly not to berate or chastise people, still less to menace them, still less to belittle them on a daily basis by rubbing their noses in their implicit inferiority to incoming migrants; their subordination to the demands of corporations; their worthlessness in the face of the machinations of rich, self-imagined overlords; and their powerlessness to resist the most radical and draconian attacks on the ways of life and being that had endured in human society for hundreds of years. For this, 30 years after Handy took a stab at sketching out a better future than the one he saw coming in 1994, is what we have now arrived to.

The even more chilling thing is that this state of affairs has been permitted to settle in upon us by a process of unspoken consensus. It appears to be taken for granted now by virtually everyone in the crucible of public conversation that the human race, as a whole — though especially its pasty-faced Caucasian incarnation in Europe, Australasia, the Americas and South Africa — deserves to be constrained, divested, disparaged and punished. It is as a child who has been naughty and is therefore cast into disgrace and disapproval, though it is unclear who is arriving at these judgments — most of the time it is as though the culture is constructed in such a way that the errant 'child' itself is required to be his own judge and dean of discipline. The population is reduced to a sullen silence, and yet is characterised by symptoms reminiscent of masochism and Stockholm syndrome, whereby the 'leaders' contrive to be cast in the roles of reluctant enforcers, who deliver the news of each successive privation in a tone of 'this is going to hurt me more than it hurts you.' And yet the snarl is always discernible behind the ostensible measured utterances; the fangs momentarily glimpsed flashing behind the mask of rationality, the ever-present sense of a regime that is fast losing its patience with people who think that freedom is more important than order, control and some unspecified process of retribution.

We have good cause for nostalgia, surveying the long distance we have strayed from the conditions in Western civilisation in which Charles Handy wrote *The Empty Raincoat*, and even more in contemplating the abyss that separates us from the kind of world he was hoping might emerge.

Handy was — (he died in December 2024, aged 92 — JW, 2025) — an organisational guru, and that is the main focus of the book: how organisations need to adapt themselves to the unknowable future. But there is a deeper thread: the shift in the nature of work and the opportunities the future appeared at that time to offer, whereby human beings might be able to reclaim their creativity in an emerging freelance economy in which no one would be confined to a singular mode of economic functioning, but each would have the possibility of maintaining a 'portfolio' of options. Deeper down, he digs into the question of existential self-sufficiency, the democratic yearning for possession of the means of human sustenance, which at the time was treated as something to be taken for granted, but has since revealed itself as though terminally problematic as a result of the circumstantial transfer of the ownership and control of technology out of democratic hands.

When I worked as a newspaper columnist in the 1990s, these were intermittent themes of mine also, as they had been going back at least a decade before, to the time when I edited and wrote for a number of alternative magazines — generally left-leaning — in which these questions, and associated topics such as Universal Basic Income (then quite a benign proposition to provide a bedrock, no-strings, subsistence income for everyone) and the looming technological revolution, were rarely off the op-ed pages.

Back in 1994, Big Tech was unheard of, and to a high degree, unimaginable. Companies like Apple and Microsoft were already in existence, but the Second Coming of Steve Jobs was as yet three years in the future, and the horses of habitual expectation remained undisturbed. At the time, the chief concern was with the conundrum of redistributing wealth and resources in a situation whereby machines might be doing most of the necessary work. There was some talk about 'meaning' and 'human dignity', but not much about ownership and control. Indeed, there appeared to be a sense — perhaps arising from an exaggerated sensitivity provoked by the fall of communism — that technologies, regardless of their potential reach or effect, ought naturalistically to fall within the ownership of their creators. This, after all, had pretty much always been the way. There simply was no grasp of the implications of this proposal in the context about to dawn, or that what had always been so might no longer be sane.

In this context, we should recognise that Handy's call for a ramping up of 'sympathy' was something more than a pious injunction. Already, a new wave of prosperity was sweeping across America, rendering it possible for markets to cater to the majority. Interest rates were falling from a spectacular high. There was a generalised expectation (spurious, as it turned out) of a democratisation of opportunity, that the rising tide would raise (nearly) all the boats. In these conditions, the traditional preacherly injunctions to 'be kind to others' were already losing traction in an increasingly ideological world. Handy went on to bemoan the prevailing economic climate as one in which 'the rich still get richer and the poor still get poorer,' but his words ring hollow now, in a world where this process has, in the interim, escalated to such a monstrous degree that the words seem almost pitifully inadequate to capture the extent and scale of today's abyss between the increasing stashes of the plutocrats and the diminishing chump change of the plebs. The roots of this problem rest not in an absence of compassion or charity, so much as in a deficit of observation and a paucity of thinking. The human race, taken altogether, took its eye off the ball and directed it elsewhere.

Handy captured the unspoken fears, inciting through his remarkable title many more readers than might ordinarily have read such a book. Although his title seems to contain a warning of what has since occurred, the book does not today read as though its author had more than a general and limited sense of what was going to unfold. His prognosis is rooted in its own time; it is not a foretelling of the future in which we have arrived. And yet, today, it reads as a sad record of a time when it was assumed that the human race, *qua* human race, would retain control of the means of its own survival and prospering, and that this was to be regarded as self-evidently necessary and beneficial.

On the question of prophecy, he wrote:

'Prophets, in spite of their name, do not foretell the future. No one can do that, and no one should claim to do that. What prophets can do is to tell the truth as they see it. They can point to the emperor's lack of clothes, that things are not what people like to think they are. They can warn of dangers ahead if the course is not changed. They can, and often did, point their fingers at what they thought to be wrong, unjust or prejudiced. Most of all, they can offer a way of thinking about things, a way to clarify the dilemmas and concentrate the mind.

'What the prophet cannot, and should not, do is to tell the doers what to do. That would be to take the power without the responsibility, the prerogative of the harlot, they used to say, not the prophet. It would be to steal other people's decisions. The prophet can provide a chart but cannot dictate where or how the vessel should sail.'

The chief value of the book for us today is in providing a point of solidity from which to engage in a measurement of the distance we have travelled under different headings, and using this to calculate where the most serious mistakes might have been made. Throughout its text, *The Empty Raincoat* seems, almost naïvely, to assume that human society will always remain concerned about ensuring that the processes of work and production will remain centred on the well-being and furtherance of the human race, and the management of its endeavours on behalf of its own advancing and progression. This notion emerges from the text not so much as a stated verity but as an axiomatic assumption that needs no explicit articulation. It is 'obvious' — is it not? — that work and business will always occur, foremost and exclusively, for the good of humanity as a whole?

The central themes of the book include: the propositions that efficiency and profitability ought not be valued above the needs and deeper desires of human beings; that, in pursuing the ends, we should not ignore the damage often wrought by the means; that increasing consumption creates as many problems as it seems to ameliorate. That there is more to life than 'winning'; that a stable society is based on people having regard for their neighbours. Time, he suggested, is of the essence — the same concept having opposite meanings for two categories of people. For the rich, time is money — they spend money to save time; for the poor, time is something they have to excess, something, as you might say, that they must 'kill'.

Some of Handy's thoughts now seem archaic and almost quaint, and yet he moves always to the centre of things.

'We were not meant to stand alone. We need to belong to something or some-one. Only where there is a mutual commitment will you find people prepared to deny themselves for the good of others. We, however, in our belief in liberalism and individualism, are wary of commitments. We look suspiciously at words like "loyalty" and "duty" and "obligation".

'Independence, whether we seek it or not, is being thrust upon us. Modern society knows no neighbours, said Disraeli more than a century ago, and it has been no different since. Loneliness may be the real disease of the next century, as we live alone, work alone and play alone, insulated by our modem, our Walkman or our television. The Italians may be wise to use the same word for both alone and lonely, for the first ultimately implies the second. It is no longer clear where we connect or to what we belong. If, however, we belong to nothing, the point of any striving is hard to see.'

Chiefly, the material of the book centres on what Handy deems the 'para-doxes' of human economic endeavour, first and foremost among which is the understanding that 'if economic progress means that we become anonymous cogs in some great machine, then progress is an empty promise.' In this sentence, we can sense an implicit warning of a possible calamity that may befall us unless we are careful — the surrender to the technical, to the technolo-gisation of the human; the amnesia about 'peripheral' issues of dignity and meaning; the sidelining of qualities like sympathy and empathy. Handy believes that every individual has to accept the challenge of filling their empty raincoat, which is to say, make life meaningful in the context of what they do with their time. But there is no precise anticipation here of the scale of the impending collapse into a form of digital enslavement, whereby our entire lives would become as though directed through the prism of technological progress, and the apparatus of this process would come to be owned by a tiny elite of utterly insane despots and dilettantes who would come to regard the human race as just so many lab rats for their own use and amusement. Handy did not see this coming, and nor did anyone else; but Handy, nevertheless, by sensing something urgent that went beyond what was knowable, captured something that at least provides us now with a point of reference. In fact, at the core of his book is the argument that life is so full of paradoxes that future drifts cannot adequately be grasped or understood. In many respects, his book might be read as perhaps the last remonstrance of the old world that we so manifestly failed to pay sufficient attention to in its passing.

The purpose of this short series of chapters on Handy's book is rather a modest one: to draw attention to things that are either fairly obvious or discernible in plain sight, but also to underline the fact that what is 'obvious' has ceased to be the conventional wisdom, and that 'plain sight' has been replaced by a kind of hologram, chiefly conveyed by words and thoughts, that prevents many people seeing through to what is there — in other words, the 'pseudo-reality' of our frequent invocation, which draws us into the Lie and blocks us from seeing what is really happening. Charles Handy's is not necessarily the best exhibit to attach to such a thesis, since, as he says, his work is not (or was not) prophetic, at least not in the 'normal' (i.e. abnormal: 1984) way. But in another sense, that is why I find it such a good example, since its predictive and sombre implications are, in a sense, 'accidental'. Handy was clearly presuming that Western civilisation would continue more or less as it had. He did not anticipate the present moment of rupture — very likely, such developments as we have seen in recent years would have been unthinkable to him at that time. But herein resides the beauty (the word is not too strong) of his book for us now. For let us be under no illusion but that the Combine and their willing Creeps have the means of persuading the vast majority of the West's population that, before the advent of post-Covid tyranny and toxicity, there was nothing but the same, going back into the mists of history, and Charles Handy's memo to posterity tells us otherwise.

There are probably lots of books that are worth buying that provide a similar effect, though perhaps in subtly different ways. We should be especially alert for them in these troubled times, slipping into charity shops and jumble sales in the hope of finding who-knows-what. In a sense, what we are talking about is reversing the concept of the fictional dystopia so that the benevolent past, offering a kind of summoned-up makeshift 'utopia', becomes available to be remembered or reimagined. This, being a matter of cultivating a new consensus, is different to nostalgia, which is largely a personal thing, and yet it has the power to merge and blend with that much-disparaged emotion of backwards-looking sentimentality, as a way of reassuring us that we aren't wrong in thinking that the world was not always a comprehensively evil place, that there is nothing 'new' or 'normal' about neo-feudalism, and that 'normal' is — precisely — what human beings do when they do not *have to* do anything, i.e. when they are not 'compelled', 'coerced', or bullied into doing things inimical to their collective happiness and well-being.

CHAPTER 33
THE EMPTY RAINCOAT, PART II: THE EMPTY GREATCOAT & OTHER STORIES
21-01-2024

Altogether, Western society, as it presented itself in 2020, was as ready as it would ever be for a revolution that depended on the cowardice of men and the malleability of institutions.

As noted in the last chapter, Charles Handy did not, in his 1994 book, *The Empty Raincoat*, anticipate the kind of dark world we have entered now. He anticipated some turbulence, to be sure, and proposed a number of precautionary strategies, but his outlook was too humane, too liberal, too decent to even contemplate what was actually going to happen before his book was 30 years old.

The world we have inherited is quite unlike the one that Charles Handy implicitly desired. I do not say 'the world he envisaged', for it was not, by definition, his intention to prescribe a particular way of doing things, still less a particular set of outcomes. What concerned him was to retain, at the core of the forward march of humanity, an imperative that the ministering to human needs in the context of human endeavour would be foremost of all considerations. Clearly, nothing could be further from what we now observe, 30-odd years later, when the demeanour of those we have elected to manage our affairs is such as to bark at and barrack us as though for the sin of actually existing. 'Are you still here?' they seem to ask, as though on behalf of some absent/external protagonist. 'What do you think this is — a democracy?' After lifetimes of sucking up to the People for permission to represent them, they now appear able to see the People solely as obstacle, as problem, as nuisance, seeking to express opinions and influence outcomes of important decisions, whereas — clearly—that day has passed some time since.

Yet, there is a remarkable chapter in *The Empty Raincoat* that carries within itself a strange and unintentional prophecy of the world facing us now. The chapter is titled 'The Sigmoid Curve', and it describes the method whereby the prudent head of an organisation might strive to avoid a future plummeting into decline by acting to implement change even while everything appeared to be going swimmingly. The Sigmoid Curve, Handy explains, 'is the S-shaped curve that has intrigued people since time began.' It is the story of life itself, he says: 'We start slowly, experimentally, and falteringly, we wax and we wane.' It is the story of empires, epochs, corporations, dynasties and brands. It tracks the fates of love and relationships. Things blossom and fade, flow and ebb, rise and fall. The Sigmoid Curve contains a prediction that bears down on everything: *One day it will all come to grief.*

But, says Handy, there is life beyond the curve. The right place to start that second curve is before the first one peaks, because beyond the peak is an unavoidable trough. The problem, as Handy — above all an organisational expert — explains, is that the point at which the curve requires to be renewed is also the point at which 'all the messages going through to the individual, or the institution, are that everything is going fine, that it would be folly to change when the current recipes are going so well.' Everything we know of change, be it personal or change in organisations, tells us that the real energy for change comes when you are looking disaster in the face [at the descent stage of the first Sigmoid Curve]; but that point is much too late, because the energy of the enterprise has already started to disintegrate, the leaders have lost credibility and shot their bolts, and morale is already on the floor. Starting the new curve earlier, he stresses, offers a 'Pathway through Paradox' — the way to build a new future while maintaining the present rate of acceleration.

The secret of constant growth is to start a new Sigmoid Curve before the first one peters out, where there is the time, as well as the resources, and the energy, to get the new curve through its initial explorations and floundering before the first curve begins to dip downwards.

I was unable, re-reading this nearly 30 years after I must first have come across the Sigmoid Curve concept in Handy's book, to avoid the realisation that what he is describing might, superficially at least, be taken for the working formula of the Great Reset, which might well be deemed the Sigmoid Curve of human advancement, but without human empathy. Or at least it might seem to be so to someone who thought of the world as an organisation, which most of our generally technocratic-minded politicians and entrepreneurs do nowadays. I do not imagine that Charles Handy thought of the world, or even the cutting-edge Western part of it, in organisational terms. But, in effect, what is happening now is an attempt to coerce the world into a new curve, though without democratic oversight or permission, but with the failed leadership of the past still in place, and without any persuasive evidence that we are anywhere near the point of the first curve petering out. There is — undoubtedly — a sense of urgency, but it is a contrived and imposed sense of urgency which, if we add into the equation of comprehension the fact that we are simultaneously looking at a colossal crime scene — the remnants of a half-century of systemised plunder, interrupted by a *coup d'état* and a suspension of the economic and financial systems — all of which has served to kick the consequences of these toxic initiatives down the road so far that the rolled-up tab will not be picked up short of the third generation, by which time several other rolled-up balls of debt will have gone scudding across the sky, over the heads of the transitory human quotient, into the continuingly unknowable future.

Handy was not naïve. He understood how business worked. 'For a long time, now,' he observes, 'corporate chairmen have been saying that their real assets were their people, but few really meant it, and none went so far as to put these assets on their balance sheet. That may change.'

He understood that we were heading for a world with fewer, albeit more productive and expensive, jobs. One exponential factor he was at the time unable to name or quantify was artificial intelligence, which — as we are now able to see — has the capacity to destroy his model of an exploding creative economy. But he also, along with most decent and sentient humans, had no capacity to anticipate or comprehend the notion of the world becoming an utterly rigged deck. He understood that the drift towards greater and greater demand for more and more intelligence had the capacity to divide society — 'unless we can transform the whole of society into a permanent learning culture where everyone pursues a higher intelligence quotient as avidly as they now look for homes of their own. A property-owning democracy is exciting, though with this new definition of property.'

A recurring motif of the book is the author's unmistakable tone of protectiveness for the human race. Reading it, you retain from the first page that this guy actually cares about the future and is anxious to make sure it is better than the past. Not that he is saying the past is 'bad', but that he is anxious to improve things. How ordinary this was then; how extraordinary it is today, when the entire thrust of public discourse is such as to attack the human race in a manner that makes you question the very humanity of the attackers — to blame and shame people for being people, for living ordinary lives; to warn them in the sternest terms about their expectations, excesses (of certain kinds); to set out a lengthy charge-sheet concerning self-indulgence and misuse of earthly resources; to warn in apocalyptic terms of the ultimate consequences of all this if left unchecked; and then, the pause, the severe silence, in the manner of a sadistic headmaster who says he will postpone punishment for a time until he has deliberated on all the possibilities.

If we are to attribute an error, or an oversight, to Charles Handy, then it is one he shares with most of his race, i.e. the tendency to take for granted that human beings, after 2,500 years of various gradations of democracy and freedom, must remain — as they have long been — still in control of their own destinies. Not that he bothered to say this, for there was no occasion to. He assumed democracy as a minimal condition of all discussion about the human enterprise, or at least the Western manifestation of this. At the time, nobody argued with him about this, and why would they have? But *now* . . . ? Now it is by no means so clear. Or perhaps it is all too clear: All's changed, changed utterly. A terrible ugliness confronts us.

There are multiple reasons why the Great Reset would not have been conceivable in 1994, or for a good few years afterwards. Some of these reasons are conspicuous, obvious and glaring; others are subtle, microscopic and all but invisible. All we can do as yet is draw rough, light lines on a page.

Broadly, there are perhaps three main categories: cultural, economic and technological. The three headings, of course, are interconnected, and may, as we now begin to appreciate, have been subject to manipulation, manoeuvring and nudging — and perhaps for over a longer period than we are even yet beginning to understand. This is to say that although the concept of a Great Reset was not foreseeable or conceivable within the scheme of general culture, it may well have been the subject of secret machinations at a subterranean level.

Certainly, I would say that almost anyone who was alive in 1994 and mature enough to make a judgement, would agree that, culturally speaking, it would have been impossible to pull the Covid stunt at that time. It is not immediately obvious why this is so; it is merely axiomatic, which is to say that, even ten years ago, it would have seemed an unthinkable idea. It is impossible to imagine the people we knew, or lived beside, or worked with then, standing for it for more than ten minutes of polite immobilisation.

The chief reason for this has to do with manhood — the solidity provided to culture by the presence of men of purpose, discretion and courage. Until a relatively short time ago, Western man remained relatively upright and unbowed compared to what, by a process of retrospectively observable osmosis, he was to become. There are innumerable sources to which one might repair in order to draw a sketch of these cultural conditions. I will use three books by three authors: the German psychiatrist, Alexander Mitscherlich (1908-1982); the American poet and essayist, Robert Bly (1926-2021); and the contemporary American writer, R.R. Reno, who is a friend of mine.

In 1963, Mitscherlich published his classic work, *Society Without the Father*, a rich, teeming but somewhat dense and often impenetrable volume in which he diagnosed, or prophesied, the looming demise of the historical Great Father, which he predicted would lead to a new kind of civilisation, which he called 'the sibling society.'

It was already in train when he published his book, barely into the era of Peace & Love. Temperamentally and affectively, he said, the father continued to exist, but his teaching powers, stretching back to the earliest times of the species, had been usurped. Worse, the father as constant presence in the lives of his children, had been assassinated. The presence that 'gave things the stamp of "home"' was now missing; the father had become 'invisible,' the prior fatherly aura of moral authority, having lost its incarnate reality, became invisible and abstract. This had never happened before in human history. It did not mean simply that the father had been rendered absent by separation or divorce or war, but that 'the father imago so closely associated with the roots of our civilisation, and of the paternal instructive pattern,' had disappeared from human culture. This, in many respects, had been a relief, for the father had often been a hard taskmaster, and it was now an occasion of satisfaction that his cough had been softened. Now he was reduced to a mere bogeyman, a kind of Dean of Punishments, at the behest of the mother, who became the largely unchecked and unmediated guide of her children, who now had access primarily to a singular mode of being — the feminine mode. This, Mitscherlich warned, had been followed hard by a 'socialised hatred of the father,' which had a profound unconscious effect on the father's offspring, who had fallen into a spiral of regression, alienation, anxiety, aggression and loneliness. The banishment of the father created in the children a sense of rebelliousness that had no means of reconciling itself.

Authority had lost its substance, its affection, becoming a spectral presence in the home, now stripped of its affective dimension. Beyond the home, by a process of overspill, the society in which the father's word had been law was becoming subject to other sources of order and coercion. This led to the replacement of the father-led society with what Mitscherlich calls the 'mass society,' in which the role of the father as guide and mentor is taken up by the media. Among the consequences of this, he predicted, would be 'loveless childhood and lifeless old age.'

This new type of society, he clarified, had emerged mainly out of an increase in work specialisation, which itself had arisen from the industrial revolution, which removed the working father — a competent or tolerable 'jack-of-all-trades' — from the presence of his children, and deposited him on a production line, into a work cubicle or behind a desk. 'The fatherless (and increasingly also motherless) child grows up into an adult with no visible master, exercises anonymous functions, and is guided by anonymous functions,' he wrote. 'What his senses are aware of is individuals similar to himself in huge numbers.' The repetitive and tedious nature of his work sends the individual home to the embrace of his television, which he uses as a counter-stimulant to release the tension that has built up during the day. Thus is consolidated what Mitscherlich calls the 'ideological mass identity,' whereby the individual is imbued with mass thoughts and values, and programmed for automatic mass obedience.

The sibling society stands in contrast to that which preceded it: the father-organised society in which the father was unafraid to speak or announce his authority and risk being despised by the young for so doing. A working definition of authority might be: the capacity to endure unpopularity in the interests of good, and a defining quality of fatherhood through the ages was a preparedness to be resented. The father was the guarantor and custodian of civilisation and even malcontented youth looked to him for guidance, free to remonstrate in the knowledge that affection would not be withdrawn. The Sixties tore up that Oedipal contract, and now the young looked only sideways, and warily: the father was absent or suspect, the state had become a multi-breasted mother, and the hole in the human psyche where the father once manifested was invaded by demons.

'Mass society,' he wrote, 'with its demand for work without responsibility, creates a gigantic army of rival, envious siblings. Their chief conflict is characterised, not by Oedipal rivalry, struggling with the father for the privilege of liberty and power, but by sibling envy directed at neighbours and competitors who have much more than they.' This is a syndrome expanded upon by the British psychologist, Oliver James, in his 1997 book, *Britain On the Couch*, in which he graphically proposed one of the core cultural changes in post-war Britain as being the expansion of the pool of status-comparisons available to the average person. Back in the 1950s, the average citizen 'knew' perhaps a couple of dozen people, with whom he had the occasion to compare himself. Moreover, the intimacy of his cohort group enabled a degree of perspective to mitigate such comparisons: He could discount his own inadequacies against perceived deficiencies in the attainments or resources of the other. His neighbour might have had a bigger car, but was not so handsome, and so forth. By the end of the twentieth century, however, the pool of comparison available to the average citizen had become virtually unrestricted. Every waking moment, he was confronted by comparisons with celebrities, royalty, even fictional characters, who seemed to possess everything the culture adjudged to render human beings fulfilled. James linked this phenomenon to the growing unease in British society, as expressed by various indicators, including what is called depression.

In such circumstances, a process of mutual emulation sets in, rendering the young increasingly individualised and yet lacking individuality, more and more dependent upon fashion and popular culture, and ultimately subservient to the state. Politicians become mere affable actors, first among equals in an anonymous mass. 'When "no identifiable individual" holds power in his hands,' as Mitscherlich put it, 'we have a sibling society.'

In 1996, the year my daughter was born, Robert Bly published *The Sibling Society*, one of the most prophetic books of the last century. Bly took Mitscherlich's ideas and simplified them without losing anything and adding more than a little. Merging Mitscherlich's clinical understandings with his own work as a tireless cultivator and curator of manhood, he spelt out a scenario, two years after Charles Handy's hypothesis of the 'Empty (or "Empathy") Raincoat,' that deserved a lot more attention than it received. It struck me instantly as a book that ought to have become central to the West's discussion of its own putative future, but largely came and went unnoticed. I recall reading it on the London Tube in the weeks after my daughter was born, and being riveted by its descriptions of the imminent society of envious siblings 'pummelling the chests of their fathers and calling them fascists,' at a time when I was just beginning the process of running-in my own new greatcoat.

Bly, borrowing his central concepts from Mitscherlich, warned of the approach of a Peter Pan world where nobody would ever grow up, where adults regressed towards adolescence, where 'generations of half-adults' would try to pass themselves off as grown-ups. This process of regression, he had already argued in his seminal Foreword to a 1992 reissue of *Society Without the Father*, is centrally characterised by a turning away from the vertical plane, comprising tradition, service and devotion, in favour of the horizontal plane, with its self-referential culture of the young and the wanna-be young.

At the heart of this process is a vacuum left behind by the departed figure of 'The Great Father'. In the consciousness of humanity there are three layers of fatherhood: God the Father, the State Father and the Great Father. All three were now deceased. They have been killed off, according to Bly, by Elvis Presley, the Beatles and the Rolling Stones, Woodstock, Flower Power, the Pill, feminism, abortion and all the sundry voices of post-1960s rebellion and protest. Bly painted a devastating portrait of cultures obsessed with youth, suspicious of forms of authority that might seek to deprive youth of its 'freedoms', intent upon destroying the heritage of what Mitscherlich called 'vertical' culture. The replacement 'horizontal' culture of pop music, movies, television, student-style politics and — latterly — social media, is now universally cleaved to not just by the young, but by all the generations born since WWII. The sibling revolution had no time for glory, or effort, or justice, or greatness, or duty, or patriotism, but was content with consumer durables, celebrity and shallow forms of freedom. The father's role of stoical, authoritarian receptor for society's anger and outrage had not been filled, and so the rage of the young flew off in every direction, unfocussed and unfathomable — hate biting its own tail. Since there was no longer a father to stand rock solid while his children pummelled his greatcoat, the escalating communal rage threatened to pull everything down. Hence the growing contempt for tradition, wisdom, truth, renunciation, learning, and the resultant hollowing-out of education systems, which no longer challenged or satisfied.

This revolution had some deeper roots — in the context described by R.R. Reno in his 2019 book, *Return of the Strong Gods*, (as outlined in a previous chapter) which explores the foundations of the period of 'disenchantment' in Western culture from the end of WWII, initiating a retreat into the woolly, therapeutic safetyism that followed. To briefly reprise, Reno outlines how Western society rewrote its own programmes in the wake of World War II to prevent a return to such forms of authoritarian rule. Citing a cross-sample of such contributions — Karl Popper, Albert Camus, and the economic hyper-individualism of Friedrich Hayek, Milton Friedman, and others — he demonstrates how such writings dismantled a culture rooted in strong loyalties — to God, fatherland, nobility, nation, heroism, justice, home — and supplanted them with weak, therapeutic ideals like 'diversity', 'tolerance', 'equality', and 'openness' — all constructs that inspire nothing but self-interest. According to the post-war consensus, stable convictions and strong passions had to be jettisoned in order to avoid further descents into authoritarianism, and the great human passions of patriarchy, patriotism and piety banished and forgotten. Reno's description fleshes out Robert Bly's outline of how the Industrial Revolution had destroyed the four-million-year-old Great Father, by removing him from the home and making his powers invisible, and then removing his political equivalent from the public square. It was not, Bly observed in a passage that summons up the ghost of the Western world's dead fathers, a premeditated killing: *'Industrial circumstances took the father to a place where his sons and daughters could no longer watch him minute by minute, or hour by hour, as he fumbled incompetently with hoes, bolts, saws, shed doors, plows, wagons. His incompetence left holes or gaps where the sons and daughters could do better.'*

For Bly, this disappearance of the father from the domestic sphere prefigured what would follow in the public sphere. There had resulted three absences: the physical absence of the father from the vicinity of his children; the psychic absence of the father from the human heart; and the spiritual absence of the very idea of 'father', once represented by a Loving Father called 'God', from the human being's sense of his own soul. These absences were soon to be replicated at the level of political leadership.

All true, human-centred societal growth, which is to say reliable change, demands a process of renunciation, which in turn requires a strong, safe, generous agent to act as buffer and punchbag. In other words, a person of benign authority. In the normal cycle, the natural and inevitable revolt of the child is managed within a relationship rendered safe by the father's firm guidance and resolve. Within this relationship, the child imagines himself to have a genuine problem with the father, perhaps even, for a time, to hate him. The child says 'I want', 'I want to', and the father says 'No'. The child says, 'I hate you, I didn't ask to be born'. But the steadfastness of the loving father allows this natural process to work itself out. In time, like Mark Twain, the child comes to wonder at how much his father's thinking has advanced over the course of a few short years. But when the father is absent, this does not happen. Instead, the child's emotions, deprived of a legitimate target, lack the safe provocation that nature intended. The role of the stoical authoritarian receptor for society's anger and outrage has been decried and displaced, and with it, many of the positive values of father-organised society, like security, order, risk and fair play.

In the post-father society, there is nothing at which to target our anger, which turns inward against ourselves. Moreover, since there is no longer a father there to withstand our anger, to stand rock-solid while we pummel his coat, to calm us with a pat on the head and a stern admonition to go away and be better, our anger destroys everything regardless of virtue. Without the Great Father, we cannot tell right from wrong, good from bad, or truth from mere information. The only requirement of our appetite for destruction is that the instant object in our sights be the creation of the father, and have proved its merits through time.

The so-called patriarchal society was tough, straight, straight-talking and demanding of its citizens, did not waste energy in communication, but made clear, in a minimalist way, what its expectations were. Now the state is 'tolerant', 'inclusive', indulgent, talkative, given to explaining itself in detail, as though mostly longing to be liked (but increasingly quite the opposite!). Think of the contrast between the sobriety of the founding fathers and the affable acrobats who occupied the swivel chairs of office in the recent past of mincing, grinning, yet menacing regimes, not burst out in full-on tyrannical demeanour.

The effect on males is worse than on females. With increasing industry and zeal, we build a society where fathers have no words to speak to their sons. Masculinity is demonised, and our education systems impress upon adolescent males that their fathers are inappropriate role-models. The result, by Bly's analysis, is the creation of generations of young men who are numb in the region of the heart. The umbilical cord has been severed, but no more than that. The father can find no way of protecting or guiding his son, who remains tied to his mother's apron. Still, deeply aware of his maleness, he shies away from adopting the emotional life of the female, and chooses to have no emotions at all. Thus, the male becomes incapable of taking on the father role himself, and the cycle gathers speed.

The paradox of this situation is that men now stand where they would if they had retained the stature of the Great Father, but without any of the strength or resilience that allowed him to withstand the onslaughts fathers have dealt with from the earliest days of humanity. Today's man stands accused, pummelled, denigrated, not on account of his greatness but because he is weak and refuses to carry the burden of society's grievance. His position is understandable: 'You have taken my power away, and so cannot expect me to absorb your resentments.' This double-bind is visible in the domestic arena of the home, where the father carries the dilemma in his very gut. As a child of the post-60s era of what is called freedom, his instinct is to spurn — forfeit — the authority which his own children still expect him to wield. It is also visible in the public arena, where the only successful leader is one who panders to the most immediate desires of the electorate, promising reduced taxes, increased public spending and solutions to everyone's problems, but then cracking his whip when the word comes through on the wires.

At the time Bly wrote his earliest elaboration on Mitscherlich's thesis, the effects of the society were already well in train. He reckoned that the sibling society was, at the time of that writing (1992), 'about forty or fifty years old.' That would date it, more or less, from the end of WWII, and, accepting that date, we note that, in 2020, the year of the global coup, it had attained a vintage of approximately 70 years, a human lifetime. By now the third-wave feminist revolution, with its added doctrines of intersectionality, transfeminism and ecofeminism, had for three decades been building on common ground with other affected groups among the victimologies which had become known collectively under the rubric of Woke. These included gay and race activists, who had moved ahead of the feminists in seeking to demolish the allegedly outmoded institutions of Western society. Marching through the institutions of every Western society, they had left a trail of destruction and demoralisation, having infiltrated and captured academia, media, the arts and the legal and democratic systems, rendering them the instruments of their lethal programme.

All this made what was impossible in 1994, a dead cert just 26 years later. Altogether, Western society, as it presented itself in 2020, was as ready as it would ever be for a revolution that depended on the cowardice of men and the malleability of institutions. The emasculation of the male quotient of the population had reached a pitch of advancement that would have been unimaginable when Charles Handy published *The Empty Raincoat* in 1994.

The other two planks of the assault were technological and economic, and these had come to depend on one another in a very interesting way. In 1994, as Handy's book illustrates by its very existence, there was a healthy public conversation about the implications of an imminent technological revolution. The chief issues to be resolved by this discussion included, first and foremost, the question as to who should own and control the technology. From whatever would emerge as the answer to this question would flow a series of lesser questions, mostly concerning the distribution of income in a highly automated society, and the kind of cultural interventions that might be required to rebalance the 'meaning' and 'dignity' elements so as to ensure that the society might be recalibrated in a manner that maximised the welfare of its human quotient, and the chances that the purposes of economics continued to include ministering to the needs of human beings.

Enter 'prosperity'. The American economy had been in boom mode since the early 1980s, as a result of the low taxation policies of Ronald Reagan, the collapse of communism/ending of the Cold War, the burgeoning tech revolution, the miraculous reduction of government spending and deficits under Reagan, Bush and Clinton, deregulation, and steady hands on the Fed tiller (Paul Volcker and Alan Greenspan) for 27 years (1979 to 2006). The European boom took off from the late 1990s, on a wave of optimism prompted also by the collapse of communism and the disappearance of the nuclear threat, the introduction of the Euro, the advent of Blairism, which would become the adopted leadership model of the World Economic Forum through its Young Global Leaders programme. By 1998, there were signs already of the trend towards Blair fanboys in, for example, Germany (Gerhard Schröder) and Ireland (Bertie Ahern).

A brief sketch of my own country's trajectory, since it is what I know most intimately: In Ireland, the boom began to manifest just post the mid-1990s, and quickly became known as the Celtic Tiger, which was written up all over Europe in magazines and newspapers as the greatest miracle of the post-euro era. It was clear from the outset that the 'boom' was fraudulent, being largely based on runoff from Ireland's profoundly corrupt tax system, which offered fiscal asylum at the lowest rates of corporation tax in the world, while the indigenous economy struggled and stagnated for want of investment or ideas. During this period, public debate more or less ceased on every important matter: economic questions were deemed beyond all criticism, and anyone who might have had an alternative vision for Ireland's future was advised to keep it to himself. It was not possible to argue with 'success'.

In 2008, however, the tiger came a cropper, as the Irish economy collapsed in a mess of bad debt and unprecedented deficits. It became clear that the entire thing had been an orchestrated boom-bust set-piece designed to asset-strip Ireland and leave it on its uppers, creating an unprecedented paper debt that stood no chance of being repaid within the imaginable future of the country.

The problems facing Irish society included not just the loss of prosperity but the fact that this prosperity, while it lasted, had served to suppress real thought and discussion about how our nation sought to move forward. The fact that the Celtic Tiger had not been built on solid native foundations has even yet failed to emerge as a coherent or definitive idea: Most people still believe that we lost something real and immensely valuable in 2008, and that there is, accordingly, no alternative to a policy of foreign direct investment. In many respects, what happened was not merely inevitable but an intrinsic consequence of the kind of progress and prosperity pursued by those highly unsuited and inadequate players who found themselves in charge of Ireland's destiny over the past half century or so. It was easier to farm out the imagining of Ireland's future to interests who — it should have been obvious — had no love for Ireland or her People.

In the past 50 years, Irish life has been dominated by a series of battles between traditionalists and modernisers on various iconic questions which seemed to define two opposing versions of reality. On the one hand, the alleged traditionalists — those who followed the light of the founding fathers and mothers — clung to an idea of a pious and God-fearing nation, which eschewed materialism and valued itself mainly according to the principles of a simple faith and limited ambition, which sought, by and large, to shut out the menace of the modern world. On the other hand, there were the increasing ranks of those who argued that, to become a vibrant and prosperous country, Ireland needed to turn its back on the simple verities of the past, to embrace equality, diversity and what was called 'progress'. By attacking Irish attachments to tradition, nationalism, faith and family, the revolutionaries succeeded in opening Ireland up to the outside world, and creating an economic model based on this purported openness. But what they did not anticipate was the extent of the vulnerability this would bring with it. Their ideological struggle presented a false choice, implying a moment of severance between past and future, which, having been insinuated into the culture, had made it almost impossible to retain a successful line of continuity with the past, with tradition and with the essential languages of patriotism and self-realisation employed so effectively a century before in the project of national liberation.

In this period — from the 1960s to 2007 — the core idea of the modernising project — that Ireland could become self-reliant, wealthy and self-confident by jettisoning its internal objections and national sentimentalities, adopting an imported model of modernity and opening itself up to the global capitalist system — seemed, for all its obvious contradictions, to become irrefutable. By the early 2000s, Ireland's chief products were pharmaceuticals and online chatter, with the top ten of such enterprises accounting for nearly half of 'Irish' GDP.

What collapsed in 2008 was actually the materialist model of Ireland that was constructed as a reaction to a traditionalist Ireland previously regarded as having failed, long banished behind a curtain of scorn. The problem was that, arising from a poor understanding of the workings of tradition in modernity, the favoured policy had amounted to a kind of cultural scorched earth, which had left almost nothing behind out of which a new beginning might be effected. Additionally, there had occurred in the course of the battle a bifurcation of the national 'we', whereby Irish people continued to describe themselves as before, while at the same time feeling increasingly alienated from what was being presented to the world in their name(s). There was, to a degree, a surviving collective 'we', but it was not, *is not*, the kind of 'we' that is capable of summoning up its own collective energies. We say 'we', but only because there is no other word to describe a collective that is not a community, a state that is not a nation, a population that is not a People.

A similar picture could by then be observed right across the Free World. The constructed booms that swept across the West in that period were to last, in America, for a quarter of a century, in Europe for approximately half that. Both ended together, however, in the meltdown of 2008, and were, in all instances, followed by a period of mourning and recrimination that offered an extension of the period of public distraction from meaningful engagement with public affairs, perhaps for another decade. By the time the human race in its Western manifestation had emerged from this prolonged tantrum, the configuration of the future was more or less a *fait accompli.*

In retrospect, we are able to observe the remarkable coterminosity of this period of 'prosperity'/meltdown with a massive burst of progress on the tech front, when many of the innovations that were to transform the world of personal communications in the early 2000s were refined and brought to market, and the infrastructure brought into being that would manage this on what now reveals itself as a highly concerted and quasi-monopoly basis.

By way of a clumsy sketch, one might etch out that what happened was that, in a period of constructed prosperity (which was to culminate in massive and widespread indebtedness of countries and individuals) the path of civilisational development, if not of human evolution, went underground, like a river forging its way through a mountain, so that, out of sight, its existence was temporarily forgotten. The discussion that had begun in the 1980s about the future of work, income, leisure, meaning, and dignity — all that disappeared from plain sight at the point where the democratic questions had been tabled but left unanswered. Then the party took off. Two decades later, the river burst up through the floors of our living rooms, its decisiveness announcing that all questions had been answered and everything already decided.

These questions included: Who should own (i.e. control) the emanations of the technological revolution which for two decades had been at full tilt underground? Should this amount to public ownership, and if so, how might this be framed and regulated, and how might it be rendered democratically accountable? Were there boundaries and limits on the potential of technologies to alter human existence out of recognition and/or in a manner as to affect the functions of human tools so as to change the nature of their utility and 'responsivity' / 'answerability' to human desiring? In other words, were there things that might become possible that ought not to be developed because they would, in time, defeat the very function of scientific progress as an instrument of human development, well-being, happiness and security?

But these questions, which had osmotically started to raise themselves in the mid-1980s, were no longer anywhere to be heard. Instead, the new communications technologies that had been hatching in Silicon Valley for the past couple of decades were launched as conduits for the anti-culture of the Sibling Society, extending platforms and klaxons to the generations of the young, still frenziedly pummelling the chests of their fathers and calling them fascists.

In 1994, Charles Handy had observed many signs that conveyed to him that we were entering uncharted skies. In *The Empty Raincoat*, he cites Francis Fukuyama's thesis, outlined in his 1992 book, *The End of History and the Last Man*, in which he prognosticates that by then we had entered an epoch in which imagination, daring, courage and idealism would be supplanted with 'economic calculation, the endless solving of technological problems, environmental concerns, and the satisfaction of sophisticated consumer demands' — on its face a fairly accurate summary of where we have fetched up in our societies now,

In the post-historical period, Fukuyama predicted, 'there will be neither art nor philosophy, just the perpetual caretaking of the museum of human history.'

Handy interpreted Fukuyama as meaning that 'liberal democracy, the tolerance which it brings with it and the affluence which made it possible, have removed the will to fight great causes.'

This was an astute, almost uncanny perception, suggesting perhaps an intuition that liberal democracy was already manifesting the seeds of its own destruction.

If there is a singular note within the clamour of 2024 society, with its abandonment of values and virtues in favour of bogus varieties of diversity and inclusivity, it is the avoidance — even repugnance — of great causes. Whereas the young of 1968 or 1975 or 1984, or even 1996, were preoccupied with expounding variegated values rooted in freedom, justice, truth and solidarity — and all this tending towards a babble of relatively constructive disagreement — the young of 2024 appear to eschew any value that does not come shrink-wrapped in the ideological packaging of what is called Cultural Marxism and/or Woke. These values, if such they can any longer be termed, are not independent, self-standing quantities that may be weighed in the balance and sliced and diced like platefuls of edibles gathered from a buffet, but resemble more a fridge full of ready meals to be opened, microwaved and eaten in front of a TV set that renders their contents and taste a secondary matter to ticking the box marked 'Dinner' and getting back to passive (in)activity.

On the face of things, we may have to concede that, as concerns the granular detail of things, Fukuyama was closer to the mark than Handy. As the second millennium gave way to the third, this was to become ever more clear.

Just as the internet was supposed to unleash a utopia of free-thinking and free-speaking, so, as per Handy's thesis, it was going to liberate humanity into an orgy of creativity and imagination. Freed of the burden of material self-sustenance, mankind would blossom and expand exponentially in all directions. Now, of course, we observed the opposite of both of these promises: the opportunities of the world wide web for individual humans being closed down, one by one, as power moved in to utilise the technology instead, for an entirely opposite purpose — not least the covering-up of crimes committed in the Covid episode. One sunny, dark day around the Ides of March 2020, we awoke to find that freedom had been abolished, and nobody seemed to mind. We raised an eyebrow and were shouted down: Freedom, we were told by people whose middle name was Liberal, was 'a far-right obsession.'

So it was, too, more or less, with hopes for a richly creative future for mankind, which had been snatched away by the robber barons who, like prospectors for precious metals, laid claim to the capacitors and algorithms that might have made this future possible. Long before we had gotten to the ChatGPT stage, it was clear that technology was usurping far more human functions than it was enabling. The benefits for the freelancer of the 'gig economy' were largely transitory — a bit like a building boom as a booting-up economy starts to emerge. Once everything is built and in place, the necessity for mere labour decreases as business becomes more streamlined. Handy understood this principle well, citing the chairman of a large pharmaceutical company who once summed up his economic policy as '½ × 2 × 3 = P,': 'half as many people in his core business in five years' time, paid twice as well and producing three times as much, that is what equals Productivity and Profit.'

All this happened outside of the remit or oversight of democratic society, distracted by the explosion of prosperity that just so happened to 'coincide' with this moment of possibility or its absence.

A volume (just by way of an exemplary indicator) was published at the start of 2022, that was really not so much a book as a communique. It was titled *The Age of AI And Our Human Future,* and credited to no less than three authors —

Henry A. Kissinger, Eric Schmidt, and Daniel Huttenlocher — my *First Things* review of it from January 2022 is called 'Morality In The Age of Machines'.

Really, it amounted to the announcement of a victory in a war that had never been declared, the silent war for the future of the machine that had persisted from roughly the time of the publication of *The Empty Raincoat* in 1994, and continued until the middle-teens of the first century of the third millennium.

In my review I note *inter alia*:

It goes without saying that the 'risks' associated with AI have nothing ultimately to do with the inert pieces of metal and plastic comprising the attendant technology, but with the people who will control it. The most important question is: Who should manage this epoch-making moment?

Big Tech already controls the world via the internet, through data harvesting, intimate surveillance, and censorship. Now it moves toward the final stage: the unity of humans and machine, but not on the terms of the human, or at least not the human race. Instead, as usual, the plan is for things to be handled by placing the self-anointed few over the befogged many, in the name of progress.

And further:

Some scientists acknowledge, rather blithely, that the moment of Technological Singularity may well result in the obliteration of virtue, conscience, and morality, and even the final exit of the human species from the world, as human beings lose the battle to justify their existence against the claims of vastly more intelligent 'beings'. Against these risks, scientists posit benefits like increased cognitive capacity and processing speed, leading to the possibility of more and more scientific discoveries, but rarely do they get to the question: to whose benefit?

And further still:

AI ultimately will either be a new beginning or a final ending. There is a view in tech circles that, since the human race faces extinction thanks to its own behaviour, some kind of absorption of humanity by the machine may be the only way of maintaining an intelligent, albeit mechanical, human presence on earth. Thus, this thesis expands, the biological essence of humanity might have to be sacrificed, and the species maintained in the only form by that stage possible: posthumanist 'man'. Conversely, there is the hypothesis that the moment of Technological Singularity will bring with it a radical threat to natural selection: The machine will elevate humans according to values different from those of nature — a Superman. Where have we heard that before?

All this, one might advisedly speculate, was at play among the core agendas of the brief period of pseudo-prosperity. The underground activity took the form not of the coursing of water but the machinations of self-interested actors seeking to ready-up the future in a manner congenial to themselves and their associates. I choose/chose this book (Kissinger *et al.*) not so much for its intrinsic merits or centrality but because it is emblematic of a syndrome we have observed now for roughly a decade — whereby, from the moment the aftershocks of the economic collapse of 2008 had started to abate, there was a profound and widespread sense of a new era being announced, an era in which technology would become dominant in a manner that hitherto had been the province of science fiction, but which was now on the point of realisation and execution. The book is, of course, remarkable for the presence among its authors of Henry Kissinger (since deceased), a figure who had flitted around the super-structure of geopolitics for, at the time of the book's publication, close on seven decades, advancing ideological programmes and keeping the world safe for globalism. Kissinger, more than any other contemporary figure, had represented the shadowy forces in the background to the theatre of the planet's political life.

Those who know what is happening are always in a better position to know what is going to happen, and, by controlling the rollout of technology under cover of a fake prosperity, which ensured the limiting at the same time of the scope of the collective conversation, the robber barons were able to ensure their own future enrichment by a careful elision of inconvenient factors like democratic input, sovereignty and accountability. By polluting academia with poison and nonsense, they blocked one channel of collective comprehension. By rendering journalists dependent on centralised funding, they gained effective control of almost all media output. For the wealthy who had their hands on the levers of future tech, this amounted to a form of insider trading, whereby they could not only predict the future, but be the ones to create it, first in words and then in algorithms and neural networks.

Charles Handy foresaw this in a different way, almost as a feeling concerning some lack that was emerging in the human spirit. 'We are slumped in comfort,' he writes in *The Empty Raincoat* (three decades ago, remember?). 'When we compete, it is for the World Cup or gold medals. Such things do not bring forth great art or noble deeds, they don't stir the heart more than momentarily, nor do they foster revolutions. Like dogs, if we are well fed, we are content. When scientific and economic progress lead more and more societies into the content-ment stage we shall see the end of history.'

Handy cites De Tocqueville's famous passage, published the greater part of 200 years ago, about the atomisation of America, the future man (i.e. today's contemporary citizen) who is close to his neighbours but does not see them, 'touches them but does not feel them':

'He exists only in himself and for himself alone; and if his kindred still remain to him, he may be said at any rate to have lost his country. Above this race of men stands an immense and tutelary power, which takes it upon itself alone to secure their gratification and to watch over their face . . . it is well content that the people should rejoice, provided they think of nothing but rejoicing.'

Towards the end of his book, Handy touches tentatively on the possibility that democracy contains the seeds of its own undoing in the context he is describing. 'Democratic societies,' he writes, 'are tolerant; they do not tell their citizens how they should live, or what will make them happy, virtuous or great. It is not an accident that people in democratic societies are preoccupied with material gain and with the myriad small needs of the body.'

Then he cites Nietzsche, on the world after God, with the 'last man' departed 'the regions where it is hard to live, for one needs warmth':

'One still works, because work is a form of entertainment. But one is careful lest the entertainment be too harrowing. One no longer becomes rich or poor: both require too much exertion. Who still wants to rule? Who to obey? Both require too much exertion. No shepherd and one herd! Everybody wants the same, everybody is the same: whoever feels different goes voluntarily into a madhouse.'

Here again, Handy seems to be, perhaps instinctively, provoking the Combine with thoughts that might, in time, lead them to attempt their Great Reset, taking literally the notion that democracy — and with it too much freedom — is at the heart of the problem of the levelling out of man's potential and desiring. Why not then decide, as Larry Fink has decided, that democracy is no longer a fit for the kind of capitalism that is best adaptable to modern and future needs — that 'totalitarianism is better'? Perhaps the Secret Unknowns of the Combine reflected that it was time to tell people how to live, and what would *really* make them happy — 'owning nothing', for example, which by happenstance would make the Combine happy too? Perhaps the world had become too tolerant of things that were bad for the kind of business needing to be done, in all the circumstances prevailing?

Handy, channelling Hegel, observes:

'In 1806 [Hegel] wrote, "We stand at the gates of an important epoch, a time of ferment . . . when a new phase of the spirit is preparing itself. Almost 200 years later we are in another time of ferment, another dark wood. It may not be the end of history."'

Humanity in 1994, writes Handy, in their lack of idealism, or passion, or pride, their dearth of desiring, were 'all last men now.'

Maybe, maybe not: Perhaps we/they — as we, today — were/are the last men before the quasi-men to come, the posthumanist cyborgs whose imagining puts the twinkle in the eyes and the pep in the step of Ray Kurtzweil, Eric Schmidt and Yuval Noah Harari?

Or perhaps Hegel had been right in anticipating that the human need to feel pride would not be satisfied by the peace and prosperity that accompany the end of history? And that way, by the Combine's way of thinking, lay trouble. The problem with having everything you think you need is that the next stage is getting the things you think you want. Finding a purpose, meaning, in existence is not something to be taken for granted, as it may well become when the purpose of existence is merely to exist. And humanity, satisfied of belly and libido, seeking other forms of satisfaction, is a baleful prospect for criminals who have — or whose forbears have — plundered the world for decades and centuries, and now look to the prospect of its human quotient (themselves excluded), possessed of a surfeit of leisure time in which to ponder and wonder, as a rather ominous development.

Handy cites an unlikely philosopher — Laura Ashley! — explaining why she became a designer of homesteads for humans: 'I sense that most people wanted to raise families, have gardens and live as nicely as they can.' Handy speculated that Ashley's business had prospered in the 1970s and 1980s because it caught the zeitgeist of the times, 'the generation of the last men.' In the coming time, he said, nice things and passionless aspirations would reveal themselves as insufficient. Here, he predicted, in outline form, a coming era of ideological obsession — 'a growing search for meaning and authenticity . . . a sense of purpose, a search for identity, dignity and a quality of life prior to lifestyle (aesthetics and harmony).' The return of the strong gods?

Perhaps this is the core foresight of Handy's striking book: that humanity — he is speaking chiefly about Western humanity — having attained sufficiency as to material needs, would become restless and begin to search for causes, a 'purpose beyond oneself.' This, if you are a cunning member of the elite predator quotient, is yet another dangerous trait to be curbed, sat upon and ultimately diverted.

'It is hard,' Handy concludes, rather morosely, 'in the conditions of comfortable democracy, to find a cause which lifts the efforts of the comfortable ones. That is why some fear a return to war as a way of putting some energy back into our peoples. Making money, not war, has turned out to be less inspiriting. Another war would be a tasteful way to disprove the end-of-history thesis.' It was pointless to look to the leaders of nations, he added, for nations were 'too big, the connections not strong enough, the commitment to the future not long enough.' He proposed we 'look smaller' — to local communities and organisations, to families and clusters of friends, 'to small networks of portfolio people with time to give to something bigger than themselves. We have to fashion our own directions in our own places.'

Handy ends his book with a Postscript, which in turn concludes:

'Our people are clever, many of them. Most people are decent, given half a chance. They are not uncaring, if only because they know that a world which crumbles around them will do them no good at all. But first there has to be a general acceptance that the world has changed. The end of communism does not mean that capitalism, in its old form, is therefore the one right way. The triumph of the democracies over totalitarianism does not mean that everything in those democracies is thereby validated. The huge strides made by science in the last decades does not mean that scientists have or could have the answer to everything and that the rest of us need not bother.

'It is also the end of the age of the mass organisation, the age when we could all confidently expect to be employed for most of our lives if we so wanted, and over 90 per cent did so want. Work will still be central to our lives but we shall now have to rethink what we mean by work and how it might be organised. At first sight, the challenge is daunting, but work in those mass organisations has never been unalloyed bliss for all. The mass organisation has not been with us that long. We should not think of it as a law of nature. Maybe we shall be better off without it.

'The hope lies in the unknown, in that second curve, if we can find it. The world is up for reinvention in so many ways. Creativity is born in chaos. What we do, what we belong to, why we do it, when we do it, where we do it — these may all be different and they could be better. Our societies, however, are built on case law. Change comes from small initiatives which work, initiatives which, imitated, become the fashion. We cannot wait for great visions from great people, for they are in short supply at the end of history. It is up to us to light our own small fires in the darkness.'

What is ultimately most striking about Handy's book is that its content, its analyses, its aspirations and its warnings are, in their particularities, so refined, so delicate, so filigreed with a form of sophisticated desiring that they summon up a moment of extreme contentment, even complacency, whereas the sketch that underlies the book carries a warning precisely about that complacency. It is, on the one hand, as if nothing much requires to be done not merely to avoid disaster but to attain a kind of perfection, and yet there is the cautionary note about getting it all completely wrong. What happened was something entirely different: We simply took our eye off the ball and allowed the predators to slip in behind our backs and build their new world right under our noses, like the robbers who, dressed in workmen's overalls, dismantle the ATM built into the bank's frontage, and even borrow a screwdriver from the doorman to enable them to complete their 'maintenance operation'.

Handy, like every other thinker and commentator of the time, assumed that the worst that would happen is that we would fail to achieve our own high expectations, perhaps by virtue of an overdose of complacency; he did not envisage — nor did anyone else —that, before his book was 30 years old, the entire structure of Western civilisation would have been dismantled and marked for transportation to the landfill, and the world loaded up for transportation back to the Middle Ages.

Perhaps the limits of Handy's tender thesis have ultimately to do with the idea of seeing human reality as in any way conforming to the laws of business. Businessmen, I have often noticed, can be extremely ingenious in their capacity to manipulate the world in order to generate wealth for themselves — and therefore benefits for others —without understanding much about how things work beneath the superficial level they need to operate within. Almost by definition, tunnel-vision is a prerequisite of wealth-generation. The entrepreneur seeking to manipulate specific instruments or circumstances so as to liberate wealth from them must adopt a disposition of relative indifference towards the world beyond those specifics. One example is ecological damage, an issue that has, over time, provoked the necessity for environmental protection legislation. Once, not long ago, businesses employed lawyers and other advisors to advise them how to skirt around such legislation and so pollute to their hearts' content. The modern entrepreneur must take steps to minimise such damage, and also turn this into a public virtue, while privately regarding it as a drag on his ability to maximise the potential of his wealth generation.

To some extent, as well as seeking to exploit circumstances for immediate profit, the businessman must remember also that profit can only be maintained over long periods by the exercise of prudence and restraint in the short and medium terms. This is a way of avoiding or delaying the inevitable operation of the law of diminishing returns. Those who seek always to cash in without nurturing and rebuilding are doomed to destroy that on which they depend for their continued good fortune. In certain periods of human endeavour, these ideas have ebbed and flowed, sometimes favouring prudence and discretion, at other times celebrating unrestrained avarice and ecological recklessness. This latter 'ethic' was perhaps best articulated by Gordon Gekko in the 1987 movie Wall Street:

The point is, ladies and gentlemen, that greed — for lack of a better word — is good. Greed is right.

Greed works.

Greed clarifies, cuts through, and captures the essence of the evolutionary spirit.

Greed, in all of its forms — greed for life, for money, for love, knowledge — has marked the upward surge of mankind.

And greed — you mark my words — will not only save Teldar Paper [his corporation] but that other malfunctioning corporation called the USA.

We ought perhaps to avoid becoming too moralistic about this, since there is an essential truth in what Gekko says: Even the capacity to make two blades of grass grow where only one grew before does, in fact, require a certain arrogation of divinity, even a degree of ruthlessness. There will always be times and senses in which what Gekko says will remain right and true. But this rightness and trueness are not constant, absolute or eternal conditions. What we call 'greed' is a necessary instrument of propulsion for the human dynamic in action in creating more and more wealth. Up to a point, this is a valorous process, since it helps to maintain the edifice of capitalism upon which all economic activity ultimately depends. The problem is that the action of greed in economic activity can only continue to function without causing damage so long as it respects, at some level, the process of ecological accountability that economies require in order to sustain themselves. The instinct of the speculator is like that of the scrap merchant: he moves in to salvage whatever he can from the debris of failure and obsolescence. But this implies and requires also some degree of mindfulness concerning renewal. In order to minimise the risk of imposing consequences of its own, the speculative move must respect the edifice of business and, therefore, place a limit on greed. Profiteering can be relatively painless, but it is a matter of timing, of sporadic opportunism rather than wanton exploitation. This works best on a transitory basis, i.e. it works when it occurs as an occasional process of cleansing, tidying-up, after which the wealth-generating machine must be enabled to tick on for a further while in a more or less routine fashion, benefitting in small ways those who are happy with smaller rewards.

What is happening now is quite different: it is terminal. It is an attempt to cover up the crimes of the five decades since the final abolition of the Gold Standard and the reinvention of the global economy as a roulette table, the action upon which became infinitely more important than the mere endeavours of human beings. What is happening now is the application of the logic of transitory greed to the entirety of the economic systems of the world as a kind of final process of plunder before the entire edifice is changed from one in which human work remains at least nominally central to one in which the human involvement is terminated and supplanted with Central Bank Digital Currencies (CBDCs), social credit, Universal Basic Income (UBI), surveillance and, in effect, a total transfer of the ownership of the means of production from humanity in general to a tiny slice of that species (which I call the Combine, but if you prefer, 'the FEW', the reversal of the acronym 'WEF'). The idea is that, in the future, most people will own nothing, and will rent whatever they need from the Combine, which will finally become omnipotent and virtually deified.

The strange thing is that those who are responsible for this ludicrous plan are never done with talking about 'sustainability'. And the deep problem about this moment, from the viewpoint of genuine sustainability, is that it is a once-off moment that is being mistaken for the first of a series of recurring opportunities. In other words, the perpetrators appear to think that, despite their having dismantled the world to break it up for scrap, it will somehow magically continue in the approximate forms it took before they started the breaking process.

They are so drunk on the prospect of their imminent gains as to be unable to see that, whereas — for certain — in that singular moment, there will undoubtedly be the opportunity for unimaginable self-enrichment by those who already control the levers of finance and corporate business, this moment will be brief and terminal. Those who lick their lips about the coming windfall are so drunk on the prospect of their exploding bank balances that they overlook to consider what will happen afterwards, which will include the turning of their bank balances to meaningless digits. They forget that, in pulling off this *coup d'état* against the human race, they, in effect, initiate a process of disintegration which will cause the entire edifice of the global economy to collapse, and their own empires with it.

A handful of years back, before the Covid crimes began, my wife and I were at Dublin Airport one morning to catch a flight to the United States. New machines had been in place for some time, to 'assist' passengers in checking themselves in, but now there were machines to check in your baggage as well. At some of these machines, there were people in airline uniforms helping people to negotiate the new system. With their help, you could carry out the entire process yourself and then deposit your tagged bags at a desk over in a corner of the check-in lounge. There were still people behind the check-in counters, presumably to assist those who were unable to figure out the machines, and also for people whose bags had failed the weight test or some such.

I was fascinated by the huddle that surrounded each of the machines, with travellers being coached in operating them by uniformed staff members. This at first struck me as absurd, but then I remembered that, of course, it was an interim, transitory measure and that, in time, the airline would be able to dispense with the supervisory staff members and trust its passengers to operate the machine on their own, or, at a pinch, with the guidance of other passengers. In other words, the uniformed staff members had been conned into becoming the allies of their own economic gravediggers.

But then something even more interesting occurred to me. Glancing at the check-in desks, I noticed that there were no queues. That made sense: all the functions once carried out by the staff behind these desks were now being done out on the floor, mostly by the passengers themselves. There were still several — I think I counted eight or nine — staff members manning the desks, but they were standing around chatting to each other. They had no work to do. I turned to my wife and pointed out to her what was happening; 'Look,' I said, 'there is nobody outside the counter.' 'Yes,' she replied, 'that's because of the new machines.'

It struck me that we were moving closer to a moment when there would be nobody behind any of the counters, just people milling around in front, carrying out the airline's work for it (while still paying the market price of an air ticket). My first thought was, 'Progress!' or some such. My second thought was that there was a problem here, not at first sight for the airline, but for the society at large, which went something like this: Since the people inside the counter would also become, at other moments, the people standing outside other counters, and they, in being rendered obsolete, would lose some or all of their consuming capacity, the overall effect of all this was not a saving of costs but a shrivelling of total economic activity. To put it another way: If you eliminate the people behind the counters, you eliminate also the counters, which is tantamount to eliminating the economies they cumulatively comprise.

I said: 'It seems to me that unless you have people on both sides of the counter, there will very soon be nobody on either side. What we are observing is a staging-post on the way to a total evisceration.'

This is something that businessmen do not seem to see, perhaps because it is not in their immediate interest to see it. For many decades now, the fashion in business has been to increase profits by what is called 'rationalisation' — essentially a constant process of cost reduction, trimming and downsizing. This helps the bottom line in the short term, but eventually the law of diminishing returns begins to work its black magic. Rationalisation eventually reaches the outer limit of its useful potential, and, after that, exposes the company to risk of inefficiency and uncompetitiveness. An obsession with cost-cutting may increase profits for a time, but eventually it kills the goose that lays the golden egg. In other words, what they can look forward to is a once-off — undoubtedly lucrative — payday, followed by the utter disintegration of the economic model, and, thereafter, perpetual penury.

And this rule applies in spades to what is happening now. Those orchestrating this coup seem to forget that, in rationalising the world, they are essentially reducing most of the human race to a mendicant serf-class of redundant operatives who will, by virtue of losing their capacity to generate income, become all but useless as consumers also. Before long, there will be nobody outside the counter, and, soon afterwards, no one inside it. They may well replace those people inside the counter with machines and AI, but this will not work with the problem they face on the other side of the counter. Thus, their windfall of wealth — fabulous though it may be — will be a short-lived and once-off boon.

These things are so self-evident that it is a little absurd that they still require to be said. What is happening is, in effect, an attempted plundering of the world's financial resources with a view to commandeering the hard assets later, for a song. And it is being effected with the cooperation of the 'people's representatives' — the political classes — the supposedly democratic media, the police forces and judiciaries paid for out of the public purse, and with the connivance of most of those who have purported to be the watchdogs on ethical economics and human freedom since Adam was a boy. It ought to be obvious: It is neither possible nor wise for members of the human race to seek to impose a terminal seizure on the functioning of human existence, or to corral their fellows in slavery in the process of stealing the fruits of their labours and ingenuity. That is not a good idea, and it always ends up badly.

Within the logic of the system as it stands, it is possible to see how those in charge of the levers have come to feel that there is no other way. It is not even that they seem oblivious that there is no way of achieving their desired outcome that will not in time result in their losing everything themselves, but that the system has been constructed in such a way that its reorientation involves incalculable risks that might result in its implosion into nothingness.

Nevertheless — perhaps — they legitimately feel that there is 'no viable alternative.' In a sense, they are correct: Outside of the logic they have been applying, the sole alternative is an unprecedentedly radical one: tell the people what the problem is; set in train a plan to replace the system at a chosen moment, in accordance with democratic principles, acknowledging that human beings have jointly held interests and equities in the economic and monetary systems that grew out of the totality of human endeavour and ingenuity through time; and commence, enable and conduct a democratic discussion as to how this might be managed to create a genuinely new kind of world — in particular, though not exclusively, tackling the vexed question of how to bequeath to the people their just entitlement of a 'dividend' from the final onset of the AI economy, which would in effect put the entire species into a largely involuntary retirement.

This recourse may pose many taxing problems, not all of them economic. There would be, for example, the problem of how to 'reinvent' human cultures and societies for an age in which the meaning and dignity of human existence was no longer bound up with paid work. This might have involved something along the lines of what I have called a 'redistribution of dignity', so as to valourise activities of the human that are currently deemed to be 'social', 'volun- tary', or 'recreational'. Even writing that down, one has a sense of its impracti- cality, even *naïveté* — I mean not its intrinsic difficulties but more the effrontery of imagining that the 'proprietors' of the system as presently constituted, were ever going to hand it over to the people out of the goodness of their hearts.

Right now, we seem to be moving towards a kind of serviced slavery. But how long can that last — the 'serviced' element, I mean? Things change. For the initial period, yes, as the new oligarchs sneakily rub their hands in glee at the idea of getting away with it, the people may find themselves indulged, and the atmosphere may be, for a time, more Huxleyan than Orwellian. But then, ever so slowly, the temperature may change. The oligarchs, controlling public opinion as much as everything else, may be able to impose on the public mind, and on the minds of its constituent members, a sense of their uselessness, then of their superfluousness, then of their pointlessness. Gradually we may move towards a kind of constructive culture of self-liquidation. In five years, ten years, the oligarchs of the Combine may well ask: *Why are we paying these people to just sit around guzzling beer and stuffing their faces with pizza?* If you think this fanciful, the chances are that you haven't been paying attention.

We come back here to a point of discussion which, though in a certain sense ridiculous, is one that we now know cannot be taken for granted. This is that human civilisation, built with the sweat and toil of human beings, exists for one purpose and one purpose only: to make the future better for humanity, to remove as far as possible the causes of continuing misery and evildoing, to ensure that the benefits of human endeavour are directed at these objectives and aspirations, and most certainly to ensure that these resources not be diverted to the stashes of hoarders and misers, for whom the human race, when it can no longer contribute to their enrichment, is an albatross and a drag.

This is why, stumbling across Charles Handy's now peculiar book from 30 years ago, I have been moved to raise its significance to us now as a mnemonic and a bromide-print of thinking that seemed axiomatic just 30 years ago, but is now so far removed from the content of our culture that I am moved to wonder if what is in train is not some profoundly-situated, osmotically-organised suicide pact by a People — the People of the West — who no longer know what is the purpose of their presence on this planet, or even why they ought to get out of bed in the morning.

CHAPTER 34
BEWARE THE IDES OF MARCH, PART I: GRAND THEFT AURUM
17-03-2024

Two short chapters to mark the fourth anniversary of the widely-misunderstood revolution that is likely to make a Hell of human reality unless we come to understand its true nature.

A couple of months ago, when the President of Argentina, Javier Milei, addressed the motherWEFfers in Davos, he had the Resistance wires vibrating with exultant celebration, but mainly on the basis of a misunderstanding shared by the president and his admirers.

In the wake of his election last November, he was touted as a 'far-right libertarian' — an accusation that seemed to be contradicted by his willingness to go to Davos in the first place. Did he not understand that this body is a planetary club for quockerwodgers — i.e. the marshalled puppets who have been planted throughout the global political firmament? He knows, surely, that, being completely unelected and utterly without mandate, the World Economic Forum lacks all moral or political authority? Did he not know that he was going into a nest of globalist vipers? And, if so, why did he not simply rattle off a few observations along these lines and take his leave?

These questions occurred to me, but still I allowed that he might just be playing the game, as I had assumed Putin had been doing for a while, to get the measure of their agendas and capacities, with the clear intention of giving it to them up the Günter at the first opportunity.

The main reason people on our side were celebrating President Milei's speech was that it was critical of socialism/communism. One reader sent me a text saying he thought Javier might be crossed off 'Uncle Klaus's Christmas card list,' a line that neatly captured the general sense of glee among members of the Resistance.

But do they/we really believe that the motherWEFfers are interested in pushing a communist programme on Western society?

The motherWEFfers are the agents of the FEW ('WEF' in a mirror), which is to say the richest of the rich, which chiefly means people who have never shown their faces, even in Davos, because they do not need to: Their puppets go there and report back.

We need to be clear that neither the people who go to Davos, nor the interests they represent, are either communists or capitalists. Insofar as they have any ideology at all, it might be called a radical brand of monopoly acquisitiveness — totalitarian by nature — plugged into something that might accurately be termed the 'monetary monopoly power grid', which is closer to Benito Mussolini's brand of fascism than to anything else in the ideological firmament. Of course, in promoting this agenda, the proxies of the FEW like to bandy about socialist or Marxist tropes and even 'principles', as though they were fanatically intent upon achieving equity for all persons, or justice for the downtrodden, or a more secure future for those threatened by 'climate change'. This, indeed, is something like the seeming subtext of their rhetoric, but it is all mere theatre in the cause of misdirection. The WEF has no belief in anything other than profit and plunder. In the motherWEFfer worldview, ideological programmes are merely software; they do not serve as enduring maps of the kind of human future that is implicit in the WEF worldview, nor in the actions and programmes the WEF seeks to implement. They are mere bait designed to hook the gullible who have been conveniently soaked in ideology through most of what is laughably called their 'educations'. In the packed hall of the Davos Swiss Alpine School, Javier Milei was not so much confusing the dancers with the dance, but rather allowing the soundtrack to dictate his understanding of the movie's plotline.

There is a strong and strange parallel in many Western societies between socialism and religious faith. In our cultures, for pretty much all my sentient life, people in Western societies have thought about socialism more or less as conterminous with Christianity, or in doctrinal terms with liberation theology, whereby to be Left is to be kind, compassionate and generous, whereas being 'conservative' or 'Right-wing' is selfish, greedy and mean-spirited. Thus, when our cultures 'think' or talk about socialism, it is nice-sounding concepts like equality or solidarity that spring immediately to mind or tongue. This is what the motherWEFfers are trading off — all the things many young people find attractive in politics (when they do), and indeed all the things which so many children of the Sixties and their aftermath(s) — the 'Boomers' — have clung to all their lives — Mao, Stalin, Pol Pot and Hitler notwithstanding — and continue to regard as representing what is most virtuous and 'progressive' in the political warehouse, and possibly in the human heart. The motherWEFfers have weaponised all these confused sentiments and energies, and intend to trade off them to bring about an ideological destination about as far from equality and inclusivity as it is possible to imagine — unless, that is, you regard 'equality' as the vast majority of humanity being equally poor and 'included' among the ranks of the destitute, and a tiny self-styled 'elite' owning everything and being as happy as psychopaths are ever likely to be.

Thus, what people on our side have been mistaking for a leftist orientation on the part of the motherWEFfers is merely a mirror image of the time-warped misconceptions of the leftist useful idiots who support the WEF agenda without knowing what it is, largely because of being misled by the 'progressive' camouflage designed to misdirect those for whom uttering virtuous noises is the most important thing.

Without doubt, more than a few of the puppets, apparatchiks and functionaries in use by the 'elite' predator classes are either openly or secretly leftist in tilt and stamp. This is because, although they are the least likely revolutionaries in their demeanours and lifestyles, they have, at certain moments (such as now), a need for revolutionary input so as to further and enforce their agendas. Many agents of the American Deep State, for example, are Communists, Trotskyists, Maoists and the like, as are members of the terrorist goon squads sent on to the streets of Western cities to put manners on the more uppity or reluctant citizens, but this manifestation of useful ideologues, aside from being operationally effective, is also a use of theatrical misdirection. We ought not be misled by the ideological pantings or antics of such actors: At most, they are merely 'useful idiots' of a slightly higher rank.

It was surprising to note that President Milei appeared to be taken in. In Davos this recent January, he called on business and political leaders to reject socialism and instead embrace 'free enterprise capitalism' to bring an end to world poverty. A worthy thought, but where in the motherWEFfers programme is he observing egalitarian inclinations? Milei harangued the Davos meeting for what he perceived to be the WEF's 'socialist agenda,' which he said would 'only bring misery to the world,' but had he read the body of crypto-literature produced by Herr Klaus Schwab? The leftist leanings of contemporary Western politics are designed to mislead the young who, out of ignorance of history, find leftist ideas attractive, but they have next-to-nothing to do with the ambitions of the people who were sitting in front of Javier Milei.

'The main leaders of the Western world have abandoned the model of freedom for different versions of what we call collectivism,' he said, speaking here with more accuracy, for 'collectivism' is not the same as socialism. All socialists may be collectivists, but all collectivists are not socialists. His country had had enough of this brand of politics, he continued. 'We're here to tell you that collectivist experiments are never the solution to the problems that afflict the citizens of the world — rather they are the root cause.' There is a great deal of truth in this, of course, but, at least in the manner he was couching the point, it had little or nothing to do with Davos or its parachuting occasional denizens. Who ever suggested that the motherWEFfers were interested in solving the problems of the world? They are interested solely in solving the problems afflicting themselves and their clients and fellow travellers.

But Javier Milei is 100 per cent correct in saying that 'the Western world is in danger,' though he could not be more wrong in adding that this is because 'those who are meant to defend the values of the West have been co-opted by a vision of the world that inexorably leads to socialism.' His remarks about the continuing contrived war between men and women, the current spurious notions of social justice, and the rise and rise of environmental fundamentalism, were well-aimed and hit at several of the sacred cows of the Davos crowd — but they amounted in the end to low-hanging fruit.

I found it interesting that his speech was, superficially at least, a rehash of the main points — or perhaps I should say *the chief contemporary interpretations, which is to say 'misunderstandings'* — of Friedrich Hayek's 1944 book, *The Road to Serfdom*, which marks its 80th birthday this year. In this seminal statement concerning human freedom, Hayek warned the people of his adopted nation, England, about the dangers of what he intuited to be their flirtation with socialism in all its diluted manifestations — democratic socialism, social democracy, 'Christian' democracy, *et cetera*. I listened to President Milei in the English translation, and was struck by hearing Hayek's (and before him Alexis de Tocqueville's) word 'servitude', which is certainly apposite in the context of what Uncle Klaus and his mates have planned for us. I was also paradoxically encouraged to hear the underwhelming round of applause that followed Milei's remarks — not so much disapproving as perplexed. But, even on its chosen terms, his analysis was riddled with holes: in particular his failure to stress that the dangers we face now arise from a set of objectives that take the outward form not of socialism but of rampant, unmoderated capitalism — though not of the market-driven variety he himself favours. Instead of a Communist Utopia, what is being constructed is a totally globalised planned economy, run to technocratic principles, with ESG scores, UBI payments, CBDC currency (tokens, not money), all based not on competition and free markets but on artificial intelligence (AI), data harvesting and surveillance, the micro-managing of every citizen's existence, the seizing of the natural environment — including its capacities for food production — the tokenisation of natural features, (such as land, lakes, mountains, forests, and of livestock — though also of humans themselves), so that everything — every blade of grass, drop of rainwater, leaf, rock and grain of sand — and everyone, every human life — will be 'managed' and, indeed, 'owned', under the munificent kingship of Emperor Larry Fink, by his company BlackRock, the world's largest criminal org . . . sorry, 'asset-management company'. This would, or will, amount to the total reinvention of human existence, which is one of the reasons the populations of all Western countries are currently undergoing a process of replacement (the natives would be likely to object to these modifications) and why utterance of the term 'replacement' is being refashioned as a 'hate crime'.

But I was struck by President Milei's apparent lack of awareness that the cardinal problem we face at the hands of the motherWEFfers is not socialism — nothing like it, in fact — but a bid to create a neo-feudal world camouflaged with weaponised Marxist dog-whistles to draw in unsuspecting leftists. It was as if President Milei had formed his view of the World Economic Forum from reading the *Economist* or the *Financial Times*. He had nothing to say about LGBT goons, child grooming, legalised genital mutilation, land-grabbing, population culling, mass migration, or the censorship programmes designed to pull a curtain on such enterprises, as well as on recent crimes and their cover-up. I'm not sure why. Perhaps he does not understand — and yet he has come across, in various interviews, as a highly thoughtful and intelligent man. He seemed unaware that the sole element of the Marxist toolkit that interests the motherW-EFfers is the adoption of a technocratic digital tyranny, whereby the population of the world, though primarily the West, will be imprisoned and enslaved.

I would highlight also President Milei's apparent failure to grasp that the statistics he purveys in support of his claim that market capitalism is the most effective model of economic operation are, in respect of at least the past five decades of Western economic life, contaminated by the deceptive action of funny money, generated out of fiat currencies and powered by fractional reserve banking, which is essentially a mechanism designed for whole-scale plunder. I would certainly have expected an Argentinian whose name is not Bergoglio to understand and reference that. Having the attention of the world beyond the Davos Swiss Alpine School, he might usefully have sketched all of these relevant conditions, but instead he stuck to a stale ideological analysis, for which he was widely and ludicrously praised by people who ought to know better.

We all surely know by now that what interests the people Milei was addressing is not egalitarianism, but the creation of a Trojan horse seemingly stuffed with good intentions, which is really designed to deliver the world to a Hell of centralised totalitarianism — the very conditions invariably spawned by attempts at total planning and control such as Friedrich Hayek defined as the engine of the socialist programme, and rightly anathematised. Hayek's rejection of socialism was not an aesthetic or 'economic' one; what he warned of was its deep nature rather than its bells and whistles. What he highlighted was the fact that its incoherence and ultimate unworkability inevitably lead to a tightening of control. Issuing warnings about socialism in his time, he did so mainly because he could see that it represented the thin end of totalitarianism. And, just as it would be a misreading of his message to search the present merely for signs of such ideological regression — ignoring his deeper concern, which was the accompanying threat of the will-to-power, one man over others — it would be a mistake to decide that *The Road to Serfdom* has limited relevance for us now that the concepts of 'Left' and 'Right' have migrated to new and more lucrative territories, and both capitalism and socialism taken on different forms than they used to inhabit. Capitalism, it is true, has degenerated into a form of corporatism, which now pursues not market freedom but centralised control, protectionism and ultimately the very characteristics of mid twentieth century socialism that Hayek warned about. Socialism and socialist activism, too, have shifted ground, becoming as operational adjuncts of this corporatism, rather than offering any form of resistance to it. This, I think, is what President Milei may have been seeking to describe, though I believe he had failed to think it through in its granularity and relative novelty. Whereas I suspect that his intention was to differentiate different styles of capitalism, his remarks came across as simply contrasting left-wing with right-wing philosophies in the time-honoured fashion, and accordingly drawing the ideological dividing-lines in the wrong places.

President Milei favours what he calls 'market-driven capitalism,' as did Friedrich Hayek. By setting it in opposition to 'socialism', he is falling into an old trap — precisely the one the motherWEFfers had set for him, and it is precisely the same trap that has captured virtually the entirety of the Western liberal world, causing self-styled left-liberals to stare into the middle-distance while their governments trample upon the West's 3,000-year history of freedom. This, I suspect, explains why Klaus Schwab gave President Milei such an unequivocal welcome, declaring that his 'more radical methods' had delivered 'a new spirit to Argentina.'*

Had he wished really to call out the motherWEFfers's agenda, President Milei might have concentrated on the later sections of Hayek's book, especially the chapters titled 'Economic Control and Totalitarianism,' 'The Socialist Roots of Nazism,' 'The End of Truth,' and, above all, 'Why the Worst Get on Top.' In these sections, I suggest we get to understand the deeper significance of Hayek's philosophy, which is all too often written off as anti-leftist prejudice, i.e. in ideological terms mere reactionism.

The Road to Serfdom does, of course, proffer a strong warning about socialism; but deeper down it is a warning about suppressing the human instinct for spontaneity in the interests of efficiency or order. And this is where it comes into its own in the present moment, for, with a couple of minor edits, it might well be adapted as a blueprint critique of what is happening in the world now. While it is usually valid to invoke ideological categories to track and critique the move-

---

* The video if his speech can be found by searching for 'Special address by Javier Milei, President of Argentina | Davos 2024' (it starts at about 4 minutes in).

ments of 'useful idiots' deployed by whatever tyrants may be on the prowl, it is not, in this case, valid to see as ideological the threats, plays or ploys of the WEF, on behalf of its unseen clients (the FEW). The objectives of these actors are, first and foremost, of an intensely tyrannical nature, and, as already stated, are almost utterly devoid of ideological content.

Friedrich Hayek's emphasis on socialism had mainly to do with the timing of his writing of *The Road to Serfdom*, which emerged in the middle of the Great Depression and near the end of the Hitler war. Socialism he defined as all those ideas devoted to empowering the state. Although he had much to say about the baneful content of socialism, his emphasis was on the methods and practice of its execution, his underlying thesis focussing on the propensity of collectivist systems to destroy human spontaneity by virtue of their insistence on centralised planning and control, and their habit of summoning up distorted forms of science in order to pass themselves off as 'modern' and 'rational'. This, precisely, is the aspect of the motherWEFfers' machinations that should most concern us, for what they have in mind for our futures is a collectivism most unsocial, a 'cooperative' of the idle-enslaved under the silicon thumb of technology, and a state of 'equality' among populations achieved, as already observed, by rendering everyone equally bereft of property or wealth or freedom of any meaningful kind.

Hayek's chief preoccupations at the time of writing *The Road to Serfdom* were to draw attention to a prevailing backlash against free-market capitalism due to the growing sense that it had failed, and his desire to avoid in Britain a post-war continuation of the policies which had, of necessity, dominated the previous few years of WWII. Every time there's war he dryly noted, the size of the participating governments gets bigger and bigger. These thoughts came to him when he was a lecturer at the London School of Economics — itself a leftist stronghold, though open to alternative ideas. At the height of the Blitz, when the college evacuated its operation to Peterhouse College, Cambridge, Hayek became a regular volunteer lookout, sitting on the roof in the small hours, keeping watch for German bombers. It was this experience that, contemplating the putative aftermath of the war, caused him to fear that even an allied victory would result in the continuation of the wartime policy of centralised control of economic and social affairs, with the state owning, planning and controlling everything, and the people looking state-wards for answers and solutions: *'As in war, so in peace.'* This, above all, is the context in which his warnings about socialism require to be read — as the expression of a fear that victory and defeat would amount to the same thing, in effect an imposition of state power and control that would lead the allied West willy nilly to National Socialism, with the retention of English being the sole and small 'consolation'.

His emphasis on socialism was, to an extent, a secondary aspect of his thesis — German National Socialism being, at the time, the most visible manifestation of an ideology of centralised control, with Soviet Communism a close second (and Hayek made minimal ideological distinction between them). At that time in Britain, the conventional wisdom was that socialism offered itself as a kind of halfway-house between capitalism and fascism, whereas Hayek understood 'Nazism' as a close relative of what had emerged in the East, with tyrannical centralised control being the most ominous common factor.

One of the striking things about ideological conversation through history is its consistent refusal to bend with the times, or acquire the necessary suppleness to capture the ebbs and flows of reality. It is as though concepts like 'Left' and 'Right' have constant, eternal meanings, unaffected by proximate conditions or developments. Thus, the 'conservative', the 'capitalist', the 'right-winger', will mount the same critique of socialism/communism in 2024 as his father mounted in 1984, or his grandfather in 1959. In his turn, the leftist will respond with the same defences of the working class values of equity, compassion, decency, inclusivity, solidarity, and other claimed virtues of the socialist disposition, as though nothing much had changed, when in fact, the entire focus of leftist agitation has shifted from the working classes to the Woke classes — two utterly divergent and incomparable social, ideological and moral categories.

These conditions of thought-sclerosis have supplied an entirely new camouflage for the predator class, who want simply to own everything and everyone. And, because we think of capitalism as the expression of greed expressed economically, we fall into the trap of hearing only the old drumbeats, whereas the dance has taken on an entirely different form.

In these sclerotic thought-streams, the capitalist/conservative will warn ominously about the dangers of government overreach emanating from the Left, the destruction of individual choice as a consequence of command economics, the elimination of incentives arising from policies of redistribution, and so on — always with the implication that such evils will be avoided by simply taking a walk on the Right side. Leftists awaiting their turn will come back with lectures about avarice and the evils of unrestricted competition. No matter what the political or economic climate, it's the same old Punch and Judy show. And so it goes, even into 2024, when it must surely by now be clear that the menaces and dangers facing the world have nothing to do with any of this, but relate to the unprecedented convergence of power at the top of the former capitalist structure, and this arising neither from ideology nor from familiar strains of authoritarianism but directly as a consequence of the effects on our cultures and systems of the past five decades of funny (which is to say 'fake') money. This half-century has witnessed the seeming apotheosis of usury and the alienated essence of man's work and purpose, which, being of late times insinuated as his sole tangible reason for existing, casts doubts over his very future existence. The culture of fake — 'funny', not funny — money is a culture of looting, of turning tricks in which a procedure of *ex nihilo* resubstantiation renders unto the trickster the assets of his neighbour and leaves his neighbour with worthless paper soaked in tears. This, all but literally, amounts to a form of magic, which though it leaves its victims bereft, retains about it an aura of righteousness, of work ethic, of 'success'. And this 'success', paraded on the world's power stages, willy nilly translates into more power, so that rapidly the world moves not towards the Left or the Right, but toward a form of monopoly criminality.

The danger facing the world now arises not from socialism *qua* socialism, or even communism *qua* communism, but from an edifice of hyper-capitalism that feints in a leftish direction while drawing to itself the greatest convergence of wealth the world has ever seen. I'll say it slightly differently: The threats to human reality, life and existence today derive not from any prospect of state socialism, but from state-supported bureaucratic corporatism (fascism), posing as mainstream capitalism while keeping itself wrapped in a cloak of progressivism to camouflage the ancient art of looting in a virtuous robe. Even more so, the problem requires to be perceived in the context of the unprecedented access to virtually unlimited power afforded this behemoth courtesy of fake money, which has enabled it to impose its will upon reality while blocking the access of human culture to thought of the implications or consequences for humanity, or the future of human reality.

Its ability to do this arises in the first place from the severing of the connection between money and human endeavour arising from the outright abolition of the Gold Standard in August 1971. This meant that money was no longer in any degree accountable to those who depended on it for the exchange of the essentials of existence, or other necessities or benefits directed at furthering human existence, or for rewarding work and creativity, or for measuring the relative values of the goods and services on which human flourishing required to count. After the abolition of the Gold Standard, money became a free-floating entity, generated by banks under loose state licence, which predictably enabled the money systems of human society to fall into the control and effective ownership of those who already had access to the citadels of gambling, which had hitherto existed as marginal phenomena leeching off the toil and invention of the mass of humanity, but latterly incrementally turning into the veritable crucible of 'meaningful' economic activity. In the beginning this phenomenon had been bound by the protocols of a residual culture born of a time when money existed as nothing more than a cypher of exchange in concrete matters concerning essential human functions; but gradually these protocols began to wane in relevance to 'wealth'-generation, and this process was to accelerate when the limited natural life of this system of generating money as debt, by state fiat, came into view, as it did especially since the financial meltdown of 2008. Unlike the old system, which saw money as a material representation of tangible goods and services, the life of which was limited only by productivity, i.e. the human willingness and capacity to work, the new system operated by exploiting residual dynamics from the old patterns of operation, in particular the maintenance of phantom quantities of confidence and trust that had no concrete basis other than in the idea that no one in the system could possibly desire it to fail. For many years, with occasional hiccups arising mainly from temporary loss of faith, this system continued to succeed to excess, delivering to its participants unprecedented wealth — in the first place on or of paper, and subsequently in the capacity to exchange this paper for true wealth, the actual 'stuff' of reality — land, buildings, objects, patents, intellectual property, *et cetera*. But, precisely by virtue of its nature and capacity to deliver spectacular outcomes, this system was as though an expanding star accelerating towards its supernova, a moment that cannot be much longer delayed. Paradoxically, as the moment of explosion approaches, the power of the star increases exponentially, which in the instance of the present metaphor means that, although there is now almost unlimited 'money' with which to play, in the end, it will all be worthless except whatever has been transferred into concrete assets. By accident or design, therefore, the terminal nature of these moments provides, while it lasts, a perfect mechanism for turning paper assets into tangible ones, which is to say plundering the real world by means of worthless tokens, in the manner of a small-time confidence trickster, whose hands move faster than the speed of light.

The ostensible mystery is how this process was enabled to continue all these years without coming to the attention of those most in danger of being dispossessed by it — this being the vast majority of humankind. In part this was down to the corruption of public conversations, the bought blindness-to-corruption of most of those occupying roles as 'experts' and commentators, and the vested interest of the institutions involved in managing and policing the system, whose managers themselves became, or imagined they had become, minor players in the game of winners-take-all.

An additional factor was the level of distraction afforded in recent years — but especially since the final-warning collapse of 2008 — which served to divert public attention from the eye of the coming storm. The central element of this programme was the insinuation of a condition of intense irrationality into the public realm, whereby concepts that might previously have been thought insane or deranged were presented more and more as perfectly everyday and unexceptionable (men winning women's sports events, children being taught about anal sex, and so forth). For as long as a state of near-outright irrationality could be maintained, there was every chance of delaying the supernova beyond any definite period, so that its timing could be arranged to the maximum benefit of the main players. This is why there is so much money available now for apparently ridiculous and destructive purposes — nonsense, filth, craziness — because these quantities create not just helpful divisions, but also diversions which have the appearance of a kind of carefree extravagance, of nonchalance, of crypto-drunken abandon, which in turn distracts the human race from the kind of introspective brooding which could have the consequence of destroying trust and confidence in the fake money-driven pseudo-reality as it plunges towards its doom. The 'logic' of this has to do with the cultivated presumption that nothing truly bad or seriously damaging could be imminent if the state and government can find so much time for nonsense.

Participation in this game of existential brinkmanship — because it involves the diversion of money from its proper course through the channels of human endeavouring — amounts to a form of hoarding, once regarded as a cardinal sin of economic husbandry, the 'private virtue' that becomes a 'public vice'. Indeed, it is much worse than that once notorious economic sin: It is virtuous in neither realm, for in the private realm, it serves only to feed avarice and nugatory trading, and in the public realm acts to starve true human striving of necessary sustenance, or renders these processes impossible through inflation, high interest rates or other conditions bequeathed by the roulette tables, but with purely destructive powers in what was once the 'real' economy.

But, far worse than a mere vice or sin, what is being done is a crime against humanity, a crime that cries out to Heaven for vengeance. The burning out of the star will bring into unambiguous view a crime that started slow and is likely to end sharply and with extreme prejudice. Its end will have been inevitable from the beginning, and none of those implicated may be deemed entirely blameless. From the beginning it had been an attempt to ignore the laws of physics, to make substance out of nothing, but without recourse to traditional magic. The crime will relate to the usurpation of the money system in the first place, an event that will emerge as having occurred a long time before — perhaps 53 or 54 or 55 or more years ago, though probably not much more. This 'grand theft aurum' will amount to the strangest crime in history, for though undertaken with knowledge aforethought, it will have continued for more than half a century relatively undetected, and will have become manifest as catastrophe only in its culmination, when the consequences will be visited upon all but the entirety of the human race. For then it will become clear that the whole thing was from the beginning a kind of three-card trick, whereby men in suits had methodically enriched themselves by asset-stripping the world, using a fraudulent form of currency to imply substance and value, while in reality, it bore no relationship to either. These players had 'borrowed' (i.e. stolen) the instrument of measure, exchange and reward upon which the human race had depended, and misappropriated its logic and licence to multiply their own wealth — first in paper form and later tangibly — but in a manner replicating the action of a cancer in the biological realm, that now threatens the happiness and health of the great majority of humanity.

At the moment of the implosion, the criminals stand to be winners, but only if their crime remains unstatable, if the world continues to maintain its innocence as to what has been happening, and this can only be achieved by the maintenance of a mendacious culture in which nothing is permitted to be stated truly, or at least loudly enough to be widely heard, which is why arrangements have been in place to ensure that every purchasable voice might be compensated for maintaining silence, and the remainder frightened into the same state without monetary cost, which is achievable only by an unprecedented coercion

This is the mission that set sail in or around the Ides of March 2020, four years ago, more or less to the day.

Actually, the real commencement of the final Act of this long-running crime series was the intervention on August 15th 2019 (Assumption Day, in the Christian calendar) by BlackRock, the world's largest criminal organisation ('asset-management company' in funny-money parlance, *haha*), to instruct the world's governments and their superiors that BlackRock wished the economic life of the planet to be placed in an induced coma, so as to avoid its clients losing anything, or as little as possible — that not a drop of their wealth be spilt in the financial collapse then believed to be imminent. Assumption Day is a Christian feast day, commemorating the taking up, or reception, or 'assumption' into Heaven of the human body of the Blessed Virgin, to be reunited with her soul rather than to remain on Earth and undergo the same process of decay and degeneration as the bodies of mortals. It would be foolish of us to imagine that this timing was purely coincidental, for this was to be the beginning of the process whereby Emperor Larry would be assumed into a state of *de facto* kingship of all reality. The word 'assumption' has other connotations also — indicating something that 'is certain to happen', i.e. inevitable; something that is 'accepted as true without necessity of proof'; a 'presupposition' or 'presumption', 'an action of taking on power or responsibility' — and that day, BlackRock invoked all of these meanings, with the *de facto* outcome that its CEO, Larry Fink, laid his claim to displacing the democratic powers and sovereignties of what had hitherto been the Free World, and took possession of the conch that had been held by the People for — variously, depending on the location — hundreds or thousands of years. It took another seven months for this demand to come to realisation, but in or around the Ides of March 2020, Laurence Douglas Fink was investured as Emperor of the Whole World (though especially the Western part), albeit not explicitly on his own behalf, rather as the earthly representative of unseen unseens and unknown unknowns who held the chits of the near half-century-old roulette game in their breast pockets and were anxious to prevent reality getting in the way of their ultimate payday.

In trying to comprehend — and afterwards, hopefully, explain — what had been happening through the middle years of my life to prepare us for what is now unfolding, I have stumbled upon a metaphor that I think at least promisingly apt. When I say 'prepare us', I don't mean adequately from our viewpoint; I mean from the viewpoint of the 'preparers' (or should that be the 'preppers'? Probably not).

The issue is this: All our livelong lives we have been present for a kind of continuous social or 'cultural climate', which might be termed 'liberalism', 'progressivism', 'Enlightenment liberalism', 'democratic liberalism', or perhaps a half-dozen other variations on that familiar and singular theme. You will understand what I mean: the general sense that we lived in a society in which the People were sovereign, at least nominally, but in which, at a minimum, the licenced governing power flowed upwards— in the manner of a light — from the People, in which the broad approach was to leave citizens alone unless they broke the law in some way; in which everyone was deemed equal under the law; in which privacy and liberty were optimal values; in which what you did in bed was your own business so long as coercion or minors were not involved; in which you were entitled to accumulate as much wealth as you could manage, provided you paid all due taxes; and in which, above all things, it was axiomatic that each citizen was entitled to speak his mind, with minimal qualifiers ('Fire!' in a crowded theatre, *et cetera* — unless there actually was a fire, in which case even this indulgence was permissible), and no matter how much anyone else might be offended. And the even more critical thing was that any individual member of that society was deemed to be entitled to dissent from any, or most, or even all of those principles, philosophically speaking — which is to say, in his own mind, in his family or group or community, even in public — provided that, in his actions he extended, however reluctantly, token acquiescence to the general thrust of the democratic liberal project thus described, for as long as its fulfilment remained the desire of a majority of his compatriots, and insofar as mere observance of the law and acceptance of the government's functional authority were concerned.

And this dispensation was protected by a constant conversation — by no means always polite — which acted as a kind of sentry-detail on the superstructure of the culture in which this system or dispensation was apprehended, managed, cherished and implemented. By the process of constant talking — and occasional shouting, sometimes tearful or overwrought — the intermittently-developing weaknesses in new proposals were identified, thrashed out and mended, by way of ensuring that bad ideas did not get implemented in the public square. This conversation was a chaotic, stochastic process, in which the 'rules' were implicit and intuited rather than expressly understood. Argument was the chief mechanism, and this was subject to unwritten rules of engagement, arrived at over only God-knew-how-long. There was no fixed locus or forum, and anyone could have an input so long as he could persuade at least one other citizen to listen. Between adversaries, there was a time for hate and a time for cantankerous disharmony and even occasionally a time for agreeing to differ — and all these conditions were regarded as equally valid and vital. It was never thought either necessary or particularly beneficial that agreement or consensus be reached; the talking was everything because it alerted each and every factional viewpoint to the red lines marking off the potentially dangerous hazards and frailties in each instant proposal, so as in time to be fenced off by more moderate opinion, and in general, on a day-to-day rolling basis, to be addressed by a process somewhat resembling that of a colony of ants nibbling at a stray potato crisp.

In this informal crucible, the general experience was that there were fundamental points of agreement, though not necessarily many. One of them was that the exercising of power needed to be carefully monitored and kept in check. Certain dangers were recognised in this respect, above all that power took many forms, the most dangerous of which was the potential for distortions arising in the system due to the influence of large amounts of money, which had the power to purchase distortions of spontaneity and pass them off as freedom, and that this was something that everyone, including the financially endowed, had an interest in curtailing in the interests of the cohesion of the overall model. This caused, almost by way of an adaptive immune response to an exogenous interloper, a high degree of suspicion to develop in the sentry-culture concerning the relationship of monied interests or individuals to elements within the governing system. This healthy suspicion, indeed, was close to being the core principle directing this chaotic system of thought and self-governance. As a consequence, almost all the argumentational factions that emerged within the culture of the system were distinguishable by their attitudes towards — and positions on — questions relating to money: how should the society's internal flows of wealth and income be organised?; what were the limits that might properly be set on the capacity of money to buy power or access or privilege within the system?; how was the question of ensuring freedom to operate economically (a good thing) to be separated from the risk of having the system of power distorted by the necessity to protect this 'good thing' from the natural human urge to game the system?

Virtually everyone involved in the conversation could pretty immediately be identified on a spectrum emanating from the importance and urgency of these questions. There were people who called themselves capitalists and people who called themselves socialists. They did not agree on many things relating to how the benefits of the endeavours of people within the society might best be organised, but they were pretty much unanimous on the idea that it was not a good idea to allow success in the economic sphere of a particular actor or group to be a factor in tilting the scales of power in one direction or another.

In or around the ides of March 2020, all this changed out of all recognition, and the world has yet to come to grips with the implications.

CHAPTER 35
BEWARE THE IDES OF MARCH, PART II: THE LEDGER OF EVERYTHING
24-03-2024

'How can you buy or sell the sky, the warmth of the land? This idea is strange to us. If we do not own the freshness of the air and the sparkle of the water, how can you buy them?' — Chief Seattle

---

Pragmatism and moderation are two of the essential virtues of democracy. If we think of the 'power-source' of our civilisation as having been, in some slim sense, 'democratic', then we may imagine a three-pronged plug ('liberty, equality, fraternity', *haha!*) connected via a thick cable, plugged into the psychic vibration of the People as the source of its energy. It seems probable now that this was largely a pretence, if not an illusion, though for a long time — perhaps all our lives, until the Ides of March 2020 — we believed in it, after a fashion, while drily regarding it as the 'second best' system of government, the 'best' having forever remained elusive. Notwithstanding our occasional disgruntlement and scepticism concerning this arrangement of our collective affairs, we continued to pay it both loyalty and tribute, always mindful that the jungle lay behind, where dark monsters with names like 'fascism', 'totalitarianism', and 'neo-feudalism' lurked menacingly and patiently, ever-ready to re-emerge. Actually, no: We didn't really think like that; on the contrary, we thought of ourselves as having acquired immunity to such resurrections, not least because the levels of 'education' and connectivity suffusing our societies were such as to make us hyper-aware of such phenomena as having occurred previously through history, and of (we imagined) the reasons why, and, in many cases, we imagined ourselves 'expert' in them, and in the reasons they could not possibly happen again.

Not only were we, as a People (as Peoples everywhere in the West), so hyper-aware of these histories as to imagine ourselves to have 'evolved' beyond them, but the theoretical locus of the hypothetical threat had become so 'civilised' that it no longer counted as such.

In the past, the threats had arisen from external invasion, or the ambitions of the rich and powerful within, especially when they went to war, one against another. But now, we in the West felt protected by our big, strong Sugar-Daddy, the US of A, and the risk of such an intrusion was non-existent and laughable. As for the possibility of an internal eruption of predatory ambition — from the wealthy and powerful within — this idea was so preposterous that it never occurred to anyone. The rich were now our benefactors! They were altruists and philanthropists, who valued democratic freedoms even more than did we, the not-so-rich and the poor, if only because these were the source of their continued good fortune. Indeed, we imagined, the capitalist system was part of the infrastructure of freedom! Did we not call its engine 'the free market'? We might — as 'socialists', 'rebels', 'hippies', or 'counter-culturalists', rail against the dominion of 'The Man', or make occasional disparaging remarks about 'capitalist pigs', but we — and they — understood that this was pure theatre, all huff and bluster. 'The Man' had been tamed, long since, and was now 'one of us', albeit richer (by far), narrower of outlook than ever, fixated on accumulation rather than contemplation, and convinced of consumption above all. In truth, we imagined, The Man was too busy coining it to be bothered with controlling or even gaming the 'system'. He shared our values, more or less, albeit at a more concentrated level of material engagement. Capitalism had become not merely benign, but essential to the common weal — the well-being of all. Indeed, in the wake of the collapse of the Berlin Wall, it had become the only show in town. The Punch-and-Judy theatre of Left-Right politics continued, of course — *down with this or that*, and *'equality for all!'*, and very occasionally, *'let's soak the rich!'*, but it was all in good temper and in the best possible taste. What once had been a class war seemed to have turned into a sort of game in which the sides parried and feinted in good-humoured fashion — by way, perhaps, of preserving or safeguarding cultural mnemonics that, really, nobody seriously considered any longer necessary. History had ended, after all — hadn't some smart Yankee-Jap written a book that said so?

Then, one day in or around the Ides of March 2020, we awoke to find the whole thing had flipped overnight. It was as though someone had pulled out the three-pronged plug that linked the power cable of civilisation to the socket labelled 'the People', and plugged it into the jack marked 'Money talks'. The entire grid had been inverted — back to what it had been before the advent of this famous era of 'democracy', but with not as much as a *ping!* becoming audible above the admonitions to *'Stay home, stay safe!'* and *'Let's leave no one behind!'*

The stranger thing was that, even yet, four years on and counting, and judging by the collective conversation, almost no one understands that this is what occurred. Like someone flipped an egg-timer in the middle of the night, the configuration of demonstrable power inverted itself and seemed to start up again in a different gear, and from a new point of departure, without anyone but the odd remote crank noticing or describing it in such terms. The hourglass was inverted, so the power had swung to the top — contrary to every former instinct of the guardians and custodians of the system — and the thin grains of an unmistakably unfamiliar dispensation had commenced their (New World) ordered spillage into the neck of the future. Perhaps, by the time the word went out of anything happening at all, the sand had already completed its flow into the lower chamber, which was now full and waiting to be flipped again to cue the beginning of a whole new epoch? If so, no one had issued any warning or instruction concerning this moment, nor was there any evidence of an understanding of its — as it were — *moment*. No germane commentary preceded or accompanied it. No great puzzlement was expressed as to how it could even be possible. Any notice that was taken of something untoward was almost filed under headings relating to the pretext, which was, we were assured, health-related. And, indeed, if seismic changes were afoot, then clearly it was because they were inevitable — the march of progress. No one spoke of a natural ebb of civilisations, to be perceived in the grain of history, from times of freedom to times of its antithesis. This was unthinkable, and therefore, unthought, and, in any event, no existing single human being had lived long enough to be aware of this danger other than as a theory.

All that being as it might, as we now begin to observe from all the visible signs and from the demeanours of various actors — politicians, scribes, philanthropists, economic theorists — it appears that, at normative rates of flow, it might well take half a century for the sand to complete another cycle, for this new era to play itself out, and for its driving force, whatever that may be like, to weaken or recede. As far as we know — which, realistically, we cannot.

Thus it was that, in a private ceremony, in or around the Ides of March 2020, a new king was crowned in secret. His name, as already intimated, was Laurence the 1st, of the family Fink, of the principality of BlackRock. With little or no notice to the implicated public, he came to the top of the stairs and looked down. No one looked up, but King Larry stood there anyway, in his cockaded robe and golden crown, gazing down upon his people — the new, and this time literal, 'Master of the Universe'.

For those few bystanders who noticed, what appeared to have happened was inconceivable, and therefore, could not conceivably be true. And yet, the elements within the system that ensured its operation and defences had all, as though instantaneously, jettisoned their prior functioning and logic and started to operate as if the new dispensation had been in place from some long-ago beginning. The political puppeticians and apparatchiks — long since having handed over all claims to actual leadership — immediately began ostentatiously to serve the new master. The judges on the benches slipped from implementing the rule of law to implementing the will of Emperor Larry. The police went out to enforce the new Kingdom of BlackRock diktats, with no absence of gusto. The scribes began to describe the new world as though it had always existed in this form, or as if anything that seemed to be amiss was, in fact, an improvement. In their spare moments, the scribes turned to attack those who continued to speak of the 'old days' of 2019 and before.

While this was happening, nobody from among the conventional custodians of democracy and freedom spoke out. The 'liberals' were silent. The 'civil libertarians' were preoccupied with quotidian matters, such as cashing the cheques from the Open Society Foundation. The human rights lawyers were on leave, having been paid in advance for an unscheduled vacation from their vocations.

Of course, the coup (for such it was) was not advertised in these terms. There was a 'health emergency' arising from a 'deadly disease'. The platforms of public discourse were suddenly crammed with sundry experts, none exhibiting signs of undue poverty, or indeed ill-health, who drew the collective conversation away from mere bagatelles like rights and freedoms, now suddenly deemed to be luxuries in the times that were said to be in it. The 'Emergency' was on everyone's lips, and virtually all agreed that its management was such a priority as to render talk of lost liberty a dangerous indulgence that might properly and wisely be postponed to a less troubled and threat-filled future day.

In a certain acoustic, it seemed that, at the crucial moment, almost all the watchdogs of freedom developed a sudden condition of contagious lockjaw. Only the mavericks, waifs and strays had anything to say, and why would anyone listen to them? Those who did were cattle-prodded using the spell-words issued in the form of a list in a separate communication from Emperor Larry's palace:

farrightwhitesupremecistconspiracytheoristantivaxxernazi

Multiple explanations have been essayed for this sudden and virtually universal capitulation. In this or that instance, it has been mooted that perhaps no one had properly understood what was afoot. Fear might have been a significant factor — but fear of what? Fear of consequences, perhaps? But consequences of what? The entire edifice of the — as now we may call it — *conspiracy* seemed to be sustained by an internal compact of *omertá*. In the greasing of this, there were, undoubtedly, inducements — the benefits of limitless 'free' money, now becoming available as the star of Western civilisation plunged towards its supernova. But there were other motivators also: the risk that, by not playing along, any particular actor might become the scapegoat of what was, after all, the Most Heinous Crime in All History. What was being brought in to land was no less than a history encompassing multiple decades of plunder. And the most important thing about the handling of this landing was that the word 'crime' not pass the lips of anyone who had the remotest chance of being taken seriously. It was no less than wise to be *afraid* — to play along rather than rock the rocket ship.

As regards the political class, the supposed custodians of the democratic structure and values being usurped and bypassed, in the more benign hypotheses it was as if it had been decided that, by adopting the correct demeanour of acquiescence, this phase might pass quickly, and democratic rule be restored within a reasonable time. But, as time passed and this did not appear to be a pressing matter for those now fronting-up for the new Regime, the response of the People themselves was neither chagrin nor agitation, but silent acquiescence, as though something had been wordlessly understood about the permanence of what had occurred. Or, perhaps it was something as crude as the primary rule of human intercourse as conveyed by our old friend, Deep Throat, in that underground car park: *Follow the Money?* There was the fake money, of course, the furlough schemes and the Pandemic Unemployment Payment, and the usual bribes and inducements, albeit more generous than was customary. The People, too, had been bribed and intimidated, and therefore induced into a mindset of self- or mutual policing.

The bottom line was, as usual, all that mattered, and the bottom line declared that Emperor Larry was the new boss who, contrary to the assertion of the bumper sticker, was not in the least like the old boss. Everything relating to the nature and structure of democratic society that had persisted in human culture up to the Ides of March 2020 had been history-binned, as though someone had tipped that unseen sand-timer and set our civilisation back to more or less the moral point at which it had begun, many centuries before. Something had happened in the world that rendered the old arrangement — whereby the People were the arbiters and architects of their own affairs — as though now an unfathomable and distant recourse, perhaps no more than a rumour of some odd predilection of some ancient, extinct tribe, and no longer worthy of defence or advocacy by right-thinking people. As King Larry put it: Democracy was no longer a 'fit' for the kind of capitalism that was necessary going forward — *'totalitarianism is better!'* Almost everyone nodded in a mature fashion. Very soon it became implicit in everything — in the tone of the media, in the visages of the puppeticians, in the acquiescence of the executive and legislative branches of governments, in the twisted, evasive subtexts of the judicial marionettes — that not only the political power, but the liberties and rights of the People also, had been rendered forfeit. Democracy had been ended without announcement. The new Power was naked in every way, not least in its intentions and its clarity of purpose, but there was not even the occasional little boy willing to step up and say so. The constitutions, charters and conventions of the former Free World had been 'suspended', as though instanter and *sine die*, and replaced with an unspoken though implicit new maxim: *Money talks; bullshit walks.* To those who saw, with the eyes they had used before, the monsters imperilling them from behind, wearing what looked like the masks of vaguely familiar idiot faces, had no reference for what they saw except in stories of ancient, remorseless invaders, and incongruous but compelling fictional tableaux of rationally implausible comparison. In any event, such observers were few. The sovereign citizen had died suddenly in his sleep, awakening, Lazurus-like, with a new cry upon his lips: *Long live the King! Long live the King's money!* The advent of neo-feudalism had been announced with an absence of abashment, and little or no protest. The inversion of Western civilisation, the word went quietly out, was to be regarded as a new form of progress, which only the most loathsome of reactionaries might oppose.

An eBook was published in the middle of last year which describes this crime in explicit detail, outlining not merely its nature but its method and its brazenness. The book is *The Great Taking*, by David Rogers Webb — an American investment banker, hedge fund manager and financial analyst. Webb delves into what I have been calling The Most Heinous Crime In History, i.e. the ongoing project to impoverish vast swathes of humanity by transferring their assets to the clients of Mr. Larry Fink.*

Essentially, *The Great Taking* is a forensic diagnosis of the current actual financial state of the West — and, implicitly, beyond that, of the whole world — underneath the spin and pretence and lies spun by politicians, bankers and the setaside media. The roulette table, which has been at the centre of our financial affairs for more than half a century, is creaking under the weight of the multiplicities of bets usurping a decrementally dwarfing store of collateral used to justify the creation of more and more debt, which exists in loops within loops to the point of untrackability. This Ponzi edifice is about to come down, bringing to an end the five-decade three-card-trick that has enabled several generations of pseudo-entrepreneurs to move from asset millionaires to paper trillionaires, without adding a soupçon of benefit to human circumstances, by doing nothing for human society except strangle it in debt and use this debt to transfer its actual wealth from the citizenry to themselves.

As you may observe on reading the book, it deals in pretty dense material, but the general picture is not hard to grasp. Those who were paying attention during the crash of 2008 and its aftermath will surely have a shrewd sense that the people who control the Ponzi scheme are not the types to shrug off losses, and all the less so when they stand to lose pretty much everything they believed themselves to be 'worth'. Instead, they have decided that, since they have come

---

* The audio of this book is available free on the internet.

this far, there is no good reason why they should not hoover up everything. This, to all intents and purposes, is to be the final divvy-up.

It need hardly be said that their 'wealth' is entirely bogus, being the payoff of a series of multiplicatory tricks in which assets are given different euphemistic names to enable them to be switched, shuffled, swapped and cut like an oily deck in the hands of a skilled shark. It is important to understand and re-emphasise that this predator class has contributed nothing to the well-being of humanity or human society — *ever*. This has nothing to do with what we speak and think of as economics. They are thieves, essentially, who have used power, connections, graft, access to the levers of fiat currencies, and the rigging of every deal, to multiply paper assets, which in a sane and decent world would long since have been declared worthless. They deserve to be stripped of every bogus cent of their 'wealth'. Instead, it is the human population that stands to be impoverished, to be plundered of the actual collateral that sits diminishingly at the bottom of this dungheap. What is collapsing is not the world, but this bogus house of cards, constructed to enable the accrual of paper wealth to this predator class as we approach the end of the span of time (53 years to date) when the bogroll-in-waiting currencies of the West could still be exchanged for real assets. Now, as the value of currencies begins to slide towards oblivion, they seek to cash-in everything in final exchange for the collateral that amounts to, in effect, everything still worth owning. Those who have inhabited the economy of work and produce, measure and reward, will be stripped of everything they had imagined themselves to be working for all their lives; the three-card-tricksters will inherit ownership of the whole of the Earth.

As David Rogers Webb outlines, they have prepared the way by nobbling the political, media and legal systems of multiple countries, to ensure that their claims will override all others. The details of this, though likely to seem arcane and labyrinthine to the layman, are important to gaining an overall sense of the patience and preparation that has been invested in this crime of all crimes.

David Rogers Webb explains in immense and precise detail what is intended to happen: the human race is set to lose; the predator class is set to win — (*unless, unless, unless . . . !* — and we are running short of unlesses!). Those who hold the chips, and are determined not to lose them, have already rigged the game — legally speaking, above all — to ensure that when the star blows and the house of cards comes tumbling down, it is the actual owners of the collateral at the heart of the subterfuge who will lose everything. A 'protected class' of secured creditors will have prior claims over all others, including those who imagine themselves to be the owners of the collateral that has been misused in this corrupt system. What is planned is a kind of Mother Of All *Ex Nihilo* Transubstantiations, by which all forms of property rights have, *de facto, de jure* and in secret, already been abolished in every jurisdiction in the world, so that every piece of collateral that falls within the purview of the banking system is forfeit to the 'higher' interest of the liquidity of particular banks, and the solvency of their premier customers.

Essentially, the things we think we own are ours only for as long as 'they' — the predators — permit us to believe so. Even though you have paid for the property you believe to be yours, the bankruptcy of the bank to which you have entrusted that asset to secure a loan will ensure that its value transfers to others who have established a stronger claim than yours by virtue of being in the know and in the right bank.

David Rogers Webb elaborates:

'And they have now established legal certainty that they have absolute power to take it immediately in the event of insolvency, and not your insolvency, but insolvency of the people who secretly gave them your property as collateral. It does not seem possible. But this is exactly what has been done with all tradable financial instruments, globally! The proof of this is absolutely irrefutable. This is wired to go now.'

A useful way of seeing the final divvy-up might be that the spoils being divided at the roulette table will no longer be the chips, but the real, three-dimensional assets — properties, cash, shares, bonds, *et cetera* — that have been left lying around as bedrock collateral, largely ignored while the 'game' was the promulgation of digits —in other words, the time is approaching when what will be traded will not be chips or chits, but the actual wealth of the world.

To a mere murmur of commentary, the past half century has seen the debt quotient in the global economy expand, from approximate equivalence with aggregate GDP, to a level more than 20 times the capacity of human society to pay its way as it goes. This bizarre circumstance remained either unremarked or, when occasionally mentioned, was deemed an inevitable and unworrying aspect of 'modern' economics. All that really meant was that the Day of Judgement was being postponed, but now it is arriving.

And so, the plan goes, the heist will be achieved by liquidating all the smaller banks, and 'burning' all their account holders, to the benefit of a handful of bigger banks, where the pseudo-wealth of the FEW will be augmented and protected. This time around, banks will be closed rather than nationalised. Instead of bail-outs, there will be bail-ins, in which some or all of the cash assets of depositors will be confiscated. Gold and silver deposits, too, may be subject to seizure, and those who refuse to hand these over liable to imprisonment. Only the 'protected classes' of secured creditors will retain their wealth, and they will retain as much as possible of what the chits say is theirs.

After what David Rogers Webb calls the 'Everything Crash' that follows inevitably on the heels of the 'Everything Bubble', there will be nothing left of what we consider 'our' property. And not only will there be nothing left, but as I have emphasised several times in the past year or so, even after accounting for every blade of grass, every grain of sand, and every drop of rainwater in our countries, the paper value will come nowhere close to the sums that are owed to the clients of Larry Fink, the Emperor of the Whole World and Everything In It (nominally, at least, but also *de jure*). In this Ledger of Everything, we will all remain burdened by debt, but in a sense, this will be academic because the predators will by then own anything of any value — including the whisper of the wind and the ripple on the stream — and will be ready to start off their 'game' again once another financial system is launched — by all accounts by means of a global Central Bank Digital Currency (CBDCs), using programmable digital 'money', social credit scores and universal basic income (UBI), 15-minute cities, pods, surveillance and delivery drones, and bug sandwiches for lunch. This time, we, the former People, will be — at best — spectators, but mostly we will be the newly-indentured serfs that Friedrich Hayek feared we might one day become.

As *The Great Taking* 'went to press', less than a year ago, central banks in 114 countries representing 95 per cent of the global economy were working on CBDCs, with all G7 economies and 18 of the G20 countries having arrived at an advanced stage of preparation. Through this system, the losers under the old dispensation will be 'compensated' on a take-it-or-leave-it basis, with UBI, starting with token lump sums being lodged to their digital accounts to get them up and running with a currency that will be programmable and contingent on behaviour and attitude, and therefore a central instrument of the totalitarian system that will take up where the Covid tyranny left off.

This, writes Rogers Webb, is the planned endgame of the accumulation of debt that has characterised Western economies for half a century.

This is being executed by long-planned, intelligent design, the audacity and scope of which is difficult for the mind to encompass. Included are all financial assets, all money on deposit at banks, all stocks and bonds, and hence, all underlying property of all public corporations, including all inventories, plant and equipment, land, mineral deposits, inventions and intellectual property. Privately owned personal and real property financed with any amount of debt will be similarly taken, as will the assets of privately owned businesses, which have been financed with debt. If even partially 'successful', this will be the greatest conquest and subjugation in world history.

To achieve these ends, we have been for some time, says David Rogers Webb, in the midst of a 'hybrid war' — a combination of forces, public and private, using a multiplicity of weapons — directed at humanity in general, which is to say everyone apart from the tiny FEW represented by the WEF: brainwashing, soft tyranny, the suspension of charters, conventions and constitutions, mandates, cancellation, censorship and the minting of new legal concepts, such as 'domestic terrorism', to deal with those who insist on objecting.

This time, what the thieves will take is all of your property, or what you thought was your property.

Webb puts it like this:
'Here is your Central Bank Digital Currency deposited on your smartphone, so that you can buy milk. Noblesse Oblige!'

What is coming, as he describes it, will be merciless — to the outer reaches of the meaning of that word. The world has never seen anything like it. This is what has been in train for the past 48 months: the orchestration of the Great Taking. This is the reason for the lockdown, the propaganda, the bogus PCR tests, the fomenting of the Ukraine war and the slaughter on the Gaza Strip. This is why they need 'hate speech' laws: to stop us speaking publicly about what they have done/are doing to us. To complain is to hate. And it all started with a head cold.

In this respect, David Rogers Webb tells us nothing new. But he summarises effectively, lest we misunderstand anything:

'Governments broadly abused fundamental human rights using as justification prevention of the spread of infectious diseases, which are, in truth, a great many, ever-present, and continually evolving. And so, this justification, if allowed to stand, affirms the end of democracy and the continuation of openly despotic government.'

And the WHO 'pandemic treaty' — likely to be implemented by a majority of governments throughout the West within a couple of months — is set to make these conditions permanent, creating a state of implicitly permanent 'Emergency' (invocable by an external body at the drop of a needle) throughout the former Free West and beyond.

In a certain light, as already noted, what is happening now has strong roots in the early 1970s, and before that into the mists of history. But the scale of what is about to happen exceeds anything ever conceived of in the public discourse, economic hypothesising, academic literature or ideological argumentation of the mass media era. What is planned amounts to a deliberate and unabashed takedown of not merely the financial and economic systems of the world, but of all the broader and ancillary infrastructures of societies, democracies, civilisation. In short, this puts an end to the era of freedom that began with the Greeks and seemed to achieve its apotheosis after the 1960s countercultural revolutions, whereas in truth the star of Liberty was already generating an excess of the wrong types of freedom, and consequently taking in energy from outside, causing the edifice of Western civilisation to fall in upon itself.

The scale of the resulting reversal is total and, by now, possibly irreversible. Never before has a system benefitted so few at the expense of so many, with the few continually becoming richer and fewer, and the many reducing to a great mass, drifting towards subsistence or much worse.

The people behind this, says David Rogers Webb, are the same people — in the sense of 'the same stock' — who orchestrated the great wars of the twentieth century, who have never been investigated or called to account. What has been happening in Ukraine and Gaza is in line with the historical patterns — and the world has fallen for it again. The people behind the wars are 'quite literally, lying, thieving killers, and they know it,' he writes. They will leave nothing behind, especially not witnesses to their crimes.

It should be clear to us that only a miracle can now prevent this catastrophe unfolding until it consumes the world as we have known it.

Webb writes:

'We are in the grip of the greatest evil humanity has ever faced (or refused to acknowledge, as the case may be). Hybrid war is unlimited. It has no bounds. It is global, and it is inside your head. It is never-ending.'

Strangely, after all that, he is hopeful. The collapse of the star that is Western civilisation has multiple unpredictable characteristics.

'We have witnessed designs and real attempts to exert physical control over every person's body, globally, and this is continuing. Why is this happening?

'I will make a startling assertion. This is not because the power to control is increasing. It is because this power is indeed collapsing. The "control system" has entered collapse.

'Their power has been based on deception. Their two great powers of deception, money and media, have been extremely energy-efficient means of control. But these powers are now in rampant collapse. This is why they have moved urgently to institute physical control measures. However, physical control is difficult, dangerous and energy-intensive. And so, they are risking all. They are risking being seen. Is this not a sign of desperation?

'Where will they hide when they have all of the assets, when they have damaged all of humanity, and caused billions to awaken through suffering?

'They promote the belief that they are all-powerful. They are not. All they have had is the power to print money. The rest, they have usurped from humanity.'

And again:

'Antipathy for humanity is aberrant. For 99.99% of human history, sociopaths like these would not have survived the next winter. Their nature was seen and they were ostracized from the village, to save the village.

'They operate today through anonymity enabled by inhuman scale of social organization. Even so, this will not allow them to continue indefinitely. We have entered a time in which their nature is being recognized. Knowledge of their existence has become unavoidable. Their grasping will come to an end, because all of humanity cannot allow it to continue. Once it is recognized, humans will bond against a common existential threat. People from all walks of life will join in common cause. We have witnessed this already.'

What we contemplate here is both 'fictional' and all too real. It is, as already stated, the usurpation of the economy by gangs of feral predators who have been living and prospering off the system designed for human protection, preservation, endeavouring, development, enrichment and enhancement, for half a century and indeed long before that, in multiple other ways. Nothing of this has contributed as much as a cent or a spud or a cake of bread to human prosperity or well-being. What we speak of are parasites, and like all parasites, they are not content with merely leeching — they must also invade and commandeer. It is important that we firstly understand this, if we are to have any chance of overturning what is occurring: that these are criminals, just like bank robbers or kidnappers or gangs of rapists — only a billion times worse. In truth, they are the controllers of the world solely through processes that enable them to usurp our power by appropriating the instruments of democratic power and its attendant instruments of coercion — by corrupting those to whom we entrusted that power by making them our 'representatives'. Otherwise, these are just pathetic leeches and bloodsuckers.

And this is why they are flooding our counties with unvetted, unidentifiable military-age men — so they will have willing, stakeless agents to carry out their dirty work when the marquee finally comes tumbling down.

The parasite was a standard character of Ancient Greek drama. The literal meaning of the word 'parasite' is 'beside food', a Greek word for 'waiter', which subsequently came to mean a hanger-on, referring to a sponger who plied the wealthy with charming conversation in return for comestibles. In due course, the word teleported to biology, where it became *inter alia* the source of multiple metaphors of leeching and blood-sucking. Biological parasites use all kinds of tricks to fool the immune system of the host into providing them with the conditions ideal to their existence.

The phenomenon of economic parasitism has featured as a topic of writers for more than a century. In 1898, an American writer, John Brown, published a book called *Parasitic Wealth to Money Reform: A Manifesto to the People of the United States and the Workers of the World.* He complained that two-thirds of American wealth was concentrated in the hands of six per cent of the population. 'With the refinement of innate cruelty,' he wrote, 'these parasites eat their way into the living substance of their living but helpless host, avoiding all the vital parts to prolong the agony of a lingering death.'

This metaphor blends into literalism as treated in *Parasite Rex*, the 2000 book of biologist Carl Zimmer, subtitled 'Inside the bizarre world of nature's most dangerous creatures', meaning the biological parasites that infest the bodies of animals and humans. It is an extraordinarily detailed and graphic book of biology, but the contents page is instructive as to the metaphorical value of these comparisons in our present context:

Chapter 1: *'How parasites provoke, manipulate, and get intimate with our immune system';*

Chapter 3: *'How parasites provoke, manipulate, and get intimate with our immune system';*
Chapter 4: *'How parasites turn their hosts into castrated slaves, drink blood and manage to change the balance of nature'.*

Zimmer elaborates:
'A parasite lives in a delicate competition with its host for the host's own flesh and blood. Any energy that the host uses itself could go instead to the growing parasite. Yet, a parasite would be foolish to cut off the energy to a vital organ like the brain, since the host would no longer be able to find any food at all. So, the parasite cuts off the less essential things. As *Cotesia congregata* robs the caterpillar of its fat stores, it also shuts down its host's sex organs. Male caterpillars are born with big testes, and normally they channel a lot of the energy from their food into building them up even more. When a parasitic wasp lives inside the male, however, the testes shrivel up. Castration is a strategy that any number of parasites have hit on independently — *Sacculina* does it to crabs, and blood flukes do to the snails they invade. Unable to waste energy on building eggs or testes, on finding a mate, or on raising young, a host becomes, genetically speaking, a zombie: one of the undead serving a master.'

Zimmer elaborates on aspects that resonate with the present, early-21st-century parallels between parasitism in nature and in inter-human relations:
'In attacking humans,' he warns, 'a parasite can manipulate its host in ways that dispose it better to their desires and demands. Psychologists have found that *Toxoplasma* changes the personality of its human hosts, bringing different shifts to men and women. Men become less willing to submit to the moral standards of a community, less worried about being punished for breaking society's rules, more distrustful of other people. Women become more outgoing and warm-hearted. Both changes seem to break down the fear that might keep a host out of danger.'

Interestingly, biological parasites use serotonin-boosting molecules to adapt their hosts and make them less wary — for example, persuading a male host that it's having sex, or convincing a female host that she is the male. Zimmer advises that parasites 'come equipped with a big pharmacy full of drugs ready to be dispensed [to its victim] at different times during the parasite's life when it needs different things.'

In a certain light, the above may be read as a kind of metaphorical summary of Western culture in the post-1960s era.

As observed in the last chapter, the WEF is not fighting for equality or inclusivity or justice, any more than it is comprised of environmental fanatics lying sleepless at night thinking of the future of Planet Earth. The motherWEFfers are not seeking to divvy up the Earth's resources on a more equitable basis; quite the contrary. BlackRock is not a bleeding-heart operation. Instead, it now seems clear, the plan is to present the world with a Hobson's choice: slavery under a unipolar system — a continuation of US/EU/NATO hegemony — or the same under a 'multipolar world' led by Russia/China, a fake alternative that is no kind of alternative at all. This has been the meaning of the hot wars of the past two years — in Ukraine, Gaza and Yemen: to create a constant sense of the world plummeting towards a disastrous conflict that will alter our lives out of all recognition no matter who wins. The Woke element, being born out of the Sixties 'freedom' revolution (sex is everything!), is a distraction put in place to capture the imagination of the West in a manner as to demoralise it and perhaps make it grateful if Russia/China finally wins. All the stories we have been told, which we have been telling ourselves, are planted to serve this ultimate agenda.

It now seems as though every player in these dramas is, in some sense or another, a kind of actor. I resisted this thesis for a fair while, but now I begin to believe I was wrong. I do not claim to understand how Vladimir Putin — for example — could be such an actor. If so, he is a rather good one. In fact, in piecing together my 'dry stone wall' of understanding, I have been arguing that this is not possible, that he seems utterly sincere, that his disgust of the drifts of the West is too real to be invented, that he would not bet the best of Russian manhood in the service of such a project; but now I think I may have underestimated the mentality that it nowadays takes to lead a country in the first place: The prize is too alluring for any political leader, who must perforce make pragmatic decisions all the time, not to be prepared to lay down these wagers and live with the outcome on the basis of whatever rationalisation suggests itself as plausible.

If this hypothesis is correct, then everything we have been watching is indeed part of the drama, and the behaviour of all the layers begins to make more sense. By this (unproven, possibly unprovable) hypothesis, Tucker Carlson had to leave Fox News in order to do his Putin interview; Elon Musk had to buy Twitter in order to be seen to be the Hero On A White Charger, shouting slogans about freedom as he rode into town.

For the several years since I started delving into these matters, I have been subject to particular drips of information from various quarters, which half the time I believed and half the time I did not. Now, I understand that, in the generality of this material, I was being fed information in which the truth was buried — i.e. not to be found in its literal content but in the runes of what I was being exhorted to believe and relay, which in most instances was intended as planted misdirection. The truth was neither what I was being told, nor what was, in whatever context, being explicitly or implicitly refuted — i.e. neither thesis nor antithesis — but in a synthesis of these. Very often it confused me on account of its surface lack of coherence. But I was reading it wrongly — for raw facts and indicators and directions, rather than for what it was: a leaked movie script in which the false dichotomy was being peddled by way of a narrative tease: Bad

Guys within and White Hats without. I even published some versions of this narrative, though studded around with caveats, and now I must revisit these to clarify not so much their veracity as their correct place in the plot. To be frank, more and more, I was leaning towards the idea that the West had become so evil that Russia/China must perforce represent a better alternative. From any sane evaluation of, say, the past history of Western civilisation, this should rightly be regarded as seriously dangerous thinking, and yet now — in these unprecedented moments — it seems almost prudent to contemplate it. And yet, hold on: Mao, Lenin, Stalin, *et cetera*? Get a grip! — no?

And doesn't even the validity of that question betray a sneaking residual belief that nothing quite as bad as all that could happen in the 'democratic' West? And how delusional is that, after all we've come through?

The official narrative of Western society has for several years now been promoting a version of our future that amounts, in truth, to a version of the West in which it turns into Russia/China willy-nilly — or something akin to that — Hobson's choice, with the sole element of 'choice' being how we, the People, decide to deal with this. Will we resist and bring the wrath of the New Masters down upon our heads, or acquiesce, make the best of it and knuckle down to a life of neo-feudal unfreedom? In truth, the planned ultimate outcome amounts to the same thing: democracy ends, and digital slavery begins.

Ultimately, I believe, the Plan is Plan A: that we shall 'cling to nurse for fear of something worse' — that the tyrants have anticipated that we will opt for the devil we know rather than the one we only *know of*, but with the 'software' of our future existence being indistinguishable, one way or the other.

A couple of years back, as Elon Musk was beginning to emerge as some kind of one-man cavalry driven by something like the values we had watched being torched for the previous two years — I described him as a 'hero on a zebra', a phrase no one appears to have interpreted as I intended it. I thought it obvious that it was intended to convey a man on an ambiguous steed — neither a black stallion nor a white charger — and therefore not so easy to pin down, and accordingly probably to be regarded with suspicion, no matter how persuasive his patter. I have long been sceptical of Twitter, which, being a central element of the mechanisms of the takedown of our civilisation, is unlikely to be any kind of solution, and so, while acknowledging at least the surface desirability of his assuming control of the platform he rather ludicrously dubbed 'the public square', I cited as evidence of a countervailing darkness his involvement in surveillance satellites, the development of driverless cars and technological enterprises that strive to connect human brains to computers. I say this as someone who is as captivated by Elon Musk's charism and charisma as just about anyone. I have listened to dozens of hours of his interviews online, and find him profoundly engaging, intelligent, seemingly humane and idealistic, and extremely entertaining, even allowing for my suspicion. Having listened to him very carefully for many months, and especially in his unpicking of Twitter corruption last year, I am now more than ever certain that Musk is not what he seems. However uplifting or entertaining his presence becomes, he still doesn't seem to be achieving anything that might be deemed useful in the circumstances I am trying to describe.

A dark thought occurs to me, as it has occurred to others, and will not go away: What if Musk is one of the Combine's creatures, but carefully choreographed to appear to be something like a 'white hat', who has come to rescue us from the villainous Schwab and his scheming, evil-laughing minions? What if this is the true Plot? I have wondered many times about their pushing of Schwab, the dead spit of a pantomime villain, to the forefront of their Great Reset, and asked myself: What if they are making a movie, in which wicked old Klaus is being set up (probably knowingly, since he plays it with such gusto!) as the fall guy — i.e. the story of a plot to take over the world that is destined to fail because the 'cavalry' arrives just in the nick of time?

And then what? After the celebrations, we all sit around ('democratically', as in the olden days) and discuss what to do. Nice Mr Musk has an idea: Why don't we introduce a social credit system using his satellite surveillance network, get our brains chipped and each receive a free driverless car? *Whoopee! Elon — yes, let's!*

By way of evidential submission: Whereas Musk was last year vociferously stating that he would fund any litigant who sought to challenge the proposed Irish 'hate speech' laws (all but universally deemed to be the most draconian ever tabled in the former Free World) but more recently (and to remarkably sparse commentary) has appeared to resile from this offer and meekly stated that Twitter/X will 'obey the law'.

Right now, it appears that, although the Combine appears unstoppable, short of a miracle, its 'victory' on the present trajectory would, as David Rogers Webb has postulated, be a Pyrrhic one, because it would have been achieved mainly through coercion and a degree of Bad Guy-inflicted ugliness, such as we have observed, in trial-mode, over the past 48 months. Far better to create a plot-twist at a late stage in the action, making it appear like the evildoers have been defeated by a shining new hero who arrives promising freedom and progress at the same time. What I am suggesting is a third-act shift of narrative, in which the one-man cavalry comes over the hill (on his zebra), and everyone breathes a sigh of relief and goes back to watching Netflix. And then, the surveillance and the process of human electrification and the centrally-controlled electric vehicles will be ramped up again, but this time in a climate of renewed complacency and celebration. It is certainly a movie I might like to watch, though not to be trapped in.

Paradoxically — and regardless of which fork in the road we drive or are driven down — as we approach the *denouement* of this criminal campaign, there will be a fleeting opportunity to arrest it, and possibly even its parasitical perpe-trators. Already, there is a growing consciousness about the true nature not merely of this crime but all the associated crimes which have been committed in order to keep this primary crime under wraps. This, as described, is why the world economy was placed in a coma in March of 2020, on the rumour of a respiratory infection. This is why martial law was introduced at that point — both as precautionary measure in its own moment and a rehearsal for a future more ominous one. This was why millions of people (between 20 and 100 million, by various estimates) were designated to die from stress, grief, seda-tives, ventilators, experimental injections, lack of medical attention, despair, and multiple other causes. This is why the public conversation had to be compro-mised by the purchasing of journalism. This is why Mr Larry Fink, the CEO of BlackRock, was heard to muse about totalitarianism being possibly a better fit than democracy for the 'modern' forms of capitalism. This is why democracy was put on ice with a view to its final dismantling — all while more than a few of those who stood to lose everything from the 'success' of this initiative were going around abusing one another for not wearing face coverings.

Our immediate instinct is both rational and unthinking: Why not simply arrest these malefactors now, before it is too late? It is a good question, but there is a problem. Normally, once a crime is detected and described, it is merely a formality to carry out the processes of arrest, prosecution, conviction and sentencing of those found to be guilty. But this is also a unique category of crime, and in more senses than one. Apart from its scale and duration, this crime is distinguished by the fact that it is one in which the power to prosecute is all but entirely trapped within the criminal fraternity. Because those designated by society to investigate, prosecute, judge and punish such crimes, are this time themselves, virtually without exception, implicated (as perpetrators or accom-plices), it is by no means clear how this particular set of crimes would be defined and treated as such by anyone but its helpless victims. Accordingly, the inevitable outcome of this situation, as things stand, is likely to involve the victims themselves being deemed the perpetrators, and punished accordingly.

How might this be avoided? I suspect the answers may lie in *The Road to Serfdom*, Friedrich Hayek's most famous book — mistakenly remembered as an economic treatise, and often perceived as an extremist ideological tract — really a work of political philosophy directed at identifying the core nature of human freedom. In my view, among all of the dystopian expositions/narratives we have inherited, this is the one most relevant to our present situation — in the main because it penetrates beneath the ideological standpoints and rigidities to the existential level at which true human feeling might be invoked in the inter-ests of a true liberation. It may not be too late to (re)read it.

CHAPTER 36
SATANIC PLAYGROUND
06-12-2024

What if Covid was, at some level, a kind of game, that this was necessarily part of the logic of its construction and implementation, and self-evident to the leading architects and technicians?

Perhaps the strangest and, to date, most unresolved aspect of the Covid 'pandemic' was the 'dancing nurses' who suddenly erupted onto the screens of iPads and smartphones in that dark and sunny spring of 2020. We had never seen anything like it before: overworked nurses, working around the clock to 'save lives' in 'overwhelmed hospitals' suddenly dropping everything, declaring a break and throwing themselves and their scrubs into elaborate dance routines that would do justice to professional troupes — and then some. The music, video to video, only slightly varied — popular disco numbers like 'Happy' by Pharrell Williams, Lizzo's 'Good as Hell', Bruno Mar's 'If I Catch a Grenade For You', Pitbull's 'I Believe That We Will Win', and, of course, 'Jerusalema' — and each routine seemingly worked out and polished to the nth degree. Even to the practised eye — or so I'm told — it was impossible to spot a fluffed manoeuvre or a clumsy shimmy. First there was just one video, then two, then a cascade. The early ones seemed to emanate from the same place, someplace oriental, to be sure, possibly China, though it was never specified, and the backdrops were similar in the way all hospitals are similar. Later on, the video became more customised, more localised, as the dance virus made its way around the world.

It's one of the most abiding mysteries of the Time of Covid, perhaps the most perplexing, not least because even yet there is no clarity as to what exactly was, so to speak, afoot. Superficially, the story went, the videos were the nurses' contribution to public morale. Despite their overworked situation, they wanted to send out messages of hope and joy. Or so they said. But a close examination of most of the videos — aside from the most amateurish — reveals a dark centre to the dance. Many of them were produced as though parodies of the circumstances they purported to address, acting out bizarre burlesques of illness and death, flinging inflated 'patients' around on stretchers in a manner less than succouring, even — in some videos — portraying a 'pretend' 'funeral' of a Covid casualty. It was as if groups of bored children had decided to make dark games out of terrifying things. The dancing nurses signalled play but communicated pasquinade and menace, a carnivalesque attack on the consciousness of humanity. The fragmented effect was of an attempt to reassure erupting suddenly into an orgy of evil clownery. No one could say who was behind these videos, or if they were some kind of spontaneous cultural trope that spread by contagion in a world of suspended disbelief.

What rendered this phenomenon even more bizarre was that it ran almost simultaneously with an entirely different video trope, whereby lone citizen-videographers wielding smartphones would wander around the insides of deserted hospitals, searching in vain for patients, nurses or doctors. These hospitals, contrary to the 'narrative', were decidedly underwhelmed. The surface optic was of overworked nurses finding time to entertain and console the public; meanwhile, in the corridor outside, the 'citizen journalist' passed the closed door of the ward where the dance was taking place, encountering nothing but speckless floors and empty beds. The laugh was a dark one, and on us.

It is strange: even five years after these strange events, there has been no serious investigation of them, no definitive account of what was going on. The dominant 'narrative' remains as it was in the beginning: a 'deadly virus' whipped up a 'pandemic' and swept across the world, killing millions and leaving millions more with 'long Covid'. Nurses danced in the spaces between 'saving lives'. Nothing of what has surfaced by way of commentary appears to be reliable — very often, such commentaries (particularly emanating from the academic zone) are unmistakable as propaganda designed to throw the curious or furious off the scent.

Who, really, were these dancing nurses? How were all these routines put together?

In an interview with Jamie Glazov on *The Glazov Gang* in November 2024, the former feminist icon, Naomi Wolf — now an eminent investigator of governmental genocide — remarked on the across-the-board sameness of the dancing nurses videos, and spoke of them in the language of occult ritual, a thought that had occurred to many but had rarely been articulated in such precise terms.

They were not, after all, casual coffee break moments. 'Those were highly sophisticated, expensive, highly choreographed, produced theatrical productions that took rehearsal time and complicated sets and complicated drone shots,' she said. 'Anyone that knows about film knows that it took days if not weeks to produce.' An expert she had heard speak on the subject, she recalled, had suggested that many of the performances had the hallmarks of Chinese communistic dance, observing that the videos and the routines were frequently similar in choreography and production values. There was, said Wolf, 'a totalitarian vibe'. This was not, she said, 'the Western, individualist, joyous, spontaneous forms of dance we have; it's very much the *group*.' But there was something deeper, she suggested: a dark ritualistic element that seemed to jell with a more general sense of the Covid episode as a kind of predatory assault on humanity, perhaps even an exercise in black magic. 'I'm persuaded that it's a ritual, and it's emerging more and more clearly, day by day, that there's some kind of dark, primordial, negative cultic or religious behaviour going on — globally, among the elites, among the people who locked us down — that we can't understand, that we're not familiar with.

'You know, it didn't really make sense in any kind of Judeo-Christian context, or even materialist, post-Enlightenment context. And they went back to Mithraic death-and-rebirth ceremonials, which a lot of these rituals have elements of. So the more I read about the kind of magic into which [the Irish poet, W.B.] Yeats was initiated, and other elites in the West . . . if you do certain rituals as a group, you affect group consciousness, and consciousness affects history. That's what they believe. So . . . it sure looks like there are weird rituals taking place collectively all around us. Like the last Olympics [Beijing, 2022]: crazy satanic imagery, very bestial imagery, Moloch imagery, Baal imagery. You know, you have so much satanic imagery in Hollywood, in pop culture. I [once] thought people who saw that imagery were crazy fundamentalists; now I see that in fact it's right there. . . . And now most of pop culture has themes of possession, or ironic behaviour, or compulsive behaviour, or degraded behaviour, or strange kind of Illuminati symbolism.

'And, taking a look back at what the nurses' dances were: they were people who were supposed to be healing and saving life, which is a very Judeo-Christian thing to do, but it was mocking illness and mocking vulnerability and mocking our need for healing. And they were masked, which is very common in dark ritual, and they were caricaturing the distress that humanity was going through, and that is just satanic, whatever else that was [intended] for.'

Other online commentaries highlight the Pagan or occult imagery to be observed in the backgrounds or dance-moves — referencing, for example, the Hindu 'goddess of destruction', Kalika, or the Baphomet deity worshipped by the Knights Templar. Others claim that the participants were not nurses — or any kind of medical personnel — but crisis actors, and that the conformity of the videos to a singular model suggested a centralised agency and purpose.

There are more than a few academic studies on the issue to be found, but they are invariably a disappointment, missing the point by criticising such phenomena as 'inappropriate' or 'sexually suggestive' and fretting that the videos 'could damage the professional image of nurses and downplay the seriousness of the current pandemic.' Really, the impression these papers conveyed was as interventions aimed at misdirection or camouflage: *Nothing (much) to see here.*

But what if the point of these videos was to set the tone of a certain undertow of the Covid subterfuge — a tone of frivolity and light-heartedness, with the occult elements functioning as the required admission of the deeper truth of what was afoot? Perhaps there is also here an implicit but glancing owning-up that the whole thing was a hoax — a pretence rooted not so much in lies as misdirection — and that, in this sense, flippancy was self-evidently the correct inflection for the 'pandemic' without substance.

What would that hint at? That Covid was, at some level, a kind of game? That this was necessarily part of the logic of its construction and implementation? That this aspect was self-evident to the leading architects and technicians?

It had, almost from the beginning, been widely acknowledged that the Covid scam succeeded in tapping into what has long been acknowledged as the human instinct for some form of religious understanding, some sense of the before and the after, of the ultimate meaning and purpose of existence, fleshed out in ceremonies and rituals that seem to satisfy some deep craving in the human heart.

What if there is a similar instinct that craves play? The idea is that the 'play instinct' in human beings, somewhat akin to the 'religious instinct' or 'religious sense', is hardwired in, so that it is much further 'up' in the mix than, as adults considering what makes us tick, we tend to be aware of. What if — as many who have studied the subject believe — this instinct is actually core to the very formation of the human person, a fundamental element of the bedrock of our formative influences and experiences? What if, right through our lives, play functions as a sort of secret code, whereby someone can be 'hacked' without their knowing, by the simple device of tapping in instructions which somehow invoke the childhood experience of play, which of course is continued through adolescence via games and sport, and into adulthood in all kinds of ways, including humour, mischief, various recreational activities, romance, business competition, jokes, et cetera?

Children have long mimicked adult activities in play, including playing 'house', 'shop', 'hospital', even 'funerals' in which a doll is solemnly buried; and, as noted, 'funerals' featured as part of the repertoire of the Dancing Nurses during the Covid crime. In this sense, it becomes clear that play offers a way into not merely the emotional life of humans, but into the meanings that attach to what may well be the root structure of human development. Play is central to the trunk and roots of human formation and growth; adults are the branches and leaves, but they must stay connected to play in order to stay healthily alive.

The Combine, as I call it — the 'Cult', 'Cabal' or 'Predator Class' —which seeks ultimate control over humanity, likely seeks leverage over not just the formalised element of the human make-up, but also the primitive, atavistic, primordial and savage elements, all of which would be more readily accessed through the appropriation of the play instinct, which may pre-exist even the manifestation of the religious, god-seeking impulse. The latter would operate on the leaning towards ritual and solemnity, but the former would tap into the desire for spontaneity, gaiety and diversion, catching us in our most artless state of repose. What better way to assert control than to create scenarios whereby the first human experience of rules made by anyone, other than a parent, is tapped into and weaponised? What, then, if the Covid deception was consciously engineered to exploit or embezzle the most primal human impulse of all — the desire to play? What if this, rather than solely a weaponisation of fear, were part of the explanation for why humans were persuaded to behave so childishly?

It has not been widely remarked that the Covid cult, aside from its crypto-religious, tyrannical and hypnoidal layers, also has elements of play and performance. There were, for a start, those masks. There were the arcane rules which could not be fathomed, only learned by rote. There was the 'scoreboard' on the Nine O'clock News, displaying the day's (alleged) fatalities. Those who disputed the referee's decisions were as though dubbed spoil-sports, and sent for an early shower of abuse from the waiting Branch Covidian Chorus.

Is it possible to turn reality into a more or less continuous game, but without the 'players' getting to understand that this is what is happening? If so, what are the implications? Is reality fundamentally altered or simply restored to its true disposition? Is it possible to imagine a form of 'reality' in which play might become the dominant mode of human existence — in a post-work, post-earned-income world, for instance? Was this, then, some kind of pilot scheme?

With these thoughts rattling around my head, I dug out *Homo Ludens: A Study of the Play-Element in Culture*, the 1938 book about humans and play by the Dutch cultural historian Johan Huizinga. My intuition was something like this: What if, underneath all the elements that have been leveraged by the perpetrators of the Covid desecration — latent, manipulable fears; love of authority; susceptibility to propaganda; tendency towards groupthink; residues of religiosity and ritual-istic re-enactment; propensity towards hypnoidal manipulation; covert masochism; et cetera — there was something else, something even deeper, more fundamental, more primeval?

Johan Huizinga is mostly responsible for the proliferation of the word 'ludic' — describing spontaneous, undirected playfulness — in the current multidisciplinary research discourse. In his hypothesis, play is present in most areas of human activity, being the basis for law, politics, religion, commerce, war and most other human endeavours.

Huizenga sought to distil the essence of play and demonstrate its importance to the evolution of human civilisations. He emphasised that play is a creative function of man, something that, being spontaneous and voluntary, is 'done for its own sake'. The play 'instinct' wires us deep into the animal kingdom, and is perhaps the oldest detectable reflex written up by anthropologists. Play, Huizinga is careful to emphasise, is not an 'instinct', although he sometimes uses the word as a shorthand. Play, he stresses, is more serious than seriousness, and comes before everything: culture, art, civilisation — the very basis of culture.

Huizinga describes play as:

'. . . a free activity standing quite consciously outside "ordinary" life as being "not serious", but at the same time absorbing the player intensely and utterly. It is an activity connected with no material interest, and no profit can be gained by it. It proceeds within its own proper boundaries of time and space according to fixed rules and in an orderly manner. It promotes the formation of social groupings which tend to surround themselves with secrecy and to stress their difference from the common world by disguise or other means.'

Play begins with a shrinking of the world — down to the ring, the field, the table, the 'magic circle' that becomes the entire world of the game. 'For us the chief point of interest is the place where the game is played. Generally it is a simple circle, *dyutamandalam*, drawn on the ground. The circle as such, however, has a magic significance. It is drawn with great care, all sorts of precautions being taken against cheating. The players are not allowed to leave the ring until they have discharged their obligations. But, sometimes a special hall is provisionally erected for the game, and this hall is holy ground.'

It is, he insists, one of the most fundamental categories of human existence and activity.

Play is 'pointless but significant,' in Romano Guardini's words: it is not utilitarian, and yet it has purposes, many of them opaque and inscrutable. Play, according to Huizinga, belongs to 'the highest regions of the spirit.' It is then, in several senses, 'religious' and, in this and otherwise, transcendent: it aspires to the holy; it rises above 'real' life; it enables a 'forgetfulness' about real-world problems and difficulties while it is happening. Like religion, magic and the law, play has its own marked-out spaces, possibly confirming the idea of some sacred function or aspect: a 'hallowed spot'. Play and religion occupy the same quarter of the imagination.

Play is steeped in ritual, but play came first. Under various headings — performance, dress-up, 'let's pretend', it is as though it might be somehow synony-mous with the true meaning and purpose of life, for it retains the same aura of mysteriousness. 'Life must be lived as play,' said Plato, 'playing certain games, making sacrifices, singing and dancing, and then a man will be able to propitiate the gods, and defend himself against his enemies, and win in the contest.'

Huizinga concurs: 'Ritual grew up in sacred play; poetry was born in play and nourished on play; music and dancing were pure play.' From this, he concludes that 'civilization is, in its earliest phases, played. It does not *come from play*. . . . It arises in and as play, and never leaves it.'

A civilisation, he writes, cannot exist in the absence of 'a certain play-element,' for civilisation 'presupposes limitation and mastery of the self, the ability not to confuse its own tendencies with the ultimate and highest goal, but to understand that it is enclosed within certain bounds freely accepted.' Civilisa-tion is rooted in noble play and cannot afford to neglect the play-element. Once the importance of 'play-rules' is forgotten, he says, a society falls into barbarism and chaos. Indeed, the idea of 'game' may be the very essence of the concept 'society', the engine of civilisation.

And if all this is agreed, might it be possible to insinuate that play is suffi-cient in and of itself as a mechanism to make a civilisation function? Is this not the subtext of Aldous Huxley's novel of totalitarian coddling, *Brave New World*?

Huizinga goes on to describe how play 'moves and has its being' within the 'playground' marked off beforehand, either materially or conceptually, deliber-ately or at least as a matter of ready perception. Just as there is no formal differ-ence between play and ritual, he says, so the 'consecrated spot cannot be formally distinguished from the playground: The arena, the card-table, the magic circle, the temple, the stage, the screen, the tennis court, the court of justice, etc., are all in form and function play-grounds, i.e. forbidden spots, isolated, hedged round, hallowed, within which special rules obtain. All are temporary worlds within the ordinary world, dedicated to the performance of an act apart.'

Play derives from the depths of the mind. It defies the reductionism that man seeks always to impose on his own affairs, denying the wondrous nature of his situation. Its gratuitousness poses questions irreducible by logic or reason. And yet, even the most logical and reasonable humans like to play games. 'The play-mood is one of rapture and enthusiasm, and is sacred or festive in accordance with the occasion. A feeling of exaltation and tension accompanies the action.'

Play, being antecedent to everything else in civilisation, is all but synony-mous with Being. It is irrational, and yet deeply intelligent. It is superfluous and yet fulfils some deep, inscrutable need. It has no 'function' beyond itself and yet invades every dimension of human life. It is the opposite of seriousness, and yet must be taken seriously if it is to happen at all. When children play, it is always serious. But with adults, this cannot be assumed, for they find it embarrassing to be observed doing things they no longer understand or believe in, and exhibit this tendency to drive things towards a face-saving frivolity, thus achieving the opposite of the true play-spirit. But — perhaps — there may be mechanisms for dissolving such inhibitions, for returning the adult unwittingly to the fluidity of childhood?

Play, as Huizinga defines it, 'creates order'. It *is* order.

'Into an imperfect world and into the confusion of life it brings a temporary, a limited perfection. Play demands order absolute and supreme. The least deviation from it "spoils the game", robs it of its character and makes it worthless. The profound affinity between play and order is perhaps the reason why play . . . seems to lie to such a large extent in the field of aesthetics. Play has a tendency to be beautiful. It may be that this aesthetic factor is identical to the impulse to create orderly form, which animates play in all its aspects. The words we use to denote the elements of play belong, for the most part, to aesthetics, terms with which we try to describe the effects of beauty: tension, poise, balance, contrast, variation, solution, resolution, etc. Play casts a spell over us; it is "enchanting", "captivating". It is invested with the noblest qualities we are capable of seeing in things: rhythm and harmony.'

It is in this way that playing becomes 'holy'.

'The participants in the rite are convinced that the action actualizes and effects a definite beatification, brings about an order of things higher than that in which they customarily live. All the same this "actualization by representation" still retains the formal characteristics of play in every respect.'

Play is rarely purely 'fun' (a word without a direct translation to most other languages), though it provokes something akin to pleasure — perhaps satisfaction or enjoyment. Nor does play necessarily lend itself to laughter. Since much play takes the form of ritual, it is not observably light-hearted. 'Fun' is an unstable definition. A tennis player waiting for his opponent to serve does not appear to be enjoying himself. He is tense, even anxious, possibly fearful or angry or frustrated. Yet, he is engaged in something instantly identifiable as play.

'Ritual is seriousness at its highest and holiest,' writes Huizinga, and yet it is an essential part of play. The joy it confers is not necessarily raucous and giddy. It can be quiet and introverted. It can also fester and become vengeful, neurotic, even hateful. It can be the jealous stab of the inadequate, or the slow-burning anticipation of the resentful awaiting his hour in the sun of retribution. 'Frivolity and ecstasy,' writes Huizinga, 'are the twin poles between which play moves,' but ecstasy can be born of the dark as well as the light.

Similarly, 'freedom', another of the essential characteristics of play identified by Huizinga. Freedom does not necessarily mean 'freely entered into'. Play generates its own forms of freedom 'within a structure of law and form', separate from and different to those of the 'real' world. The rigidities of the magic circle and the rules create a strange, contained kind of freedom that may only be experienced and observed in its place. It cannot be captured or transplanted.

Might Covid, in some sense — and this is no frivolous question — be *a game*? Were we duped into playing it? Have we been played, literally as well as figuratively? Is it, in different senses, play or, perhaps, 'a play'? Was the world turned into something like a 'pitch', a 'court', a 'board', a 'track', a 'ring', a 'diamond', a 'magic circle'? Were we all, of most of us, unbeknownst to ourselves, recruited as 'players', and persuaded to engage in some kind of charade in which we behave in extra-ordinary ways, while believing a flimsy fiction because that fiction supplied the stuff of the game, and the 'rules' to be obeyed — arbitrariness notwithstanding — because they were the rules of the game?

Play is a quantity much closer to the surface of modern culture than many realise. From those who have not looked into it, it is a well-kept secret; for those who know, the connection between play and everyday reality is axiomatic. Unbeknownst to the crowd, play is everywhere, and by no means just for children. The gamification of the world is well advanced, without our knowing it. (Yes, there is a name for it too!: the word 'gamification' being all the rage in business-lit a few years back, elaborated by the strapline: 'technique to encourage engagement with a product or service'.)

Virtually everything can become a 'game' according to one motivational writer, Seth Godin, who in his most recent book, *This is Strategy: Make Better Plans* (October 2024), writes:

'Getting your insulin dosage right is a game. Getting the farm bill passed in Congress is a game. Finding a job is a game as well.

'You move, then the system (actually, someone in the system) makes a move in return. There's a competition-for attention, for resources, for slots — and there are outcomes.'

'A game,' writes Godin, 'has the following elements: players, rules, scarcity, choices, feedback loops, and outcomes.

'Smart people have studied games — from nuclear proliferation and public health to poker — and we can learn from them.'

The history of games in human culture goes back to the earliest civilisations, in the traces of which have been found the carvings and drawings denoting the parallelism of play. Among the riches discovered in King Tutankhamun's tomb was a wooden surface with regular divisions that appeared to be a boardgame. Long before that, games were played by animals, having a profound connection with the skills required to hunt and survive. In human society, games have long been linked to education.

Play can be a highly creative activity. In play, children create carefully imaginary situations in which they 'test out' various adult activities in ways they are not otherwise able to experience, or might not otherwise undertake without suffering adverse consequences. Freud said of play: 'Perhaps we may say that every child at play behaves like an imaginative writer, in that he creates a world of his own, or more truly, he rearranges the things of his world and orders it in a new way that pleases him better.' Freud also claimed that adults are much less likely to play in this expressly 'psychodramatic' way. Play is therefore central to development, because it creates the 'laboratory' where children refine their capacities to understand and manage reality.

Types of games include sports, board games, card games, children's games and, latterly, computer games. Games, wrote Marshall McLuhan in *Understanding Media*, are a form of popular art, offering 'to all an immediate means of participation in the full life of a society, such as no single role or job can offer to any man.'

Doll play, likewise, has been a feature of childhood since about the twenty-first century BC, taken seriously as a means of introducing girls to the concepts of motherhood, childbirth and domesticity. In 2024, we in Ireland arrived to the point of unravelling this carefully-constructed culture, contemplating the removal of the words 'mothers' and 'woman' from the Irish Constitution. Only by a miraculous awakening was this coup against nature and reality put down, and even then, its champions declared their determination to return to the battlefield and have another go. It is as though the circus of human existence is being dismantled before moving on to a new town, even as the applause of the crowd still rings in the ears of the affable acrobats now rolling up the tarpaulins and loading them into the coloured wagons.

Play is not merely hardwired into humans but into multiple species of the animal kingdom. Until recently, 'true' play was considered a trait only found in mammals and some birds, with controversial examples in other vertebrates and invertebrates dismissed as anecdotal, anthropomorphic conceits, misinterpreted functional 'instincts', or accidental immature behaviour.

Gordon M. Burghardt writing in 2005, declared: 'We now know that behavior fitting the play criteria . . . can be found in several species of reptiles. For example Nile softshell turtles knock around basketballs and manipulate hoops, and juvenile red-bellied cooters engage in precocial courtship interactions reminiscent of play fighting in rodents. Monitor lizards grab and push around all kinds of objects, shaking shoes and retrieving soda cans like dogs. A salt water crocodile plays with a tethered ball. Dart poison frogs engage in social rough and tumble play. Mormyrid fish push around and manipulate balls and the more social freshwater stingrays play keep-a-way with them. Octopuses manipulate Legos and play catch with balls using their jets.'

Play, Burghardt stipulates, reveals itself more clearly in a bottom-up, rather than top-down viewfinder — an interesting observation in the context of Covid 'play', as the schemers were clearly keen, where possible, to pass agency and responsibility on to the people rather than using direct coercion — the better to make tyranny seem like a voluntary exercise.

A game is a closed system, a safe space in which the player is able to enter into various forms of conflict without risking loss of comfort, warmth, security, gratification or personal safety. All games have common features, above all the 'magic circle' which defines the space and logic of the game and makes of it a closed world, to which entry is voluntary but subject to certain conditions. In the 17th century, following the 'invention' of leisure time as a result of the Industrial Revolution's having drawn a line between work and social time, games acquired a new significance and popularity, drawing on adult reality for material to feed childhood dreams and fantasies. Dollhouses became a major leisure fashion in Europe, and not only for children: Grown women, especially those about to be married, offered a hugely lucrative market for such toys. In the Victorian era, paper dolls and scrapbook houses provided outlets for childish fantasies about adulthood, and these have been noted as extraordinarily faithful to the actual lives of the children who played with them. Gradually, in different parts of the civilised world, homemade dollhouses began to take on the role of reflecting the changing mores and patterns of domestic life, becoming symbols of middle-class aspiration, helping subtly to drive forward the engines of American and European consumerism by getting to their targets' hearts in the fastest way known and at the earliest possible moment. In this way an ideal was created in the 'real' world for domestic and familial bliss, facilitating fantasies about shopping, tea parties, bathing and dressing-up, upstairs-downstairs relationships, and so forth.

Play of this kind acted to reinforce rituals, traditions and belief systems, as well as preparing young girls — and boys — for the lives that lay ahead of them. Sometimes girls would baulk at the encoded 'feminisation' contained in these forms of play, leading to a trend towards subversive innovations such as family strife, divorce and death being introduced to the doll's house.

All of us have memories of play, some of playing pretty straightforward games like hopscotch and tag, others of more elaborate, even dangerous play. When I was a child, our street life was dominated by two families of older boys who jointly ran an operation they called 'the Hollow Gang', comprising several dozen boys of various ages, who engaged daily in sundry routine activities of a time-killing, disruptive or nuisance-oriented kind. These might include something as anodyne as organising football matches in the Fair Green, or, more often, actual devilment like planning a raid on Foley Bennett's orchard, or a 'battle' with the boys from Knockroe or Arm, or conducting a scoping operation on the local garages with a view to purloining tyres for the St John's Eve bonfire. One of their favourite activities was 'kidnapping' members of rival gangs, and 'sentencing' them to terms of imprisonment in a rather well-adapted loft in one of the outhouses behind our house. For several years, my father was the unwitting owner of this 'jail' in which the unlucky rival gang member would be incarcerated for a number of hours, even a whole day, perhaps as a reprisal for an attack on a member of the Hollow Gang, or some other infringement of intertribal warfare protocols. The jail was also used to discipline members of the Hollow Gang itself, who had broken the rules or who were suspected of treasonous behaviour in their dealings with members of other gangs. I became aware of this penitentiary in early childhood, hearing rumours of the goings-on that occurred there, only later learning that it was located in the garden of the house that my father was in the throes of renovating, with a view to our moving there. The 'prison' was located in the upstairs of a converted two-storey shed at the end of a line of outhouses, its tiny upstairs window looking on to the 'backroad' (one word) which ran parallel to Main Street. The 'prisoner' would be 'arrested', usually on a Saturday or during school holidays, and taken to the prison, from which the stairs had long since been removed, and there would be escorted to the upper storey via a ladder which would then be withdrawn, leaving him there at the pleasure of the Hollow Gang's leadership acting in the manner of a Supreme Court. In this way, 'child's play' can become an engagement with adult reality in the form of tribute-by-imitation, a kind of unconscious rehearsal for civic participation later on. Games, play, are about real things. Even reckless or madcap forms of play can incorporate elements of social participation and compliance. It is through play that children learn about rules, laws, negotiation, narrative, records, creativity, motivation, theatre, teamwork, goals, solidarity, community, ritual, and more abstract concepts like emotion-regulation, duty, logic, competition, symbolism, moral reasoning, fairness and justice. When people play, they transform not only their surrounding environments but also themselves.

And what if these — nowadays, eccentric or dismissed — ideas of the hidden structure of culture, were somehow to come to renewed official — or would-be authoritarian — notice? What if this most fundamental impulse or response were to be identified, latent and somewhat derelict, as betraying under-utilised promise and potential?

Some researchers have suggested that, in play, we engage multiple levels of self, whereby more deeply-seated levels of consciousness challenge, confuse, and sometimes overwhelm the cognitive faculties with their demands. In one study, rats whose cortexes had been removed were still able to continue playing by relying on deeper-brain processes, though they lacked the qualities of social reciprocity present in unimpaired rats. These experiments are taken as indicating that some play behaviours rely on the most ancient brain regions, a factor that would be useful to schemers seeking to cut human beings off from the influences of their hippocampi.

Chris Crawford, in *The Art of Computer Game Design* (1982), writes that a game is 'a closed format that subjectively represents a subset of reality.' By 'closed', he means that the game on its own is 'complete and self-sufficient as a structure'. As with a novel, no reference need be made to elements outside the game.

He expands: 'A game creates a subjective and deliberately simplified representation of emotional reality. A game is not an objectively accurate representation of reality; objective accuracy is only necessary to the extent required to support the player's fantasy.'

A game, then, is 'an artifice for providing the psychological experiences of conflict and danger while excluding their physical realizations.'

'In short, a game is a safe way to experience reality. More accurately, the results of a game are always less harsh than the situations the game models. A player can blast the monsters all day long and risk only her quarter. She can amass huge financial empires and lose them in an hour without risking her piggy bank. She can lead great armies into desperate battles on which hang the fate of nations, all without shedding a drop of blood. In a world of relentless cause and effect, of tragic linkages and inevitable consequences, the disassociation of actions from consequences is a compelling feature of games.'

Play, then, is an astonishingly broad canvas, embracing just about every human activity and emotion there is, as well as a bewildering variety of objects and settings. To the Man from Mars, it might seem an enigmatic behaviour, defying definition and yet appearing to have detectable patterns and the strong implication of meaning in virtually every move. In this sense, it becomes clear that play offers a way into not merely the emotional life of humans, but into the meanings that attach themselves thereto.

Studying how video game communities form and discuss issues can offer unexpected insight into how network audiences are built and come to share common beliefs, including 'malignant' ones. Video games are by no means neutral, non-partisan spaces in which apolitical people engage in neutral mutual play. They are growing, increasingly vibrant, contested, lucrative, politicised spaces, where hidden actors of all shapes and ideologies compete to influence the minds of an audience already regarded as captive. Today, the global video game industry is one of the world's largest culture industries. According to market research firm IDC, the global video game market topped $179 billion in revenue in 2020, making it larger than the global film industry ($100 billion) and North American professional sports (around $75 billion) combined. The growth of online streaming has further expanded the audience for video games and has had a powerful effect on culture. According to the Entertainment Software Association, 70 per cent of people under the age of eighteen play video games regularly. According to a Pew survey, almost twice as many young men regularly play games as young women, but this is changing fast. And players are by no means all young: two-thirds are between eighteen and fifty-four years old, the demographic most likely to vote.

A strange factor, drawn attention to by the games philosopher, Jesper Juul, in his 2003 book *A Casual Revolution*, is that games played and developed over thousands of years have turned out to fit the modern digital computer exceedingly well.

I am not sure that, in 2003, Juul understood the full implications of what he was saying (perhaps he does now?). Like all computer geeks, or geeks of any kind, he perceived his own obsession only in its particularities in respect of the primary nature of his interest, i.e. playing. He betrays this in his concluding sentences — first, *'The revolution in games that computers have provided is one of their strongest contributions to human culture'*; then, *'We like to play games, so now we play computer games.'*

But what if the ultimate effect of the computer, on both games and reality, will be to dissolve the boundary that exists, not merely between adulthood and childhood, but between the real and unreal, the fact and the fictional, the truth and the untruth, the game and the real? Perhaps gamesters should be more concerned about their hobbies bleeding out into the world? Already, as he notes in a footnote, games have 'fuzzy borders'. But what if the obsession with a borderless world were to culminate in the destruction of the borders that we barely notice in playing because our mechanisms of comprehending meanings are capable of slipping in and out of 'reality' as though by the functioning of automatic gears?

We have spoken a great deal in these pages in respect of the context of what has happened to the world since 2020 about 'software', invariably seeing this in terms of ideological modes or categories: communism, socialism, fascism, *et cetera*. But what if the true, most fundamental and malleable mode of software is simply *play*? Wouldn't that make a lot more sense — that super-wealthy power-hungry robber barons might wish to distract the world in the direction of harmless diversion rather than permit them to fill their heads with potentially dangerous notions of revolution or utopia?

The motherWEFfers' philosopher-in-chief, Yuval Noah Harari — in between describing humans as 'hackable animals' and airily musing to no one in particular: *'What do we need humans for?'* — has proposed his best solution to future uselessness and idleness: 'The problem,' he claims, 'is largely about boredom, and what to do with them and how they will find some sense of meaning in life when they are basically meaningless, worthless. My best guess at present is a combination of drugs and computer games.'

What better way than to turn the world into a chequerboard, governed by complex but immutable rules, with movable pieces divided into black and white?

What if the whole world might be turned into a game? What if the aim of the

game were to be defined as 'saving lives', but the purpose was somewhat different? What if the future were to comprise a constant 'game' in which each citizen
battles every other citizen for scarce portions of freedom?

Perhaps this hypothesis explains the otherwise inexplicable and illogical, filigreed, arcane rules of the Covid period: the two-metre rule of 'social distancing',
the nine euro meal, the labyrinthine regulations about wearing masks in restaurants and bars, which had no reasonable meaning in the real world, but in the
world of the rules had immense meaning, for they set limits on what was
permitted and consequences for failure to comply.

Video games, by virtue of their ubiquity and attractiveness to those
concerned with the future operation of power structures, have supplied the
main frontier of contact between politics and play, the locus where the concept
of play becomes more akin to its sociology than its ostensible appearance of
frivolity and idleness. In recent decades, there has been massive, if largely unnoticed, connectivity and interaction between politics and the video games sector.
Though ostensibly concerned with 'democratic' engagement, participation and
education, the chief purpose appears to be pursuing voter loyalty, promoting
policies and disseminating propaganda.

For most of those political actors, ideologues and would-be demagogues
who venture into the area, gamification is a way to reach out to the new generations who are alienated from politics, capturing the hearts and minds of young
people who may be sceptical or hostile towards institutions and disapproving of
the communications style of political parties. Military organisations have
increasingly been using this novel medium as a tool of recruitment and information gathering. The interactive nature of video games makes them an inherently
persuasive medium — a system of 'procedural rhetoric' that encourages players
to create abstract mental models for how systems work, and to form judgments
about those systems through the act of playing. One video game designer called
this effort to induce a certain type of player-reaction 'emotion engineering' in
the design process. This has caused a raising of eyebrows among game
commentators, who fear that military consultation in the design of such games
raises uncomfortable questions concerning why certain choices are made. For
example, one particular game, Full Spectrum Warrior, produced by a company
with the interesting name of Pandemic, began life in 2004 as a training simulator
for US Army soldiers. The game was later subjected to a commercial release
which allowed soldiers to use it recreationally while deployed. One critic
observed that, despite its marketing as 'realistic' and messaging that it was
developed with input from the Pentagon, the game-world it creates removes the
complexity of urban insurgency and substitutes simplified moral dilemmas that
portray the military in unambiguously good terms — an enjoyable setting for a
game, but hardly reflective of reality.

The Pentagon certainly views games and gamers as a high-value mode of influencing and has spent more than two decades using video games for recruitment. The most famous game to emerge from these endeavours, America's Army, was a free-to-play military FPS (First-Person Shooter) game launched in 2002 to persuade young players to enlist in the US Army. Its portrayal of army service was neutral, avoiding the grind or gory details of active service, focussing instead on details like uniforms and weapons. The game failed to provoke a recruitment boom, however, so a decade later the Pentagon returned to the drawing board, building its own team of professional video gamers, to compete in e-sports competitions in order to reach younger gamers from adolescence on.

Since early in the twentieth century, the Pentagon has been involved with Hollywood through its Entertainment Office — also known as the 'military-entertainment complex' — to create sympathetic portrayals of military and other state operations and operatives. This entity vets scripts to ensure positive portrayals of military operations and is known to turn down 95 per cent of the scripts and storylines it considers. It has long been established that certain media, such as realistic films, have produced changes in the emotional responses of the public to real-life events depicted.

Video games are where politics happens, says games researcher and commentator, Joshua Foust, in a 2021 paper, *Video games are the new contested space for public policy.* 'Video games,' he elaborates, 'began as a new way to play with computers but have evolved into rich texts filled with politics and arguments for how the world should work.' Foust argues that 'all video games do present a worldview to the player, whether it is explicit or not, and understanding that world view can help us understand what the players themselves believe.' As an inescapable part of public discourse and an enormous media market, we ignore these developments at our peril, he warns. Video games are not just video games: They are the site of political contention, of negotiation over social boundaries, and of free speech itself.

The key to understanding this bridging function of video games between the real and virtual worlds relates to their capacity to create artificial landscapes in which scenarios may be tested and observed for their effects on human actors. Take Harmony Square, a video game that supposedly operates to combat political 'misinformation'. The goal of the game is to reveal the manipulative tactics and techniques used by 'fake news producers' to mislead their audience. The game's setting is Harmony Square, a peaceful cul de sac where residents have a healthy obsession with democracy. At the start of the game, a player is hired as Chief Disinformation Officer, with the task of destroying the tranquillity of the square and exploiting the consequent societal tensions to achieve a political goal, pitting its residents against each other, all while gathering as many 'likes' as possible. Harmony Square was produced in collaboration with the US Department of Homeland Security and based on its Cybersecurity and

Infrastructure Agency's (CISA) approach to investigating foreign interference in elections and how this might be used to foment political polarisation. The object of the game is to ramp up emotions in the context of a totally benign issue, such as whether pineapple should be a pizza topping, which was the topic of one of CISA's actual campaigns. The real-life benefit is that the game helps to build cognitive resistance against forms of manipulation that people may encounter online, in something like a process of inoculation: exposing people to weakened doses of these techniques in a controlled environment. The idea of such psychological 'vaccines' was coined in the 1960s by the psychologist William McGuire and is actually called 'inoculation theory', following the medical analogy of vaccines, which involve administering weakened versions of a particular pathogen which, after being introduced to the body, induces the production of antibodies, preventing an individual from becoming sick when exposed to the real virus. Here, the purpose of the game is to create 'mental antibodies' which help build resistance to the phenomenon of misinformation when encountered later. This is achieved by exposing players to controlled doses of 'viruses' like trolling, hyperbolic or emotive language, polarisation, bots, and 'conspiracy theories' about 'a small group of people exercising control over the world'. Research into the playing of the game demonstrated that players were indeed 'inoculated' against such 'viruses', albeit in the short term only — being better able for a week or so afterwards to spot such content, though somewhat longer if players were given short reminders or 'booster shots'. The 'treatment' was equally effective for liberals and conservatives.

In an eBook, *Gamocracy: Political Communication in the Age of Play*, Alex Gekker explores the increasing role that modern game culture plays in shaping political communication and 'the ludification of culture' in the remaking of politics. He focuses on Western liberal democracies, where video games are on the increase and politics is more and more regarded with suspicion. He argues that 'the increasing convergence of traditional media with new media, together with global loss of political legitimacy, has led to media space becoming the social space where power is decided, with this space being increasingly playful.' By acknowledging that digital video games are becoming the most widespread play medium, he makes the claim that 'we must look for insights from play and game studies for reshaping our paradigms of what is the meaning of being political. This may already be implicit in the very nature of the experimentation being conducted, which increasingly acquires a symbiotic character, with politics using games as zones of virtual experiment, and weaponising the methodologies being refined in those zones to intervene in the real world.'

By way of examples, Gekker explores the activities of the online guerrilla phenomenon Anonymous and the use of new media in the presidential campaigns of Barack Obama in 2008 and 2012. In these and other contexts, he observes, mobile devices have been playing an increasing role. He also argues that 'we are moving towards a state of gamocracy,' i.e. a manner of political engagement characterised by ludic modes of action via interfaces that resemble modern age games, and incorporate gameful elements — leader boards, points, cooperative problem solving, *et cetera*. 'I speak not only of gamification of politics,' he declares, 'but also on the politics of gamification — the underlying processes of the ludification of culture that bring about gameful elements into more and more non-games environments.'

He cites prominent game developer and theoretician, Eric Zimmerman, from *A Casual Revolution*, Jesper Juul's book on the explosion of casual games that occurred in the Noughties, when, with the advent of the 'casual game' (a video game targeted at a mass market audience, as opposed to a hardcore game targeted at hobbyist gamers) 'gaming' ceased to be the preserve of young males and spread in all human directions, to men and women equally, old as well as young.

Juul himself, speaking of his motivation to write the book, had observed: 'Spending the winter of 2006-07 in New York City, I was beginning to lose count of the times I had heard the same story: somebody had taken the new Nintendo Wii video game system home to parents, grandparents, partner, none of whom had ever expressed any interest whatsoever in video games, and these non-players of video games had been enthralled by the physical activity of the simple sports games, had enjoyed themselves, and had even asked that the video game be brought along for the next gathering. What was going on?'

Juul quotes Zimmerman:

'As digital technologies and networks of information, the Internet, computers, mobile technologies, more and more pervade our lives, [and] the ways in which we socialize and flirt and communicate and work and do our taxes and engage with our government and manage our finances, and many, many other important aspects of our lives, the more I think our culture becomes primed for play and, particularly, games as the dominant form of leisure. Because games are the form of culture that is most intrinsically related to those things, to systems, technology, information, and mediated communication. It wouldn't surprise me [if] just like society in the twentieth century gave rise to cinema . . . and television, in this newer century where information technology is now being supplanted by ludic technology, . . . play becomes a more dominant paradigm for culture rather than the moving image.'

We can observe the potential of these ideas about games by considering Jesper Juul's definition:

'A game is a rule-based formal system with a variable and quantifiable outcome, where different outcomes are assigned different values, the player exerts effort in order to influence the outcome, the player feels attached to the outcome, and the consequences of the activity are optional and negotiable.' Obviously, these terminologies and definitions could quite readily be transposed to politics as it exists in a media-dominated arena. Elections, for example, involve contestants and an ultimate scoreboard, being congenitally characterised as 'battles' or 'races'. Referendums are even more precisely comparable to games, as they pit two 'teams' against one another in 'combat' on a specific political issue of contention.

My objective is different, if not utterly opposite, to that propounded by Jesper Juul. I want to show that it may be possible to break down the game-reality barrier so that humans, from their situations in 'reality', can be moved into an unannounced 'game' in which they can at once be entertained and controlled. In a certain sense, he intimates, all games are coercive. Rules are what give a game meaning. Discussing the rules of games, we may have a nagging feeling that games contain a built-in contradiction: Since we would normally assume play to be a free-form activity devoid of constraints, it appears illogical that we would choose to limit our options by playing games with fixed rules. Why be limited when we can be free? The answer to this is basically that games provide context for actions: Moving an avatar is much more meaningful in a game environment than in an empty space; throwing a ball has more interesting implications on the playing field than in an open space without markings; a Demolition of Pawns attack is only possible if there are rules specifying how attacks work; without rules in chess, there are no Sicilian Defenses, checkmates or endgames; winning the game requires that the winning conditions have been specified and met. The rules of a game add meaning and suggest actions by setting up differences between potential moves and eventualities. This creates a different kind of freedom — neither anarchic nor chaotic, but the freedom to follow a clear path with constant options and choices.

What does this signify? That, in a game, control becomes acceptable, even essential? That, in a world governed by the logic of gaming, the meanings hitherto attributed to life might well be supplanted with meanings created by turning all life into a game, thus radically redefining the meaning of freedom?

Miguel Sicart is a play philosopher and game designer, who has written a fascinating book which breaks the noise barrier between the worlds of gravity and play. It's called *Play Matters*, and was published in 2014.

It is important to stress that the analysis that follows in no way implicates Miguel Sicart in respect of either his writing of the book, or the application of its content by others to real-world circumstances, if that is what happened (which I believe it is). My suspicion is that, over the five years or so following its publication, *Play Matters* came to the attention of some dark forces which gleaned from it a method for tapping into the play instinct in humans, in order to steal their freedoms and incarcerate them under cover of a virus that nobody has yet been able to isolate.

Although *Play Matters* mostly reads as the antidote to and the antithesis of all that, it is not hard to understand why it may have attracted the attention of actors seeking ways to tap into the power of play in order to gain the confidence of humanity for the purposes of harnessing and controlling the hearts and minds of the species.

The book is actually a rather beautiful encapsulation of the potential of play to invade the world by increasing the quality of playfulness in everyday reality. Sicart focuses on computer play, which he says he believes is capable of altering human reality — though *in a good way*. The capacity of computers for processing data, he writes, has spawned a new era of 'human be-ing' in the world. Computers, he writes, without detectable irony, 'can help play take over the world.'

Sicart insists that play is a deeply serious activity, rooted in reality. For him, play can be invited into any or all of our everyday activities. 'To play is to be in the world,' he writes. 'Playing is a form of understanding what surrounds us and who we are, and a way of engaging with others. . . . It is a way of being in the world, like languages, thought, faith, reason and myth.'

Play enables us to both laugh at, and make sense of, the world: 'We play not to entertain ourselves or to learn or to be alienated: we play to *be*, and play gives us, through its characteristics, the possibility of being.'

He argues that play is not something confined to childhood, but forms and informs the entire existence of a human being and the evolution of a personality in the world. We can play even while working. Play is the appropriation of context for the player's own playful purpose. Play, in his vision of it, is a shield against some of the nasty things we have been exploring in this book: technocracy and the technical society, for example, not to mention some other words starting with 't'.

Play is capable of converting activities usually geared in one direction into unrelated pursuits and engagements. It need not always be 'fun'. 'Playfulness', however, exhibits discrete characteristics, being an attitude, a mindset projected on to events or circumstances. 'An activity,' he differentiates, 'is a coherent and finite set of actions performed for certain purposes, while an attitude is a stance toward an activity — a psychological, physical, and emotional perspective we take on.' By instilling playfulness in an otherwise routine activity, we render it more enjoyable. 'Play appropriates events, structures and institutions to mock them and trivialize them, or make them deadly serious. The carnival of the Middle Ages, with its capacity to subvert conventions and institutions in a suspension of time and power, was a symptom of freedom.'

Above all, he says, play is 'carnivalesque', by which he means that it can facilitate a kind of raid upon the normal and regimented, creating an inversion of the everyday and thus effecting a form of subversion. Play is disruptive of what are deemed decorum and order.

Playfulness is not itself an activity, and therefore is open to being mobilised in different situations, some of which may be far from the concept of play as conventionally understood. Playfulness can be managed to respect the dynamics of whatever activity it is applied to, avoiding any logistical or operational contradiction. Playfulness may, by projecting a different attitude, appropriating a context not intended for play, 'taking over a situation to perceive it differently,' letting play be the interpretative power in that context. Appropriation implies a shift in the way a particular technology or situation is interpreted. The most usual transformation is from function- or goal-oriented to pleasurable or emotionally engaging.

'Playfulness reambiguates the world,' Sicart writes. 'Through the characteristics of play, it makes it less formalized, less explained, open to interpretation and wonder and manipulation. To be playful is to add ambiguity to the world and play with that ambiguity.'

'In fact,' he writes, 'play is a fundamental part of our moral well-being, of the healthy and mature and complete human life. Through play we experience the world, we construct it and we destroy it, and we explore who we are and what we can say. Play frees us from moral conventions but makes them still present, so we are aware of their weight, presence, and importance. We need play precisely because we need occasional freedom and distance from our conventional understanding of the moral fabric of society. Play is important because we need to see values and practice them and challenge them so they become more than mindless habits.' Here, too, we pick up hints of an ominous shadow-hypothesis: that play might one day, in some way, serve to disintegrate moral and social understandings, perhaps enabling them to be "played with".'

He describes his definition of play as 'romantic theory (or rhetoric),' based on 'an idea of creativity and expression that has been developed in the highly postromantic cultural environment of the twenty-first century.' He developed his theory, he says, as a reaction to the 'instrumentalist mechanistic thinking on play championed by postmodern culture industries.' His is a theory 'that acts as a call to playful arms, an invocation of play as a struggle against efficiency, seriousness and technical determinism.' He claims that the kind of play he advocates is 'artistic' in that it has provided the creative stimulus for many works of art. He is not interested in 'the arts', however, but in 'the beauty of play'.

Play and systems he characterises as quasi-opposites: play, he claims, is autotelic — an activity with a specific intent and purpose — but also expansively appropriative, i.e. it can extend into the world, incorporating 'real' things and situations. Systems, however, are reductive. Games, he says, 'don't matter that much. Like in the old fable, we are the fools looking at the finger when someone points at the moon. Games are the finger; play is the moon.'

There may be contexts and modes in which Miguel Sicart fails to see things through to the end: that, for example, it may be possible for the play instinct to be usurped and weaponised as an instrument of harnessing and control, a darker side to his hypothesis.

Play, he acknowledges, can be dangerous, leading to lost friendships, injuries, breakdowns. Play, he claims, occurs as a tension between the Apollonian and Dionysiac instincts — the desire to create and the desire to destroy. A child builds his bricks up into a 'skyscraper' and then topples his tower while laughing maniacally.

It can also be addictive. 'Play is a dance between creation and destruction, between creativity and nihilism. Playing is a fragile, intense activity, prone to breakdowns. Individual play is a challenge to oneself, to keep on playing. Collective play is a balancing act of egos and interests, of purposes and intentions. Play is always on the verge of destruction, of itself and of its players, and that is precisely why it matters. Play is a movement between order and chaos. Like tragedy, it fulfils its purpose when it manages a fragile, oscillating balance between both.'

'Play as an affirmation of humanity occurs because we have to strive to balance it — to tie our demons and make them coexist with our passion for order without falling into the mindless focus that lures us towards structured play. We play by taking only moderately seriously the Apollonian structures of the game and not letting the intoxicating destruction deprive us of the virtues of submitting to order.'

Playfulness and laughter go together. Laughter is where the equilibrium between order and chaos, creation and destruction, is made.

If play is appropriative, might play itself be open to appropriation? It would be strange indeed if such a beautiful theory proved capable of being weaponised in support of precisely the quantities most anathematised by their creator-author. Yet, this is a possibility he is conscious of, for he also says:

'And play is not just the ludic, harmless, encapsulated and positive activity that philosophers have described. Like any other form of being, play can be dangerous; it can be hurting, damaging, antisocial, corrupting.'

In the Covid 'playground' there was neither laughter nor fun nor freedom. Could it therefore be deemed a playground? Surely not without stretching words beyond reason or gravity. How, then, could this logic be applied?

Perhaps we should remember Mel Brooks's line: 'Tragedy is when I cut my finger. Comedy is when you fall down an open sewer and die.' In a sense, you might call what occurred in the Time of Covid 'anti-play', but it may well, nonetheless, have been a construct based in part on the principles and meanings of play, seeking to tap into the buried instinct in each person for the activity or action that speaks of the child within, longing to be free as one of a team, to enter contest with opponents who become 'enemies' for as long as the 'game' lasts.

Such was the extent to which the Covid crime took on the characteristics of a game — albeit a dark and toxic one — that it is not possible to imagine it an accident. Just as in a video game, it had access to the capacities of technological connectivity, systems, rules, contestation (even enmity), the negotiation of social boundaries, narrative, non-functional activities, theatre, data. In this 'game' the logics came to be distributed on both a bottom-up and top-down basis, though the former is largely illusory, since data and surveillance tilt the balance overwhelmingly towards the controllers.

Covid was not work, but in many respects the antithesis of work. Many people were mandatorily obliged to stop working, to stay home, to accept payment for doing nothing, to 'cocoon', as though this word had always existed in this context and as though no one found it in the least strange or funny to hear themselves using it like this. If an order had been issued to the whole world to stop what it was doing and participate in a game, the instructions for which would be transmitted by TV and social media, the results would not have been significantly distinguishable. Within the 'fiction' of the 'game', the 'virus' was the initial 'opponent', but if you were to remove or stop believing in this notional 'dread', the 'game' turned instantly benign, a pretence, a charade, a harmless pastime. But the 'rules' ensured that the 'players' maintained belief in the given 'logic' of the game, so that questioning them became an irrelevancy — no more reasonable than a footballer stopping in the middle of a match to argue with the referee about the philosophy of the offside rule. 'Emotion engineering' became rife, discreetly, surreptitiously orchestrated to a centralised plan.

The unasked implicit question is: if the world were increasingly amenable to the logic of gaming, might it be possible to turn the whole world, or at least the parts deemed necessary by the orchestrators, into a board upon which the players could be compelled, or persuaded, to play parts that, though appearing naturalistic and spontaneous, were scripted well in advance of the initiation of the game? What if the purpose was to create two 'sides', one overwhelmingly more numerous than the other, but with the other being essential to the galvanisation of the will of the majority group, which was required to see the minor element as representing a mortal enemy, the marginalisation or vanquishing of which was the implied putative object of the 'game'.

Let us refresh for ourselves the definition of Jesper Juul: 'A game is a rule-based formal system with a variable and quantifiable outcome, where different outcomes are assigned different values, the player exerts effort in order to influence the outcome, the player feels attached to the outcome, and the consequences of the activity are optional and negotiable.' Every night on TV, the orchestrating officials revealed the day's 'scores', and the players watched in interest and expectation. The 'out-group' was as vital to the game as the in-group, and equally subject to the rules, except that here the 'rules' prompted some of the players to break them so as to provide matter for the enmity of the 'in-group'.

It was only a matter of time before the idea struck that, if you could replicate the real world in a video game, you might just as readily impose a game on the real world and acquire not merely a similar suspension of belief, but a willing-ness to enter into the spirit of the 'game' almost to whatever extent was demanded under certain circumstances of induced fear, persuasion, subtle coer-cion and control. Through leveraging various technologies to achieve connectiv-ity, it would become possible to achieve certain levels of mass entrancement, obedience and even recruitment to the 'cause' as dictated through the channels governed by the 'regs', and organised so as to summon as many 'players' as possible to the locus of the game at particular moments in the day. The 'console' of the game was the TV set in the corner, but the game was played out in the entire world — or at least those parts of it deemed meaningful by the commis-sioners of the game.

To be clear, Miguel Sicart is not making this case. *I am the one making it.* That his ideas were usurped for the purpose of the Covid scam, I am satisfied of, on the balance of probabilities. It is written all over his book, even though this book is 'innocent' of as much as an intonation of such wickedness. I developed this notion first of all based on intuition and suspicion, and then on reading up on a subject I had not previously had much interest in. Let me put it like this: if I had been one of the people designing a fake pandemic, I would have found unimag-ined riches in Sicart's writing, albeit turned inside out.

Sicart had asserted his belief that play drives the creation of new cultural, social, and political forms, especially in the digital and cybernautic spheres, and that this might have serious negative implications. He specifically objected to the instrumentalisation of play as a tool wielded by platform capitalism, which may be exactly what has occurred with *Play Matters.* This is utterly contrary to his personal mission, which maintains the perspective that what we need as human beings is the 'attitude' of play — 'playfulness without play'. What he does not seem to consider is that the dark aspect of play might well dominate any particular instance of play, all depending on the motivation behind its cura-tion. Sicart is a natural refusenik who sees play as a form of rebellion. And yet his ideas cast shadows of the opposite values, which might easily be weaponised to an entirely contrary purpose.

'We need to take the same stance towards things, the world and others that we take during play,' he writes. Really, I believe his core point concerns the possibility of adults adopting a childlike demeanour in the world, which can be innocent but also naïve. Playfulness is a way of engaging with particular contexts and objects that are evocative of play, while simultaneously respecting the purposes and goals of the instant context or object. That we can be playful in flirting, seduction and other sexual contexts, while still taking these things seriously; or playful in the workplace while still working; or playful with language by making puns and jokes and yet communicating; or engaging playfully with something (a 'deadly pandemic', for instance) — does not turn these activities into play. Playfulness, he insists, is 'a physical, psychological and emotional attitude to things, people and situations.' It is, one might say, an attitude separated from the actions being performed. In the Covid episode, you might specify that, in many instances, it amounted to an entering-into the fictions without actually believing them, but accompanied by a willingness to become an active player in the game being insinuated, and clinging to this as though to an absolute reality.

Is it possible that many people who engaged, on what appeared to be positive terms, with the scam of Covid were doing so not out of conviction concerning its veracity and gravity, but because their play instinct had been awoken and put in gear? The mixed signals, the censored landscape, the good weather, the paid time off work, the sense of community, the creation of a kind of schooldays sensibility, whereby people were allowed out for 'breaks', the sense of absurdity created by the dancing nurses and other factors, all these seem calculated to tap into the spirit of playfulness and to mobilise populations in particular, reasonably predictable ways. Thus, the populations of whole countries entered, in Sicart's model of human reality, 'the mode of being of play but not playing'. The availability of social media, for example, enabled individuals to become proponents and, in effect, participants in the coup by going online and adding their voices to the clamour for compliance, urging their 'co-players' not to kill their grannies. Customised masks were another example of 'playfulness', with some players exhibiting bespoke colours or slogans, turning the pandemic into a kind of personalised parade. 'Masks and disguises, merry-go-rounds and computer controllers all point to the idea that play is possible in that context,' writes Miguel Sicart. And artificially created objects or situations are a clue that play may be afoot. Like 'social distancing'? Like elbow-bumping?

We may here, too, have encountered a version of what Sicart calls 'dark play' — not exactly what it sounds like — of which he provides an example:

'Dark play is used as a playful approach to play situations, in which the disruptive nature of play can be used to break the conventions of gentrified play contexts. An interesting example of this understanding of play comes from the story of a group of friends who have played tag for twenty-three years. For a month every year, a group of old friends play a game of tag that involves, without making them players, their families, friends, and coworkers. And not only are there players who are not playing (such as wives who act as spies but cannot be It), but also players who don't know they are playing. The employers of these men did not necessarily know about the game being played and involuntarily become pawns in the game. Imagine if the people around you were in fact playing a game you were not aware of. Imagine those multiple worlds being experienced at the same time.'

Imagine!

Perhaps we have already lived in such a 'game' for months or years. Perhaps Covid was a top-down appropriation of the total reality context in which people were suddenly required to live for an extended period — in many instances two whole years, but which also weaponised multiple 'bottom-up' energies which made of the 'pandemic' an undiagnosed 'game'. At the height of said 'pandemic' there was an 'emergency' in which people were put in fear for their lives, but there was also a 'game', in which people 'volunteered' to be the eyes and ears of establishments, regimenting and intimidating their neighbours and imposing judgements and potential punishments upon them, reporting breaches of the 'rules' via snitch-lines in a manner that would instantly have seemed an unthinkable obscenity had an implicit designation of 'play' not been in train.

Play and gaming seem, as though by their nature, to encourage conflict, even rageful conflict, between players, and not just in the stereotypical context of violence-ridden video games, an area showing mixed results. Several surveys have found that more competitive games produced greater levels of aggressive behaviour, irrespective of the amount of violence in the games. Frustration and anger, even physical aggression, can be sparked by things going badly, own in-game failure, elimination, cheating, disruptive play by an opponent, incompetence of a teammate, technical problems, trash-talk, humiliation by another player, out-of-game interruptions, or even plain 'having a bad day'. The 'climate' of the game seems to create the conditions whereby 'gamer rage' — i.e. responses that might otherwise be unthinkable — seems to occur as though routinely and spontaneously. This very description evokes memories of a phenomenon we were witnessing, perhaps without any clear realisation of its nature, in 2020 and 2021, with minor breaches of Covid rules or etiquette provoking outbursts of often extreme anger from bystanders who might never respond in that way in other situations.

In the Covid 'playground', the 'players' moved in mysterious ways, circling around one another at elaborate distances, stopping to speak in groups separated as though by large, invisible squares and circles, having conversations while seated at opposite ends of park benches. Sometimes a shrill voice from a hidden tannoy might interrupt, like the voice on Orwell's telescreen, barking orders concerning the rules of the 'game'. The effect was to combine recreation with a constant reminder that the reason for the distancing was not merely rooted in the rules, but had to do with the infectiousness of the human condition, the fact that I represented a danger to my neighbour and *vice versa*. In speaking, we anathematised one another, though not by choice — because we were compelled by the 'regs' to do it, and each in turn were unquestioningly obeyed.

Differentiation and, it sometimes seemed, competition between PCR tests and Antigen tests (the first 'official', the latter suspect) seems to have been another game, this one using 'toys', which Sicart describes as 'the materialisation of play.' The test, particularly the at-home kit versions, provided for a ritualistic participation in the communal sacrament of make-believe, i.e. 'make ourselves believe'. Toys, Sicart observes, become the physical manifestations of the 'game', embodying the activity of play. 'Through the toy, play is concretely formed, and it assumes a material form.' Toys, he reminds us, play a fundamental role in our sentimental lives, 'They can embody times past, of childhood and also of times when we played with others.' A test-kit may not seem like a plaything, but it conveys a hint of the tactility of toys and also has within it a magical capacity to change reality in an instant: to render us ill or well, without another human — an authority figure, for example — being present to make the call. It is like a game of chance, the toss of a coin, the turn of a roulette wheel, or the cylinder of a gun in the Russian form. Toys, being objects, convey the meaning of the activity, and therefore bolster the imputed meaning — to seduce us, anchoring us in time and space, trigger emotional responses, play a role in memory and culture, and help us devise situations so that play can take place. . . . They help us locate, touch, feel, express and share the ideals of play.

In video games, a 'level' is like a 'floor' in the 'building' of difficulty. In general, the goal set with each 'level' requires the players to reach the end by navigating through various obstacles and overcoming sundry enemies. The higher you go, the more difficult it becomes to survive. At each level, there are set boundaries indicating the space the players are required to move in and interact. So it is with the 'game' of fake pandemics.

In September 2020, at the height of the lockdown frenzy, a new system of 'levels' was introduced into the game of Covid, whereby various 'rewards' or 'penalties' were to be imposed on individuals and families on the basis of a system in which levels one to five would decide on the numbers of people to be permitted at various family-related events, including gatherings in the home of a private citizen. Under this system, the Irish government was to decide on moving between levels based on advice from the National Public Health Emergency Team (NPHET), under the supervision of various unelected factotums and 'experts'. For example, people were 'permitted' to have as visitors to their homes at any one time a maximum of ten people (from three households) at Level One; six from two or three households at Level Two; one member of one other household at Level Three; and beyond that (Levels Four and Five) no visitors at all. Similarly, for weddings, people were permitted to have 100 attendees at Level One; 50 at Level Two; 25 at Level Three; and six at Levels Four and Five.

The levels were to be ordained on the basis of criteria including recent breakout rates, numbers of 'cases' and 'clusters', number of recent deaths, 'capacity to manage outbreaks', the international situation, and information gleaned from testing and contact tracing. Thus, at a moment when the initial energy of the 'game' was beginning to flag, there were more 'rules' to be absorbed and accepted by the 'players', which for the most part they were.

This was not a game purely in the sense that we were unconsciously playing it, but in the sense that we were the objects of the game, of a burlesque of our very natures and bodies. We were a festering mess of microbes who, in a civilised society, would not be allowed outdoors at all. Thus, the 'game' — like the face mask — prepared us for a renegotiation of our freedoms; for an acceptance of the indictment of our noxious natures, and even for death or injury as a collateral outcome of the 'game'.

You can see some of the effects and consequences of this distorted apprehension in the responses of those afflicted or bereaved by vaccine injuries and deaths arising from the 'pandemic', whereby far from evincing anger towards the authorities who brought these catastrophes down upon their heads, we find instead indignation directed at those who seek to draw attention to such possibilities. I came across one such case in which a mother who had herself, along with her several small children, suffered vaccine injuries, declined an offer of legal advice on the matter on the grounds that *'We all had to take it.'* Somewhere in the depths of her sorrow seemed to lurk an attitude akin to what applies with a sportsperson injured in the course of a game, who understands that injuries on the pitch are to be regarded, not in the manner of injuries in 'real life', but rather as the natural and unavoidable attrition of play. Very often, especially in the midst of the 'pandemic', such affected 'players' would discount their injuries as if they were nobody's fault, and become angry with anyone who insisted on moralising about them, thereby repudiating the suggestion of anything nefarious or even blameworthy; and implying that there would be something 'unsporting' about making a fuss. Far from wishing to be defended against the forces that had destroyed their or their children's health, or brought about their relative's death, they become angry with anyone who insisted on talking about it, suggesting that they continued to see such people as their 'opponents' in the game and were more outraged at their 'spoilsport' attempts to disrupt it than about the murder and injury of their beloved.

Here, the word 'dark' acquires a split meaning: Sicart's concept of what we might call 'uninitiated play' and the deeper, darker intimation of the appropriation of play for a dire and sinister purpose — perhaps approximating what Johan Huizinga calls 'false play', though here we may require a different epithet, perhaps 'Satanic play'.

Play can be political, Sicart acknowledges, and political play takes place when a plaything 'harnesses the expressive, creative, appreciative, and subversive capacities of play and uses them for political expression.' But he seems to assume that this can only occur in a bottom-up fashion. He references the Occupy movement, the hacktivists of Anonymous, and the brief flowering of the

Arab Spring. He talks about the 'popularisation' of 'kettling', the police manoeuvre whereby in 2010, British riot police would surround and corner groups of protestors, either to arrest or baton them, which inspired a satirical board game called *Metakettle*, 'a game to play when you're being kettled' — the only circumstance in which the game would actually be political, as Sicart observes. The sole technology required is a printer, which might be problematic in most kettling situations.

'Play is political in the way it critically engages with a context, appropriating it and using the autotelic nature of play to turn actions into double-edged meanings: they are actions both in a play activity and with political meaning and are therefore heavy with meaning.'

Political play, he says, takes place when the focus of the play activity is set on the appropriation of play 'and how that appropriation can be used creatively to subvert the establishment, institutions, or other forces.'

Yes, or — on the contrary — used by establishments, institutions, or 'other forces' to 'subvert' the freedom of the people, so as to render them to restriction and denial of basic human rights and freedoms. Play as a political phenomenon is always ambiguous, Sicart says, as between the play and political activity elements.

In the Covid episode, the 'play' element was never rendered explicit, but existed only as a subtext, perhaps an unconscious reflexive response implanted in each affected individual. 'Because it is play,' Sicart concludes, 'it can thrive in situations of oppression; because it is play, it can allow personal and collective expression, giving voice and actions when no one can be heard.' Or, on the contrary, it can thrive as a discreet and subtle instrument of coercion-by-seduction, on the mere account of having an undertone of play. It can facilitate authoritarian imposition under the guise of 'solidarity' and the 'common good' in circumstances where few have the courage to break with the logic of the 'game' to articulate the true nature of what is happening.

The computer, along with a ragbag of residual media instruments, carefully acquired and controlled, also offers the means by which a pseudo-reality — a self-suggesting playground — can be constructed to fool almost everyone. But it is, at the same time, necessary to persuade people to enter the pseudo-reality, and here it is necessary first to invoke the play 'instinct', which is already much more than that, being conditioned by childhood play, games, sports (participation or watching), which create a latent mindset that can be activated by certain cues — dancing nurses, for example.

There is more than the world to playfully take over now, Sicart innocently cautions: 'there's the world, the machines, and the way the machines make the world exist.' But he does not seem to perceive all the risks inherent in this, including the opportunity which the marriage of computing and games can give to those who, themselves far from playful, seek to 'play' us using our own innate and predominantly self-starting desire to play in a world where electronic 'toys' of communication are ubiquitous.

There is a moment in *Homo Ludens* in which, without elaborating, Johan Huizinga makes an intriguing suggestion:

'But at any moment, even in a highly developed civilization, the "play-instinct" may reassert itself in full force, drowning the individual and the mass in the intoxication of an immense game.' And this, too, has the capacity to move towards the light or the dark — towards play or 'false play', this being his characterisation of the tendency of rulers to tap into the play instinct of their subjects for a nefarious purpose, to unleash a 'play' so that the citizens may, in participating in its logic, lose touch with reality and become malleable.

Might something like this be 'at play' in the Covid exercise? True play has no ulterior motive, no point but itself. Man engages in it sometimes for reward, but that is never the primary aim. It is gratuitous, unnecessary, but not without purpose. Indeed, purpose is at the heart of play — a certain focussed goal is the point of every game: to put the ball in the net, to clear the highest raised bar . . . to 'save lives' . . . to gain the approval of others for such virtuous conduct?

But soft! Perhaps even 'saving lives' or being exalted for it, is not the 'exalted purpose' of the Covid game. These are the pretexts, yes, but the tension and action of the game, looking back at it five years later, seems to reside elsewhere. In the beginning, we noted, the 'opponent' was 'the virus'; later, however, we might say that the opponent became the one who disputed the existence or gravity of the virus. The 'object' of the game, therefore, now resided in identifying and chastising those miscreants who refused to play the game properly or at all. And this hints at a lower purpose, separate to the play and inimical to the true play-spirit. The loss of virtue was implicit in the 'game' from the start, the Covid equivalent of *going back to square one*; but here there was another dimension: not merely a loss of advancement or points, but a casting out not just from the 'game' but from reality itself, which had become the 'board', the 'pitch' and the 'magic circle'.

In the game, the 'spoilsport' is someone who trespasses against the rules or ignores them. He may, or may not, be a 'player'. Huizinga notes: 'The spoilsport is not the same as the false player, the cheat; for the latter pretends to be playing the game and, on the face of it, still acknowledges the magic circle. It is curious to note how much more lenient society is to the cheat than to the spoilsport. This is because the spoil-sport shatters the play-world itself. By withdrawing from the game he reveals the relativity and fragility of the play-world in which he had temporarily shut himself with others. He robs play of its illusion — a pregnant word which means literally "in-play" (from *inlusio, illundere* or *inludere*). Therefore, he must be cast out, for he threatens the existence of the play-community.' In this construction, we perhaps see a dimension of the Covid game that made it unique: the 'stakes' of the 'game' related to real life: to lose was to lose more than the game; it was to lose face, place, respect, affection, even material well-being, in the real world.

The objectives and rules of a game of Covid can seem inscrutable to the uninitiated. It will be noted that players are sometimes masked with cloth strips placed over their mouths, and tied to their ears. The masks are coloured, though to no discernible pattern, a pale blue being by far the most common. Occasionally, a player may wear two or more different coloured masks, though again, the logic of this is opaque.

The players tend, in general, to move around one another, leaving approximately two metres in between, though sometimes more, often moving in very wide circles around the others, occasionally pausing to wash their hands using potions from bottles that are distributed haphazardly around the places where the game is played.

In queuing up outside various facilities, players tend to keep the same two-metre gap between themselves and others, moving forward one at a time, preserving the distance and tugging at their face masks, pulling them more tightly over their noses or down on their chins. Sometimes, a player who is not wearing a face mask, or wearing one in an unapproved fashion, will be accosted by another player or players, and a confrontation will ensue. This appears to be somewhat close to the nub of the game's purpose, for it is here the players become most animated.

The rules concerning face masks are even more impenetrable than under other headings. In certain areas, for example, players must wear face masks when walking between one point and another, but may remove them when sitting down. In other situations, a player must wear a face mask while either sitting or standing, but it permitted to remove the mask to eat or drink. A player who deviates from the correct routine — for example, omitting to don a face mask to walk across a room from a doorway to a chair — may be loudly assailed by other players, and sometimes either debarred from the room or other areas, or occasionally forcibly removed by uniformed referees or stewards.

The routes and paths of the game are laid out with yellow markings — arrows, lines, symbols and other enigmatic signs. The players follow the general instruction of these signs, though somewhat haphazardly. Sometimes, on encountering and recognising another player or players, one player or more may engage in a jerky dance in which the participants touch elbows or clench fists and gently push them together in a show of mutual affection or solidarity. This appears to be the aspect of the game offering the most explicit 'fun' element, as the players giggle and titter as they touch fists or elbows. It is evidently forbidden to touch mouths or open hands, though sometimes, as an alternative to elbow or fist contact, players may throw or blow kisses at other players. Generally, this ritual involves one masked player and another, unless one player is unmasked but in an approved situation, such as holding a cup of beverage in the vicinity of his mouth while either sitting down or walking towards an approved destination (for example, a vacant chair).

But what, in the Covid game, equates to the 'magic circle'? It is a good question, for at first sight the most 'obvious' answer seems to disintegrate the entire hypothesis, for did not Covid take over everything for the duration of itself? Perhaps this is not quite the case: The lines and arrows and signs and PA announcements appeared to be total, but in reality they were always still striving so to become. It is true that they designated and partitioned separate spaces within the 'real' world, in a sense colonising them for the game, but this encroachment did not (yet) amount to the entire world. Though totalitarian in ambition, Covid was not yet total. The imaginative 'space' of the Covid game was the State, which was seeking to intrude upon and conquer all space and time. This is an aspect of which the players were at best dimly aware, for in their minds the game was already total, as it needed to appear. Covid came replete with a kind of 'roving' magic circle, which enabled the 'game' to erupt in virtually any location at any moment, and there acquire 'jurisdiction' to impose its penalties on losers, cheats and spoilsports.

Another sign of the presence of the 'false play' syndrome in the Covid 'game' might be the way the rules changed all the time, purportedly for good and rational reasons but really to fuel the sceptic on his unbelief and, at the same time, confuse the believer, so the two might go, with fresh vigour, at one another's throats.

Covid also abolished all other forms of play. In the beginning, the Covid regimens stopped all singing, dancing, swimming at the seaside, golf — and only grudgingly restored some of these on a qualified basis. By way of compensation, it created less familiar forms of 'play', which were not so recognised and yet seemed for many people to fill the gap. The Covid game became, in some respects, like a form of hopscotch for grown-ups, or perhaps for slow-learners: it marked out parts of the pavement and claimed them, so that even when the game was in suspension, Covid remained before the imagination. Sometimes, in certain lights or acoustics, it seemed like Covid was a 'replacement' game, seeking to supplant all others.

In a 'real' sense, the Covid illusion had this capacity to be at once real and not real. The intrinsic human attraction to play allows for a blurring between the fictional and the actual, so that, like children, adults can engage in the game via a kind of quasi-total belief, while still seeing the rest of the world as separate — for the frozen moment of the game. This contains within its 'logic' the possibility that the ever-present hypnosis, created in the Covid era to enhance the experience of the 'game', might allow people to return to 'normal' and regard the whole episode in the way they might a particular day's golfing, or a pop concert, or a game of hide-and-seek with their grandchildren in the park. But they might just as readily come to accept the 'game' as permanent, as a new reality, a 'new normal'. It all depended on who 'won' — the believers or the spoil-sports. And there remains a sense, even now, that the game is not yet over, that it must recommence at some unspecified future time, perhaps with a new name and slightly different rules.

The Covid 'game' was therefore both a game and not a game. This dualistic sense of its meaning is intrinsic to play. The player abandons himself to the game and the consciousness of its being 'merely a game' melts into the background. You might, then, observe that Covid represented 'a temporary constriction or part-abolition of the ordinary world', a concept which Huizinga says is 'fully acknowledged in child-life, but it is no less evident in the great ceremonial games of savage societies.' In both contexts, the 'real' and the 'play' become part of the same magic circle. The players are like actors in a play. They know it is a play and yet they are utterly diverted by and immersed in the parts they are playing.

And yet they are always, in a certain sense, not playing. One time, at Halloween, I watched my wife playing with her then six-year-old granddaughter. They were playing seasonal games, and in one of these my wife covered her head with a sheet and pretended to be a ghost. Her granddaughter, who adores her Nana, watched her pull the sheet over her head. They were both laughing, close to hysterically. Nana, making 'ghost noises', approached her granddaughter, 'Poppy', her hands raised in the sheet. Reaching her, she brought her hands down as though to grab her granddaughter, who screeched for all her worth, but then instantly reverted to laughing. She was both in the game and not in it. Poppy knew it was her Nana under the sheet, but also, engaging fully in the 'let's pretend' dimension — a special capacity acquired in early childhood — she was in some sense 'scared'. She saw the sheet, could call it by its name, yet momentarily believed it to be something else. Huizinga's words from another, more traditional context, seem to fit: 'Whether one is sorcerer or sorcerised, one is always knower and dupe at once. But one chooses to be the dupe.'

He cites R.R. Marett, from *The Threshold of Religion*: 'The savage is a good actor who can be quite absorbed in his role, like a child at play; and also like a child, a good spectator who can be frightened to death by the roaring of something he knows perfectly well to be no "real" lion.'

It is as though play accentuates some otherwise unremarked bifurcation of human responses, a flitting between the 'play' and the 'real'. In the same spirit, we may 'pretend' to be afraid, 'act out' the emotion required by the script — because it is, after all, at some level, a game. And yet, in a different sense, the emotion — of fear or rage — is somehow also 'real'.

These quirks of play seem, too, to achieve some resonance with the function of the face mask in the Covid game, which somehow equated to the sheet over Nana's head: Huizinga says: 'Even for the cultured adult of today, the mask still retains something of its terrifying power, although no religious emotions are attached to it. The sight of the masked figure, as a purely aesthetic experience, carries us beyond "ordinary life" into a place where something other than daylight reigns; it carries us back to the world of the savage, the child and the poet, which is the world of play.'

It is hardly accidental that the core of the Covid subterfuge seemed to manifest a mechanism along these lines: It imbued intense belief at the same time as an agnosticism essential to everyday continuity. People believed in the 'disease', were 'frightened' by it, yet, believing that, if they followed the rules, they would remain safe; they were more afraid of those who were not afraid, for it was they who threatened to break the spell and bring perdition — or reality? — (back) down upon everyone.

'The play-mood is labile [constantly undergoing change] in its very nature,' says Huizinga. 'At any moment "ordinary life" may reassert its rights either by an impact from without, which interrupts the game, or by an offence against the rules, or else from within, by a collapse of the play spirit, a sobering, a disenchantment.'

Let's 'pretend', then, that, wiring into the play 'instinct' in human beings, the plotters of our hypothesis have created a fantasy that finds its energy in the residual 'pretend' life of infantilised adults, and yet at the same time have weaponised all the real-life emotions of the 'players' in much the way that the participants in a savage drama, or the viewers of a horror movie, experience real fear and shock at things they are, at the same time, able to 'see through'.

The player, once within and accepting of the 'magic circle', accepts also the total logic of the game and is able to close out the 'real world' outside. A footballer may be carrying griefs or worries from his everyday life, and yet be able to put in the performance of his life on the pitch. This facility, too, was leveraged by the Covid scam. The sometimes opaque, complex or absurd character of the rules was as though designed to maintain the illusion by keeping 'reality', with its 'logics' at bay. Here, in fact, the elements of complexity/absurdity assisted in focussing the player exclusively on the content of the rules, to the exclusion of logic or meaning. The game created its own centre-of-gravity, which drew the players to it, maintaining the spell, keeping them in their trance. The 'logic' of the rules did not matter — the rules were there to support the coherence of the game, and could not be analysed by the logic of the 'real' world. It is as though the rules were handed down by a superhuman force, a quasi-deity, all-seeing, foreseeing, all-wise, who could be trusted to have the best interests of the players at heart at all times. If you played, you accepted the rules in their totality; there was no point in not doing so, just as footballers do not stop to argue the foundational logic of the offside rule with the linesman; they accept it and its contradictions as a given condition of playing the game. It is something with no currency or traction in the 'real world', but that world has little traction or currency while the game persists, unless some sudden intrusion of reality — a bomb scare or a sudden pitch invasion — brings the illusion to a disgruntling halt. Even a sudden downpour at a football match has little or no impact. The players continue as though nothing has changed. In motor racing, rain provokes a pit-stop and a change of tyres, but even then, the continuity of the game is preserved, since the speed of the change may prove a vital element of the game. So it is with Covid: the labyrinth of rules provided a constant reminder of the game's continuance, and also a distraction from 'real life', in which these rules did not apply, and did not need to make sense. The game became a warm place of community, notwithstanding the hardships, a bit like a place of pilgrimage where you must remove your shoes and walk on sharp stones, or a triathlon where the players endure freezing water and wet clothes and yet remain focussed on the prize. Thus, the 'fun' of the game becomes likewise something particular to the play: to go around in wet clothes in the 'real world' is a defini-tion of misery; in the game it is part of the joy. To lose your human autonomy but gain the camaraderie of the play-group in the mission to 'save lives' and oppose 'deniers' and 'anti-vaxxers' is, on balance, not a bad bargain — espe-cially when, between ourselves, you have no choice except cancellation.

In the Covid game, there were two adversaries: the virus and the spoilsport. The virus represented a constant, invisible threat, and the nightly scoreboards on the TV News allowed the players an approximate monitor of how they were progressing in avoiding this risk. But they also had to contend with the sceptic, who tried to break the play-spell by suggesting that the 'game' was not real, to jerk them back to 'reality' and spoil their satisfaction or, yes, in a certain darkly rapturous sense, their fun.

But why?

- To create a context — a space and time — in which rules, regardless of logic or coherence, would be accepted unquestioningly.
- To create a sense of order, albeit rooted in a kind of game, that might function as a 'rehearsal' for something more serious.
- To create 'teams' which might, by opposing one another, serve to police the rules and thereby sustain the game through various trials of opposition or dissension, to 'victory'.
- To break the spirit of the 'spoilsports' by compelling them to surrender and stop trying to break the spell of the game and, above all, to take the vaccine — so as to be re-admitted to the magic circle — the ultimate victory?
- Ultimately, to see if it was possible to convert the entire world — or something close to that — to join a magic circle in a game that might possibly never end.

It was, of course, a travesty of play, just as it was a travesty of health, science and life. But that in itself does not gainsay the hypothesis that such a primal element of the human make-up might have suggested itself to would-be evil-doers as a means of drawing in and trapping humanity in the tangles of its own structure and dynamism. Clearly, beings exist who are well capable of such cynicism.

And nor is the thesis destroyed by the occasional discordance with the definitions of play as set out by Johan Huizinga, or Miguel Sicart, or any other expert in the field of play. It may well be that the forms of 'freedom' afforded by the lockdown play did indeed liberate certain categories of the human from fear of death or sickness, reassure them that their government was in control (and how!), and enable them to enter into a, yes, cocoon of quasi-certitude as to their security and correctness, their moral uprightness and indeed superiority to more lackadaisical or truculent folk. This is the freedom of the bird in the cage, but this seemed not to compute in the minds of most players.

Nor can it be said that there was much 'fun' as normally understood to be had on the lockdown frontline — venturing to the shops for milk and bread or trying to obtain a takeaway coffee without humiliating oneself along the average high street. The 'fun' to be had here was indeed perverted; it was the 'fun' of the sub in the master-slave BDSM scenario; albeit perhaps punctuated by the brief occasional moment of rapture when the sub finds himself temporarily endowed with the powers of the Master to chastise a random miscreant along the way. Huizinga says: 'The joy inextricably bound up with playing can turn not only into tension, but into elation. Frivolity and ecstasy are the twin poles between which play moves.'

The hypothesis is not hermetically sealed. But the fact that such quantities as freedom and fun are perverted within the logic of the rules and the play does not take substantively from the likelihood that the overall architectures of the play-ethic and play-space had been appropriated for the most malign and misanthropic reasons imaginable. The overall structure of what feels like a metaphor, but probably isn't, holds firm: the usurping of the most primeval and profoundly joy-making capacity of the human person in the achievement of his enslavement.

Huizinga sternly reminds us that such perversions are not 'play', but a new tendency he identifies in the early twentieth-century modern moment which he believes to be deeply antithetical to the play-spirit, resulting in what he deems 'false play', which he says arises when certain play-forms are used, consciously or unconsciously, to 'cover up some social or political design.'

He does not elaborate, but it seems that here he is returning to the theme touched on earlier when he alluded to the danger of the play-instinct reasserting itself 'in full force, drowning the individual and the mass in the intoxication of an immense game.' Without doubt, it is this form of 'play' that we are confronted by in the Covid deception. And this can become dangerous precisely because of the ambiguity it fosters, whereby the aggression and 'kill-element' of the game may overflow into real life.

To the underpinnings of the 'false play' tendency, Huizinga also gives the name 'puerilism', a form of childishness that lacks both the spirit of childhood and the associated true impulse towards playfulness.

Without doubt, the 'play' taking place intermittently in the past five years, and still bubbling under, is indeed, as by Huizinga's analysis, mostly 'false play', rendering it difficult, as per his definition, to say where play ends and non-play begins. This is the core of the Covid trick: the creation of a world-within-the-world in which a logic has been planted that could be at once real and unreal, serious and not, in which the 'virus' might exist only in certain places, at certain heights and times, in a certain frame of mind — to infect or not to infect — or on TV only, where the scoreboard manifested on a nightly basis, but with sufficient impact to propel the game for another night and day. And yet, and yet, having the power, scope and appeal to become a total preoccupation of humanity, a state of being that overcame and sidelined virtually all others.

Real civilisation, as Huizinga reminds us, cannot exist in the absence of a certain play-element, which implies various indispensable qualities: the limiting and mastery of the self; the player's capacity to accept voluntary subordination to 'the ultimate and highest goal', which must remain distinguishable from personal responses or instincts. The human mind, says Huizinga, can only disengage from the magic circle by turning towards the Ultimate. All man's thoughts, acts, judgements, pronouncements are imperfect, and it behoves us to remember this. In play, properly ordered, man is safe from himself and his own flaws and darknesses, though only for a while.

These characteristics must apply also to those seeking to instrumentalise play as a means to some other end, and most of all a dark one. Even more important to play than self-mastery and humility is fair play, which as Huizinga observes 'is nothing less than good faith expressed in play terms. Hence, within the normative play paradigm, the cheat or the spoil-sport shatters civilisation itself.' How much greater might we expect the consequences to be when play is being weaponised for a nefarious purpose?

When, as in the Covid 'game', the 'play' is false, deceptive, it becomes a travesty of the 'real' thing, and what results is a perversion of something both primal and sacred, with enormous power to move the mind of man in the wrong direction. 'To be a sound, culture-creating force,' Huizinga warns, 'this play-element must be pure. It must not consist in the darkening or debasing of standards set up by reason, faith or humanity. It must not be a false seeming, a masking of political purposes behind the illusion of genuine play-forms. True play knows no propaganda; its aim is in itself, and its familiar spirit is happy inspiration.'

Telling play from false play requires a wisdom that appears to have flown the coop of modern society. Whether we have surrendered to the game or seek to stand outside it, we have all been played by the evildoers behind the continuing and most fundamental attack on human life, mind and culture. At the most basic and banal levels, we have been pitted against each other so as to induce fears and hatreds with matching toxicities. We have been conditioned to think that the other 'player' is our enemy so that we will overlook where the true enemy lurks. This, above all, is what we need to see through: the working of the false play. Mistaking the false for the real thing delivers us into the path that takes us towards darkness, where all the villains are devils, and the screams are never followed by the laughter of relief.

CHAPTER 37
REREADING 'NINETEEN EIGHTY-FOUR' POST 1984

04-11-2024

Sally Minogue says that *Nineteen Eighty-Four* 'presents us with a *reductio ad absurdum* of totalitarianism.' I'm not sure how one could write such a sentence in 2020 and not pause for a long time.

I've finished rereading Orwell's masterpiece, *Nineteen-Eighty-Four* (and it is) — forty-four years after I first did so. I cannot say I 'enjoyed' it, for it is a scarifying read, and all the more so now we understand that our presumed immunity to the kind of tyranny it depicts has been delusional. Reading it again, I was mindful of several factors that I did not have access to the first time, in particular, the fact that he did the final rewrite and typed the manuscript while dying of tuberculosis. It is a breathtaking achievement, for the book lacks any (or at least much) trace of agitprop or didacticism. For such a political writer, he was one hell of an actual writer, a seemingly effortless stylist with a powerful imagination and capable of creating believable dialogue in describing even the most unthinkable situations.

What struck me most forcibly on rereading the book was the strange dualism of response between what I was experiencing in the course of reading it again and what I recall from the first time. But before that, I was impacted by the clarity with which I remembered almost every detail of the book, even the flow of the sentences. The opening sentence, for example — *'It was a bright cold day in April and the clocks were striking thirteen.'* — I practically finished that sentence in my head before I got to the end. Having been in my mid-twenties the first time, and since I have in recent years found myself three-quarters of the way through a book before realising that I've already read it, I presume this has to do with some capacity of the brain to preserve more effectively material it encounters when 'newer'.

What interested me in rereading *Nineteen Eighty-Four* was primarily, if not entirely, these questions: What, after 56 months of living with a tyranny that seemed impossible at the time I first read it, might be said now about (a) Orwell's prophetic capacities, and (b) our previous smugness in regarding ourselves as inoculated against his predictions?

I first read it back in 1980, after I decided to repeat a couple of Leaving Cert subjects (English and Economics, as I recall) with a view to obtaining the neces-sary two honours and getting into Trinity College, Dublin, to study either English or Philosophy. In any event, instead of adopting a strategic approach, I decided to pick out certain writers and learn as much as possible about them. The three I chose from the syllabus were Orwell, Patrick Kavanagh, and Dylan Thomas. I'm not even sure *Nineteen Eighty-Four* was on the syllabus — it may have been *Animal Farm*. But, in any event, I decided to read not just everything the three writers had written but everything I could find that others had written about them. So I became, for a time, 'expert' in all three. I never got to Trinity, instead landing my dream job with the music magazine *Hot Press*, the following spring, whereupon I abandoned my academic trajectory, which seemed ill-starred in any event. I would say that those three authors amounted to the foun-dational core of whatever I would nowadays describe as my 'formal education', and all three have stood me in good stead: Kavanagh for the spiritual plane; Thomas for linguistic euphony; and Orwell for just about everything else.

So, I first read *Nineteen Eighty-Four* in the 'before' years — before the date that Orwell chose as the title of his prophetic novel, and at a moment when it was beginning to loom large as a cultural trope that could not be ignored.

There are various tellings of the reasons he chose that year as the title. One is that he called it *1984* as a reversal of '1948', the year he completed the writing of it. Another more substantial explanation relates to a poem written by Orwell's first wife, Eileen O'Shaughnessy, in 1934, a year before she met her husband-to-be. The poem, written to mark the fiftieth anniversary of her old Sunderland high school, ponders the question as to how things would be in the world in another fifty years — the 'end of the century' of her old school.

To add a conspiracist element, a friend who likes to drill deep into things writes me the following somewhat less poetic and also less prosaic explanation:

MI5 Fabian George Orwell was an insider who used his novels to warn mankind about the concrete plans of his own Fabian Society (dubbed 'Ingsoc'), for which his employer, the BBC, worked as a key propaganda organ. The title of his novel 1984 was based on an old Fabian boast that it would only take it 100 years, since its founding in 1884, to utterly turn Britain on its head. In the event, it may take the Fabian Society 140 or 150 years to realise all of its collectivist aims, unless, of course, the slaves finally move to foil the worst-laid plans of 'Team Antichrist'.

This year, 2024, is the fortieth anniversary of the actual year Orwell fired his dart into. Meditating on these two dates, the current year and its iconic antecedent of four decades ago, I am moved to make an adjustment. Something is wrong with their arrangement or chronology — one in the receding past, disparaged and defamed by presentism, hubris and dystopian prophecy; the other in the present — tyrannised, propagandised, gaslit, devoid of meaningful culture or conversation, sorrowful. What can it all signify? Then it strikes me again: *They are in the wrong order*. If a Man from Mars, shown some clips from each of the two years and perhaps some writings by way of evidence, were asked to undertake a brief stab at a comparison between their qualities with a view to declaring one or other the more advanced, hospitable, open, interesting and vibrant — accounting for everything aside from, say, fortunes defined economically — he would undoubtedly elect 1984 as by far the more enviable year, and accordingly the obvious choice to be, paradoxically, the more 'progressive' and 'modern' year of the two. By rights, had progressivism been a true thing, we should by now have progressed to the way Ireland was (other than economically, perhaps, though not necessarily) in 1984.

It is strange that, in cultural terms, 1984 has become an iconic year due its associations with literary totalitarianism, for here is the clanging irony: The present year, 2024, is the tyrannical one, the one in which the public life of the onetime 'Free West' has been stripped of all human tenderness, this having been replaced with an ersatz compassion rooted in a fiendish, murderous and grasping ideology, all backed up with the constant implicit threat of state coercion and, ultimately, violence.

When I hark back to (the real) 1984, I enter not so much memories as feelings. The overwhelming sense I have is of a moment of expectation. It is a strange thing, but the celebrations we engaged in that year on account of Orwell and his book were exuberant and ebullient precisely because we felt certain that nothing of what Orwell had imagined could ever dampen our ardour for life and the future, both guaranteed by the escalating scent of freedom and possibility. This, after all, was the Free World!

In a strange dissonance, the public events of that year — dark or light of them — are of little or no help to me in connecting with those feelings and rendering them present. That was the year that Ronald Reagan came to Ballyporeen, County Tipperary, the alleged home of his ancestors, and met with a mixed reception. I am back there in the moment on Eyre Square in Galway, when his eyes connected with mine over my clenched fist, as his car swept through our Western capital, celebrating its 500th birthday, a town we adored more than any place on Earth, now reduced to a ghetto teeming with hostile outsiders who constitute nearly half of its population, from a standing start three decades ago. 1984 was also the year of the UVF's attempted assassination of Sinn Féin leader Gerry Adams, whom I'd interviewed for *Hot Press* in his lair

in West Belfast just the year before. It was also to be the year that the Irish State
released Nicky Kelly, wrongfully convicted of participation in a train robbery at
Sallins, County Kildare. In November 1984, as I was interviewing the Leader of
the Irish Opposition, Charles Haughey, in his office in Leinster House, we heard
of Margaret Thatcher's since infamous 'Out, out, out!' rejection of the report of
the New Ireland Forum. Politically, sociologically, a varied but overall uninter-
esting year, and yet a year which would stay with me for the rest of my days as
the one in which I began to feel that just about everything good and positive
was at last possible for my dear land, now sloughing off the limits and weights
of its constricted and sometimes monochromatic past.

The sole area where the pace of *Nineteen Eighty-Four* seems to flag (as a
narrative, I mean) is in Orwell's reproducing of sections of what he refers to as
'the book', a fictitious volume attributed to the mythical enemy of the 'Party'
and the State of Oceania, Emmanuel Goldstein, a section that is in many ways
otiose by the time you get to it. I am not sure of the historical solidity of this
assertion, but my suspicion is that 'the book' was a piece of scaffolding
constructed by Orwell in advance of writing the book proper, and utilised here
— 25 pages inserted just beyond the middle of *Nineteen Eighty-Four* — as an
insurance policy against his having overlooked, in his race against tuberculosis,
any vital element of plotting or background. In fact, the 'book within the book',
which Winston Smith sets to reading just before the novel reaches its inevitable
but nevertheless chilling climax, contains almost nothing that Orwell has not
already embedded in his narrative. The sole point of its inclusion seems to be
when O'Brien — Winston's Great-Hope-turned-tormentor — tells him that he,
O'Brien, is the book's actual author, before describing its conclusions as 'nonsense' — Orwell foreseeing the age of the psyop, in which the Regime acts as
both establishment and opposition.

In the first chapter, there is a description of Winston, after much prevarication, starting a diary, an activity he pursues in an alcove which he imagines puts
him out of the line-of-vision of the telescreen, which can receive as well as
broadcast. 'For whom, it suddenly occurred to him to wonder,' the voice of the
omniscient narrator intones, 'was he writing this diary?'

Winston answers himself: *'For the future, for the unborn.'*

This might have been Orwell speaking. The book, he was to explain, was a
warning, not a prophecy. Seeking to clarify his intentions, in the wake of a backlash from fellow socialists after its publication, he emphasised that it was an
attack on totalitarianism — especially the centralised economy — and not on
socialism.

He continued:

'I do not believe that the kind of society which I have described necessarily
will arrive, but I believe (allowing, of course, for the fact that the book is a satire)
that something resembling it could arrive. I believe also that totalitarian ideas

have taken root in the minds of intellectuals everywhere, and I have tried to draw these ideas out to their logical consequences.'

Another thing strikes me forcibly about *Nineteen Eighty-Four*: that, despite its foreshadowing our present situation, the book still reads as a story. You cannot but be involved, even though you may know how it ends. Winston Smith's description of his existence is uppermost, and everything else reads as backdrop. Nevertheless, it is also one of those rare novels that manages to be both political and imaginatively convincing. In her rather excellent Introduction, Sally Minogue notes that readers had been drawn to the book 'for over seventy years now', adding that its 'imaginative verve' and 'endless ability to reinvent itself for its current context', may help to explain its enduring popularity.

There is something possibly odd here: the Wordsworth Classic edition, which I read this time around, was published in 2021, the second year of the Covid coup. This and Minogue's reference to 'over seventy years' (since the novel was first published in 1949) would seem to imply that she wrote and delivered her Introduction to the publishers sometime in 2020, the year the Free World was dismantled using deceit and coercion. Nowhere in her Introduction, or about the book itself, is there any reference to this or to the fact that, at no time in those seventy-plus years has there been another moment that came remotely as close to realising Orwell's foreboding than 2020. That was the year when *déjà vu* came to call, wearing jackboots and carrying a big stick.

Earlier, Minogue says that *Nineteen Eighty-Four* 'presents us with a *reductio ad absurdum* of totalitarianism.' I'm not sure that's any longer sustainable; indeed, I am not sure how one could write such a sentence in the circumstances of 2020 and not pause for a long time.

It has repeatedly been argued in the past nearly five years that the more accurate prophecy of this totalitarianism we now experience is to be found not, as is often suggested, in Orwell's *Nineteen Eighty-Four*, but in Aldous Huxley's 1931 novel *Brave New World*. This is because, whereas Orwell anticipated a world dominated by torture and terror, Huxley foresaw humanity imprisoned by seduction, sedation, and diversion. The society of *Brave New World* is run as a benevolent dictatorship, its subjects kept in a state of pseudo-contentment by conditioning and a drug called Soma. Set in London in A.D. 2540, Huxley's novel anticipated subsequent developments in sleep-learning and psychological manipulation being used to impose the will of the few upon the many.

Thus, perhaps what we were assailed by from early 2020 was a new form of tyranny, one which 'oppresses' man by cosseting him — Huxley rather than Orwell? But no: I believe it more accurate to speak of the Orwellian fist in the Huxlean glove, two parts Orwell to one of Huxley.

In Huxley's vision, people are manipulated in ways that are infinitely more subtle and refined than the brutal methods used in post-totalitarian societies, but the processes of capitalism, materialism, advertising, commerce and consumer culture all combine to repress in the human being the questing for the 'something' that defines the human. But it's not that simple, as we shall observe. No such system could ever be introduced without the implicit, occasionally explicit, threat of state coercion, which is to say thinly veiled violence.

If Orwell, instead of calling his book after the future year 1984, had opted for, say, 2054, would any of what has befallen us have even happened yet? I think there's a certain sense in which, once the year of its title came and passed in reality, there occurred an almost inaudible sigh at the core of our culture and a whisper of, *'Well now it can't happen!'*, and societies became, they imagined, inoculated, and accordingly complacent about the warnings Orwell had worked into his book. There was even a slight sense that Orwell had gotten it wrong, and now we could all relax. This and Michael Esfeld's theory that the fall of the Berlin Wall made Western totalitarianism inevitable, takes us more than halfway to an understanding.

By the same token, there is a strong possibility that, for at least forty years, Orwell's book functioned as a kind of cultural brake on the eruption within the Collective West of any form of totalitarianism such as it depicts. In this sense, although what has happened now appears superficially to adhere more to the Huxlean blueprint of tapping into human desires, instincts and vices in order to draw humanity into an essentially digital/cultural prison and keep it there, it is the Orwellian model that has remained uppermost in human consciousness and apprehension. This is because of Orwell's depiction of both the potential of authoritarian state violence and the psychological reality that emerges in response to its presence or threat — i.e., the actuality of the fear of violence, which is, as he also conveys, even more powerful than violence per se. In O'Brien's electrical torturing of Winston Smith, it is clear that, once he has established the potential of the technique for imposing pain, Winston's will falls to pieces, and any residual resistance is swept up by the mere threat of 'the worst thing in the world' — a different fear for each individual human — in the dreaded Room 101.

Having started rereading *Nineteen Eighty-Four*, I decided that I would read in parallel a book I had made several attempts to read in the past but mysteriously failed to progress far into. This is another legendary book about totalitarianism — non-fiction this time — the 1951 essay of the Polish writer and poet (I don't regard poetry as writing, but something else), Czeslaw Milosz, *The Captive Mind*. Orwell's book had been published three years before it and may well have inspired Milosz to write his meditation on the mentalities of totalitarianism as observed in his time living within the Soviet bloc (he wrote it in Paris, where he arrived seeking asylum). The two books criss-cross the same territory and, for that reason, are somewhat complementary, but Orwell's is, as I say, an unambiguous story, whereas Milosz's is as though an expansion or explication of Orwell's backdrop, though without overt mention of it.

Milosz is a more difficult read than Orwell, who writes fluent prose in a manner that bears no stamp of a former era, but is as though written yesterday. Milosz, being translated from the Polish, has a rather more convoluted style, though — strangely — mostly in the first section of the book. A Polish friend of mine tells me that I am not alone in finding his prose difficult — Poles do as well, and he speculates this will not have been improved in translation. Actually, Milosz's style reads very elegantly in English; the difficulty arises from the syntax, which creates entirely different constructions than one tends to find anymore in non-fiction books in English. Half poetic, half what reads like a literal translation, many of his sentences require multiple rereadings in order to release their correct inflexions. Yet, every effort is handsomely rewarded, and it is certainly not that one can read one of his sentences and immediately say how it might have been rendered better. He says complex things in a pretty unambiguous fashion, and always you have the sense of being in the hands of a master.

One of the most interesting sections deals with an obscure condition of totalitarian societies which Milosz calls 'Ketman' — a kind of practised doublespeak which can be developed as a form of armour against what George Orwell calls 'vapourisation' (liquidation), a standard feature of advanced tyrannies. From Milosz's description, the concept appears to be of Islamic origin, being somewhat related to that of *taqiyya*, or 'holy dissimulation', a technique attributed to Muslims for concealing and mystifying their beliefs in situations where professing them openly might be dangerous or counter-productive. Muslims also refer to a related syndrome, known as *kitmān*, which literally means 'to conceal' or 'prevaricate' or 'dissimulate', and was especially, as with *taqiyya*, a feature of the Shia sect, which tended to experience more persecution as a religious minority. Courtesy of *kitmān*, Shias are even permitted under Sharia law to pretend to convert and practice another religion while remaining Muslims 'in their hearts' if, by doing so, they can gain an advantage. In Shia theology, *taqiyya* and *kitmān* are permitted in situations where there is a threat to life or property, and no denial of fundamental principles arises from a pragmatic, self-protective selectivity of speech.

Milosz stumbled on the concept of Ketman out of a necessity born of detecting and observing his own duplicity when asked, as a cultural attaché in America in the late 1940s, about the terrible things happening in the Soviet Union and the Soviet Bloc. He was there at the time representing the Communist Polish government — having been a lifelong socialist until the atrocities of Stalin. In his 1989 memoir *Native Realm: A Search for Self-Definition*, he described the way when, working in Warsaw under the Soviet regime, whenever asked by people who were admirers of the Soviet experiment for 'a few kernels of lying propaganda', he would find himself speaking evasively or remaining silent.

Milosz adapted *kitmān* to the communist world, as 'Ketman', applying it to the forms of prevarication and dissimulation that developed in 'the peoples' democracies' of the Soviet bloc during the tyrannical reign of Joseph Stalin — a form of forked-tongue speech whereby writers would evince a studied ambiguity in respect of the political situation, so as to avoid attracting official attention and at the same time shield their integrity as writers.

Hannah Arendt had described people under the influence of totalitarianism as people 'for whom the distinction between fact and fiction no longer exists', but Milosz noticed something to the contrary: that totalitarianism seemed to nurture a skilled evasiveness, casuistry and sophistry that would put a Jesuit to shame, a divided mind that became inured to its own self-contradictions. His gaze on this condition was refined in post-war Poland, a country revolutionised by an external power and, soon after its Nazi-inflicted horror, subjected to radical Stalinist interference and menace. Ketman was the phenomenon of his fellows succumbing to the new tyranny but pretending that they were doing so willingly. What distinguished Ketman from other forms of dissembling was that it deceived the deceiver as well as the deceived. Ketman was a performance, as much for the performer's benefit as that of the audience. Ketman enabled one to be fleet of foot and tongue, to adapt to all contingencies and, above all, to satisfy the looming tyrant with what had the outward appearance of compliance.

George Orwell unveiled in *Nineteen Eighty-Four* another word for much the same syndrome: 'doublethink':

'To know and not to know, to be conscious of complete truthfulness while telling carefully constructed lies, to hold simultaneously two opinions which cancelled out, knowing them to be contradictory and believing in both of them, to use logic against logic, to repudiate morality while laying claim to it, to believe that democracy was impossible and that the Party was the guardian of democracy, to forget whatever it was necessary to forget, then to draw it back into memory again at the moment when it was needed, and then promptly to forget it again: and above all, to apply the same process to the process itself. That was the ultimate subtlety: consciously to induce unconsciousness, and then, once again, to become unconscious of the act of hypnosis you had just performed. Even to understand the word "doublethink" involved the use of doublethink.'

Parts of Milosz's definition of the Ketman method might well be added on:

Before it leaves the lips, every word must be evaluated as to its consequences. A smile that appears at the wrong moment, a glance that is not all it should be, could occasion dangerous suspicions and accusations.

Milosz used the word 'Ketman' to refer to the capacity of the private dissident to keep his true convictions and feelings hidden in circumstances whereby exposing them might risk severe punishment, even death. Sometimes, mere silence is enough to avoid trouble, but often it is not, and then it is necessary not only to deny one's true opinions but to 'resort to all ruses in order to deceive one's adversary'.

Everyone is an actor. Everything must be accompanied by the appropriate emotion; fervour, hatred, rage, lest its absence be detectable by someone liable to alert the authorities. This is a predicament that Winston Smith refers to continually, especially his fear that any lapse of attention concerning his facial expressions may be picked up by the telescreen.

The art of Ketman is a form of brinkmanship and verbal acrobatics by which, with increasing proficiency, the practitioner can enable himself to negotiate the risks of a regime he secretly repudiates, without fear that his statements will let him down. The most adept are able, in speaking publicly, to maintain a line of thought that is in some ways incongruent with the dominant ideology, even to the point of outright heresy, but with such an adroit delivery that this escapes official notice. This is achieved by delicate obfuscation and ambiguity so that the speaker is able to communicate relatively truthfully while avoiding liquidation. Sometimes, this requires a slow process of evolution in his public pronouncements, from strict orthodoxy and even fanaticism, via ambiguity, deviation, self-contradiction, fallacy, hair-splitting concerning certain orthodoxies, and other devices, to the point where such is the speaker's acquired reputation for reliability that he can publicly contradict the authorities without a negative interpretation being applied, and therefore without adverse consequences for himself. You might call it casuistry, but it is really a form of pragmatism designed to retain self-respect while also avoiding the kinds of risks that might lead the speaker into perdition.

Ketman involves the adoption within a context of tyranny of a Janus-faced disposition of compliance and, simultaneously, an implied dissension, the first for the sake of safety, the second in the interests of maintaining dignity and a form of intellectual and moral pride.

Ketman is essentially the condition diagnosed by Václav Havel in his account of the actions of the Prague greengrocer in 'The Power of the Powerless'. It amounts to an insurance policy that protects the actor from the consequences of detectable dissidence or wrongthink.

Ketman is a means of preserving an image of integrity, while publicly conforming to the mandatory line. In a sense, it consists in a performative compliance with the official narrative which is inwardly rejected. Ketman is a kind of mask that allows the wearer to fit in.

Milosz lists multiple categories of Ketman: 'nationalist Ketman', 'professional Ketman', 'aesthetic Ketman', 'sceptical Ketman', 'ethical Ketman', 'the Ketman of revolutionary purity', 'metaphysical Ketman', et cetera. In all of these, the objective is a constant and simultaneous process of compromise and circumstantial best-endeavours, with the ultimate aim of staying, simultaneously, relevant and alive.

He describes it thusly:

'To say something is white when one thinks it black, to smile inwardly when one is outwardly solemn, to hate when one manifests love, to know when one pretends not to know, and thus to play one's adversary for a fool (even as he is playing you for one) — these actions lead one to prize one's own cunning above all else. Success in the game becomes a source of satisfaction.'

For example, under the rubric of metaphysical Ketman, it was necessary for people of religious mindset not merely to conceal this from the communist authorities, but also to avoid any hint of allusion to modes of spiritual transcendence such as 'beauty', 'awe', 'wonder' or 'uplift', which were equally likely to occasion flashing red lights. Even a liking for certain kinds of music was suspect. Polish writers, including those who had been Catholics before the occupation, had to recognise the all-knowingness of Comrade Stalin and refrain from the public acknowledgment of their religious faith. There was, however, some wiggle room. The Regime, though ideologically committed to its secular atheism, was also pragmatic and would tolerate Catholics as a necessary though temporary evil, regarding this as a transitional imperative pending the total wiping out of religion, provided they played the game. An example of the outworking of metaphysical Ketman might be that Catholics, though privately clinging to their faith, would become additionally zealous in their public work, for example, by joining the secret services and suspending their Catholicism in the course of carrying out their duties without undue attention to moral scruples.

Ketman, it strikes me, may be only in its infancy, with the neophyte version described by Milosz having some potential for expansion into a more generalised usage, even in the present situation of countries like our own, not by the dissidents of tyranny but its very architects and stewards. Ketman, let us reprise, is first and foremost a demeanour adopted in the face of an implacable and unassailable power, whereby the advocate of high principle contrives to protect himself from publicly straying into heresy with potentially damaging or unpleasant consequences, and thus to survive within his traumatised culture and country when this seems unlikely or impossible.

Ketman has also been described as 'a form of self-gaslighting' whereby the 'sufferer' espouses views diametrically opposed to his actual beliefs, a demeanour adopted in the face of an unassailable power, whereby the advocate of high principle contrives to protect himself from publicly straying into heresy by dissembling and equivocating in a manner that leaves open the interpretation that he does not seek to offend the dictates of the Power/Regime, while at the same time persuading his dissident admirers that he remains as principled as ever. The practitioner of Ketman manages to have it both ways, to adhere to the concepts — freedom, truth, decency, reason — he has exalted all his adult life, but at the same time avoiding intruding upon the implicit 'correctness' and 'morality' of what the Regime values.

Ketman is therefore resonant of a certain bifurcation which enables a dualism of outlook and implication reminiscent of the capacity, within a game, to believe two things at once, even, as we have seen, to experience two conflicting emotions (laughter and terror, for instance) at the same time, and to adhere to the logic and rules of the game and yet remain, at another level, aware that it is not real.

This may be achieved by dissembling and equivocating in a manner that leaves open multiple interpretations, thus enabling coded dissident communications while at the same time providing reassurances to the listening Regime that the speaker does not seek to offend its dictates, while insinuating to partisans or neutral observers that he remains as steadfast as before. This provides him with a reasonably reliable means of maintaining a sense of self-respect and contact with meaningful activity, while publicly conforming to the mandatory line, and accordingly retaining his income and his health and life.

Now, let us hypothesise that it might be possible, in the totalitarian conditions of the future, to adapt Ketman to instead anticipate and include it in the very model of tyranny being applied, the 'beauty' of this being that it upstages and queers the pitch for the dissident from the beginning by hacking his refuge and shorting out its mechanisms so that it is laid bare from the outset, putting him at risk of being shot at by both sides, his own and the Regime.

To the list of Ketmans proffered by Milosz, I would add the still evolving phenomenon of 'Covid Ketman' — which can be detected by those with attuned senses, right across the Western world. Since the Covid coup had nothing to do with anybody's health, and since its nomenclature has become an iconic synonym for 'soft' tyranny, it may be said to have created a blueprint for a more generic new phase of totalitarianism — the 'hydra-headed' kind described by Michael Esfeld. It is, therefore, vital that we seek to plumb and decipher its undertows before it returns in a changed form.

The Ketman of which Milosz wrote emerged under the old dictatorial form of totalitarianism, whereby the Orwellian brand was eternally poised to land with extreme prejudice its stamp on the reticent or unrepentant human face. In the Huxlean or hybrid forms of totalitarianism, the dynamic can be deciphered as radically different.

The circumstances arising in the Covid totalitarianism experience are therefore somewhat different from those described by Milosz, or foreseen by Orwell. For one thing, the Covid hydra-headed tyranny, being relatively 'young' has not (yet) attained the competence with terror-inducement and death-dealing of a Stalin or a Mao, although in fairness the learning graph has been steep. This has at least liberated dissidents from having to become dissemblers while still trying to work out how a civilisation could go overnight from democratic principle to jackboot tactics. For the moment, the role of the dissident resides in diagnosis rather than dissembling and diversion.

The necessity for the adoption of Ketman manifested only in recent times in the once free West, as a result of cancel culture, which in turn erupted following the launch of Twitter in 2006, whereby the mechanism of shaming, doxing and show-trialling ideological wrongdoers became a favourite weapon of Woke 'social justice' warriors. Cancel culture has since made Ketman an all-pervasive but unidentified and unnamed element of contemporary Western culture, as the deranged desire to seem politically correct has caused previously sane people to sign up to views involving approval of self-mutilation, child abuse and the destruction of female sports, and the fear of being called 'racist' resulted in the surrendering of whole continents to alien hordes. The action of Woke/Cultural Marxism has created conditions that, albeit not necessarily involving overt state coercion, are somewhat analogous to the background radiation of totalitarian societies, such as the Soviet Communism and German Nazism of the last century. This took on a new lease of life during the Covid coup, when the intimation of a lethal viral threat to human life and health was used by governments and health establishments to shame dissident scientists and other critics of lockdown policies into either compliance or marginalisation.

To date, almost five years in, those requiring to become adept at Ketman skills have turned out to be not the dissenters to Covid and its works and pomps, but mainly the public faces of the prior establishment 'liberalism' and its mirroring 'conservatism', who were required overnight to change horses in mid-air, and duly did so, the sole surviving source of opposition being rather unexpected pockets of miscellaneous mavericks, non-conformists, bohemians and reactionaries, who did not seem to fit any of the conventional Ketman categories.

Of course, almost by definition, all public figures, having been advocates of 'liberal' policies and 'values' a great deal more rarified than the basics being trampled on between the spring of 2020 and that of 2022, were at a loss, in theory at least. How to explain their own radical autocratisation? This required a form of Ketman quite different to anything encountered by Milosz or imagined — as 'doublethink' — by Orwell. Simply telling the truth would have been unthinkable: *we have decided to bin everybody's rights and freedoms.* Instead, the Covid subterfuge was created to get them off that hook by insinuating a superior 'value' — tenuous, yes; fragile, certainly; implausible, very — but nevertheless adequate, when accompanied by torrents of propaganda and fear porn, with the help of bought and paid for journaliars, to meet the needs of a population simultaneously being induced with fake money and presented with the opportunity for a break from quotidian troubles for an extended period. All that was required of the political class was a slight hardening of neck and a modicum of coaching, then yesterday's 'liberal' would today be fit to repeat the scripted mantras about 'flattening the curve', 'saving lives', and 'leaving no one behind' — the purest Ketman, under cover of 'the common good'.

Accordingly, during the past four and a half years of life in our formerly democratic countries, Ketman has manifested mostly in institutions like politics (to begin), journalism, civil libertarianism; religion; academia; literature, theatre and the other artforms; as well as in the more diffuse context of personal and neighbourly relations, where its influence is probably cumulatively stronger than in the crucible of public opinion.

The typical Western 2020-2024 practitioner of the 'art of Ketman' might typically be identified as a lifelong 'socialist' who had been a 'rebel' and perhaps even a 'thorn in the side of the establishment' (though chiefly in his own head) for many years, a theoretical revolutionary in a stable society in which insurrection was as likely as flying sheep, so that he was therefore never called upon to put his mojo where his mouth was, but was able to posture shamelessly while incurring no risk whatsoever.

In conditions such as have descended on the former Free World in the past 56 months, this practitioner of Ketman continues to have it both ways: to adhere to the concepts — freedom, truth, decency, reason — he has exalted all his adult life, but at the same time contriving not to cast any doubts upon the implicit correctness and morality of what the Regime imposes, preaches and demands. Thus, the lifelong 'left-liberal', perhaps recognising something in the early events of the spring of 2020 to indicate that what was happening would not result in any diminution of his own living or working conditions, and indeed might be actually beneficial to his personal ideological outlook, was an early enthusiast for lockdowns, even though these seemed to contradict everything he had ever previously seemed to stand for. Open-mouthed, we have observed him, throughout the Covid bioterrorism episode, paying lip-service to the 'common good' while at the same time clinging to his 'liberal socialist' ethos, with its alleged 'concern' for civic virtues like justice and fairness and the rule of law. This contemporary exponent of Ketman constantly bleats about democracy but does not acknowledge (or even realise?) that the would-be all-powerful usurpers of democracy and freedom have redefined these concepts to vacate the idea of a sovereign people, replacing this 'redundant' concept with the bracing ideas that 'democracy' amounts to the secure tenancy of the incumbent (imposed) regime, and anyone who in any way questions this becomes automatically and instantly an 'enemy of democracy' and 'a threat to freedom', and very likely some kind of terrorist.

Take, for example, a stellar commentator who for many years has maintained a reputation for impeccable ideological integrity by adhering to positions of opinion and advocacy which, though not widely comprehended in their undertows, details or full implications, are regarded by the society as respectable and highly ethical. Propounding highly virtuous values of honesty, decency and love of justice, and paying lip-service to equality, democracy, egalitarianism and many other such dispositions, our hero has acquired in the society a moral stature that once was reserved for archbishops and retired presidents. Then, along comes a set of circumstances which, as is made clear to him, requires his adherence to a set of 'values' contrary to everything he has ever uttered or written, including support for the tyrannical imposition of a mendacious programme of social control, coercion, intimidation and propaganda, to be followed by all manner of intrusion and interference in the private lives of the people, and topped off by the promotion of quasi-mandatory injections, contrary to the principle of the Nuremberg Code, while simultaneously assisting in the demonisation of dissident voices seeking to question or denounce these initiatives.

This places our hero in a dilemma. To fail to support this programme may well result in him losing his position, or at least incurring the displeasure of his employers and the Regime, and being cast out into the wilderness like the most dreadful reactionary. Yet, he knows also that defending this programme and providing it with the covering fire of his weekly commentary will offend against every principle he has ever uttered. What to do?

There is a solution: Ketman, which in this context means the jettisoning of principle and the adoption of a disposition of subtle equivocation and moral righteousness couched in elevated concepts of the 'public interest'. To adapt to the changed circumstances, our hero merely requires to have a minor and painless 'operation' in which he is fitted with a forked tongue (presuming he doesn't already have one!), which will allow him to give coded support to the tyranny as demanded by his employment, while at the same time paying continued lip-service to the values of democracy, egalitarianism, and so forth. Although for many years he has excoriated those who spoke from both sides of their mouths, those who helped to cover up wrongdoing or supported abuses of human rights or freedoms, he now settles quite easily into this new role, which, for the sake of clarity and specificity, we might usefully recast as 'KETMAN-19', sliding soundlessly and smoothly into the role of guardian of the common good. It is inevitable that our hero will be led half-blindly across lines that rattle uncomfortably against his previous 'liberal' stances: wrongful discrimination, coercion, health apartheid, et cetera, but any awkwardness arising therefrom is fairly easily offset by the summoned spectre of some nefarious internal enemy who might take succour from a failure of resolve and seek to make political hay for himself, and whom therefore must be defied. To these ends, the practitioner of KETMAN-19 will do whatever is necessary, including the exaltation of political figures he has previously excoriated, to distance himself from such 'enemies of democracy' or 'far-righters'. All previous objections have evaporated and his even recent targets in politics and government — the onetime 'gombeens' and 'chancers', even the 'beggars on horseback' — are now to be treated as exemplary statesmen, their every word as gospel.

And there is, somewhat piquantly for the wry observer, another category, whose constituent members were called upon during the Covid episode to reprogramme themselves to supply a different kind of cover for official arbitrariness, lawlessness and brute force. This is the 'conservative' commentator/activist, who for as long as anyone can remember had been daggers-drawn against the liberal socialist, with whom he was now, at last, able to find common purpose. Despite this history of being, in a certain ideological sense, 'opposites', the 'liberal' journalist/activist and the 'conservative' commentator found it equally congenial enthusiastically to cave into the new dispensation, talking up the virus and lockdowns with just slightly more or less muted enthusiasm, but in a manner decisive, nonetheless, in bringing their respective constituencies of perspective on board. Being, in the main, like his erstwhile 'liberal' opposite number, part of the national communications apparatus, and therefore increasingly, for reasons of economics and a declining business model, almost utterly dependent on state subvention, the 'conservative' commentator was presented with a simple choice: comply or join the dissenters in their sin-bin. Abandoning their objections to state overreach, such actors joined in the chorus of 'deadly virus', while maintaining their demeanours of conspicuous conservatism under other headings, though for in-house consumption only, and in a suitably toned-down manner.

It is as if the architects of the Covid scam built into its design a form of Ketman — in the sense of sophistry, doublethink, 'self-gaslighting' — that rendered it resistant to the variety that had worked to provide some relief to dissidents under the previous totalitarian dispensations. There manifested also a number of odd quirks of the Covid subterfuge which strangely seemed to lend itself to the ethos and character of Ketman in ways that had neither previously arisen in reality nor occurred to real-life observers like Milosz. These seemed to presage some deeper, darker element of putative future iterations of the hybrid form of totalitarianism sketched out by Michael Esfeld, perhaps pertaining especially to the very essence of the new brand of totalitarianism manifested by the Covid conspiracy. These might be filed under a category headed along the lines of 'Constructed Doublethink', to include — as intimated in fictional terms by Orwell — contradictions, repudiations of morality, amnesia, illogic, mental acrobatics, hypnoidal legerdemain, and lies.

There was, for example, an odd dimension of the Covid laws and 'regs' (chummy tyrant slang for 'regulations') which invited a recourse to Ketman and yet made this impossible for anyone but those shameless or indoctrinated enough to take the side of the tyranny. For example one strange and deeply troubling aspect of the Covid 'regs' was the manner in which they were quite openly directed not at preventing the spread of disease but at controlling people's movements as though for the sake of that only. In Ireland, the foundational piece of legislation, on which the totality of the 2020 laws, statutory instruments and regulations were purportedly founded — the Health Act, 1947 — had in its own time been directed exclusively at preventing the spread of disease. In 2020, however, all the 'regs' and 'measures' concocted to be raised up on top off the 1947 legislation were applied not specifically to infected persons, but *to all persons and citizens*, without any burden of proof or evidence being imposed on the relevant authorities as to whether people might be infected or otherwise, but still with apparent carte blanche to employ the full weight of state force and coercion to enforce these often arbitrary rules. In particular, the manner in which the newly framed legislation and ancillary elements impinged upon the fundamentals rights of people and citizens to free movement, right of association, assembly, protest and the inviolability of the home and household, and this in circumstances where no proof or evidence of infection was required, amounted in effect to an inversion of presumption in respect of the spirit of the Health Act, 1947, which stipulates certified infection or the suspicion of infection as the necessary basis for restriction.

Section 30 of the 1947 Act provides that it is forbidden and a criminal offence for a man or woman who knows he/she has a dangerous infection to act on purpose in a manner that might spread the infection to others. In other words the focus of the legislation is on preventing the *spread* of disease, and therefore on curtailing only those who are already infected — i.e., rather axiomatically, someone must *have the infection* in order to *spread* it. All medical staff are required by the Act to notify the Minister for Health of the names and addresses and symptoms of every man or woman or child who is suspected of having the infectious disease. It is the duty of the Minister for Health to regulate infected persons, and to quarantine them from the unaffected population. In circumstances of infectedness, the loss of constitutional rights is accepted as being proportionate and for the common good, but also counterbalanced by virtue of the sufferers from illness being treated and cared for, albeit that it is forbidden under criminal penalty for infected persons to break the quarantine and endanger anyone else.

Despite the pretence of their being based in the 1947 legislation, the 2020 Covid laws, purportedly raised up on those foundations, did not seek to prevent, limit, minimise or slow the spread of the virus SARS-CoV-2 or the infectious disease known as Covid-19, but ostentatiously to regulate people concerning whom there existed no evidence of their being infected or having been in intimate proximity of someone thus affected.

Under the laws introduced in 2020, measures were applied to all persons and citizens, without any burden of proof or evidence being imposed on the relevant authorities as to whether people might be infected or otherwise, extending apparent uninhibited licence to employ the full weight of State force and coercion to curtail the freedoms of just about everyone. This *de facto* violated the constitutional rights to freedom of association and assembly, freedom to travel, right to family life and right to manifest religious belief, and not just of one, several or a number of people, but *of the entire unaffected population*. And here there was no balancing of rights, no equivalent of medical care as in the case of someone who might have been quarantined under the original 1947 legislation, and therefore no proportionality. The unaffected did not require and were not provided with medical treatment, and nor were they in a position to commit a crime under section 30 of the Act of 1947, and so should not have been in any regard subject to the Act. The detention and derogation of rights of the unaffected was entirely without rational purpose, as was the suspension/deletion of the constitutional rights of the vast majority of the population. (There was one marked breach of this pattern, a six-month period between March and September 2021, during which people arriving in Ireland, or returning to it from certain designated countries without proof of vaccination, or a negative PCR test, for SARS-CoV-2, were subject to a mandatory period of hotel quarantine, at their own expense. The nadir of this enterprise was when the then Tánaiste {deputy prime minister}, Leo Varadkar, was heard mumbling to himself, as though channelling Adolf Eichmann, about the burden of providing 'secure transport' for such happy campers from the airport to their designated concentration camp accommodation.)

Here, under the logic of the old totalitarianism, one might anticipate that the practiced practitioner of Ketman might find himself required to show willing on the fundamentals: lockdown, masks, 'vaccines', et cetera, dressing these up as virtuous acts of solidarity in the interests of the common good, while slyly winking at his fellow initiated. He might accordingly wish simultaneously to retain his integrity while also avoiding falling afoul of the regime. Aside from wearing masks, Ketman might be acted out by wearing two or three masks at a time, publicly banging pots and pans in tribute to the frontline workers, walking elaborately on to the middle of the road on encountering neighbours in the street, standing in military fashion six feet away from a friend or acquaintance in a conversation on the street, or publicly excoriating someone on social media, or in public, for not doing one, more, or all of these things when required.

There is something in the depths of these circumstances suggestive of a sensibility strangely akin to that of the spirit of Ketman as described by Czeslaw Milosz. Here, however, this spirit manifests not in the demeanour of the dissident, writer or artist, but in the very entrails of the programme of repression, conducted by the most egregious of its perpetrators. Here, the devices of the Ketman technique — the prevarication or dissimulation — rather than emerging as protective mechanisms against the tyranny, are as though a shadowy inbuilt element of it — a form of structural dissembling designed to 'gaslight' and confuse, while at the same time obstructing any initiative aimed at the normative purposes of Ketman. The entire edifice is as though conceived in a spirit of Ketman, as though anticipating the response which has been shown to function as a cultural prophylactic against coercion, though here to protect not the dissident but the tyrants themselves.

This, obviously, involved a kind of inversion of the normative Ketman disposition, whereby the individual in question implicitly and explicitly denies demurral or wrongdoing by implying adherence to ideology, narratives, et cetera. Here, the citizen was required to admit to a form of 'guilt' diagnosed in advance, and to forfeit all rights, without complaint, on that account. And this process was culturally enforced by an induced state of perverted Ketman, which in this case involved a total self-abasement of the formerly sovereign citizen, who was, out of the blue, required to accept a categorisation of arbitrary rightlessness and, in effect, worthlessness and diminution of dignity, and to direct his Ketman energies in a form of masochistic renunciation of virtually all human self-respect and entitlement, acknowledging 'guilt' in the form of a biological state of putrescence in something like an imposed process of voluntary self-gaslighting — human susceptibility to infection as a kind of biological 'original sin', to which the 'sinner' must 'confess' by compliance with the 'regs'.

These conditions enforced a situation amounting to the equivalent of the inversion of the principle of 'innocent until proven guilty' on which the legal system of Western civilisation rests, albeit in circumstances where virtually no question of moral fault could possibly arise in the mind of anyone whose apprehension of reality was governed by normative cultural understandings of the natural condition of being human.

There was, here, an intimation of guilt on the basis not of infection but of existence itself, the insinuation that by being alive someone was a courier of death — an existential 'crime' that had not yet been either committed or contemplated. People were encouraged to think of themselves as dangerous to their fellows, who were in turn a danger to them — just as their fellows were encouraged to think themselves a menace to everyone else. In a sense, the entire human species stood indicted by this gigantic exercise in mass Ketman, the venerable licence to dissimulate turned backwards on those who might well have thought to adopt it as a defence mechanism against the very tyranny it was now serving to support.

Out of these involutions flowed all kinds of other 'subtleties', tricks, snares, booby-traps and double-binds, which, extending the anti-principle of 'guilty (of putrescence) until proven innocent', rendered it impossible for the dissident to remain within the corpus of the community he was seeking to protect. The novel, hydra-headed genre of totalitarianism came with a new brand of Ketman — in pilot, KETMAN-19 — thus reversing the logic of the original by adopting a mechanism that served to divert the Ketman energies away from a defensive disposition into one of self-entrapment in a logic inimical to freedom, precisely by anticipating, hobbling and nobbling the Ketman instinct before the fact.

The concept of Covid Ketman — KETMAN-19 — accordingly, was a symptom of the corporate structure of the enterprise from the outset, and came to have in large part to do with the 'rules' — the displacement of discussion, from areas such as the believability and substance of the 'virus', and 'pandemic', to the 'rules' and logic of the 'game'. This enabled the controllers to create vistas of confusion arising from the bifurcation between the 'objective' of the 'game' (saving lives) and the 'rules', and also allowed sceptics to disguise their scepticism (by focussing on the 'rules'/'regs' rather than the 'objective'), and at the same time unwittingly protect the threadbare narrative from overly close scrutiny. Strangely, although the Covid sceptic was to become the bête noire of the bespoke Covid groupthink, there was an implicit permission to dissent and be sceptical, provided this was narrowly focussed on rules rather than substance.

In a sense, then, the Covid programme of enforcement (the word is not too strong) was constructed around a novel form of Ketman, which was entirely concerned with semiotics. Ketman, remember, is a means of maintaining full functionality while publicly conforming to the mandatory line, and simultaneously preserving an image of integrity. In a sense, it consists in a performative compliance with an official narrative which is inwardly rejected. Ketman is therefore a kind of mask that allows the wearer to fit in, and thereafter to be free to believe what he pleases in the privacy of his own head. The Covid face masks enabled a literal public exhibition of this form of obedience, an actual physical mask that compromised the wearers so that his compliance had a visible aspect, while he remained entitled to his own private thoughts.

The practitioner of Ketman seeks at all times to send out mixed signals, to imply dissidence without going too far to alarm the regime. This became easy since the 'regs' were mainly directed at phantoms, so that it was possible to comply while knowing 'in your heart' that the pandemic was a hoax, taking the 'rules' with a grain of salt, while not getting worked up about the implications of the big picture. We shall probably never know how many of those who appeared to be devout Branch Covidians were actually hiding their scepticism behind their masks. The controllers didn't seem to mind so long as these patsies continued to wear them.

As we have seen, the 'regs' were directed against the healthy and well, rather than the infected or ill, a ploy to deem everyone ill until proven well (next to impossible in the sense of 'getting a clean bill of health'). Everyone therefore remained 'guilty' until the trial that never started, but moved inexorably into the future, like the end of a rainbow 'moving' across a vast plain. Bizarrely, this ostensible injustice paradoxically enabled people to feel free to observe the laws and 'regs' in the knowledge that they were not serious, but part of a 'game', which in retrospect reveals itself as a massive confidence trick. There were no

laws or 'regs' about coughing or sneezing or sniffling in public places, no prohibitions on being in public while exhibiting any of these symptoms, no regs
about carrying handkerchiefs in your pocket or nasal sprays in your handbag.
People were urged, by way of a public mantra, to 'stay home, stay safe', but
nobody cared about ensuring that the unwell did so on account of being unwell
rather than for the same stupid reason as the well. The implicit presumption of
all 'regs' was that virtually no one had yet become ill (which, as it happened,
was broadly the case), and at no point did this emphasis seem to change or
abate. It didn't matter: wellness had implicitly been declared a dangerous condition, and that was sufficient to keep the 'game' going.*

Covid was a pandemic not characterised by symptoms, but overwhelmingly
by symbols. The well, not the sick, were targeted, to the extent that the most
emphasised 'symptom' of Covid was having no symptoms — i.e., being asymptomatic. The arcane and absurd 'regs' about wearing masks in restaurants (only
while standing up or walking across a floor space) were clearly directed at the
healthy, and had no function but, it seemed, a twisted form of satire. What was
mandatory was actually the semiology, which had no purpose other than for
show, which is to say that Ketman became obligatory: everyone was obliged to
dissemble and pretend belief in things that made no objective sense, but they
did so because the 'regs' said they must. The public was nudged and coaxed
and — if resisting — coerced into a condition of KETMAN-19, as though what
was invited was not a state of vigilance but of pretence. You could walk around
in public places all day and never meet, see or hear about a person who was
actually ill.

In this regimen or scenario, there was minimal room for equivocation or
objection, and the constructed lintel for tolerance was extremely low. The central
trick of reversal, though easy to describe, remained strangely remote from detec-
tion, due to some of the quirks of reportage and discussion that we have dealt
with in previous articles/chapters.

But there were also, at the same time, coercive mechanisms directed against
Ketman of the old kind — i.e., against blatantly behaving as though it was obviously a hoax, while paying lip-service to the 'pandemic' or 'measures'. The
imperative of maintaining the fiction of the 'pandemic' made it vital to keep
people in a state of inactivity, so as to maintain the atmosphere of emergency.
Hardware stores, for example, could remain open but were required to close off

---

* Recently, in the course of editing this chapter for publication, five years from the epicentre of the
'pandemic', someone sent me a video just recently taken at the entrance to one of the bigger Irish
hospitals, which was — in mid-March — overwhelmed by flu sufferers. In the video of the entrance,
you could hear a voice on a tannoy saying, *'Do not come into the hospital if you are ill!'* Funny, but also
telling. it struck me that no one had thought of having such an announcement during the 'pandemic', in large part because the hospitals were empty, but also because someone being ill was the last
thing anyone seemed to think of.

the parts of their stores that sold carpet, flooring, furniture, garden supplies, and paint. Food stores, likewise, were permitted to remain open but only for the sale of groceries, medical supplies, or items necessary to maintain the safety, sanitation, and basic operation of residences. The 'regs' prohibiting people travelling between their habitual residences and holiday homes made no health-related sense either, the point being purely to create an atmosphere of ghostly quietude on roads, motorways and other public spaces. People were arrested or fined for having family picnics on isolated, deserted beaches, obviously for the sole purpose of avoiding an impression being given that any location was safe, when in fact pretty much *any* place was safe. To see someone painting a gate, having a picnic, or arriving from some great distance to their holiday home, would have broken the spell and endangered the trance.

The nature of the required demeanour to be adopted in the face of the 'pandemic' was such as immediately to announce the compliance of the complier and the dissidence of the denier. This provided a visibility of obedience which functioned to minimise opportunities for 'traditional' Ketman. In fact, here, in a sense, each individual was invited to eschew Ketman by dissembling against his own 'innocence'. The highly visible nature of the 'measures' — masks, 'social distancing', hand sanitising, et cetera — called for a constant public avowal of obedience. Minds were divided not on the basis of outward compliance and inward dissent but on the question of the willingness to 'play'. There was no means of dissenting without standing out, no sneaky withholding of acquiescence, no opting out without consequences. This provided a mechanism that would have been unavailable in previous totalitarian models, whereby the fundamental 'article of faith' — here, belief in the primary ideological 'virus', in the 'pandemic' — became secondary or actually unimportant. Provided someone was obeying the 'regs', even though these were directed at the absurdity of indicting wellness rather than sickness, he could avoid becoming a 'person of interest'. It wasn't as if people needed to go around hiding their symptoms — coughing, sniffling, et cetera (sneezing was said not to be a symptom of Covid!) — they were simply required to show that they were accepting of the mandates, which had nothing to do with actual illness. This strategy, very cleverly, removed the most important aspects of the matter — did the virus actually exist?/ was this actually a pandemic? — out of the range of immediate public scrutiny. It was, in a sense, a gigantic exercise in dissembling, and therefore of a kind of reverse Ketman. Not only was no one required to conceal illness, but neither was anyone even required to believe in the 'virus'. Compliance was confined to an earlier compartment of willingness to 'serve the common good' by playing the 'game'. There is no knowing how many of those who wore masks, socially distanced, and excoriated their neighbours for laxness under these and other headings, knew perfectly well that the 'pandemic' was a colossal scam, but, by taking the offered opportunity to exercise a form of reverse-Ketman, managed to keep themselves out of danger, participating in the 'game' but without investing in its inner logic.

In a sense, in these conditions, the old style of Ketman became impossible for the Covid dissident, because there was no escaping the reach of the laws and, being cast out as a 'spoilsport', he had no 'audience' on whom to impress the virtues of dissent. On the contrary, the culture bore down upon the dissenter and tried to break his spirit by compelling him to accept the legitimacy and logic of the 'game'. He, the 'spoilsport' was depicted as a moral degenerate, while the scrupulous complier was hailed a hero, while really behaving as a spineless masochist. But it must also be noted that the main reason why there was minimal recourse to conventional Ketman was that so many of the minority who dissented from what was happening were prepared to speak out regardless — not by dint of any tenderness or decency on the part of those imposing this newly hatched tyranny, but because they had confidence in the beliefs which they — and so many of those who had now fallen silent — had inherited and rehearsed all down the years of their lives. Believing themselves still to inhabit the (as far as we knew) greatest civilisation the world had ever seen, the dissenters and dissidents said 'No, we're not doing it!' And then, assailed by all manner of threat and intimidation — from mask mandates to rumblings about mandatory vaccines — stood their ground. We who opted to resist went to court and were predictably rebuffed and insulted by purchased judges, but did not give up. We were smeared and pilloried by some of the lowest forms of life on the planet, but we did not yield. We spoke the truth and spoke it loud. KETMAN-19 was the last thing on our minds. Perhaps because things had not (yet) got to the pitch of 1930s Stalinism, it took some among us time to realise the enormity and evil of what was happening, but all of us seemed to sense that, once it reached that pitch, it would be too late to dissent. With the greatest of respect to Milosz, we understood that, if we wished to avoid our societies and countries descending to the depths of the Soviet Union under Stalin, we needed to stand and speak up at an early moment, and to stay standing as long as necessary, until death did us dispense with. This we continue to do, and will do for as long as it takes, or until the Lord takes us, whichever may be sooner.

From all this we can observe that, under the novel genre of totalitarianism, the nature of Ketman acquires a symbiotic quality. Totalitarian power of the contemporary kind works in both directions: tyrants bearing down on the tyrannised, but also in the opposite direction as a kind of extended affirmation or permission from the subjugated, without which, paradoxically, the regime would be unable to function or continue for long. Thus, there is a requirement for two forms of Ketman — that of the Regime, seeking to bully and coerce its victims but in a manner that avoids an excess of overt force, and that of the victims seeking to deny their total obedience or state of subjugation by engaging with the tyranny in something like a mode of 'false play'. All this appears somehow to have been built into this newest form of totalitarianism.

Moral blackmail is the mainstay tool of the official Ketman, and avoidance the instrument of the victims who wish to deny this description of themselves. The two work in harmony because both the regime and its victims desire the same outcome, i.e., a denial of the true conditions to which the population had been reduced.

We see this condition of cultural schizophrenia writ large in 'modern' Ireland now. It is not impossible (though unlikely) that the judges who caused a young Irish teacher, Enoch Burke, to be jailed for more than 500 days for refusing to call a young male pupil 'they', and subsequently to seize his life savings in 'fines', might be daily mass-goers, or admirers of the Dalai Lama. By the same token, an occasional perusal of the contents of the output of 'conservative' columnists will confirm that, here too, these are, and feel, permitted to continue with their conspicuous 'conservatism' provided they remain sound on the big questions — for example, being 'pro-life' but refraining from calling bioterrorism by its name, or worrying about 'assisted dying'; while dismissing interest in excess deaths and other 'conspiracy theories'. Thus, many supposedly oppositional voices are able to survive in the mainstream even in times like these, avoiding giving offence to the batshit crazy 'progressive' regime of the day, while also reassuring their followers and supporters that they remain onside for the 'conservative' agenda. The very idea, of course, is utterly absurd, for what is 'conservatism' in a time when reality is already turned upside down? The conserving of madness — the ultimate triumph of totalitarianism.

It is therefore with an explosive sense of irony that we might read such a passage as this from *The Captive Mind* (addressing the circumstances of Paris, 1951, but equally fitting to the mood and circumstance of a citizen of Ireland visiting, perhaps, the republic of Hungary, a quarter of the way into the twenty-first century):

'A visitor from the Imperium is shocked on coming to the West. In his contacts with others, beginning with porters or taxi drivers, he encounters no resistance. The people he meets are completely relaxed. They lack that internal concentration which betrays itself in a lowered head or in restlessly moving eyes. They say whatever words come to their tongues; they laugh aloud. Is it possible that human relations can be so direct?

'The inhabitants of Western countries little realize that millions of their fellow-men, who seem superficially more or less similar to them, live in a world as fantastic as that of the men from Mars. They are unaware of the perspectives on human nature that Ketman opens. Life in constant internal tension develops talents which are latent in man. He does not even suspect to what heights of cleverness and psychological perspicacity he can rise when he is cornered and must either be skilful or perish. The survival of those best adapted to mental acrobatics creates a human type that has been rare until now. The necessities which drive men to Ketman sharpen the intellect.'

Now, twenty years after the death of Czeslaw Milosz, these symptoms and conditions have arrived unannounced in the Western countries, having largely disappeared from the former Soviet bloc. Now, the people of the former Free World are the ones with the lowered heads and the restlessly moving eyes. No longer do we utter the words that hover on the tips of our tongues, but instead require to cogitate prohibitively before acknowledging a joke with our laughter. Daily we live with the internal tensions of having to second-guess each and every bystander before expressing an opinion. We have not yet become sufficiently adept at mental acrobatic or psychological gymnastics to acquit ourselves in the court of Ketman. But we are improving, and soon we shall put on shows of doublespeak that will make the diminishing ranks of the survivors of Stalinism gasp in wonder at our proficiency in the arts of dissimulation and evasion.

Those responsible for this developing dystopia will, of course, immediately begin issuing their rehearsed snorts of derision at the very idea of a comparison between either any historical event or George Orwell's dark vision and the egregious and unpardonable events of 2020. We cannot be serious! They, after all, were 'saving lives'. They forget that tyranny nearly always clothes itself in virtue, that the 'Party' in Orwell's fictional dystopia was also engaged in the selfless philanthropic work of improving its citizens. And yet, at the same time, it is possible to be sympathetic to their pleas of innocence on the grounds of the implausibility of the idea that anyone who had read Orwell's book — and who hadn't? — would be capable of becoming embroiled in the kinds of things that were done in innumerable countries claiming democratic status in those dark sunny days of March/April 2020. In other words, were not those who failed to lift the heavens with their roars of refusal almost as guilty as those with the actual blood of innocents on their hands?

This silence, and related questions, have been the most puzzling aspects of the Covid crime: how (for example) by, at the latest, May 1st 2020, any inhabitant of one of the multiple Western societies that had been washed in the futuristic predictions of seers like Orwell and Huxley could possibly find themselves uttering a single sentence suggestive of prior knowledge of such prophecies — never mind engaging in any resonant action in support of the emerging tyranny — without either freezing in self-disbelief or bursting out laughing at their own momentary myopia?

I turned 29 in the middle of the actual year 1984, and remember with extreme clarity the sense of superiority that accompanied the marking and celebration of that occasion. Western peoples had a vague idea that such things as

Orwell depicted could indeed happen — *but to other peoples in other, distant lands.* Something like the events he described might even have happened in Russia and the Soviet bloc, but that was because they were less civilised than us. Even if we could not — in necessary liberal humility — claim to be more 'civilised', we could certainly claim (couldn't we?) to be more knowing, having been forewarned by these writers whom we regarded with such respect and solemnity.

No, no, it was unthinkable. Not that we even deigned to think about it — perish the thought! — a few troublemakers and hysterics excepted.

Orwell's vision, in particular, by virtue of its constant undertone and descriptions of more than occasional outbreaks of violence, seemed especially remote. Think of those extraordinarily imagined scenes in the Ministry of Love, when Winston is waiting following his arrest, which read as though episodes from an extreme horror nightmare.

While Winston is waiting to be interrogated, Orwell describes in graphic detail the countenance of another prisoner who is brought into the room, sending 'a momentary chill through Winston'. The man is emaciated, his face that of 'a skull', the eyes 'filled with a murderous, unappeasable hatred of somebody or something'. The man, Winston realises, is dying of starvation. Another prisoner, overcome with pity, takes his life in his hands by trying to pass to the skull-faced man a grimy piece of bread he has secreted in a pocket of his overalls. A voice roars from the telescreen, and two guards, one an officer, enter the room. At a signal from the officer, his underling lets loose a savage blow to the face of the man who has offered his last piece of bread to the dying prisoner.

The force of it seemed almost to knock him clear of the floor. His body was flung across the cell and fetched up against the base of the lavatory seat. For a moment he lay as though stunned, with dark blood oozing from his mouth and nose. A very faint whimpering or squeaking, which seemed unconscious, came out of him. Then he rolled over and raised himself unsteadily on hands and knees. Amid a stream of blood and saliva, the two halves of a dental plate fell out of his mouth.

Nothing like that, it will be said, has happened in any Western country arising from the Covid episode or subsequent shifts in political culture (echo asks: *What shifts in political culture?*), and nor could it ever happen here, now; it is unthinkable. Totalitarianism is a matter of violence, of brutal repression, of industrially generated terror. Ergo: Orwell's vision has no relevance for us today.

But there are differing forms of violence, just as there are differing forms of pain. We need to be mindful of something about state coercion that has always been true, but is not obvious in the quotidian context: that its very existence is in the vast majority of cases sufficient to do the heavy lifting of coercion. With most people, even the ones who have seemed to be indomitable, the very capacity or exclusive entitlement of the state in the exercising of democratically sanctioned coercion — force, licensed violent force — is itself, in all but the rarest of cases, sufficient to break the will of the dissident or refusenik. It is rarely necessary to turn up the dial on the shock treatment more than once or twice in order for the fear of its potential to induce total submission in circumstances of complete deniability.

This issue has been a concealed element of the Covid crime. As Sally Minogue beautifully exposes in her Introduction to Orwell's novel, the two central relationships depicted in *Nineteen Eighty-Four* — between Winston and Julia and Winston and O'Brien, are both 'affairs of a sort' — both of his 'lovers' seeming to seek Winston's ultimate wellbeing, Julia through affection, O'Brien through torture; both 'relationships' starting with a meeting of eyes, and both operating at a level of intimacy Winston has not experienced before; both figures growing in his imagination as 'revolutionary comrades'. In fact, of the two, he is 'attracted' to O'Brien much more immediately than he is to Julia, whom at first he believes to be spying on him on behalf of the Thought Police, and whom he quickly begins to forget about when his experience of grief and pain starts to escalate.

Although Orwell does not imply the term, there is an intimation in Winston's relationship and interactions with O'Brien of something that was to surface as a strong subtext of the Covid coercion in 2020: a kind of sadomasochistic insinuation in which Winston's 'treatment' by O'Brien consists in an alternating of torture and morphine, a process in which he — superficially, perversely — comes to trust and even love O'Brien: *He had never loved him so deeply as at this moment, and not merely because he had stopped the pain.*

This rather familiar syndrome seems to work off the imputed guilt of the suspect, and is perhaps a quality of the newer forms of tyranny, which have at their cores some perverted sense of the 'common good', in which the coercive authorities-without-authority purport to act not merely on behalf of power and the law, but also for the good of the suspect who has been led woefully astray. In this scenario, the jailer/torturer becomes, simultaneously, a reluctant administrator of state coercion and violence, and also a benign figure who administers punishment 'reluctantly' for the good of the victim. In this sense, the modern forms of totalitarianism differ from tyrannies involving an individual dictator, becoming a form of 'conspiracy' between the oppressors and the oppressed — indeed, a form of sadomasochistic intrigue in which both participants crave that which they experience, and the victim most of all.

I have recalled before how, in Dublin's Phoenix Park on May 25th, 2020, at the very height of the lockdown, the (exhibitionist homosexual) leader of the then Irish government, Leo Varadkar, was filmed participating in a picnic in the park and cavorting with his mates, at a time when picnics were forbidden by Varadkar's own government. There was afterwards what superficially seemed an attempt to explain this away by claiming, in a manner that would have made

Orwell chuckle dryly, that there had in fact been no ban on picnics, but this was almost certainly a way of twisting the dial a little further, for the real message had to do not merely with the power capacities of Varadkar's government but with a consciousness in the air that, in a certain sense, the public *liked* being treated in this contemptuous manner. The relationship being briefly exposed — almost in the manner of a stripper's tease — was that of 'master and subs'.

It is easy to forget, because of a lack of emphasis at the time, the kinds of things that happened in 2020: people being shunted out of public parks by police officers because they had paused to sit on a bench to enjoy the sunshine; maskless people being dragged out of trains and buses and into squad cars; drivers turned around on the road because their proffered rationales for being out driving fell short of the protocols; demonstrators being truncheoned in the street for daring to protest their right to freedom, or even for kneeling in prayer.

There were also the elderly people who died alone in nursing homes and other institutions, refused contact with their most beloved family members. Was this not violence? Was this not also a total denial of mercy? In what sense can the perpetrators of these obscenities claim to be better than the thugs imagined by George Orwell?

And what about premeditated killing by poison injection? Might we call this manslaughter? Democide? Genocide? Well, in Ireland, the level of excess deaths has this year [2024] increased to 19 per cent, bringing to approximately 20,000 the number of additional deaths in the past 46 months — i.e., multiple orders of magnitude over and above what would have been regarded as a serious health crisis just five years ago. Meanwhile, Ed Dowd's latest international research indicates that one in five people worldwide who took any kind of (alleged) Covid vaccine has been adversely affected. Approximately five billion people on the planet accepted a vaccine of some sort. Applying the scale of the death rate in the United States to the wider world, Dowd estimates that deaths from these injections worldwide is somewhere between 7.3 million and 15 million. By the same exercise in measurement, disabilities arising directly from the injections are estimated at between 29 to 60 million globally, and sundry forms of injury at between 500 million and 900 million. For the avoidance of doubt, all these people received at least one of some kind of Covid-related injection; most are of working age.

Might we call this genocide? The legal definition of genocide is the committing of acts with the intention to destroy a people. Maybe the level of slaughter has not yet reached the level of a demonstrable attempt to obliterate a particular population, but overall, it amounts to a level of homicide that has no parallel since WWII — which ended just four years before Orwell's most famous book was published.

Another phenomenon an attentive younger reader of 2024 might raise an eyebrow to in *Nineteen Eighty-Four* is snitching: citizens taking it upon themselves to report to the authorities any infractions against the narrative, the 'measures' or the Regime. While waiting to be tortured and reconstructed in the Ministry of Love, Winston runs into a colleague called Parsons whom he has known as a grovelling lickspittle of the Party and the regime. He asks Parsons if he is 'guilty', and Parson replies, *'Of course I am guilty. You don't think the Party would arrest an innocent man, do you?'* His crime, he relates, is that he has uttered the ejaculation *'Down with Big Brother'* in the course of a dream. *'Thoughtcrime is a dreadful thing, old man,'* he elaborates. *'It's insidious. It can get hold of you without your even knowing it. Do you know how it got hold of me? In my sleep.'*

Luckily, his six-year-old daughter, who overheard this slumberous outburst while listening at the keyhole, immediately reported the incident to the patrols. *'Pretty smart for a nipper of six, eh? I don't bear her any grudge for it. In fact, I'm proud of her. It shows I brought her up in the right spirit, anyway.'*

If this seems funny or cartoonish — *a reductio ad absurdum?* — let us not forget some of the things that happened in our 'modern', self-satisfied 'democratic' 'republics' in the early years of the Covid crime. I have not been able to discover with certainty if Ireland had a formal 'snitch line' during the Covid period, although there is evidence that such may well have existed. One of the tiny number of dissident voices of formal Irish political opposition raised against the escalating tyranny of the past 56 months is that of Tipperary TD, Mattie McGrath, whom I have cited previously in a different context. In a debate on the Health and Criminal Justice (Covid-19) (Amendment) (No. 2) Bill 2021 (Second Stage), an appalled McGrath told Dáil Éireann — the lower house of the Irish parliament (Oireachtas) — on December 3rd, 2021, that he had heard members of that very House demanding the introduction of snitch lines. 'That has come from parties I am very surprised with. They are looking for people to report on people and so on. We are dividing society and creating an apartheid, and it is totally wrong.'

In late March 2020, such a 'snitch line' had been established in London, and citizens were invited to report observations or concerns about 'non-essential businesses that aren't closed, activities at closed outdoor structures including playgrounds, multi-use courts and skate parks, residents gathering in large groups, and individuals not following self-isolation orders.'

A month later, the *Guardian* was reporting that the police had received 194,000 calls to the line. A female deputy chief constable was reported as saying that the 'troublesome spots' included 'beaches and rural communities in the countryside where people want to walk.'

In America, too, the business of informing was proving very popular. Between March 23rd and April 8th, 2020, a dedicated 'tip line' in Kentucky received roughly 30,000 calls from people concerned about the alleged social-distancing breaches of individuals and businesses. In mid-April 2020, the Mayor of New York, Bill de Blasio, was reported in the *Washington Times* calling on

THE ABOLITION OF REALITY 597

people to turn in neighbours who failed to follow social distancing rules, encouraging them to text photos of violators and report their location to a government hotline. Tucker Carlson responded on his Fox News programme: 'The mayor of New York . . . has asked all eight million New Yorkers to become informers, to snitch on their neighbours. Sounds a lot like East Germany actually, except now everyone has a smartphone.'

These levels of abuse of long-held understandings of proper civil behaviour had profound effects on social solidarity and neighbourliness carrying consequences which remain incalculable for our cultures. It was as though the programming of the human being in culture was being rewritten to reverse some of the most fundamental lessons we had learned as children — *Don't be a squealer* or *a stool pigeon!* — turning it overnight into its direct opposite. This resonates with one of the most scarifying elements of Orwell's recounting of the misadventures of Winston Smith, when O'Brien demands that he rethink his perception that 2 + 2 = 4.

We remember that scene from the book as stretching credulity. It is unthinkable — is it not? — that anyone could become confused as to the answer to this most rudimentary of arithmetic conundrums. A child could answer it. This is to miss Mr Orwell's point, which is that this knowledge is not achieved in the first place by reason, but learned by rote as part of our two-times tables. In this sense, it is one of the most foundational pieces of knowledge we glean as little schoolchildren. Having received it in this way, it becomes almost an article of faith, a foundational calculation upon which all others are constructed. As long as such knowledge remains approved, there is no issue; when the Regime decides that the answer '5' would be better, everything changes.

Orwell's point is that it is possible, by the use of propaganda and fear, to undo even the most rudimentary elements of our knowledge of the world.

The question arises in the course of Winston's interrogation because he has written in his diary: *'Freedom is the freedom to say that two plus two equals four'*.

O'Brien holds up his left hand to Winston, with the thumb folded under and the four digits visible. 'How many fingers am I holding up, Winston?'

'Four.'

'And if the Party says it is not four but five, then how many?'

'Four.'

Orwell continues:

The word ended in a gasp of pain. The needle on the dial had gone up to fifty-five.

This, as Sally Minogue writes in her Introduction, 'is the black heart of the novel.'

As O'Brien explains to Winston: 'Obedience is not enough. Unless he is suffering, how can you be sure that he is obeying your will and not his own? Power is in inflicting pain and humiliation.'

This, obviously, couldn't happen here? Or could it? How 'obvious', really, is the notion that it couldn't? As 'obvious' as once was the belief that human rights were inalienable? What if it were suggested that even worse things are happening, and that the vast majority of observers — even many who have passed with honours examinations in which their comprehensive knowledge of George Orwell's work was a vital factor — seem not to see this?

What about Enoch Burke, the Irish teacher who, at the time of writing, has already spent going on for 500 days in an Irish jail because he refused to address a pupil as 'they'? Is not the idea that there are two sexes — men and women, boys and girls — not at least as fundamental as the adding of two and two?

Oh no! goes up the Pavlovian shout: *he was jailed not for that reason but because he refused to 'purge his contempt' for which he was convicted on the grounds that he refused to stop attending at the school from which he had been suspended.*

Yes, and all of that is as useful as a handful of boiled snow without it being noted that he was suspended in the first place for declining to be told what he must say: *that the boy standing in front of him is in 'actuality' a girl.*

In other words, metaphorically and symbolically, Enoch Burke refused to say that two and two equals five.

Yes, O'Brien interjects helpfully: *'Imposing the will of the Party is easier when people do not understand it.'*

'The Party is not interested in the overt act; the thought is all we care about. We do not merely destroy our enemies; we change them.'

And again:

'You are a flaw in the pattern, Winston. You are a stain that must be wiped out. . . . When finally you surrender to us, it must be of your own free will. We do not destroy the heretic because he resists us; so long as he resists us we will never destroy him. We convert him, we capture his inner mind; we reshape him. We burn all evil and all illusion out of him; we bring him over to our side, not in appearance, but genuinely, heart and soul.'

This is what is happening, and understanding this is so vital to the future that we must make no mistake about it. This is the meaning of the attempt to break a brave and honest man like Enoch Burke.

'Power,' O'Brien explains to Winston, 'is in inflicting pain and humiliation. Power is in tearing human minds to pieces and in putting them together again in new shapes of your own choosing. Do you begin to see, then, what kind of world we are creating? It is the exact opposite of the stupid hedonistic Utopias that the old reformers imagined. A world of fear and treachery and torment, a world of trampling and being trampled upon, a world which will grow not less but more merciless as it refines itself. Progress in our time will be progress towards more pain. The old civilisations claimed that they were founded on love or justice. Ours is founded upon hatred. In our world there will be no emotions except fear, rage, triumph and self-abasement. Everything else we shall destroy — everything.'

There are resonances here with Michael Esfeld's descriptions of the undertows of the Covid episode as the initiating event in a new form of totalitarianism, which as we have seen is multi-faceted and hydra-headed, in which the purpose is not ideological for the sake of ideology, but purely a code, a software, by which to purvey a tyranny that is its own end-product and exists purely for its own sake. It can be either fascist or communist or both at the same time, but ultimately it is both and neither, because these categories are redundant and otiose, being superseded by the imperative to control for control's sake.

Who, having paid attention to the world and its devolution in the past 56 months, could assert now that this description of 'the future' from the mouth of O'Brien, is not the design of those who baselessly claim authority over us?

'We have cut the links between child and parent, and between man and man, and between man and woman. No one dares trust a wife or a child or a friend any longer. But in the future there will be no wives and no friends. Children will be taken from their mothers at birth, as one takes eggs from a hen. The sex instinct will be eradicated. Procreation will be an annual formality like the renewal of a ration card. We shall abolish the orgasm. Our neurologists are at work upon it now. There will be no loyalty, except loyalty towards the Party. There will be no love, except the love of Big Brother. There will be no laughter, except the laugh of triumph over a defeated enemy. There will be no art, no literature, no science. When we are omnipotent we shall have no more need of science. There will be no distinction between beauty and ugliness. There will be no curiosity, no enjoyment of the process of life. All competing pleasures will be destroyed. But always — do not forget this, Winston — always there will be the intoxication of power, constantly increasing and constantly growing subtler. Always, at every moment, there will be the thrill of victory, the sensation of trampling on an enemy who is helpless. If you want a picture of the future, imagine a boot stamping on a human face — for ever.'

This, when it is even in danger of occurring, even its remote possibility, ought to be news.

But there is a strange dislocation concerning the events of 2020, arising from the fact that they are not reported or remarked upon by our society in the ways that events of their magnitude would normally merit. This is because the media were essentially paid for (*inter alia*) not mentioning them, the 'sentries' on our freedoms bought off for maintaining silence about criminal activity, for failing to give evidence, for displaying loyalty to the oath of *omertà* that nowadays governs virtually all 'public' matters in our one free societies.

This amounts to a special kind of violence, because it adds to the original evil the crime of denial, implying not merely that the atrocity in question did not occur but that it *could not have occurred*, that, if it is 'remembered' by anyone, that memory is false and therefore a delusion or a lie cooked up in the disturbed mind of the individual, or acquired via channels spreading 'disinformation' on the (as yet) inadequately censored internet. This is an obscenity beyond anything that Orwell describes, for at least those dragged into the Ministry of Love, and thence into Room 101, were given truthful accounts of what was happening to them, as well as of its aims and purposes, and, like Winston Smith, given time to put their affairs in order before being shot in the back of the neck.

APPENDICES

INTERVIEWS WITH DR MATTIAS DESMET

TRUTH SPEECH IN A TIME OF INDUSTRIALISED LIES

12-06-2022

DR MATTIAS DESMET is a professor of clinical psychology at Ghent University (Belgium) and a practising psychoanalytic psychotherapist. His previous books include *The Pursuit of Objectivity in Psychology* and *Lacan's Logic of Subjectivity: A Walk on the Graph of Desire*. Professor Desmet is the author of over one hundred peer-reviewed academic papers. In 2018, he received the Evidence-Based Psychoanalytic Case Study Prize of the Association for Psychoanalytic Psychotherapy, and in 2019, he received the Wim Trijsburg Prize of the Dutch Association of Psychotherapy.

The interview opens with John Waters introducing Desmet's recently published book, *The Psychology of Totalitarianism*.

'It's an incredible book, and, for anyone who's been listening to or watching his interviews, it'll probably be quite a surprising book, because it really expands the thread of what he was talking about — mass formation, totalitarianism — in these interviews, into a much broader frame, and really elucidates the context, and maybe even the destination of all this, and perhaps then, furthermore, what we need to start thinking of doing about it.'

John Waters: This is not the kind of book you might expect. It's not a clinical book. It's much more than that. It's not even a psychology book. It's not a book about psychology. It's a book about pretty much the moment we're in and about something that has been deeply hidden, perhaps, in our lifetimes, in our culture — that we've heard about before, going back. . . . You've talked many times in your interviews about Hannah Arendt and Gustave Le Bon, and so on, and the mechanics, as it were, of mass formation, as you call it. And we'll get into that in a little bit. But this book, really, seeks to put all this in a context that is, I think, broader than anything we've seen before, in that it really brings Arendt's and Le Bon's thinking into the present moment, and particularly in the context of the Covid-19 . . . whatever we call it — 'situation'. So, to begin with, I'd like to ask— where do you come from into this subject? How did you arrive at this subject? How did you begin to formulate ideas about this . . . general topic, first of all, and more broadly? Was it the Covid-19 thing that triggered it, or had it been something that you had been pursuing in your own thinking for some time?

Mattias Desmet: Yes, well, I started my academic career in 2003, I think, and I was immediately fascinated by the fact that most publicised research findings were false, as [Dr] John Ioannidis articulated it in the title of one of his articles. Most publicised research findings are false. I started to do academic research in the field of psychology, and I immediately had a dissatisfaction with the research methods used there. And I asked my professor for permission to research the research methods themselves. And four years late, I presented a PhD in which I claimed that most research methods in psychology cannot other than lead to useless results. And from there, I started to explore research in other domains as well, and in 2005, there was a happy coincidence. In 2005, the so-called 'replication crisis' started in the sciences, which revealed that over 85 per cent of the published research articles in domains such as the medical sciences could not be reproduced, which actually means that they lack any scientific validity. And I started to write a small book, which you referred to in your intro-duction, *The Pursuit of Objectivity in Psychology*, in which I tried to show in as concrete a way as possible why most research methods cannot yield valid results, or lead to reliable conclusions. And I started to talk about this at all kinds of scientific meetings, and to my surprise, although the examples that I was giving were very concrete, and really showed in a very concrete way what the problem was with most research methods, most of my colleagues refused to open their eyes, and to the contrary they became angry. And it was at that moment that I started to be interested in the question as to how it's possible that people can continue to believe in absurd theories, even when confronted with clear-cut proof that what they believe in *is* absurd. And that brought me to the topic of mass formation. So the first part of my academic career — I have a masters in clinical psychology, but in my PhD, I also got a master's in statistics. In the first part of my academic career I was constantly involved in statistical research, in statistical questions, and at the same time, I was also writing and publishing about more conceptual things, such as Lacanian psychoanalysis and other more conceptual theories. But my focus in the first part of my career was on statistics, and on the validity of research methods. And because I noticed that no matter how concretely and clearly you show that certain research methods are completely absurd, people refused to open their eyes and see why these methods were absurd, I started to try to focus on the question: what could make people so blind? And that's how I entered the field of mass psychology. I noticed that the only phenomenon, or the only thing that can explain why people in certain situations become radically blind to everything that goes against their own beliefs — or one of the major things that could explain that — is the phenomenon of mass formation. And somewhere back in 2017, I think, I started to lecture on this phenomenon of mass formation, and all kinds of other group dynamics as well. And when the corona crisis set in, I immediately had a feeling that the statistics were wrong. And I started to study the statistics a little bit — all the statistics about mortality rates of the virus, and I immediately had the impression that, look, these statistics are dramatically overestimating the dangerousness of the virus. And together with me — very remarkable — John Ioannidis of Stanford also claimed that most statistics in the crisis were blatantly wrong. And [this was] John Ioannidis, who had been one of the major scholars investigating the replication crisis in the sciences fifteen years before. And in my opinion, by the end of May 2020, this was actually proven beyond doubt. The initial models on which the entire corona measures were based were the models of Imperial College in London, and these models predicted that, in a small country such as Sweden, over 60,000 people would die if the country didn't go into lockdown. And the country *didn't* go into lockdown, and by the end of May 2020, about 6,000 people had died, and to arrive at that figure, we had to count in a very 'enthusiastic' way — that's what they often say. So, at that moment, it was clear for everyone who wanted to see it that the initial models dramatically overrated the mortality of the virus.

From the first week of the crisis, I started to speak out in the public space. I wrote an opinion paper in the first week of the crisis, and the title of the paper was 'The Fear of the Virus is More Dangerous Than the Virus Itself'. And I had exactly the same impressions during the crisis as during my PhD, when I tried to show people what the problems with the research methods were — namely, no matter how concretely or how clearly I could show that the statistics that were used in the crisis were wrong, it seemed that nobody wanted to see it. And from then on, I changed my focus, and I decided to try to make people aware of the psychological processes that were going on in society — in other words, of the huge, large-scale phenomenon of mass formation that was going on in our society during the corona crisis.

JW: Yes. And, bringing all those things together, as you do in the book, you identify some kind of almost what I might call a pathology within science, of what has become more like scientism, and the way it permeates the world, a way of thinking that seems to be absolute, and is taken as absolute, that it is something for experts, that lay people cannot have an opinion on it, or express an opinion about it. So this kind of traps humanity in a certain mind-frame which they have no control over, or indeed no authority over. And this is then harnessed in a way that can actually bear down upon them. But there's a really interesting — to go into this thing about science, which really fascinates me — there's an amazing, to me, quote in the very first chapter in the book, about science, the nature of science: you say, 'Most are of the opinion that science consists of making dry, logical connections between directly observable facts. However, science is, in fact, characterised by empathy, a resonant affinity between the observer and the phenomenon under investigation. As such, science stumbles on a noble and mysterious essence that escapes logic and explanation, and which can be explained only in the language of poetry and metaphor.' Like, that's an amazing insight, and I don't entirely understand it. But I have a feeling, as it were, an 'empathy' that it's somewhere . . . From my own experience of reading science and listening to scientists, there's always something missing, always something that they're trying to align to keep certain paths going. I wonder, like — 'empathy' — in what sense can this . . . because it seems such a counter-intuitive idea in the context of the rationalist age that we live in, that something to do with science could have anything to do with empathy, or that empathy might be a useful tool of apprehending what a scientific proposition might mean?

MD: Yes, yes, yes, yes. Well, you know, on the one hand, you could see science as a kind of an accumulation of rational knowledge. That's what science does. Science studies the world in a rational way, and throughout the last few centuries, you've seen this accumulation of rational knowledge about a set of phenomena. So that's true. Science is an accumulation of rational knowledge, to a certain extent. But at the same time, science is also a *process* through which, while scientists are following logic and rational understanding, they stumble on the limit of rational understanding. All major scientists have concluded that that part of reality — and I will quote René Thom, one of the most famous mathematicians of the twentieth century, literally — René Thom said: 'This part of reality that can be understood in a rational way is extremely limited, and the rest of reality' — he said — 'we can only know by empathically resonating with it.' And you know, it took me until I was about 35 years old before I really started to understand that. Indeed, what we call 'the facts' — nature around us, everything around us — essentially behaves in an irrational way. And I suddenly understood that while I was studying systems theory, because I was trying to understand the basis of the measurement problems in the sciences, and suddenly I stumbled on this amazing insight — that if you look at a complex and dynamical system, which is like most phenomena in nature, you will see that intrinsically they behave in an irrational way. In a paradoxical way, systems theory proved in a strictly rational way that complex dynamical systems are irrational — literally, that they behave as irrational numbers. That, for instance, they show no periodicity in their behaviour. They never repeat the same pattern, for instance. And even with a formula which determines these systems in your hand you will never be able to predict how they will behave, not one second beforehand. So, nature — the core of nature — escapes rational understanding. And that was an insight so profound for me that I think it changed my life, or the direction of my life. That's also what Niels Bohr, the famous physicist, who studied elementary particles, meant when he said, 'When it comes to atoms, language can only be used as poetry.' And he was dead serious when he said that. He really meant that the behaviour of elementary particles — subatomic particles — is so absurd, and can never be grasped by any rational theory, any logical theory, that only poetry can resonate with it. That only through poetry you can understand something, or you can grasp something of the fundamentally strange and irrational behaviour of elementary particles. And, that so, we feel a kind of tension between two kinds of knowing, two kinds of knowledge. On the one hand, there is a rational knowledge, a logical knowledge; on the other hand, there is a knowledge that is not really rational, but that is much more a resonating knowledge. I think you could compare it to a craftsman, to craftsmanship: When someone is trained as a craftsman — in the beginning, he can learn this craft in a rational way. Someone can teach him the procedures he should use to produce a certain object, for instance, and that's the rational stage of the education, of the training. But, after a while, as the training continues, and the student is getting better, slowly he will start to have a certain feeling with what he is doing. He will *feel* what he is doing, and that's when he will really become a craftsman. In Japan, there is a wonderful proverb that says: 'First you have to protect the rules of an art for a long time, and then you have to break them and leave them behind.' So the first stage is always a rational stage, but the goal, the purpose, of this rational stage, this rational understanding, is that it should lead to a different kind of knowledge, a much more resonating kind of knowledge, a kind of knowledge that *feels* the knowledge. And the ancient Greeks also had a specific word to indicate this kind of knowledge: they called it 'tekhnê', which is a kind of technical knowledge that is more than technical and rational knowledge, which has to do with a *feeling* towards a certain object that transcends any logical and rational understanding. And the more you understand that, the better you know that the entire project of the tradition of Enlightenment — namely to accumulate rational understanding, and this entire belief of the tradition of enlightenment — that rational understanding should be the basis of human living together, and of human existence, is an illusion. Rational understanding is extremely volatile — it changes all the time. You can never use rational understanding as the basis for our existence, as the basis for the organisation of society. That's impossible. If you try to use rational understanding as the basis to organise human living together, you will end up in an ever-varying, always-changing, chaotic set of rules, which will destroy ultimately all humanity and society, and that's exactly what happens in a totalitarian system. That's exactly the problem of a totalitarian system, because it tries to rely on a kind of pseudo-rational ideology, which, in the end, creates a chaotic state in which all humanity is destroyed.

JW: Yes. It's a very beautiful thesis, and it does, obviously, resonate with what's happening now, in terms of offering a critique and maybe an alternative way of seeing the world, which would be at least a start. However, it also appears in this moment, in the prism we have created for ourselves, of rational thinking — of pseudo-rational thinking, as you would see it — that it seems to describe a parallel universe. It seems to describe something that is unattainable, because our idea, encroachingly in our cultures, our societies, is that this rational form of science is absolute, and unassailable, and non-negotiable, and that it is actually naturalistic; it is actually organic; it is actually 'the truth' — it is reality — and therefore that the best you can do, in a certain sense, is to scratch at the knees of this model, with this different kind or thinking. Because it's almost impossible to imagine a trajectory into the future in which we would correct the present thrust. Is that an excessively pessimistic view, or do you think there are signs that we might be on the verge of . . . I know that we're jumping to the end of the discussion here, but I think that, before we go back, it's important to set out this, because it's a very beautiful part of your book and the whole thesis that you've expressed about this is really, really — I think — hopeful, and enlightening for people.

MD: Yes, well, I think that what you witness now is the emergence of a technocratic system, a technocratic society, which is no longer led by democratically elected politicians but by technical experts. We've witnessed the emergence of such a society and we very soon will witness the collapse of this society. And in this period, I think it will become clear to everyone that rational knowledge is highly relative, that you can never use it as the guiding principle in society. And then, now the democratic leaders are replaced by technical leaders — you've seen it actually during the corona crisis, where the true leaders of society were no longer the politicians, but the experts. And when the experts said we should do this or that to prevent the spread of the virus, then the politicians could only obey because, if they would go against the experts, they could be held responsible for the deaths of everyone who died of the virus — just because they had this hubris to think that they knew better what the virus could do, than the experts.

In Belgium, we have this new committee of experts now which will have to guide us through the emergent economic crisis. And it will be the same story, of course. If the economic experts think that we should take this or that measure to counter the economic crisis, what politician will pretend that he knows better than the experts what they have to do? Of course, he *might* know it better, but in our current view of man in the world, it's just logical that society should be led by technocratic experts. I think that as soon as we adopted this mechanistic, rationalist view of man in the world, believing that the entire universe is a kind of material machine that functions according to the laws of mechanics, and that it can be understood and described in a strictly rational way — as soon as you take this as your starting point, as soon as you start from this view of man in the world, the logical conclusion is that the technical expert, who knows the material machine, should lead society. Why not? 'Why would you ask a democratically elected politician, a politician that is elected by the crowd, who is stupid and irrational, why would you believe that such a politician would be the best leader when we are confronted with a crisis — an economic crisis, or no matter what crisis?' What we are facing now is the ultimate and logical consequence of this mechanist, rationalist view of man in the world that started to become dominant from the sixteenth century onwards. Now we see the logical conclusion, namely: we should leave the leadership of society in the hands of technical experts who have the rational knowledge of how to repair the machine, so to speak. And now, at this moment, at the same time, we will see that this system will fail. We've seen it in the corona crisis, actually, that it's doomed to fail ultimately, but we will see it even clearer as it continues. And then, I think that, after that period, we will be ready for a new type of leader, I think, a new type of leader who will no longer pretend that he can lead society on the basis of rationalist understanding, but who went through a long period of rational training and who could then transcend his rational understanding, and arrive at something that the ancient Greeks called 'truth speech'. My next book will be about truth-speech — I'm writing it now — about the contrast between indoctrination and propaganda on the one hand, and truth-speech on the other hand. The ancient Greeks distinguished between four kinds of truth-speech: prophecy, wisdom, *tekhnê*, and something they called *parrhêsia*, which is a kind of courageous, bold speech in public space. And these four types of truth-speech were all characterised by the fact that you cannot reduce them to rationalist understanding, or logical speech. They are four types of truth-speech which are not *ir*rational, but which transcend rationality, because the speaker is in touch in a resonating way with the object he's talking about. That's truth-speech, and that should be the guiding principle in society. We should re-appreciate the phenomenon of truth — not in a naïve way, not as the fact-checkers do now, who seem to believe that they have all the facts in their pockets, and that they can just compare every statement to the facts. No! — truth is something completely different. Truth has the capacity to resonate with the object you're talking about and to speak in a way that transcends all rational understanding.

JW: I think we already had a leader like that, and it was a very interesting thing — maybe an early experiment in what you're talking about, and that was the experience of Václav Havel in Czechoslovakia and the Czech Republic, because he had this idea of creating what he called 'post-political politics' which would be very much like . . . this is the way he used to talk about things.

MD: In what book? Can you tell me?

JW: Yes, 'The Power of the Powerless' is one of his most famous essays. He wrote an essay as a letter to the then President of Czechoslovakia, which explains many of these concepts . . . but, to tell the story then to the end, it's a kind of a tragic story, in a way, because . . . He became President himself, and at the end, he wrote a book about being President, called *To the Castle and Back*, which is really a kind of diary of his presidency. And it's quite a downbeat book, you know, because he's more or less describing himself being swamped by bureaucracy and ritualistic behaviours, as the President. And that he can't . . . he spends most of his time writing speeches which he has to deliver — himself — because he doesn't trust anybody to write the ideas that he's trying to express himself — nobody else can do it. And so on. So, in that sense, it almost seems that, in the present age at least, the conditions that you're talking about — and we'll get back to the beginning of this again in a moment — but the conditions that you're talking about come out of a totalitarian culture, and he was trying to reform it and recreate it as a new culture, exactly as you say. His thinking is really close to what you're describing. But in the end, he kind of had to admit defeat, in a sense. And he died alone. . . . He had been feted by rock stars and everyone as President, but he died alone in his holiday home just before Christmas in, I think, 2011 — on his own. He was looked after by some nuns who had a convent up the road, and they brought him his meals, but they found him dead in his bed. So it's a really dark story of our time, of what you say. He used to speak of 'living in truth' as being the most important thing — exactly what you say. And there's that famous essay, 'The Power of the Powerless', in which he describes the greengrocer's window in the communist era, and in the middle, there's a sign that says, 'Workers of the World Unite!' and he analyses the meaning of this sign in the context of the greengrocer's window. What does it actually mean? Well, it's a mechanism, actually, to deflect the attention of the Regime away from the greengrocer, essentially, to stop them asking him why he's not furthering the revolution, and so on. So it's exactly what you're talking about. And it brings us to the context of what you're talking about, because totalitarianism — the word means for people, I think . . . it's a synonym for authoritarianism, but of course, that isn't what it is at all. The way you describe it is very far from that. Well, okay, as a layperson, I will try to sketch out where I see what you've described. It's like a . . . I would say a pathology of modernity — of some kind — of the rationalist thinking you describe. Also, I would say — and possibly you don't go into this too deeply, but I would say the whole issue of mass media and the effects of mass media on the consciousness of the person, the generation, then, of a mob mind that isn't visible — that is present, but people aren't aware of being part of it, but they are part of it. That it saturates their thinking, that their thinking is all received — that kind of thing.

I'm very interested in the way you talk about the symbiotic relationship between the leaders and the led, because it's a different dynamic entirely to that of the authoritarian dictator and the subject, as it were. You have described very well how in the kind of mechanistic society we have developed, that these very symptoms, like atomisation, and alienation and 'free-floating anxieties', and what you call 'bullshit jobs' — that so many people are doing — jobs that don't satisfy them, and so on — that these create a ripeness of the possibility of totalitarianism. So, can you, in a general sense, offer a diagnosis of totalitarianism because we had Hannah Arendt talking about it back in the, I think, early 1950s — 70 years ago. It has changed. The underfoot conditions have changed radically since then, haven't they? She got the essence of it, but when you think about it, Hitler and Stalin — they were almost, I would say, somewhere in as though a transitional phase, somewhere between the authoritarian and the totalitarian model. Would you agree with that?

MD: Yes.

JW: But, you know, they had radio and lord Haw-Haw, and, you know, there was cinema — a little bit. There were posters, speeches, big rallies. But other than that, there was nothing like what we have now, which is like minute-to-minute connections between the leaders and the led, and between the masses of people themselves, fermenting and fomenting their groupthink, their mass thought patterns.

MD: Yes. In this book, *The Psychology of Totalitarianism*, I focus on the formation of the masses themselves. I was fascinated by the question: Why mass formation? Why the masses or the crowds became stronger and stronger and stronger throughout the last few centuries. And then . . . That has been observed and described by many scholars, but nobody explained *why* they became stronger and stronger and stronger. That was a major challenge of my book — trying to understand why the masses became stronger — and I had some indications: people like Hannah Arendt, for instance. Without a doubt it had something to do with the fact that there were more and more people who lived in a disconnected state, an atomised state. They felt disconnected from their natural and social environment, and that, in one way or another, made them more vulnerable to mass formation. But the ultimate cause, in my opinion, is this mechanistic view of man in the world. It is clear that it is this view that, in itself, disconnects people already from their environment. When you think in a logical way, you connect from one logical idea to another, and you literally build a kind of wall around you, which isolates you from the real object that is out there. You reduce every object, on the beforehand already, to the categories of your own logical thinking. And in this way, you end up in a kind of mental prison without knowing it. You constantly believe that the categories of your own thinking will be sufficient to truly understand what is outside of you. So that's the first step. Mechanist thinking, rationalist thinking, in itself, has already a disconnecting and isolating effect. I described it in much more detail in my book. But then, in a second step, starting from this mechanist thinking, we manipulated the world, we industrialised, mechanised the world. We started to use, in a very excessive way, technology, and that — I give several examples in my book to show that almost every step forward in the direction of industrialisation, mechanisation, and the use of technology, leads to a reduction between the human being and his environment. And it's this disconnected state, this atomised state — to use a word that was also used by the Frankfurt School, and by Hannah Arendt — that makes people vulnerable to mass formation. And it's this mass formation that leads to totalitarianism. Because the difference between a totalitarian state and classical dictatorship is exactly this — that classical dictatorship is extremely simple from a psychological point of view: people are just scared of a small regime, of the aggression of a small regime, but a totalitarian state is based on the phenomenon of mass formation. So first, there is this mass that emerges in a society, which is fanatically in the grip of a certain ideology, or a certain narrative, and then there are some leaders of the mass, that can use the masses, the crowd, to seize control over the state. That's one part of the story. There is a second one, of course, and this second one I will describe in much more detail in my next book. And it is that, on one hand, throughout the last century, the phenomenon of mass formation became increasingly strong, the masses became larger, lasted longer, became stronger, because the conditions for mass formation were more and more met, were more fulfilled in society. There was more and more loneliness, more and more disconnectedness, more and more lack of meaning-making, more and more freely-floating anxiety, frustration, aggression, and that was what prepared society for a larger and larger phenomenon of mass formation. That's true. There's that aspect of totalitarianism, but there's a second one, of course, and it is that we also saw a specific development at the level of the elite. The elite became smaller and smaller, had more and more means at its disposal to manipulate the population. Mass media is a necessary ingredient for every long-term phenomenon of mass formation. Mass formation usually will not last very long if the masses are not constantly re-hypnotised through the mass media by the same messages, time and time again.

JW: The concept of hypnosis is very interesting because you say it's identical to mass formation, more or less. But it's again a counter-intuitive idea. People find it really hard, when you explain it to them, because they think of hypnosis as some kind of deep state created by an expert, or a game people play, a kind of fun thing, a show just for laughs. They don't really understand — and I don't understand — what hypnosis really is at its core. Do you, first of all, understand what hypnosis is, of its essence?

MD: Yes.

JW: What is the state that we're transported to in hypnosis? And have you ever done hypnosis or been hypnotised? Have you got that close to it?

MD: I've not been hypnotised. But I once hypnotised someone without knowing it. I will tell you the story. First, I think I can describe in a very precise way what the mechanism of hypnosis is. In a hypnotic procedure, the procedure is actually very simple. Someone — a hypnotist — who has a natural skill to withdraw, to detach people's attention, someone's attention, or someone's psychological energy, you could say, from the environment, to withdraw it and to focus it on one small aspect of reality, which can be an object that is swinging on a small chain, or just a set of representations or ideas that are presented by the hypnotist. And once the hypnotist can take someone's attention away from the environment and focus it on one small point, something very strange happens. It is as if all the rest of reality stops to exist. And you simply have to think about this as if all the energy is withdrawn from all the mental representations of reality, and focusses on one small set of representations. That's what happens in a hypnotic procedure. And this effect is extremely strong. Once people's attention is focussed on that one small aspect of reality, even the smallest stimuli that is outside that small focus of attention starts not to exist anymore. For instance, a simple hypnotic procedure is sufficient to make one completely insensitive to pain — a hypnotist focusses the attention of a patient so much on one positive mental representation that a surgeon can start to perform a surgical operation, and start to cut through the skin, through the flesh, even to cut straight through the breastbone, to perform an open-heart operation, without the patient noticing. And the procedure is really extremely simple. The professor-hypnotist says something like, 'Okay' — he was talking in the following way: 'Well, we will go together to a place that you like very much, okay, and you will feel the sun on your face, you will feel the sand under your feet' And then, while he was talking like this, he suddenly gave a sign to the surgeon, 'You can start', and the surgeon could cut through the flesh and the bones of the patient, and the patient didn't notice it. And one time, I was talking about this, during a lecture at university, when one of my students just dropped down from her chair! And I first didn't know what was going on, and I went to her and asked her what happened. She didn't understand me; she was just out of consciousness. And I said, 'I will call a doctor', and she suddenly woke up and said, 'It's okay! It's okay! I'll go back to my chair.' And she went back to her chair and I continued with my story. And I said, "Well, we will go together to a place you like very much; you will feel the sun on your face, you will feel the sand under your feet,' and she dropped from her chair again!' I then realised that she was hypnotised.

So hypnosis is a very strange phenomenon — it's very simple, it can happen in a very spontaneous way, It just means that someone can take all the attention and focus it on one small aspect of reality, and then all the rest disappears. That's exactly the same as what happens in a mass formation. Exactly the same.

JW: So, how does it work in a mass formation? Is TV the primary instrument? Is there more to it than that? Is it propaganda in general? How does that work?

MD: TV, radio, it doesn't matter. The most important thing is that, well, the population should be in a very specific condition to provoke a large-scale mass formation. And the core characteristic of this condition is that many people should feel disconnected, should feel lonely. And that was definitely the case just before the corona crisis. Over 30 per cent of the population worldwide reported that they didn't have one meaningful relationship, and that they only connected to other people through the internet. So that's a core condition, disconnectedness. And then, once people feel disconnected, they will typically experience a lack of meaning-making in life. And that was also definitely the case: 60 per cent of the people reported that they considered their own job to be a bullshit job — so that they didn't know what the purpose of the job was. And then, once people feel disconnected, and suffer from a lack of meaning-making, they will typically be confronted with freely-floating anxiety, frustration and aggression. That means that all their affects and emotions, all their psychological energy, will detach from their mental representations. They will start to feel anxious, frustrated and aggressive, without knowing what they feel anxious, frustrated and aggressive for, and that's an extremely adverse mental state, just because if you're anxious and you don't know what you're anxious for, you feel out of control. You cannot protect yourself from your anxiety; you don't know what you should run away from. And in this state, something very specific might happen, so at that moment you're in the first stage of the hypnosis. That means all the psychological energy and the tension is withdrawn from the environment; it's freely floating, and if people are in this condition and a narrative is distributed, or disseminated, through the mass media, indicating an object of anxiety, and at the same time providing a strategy to deal with this object of anxiety, then suddenly all this freely-floating anxiety might suddenly connect to the object of anxiety, and there might be a huge willingness to deal with the object of anxiety, just because, in this way, people feel that they have a little bit of control again over their anxiety. They can connect it to something, and they can fight it with a strategy. For instance, a virus as the object of anxiety and the lockdown as the strategy to fight the object of anxiety. Or a witch as the object of anxiety in the witch trials, as the strategy to deal with the object of anxiety. All major mass formations, whether we are talking about the Crusades, the witch hunts, the French Revolution, Nazism, Communism — all major mass formations follow the same mechanism. First, people were in specific mental states, then someone put forward an object of anxiety and a strategy to deal with it; and consequently, there was a huge willingness to participate in the strategy to deal with the object of anxiety. And the first advantage — psychological advantage, of course — is that people can control their anxiety in a better way, and that they have an object for all their frustration and aggression. And that's the first step. And then, in the second step, something even more important happens, because many people at the same time participate in the heroic battle with the object of anxiety, people feel connected again. And that's the real reason why people buy into the narrative. Not because they think it's right, or accurate, or no matter what. It is because it leads to this new social bond, and because it allows them to direct all this frustration and aggression at something, and because it allows them to control the anxiety of the people. So that's the mechanism. And the problem of course, with the mechanism is that this new social bond is never a social bond between individuals; it's a social bond between every individual separately and the collective. So the mass, or the crowd, or the group is formed, not because the individuals show a strong solidarity with each other — no, because each individual separately shows a strong solidarity with the collective — and the longer a mass formation exists, the more all the psychological energy is sucked away from the relationship between individuals, and it invests in the relationship between the individual and the collective . . .

And that's why, during the corona crisis, for instance, while everybody was talking about solidarity, people did accept that if someone got involved in an accident on the street, they were no longer allowed to help — unless they had a surgical mask and surgical gloves at their disposal. The websites of the Belgian and the Dutch governments, all the European governments, mentioned it like that. And that's also why, at the same time, people accepted that, if their parents were dying, they were no longer allowed to visit them. No, they should die alone. So that's a strange solidarity, the solidarity of the masses. It is a solidarity with a collective ID, and never solidarity with other individuals, and that's, of course, why every totalitarian state, which is always based on mass formation, ends up in a radically paranoid atmosphere in which every individual is willing to report other individuals to the state. No — not every individual — about 30 per cent of individuals, usually. I've had this conversation with a woman who lived in Iran during the revolution in 1979 — this revolution was a large-scale phenomenon of mass formation — and she told me how she witnessed with her own eyes a mother who reported her son to the state, and how she hung the rope around his neck, just before he was hanged, and how she claimed to be a heroine for doing so. And that's so typical. Even the strongest relationships between individuals deteriorate in a mass formation and inevitably become less strong than the relationship between the individual and the collective. Totalitarianism and mass formation are extreme examples of collectivism, usually.

JW: Yeah, there seems to be this paradox. On the one hand, they suck people into the bubble of thinking of the crowd — or the bubble of feeling, more, is it really? — because it seems to be a low level of thought, a very simplistic and simple and pious form of thinking, and very hard in its responses compared to normal life. So, is it true to say that, generally, our culture does not understand the extent to which our individuality is all the time merging and morphing with crowds, and with a commonality of thinking, and so on — that that's a kind of unexplored area? Because, on the other hand is an assumption in our culture that we're individuals, when we speak, we speak as ourselves — 'It's my opinion . . .' you know: 'This is your opinion'. We exchange *our* opinions. We have discussions and debates. But, in reality, we are very often acting within a mass, which is acting our roles that are allocated within that mass.

MD: Ah, definitely! Thinking and speech became much more uniform throughout the last century — without people knowing — because people all were in the grip of the same propaganda and the same narratives that are distributed through the mass media. People such as [Wilfred] Trotter, [Walter] Lippmann, [Edward] Bernays, the founding fathers of modern public relations — which is a type of propaganda — all explained that — that the purpose of propaganda is to make everyone think in the same way. So, of course, while we believe that we become more rational, and that we think for ourselves, we actually more and more — increasingly — start to think in the same way.

That's also interesting: that the higher the level of education, the more vulnerable people are for mass formation, and that's exactly because education — what we call education now, the school system — is actually one kind of propaganda. Jacques Ellul, one of the most prolific and most intelligent writers about the phenomenon of propaganda, said that without our educational system, propaganda wouldn't be successful. Very often, we tend to think that our educational system teaches people to think in a critical and rational way. But in the first place, it teaches everybody to think in the same way. And that's so dramatic, so clear, that the higher the level of education — this was described in the nineteenth century already by such people as Gustave Le Bon — that the higher the level of education, the more vulnerable people are for mass formation.

JW: I wonder why that is. Is it because of the level of specialisation, the compartmentalisation of disciplines and specialities, that create experts in a singular area, but there isn't necessarily any connectivity between that area and the broader world — or with other disciplines? For example, it is interesting that you have not just psychology but also statistical training as well, and perhaps that was a factor that allowed you to break out of this singular epistemology of the world that afflicts a lot of scientists and experts in other areas? What do you think about that?

MD: I don't know. It can have many reasons, I think. Why more highly educated people are more vulnerable to mass formation can have many reasons, I think. It can have to do with the effects of education on the way people think. But it could also be a selection effect. It could also be that people want to conform to socially shared ideals, and group ideals — ideals shared by the group — the more and the longer they will do their best to agree, and the longer they will remain in the educational system. I don't know. I don't know, actually, why more highly educated people are more vulnerable. It's hard to say. Maybe, yes, the fact that education is more fragmented and focussed can be a reason. But I don't think that, for instance, the fact that I continue to speak out or swim against the tide . . . I'm not sure — I don't think it has something to do with the fact that I have a double degree.

JW: Not necessarily that, but that you are not a singular specialist. That your range of attention varied across a spectrum of ideas. The duality of the two degrees would be simply a symptom of that. But that it's a different way of seeing the world. It's almost like, if you have only one language . . . if you can learn a second language as a child, it becomes easier to learn other languages when you're older. Even just having that one other language, whatever that language may be . . .

MD: Oh, okay! Yes, maybe.

JW: The process of comparison, or something, allows for a multiplicity of understandings and possibilities to enter in . . . for the meaning of words and the meaning of concepts. I dunno — something like that, perhaps?

The mass formation thing: the elite, as we call it, and the mass — I'm very interested in your thesis about this because, in some ways, it goes against the grain of a lot of the understandings that have risen up in the last couple of years, about, y'know, a highly manipulative elite, puppet-mastering the world and running the whole thing. And you describe a process that really is potentially much more organic — that it really erupts organically from the context that you have described, and that, in a sense, it really is not accurate or reliable to see it as simply, you know, the 'Illuminati' or 'the cabal' manipulating everything on some kind of downward pyramid of control that operates on a series of hand-ings-over of power and authority, and instructions — downwards . . .

MD: No.

JW: Can you elaborate a little on that? Because that, I think, would be against . . . certainly a lot of people watching these kinds of broadcasts would probably have a different view than that. I don't think you're saying that there is no possi-bility of some kind of overarching influence on this, but that it isn't actually enough to make it work. Something like that, is it? I'm not sure.

MD: Well, I think one thing is sure: of course there is an elite, and of course there are institutions that have ideological plans they want to impose on society. Of course there are all kinds of influential people who dream of reshaping society according to a technocratic or transhumanist ideal. All that truly exists, I think. But even then, we can conceive the role played by the elite in very different ways. I believe that the root cause of the problem we are dealing with now is not the elite. That's so typical of a totalitarian system. Even while the elite is manipulative and has a huge propaganda machinery at its disposal, and so on and so on, the strange thing is that it doesn't make sense to try to destroy the elite. At least, if you destroy a part of the elite, the problem won't be solved. The elite will just be replaced, and the system will continue as if nothing happened. That's one of the major differences with the classical dictatorship. In a classical dictatorship, if you destroy a part of the dictatorial elite, usually the system collapses, the dictatorship collapses. If, in a totalitarian system, you destroy a part of the totalitarian elite, it just continues. That's what Stalin perfectly knew — that he could liquidate, eliminate 60 per cent of his own Communist Party members, and that they would be replaced, and the system would just continue as if nothing had happened. And that's just because the point of gravity of a totalitarian system is not an elite — it's the masses – or [exists] in a diabolic pact, as Hannah Arendt said, between the masses and their leaders. So the root cause of the problem is not one or another elite; it's this ideology. And in the end, ultimately, this mechanist ideology that not only prepared the population for mass formation in the way that I just described, but that also prepared an elite for the totalitarian role. So, the only thing that can truly allow us to overcome the problem, the symptoms of totalitarianism, is the emergence of a new view of man in the world that goes beyond, that transcends this rationalist view of man in the world. Ultimately, that's the only thing we can do.

JW: Yes.

MD: And that's clear, that's clear. That's also a problem with most types of conspiracy thinking: that it is as if all the evil in the world is concentrated in a small elite, which manipulates and steers the world from behind a curtain, or the dark. Solzhenitsyn described this in a very beautiful quote: he said; *'The Line dividing good and evil . . . It would be easy to believe that the line dividing good and evil runs between people, but it runs through every human heart.'* And that's true. Everybody has a bit of evil and a bit of good. We are all struggling and suffering. One is more evil than the other, of course, but I think it makes no sense to believe that all the evil in the world is due to a small elite. No! If you look at the way in which the elite emerged — for instance, if you read the books written by the founding fathers of propaganda, you will see that they all believed that they developed their propaganda machinery for the better good. They all believed that if you don't manipulate the population, it will be self-destructive, it will be irrational, and so on. They believed that the masses had to be manipulated in order to prevent them ending up in radical destructiveness and radical irrationality. And in a certain way, that's true: masses *have* a tendency to be self-destructive and to be irrational, but of course, I really don't believe that propaganda and manipulation are the right solution to that problem. That's where I differ from these people — Lippman, Trotter, Bernays, and from totalitarian leaders, of course.

JW: Yes, and also seems to be a tendency in masses, or in the ordinary individual, to enter into Faustian pacts with power, for the sake of convenience. For instance, the mobile phone, which is now used as an instrument of control, despite the fact that people are aware of the dangers of it. The convenience of it is too tempting and too seductive for them to say, No, we can't use it anymore. That seems to be a paradox of our desiring to retain our freedoms, while at the same time wanting to retain all the baubles of technical civilisation.

MD. Indeed. Exactly. Mechanist thinking has this enormous grip on the population — on everyone, leaders and followers, because it always promises to make life more comfortable and easier in the short-term. And that makes us forget that it takes away some of the essentials at the core of our lives and of humanity in the longer term. That's a strange thing. That's how mechanist thinking seduces the human mind: it always promises more control over the world, that'll make our life easier. Every new technological device seems to make our lives easier, more comfortable and so on, and that makes us blind to the fact that it also takes something away. It comes with a price, and this price is always that it destroys more and more our truly human connection, our resonating connection with everything around us.

JW: What do you think is it that enables some, a small minority, to remain immune to this thinking? You talk about the Asch experiment, where one section of the participants are absolutely certain that they know what is the right answer and are therefore not sucked into the trick. What is it that makes that . . . Have you identified any characteristics in those people that can be said to be a generalisation even?

MD: No. It has probably something to do with ideological preferences. If the narrative that leads to the mass formation . . . If the ideological basis of the narrative that leads to the mass formation is not in line with your own ideological preferences, you probably will be more resilient, and you will probably be less sensitive for the phenomenon of mass formation. But that doesn't explain everything, because someone like [Joost] Meerloo — who wrote this very interesting book, *The Rape of the Mind*, on totalitarianism, and propaganda, and brainwashing — described how he observed, just before the Second World War, how certain people who, before the emergence of Nazism in Europe, were very critical of all kinds of race theories and all this Nazi discourse, how they suddenly, when the Nazi Party became the dominant party, started to think in a different way. They suddenly started to see the advantages of this kind of ideology. And that was the phenomenon that Meerloo calls 'the rape of the mind' showing that ideological preferences definitely do not explain everything. As to answering the question, as to why some people go along with the masses, whereas others do not fall prey to the process of mass formation, I think that, in the end, it all depends on the most fundamental choice a human being can make. As a human being, we constantly have to choose between going along with the largest group of people, the dominant group, the dominant thinking in society, or we can try to stay loyal to something that we consider sincere, honest, truthful, and taking the more difficult road in which we have to swim against the tide — in which we have to go against the current. That's a very fundamental choice, and probably the most fundamental choice a human being can make, and if, throughout your life, you prefer the second type of satisfaction, namely — in one way or another — staying true to something you truly consider sincere and honest and so on, I think if you make that choice enough, if you can stay in touch with what you believe is true, then you might have a better chance to escape the phenomenon of mass formation when it emerges around you, and to stay awake. That might be . . . you know, this question has been asked around the last 200 years; it has been asked so often — so many people have asked, 'What the hell makes small groups of people invulnerable to mass formation?' because, in every episode of mass formation, it was clear that there was a small group, a percentage of the population, that was immune to it. But nobody has really succeeded in explaining it.

JW: One possible theory is that it has something to do with the residue of religion in a post-religious society. That the totalitarian phenomenon seems to be a symptom of post-Christian, post-religious societies, in many respects. And I certainly noticed, in the context of the Covid thing, that many of the people on the dissident side tend to be religious people of different kinds — and very intensely religious people in many instances. But with maybe a particular anthropological insight into things. So, in a certain sense, what they're confronted by in the mass formation and the tyrannical aspects of Covid is so counter to what their fundamental beliefs are telling them about their humanity, and the dignity of the human person, and the freedom of the human person, and so on, that that's actually the trigger that galvanises these people. And I was interested in that concept in the context of your book, in *The Psychology of Totalitarianism*, a lot of the time — and it isn't a religious prognosis or anything like that, I wouldn't put it like that at all — but nevertheless, your solutions are moving towards the mystical area. They are what used to be . . . a kind of pre-religion religiosity of the human race, the desiring of the human race for a more exalted state of being in the world — that that's what you're describing, even though I wouldn't try to characterise it in any way as a religious prescription. It isn't — but it is, nevertheless, into that area, and also into the area of poetry, as it were, the poetic mindset, you know, that the two things — religion, and . . . or spirituality, shall we say — and poetry, they're very much aligned in that area. And yet both are in decline, in a certain sense, in our culture, in the mainstream of our culture now. And that maybe has to do with the mechanistic . . . well, it *has* to do with the mechanistic worldview and all of that. But I wonder what would you say about that whole area, because it seems that the big problem of our age, in so far as religion is concerned, is that our rationality has made it impossible for many people to believe in the kind of mythology, shall we say, that their parents and grandparents took for granted, and which functioned as a way of enabling their whole existences to run in a certain way, to accept certain realities, and to move through reality with a certain certitude that isn't available now to people.

MD: Mmmm. Yes. I think that religion, mysticism, poetry, are three examples of practices, or . . . kinds of discourses, that transcend rationality. You know, Max Planck, the famous physicist who won the Nobel Prize, wrote something wonderful about this. He said, 'I've dedicated my life to science and to scientific research in the laboratory, and I came to the firm conclusion that in the end, science arrives where religions once started: in an original contact with something that transcends rationality.' And he called that 'something that transcends rationality' . . . ah . . . 'a personal God'. And the difference is, he said, that for a religious person, he said, 'God is the basis of everything'. And for a scientist, he said, 'God is the conclusion of everything.' [He laughs.] It means that, for Max Planck . . . he said, 'If you really follow rationality — the *ratio* — in an honest and loyal way, in the end, you will arrive at the point where you will see that you arrive at the border, at the limit of rationality. Then, beyond that point, there is something that can never be understood in a rational way, but is alive. It speaks; you can resonate with it; and it will make you see things constantly in a different way. And that's how Max Planck describes it. So I also believe that . . . I don't think we can go back to institutionalised, dogmatic religion — that wouldn't be a solution. But the seminal, the original religious experience, is probably the same as the kind of experience the mystics were talking about, probably the same as the kind of experience Max Planck was talking about, and every time it's the same experience. It's an experience with something that transcends all rational understanding, and that touches you in the core of your being. The crucial precondition to experiencing this kind of knowing, this kind of resonance, is, I think, that you accept the limitations of your own logical understanding. That's the crucial precondition. It is at the moment I experience this clearly in my own life, is the moment I become aware of the fact that logical understanding will never grasp the essential, the core of life. It is at that moment that, almost literally, all these logical ideas that you were connecting to one another — they will never be sufficient to teach you what life is, and what the core of our existence is. And it is at this moment that you can stop obsessively trying to understand in a logical way, that all these logical ideas that you were connecting to each other will open up and — literally — something of the eternal music of life that vibrates in everything around you, can go through the logical wall and can touch the strength of your own being, and can make you resonate with the eternal music of things around you. Almost literally. In my book, I compare the human body, and to a certain extent the human consciousness as well, with a stringed instrument — almost literally: that the muscles that are on the skeleton are all on a certain tension, and they are capable of resonating with a certain frequency outside, and the more you're aware and you can accept the limitations of logic, and logical understanding, the less you need an ego, and identification with a visual self-image; the less you invest your energy in the ego, and the less you need logical thinking to protect you from the mystery of life, the more you are capable of resonating with something eternal around you. And that's the moment when we see this other kind of knowledge, which connects us to the essence of life, and which also makes that we can tolerate better and better the idea of death and dying, for instance. That's something that I notice. As soon as you develop this resonating knowledge, you feel that you're part of something eternal, and death is not so . . . well, the idea that you once had that your life would stop, that your life would end, is not as unbearable anymore. So . . . well . . .

JW: Yes. One of the words you used in there — 'mystery': It has always seemed to me — or at least for a long time it seemed to me — that our culture misses this entirely. That all of us, you know, we live in a mysterious reality — even the scientists. Each scientist, in his own way, has a certain knowledge, but no matter how large or broad that is, it's minuscule as compared to the total mystery of reality. And, of course, for the layperson — it's multiple times that. And to think that that mystery extends also into ourselves, our very beings, our minds . . . *What is the mind?* And so on. And yet we pretend. We objectify the world and objectify ourselves and pretend that we understand everything now because Charles Darwin told us how it all worked, or whatever. And it seems to me that this causes a huge space to open up in the human person, in modern culture, that that part of the mystery is being denied. That part of everything that is mysterious is being denied, and so we carry around this gaping hole in ourselves that we are not allowed to think about or talk about. But to dismiss — and even the idea of religion now has become problematic in that context, because as soon as you start to touch on what sound like religious ideas, the alarm bells start to go off all over the place, and people become edgy, you know, because they think you're trying to preach to them, or proselytise them, or what-ever. And so it seems that increasingly humanity is becoming ripe for all kinds of manipulation, for anything that will fill that hole that they don't even know exists.

MD: Definitely. Definitely. Yes. Of course.

JW: So what then? You talk about the way that man might live in the world. Do you think it's a realistic proposition . . . I mean, I'm not asking you to put a time-frame on it, but can you envisage that kind of a shift in culture, or do you see signs that we are already coming to the end of this phase? You seem to suggest that this [present phase] will burn itself out, or that it will blow up . . .

MD: It will. It will. That's a cynical advantage of all totalitarianism and mass formation that it is always self-destructive. In the end, it always becomes — to use the words of Hannah Arendt — a 'monster that devours its own children.' So that's true. When that will happen, nobody knows. My gut feeling tells me that it will last seven or eight years or something. But that's just a gut feeling; I have no idea why I think it. It could be seven or eight years. But I also think that maybe we shouldn't lose too much energy trying to predict how exactly things will evolve and what exactly will happen. It's probably better to focus on the only thing that we can be sure of, and that we can be certain of — namely, that we will stay loyal to our own principles, to certain ethical principles, the princi-ples of humanity. Because that's what this resonating knowledge allows. It makes that we can feel the eternal principles of humanity again. Principles are something that can never be articulated or grasped in logical formulations in a definitive way. We also need to reinvent them, to re-formulate them, to re-articulate them, and I think that this resonating knowledge can allow us to feel what the important principles are that are crucial and essential for a life that is truly human. And, you know, it is these principles — not so much rational understanding — it is these principles that can be the true guiding forces in a truly human society. You know . . . I don't know if you are familiar with the work of Aleksandr Solzhenitsyn . . .

JW: Yes.

MD: The guy who wrote the — his book is here on my desk — the guy who wrote this wonderful book, *The Gulag Archipelago*.

JW: I have one here as well. [I show him my copy of some collected essays of Solzhenitsyn.]

MD: [Laughing] Well, Solzhenitsyn describes in a certain chapter how, in the concentration camps, in the gulags . . . I don't know, I think he has been in the gulags for 15 years or something, or at least for a very long time, and he describes how, in the gulags, most prisoners became really beast-like — they began to behave in a truly beastly way. They were crushing each other's skulls during the night to steal each other's food or clothes. They became even worse for each other than the guards were already for them. And he described how a small percentage of prisoners evolved in exactly the opposite way — how, in this pool of darkness, they became more and more human. They preferred more and more to stick to certain ethical principles, to just make sure that there was a small light of humanity in this pool of darkness. And Solzhenitsyn described this . . . refers to one prisoner in particular. I believe that his name was Ivanovich Grigoriev, actually. I refer to this guy in the last chapter of my book — who entered the concentration camps, the gulags, suffering from several medical conditions. He was rather sickly. But, as soon as he arrived there, he refused to do things which went against his ethical principles, in a very determined way. He refused to do anything that he considered unethical. When someone stole his food or his clothes during the nights, he refused to steal food or clothes from someone else. When the guards commanded him to do something that was against his ethical principles, he refused to do it, no matter what the punishment was. And so on. And so, Solzhenitsyn describes how this guy, throughout his stay in the gulags, became stronger and stronger. Also physically! And Solzhenitsyn said that you can never understand something like that if you think in a materialist way, or in a mechanist way. But these things show us how important, how crucial, principles are for the human being. And principles are not just rules or protocols we should follow. Principles are something more — guidelines which transcend every rational understanding, and that we can never articulate in a final definitive way. We should always reinvent them; we should always stay in touch with them and reformat them, reinvent them in every new situation. And awareness — being aware of principles is something we cannot learn. We can just . . . become aware of them; we will get in touch with them. If you are prepared to follow them, even if it means that we will lose things, certain possessions, certain success in society, certain social status, and so on — if you are prepared to sacrifice certain things in order to stay loyal to certain ethical principles, we will become more and more firmly aware of them, will become more and more concretely in touch with them, and that's, I think, the future of society. And that's also part of this new society — or this evolution — we have to go through in order to really overcome the problems we are dealing with now.

JW: I think that's the area where your book stretched into a new vision of what we might do about our situation, because, like, Solzhenitsyn, in that situation, conducted an inventory of himself — to ask himself . . . He went through his life in order to see at what point had he acted in a way that was counter to his own ethical principles.

MD: Yes!

JW: And, you know, he tried to atone for these, and to identify them. Now that's really interesting, because that isn't in any way trying to present yourself as any kind of ethical or moral person. It's simply an exercise for himself, which he believes is crucial for his own soul and his existence and his being. Right? And this is something that I think . . . an aspect of the religious experience and the religious life that we've lost completely is the side that there's a purpose for it, that it's real, that you're dealing with real things. It's not for show. It's not to be *seen* to be good. It is to be genuinely good. Because, as Solzhenitsyn said about the line of evil running through the human heart: that's something we need to be so conscious of. You know? That, as you say, a lot of these people [tyrants] felt they were doing good. It's very hard to argue with people on the other side because they're convinced that they're good and you're bad.

MD: Yes! They were so convinced that they would create Paradise that they thought it was justified to kill millions of people for it! That's the mechanism that . . . yeah!

JW: This is a really difficult thing for each of us — all of us — to grasp. Because we tend to assume that we're right about everything. And to assume that the responsibility for everything lies elsewhere, with other people. But what your book is really saying is . . . It's a challenge to us all to look at this whole thing, this whole society, this whole culture, and ask ourselves, *'How do I fit into this? How do I participate in this?'* Maybe I participate more willingly in this mass formation than I'm aware of? And so on. So that it's a really, really extraordinary book and really timely. Can you tell us again what your next book will be about? Because I just got a tentative grip of what it is. It seems to follow on from where you are now. Could you take us through that idea again?

MD: Yes, I described in *The Psychology of Totalitarianism* how the mechanist, rationalist view of man in the world led to social fragmentation and disconnectedness and then to a fanatical belief in numbers and rational understanding, and how from this situation mass formation emerged ever stronger and stronger, and how it was this process of mass formation that made a large part of the population — *and* their leaders — blind for the absurd characteristics of the narratives they bought into. And then, I describe how the real solution for totalitarianism is exactly to overcome this mechanist view of man in the world, and I give several examples of how we might be able to overcome this view of man in the world. And what I announce in my last book, *The Psychology of Totalitarianism*, is that it is the phenomenon of truth-speech that can be the basis of a new kind of living together, which will transcend the kind of society we are living in now and all the problems we are facing now. And in my next book, I want to really focus on the different ways in which a human being can use speech — and I will show that, throughout the last 200 years, society became more and more in the grip of indoctrination and propaganda. And the leaders of society were convinced that they needed indoctrination and propaganda — that there was no other option but to manipulate the population through indoctrination and propaganda, for all kinds of reasons. And that's one thing. I will describe how indoctrination and propaganda emerged, how all kinds of technological machinery was created for indoctrination and propaganda, how even the media and the news, our educational system, in many respects, were examples of propaganda and indoctrination, and then I will contrast to truth-speech, such as prophecy, wisdom, *tekhnê* and *parrhêsia* speech, and I will try to show how this other kind of speech, this truth-speech, has the potential to be the basis of a new way of living together as human beings. And also how it can offer an alternative to the transhumanist society that certain people want to create. Think about Yuval Harari, probably the most famous non-fiction writer of the moment, who wrote this book, *Homo Deus*, in which he claims that the future of humanity will be transhumanist in nature, that humans are on the verge of becoming God, and how the control of the streams of information will be crucial to that project. Well, what he says actually is that a very sophisticated programme of propaganda and indoctrination will create a new society — that's what he basically says. And I don't believe that. I believe that the opposite holds true: that we need a society based on truth-speech, which is radically opposite to indoctrination and propaganda, and which does not promise that man will become godlike, or man will become God, but to the contrary, which will bring people in touch again with a God that is very human. That's exactly the opposite. And I do believe that transhumanism equals the radical destruction of all humanity and society. And it will never succeed, of course. It will fail. This entire project will fail, but it is good that we think about an alternative. The better we understand what this transhumanist ideology is, and what the limitations and the problems with it are, the more we see that the only future for humanity lies in the re-appreciation and the new respect for the phenomenon of truth-speech.

JW: And because transhumanism is really the culmination, or the apotheosis, of the mechanistic worldview . . .

MD: Yes. It's the culmination point, yes.

JW: And that is really the story, beginning to end, that we are in the midst of now. What is your general feeling, having watched this episode over the past two years? How do you feel it's panning out now? Is it tapering off? Is it in abeyance? Is it waiting? What do you think? Have we further to go down this road?

MD: Oh yes, I think that . . . well, the corona narrative disappeared a little bit into the background, but society is even more vulnerable now for new mass formations, just because the corona narrative and the corona mass formation led to a deterioration of the social bond, even much more than it was already deteriorated before the corona crisis. It's very strange to see: like now, students and personnel are allowed to come to university again, everywhere, but they don't show up anymore. Only five per cent shows up! The rest stay home, saying in one way or another that they lack the energy to leave their house and connect with other people again. So that shows exactly what I have been describing all the time — that a mass formation sucks all the energy away from the bonds between individuals, and makes that there is no energy left anymore to overcome the resistance that is always present in human relationships. So people would prefer not to reach out to the other anymore, and stay home. We've seen this at the university, but also in all kinds of companies — people prefer to work from home, and they don't reach out to each other anymore. So the problem is definitely not solved. We went through one episode of mass formation, but we see that society is very vulnerable to a new one. Think about the societal reaction to the war in Ukraine, in which you saw a little bit the same characteristics. Suddenly, there was a new object of anxiety; there was a new intolerance for dissident voices; there was this new incapability to talk, to open up, to listen to people with different opinions. We see the emergence of the narrative on the monkeypox now; probably in a few months, the corona measures might return. Here in Belgium, our Minister of Health warns us now already that in a few months it will be necessary to re-vaccinate the population. And so on and so on. I don't think it will finish here, and I definitely don't think that the tendency towards technocracy will stop here. In Europe, we will probably be confronted with the introduction of the digital ID, and all the central banks are on the verge of the introduction of digital coins. So, the tendency towards technocracy will definitely not stop now. It will continue, I think. Nobody knows exactly how this will go, but we will see — evolution. We will see more and more in the coming years how the democratic system is replaced by a technocratic system.

The most crucial thing is that we should continue to speak out. I repeat this time and time again. All kinds of totalitarianism are based on mass formation; mass formation is a kind of hypnosis, and the only thing that can disturb a hypnosis is the sound of dissonant voices. So we should continue to speak out in a quiet way, a sincere way — not thinking that you are the only ones who know the truth, no — just saying that 'to the best of my knowledge, this is what I think is going on', or 'I do not agree with mainstream opinion'. We have to continue to speak out because history shows us very clearly that it is exactly at the moment that dissonant voices stop speaking out that the cruelty starts in a totalitarian system. Masses are always inclined to commit cruelties towards the people who do not go along with them as if it is an ethical duty to do so. And they typically start to become so fanatically convinced at the moment the dissonant voices stop to speak out. And that's simply because, at that moment, the hypnotic state becomes such that the people become fanatically convinced that the people who do not go along with them are completely irrational and lack every kind of solidarity and citizenship that they think it is justified to start to commit cruelties towards them. That started to happen in 1930 in the Soviet Union, in 1935 in Nazi Germany. Each time, a few months after the dissonant voices stopped

speaking out in public space and went underground. So we shouldn't do that —
we should continue to speak out as well as possible, as sincerely as possible —
not because we think we will convince the other people and 'wake them up'.
No, not at all! We won't be able to convince them — that usually doesn't work.
But that doesn't mean that we have no effect, because every time you speak out,
you disturb the hypnosis a little bit. That's something that was very well
described by Gustave le Bon in the nineteenth century already.

JW: And that's exactly the meaning of the title of Havel's essay, 'The Power of
the Powerless', that that's the power: the power of the greengrocer to remove
the sign from his window. And for each of us to do those little things that will
signal our refusal to engage in this, to participate in this. And that cannot be
overestimated. It's really a significant thing. And it resonates too with Solzhenitsyn's idea of that personal inventory — that, even if nobody knows about it, in a
paradoxical way, it becomes powerful by virtue of having happened, having
been done — that that little gesture you make, even in private, is so important to
your demeanour in the world as you go out, and the courage that you feel that
you can walk tall in the midst of this horror.

THE 100TH HUNGRY HEART & THE SWEET POTATO OF FREEDOM

29-01-2023

This is the transcript of an exchange between Dr Mattias Desmet and me before an audience at the Button Factory in Dublin, last September [2022], exploring his latest book, *The Psychology of Totalitarianism*.

John Waters: There's a question I want to ask you about [the mass formation concept of] 'the crowd', because it's something I don't think we fully understand: the difference between the human as individual and the human in a crowd. And there is a quote here from your book [*The Psychology of Totalitarianism*] — and I apologise, because I always hate when people quote from something I've written but then quote somebody else from within what I've written! But this is a very beautiful citation from Elias Canetti:

'The crowd, suddenly there, where there was nothing before, is a mysterious and universal phenomenon. A few people may have been standing together: five, ten or twelve, not more. Nothing has been announced. Nothing's expected. Suddenly, everything is swarming with people, and more come streaming from all sides, as though streets had only one direction. Most of them do not know what has happened, and, if questioned, have no answer, but they hurry to be there where most other people are. There is a determination in their movement that is different from ordinary curiosity. It seems as if the movement of one transmits itself to the others, but that is not all. They also have one goal, which is there before they can find words for it. The goal is the most intense darkness where the most people are gathered.'

This is an amazing thing that I don't think we really understand. That the crowd is . . . we can be in a crowd, we *are* a crowd, you know, like, we can become a crowd. And it's an entirely different thing to each one of us or even the sum of all of us, isn't it?

Mattias Desmet: Yes, it is, definitely. You can compare it probably to starling swarms, swarming starlings. I think that, at a certain level, you can really consider it a complex dynamical system in which the system itself is much more than the parts that constitute the system. Definitely. And also, people also really change — their psychological functioning changes completely, once they are in the grip of an emerging crowd.

JW: And you were talking about the comparison between animals and humans, and a phrase that came into my mind was 'a murder of crows' — the way that crows congregate in the grass, suddenly, to no audible signal, move in the same direction at the same moment. And the word 'murder' in that context is very interesting, because the crowd is capable of dastardly acts.

MD: Yes, the emergence of the crowd always means that the individual psychology disappears. And it's an extremely strange phenomenon. It is as if the collective soul replaces the individual soul. So the emergence of the crowd, in one way or another, always destroys — murders — the individual souls. It's a very well-known phenomenon, which has been described since Gustave Le Bon studied 'the masses', or 'the crowds', which is one of the most remarkable phenomena in human psychology. It's extremely hard to understand. You can understand it, as long as you understand the mechanism of mass formation. But it's hard to understand that a mother is prepared to kill her son once she is in the grip of mass formation. Or if the mother is prepared to report her son to the state, knowing that he will probably be sentenced to death — she is in the grip of a mass formation. That's exactly because all the normal bonds between people disappear in the crowd, spontaneously or intentionally.

JW: Is there some dynamic, some fundamental need in the individual that is fulfilled by that — a need to be admired, to be approved of, to be loved?

MD: I think that the fundamental need that is satisfied in the crowd is that people want to belong to a collective. People want to transcend themselves; they want to be freed of the limits of their own individual existence, without realising it. That's what you do in a crowd. People suddenly . . . usually — before the large-scale mass formations of modern times — people were in the grip of an extreme individualism. They got sick of it. And then suddenly, without knowing it, they had only one desire: to sacrifice themselves in order to belong to a collective, to sacrifice themselves for the collective. So, an emerging mass and totalitarianism usually means that extreme individualism suddenly changes and switches to extreme collectivism. In one way or another, in modern times, many people have a hard time keeping the balance between individualism and collectivism. That's what is needed, as a human being, to live a life worthy of a human being, to not be too individualistic, but also not to be too collectivistic, because in both instances, there is something destructive at the level of your humanity.

JW: A concept that you rarely mention, but which comes up in other discussions of totalitarianism quite a lot, is the concept of psychopathy. There's a Polish psychologist, Andrew M. Lobaczewski, who wrote the book, *Political Ponerology: a science in the nature of evil for political purposes (2006)*.

[N.B. 'Ponerology', from the Greek word 'poneros', is the name of a division of theology dealing with evil. But Lobaczewski is not concerned with theological definitions — his work relates to the formulation of a clinical classification and deconstruction of the concept of political wickedness. Before, evil was almost solely a 'moral' question, but he turned it into something like a scientific category. 'Experience,' he writes, 'has taught the author that evil is similar to disease in nature, although possibly more complex and elusive to our understanding.'

For more about Lobaczewski's book, see my March 2022 article 'Narcissists in Lockstep':*

MD: Yes, I know it. You probably sent me the book. . . . Someone sent me the book! I even read it!

JW: It's a difficult book to read, but very interesting in this context. Is this something that you see in this context — that there is some kind of psychopathic tendency in those who seek to manipulate these forces to control people, to move people in a certain direction?

MD: That's a good question, and as a psychologist I should be careful in answering it, I think. I should answer it in a careful way. Because, first of all, I

---

* This article is now the chapter titled 'Whipnosis, Part II' in this book.

think it is unethical to diagnose someone without having spoken to him personally. I think you have to know someone in order to be capable of saying something about his personality. Usually, people like Joost Meerloo, whom you might
know — the author of *The Rape of the Mind* — and Hannah Arendt, said — and I
tend to agree with them, I think — that among totalitarian leaders, you have all
kinds of personality types. They are very heterogeneous at the level of personality. If, as a psychologist, I talk about psychopathy, I need something very
specific. Many people use the term 'psychopathy' about someone just because
they believe he is evil, for instance, but that's not enough to call someone a
psychopath, I think. The psychopath is a very specific psychological structure,
characterised by extreme narcissism, which makes the person completely incapable of empathy, and so on and so on and so on. There are very specific characteristics. And, you know, there will be psychopaths among the leaders of
totalitarian systems, but I doubt whether they are *all* psychopaths.

JW: Within the model of mass formation that you see and have described — that
kind of symbiotic model of the hypnotised masses and the leaders who are
themselves self-hypnotised, or ideologically hypnotised - do you believe that,
separately or above that, there may be a kind of super elite which may be purely
manipulative, that is not hypnotised, that is using all of its knowledge of these
forces in order to effect something that it understands implicitly and intimately?

MD: Ah, that's a very good question. I always talk about the *public* leaders of the
narrative — so, the people who articulate the particulars of the narrative in
public space. It's those people who have hypnotised themselves — by their
ideology. And also [have been hypnotised] by the masses, because the leader of
the masses hypnotised the masses by his voice, by the resonance of his voice.
But the masses also have a voice that resonates with the voice of the leaders, so
that there's a mutual hypnotic effect, I think, between the masses and the leaders. But I don't think there are just those [leaders] publicly visible to the masses.
You could suppose that there are people who are not speaking out in public
space, who manipulate the masses in society from behind the screens. It might
be the case. Yes, definitely, it will be the case. There are such people, I think. But
it can be quite difficult to know, I think, what people we are dealing with here.
Are they also hypnotised by their ideology? I wouldn't be surprised. I think they
are. I think they also believe in the transformative vision, for instance, in this
case. I think they are really one hundred per cent pure, meticulous, mechanist
thinkers.

JW: And do you think they regard themselves as 'good'? This is something that many people struggle with: that such people might imagine that they are engaged in some kind of valorous activity.

MD: Yes, I think so. I think they believe that they can become Godlike, yes. I think that's their ambition.

JW: At great cost to others.

MD: Of course, yes. That's the point. Totalitarianism is always characterised by an extreme, blind, fanatical belief, an ideological belief. The totalitarian leaders believe so fanatically that they will create the new artificial paradise that they think it's justified to cheat, manipulate, eliminate, kill, murder, torture — and so on — everyone, to realise that paradise, to make the paradise real. That's why Hannah Arendt says, 'The only problem with the totalitarian paradise is that it always looks very much like Hell!' That's exactly the problem with these totalitarian leaders: They are so convinced that they will — in the end — create a paradise where, of course, they will be the leaders; they really think that justifies everything.

JW: You said earlier that, in some sense, we need to go through this, and, in fact, earlier, when we were speaking and I gave you a book [of essays: *Stories and Totalitarianism*] by Vaclav Havel, there was a quotation that drew your attention — to that same effect: that this is a process in history that we need to move through:
   'I am unwilling to believe that this whole civilization is no more than a blind alley of history and a fatal error of the human spirit. More probably, it represents a necessary phase that man and humanity must go through, one that man — if he survives — will ultimately, and on some higher level (unthinkable, of course, without the present phase), transcend.' — *Václav Havel*

JW: And you said to me earlier something also about this being something like 'the last stages' of the totalitarian phenomenon, that we're working through now, which is a very interesting thing. And you were saying also that you had come to the end of the process of rationality when you were 35 — that you had gone through that process via mathematics, irrational numbers, and so on, which I imagine was an intensely absorbing and difficult process. So, I'm wondering . . . in that process, which a society might need to go through — which is something similar, something analogous . . . Is it possible for a society to go through that? Is it possible for a culture to 'learn' something like that? Or is that something that only the individual can do?

MD: I think it's possible for . . . maybe not for the entire society, but for a group of people in society, to go through that process, And maybe everyone will become aware of the limits of rationality, and maybe get in touch with this more resonating knowledge in his own way. Maybe not everyone has to walk the walk of science to realise, and to really stumble upon this limit of rationality, and to get to the point where he or she is capable of transcending rationality, and to get in touch with a different kind of knowledge, a different awareness of life, which is much more resonating and empathic in nature. But I do believe that there will be a group who goes to the next level, yes. I think so. I also feel that . . . It's my personal experience that, as more and more people become aware of this new kind of connection — or this new kind of awareness — the effect is stronger with a group of people who all start in the grip of the same transcendent knowledge rather than when you are [individually] aware, having this awareness.

JW: Do you think it's possible to . . . Because there's this legend of the '100th Monkey' — have you heard about this?

MD: Yes.

JW: The concept whereby . . . * Do you think there is something in this?

---

* Background note: The Hundredth Monkey is a 'hypothetical' phenomenon in which a new behaviour or idea appears to be spread rapidly by unexplained means from one group to all related groups after an indeterminate but critical number of members of one group exhibit the new behaviour or acknowledge the new idea. The behaviour is said to propagate even within groups physically remote from one another, having no apparent means of communicating. The concept results from a behavioural study experiment conducted by primatologists in the late 1940s/early 1950s on a colony of Japanese monkeys — Macaca fuscata on the island of Koshima (Kōjima), in the Sea of Hyūga off the shore of the city of Kushima, Japan. In his book The Hundredth Monkey, Ken Keyes Jr. writes about this phenomenon which, he believes, may be our only hope as a species. He describes how the scientist fed the monkeys with sweet potatoes dropped on the sand. The monkeys liked the sweet potatoes, but not the sand in which they were coated. There was a problem: how to make the potatoes palatable. An 18-month-old monkey called Imo came up with the answer. The story goes that, one day, she accidentally dropped a sweet potato into a stream. When she took it out, the sand had all been washed from it and, having eaten it, she afterwards dipped all her sweet

MD: Of course! You know, Rupert Sheldrake described this very evocatively and in a very concrete way in his book, *The New Science of Life*. And it shows experimentally also, that if a set of animals learns to solve a certain problem — in Japan, for instance — the same animal in America will be capable of learning in a faster way to solve the same problem, just because, according to him, the first group of animals changed something in the morphogenetic field, and the other animals in one way or another can use the information that is in the morphogenetic field to solve the same problem in a quicker way. I'm inclined to think that this is true. Sheldrake studied this in a very experimental . . . in a very rationalist way, actually. And he also showed that these characteristics really seem to exist.

JW: And it strikes me that there is a possibility that, at the moment, we are blocked from perceiving these realities by the mechanistic thinking you talk about in *The Psychology of Totalitarianism* . . . ?

MD: Yes, that's true. Yes.

JW: One final question — about your profession, psychology: you use the

---

potatoes in the water, and taught her mother to do the same. Likewise her playmates, who also passed the trick on to their mothers. Scientists watched as this discovery was relayed through the colony of monkeys. In the course of the next six years, all the young monkeys learned to wash the potatoes in this way. Only those adults who imitated their young learned to wash the potatoes; the remainder continued eating them with their coating of sand. Then, wrote Keyes, something startling occurred: 'In the autumn of 1958, a certain number of Koshima monkeys were washing sweet potatoes — the exact number is not known. Let us suppose that when the sun rose one morning, there were 99 monkeys on Koshima island who had learned to wash their sweet potatoes. Let's further suppose that later that morning, the hundredth monkey learned to wash potatoes. Then it happened.' By that evening, almost every member of the colony was washing the potatoes prior to eating. The point of the story? 'The added energy of this hundredth monkey somehow created an ideological breakthrough.' In other words, with the winning over of the hundredth monkey, some kind of critical mass point had been reached.

There was more. 'The most surprising thing observed by these scientists', wrote Keyes, 'was that the habit of washing sweet potatoes then spontaneously jumped over the sea — colonies of monkeys on other islands and the mainland troop of monkeys at Tàkasakiyama began washing their sweet potatoes.'

The meaning of this? When a certain number achieves an awareness, this new awareness may be communicated from mind to mind, even among those who have had no direct conscious knowledge of the phenomenon in question.

The 'hundredth' aspect is random and somewhat arbitrary: Although the exact number may vary, the 'Hundredth Monkey' phenomenon means that when only a limited number of people know of a new way, it may remain the conscious property of these people. But there is a point at which, if one more person tunes into a new awareness, a field is strengthened so that this awareness reaches almost everyone.

science of psychology to great effect, in a very positive way. But at the same time, the same science is being used in the most negative way by health agencies, governments and media, who use techniques which are deliberately calculated to manipulate people and enslave them, actually. What is your view of the moral status of psychology in this context? I understand that it is a naïve question in a way, because all professions, all sciences, have negative aspects, and we cannot hold each practitioner responsible for the wronging of others. Nevertheless, isn't it the case that the behavioural sciences, as they have developed in the past century, the manipulation of minds through marketing and so on, the capacity now to reach into people's homes and grab them in a way that, really, they're imprisoned by — that is something that is very dangerous, and needs to be addressed — if we ever get out of this [situation]— almost as a priority.

MD: Yes, I agree, of course. Like Gustave Le Bon described the mechanism of mass formation, or certain aspects of the mechanism of mass formation — at the end of the 19th century and the beginning of the 20th century, it was used by people like Edward Bernays as the basis of modern propaganda and indoctrination. So, I think, indeed — that it is an abuse of the science of psychology. In my opinion, the unethical thing about propaganda and manipulation is exactly that it uses psychology to reduce and destroy the space in which the human being can become its own master. And, to the contrary, it uses psychology just to enslave people, even without [them] knowing it, to a master, to someone else, who will become their master. Psychology should always be used to free people, to give people the capacity to become the masters of their own lives.

JW: Clearly, it has shown politicians, et cetera, that they can have this power. We really cannot afford to allow it to go any further, can we? We have to address this really rapidly, as soon as we get an opportunity.

MD: Yes. Definitely.

JW: Your next book — what is it about? How is it progressing, and when might we expect it?

MD: In my next book, I will first describe how our entire public space is saturated with indoctrination and propaganda, very often without us realising it. Even our entire educational system, the school system, is a kind of indoctrination. And I will then try to reintroduce the concept of truth-speech and truth-telling. Because, in one way or another, it seems as if people have forgotten what truth means for human beings — how crucial it is. The ancient Greeks knew how crucial it is. They distinguished between four types of truth-speech: something they called *tekhnê*, and then wisdom, prophecy, and something they called *parrhesia.**

And they were all very necessary. Without people practicing these four types of truth-speech, the ancient Greeks believed that a society could not continue to exist. And truth-speech is exactly the opposite of indoctrination and propaganda. So that's one thing my [forthcoming] book is all about. It's all about the question of why we seem to have forgotten that truth-speech is crucial to us. And then I also try to address the question of what is the difference between the two: What distinguishes truth-speech from indoctrination and propaganda? And also, at the same time, I will critically examine transhumanist ideology, which is very much related to the same ideology as is at the basis of indoctrination and propaganda. Indoctrination/propaganda, in itself, is just a part of the mechanist/rationalist view of man in the world. Indoctrination and propaganda start from the idea that you first have to rationally understand the psychological processes in society, and then try to manipulate and control them. Indoctrination and propaganda start from a certain interpretation, a certain theoretical understanding, of mass psychology, of group psychology, and it then, on the basis of this understanding, tries to use all kinds of linguistic techniques to control and manipulate these psychological processes. This is exactly what mechanist/rationalist science always tries to do. It tries to understand the reality . . . and that's not a problem in itself — the understanding is a good thing — but then, the scientist tries to use that rational language to manipulate and control reality, or a certain phenomenon, for instance: mass psychology. So, it's exactly, in this respect, that the transhumanist ideology is exactly the ultimate kind of mechanist/rationalist thinking. It is the idea that, through all kinds of technological devices, we will be capable of controlling, manipulating, the entire human being, both at the mental and the physical level. So it's all part of the same ideology: this indoctrination, propaganda, brainwashing, and this transhumanist idea. It's all part of the same rationalist ideology. It's part of the same delusional belief that, through rationalist understanding, we'll be capable of controlling our human existence, of controlling our society to the extent that it will become like a paradise, where there is no suffering or dying anymore.

JW: The way you set it out seems to be bang-on, a necessary task. But that undertaking also goes against the grain of recent history. We've gone in the opposite direction for a very long time. The propaganda, all the dumbing down of people, this official patronising, condescending to people's intelligence, while

at the same time driving everyone further and further down into a pit of banality. Do you think it's possible? It strikes me that what you're talking about —
moving through rationalism to beyond, transcending rationality in some kind of
intellectual and emotional experience at once — is somewhat analogous to
learning to play an instrument, a musical instrument.

MD: Yes, it is. Yes.

JW: That you learn the techniques with great difficulty, you go through all that,
and then, at a certain point, you become airborne . . .

MD: Yes. Yes.

JW: . . . in your instrument.

MD: Yes, exactly, yes. You become airborne, yes. (Laughs.)

JW: But do you think that's possible, in this context, for the human race? I know
what you set out is necessary, desirable, that we transcend this mechanistic way
of thinking. But aren't we really up against it, more than ever before? Even in
my lifetime — I'm 67 years of age, and when I look back at the span of my lifetime, I find that, in a certain sense now, in 2022, it's almost as though we are
behind the 1980s . . .

MD: Well, of course! We certainly are! Because that's the problem. When you . . .
this fanatical belief in the power of the human rational mind — it leads to
exactly the opposite. It leads to an absurd irrationality. So, when you follow
rationality — step by step by step by step — some people will become airborne
at a certain moment, but others won't. It is as if they climb a tree first [his hand
rises into the air], and when they arrive at the top, and they cannot transcend
the tree, they cannot spread their wings and fly, they return [his hand, finger
pointing downwards, comes down] to the bottom, and they become completely
irrational and absurd. And that's what we have seen in the corona crisis,
because the people — those experts who believe that they represent rationality
and science, they are completely *ir*rational and completely *un*scientific. So, I

really believe that we are now more irrational than we were 50 years ago. Definitely. Because the quality of scientific research, of academic research, is also deplorable. It's a disaster!

JW: And also, most of us, frankly — you talked about your journey in mathematics to this point of understanding. But for most of us, that's kind of impossible. I did 'pass maths' in my Leaving Cert, so I'm not going to make that leap! So we're kind of imprisoned by our own incapacities and our own ignorances, and so on. And therefore, to an extent, we are dependent on that Hundredth Monkey. You are the 100th monkey, and we're dependent on *your* transcendence in order to be rescued from it.

MD: I don't think we are . . . I think we all transcend rationality and our rational mind in our own way. I believe we do. It's not because . . . Not everyone needs to understand what irrational numbers mean, not at all. I think, in one way or another, we all do it in our own way — as you said, someone who wants to play an instrument. He will first go through this technical stage, and maybe he will start to repeat and repeat and repeat the same techniques, and then suddenly, he starts to feel something and will suddenly be capable of playing his instrument in a creative way, without having to think about his technique. I think we all go through the same process in many different ways, and we all have to go through it in our own way.

JW: Yes, And before you do it, it seems impossible, doesn't it?

MD: Yes. Absolutely.

ACKNOWLEDGMENTS
WORKS QUOTED EXTENSIVELY

The Year of the Narcissistic Agenda (paper) (2021) by John Anthony
Eichmann in Jerusalem (1963) and *The Origins of Totalitarianism* (1951) by
   Hannah Arendt
Noise (1977) by Jacques Attali
Taken Into Custody (2007), *The New Politics of Sex* (2017), and *Who Lost
   America?* (2024) by Stephen Baskerville
Impossible Exchange (1999), *Simulacra and Simulation* (1981), and *Screened
   Out* (2002) by Jean Baudrillard
Laughter (1900) by Henri Bergson
Propaganda (1928) and *Us and Them* (2008) by David Berreby
Iron John (1990) and *The Sibling Society* (1996) by Robert Bly
The Politics of Obedience (1577) by Étienne de La Boétie
The Crowd (1895) by Gustave Le Bon
Letters and Papers from Prison (1951) by Dietrich Bonhoeffer
The Neophiliacs (1969) and *Groupthink* (2020) by Christopher Booker, and
   Scared to Death (1998) by Christopher Booker & Richard North
Slouching Towards Gomorrah (1996) by Robert Bork
The Art of Computer Game Design (1984) by Chris Crawford
Shop Class as Soulcraft (2009), *Why We Drive* (2020), and *Covid was liberal-
   ism's endgame* (article in *Unherd*) (2022) by Matthew Crawford
The Wilder Shores of Marx (1991) by Theodore Dalrymple
The Fear of the Virus (article) (2020) and *The Psychology of Totalitarianism*
   (2022) by Mattias Desmet
The Strategy of Desire (1960) by Ernest Dichter
A State of Fear (2021) by Laura Dodsworth
Chronicles: Volume One (2004) by Bob Dylan
Men Without Work (2016) by Nicholas Eberstadt
The Technological Society (1954) and *Propaganda* (1962) by Jacque Ellul
The Illusion of the republic (*Die Illusion der res publica*) (2021) by Michael
   Esfeld and *Restoring Science and the Rule of Law* (2024) by Christian
   Lopez & Michael Esfeld
The End of History and the Last Man (1992) by Francis Fukuyama

Gamocracy (article) (2012) by Alex Gekker
This is Strategy (2024) by Seth Godin
Mass Hypnosis Exposed (by a Hypnotist) (video) (2021) by Brian Halliday
The Empty Raincoat (1994) by Charles Handy
The Power of the Powerless (1979), *Letters to Olga* (1983), and *Stories and Totalitarianism* (article) (1987) by Václav Havel
The Road to Serfdom (1944) by Friedrich Hayek
The Origins of the Irish Constitution, 1928 – 1941 (2012) by Gerard Hogan
Homo Ludens (1938) by Johan Huizinga
Brave New World (1932) and *The Ultimate Revolution* (1962) by Aldous Huxley
Victims of Groupthink (1972) by Irving Lester Janis
A Casual Revolution (2010) by Jesper Juul
The Trial (1925) by Franz Kafka
What Is the Longhouse? (article in *First Things*) (2023) by Jonathan Keeperman
The Hundredth Monkey (1981) by Ken Keyes Jr.
The Coming of Neo Feudalism (2020) by Joel Kotkin
The Abolition of Man (1943) by C.S. Lewis
Political Ponerology (1984) by Andrew Lobaczewski
The Vanity of Guilt (article in *First Things*) (2019) by Andreas Lombard
Extraordinary Popular Delusions and The Madness of Crowds (1841) by Charles Mackay
Totalitarianism in the Postmodern Age (2021) by Piotr Mazurkiewiczstudy
The Rape of the Mind (1956) by Joost Meerloo
On Liberty (1859) by John Stuart Mill
The Captive Mind (1953) by Czeslaw Milosz
Society Without the Father (1963) by Alexander Mitscherlich
The Madness of Crowds (2019) by Douglas Murray
The Indoctrinated Brain (2023) by Michael Nehls
The Genealogy of Morality (1887) by Friedrich Nietzsche
The Begrudger's Guide to Irish Politics (1986) by Breandán O hEithir
Nineteen Eighty-Four (1949) by George Orwell
The Hidden Persuaders (1957) by Vance Packard
The Filter Bubble (2011) by Eli Pariser
L'Argent (1913) by Charles Péguy
Return of the Strong Gods (2019) by R.R. Reno
The Lonely Crowd (1950) by David Riesman
Fools, Frauds and Firebrands (2015) by Sir Roger Scruton
The Natural Order of Money (2022) by Roy Sebag
The Liberal Case Against Gay Marriage (2004) by Susan Shell
Puzzling People (2011) by Thomas Sheridan

Play Matters (2014) by Miguel Sicart

Templeton Award Acceptance Address (article) (1983) and *The Gulag Archipelago* (1973) by Aleksandr Solzhenitsyn

The Wisdom of Crowds (2004) by James Surowiecki

Houellebecq and the Death of Europe, Covid-19 and the New Death Calculus, and *Morality In The Age of Machines* (articles in *First Things*) by John Waters

Ideas Have Consequences (1948) by Richard Weaver

The Great Taking (2024) by David Rogers Webb

The Human Person and Natural Law (essay) (1970) by Karol Wojtyla (Pope John Paul II)

Parasite Rex (2000) by Carl Zimmer

www.ingramcontent.com/pod-product-compliance
Lightning Source LLC
Chambersburg PA
CBHW062107020426
42335CB00013B/886